International Business and Multinational Enterprises

International Business and Multinational Enterprises

STEFAN H. ROBOCK

Robert D. Calkins Professor of International Business
Graduate School of Business
Columbia University

KENNETH SIMMONDS

Professor of Marketing and International Business
London Graduate School of Business Studies

JACK ZWICK

Professor of Business
School of Government and Business
The George Washington University

1977 Revised Edition

RICHARD D. IRWIN, INC.   Homewood, Illinois   60430

Revised Edition

11 12 13 14 15 16 17 18 MP 5 4 3 2

ISBN 0-256-01973-8
Library of Congress Catalog Card No. 76-57332
Printed in the United States of America

Preface

ONE OF the most dramatic and significant world trends of the last two decades has been the rapid and sustained growth of international business. In its traditional form of international trade as well as its newer form of multinational business operations, international business has become massive in scale and has come to exercise a major influence over political, economic, and social development throughout the world.

This growth in business activity across national boundaries has brought with it many changes. The rise of the multinational enterprise has confronted nation states with local business units that are closely linked with operations lying outside the nations' local jurisdiction. As a result nation-states have had to grapple with a wide range of new policy issues that are not satisfactorily covered by the traditional conceptual framework for thinking about the protection of national interests—a framework primarily focused on controlling transfers of goods and money as they cross national borders. The business executive has also been confronted with new management problems. Methods have had to be developed for operating simultaneously in many different and differently changing environments, for dealing with new elements of risk and conflict, and for assessing the impact of the firm on social and economic change. The management task has expanded and changed considerably from that faced within purely domestic operations.

It was not until the early 1960s that awareness of the problems that arise when business operations extend across national boundaries began to have any significant impact on business education. By this time there was a growing realization that existing theories, generalizations, and techniques of business management that had been built up largely from business experience within the United States were neither general nor universal. More explicit attention to the international dimension of business began to appear in business curricula.

At an early stage the international business orientation frequently consisted only of selected tools and materials culled from the fields of international trade and international economics—a reflection of the newness of the field and the limited development of concepts and research. There tended to be a bias toward national issues and little direct attempt to develop the special skills demanded by the realities of multinational operations. Some courses simply joined together international aspects of conventional business courses, particularly finance and marketing, with little attempt to develop skills in assessing environmental differences.

With more than a decade of experimentation and research now behind it, however, international business has evolved into a field of study and research with its own identity. Its central focus is the set of management problems stemming from the movement of goods, human resources, technology, finance, or ownership across national boundaries. As befits a course for business managers, the field has a managerial orientation, and assessment of national issues is placed in this perspective. Furthermore, the field of international business has moved well beyond an applied international economics orientation to draw heavily upon other related fields such as politics, sociology, anthropology, and law where materials from these disciplines are relevant to the tasks of the international manager. It is now widely accepted that international business courses with this focus and integration can provide a basic frame of reference and develop the international dimension of business teaching in a way that other subject areas with their own focus and conceptual approaches are unlikely to achieve.

This book grew out of the authors' experience of teaching international business courses in graduate business schools and executive programs around the world from the early 1960s. It is a general introductory text designed for graduate level and advanced students, and with a direct focus on the development of management skills in handling the problems of multinational business. Extensive footnotes have been included as an aid to more advanced study of areas in which students may have a special interest. While the book is primarily designed for business readers, it should be useful for government decision makers who must take into account the present and future behavior patterns of international firms in designing national policies.

Students of political science who are interested in the role of international business in shaping governmental patterns should also find it of interest.

The text is divided into five principle sections. Part One introduces the new field of international business and examines the forces underlying its expansion and the patterns that are emerging from this growth. Part Two presents the monetary, trade, and regulatory frameworks within which international business transactions take place. Part Three is concerned with the goals of nation-states with respect to international business, and the controls that nations adopt to achieve their goals. Part Four deals with the assessment and forecasting of the cultural and economic aspects of the environment within which the international firm operates, and Part Five covers the management of the multinational firm, paying particular attention to the issues that are specific to international activity.

Experience in teaching has shown that a course covering topics in the order in which they are presented in the text produces a clear and interesting progression for the student. Students generally benefit from a short grounding in the terminology and concepts covering international monetary and trade transactions and their regulation. From this base the natural progression is to examine first the wider issues of the firm's relationship with different national interests. Decisions taken within individual businesses which have consequences for more than one nation must inevitably be colored by the national objectives and responsibilities of those concerned. It is also wise to examine how such actions will be viewed by the nation-states. As a next step, before moving on to examine the detailed structuring of action decisions, there is a strong case for building a more solid foundation of ability in assessing what is going on in the international environment and in forecasting changes that might influence the outcome of a businessman's decisions.

Whatever the course design that is adopted, students clearly appreciate a continual examination of the relevance of the material to the management task. Discussion exercises and questions designed with this in mind have been included at the end of each chapter. Also available at the end of the text is a series of problems and cases that can be drawn upon to support the course design adopted by the instructor. All of these materials are aimed at strengthening practical analysis and decision making skills within international business situations.

Many professional colleagues and practitioners gave the authors invaluable assistance in the long and arduous task of preparing the first edition of this book, in what was then an almost unmapped field. This revised edition has been able to draw on a much wider research base and benefit from our discussions with the growing number of colleagues specializing in international business.

A word of acknowledgment is also due to the postal services on both sides of the Atlantic—we cannot understand why they both incur losses.

May 1977   STEFAN H. ROBOCK
                                                    KENNETH SIMMONDS
                                                    JACK ZWICK

Contents

PART THREE

THE NATION-STATE AND INTERNATIONAL BUSINESS **171**

over Time: *Less Developed Countries. Smaller, More Advanced Countries. Countries with Their Own Foreign Investment as Well as Foreign-Owned Local Activity. Minority Partner Countries. Centrally Controlled Countries.* Summary.

trols. Control Problems in Relation to Joint Ventures. External Reporting and Controls. Summary.

General Policy on International Executives: *Foreign Nationals for Managing Subsidiaries. Headquarters Managers. Criteria for Choosing a Policy.* Problems of Cross-National Transfers: *New Working Relationships. Family and Social Adjustments. Career Patterns.* Recruitment and Selection of International Executives. Training for the International Executive. Compensation Policies: *Base Salaries. Premiums. Allowances.* Labor Relations in the Multinational Firm: *Work Force Management. Transnational Labor Union Collaboration.* Summary.

PART SIX

part one

The Nature and Scope of International Business

1

The Field of International Business

A DEFINITION OF INTERNATIONAL BUSINESS

INTERNATIONAL BUSINESS as a field of management training and scholarly research deals primarily with business activities that cross national boundaries, whether they be movements of goods, services, capital, or personnel; transfers of technology; or even the supervision of employees. International business has emerged as a separate branch of management training because of the growing scale and complexity of the international involvement of business firms and because transactions across national boundaries give rise to new and unique problems of management and governmental policy which have received inadequate attention in traditional areas of business and economics.

Business transactions that run between different sovereign political units are not new phenomena on the world economic scene. Some business firms have had foreign direct investments and foreign operations for many years, predominantly but not limited to companies in the fields of mining, petroleum, and agriculture.[1] Foreign trade, moreover, has a venerable history dating back to the emergence of the nation-state. But since the end of World War II a dramatic change has occurred in the patterns of international business activities. Thousands of business firms in many nations have developed into multinational

---

[1]Mira Wilkins, *The Emergence of Multinational Enterprise: American Business Abroad from the Colonial Era to 1914* (Cambridge, Mass.: Harvard University Press, 1970). This study shows that U.S. direct foreign investment prior to 1914 was not limited to extractive industries and utilities but also included "a surprising number of . . . U.S. headquartered multinational manufacturing companies. . . ." (p. ix).

enterprises with ownership control or other links that cross national boundaries. These firms that have begun to take a global view from markets back to resources and to integrate markets and production on a world scale have become predominant. International trade between essentially domestic firms of different nations has continued to grow in absolute value, but its relative importance in the total international business picture has steadily declined.[2]

Issues facing international managers and national governments with respect to their roles in this changing pattern of business activities across national boundaries have become the prime concern of the international business field. The field gives special attention to the advent of the multinational business enterprise—an enterprise based in one country and operating in one or more countries other than the home-base country.[3] International business thus encompasses but is not limited to international trade. It not only includes the activities of firms directly engaged in performing international services, such as shipping, communications, and international financial transactions, but also comprises the activities of all multinational enterprises, whether of private, government, or mixed ownership. Each business unit has a wide range of choices for adjusting business activity between different nations. Direct exporting from the home-base country is only one of them. Foreign production is a new international business concept used to describe the trend of multinational firms to establish production facilities in countries other than the home-base country in order to supply local demand in foreign countries or export to other markets.[4] Another aspect is portfolio investment across national boundaries involving the purchase of securities without transfer of managerial control.

International Business, Foreign Operations, and Comparative Business

As a new field of study develops, it is natural that ambiguities and differences of opinion will exist in defining the field. In order to clarify the scope of the authors' approach to international business, we should

---

[2]For an interesting discussion of why investment is displacing trade, see Emile Benoit, "Interdependence on a Small Planet," *Columbia Journal of World Business,* Spring 1966.

[3]David E. Lilienthal, "The Multinational Corporation," in *Management and Corporations 1985,* ed. M. H. Anshen and G. L. Bach (New York: McGraw-Hill Book Co., 1960). The term *multinational firm* was probably first used by David E. Lilienthal in a paper delivered at Carnegie Institute of Technology in April 1960.

[4]For example, see Judd Polk, Irene W. Meister, and Lawrence A. Veit, *U.S. Production Abroad and the Balance of Payments* (New York: National Industrial Conference Board, 1966).

differentiate between international business, foreign business, and comparative business. The last two concepts are sometimes used as synonyms for international business. Foreign business refers to domestic operations within a foreign country, while comparative business studies focus on similarities and differences among countries and business systems. The great merit of comparative studies in business, as well as in other fields such as politics, sociology, and economics, is the new perspective and better understanding of home institutions and environments that is frequently secured.[5] But as Fayerweather has explained, ". . . They are not properly part of international business because they focus on business processes involving only one country at a time."[6]

The three concepts—international business, foreign business, and comparative business—are interrelated and have large overlaps. The manager of international business operations may benefit greatly from many types of comparative business studies and from a knowledge of many aspects of foreign business operations. At the same time, foreign business operations and comparative business as fields of inquiry and training do not have as their major point of interest the special problems that arise when business activities cross national boundaries. For example, the vital question of potential conflicts between the nation-state and the multinational firm, which receives major attention in international business studies, is not likely to be central or even peripheral in foreign operations and comparative business studies.

An example from the field of accounting will illustrate the principal boundaries and focus of international business. A manager engaged in foreign business needs to know only the accounting practices in the host country. A comparative approach to accounting examines the systems and practices in many countries with the main objective of identifying similarities and differences among countries as well as universal patterns, if they exist. International business concentrates on the accounting needs for managing a multinational firm doing business across national boundaries. The accounting problems and techniques for international business operations are related to differences in national accounting systems. In some important respects, the accounting activities of the multinational firm will be influenced by tax and legal considerations of the specific countries in which the firm is operating. Within these constraints, however, accounting in international business is primarily concerned with fulfilling the needs of

---

[5]For example, see J. Boddewyn, *Comparative Management and Marketing* (Glenview, Ill.: Scott, Foresman and Co., 1969).

[6]John Fayerweather, *International Business Management* (New York: McGraw-Hill Book Co., 1969), p. 6.

multinational operations through an effective and uniform accounting system that cuts across national boundaries.

The Scope of International Business Activities

As international business has evolved from a situation where importing and exporting activities were dominant to the current stage of development in which multinational enterprises play a large and increasing role, there has been a strong tendency to emphasize the manufacturing activities of multinational firms. In large part, this emphasis results from the use of international direct-investment data to describe the new international business trends. Since manufacturing and other production activities are relatively capital intensive, they tend to show up importantly in investment statistics.

Inter-nation business operations, however, include a wide range of highly significant business activities in fields other than manufacturing. In addition to international trade and foreign production in mining, petroleum, agriculture, and manufacturing, extensive business transactions across national boundaries occur in service fields such as construction, hotels, tourism, business consulting, retailing, and wholesaling; in air and ocean transportation; in financial activities such as commercial and investment banking, securities and mutual funds, and insurance; in communications such as radio, television, telegraph, telephone, magazines and books, newspapers, news services, and movies; and in the field of technology through royalty and licensing agreements and research and development institutes.

The Multinational Corporation

The multinational corporation has become well recognized as a key feature of the changing international business pattern. But general agreement on the definition of a multinational corporation does not yet exist.[7] Some definitions emphasize structural criteria such as the number of countries in which a firm is doing business, or ownership by persons from many nations, or the nationality composition of top management. Other definitions stress performance characteristics such as the absolute amount—or relative share—of earnings, sales, assets, or employees derived from or committed to foreign operations. Still other definitions are based on behavioral characteristics of top management such as "thinking internationally."

Another approach has proposed a set of definitions that suggest an

---

[7]Yair Aharoni, "On the Definition of a Multinational Corporation," *Quarterly Review of Economics and Business,* Autumn 1971, pp. 27–37.

evolutionary process of internationalization.[8] In this scheme a firm is classified as international if it engages in foreign business but has made no foreign direct investments. A multinational firm would be one that allocates company resources without regard to national frontiers but is nationally based in terms of ownership and top management. A transnational firm would be a multinational firm managed and owned by persons of different nationalities. A supranational firm would be a transnational firm that is legally denationalized by becoming incorporated through an international agency, when, or if, this possibility exists.

The definitional debate is not simply a matter of semantics. It is important in the sense that it reflects the heterogeneity of the field and the reality that there are a number of different kinds of so-called multinational companies. It is also a reminder that researchers in the field need operational definitions that will permit them to identify which firms are to be included in their studies and which are not. Consequently, the users of research studies and statistics on multinational enterprises must be alert to the specific definitions being used.

In this book, the labels of multinational and international corporations will be used interchangeably. They refer to a cluster of corporations controlled by one headquarters but the operations of which are spread over many countries.

With the growing international involvement of business firms, more and more companies—American, Canadian, European, Japanese, and others—are finding that a large share of their assets are deployed around the world, that many of their employees are foreign citizens, that a large amount of their earnings are in foreign currencies, and that they are operating to an important extent outside the legal jurisdiction of the country in which the parent company is incorporated. In these circumstances, the companies have become multinational corporations, and the nature of their operations has been significantly transformed. They come to be managed as world enterprises, with international considerations dominating their decisions. The world becomes the company's market and sphere of operation, and the home country becomes but one part.

Although many U.S. firms have recently moved aggressively into international business operations, the multinational corporation is not uniquely nor exclusively an American phenomenon. In fact, if one were looking only two decades ago for examples of multinational firms, the names of European rather than U.S.-based corporations would have come to mind: the British-Dutch companies—Unilever

---

[8]S. Rolfe, *The International Corporation* (Paris: International Chamber of Commerce, 1969), p. 12.

and the Royal Dutch Shell Group, Switzerland's Nestlé, Britain's Imperial Chemical Industries, the Netherlands' Philips Lamps, and Sweden's Ericsson Telephone.

Not all international business is conducted by multinational corporations. Export and import activities, for example, do not require that a company establish and operate overseas branches, affiliates, or other units of the home corporation. The licensing of patents and technology in foreign countries can be accomplished without a predominantly domestic company becoming multinational. The dividing line to mark the stage at which a company becomes multinational, however, is difficult to determine. Many domestic companies go through a gradual evolution toward making direct investments, first establishing marketing, procurement offices, or warehouses in foreign countries. Even when a business firm crosses the imaginary and imprecise boundary between domestic and multinational, its degree of international commitment and internationalization may range over a wide spectrum.

In one sense, the emergence of the multinational corporation reflects a differential pace in the evolution of political institutions relative to business organizations. While business activities have become more and more internationalized, the development of international governmental organizations has not accompanied business and economic trends. Consequently, business corporations cannot be licensed by an international governmental agency as a world corporation. They still must be created and exist under the jurisdiction of a specific nation-state. Yet the multinational firm may have different patterns of ownership and control. In most cases, in the present stage of evolution, both ownership and control of the multinational corporation reside in the base country. In other significant cases, ownership and control are divided between two or more countries even though the enterprise is the legal creation of a single nation-state. If this trend continues, as it probably will, other patterns of control will develop.

From the standpoint of business management, multinational operations raise many problems associated with the need to deal with a wide range of environmental factors in several different countries. It also raises new internal issues in organization and operations. From the standpoint of world-development aspirations, the multinational corporation offers a nongovernmental vehicle for transferring technology, financial resources, management techniques, and marketing experience among nations at various stages of development.

What Is Different about International Business?

One can recognize the growing international involvement of business firms and the rapid trend toward multinational enterprises and yet question the need for international business as a separate field of study. The argument can be made that management principles are universal and that concepts being taught in the functional fields of marketing, finance, production, and control are as relevant to business management in one country as they are in another. The manager in the world economy, the argument goes, may need only supplementary training in the traditional fields of international economics and international trade.

Despite these arguments, a rapid trend has emerged to give explicit attention to the international dimension of business and to recognize international business as a separate field in the business area. The trend is supported by the view that earlier theories, generalizations, principles, methods, and techniques, developed in response to norms in the United States where management training has had its greatest flowering, were neither general nor universal. In contrast to purely domestic operations, business activities across national boundaries require considerable familiarity with international means of payments and involve new elements of risk, conflict, environmental adjustments, and influence over social and economic change. At best, only some of these elements are covered in traditional international economics and trade courses and have been only briefly treated in traditional management courses.

Although unique variables and considerations of business have fostered the development of the field as a separate entity in the business area, not everything concerning international business must be studied separately under that heading. Some aspects of international business may be covered effectively by extending existing fields; others can be better developed as a unified whole rather than as segmented appendages to existing fields. For example, an understanding in depth of cultural differences as they affect international business operations is more likely to develop when the subject is treated as a unified whole, than if the scholars of finance, marketing, production, and management were each to study separately the adjustment of their function to different cultures.

There are four aspects of international business activity around which new types of thinking are beginning to emerge. These four aspects overlap to some degree and do not exhaust the potential for new approaches that may evolve. Each stems from unique problems that develop when business crosses national boundaries, and each gives rise to a new area of study and body of concepts.

International Risk.   The special risk elements confronted in international business activity include financial, political, regulatory, and tax risks. They arise from causes such as the existence of different currencies, monetary standards, and national goals, but they are all measurable through their effect on profitability or ownership.

The financial risk elements involve balance-of-payments considerations, varying exchange rates, differential inflation trends among countries, and divergent interest rates. In the political area, the risk of expropriation or lesser harassment directed toward the foreign firm must be considered for many years ahead when heavy capital investments are being contemplated. The regulatory risks arise from different legal systems, overlapping jurisdictions, and dissimilar policies that influence such conditions as the regulation of restrictive business practices and the application of antitrust laws. In the tax field, unforeseen changes in fiscal policies can affect significantly the profitability of the multinational corporation. Furthermore, uncertainty as to application of tax laws frequently creates a risk of double taxation.

International economics provides essential tools for understanding the risks arising from balance-of-payments considerations, foreign exchange regulation, problems of international liquidity, tariff policies, and trade restrictions. Political theory is developing new insights into nationalistic tendencies and the preferences of different societies for varying mixes of public- and private-sector activities. Legal research on international business transactions has been expanding, and a growing amount of international tax research is enlarging the general understanding of different tax systems and practices.

But the coverage in these related fields does not meet many of the major needs of international business, and the extension and application of the materials and concepts to multinational business operations have been slow. The need is becoming recognized for a continuing business intelligence activity of considerable complexity to identify and predict international risks. Ideally, international risks should be analyzed for underlying causal forces, and projections into the future should be formulated in terms of probabilities and quantified in terms of potential costs.

Multinational Conflicts.   Of major concern to international business are the conflicts that arise because of different national identities of owners, employees, customers, and suppliers and because of divergencies between the interests of sovereign national states and the business goals of multinational corporations.[9] Some of the conflicts occur within the international firm, and others involve the firm's relationship to the external environment.

An extremely troublesome area of external conflict concerns profit-motivated decisions that result in the transfer of funds, production, and employment from one country to another. The results of these decisions may at times run contrary to the national economic policies of one or all of the countries involved. For example, extension of credit

    [9]Howe Martyn, "Multinational Corporations in a Nationalistic World," *Challenge Magazine,* November–December 1965, pp. 13–16.

to foreign subsidiaries at times when the foreign nation is attempting to dampen purchasing power through monetary restrictions and exchange controls can undermine national objectives as well as place local firms at a competitive disadvantage. The list of areas in which conflicts occur also includes such matters as contribution to local exports or reduction of imports, national interests in strengthening local research and management, or the country's international competitive position.[10]

Within the international corporation, the mixture of national allegiances raises further issues. Home-country nationals tend to dominate top-management echelons of multinational firms, and there is a tendency to retain research and administration functions in the developed countries. Disparities in wage and salary rates have also led to widely practiced discrimination on the basis of nationality. A number of nations have already placed restrictions on the numbers of foreign expatriates they will allow in local operations.

The conflict aspect of international business requires thinking that will relate a multiplicity of interests, each with different objectives and different criteria for evaluating potential outcomes. No other business field covers this successfully. The international manager trained to identify each conflicting interest and to think through the possible actions and reactions from each viewpoint, will be better prepared to plot the best strategy in a complex situation. One of the functions of international business study should be to erase any tendency to make blindly nationalistic decisions or revert to pure economic arguments. To date, efforts to construct an international framework for establishing the legal validity of claims and actions of different parties involved in these conflict situations have been relatively unsuccessful.

Multiple Environments.   The most pervasive distinction between international and domestic business lies in the environmental framework. Aside from its relationship to the elements of risk and conflict discussed above, the multiplicity of environments in international business creates a wide range of operational problems that require new concepts, analytical methods, and information. The wider the scope of the firm's international activities, the greater become the environmental diversities and the more crucial becomes the task of identifying, evaluating and predicting environmental variables. The environmental framework must be enlarged to include forces operating at a supranational level—such as the European Economic Community—and forces involving relations between pairs of countries as well as variables associated with different national settings.

One important category of environmental variables relates to busi-

---

[10]For example, see Raymond Vernon, "Saints and Sinners in Foreign Investment," *Harvard Business Review,* May–June 1963, p. 157.

ness activity open to the international business firm and to the form of business organization that must be used. Public utilities, including electric power, communications, and transportation, are not open to private enterprise in most countries. Business activity in natural resources such as petroleum and mining is restricted by many nations to domestic private or public enterprises. In some situations, the options open to international business firms require joint ventures with majority local ownership or joint ventures with government.

A second major category of environmental variables involves the diversity of the institutional settings. Labor unions, for example, are organized on different philosophical foundations and play different roles from country to country. Patterns of national, regional, and local economic planning vary greatly in scope and in their influence over business activity. Capital markets and financial institutions are in different stages of development and, in some cases, are evolving along different paths.

Another broad environmental variable involves cultural differences that affect business management. International business needs to know how cultural differences influence the behavior of customers, suppliers, and employees, and how these influences on behavior will change. This aspect of international business encompasses the full range of communication problems arising out of different languages, customs, and values.

International business has begun to develop its own body of cultural analysis following the functional division of business, with marketing questions receiving most attention. Considerable management literature has focused on the cultural adjustment of expatriate management and on the differences in foreign management and work force that might require adjustment of organizational structures or procedures. While concern for specific problems initially channeled cultural analysis along these functional lines, the common need throughout many business functions to understand cultural factors is for a more unified approach, which might be titled "Cultural Analysis for Business Decisions." Other customary segments of environmental study—educational, political, economic, and legal—might also be more effectively explored in a unified manner.

International Business and Development.　International business is frequently a major change agent, a means of transferring technology, and a key force in the economic and social development of a nation. This can be true for developed countries, such as the United States, Japan, and those of Western Europe, as well as for underdeveloped countries. Thus, international business requires new concepts that provide an understanding of what can and what cannot be achieved by the change agent and the potential contributions that international business can make to development.

The need to identify and justify the contribution that a proposed international business activity will make to an underdeveloped country has been forcefully stated by Richard Robinson:

> The reason for attempting at least a semi-rigorous analysis of what a firm proposes to do in an underdeveloped country within the context of the national interest of that country lies in the near certainty that the host government will analyze the project in similar terms—if not at first, then later. The Western businessman must be prepared to defend the utility of his local enterprise in terms of sustained economic growth and political modernization.[11]

The large diversified international corporation that has flexibility in its selection of countries and products to offer within those countries is much in need of specialized knowledge on economic development to guide its global operations. Although economists have given some attention to the divergence between social benefit and a firm's profit-maximizing alternative, they have stopped far short of the specific calculations needed by the international business decision maker. Economists have also investigated the costs and benefits to a country from foreign private investment, but they have not yet developed an adequate and objective framework for decision making on such questions by the host countries.

One facet of the contribution of international business to development that requires more attention is its role in encouraging indigenous entrepreneurship. The international firm may create new entrepreneurial opportunities external to the firm for local suppliers and merchants. It may also attract much of the entrepreneurial potential in a country and thereby inhibit the possibilities for development of other national enterprises.

The role of international business in development raises moral and ideological issues. It is frequently true that profit motivation will keep a firm away from the less developed markets. Yet the opportunity for the greatest long-term good from the viewpoint of both the corporation's home country and the developing nations may strongly favor entering the developing country.[12]

Once a corporation has entered a developing country, a whole range of new issues arise. One such issue is the degree to which the firm should become involved in the community and undertake expenditures normally the function of the public sector.[13] As a number of

[11]Richard D. Robinson, *International Business Policy* (New York: Holt, Rinehart & Winston, 1964), p. 100.

[12]Nathaniel Leff, "Multinational Corporate Pricing Strategy in the Developing Countries," *Journal of International Business Studies,* Fall 1975, pp.57–74.

[13]Clifton R. Wharton, "Aiding the Community: A New Philosophy for Foreign Operations," *Harvard Business Review,* March–April 1954, pp. 64–72.

studies have demonstrated, the paternalistic firm, which provides much of the normal functions of the public sector, can foster animosity among the local population.[14]

INTERNATIONAL BUSINESS TRAINING

Some students will study international business as a field of concentration, intending to follow a career working in foreign countries or in the headquarters of a multinational firm that uses nationals for operating foreign subsidiaries. Others will study international business as a supplement to their concentration in the functional fields of accounting, marketing, finance, and so on. Still others will be interested in international business as a preparation for working in government positions on the development and implementation of policies and programs for assisting and controlling business activities across national boundaries. For all these kinds of clientele, a minimum preparation for dealing effectively with the international dimension of business should include two goals: to develop familiarity with the body of knowledge on international business and to develop in the person special sensitivities, attitudes, flexibility, and tolerance.

The need for personal and emotional training to deal with international business matters deserves particular emphasis in this introduction because such training requires more than textbook reading. Ethnocentrism and personal parochialism can be diluted in a number of ways, some of which can be included within a broad framework of international business training. Student exchange programs can stimulate personal reconditioning through the experience of living and working in a foreign environment. When students from various countries and cultures are studying together, the students can be exposed to other cultures and values through class discussions and through team projects, if the teams are composed of different nationalities.

International managers need training experience that develops in them a special kind of personal and emotional radar to alert them to certain situations, where specific values and ways of action that they take for granted in their own environment are different in other cultures and nations. Successful international managers need enough flexibility to understand what underlies these differences and enough tolerance to recognize that types of behavior and sets of values different from their own may be valid for other people. In an operational sense, they must recognize that what are constants for domestic business may be variables in international business.

---

[14]Stacy May and Galo Plaza, *The United Fruit Company in Latin America* (Washington, D.C.: National Planning Association, 1958), pp. 240–43.

EXERCISES AND DISCUSSION QUESTIONS

1. "To deny that international business is a valid field for academic effort is to suggest by analogy that such subjects as international politics, international economics, and international law are equally not academically respectable. It is true that international business borrows very heavily from all three, as they borrow from each other, but the core problem in international business is quite different." Discuss.

2. Of the top 50 foreign companies in *Fortune's* list of "500 Largest Industrial Corporations Outside the U.S.," which would you consider to be not multinational? Why?

2

Patterns of International Business

HOW BIG is international business? How fast is it growing? What is the nationality composition of multinational enterprises? What are the industry and geographic patterns of foreign direct investment? Unfortunately, global answers to such questions must still be based on rough estimates. There is no international agency with authority to request such information from business enterprises or from national governments. The only source of factual information on international business patterns, therefore, is the statistical programs of the different nations, and only some of the investor nations have been collecting data on the foreign operations of multinational enterprises based in their countries. The governments of France and the Netherlands, for example, as of 1977 were not publishing such data. Furthermore, where statistical programs exist, they vary widely in coverage, concepts, and statistical quality. Yet despite these limitations, reasonably accurate estimates can be made to describe in broad terms the evolving patterns of international business. For the future, the data are almost certain to improve through the work of the United Nations Information and Research Centre on Transnational Corporations established in late 1975.[1] The UN Centre does not have authority for the direct collection of data but it should have considerable influence with national governments.

---

[1]United Nations Commission on Transnational Corporations, *Information on Transnational Corporations, Preliminary Report of the Secretariat*, E/C.10/11/Add. 1, January 23, 1976.

IMPORTANCE OF MEASURING INTERNATIONAL BUSINESS

How much difference will it make whether better information on international business is available? And what measurements are needed? International agencies need such data for adjusting the monetary system to the changed structure of the international economy. Nations need to know a great deal about the operations of multinational business firms in developing policies such as those relating to exports and foreign exchange earnings. The business firm interested in allocating its efforts over global markets also requires extensive information on international transactions and international business patterns.

The objective of the party using the information will, of course, influence the information required. Different requirements, however, can be satisfied from a limited range of basic statistics covering operations (current accounts) and ownership (capital accounts) of international business. On the capital side, the basic data required will be the size and source of ownership, financing and profits, and location of assets. On the operations side, minimum data will be the size, location, and destination of current production. For both capital and current accounts, comparison with noninternational business will disclose any significant differences.

A few examples can illustrate what might be shown by such information. A national government will be able to see what share of a local market is controlled by international business, what proportion of these sales are represented by value added within the country, and whether there is a significant difference between multinational firms and national firms in this respect. If the value added locally by multinational firms is small, the government might consider means of increasing the local components. On the export side, the proportion of the ultimate sales of multinational firms that exports represent may be deduced from international tabulations by industry. A country with a high level of exports by multinational firms may in fact discover that further local processing is possible. From a firm's viewpoint the same statistics would be valuable if governments were likely to use them. Also they would form a basis for marketing strategy and monitoring competitors' actions. Comparison of the international pattern from year to year would disclose changes in location and destination of production by international competitors.

The simple breakdown of statistics into national and international classifications provides the factual basis for many decisions. There are, however, many definitional difficulties involved in such a classification. This comes through clearly when examining the patchy efforts to date to provide data on international business.

Foreign Direct Investment

The most common way of measuring international business is to present figures on the size of foreign direct investment. Although definitions vary greatly from country to country, direct investment generally covers only investment in which the business is controlled from abroad. The U.S. government defines this as an ownership interest in foreign enterprises of at least 10 percent. It is distinguished from portfolio investment, which brings an ownership interest but not managerial involvement. At the borderline, though, the classification becomes rather arbitrary.

Direct investment is the easiest measure of international business activity to collect from available data. It is usually obtained by totaling annual flows of inbound investment plus profits and deducting annual outflows of capital and dividends. These cumulative totals of historical flows, however, do not show current values of assets owned. Furthermore, financing through borrowing or sale of equities locally may not be recorded. While this does not immediately appear in the traditional balance of payments, such borrowing can affect it and is an important measure of international expansion.

In describing the size of international business, one of the major limitations of foreign direct investment data is its tendency to focus only on the investments of international firms outside their home-base country. If international business encompasses the global investment of multinational firms, then investments in the home country, as well as foreign investments, would have to be included. If Unilever in Holland and IBM in the United States have become truly international firms with global horizons and global strategies, the investment in their home country should also be considered as international business investment. In the absence of a system for incorporating with an international agency, each business firm must have a nationality of incorporation. Yet, as a global business firm, it has its own worldwide goals and strategies, which may vary as much from those of the home country as from those of other countries.

If criteria could be established to determine when corporations become international rather than domestic firms, the resulting estimate of the total investment in international business would be many times that of total foreign direct investment and would represent a major share of the total business investment of the noncommunist world. The best criteria would seem to be the horizons and strategy of the company rather than the share of assets or sales outside of the home country. The share of assets or sales criteria will be biased by the size of the home-country economy and market. An international firm based in the Netherlands would tend to have a large share of its assets or sales outside the country because of the small size of the home-country economy. An international firm based in the United States, on the other hand, would probably have a relatively smaller share of assets or sales outside of the United States because the home-country market is so large.

Such an approach—to determine size and trends in the investment of globally oriented business firms including investment in the home-base country—is not merely a matter of academic interest. To the extent that such firms are maximizing international goals, their home-country as well as their foreign investments are relevant to the economic and foreign policies of nations. If *XYZ* company in the United States has a global strategy, it will protect its U.S. assets against a prospective decline in the value of the U.S. dollar in the same way that it protects its French assets against a decline in the value of the franc.

There are other omissions, too, from the usual figures for foreign direct investment. Aircraft used for international business operations are mobile pieces of capital equipment and are not classified as foreign investment. Another understatement results from special techniques such as loan-purchase contracts used by many international companies for financing minerals and petroleum projects. In such cases funds are made available for a foreign project as a loan to be repaid through the shipment of minerals or other raw materials produced by the project. In recent years, international firms have entered into foreign loan-purchase contracts totaling billions of dollars. The loan-purchase pattern is not portfolio investment, and it is not direct investment in the sense that the supplier of capital acquires equity and participates in the management of the project. As a hybrid form, the pattern results in making capital available and preempting a share of the output of the project. It does not fit the standard definitions, but it represents a significant form of international business activity.

The foreign direct investment method of describing the size of international business has still another major limitation. It does not give appropriate recognition or emphasis to important international business activities that are not capital intensive. The international operations of hotel chains, commercial banks and other financial institutions, advertising, accounting, and consulting firms, and many other types of commercial and service enterprises do not involve major capital investment and do not show up as an important element in the direct investment measurements of international business activities.

Foreign Production

More significant than the value of investment is the size of international business operations. The traditional approach for measuring business between nations is through export and import data. Since trade is essentially between business firms (some of which may be government enterprises) rather than between nations, it should be recognized that the business enterprise has options in the method it will use to supply demand in foreign markets.

Foreign production, as defined here, is the phenomenon of a business enterprise in one country moving management, technology, personnel, and capital across national boundaries to produce goods and services in another country. The goods and services may be exclusively or largely for the local market. Foreign production may also result in exports back to the home country or to a third-country market. Foreign production can be of three general types: (1) market oriented, (2) resource oriented, and (3) production-efficiency oriented. Each of these three types of foreign production is influenced by traditional industrial location economics.

In many situations, the business enterprise substitutes foreign production for exports because foreign market demand has grown sufficiently to justify the establishment of an economic size production unit. The motivation in such cases is frequently to achieve economies from proximity to the market. It is the same motivation as that involved in establishing regional production facilities within the U.S. market when demand in a region grows to a certain level. Foreign production can also replace exports when the foreign country imposes burdensome sanctions on imports through tariffs, taxation, or foreign exchange constraints, and when prospective production costs in a foreign nation are significantly lower, either because of lower factor costs or special incentives.

Foreign production and exports can also be complementary. Business firms with a global strategy may achieve economies of scale from specialization by producing specific components in one foreign plant and supplying all other plants around the world from the output of this plant. Some corporations, such as the petroleum companies, have a vertically integrated global strategy wherein products cross national boundaries while moving from one production stage to another but are still within the same enterprise. Thus the movement of goods across national boundaries becomes foreign trade even though the goods are only being transferred from one unit to another unit of the same firm.

A large and growing share of world exports and changes in export patterns are thus accounted for by internal product movements of the international company. The significance of this development is beginning to be noted by national governments as they attempt to formulate trade and tariff policies to achieve national balance-of-payments objectives. Patterns of many types of exports (particularly manufactures), which are assiduously analyzed and projected by such international agencies as the United Nations Conference on Trade and Development (UNCTAD), cannot provide any realistic insights into future export possibilities without taking into account trends in foreign production and the strategies of the global firms.

Exports and foreign production are important but they are not the only components of the international business sector. International business also includes transportation, tourism, communications, private finance, services, and the sale of technology.

For some purposes, a measurement of value added would be even more appropriate than measurements of either investment or production. The value added within the national boundaries, excluding the import content, is of great significance to governments. Statistics on foreign production would be misleading, for example, if they showed an increase while local value added was in fact decreasing. It is quite clear that the available data and the concepts used for their collection are most inadequate for the sorts of decisions needed to function in a world in which international business is so pervasive.

Size of International Investment

How much can be pieced together from available data? Can we begin to answer the question: "How big is international business?" In the world as a whole, the estimated book value of direct foreign investment was a minimum of $248 billion as of the end of 1974, as shown in Table 2–1. This total is 2.3 times the $108 billion estimated for 1967 by the OECD.[2] Some of the increase, however, was due to inflation and to improvements in statistical coverage.

The leading home-base country was the United States with 48 percent of the total, followed by the United Kingdom with approximately 14 percent. These two countries, however, publish the most complete information. If more complete data were available for the other countries, the United States and United Kingdom shares would be somewhat lower. Other important home countries for multinational business firms are Switzerland, Germany, Japan, France, the Netherlands, Canada, and Sweden. Switzerland is a special case because many firms from other countries use Switzerland as a conduit through which investment outflows are channeled. Thus the data reflect much more activity than that of truly Swiss firms.

The fact that more than half of total direct investment is accounted for by non-U.S. firms may come as a surprise to some. The ratio of

---

[2]Organization for Economic Co-operation and Development, *Stock of Private Direct Investments by DAC Countries in Developing Countries, End 1967* (Paris: OECD, 1972).

TABLE 2–1
Foreign Direct Investment by Country of Ownership, GNP, and Exports: 1974 (billions of U.S. dollars)

Countries	Total GNP		Exports		Foreign Direct Investment	
	Amount	Percent	Amount	Percent	Amount	Percent
United States	$1,304.5	32.1%	$100.0	12.9%	$118.6	47.8%
United Kingdom	171.4	4.2	48.8	6.3	34.0	13.7
Switzerland	39.2	1.0	16.1	2.1	17.0	6.8
West Germany	329.7	8.1	65.8	8.5	15.3	6.2
Japan	425.9	10.5	52.7	6.8	12.7	5.1
France	236.6	5.8	47.9	6.2	12.6	5.1
The Netherlands	58.2	1.4	36.7	4.7	11.3	4.6
Canada	120.5	3.0	30.4	3.9	8.2	3.3
Sweden.	48.1	1.2	15.1	1.9	4.5	1.8
Italy.	134.5	3.3	38.8	5.0	4.0	1.6
Belgium-Luxembourg	46.2	1.1	30.0	3.9	4.0	1.6
Australia	63.4	1.6	10.7	1.4	.9	0.4
Other	1,080.8	26.7	283.9	36.5	5.0	2.0
Total: Noncommunist countries	$4,059.0	100.0%	$776.9	100.0%	$248.1	100.0%

Sources: Total GNP: *World Bank Atlas,* 1975, pp. 27–30. Exports: International Monetary Fund, *Direction of Trade, Annual 1970–74,* p. 2. Foreign Direct Investment: United States—*Survey of Current Business,* October 1975; United Kingdom—*Bank of England Quarterly Bulletin,* June 1975; Switzerland—Union Bank of Switzerland; West Germany—Federal Republic of Germany Economics Ministry; Japan—Bank of Japan; France—estimate published by Japan's Ministry of International Trade and Industries (MITI) in Report by Council on Industrial Structure, August 1975, for 1973 and updated on basis of data released by France's Service de L'information, February 1975; the Netherlands—estimate based largely on inbound investment shown by receiving countries and balance-of-payments outflow data; Canada—Statistics Canada; Sweden—Birgitta Swedenborg, *Den Svenska Industrins Investeringar i Utlandel,* 1965–70 (Stockholm: Almquist & Wicksell, 1973) and balance-of-payments data; Australia—Commonwealth Bureau of Census Statistics, *Annual Bulletin of Overseas Investment;* Belgium-Luxembourg, Italy, and "Others" based on United Nations estimates in UN, *Multinational Corporations in World Development,* 1973.

direct investment to exports is high for the United States as compared to other countries but, as will be discussed below, the patterns have been changing in recent years with non-U.S. direct investment expanding at a more rapid rate than U.S. direct investment.

The $248 billion estimate for the book value of foreign direct investment in 1974, which approximates the value of total GNP for a country like France, substantially understates the actual situation. Book-value estimates are cumulative totals of historical cost, or values at the time the investment was made. If the effects of appreciation on the value of fixed assets as well as of inflation were included, the book-value figures would probably have to be increased from 50 to 100 percent. With adjustments for understatement of book values, exclusion of transportation equipment investments, incomplete coverage such as the omission of reinvested earnings in the West Germany estimates, and other data deficiencies, a more realistic estimate of total direct investments would probably be at least $400 billion.

Size of Production for Foreign Markets

Turning from the size of investment in international business to the value of foreign production, the statistics are even fewer. While data on imports and exports have the best quality of any international statistics, largely because of the pervasive practice of taxing trade, information on foreign production is scanty. As a result, the estimates that can be presented are highly speculative. Allowing for a wide range of error, they suggest that the phenomenon is massive in size and growing rapidly.

The movement of goods across national boundaries as exports totaled $777 billion for the noncommunist countries in 1974. Foreign production by international firms in the same year is estimated to have reached a level of about $635 billion (Table 2–2). The value of foreign

TABLE 2–2
Product Categories of World Exports and Foreign Production

	World Exports* (f.o.b.)			Foreign Production	
	1970	1974			1974
Food, beverages, and tobacco	14%	11%	Mining and petroleum		35%
Crude materials, excluding fuels	11	10	Other		8
Mineral fuels	9	21	Manufacturing		57
Manufactured goods	66	58			
Chemicals	(7)	(8)			
Machinery, transportation equipment. .	(29)	(24)			
Other manufactures	(30)	(26)			
Total.	100%	100%			100%
Total (billions of U.S. dollars) . . .	$311	$777			$635

*Excludes centrally planned economies.
Source: Export data from United Nations, *Monthly Bulletin of Statistics.* Foreign production estimates based on investment data from Table 2–1.

production, in order of importance, includes manufacturing, petroleum (production, refining, and distribution) and mining, and "other."[3]

---

[3]The estimated totals have been derived from national data on foreign direct investment using ratios of sales to investment for U.S. firms as calculated from W. K. Chung, "Sales of Majority-Owned Foreign Affiliates of U.S. Companies, 1973," *Survey of Current Business,* August 1975, p. 23. The ratio of sales to book value varied with the type of activity—manufacturing 3.2:1, petroleum 3.3:1, mining 0.7:1, "other" 4.1:1. Direct investment in trading offices, services, finance, hotels, and other nonproduction activities was not included in arriving at the foreign production estimate.

Most foreign production was sold within the markets of the nations in which the operations were located. But some of the value of foreign production represented components or raw materials brought in from outside of the producing country and thus were already included as some other country's exports. For example, 10 percent of the value of sales by foreign affiliates of U.S. multinationals consisted of exports from the home country by the parent.[4] Some of the foreign production was exported, thus resulting in another overlap with the export data.

The extent to which foreign production goes into international trade varies greatly with the type of activity. A study of the foreign production of Swedish companies—mainly manufacturing—shows that 83 percent of sales was in local markets and 17 percent was exported.[5] Data for U.S. firms as of 1973 indicated that 77 percent of the sales of manufacturing plants were local and 23 percent entered into international trade.[6] In some cases, foreign manufacturing plants are established to supply the home-country market, and in other situations the foreign plants may be a base for exporting to third-country markets. But data on these important patterns are not available.

A much smaller share of the foreign production of petroleum is for local markets. The U.S. data do not separate production and refining, but they show local sales to be 59 percent of the total. A breakdown between production and refining would undoubtedly show that the bulk of petroleum is exported from the producing area and that most refining output is sold in local markets. In the case of mining and smelting operations, U.S. data show that in 1973 only 18 percent of the output went to local markets, 36 percent was exported to the United States, and 45 percent was exported to other countries.[7]

On the basis of these figures, an overlap between exports and foreign production of about $220 billion can be estimated. It is probable that large amounts of the overlap are movements across national boundaries among units of individual international companies.

Joining the concepts and data for both exports and foreign production by international firms begins to outline a real world of international sales of goods that is far different and more complex than the obsolete image that underlies much, if not most, of the national

---

[4]"Worldwide Sales by U.S. Multinational Companies," *Survey of Current Business,* January 1973, p. 34.

[5]Birgitta Swedenborg, *Den svenska industrins Investeringar i Utlandet* (Uppsala: Almqvist & Wiksell, 1973), p. 68.

[6]W. K. Chung, "Sales by Majority-Owned Foreign Affiliates of U.S. Companies, 1973," *Survey of Current Business,* August 1975, p. 24.

[7]Ibid, p. 24.

decision making on trade policies. The size of sales by business firms outside their home country is much larger than that indicated by traditional export data. In 1974, for the noncommunist countries, foreign markets absorbed goods valued at about $1,200 billion. Probably about half was supplied by exports and half by foreign production, depending on how one handles the overlap.

Size of International Operations

The most dramatic, and probably the most significant, indication of the size of international business is the total worldwide turnover of multinational enterprises. This measure includes foreign production, home-country operations, and intangible services, as well as the production of goods.

Why focus on the total operations of the enterprises rather than on only their foreign operations? The reason is simple. If the firm pursues a global strategy, it will manage all of its activities and assets to maximize (or optimize) its global goals. Thus its activities may conflict with the national objectives of the home country as well as the host country. Performance objectives would likely lead to concentration on the largest and fastest growing markets, production in cost-minimizing locations, and avoidance of weak currencies. If a large proportion of world business follows a global strategy, even to a small extent, it is the total operations of the international companies rather than just their foreign activities that will largely shape the international economy.

The basis for classifying businesses as multinational will determine, of course, the size of the estimate. By defining U.S. multinational enterprises as those large enough to be on *Fortune's* 500 list and having manufacturing subsidiaries in six or more countries, Vernon estimated that the total sales of 187 U.S. international companies exceeded $200 billion in 1966 and accounted for between 32 and 39 percent of the total for all U.S. enterprises.[8]

As a less precise estimate and to provide only a rough gauge of the importance to the world economy of all international firms, "international" may be specified as representing all enterprises with a minimum of 10 percent of either sales or production outside their home country. On this basis, U.S. and non-U.S. multinational enterprises accounted for an estimated $1,300 billion of revenues in 1974. This was almost equivalent to one-third of the noncommunist world gross national product. Of course, GNP is estimated on a value-added basis and cannot be compared directly with revenues.

The estimate of $1,300 billion includes international revenues for

---

[8]Raymond Vernon, *Sovereignty at Bay* (New York: Basic Books, 1971), pp. 13–15.

services, thus getting away from the myopic concentration on manufacturing fostered by a theory aimed at commodities. As previously
mentioned, internationalism is widespread in nonmanufacturing.
Commercial banking on an international scale has long engaged the
interest of large banks. Many insurance companies have extensive
international activities in direct-insurance underwriting and in rein-
surance. Numerous construction firms of many nationalities operate
internationally. Television companies sell reruns of their home-
country productions to foreign countries. Hotel and motel chains and
retail and wholesale firms have expanded their activities across national boundaries.[9] Transportation and tourism are well entrenched as
international activities.[10] The sale of technology through licensing and
royalty agreements has also become a substantial source of financial
flows between nations.

PROJECTING THE OVERALL PICTURE

The five indicators of international business size that we have
discussed give the following picture:

	Estimate for 1974 for all noncommunist countries ($ billion)
World exports	777
Foreign production	635
Production for foreign markets*	1,190
Operations of international units	1,300
International direct investment	248
Total GNP	4,000

*Exports plus foreign production minus overlap

Presently available data, generally collected without any sensitivity
to the emergence of the international business phenomenon, show that
international business has become a significant factor in the world
economy. But this picture is only a snapshot at one point of time and
needs to be supplemented with data on trends.

Since the end of World War II, the international component of the
world economy has been increasing steadily, with both world trade
and foreign production expanding more rapidly than world GNP.

---

[9]See Stanley C. Hollander, *Multinational Retailing* (East Lansing: Michigan State
University, 1970).

[10]See H. Peter Gray, *International Travel–International Trade* (Lexington, Mass.:
D.C. Heath & Co., 1970); Mahlon R. Strazheim, *The International Airline Industry*
(Washington, D.C.: The Brookings Institutions, 1969).

During the early 1970s, the internationalization trend accelerated mainly due to sharp price increases for petroleum and commodities in the case of trade and to the growing strength of non-U.S. investor countries and the realignment of world currencies in the case of direct investment.

It would be unrealistic, however, to extrapolate the growth rates of the early 1970s into the future. In fact, the world recession of 1974–75 caused a slowdown in both trade and investment. Also, the international sector cannot grow indefinitely at a faster rate than the national economies. Given the magic of geometric growth rates, an extrapolation of the trends of the recent past would reach the impossible result of the international sector shortly becoming greater than world GNP. Of course, as previously noted, GNP is estimated on a value-added basis whereas trade and foreign production are stated in total revenues.

Another reason for a likely slowdown in foreign direct investment is that natural resource areas such as petroleum and minerals are becoming less and less open to foreign investment because of the restrictive national policies of host countries. Nevertheless, it is a possibility that the international sector will continue over the short run to grow as a share of the world economy and that an increasing proportion of world trade will come under the control of the multinationals.

CHANGING COUNTRY PATTERNS FOR MULTINATIONAL BUSINESS

On a global basis, the expansion of foreign direct investment has occurred in three rather distinct phases since the end of World War II. The first phase, beginning in 1946 and extending until the late 1950s, was characterized by a heavy concentration of investment in foreign petroleum and other raw materials projects and the dominance of business firms from the United States and the United Kingdom.[11] A second phase began about 1958 and extended through the 1960s in which foreign direct investment shifted toward manufacturing and trade activities heavily directed to the European Common Market and European Free Trade Association countries. This phase also saw a resumption of foreign direct investment activities by Japan and the Western European countries other than the United Kingdom, with a gradual loss in dominance by the previously leading investor countries. A third phase beginning in the early 1970s was characterized by accelerated activity by non-U.S. firms and a sharp increase in the

---

[11]United Nations, "International Direct Investment by Private Enterprise in Western Europe and North America," *Economic Bulletin for Europe, Part B—Special Studies* (New York: UN, November 1967).

attraction of the United States for foreign investment after the 1971–73 realignment of major world currencies.[12]

Total foreign direct investment increased from $165 billion in 1971[13] to an estimated $248 billion in 1974, exclusive of foreign direct investments by the Middle East and other major-oil producing countries for which data are not available. Of the total gain, 40 percent was accounted for by U.S. investors and 60 percent by non-U.S. investors. Consequently, the U.S. share of total outstanding direct investment declined to 48 percent, as compared with 52 percent in 1971 and almost 60 percent in 1960.

The estimates of outstanding direct investments are in U.S. dollars and reflect the increased dollar value of many foreign currencies. As a result of the depreciation of the U.S. dollar beginning in August 1971, Japanese and the principal European investors, other than those from the United Kingdom, were able by 1974 to buy on the average 35–45 percent more in dollar-denominated assets for the same amount of national currency. It is not surprising, therefore, that about one fourth of the total 1971–74 increase in foreign direct investment by non-U.S. countries went to the United States.

FOREIGN INVESTMENT PATTERNS BY RECIPIENT COUNTRIES

Which nations are the principal recipients of foreign direct investment and the host countries for foreign multinational firms? In general, with the exception of Japan, the industrialized countries are the major home and host countries for foreign investment. Canada stands out as the country that has absorbed the largest absolute amount of direct investment, about $33 billion in 1973, and has the largest share of total domestic output accounted for by foreign enterprises. In the early 1970s, foreign affiliates accounted for 60 percent of manufacturing output, 65 percent of output in mining and smelting, and 75 percent of Canada's petroleum and natural gas industry.

The United States is the second most important recipient of foreign direct investment—$26.5 billion in 1974.[14] But this large amount still represents a relatively small portion of the country's business activity. If the U.S.-based multinationals are included in an estimate of the share of U.S. domestic output controlled by multinationals, on the assumption that they are not truly domestic-oriented firms, the comparison with Canada is less dramatic.

---

[12]See U.S. Department of Commerce, *Foreign Direct Investment in the* United States (Washington, D.C.: U.S. Government Printing Office, 1976).

[13]United Nations, *Multinational Corporations in World Development* (New York: UN, 1973), p. 139.

[14]U.S. Department of Commerce, *Foreign Direct Investment in the United States.*

Although geographical patterns of international business are complex, two clear types of patterns have evolved. One is that of geographical proximity. The United States and Canada have become closely intertwined in international business. Almost 22 percent of U.S. exports and 24 percent of U.S. direct investment are in Canada. Conversely, the United States accounts for 51 percent of Canadian foreign direct investment and 63 percent of Canadian exports. Similar patterns prevail among the European countries. The largest investment flows from West Germany, Italy, the Netherlands, and Belgium are to other European countries, and French investments in Europe are probably only second to those in the "franc area." Much of Japan's trade and a growing share of its overseas investments are in Asia.

A second pattern is a close international business relationship continuing between the former colonial powers and their former colonies. British overseas investment and foreign trade are heavily with the Commonwealth countries, which were once British colonies. The French trade and investment relationships are predominantly with the former colonial area, now referred to as the "franc area." The United States is strongly tied in trade and investment to the Philippines.

In general, international business activity among the industrialized or advanced countries is greatest in size and has been growing most rapidly. Twelve investor countries, with less than one quarter of the population of the noncommunist world, "control" probably 90 percent of multinational business. The remaining noncommunist countries, whose 2 billion population represents three quarters of the noncommunist world, participate in international business almost exclusively through exports. In 1974, they accounted for 37 percent of total noncommunist world exports.

The less developed countries (LDC) in 1968 accounted for about one third of the value of total foreign direct investment as opposed to one sixth of world domestic product and one fifth of world exports, not including centrally planned economies.[15] More recent global estimates are not available, but the LDC share appears to have declined since 1968. Much of this direct investment was concentrated in a relatively few developing countries such as Argentina, Brazil, India, Mexico, Nigeria, Venezuela, and certain Caribbean islands. The situation in Brazil, for which recent data are available, reflects the changing relative importance of the investor countries. In 1969, U.S. firms accounted for 50 percent of total registered foreign investment. But by 1974, the U.S. share of a rapidly expanding foreign sector had declined

---

[15]United Nations, *Multinational Corporations in World Development*, p. 18.

to 34 percent as compared to 12 percent for German firms, 10 percent for Japanese companies, and 9 percent for Swiss enterprises.[16]

Paradoxical as it may seem, multinationals have also become active in the communist countries of Eastern Europe under imaginative arrangements that testify to the flexibility of the multinationals and the pragmatism of many political ideologists. In a search for better ways to secure Western technology and lower the costs of acquiring know-how, Eastern European policy makers turned to industrial cooperation agreements and "co-production" ventures with Western multinationals. At the beginning of 1973, an estimated 600 industrial cooperation agreements with Eastern European countries were in force.[17] Yugoslavia had 375 industrial cooperation agreements and 72 ventures in which foreign firms had equity participation.[18] The large bulk of these were with West German and Italian companies. Under the industrial cooperation agreements, the Western firm typically provides machinery, advanced technology, assistance in management plus the use of its world marketing channels; it is compensated by keeping part of the physical product or a portion of the foreign exchange earned through sales abroad.[19]

PRODUCT COMPOSITION OF WORLD TRADE

Manufactured goods account for the dominant share of world trade as well as foreign production. As shown in Table 2–3, exports of manufactures as a share of the total value of exports increased from 50 percent in 1960 to 62 percent in 1972. This share receded during 1973–74, however, because of the rapid escalation in the prices of agricultural products and fuels, due to world shortages in many commodities and the effectiveness of the cartel of oil-producing countries in quadrupling the international price for petroleum.

The underlying trend toward an increased share for manufactures is partially explained by world trends toward industrialization and mechanization, which have increased the demand for producer goods. Another factor has been the so-called Engel's law. The law stems from

---

[16]Stefan H. Robock, *Brazil: A Study in Development Progress* (Lexington, Mass.: D.C. Heath & Co., 1975), p. 67.

[17]United Nations, *Multinational Corporations in World Development*, pp. 21–23.

[18]Patrick J. Nichols, "Western Investment in Eastern Europe: The Yugoslav Example," in *Reorientation and Commercial Relations of the Economies of Eastern Europe* (Washington, D.C.: U.S. Government Printing Office, 1974), p. 735.

[19]For a discussion of the benefits of these agreements to the multinational corporations and to the Eastern European socialist economies, see Geza P. Lauter and Paul M. Dickie, *Multinational Corporations and East European Socialist Economies* (New York: Praeger Publishers, 1975), pp. 60–86.

TABLE 2–3
Development of World Exports and Production between 1960 and 1974

	1960	1963	1968	1969	1970	1971	1972	1973	1974
World exports									
Value (billion dollars f.o.b.)									
Total..................	129	155	240	274	313	351	417	575	(848)
Agricultural products	40	45	54	58	64	69	83	120	(148)
Minerals*..............	22	26	41	45	52	57	65	96	(224)
Manufactures	65	82	141	165	192	217	260	348	(459)
Unit value (1960 = 100)									
Total..................	100	100	104	107	113	119	130	162	(225)
Agricultural products	100	100	99	104	107	111	126	190	(238)
Minerals*..............	100	99	110	115	123	131	142	185	(450)
Manufactures	100	100	106	108	114	123	134	153	(185)
Volume (1960 = 100)									
Total..................	100	120	178	199	215	229	249	276	(293)
Agricultural products	100	111	136	139	150	155	164	158	(155)
Minerals*..............	100	120	172	181	195	202	214	240	(232)
Manufactures	100	126	205	236	260	273	300	351	(384)
World commodity output									
Volume (1960 = 100)									
All commodities	100	115	155	164	170	177	186	202	(208)
Agriculture..............	100	107	125	126	129	134	133	139	(140)
Mining	100	115	147	154	167	172	180	187	(192)
Manufacturing	100	119	169	182	188	196	211	232	(240)

*Including fuels and nonferrous metals.
Source: General Agreement on Tariffs and Trade, *International Trade 1974/75* (Geneva: GATT, 1975), p. 2.

a study of the spending patterns of 153 Belgian households carried out in the late 19th century by Ernst Engel, a German statistician, and states that as income grows the demand for food grows at a lesser rate. In statistical jargon, the demand for food has an income elasticity of less than 1. A corollary of Engel's law is that with rising income, consumers spend increasing proportions on nonfood products— generally manufactured goods. The logic of Engel's law is that the capacity of individuals to increase their consumption of necessities is more limited than their capacity to enlarge their consumption of luxuries.

Within the manufacturing category, the most important subgroups of exports are engineering products, chemicals, and road motor vehicles, which together account for about 60 percent of the total value of manufactured exports. These are also important product areas for foreign production. In contrast, two other significant export product categories—iron and steel and textiles and clothing—are significant in export trade but not as areas for foreign production.

The export of agricultural products, including food and agricultural raw materials, has been steadily declining as a share of the value of world exports, dropping from 31 percent of the total in 1960 to 18 percent in 1974. A few international business firms operate tea, fruit, and sugar plantations, mainly as a vestige of the colonial era, but direct foreign investment in food production is small and declining. On the other hand, international trading companies are extremely important as exporters and importers of food products. Agricultural raw materials such as natural fibers, hides and skins, and natural rubber as well as timber and pulp are important in trade but not in foreign production.

The share of fuels and minerals in world exports remained rather constant until petroleum prices escalated dramatically in 1974. Foreign direct investment and foreign production still remain large in the petroleum and minerals field, even though many producing countries have developed a capacity to exploit their natural resources through domestic companies frequently owned by the government.

Technological developments have affected international trade and production patterns through such advances as synthetic substitutes for natural raw materials, improved production processes, and new discovery and exploration techniques for natural resources. In the food category, synthetic materials have been substituting for oils, fats, and sugar. In raw materials, synthetic fibers have been substituting for natural fibers, synthetic rubber for natural rubber, and plastics for metals; and processing improvements have reduced the raw material requirements for a given level of output in numerous cases. Synthetic substitutes are being produced domestically in many countries as replacements for imports, often by international enterprises. Also, mineral-exporting countries have succeeded in having raw materials further processed in the country before export, with the result that raw material transfers are decreased and manufactures increased.

SUMMARY

International business activity is large and growing rapidly. Furthermore, when measurement is extended to include all the business that falls under the control of multinational firms, it already represents a significant proportion of total world business.

While it is possible to get an overview of the general size and trends in international business, the estimates and analyses presented in this chapter are of necessity rough. They do not have the precision to answer the specific policy questions of international agencies, governments, or the international businesses themselves. A determined effort to collect figures that depict what is really happening in the world today is urgently needed. A prerequisite for this effort would be a much wider realization that today's world no longer fits the theoretically assumed image of how imports and exports work. Countries do not export, firms do. It is of little use to base policy making on a fiction.

EXERCISES AND DISCUSSION QUESTIONS

1. Write a report for government officials of a specified country suggesting a program for statistical collection with a view to monitoring and controlling multinational business operations as they affect the country. Explain the concepts you think are relevant and indicate the data requirements as precisely as you can.

2. For a selected minor country, assess the size and roles of multinational business within its economy. Indicate the sources of your information and how you have arrived at your particular estimates.

3. To what extent has the expansion in world exports (see Table 2–3) been due to price increases rather than to volume increases?

4. In what ways do traditional industrial location factors differ for international projects as compared to domestic projects?

3

International Business Theories

BUSINESS ACTIVITY across national boundaries was for many centuries predominantly importing and exporting between independent firms which did not have operations in more than one country. In such a world, international trade and international business were considered synonymous. It was logical to look to international trade theory as a framework for understanding current patterns and anticipating future trends in international business relations.

With the emergence of the multinational firm and the resulting dramatic change in patterns of inter-nation business and in the structure of the world economy, trade theory has proved to be too limited for explaining the current realities of international business. Theoretical and empirical studies of direct private-investment flows have added to our understanding of the role of the international corporation. Yet the development of a theoretical basis or framework for explaining and predicting international business patterns is still in an early stage. There has been no movement to discard trade theory. But something more is needed. The task is difficult because it is no longer realistic to neglect the business firm and the way its decisions affect patterns of activity. The macro theories of international economics must be integrated with the micro theories of the behavior of the firm.

This chapter examines the limitations of traditional theories and summarizes the various new theories of international business that have been advanced. It will attempt also to provide a satisfactory explanation of the rationale for the why and how of multinational business and develop a framework for interpreting the international business patterns described in Chapter 2. The explanatory requirements imply answers to questions such as the following:[1]

Why and under what circumstances do firms "go international"?

Why do firms expand abroad by means of foreign direct investment rather than through alternative strategies such as exporting or importing, licensing, portfolio investment, or loan-purchase agreements?

What advantages do foreign investors have over local firms that enable them to overcome the inherent diseconomies of foreign operations?

Why do a few countries tend to be mainly the source of, and many others the recipients of, foreign direct investment?

Why does foreign direct investment occur in certain industries and not in others?

Why does cross-investment take place in the same industry?

RELATED THEORIES

International Trade Theory

With its long history and high refinement, international trade theory continues to shape much business thinking and, even more so, the actions of government. For this reason, the international manager needs to be reasonably conversant with it even though trade theory has only limited utility for explaining the modern international business era. Because it still constitutes the rationale for many features of the environment within which the manager must operate, it is reviewed in some detail in Chapter 6. At this point, however, the emphasis is on trade theory's limitations for explaining the forces underlying the growth of international business.

The main questions with which "pure" or "orthodox" trade theory is concerned are: Why do countries import and export the sorts of products they do, and at what relative prices or terms of trade? How are these trade flows related to the characteristics of a country and how do they affect domestic factor prices? What are the effects of trade intervention such as tariffs? What are the gains from trade and how are they divided among trading countries?[2] Within trade theory, the foundation stone for explaining patterns and gains from trade is the *doctrine* or *law of comparative advantage*. The doctrine demonstrates

---

[1]See Thomas N. Gladwin and Ian H. Giddy, *A Survey of Foreign Direct Investment Theory* (Ann Arbor: Division of Research, Graduate School of Business Administration, University of Michigan, November 1973), pp. 6–7.

[2]See Charles P. Kindleberger, *International Economics*, 5th ed. (Homewood, Ill.: Richard D. Irwin, Inc., 1973), pp. 17–104.

that if a country specializes in those products in which it has the greatest *comparative advantage* relative to other nations and trades those products for goods in which it has the greatest *comparative disadvantage,* the total availability of goods secured by the country with a given amount of resources will be enlarged. In other words, by emphasizing *comparative* rather than *absolute* advantages, the doctrine shows that every country has a basis for trade and that specialization and trade are more efficient than policies of national self-sufficiency.

But trade theory did not anticipate nor does it explain the internationalization of business in forms other than the international movements of goods. In part, this failure results from the assumptions of orthodox theory that the factors of production (land, labor, and capital) remain fixed within each country, that lack of information is not a limitation on exploiting international trade opportunities, and that trading firms in different countries are entirely distinct from each other. Furthermore, trade theory does not allow for oligopoly or monopoly, and does not explicitly recognize technology, know-how, or management and marketing skills as significant factors of production which can be the basis for comparative advantage.[3]

The limitations of trade theory also stem from the way the question is posed. Trade theory asks the question, "Why do countries trade?" This is the wrong question. Businessmen trade and, increasingly, they transfer goods across national boundaries for their own business activities without selling them outside their organization. The question should be, "Why are goods and services transferred between countries?"

When this question is answered, it is clear that the decision-making unit is the business enterprise and not the country. To be sure, decisions are heavily influenced by government actions. Nevertheless, business decisions by international corporations—not traditional trade concepts—have become the focal point for explaining most of what happens internationally. Moreover, an explanation of international business actions provides an integrated account of the transfer of investment and working capital as well as the transfer of goods.

The business firm has numerous ways besides traditional importing and exporting for supplying foreign markets or securing foreign goods. It can supply foreign demand through licensing or foreign production. It can secure foreign goods through direct-investment projects. Orthodox theory rules out these options through its limiting assumptions. It

---

[3]See Raymond Vernon, "The Location of Economic Activity" in *Economic Analysis and the Multinational Enterprise,* ed. John H. Dunning (New York: Praeger Publishers, 1974), p. 90.

also misses the rationale behind the 20th century development of marketing by assuming that commodities sold in the international marketplace are standard, basic, and transferrable—wheat, cotton, and wine, for example. Today's firms, however, are continually adjusting many dimensions of their products against their assessments of customer wants—against the market. There is no simple standard commodity.

More and more firms are putting together marketing strategies for world markets, not just their home markets. Starting from an assessment of world markets, the decision maker tends to identify his market objectives and work backward to arrive at his location of production and distribution pattern. As the markets change, so do the patterns of activity of the international firms, and these patterns loom large in the changes in the international position of individual national economies.

The implications of the multinational enterprise for international trade theory have begun to receive serious attention by economic theorists and considerable reconstruction is underway particularly to allow for some internationally mobile factors.[4] But the emphasis of the reconstruction efforts is more on ways to make traditional theory more relevant than on developing a theoretical framework for explaining the multinational enterprise phenomenon.

Direct Investment Theories

International economics has devoted considerable attention to international capital movements as well as to international commodity flows. In the capital field, issues of importance for understanding international business patterns are being considered under the heading of *direct investment,* that is, investment that carries with it decision-making control by the foreign investor as contrasted to *portfolio investment,* which does not.

The general theory of international capital flows suggests that capital will move from one country to another in response to differences in the marginal productivity of capital. In other words, capital will move from where it is abundant to where it is scarce, or from countries where rates of return are low to countries where they are high. However, in recent years the flows of direct-investment capital have been increasing sizeably and rapidly, and the general theory does not explain the patterns in a satisfactory way. For example, there are substantial two-way flows of direct investment capital. American

---

[4]See W. M. Corden, "The Theory of International Trade" in *Economic Analysis and the Multinational Enterprise,* ed. John H. Dunning (New York: Praeger Publishers, 1974), pp. 184–210.

enterprises are making large direct investments in Europe at the same time that European firms are making substantial direct investments in the United States. Furthermore, direct investment often does not involve an international capital movement. Business firms have been increasing their foreign direct investment by borrowing funds in the local country.

To explain direct-investment patterns, international economists have enlarged their framework of international investment theory to recognize the role of the multinational corporation. In effect, this is a beginning step toward integrating the micro theory of the firm with the macro theory of international capital movements.

Various direct-investment theories have been advanced by economists.[5] One view has been that direct investment represents not so much an international capital movement as capital formation undertaken abroad. Another has been the "defensive investment" concept of Alexander Lamfalussy.[6] Direct investment is undertaken where there are large and growing markets regardless of immediate profitability. In this view, where markets exist, profits will be found in the long run. Still another theory explains foreign direct investment as a currency phenomenon brought about by the market's preference for holding assets denominated in selected currencies. As Aliber argues, "If the world were a unified currency area, exchange risk and a currency premium would not exist: then the analysis of direct foreign investment would be in terms of the economics of location."[7] Imperfections in capital markets have also been advanced as factors explaining foreign direct investment.[8]

Business Management Studies

The field of business management has long had a predominantly domestic orientation. Several current lines of research in the management studies field, however, contribute to our understanding of international business patterns.

One of the most valuable lines of investigation has been the effort to identify forces likely to enlarge the geographical horizon of the

[5]See Giorgio Ragazzi, "Theories of the Determinants of Direct Foreign Investment," *International Monetary Fund Staff Papers*, July 1973, pp. 471–98; Guy V. G. Stevens, "The Determinants of Investment," in *Economic Analysis and the Multinational Enterprise*, ed. Dunning, p. 47–88.

[6]Alexander Lamfalussy, *Investment and Growth in Mature Economies* (Oxford, England: Basil Blackwell & Mott, Ltd., 1961).

[7]Robert Z. Aliber, "A Theory of Direct Foreign Investment," in *The International Corporation*, ed. Charles P. Kindleberger (Cambridge, Mass.: The M.I.T. Press, 1970), p. 34.

[8]Ragazzi, "Theories of the Determinants of Direct Foreign Investment," pp. 480–84.

business enterprise. In a utopian world the issue of geographical horizon would not arise because the business firm and business managers would be aware of and prepared to take advantage of attractive business opportunities wherever they exist. The reality is that the business firm is usually born with a geographical horizon limited to a locality, a region, or the home country. Until recently, most business enterprises did not bother to look at the possibilities of investing or establishing operations outside their home country.

As Aharoni has suggested, "Companies do not in practice reject such investment opportunities because the expected profits are not sufficient to compensate for the risks involved; they simply do not bother to devote the time and effort necessary to calculate the rate of return on such investments."[9] Brilliant foreign opportunities may have existed which the enterprise was not aware of, or not interested in, because they were beyond the geographical horizon of the enterprise.

But the horizon of the business firm is not necessarily static or immutable. Geographical horizons can be changed by forces arising within the organization and by exogenous forces stemming from its environment. We will examine these forces in greater detail below.

In a related but independent direction, other management studies are examining and classifying business enterprises by their management philosophies and policies in international business operations. A behaviorally oriented model elaborated by both Howard Perlmutter and Hans Thorelli focuses on three distinct management philosophies adopted by firms with international operations.[10] Firms are classified as ethnocentric (monocentric), polycentric, or geocentric (cosmopolitan).

The ethnocentric firm is essentially home oriented and has chosen to ignore environmental variables. The polycentric firm is mainly host-country oriented and frequently overwhelmed by the differences between its many operating environments. The geocentric or cosmopolitan firm has as its ultimate goal a worldwide approach in both headquarters and subsidiaries.

The taxonomy or classification of managerial philosophies is directly related to the topic of global strategies for international business operations to be considered in Part V. As a contribution to explaining the forces underlying international business patterns, the

---

[9]Yair Aharoni, *The Foreign Investment Decision Process* (Boston, Mass.: Division of Research, Graduate School of Business Administration, Harvard University, 1966), p. 50.

[10]Howard V. Perlmutter, "Social Architectural Problems of the Multinational Firm," *Quarterly Journal of AIESEC International* 3, no. 3 (August 1967): 33–44; Hans B. Thorelli, "The Multinational Corporation as a Change Agent," *Southern Journal of Business* 1, no. 3 (July 1966): 1–9.

classification suggests a path along which many business enterprises may be moving in their evolution from predominantly domestic-oriented firms to fully internationalized horizons.

NEW APPROACHES

The Oligopoly Model

A major advance toward developing a theory of international business came from the oligopoly model for explaining direct investment.[11] This view shifts the focus from macro theories of international capital movements to the motivations and behavior of the business firm as developed in industrial organization theory. According to the oligopoly model, the business firm makes foreign direct investments to exploit some quasi-monopoly advantage it holds. The advantage of a foreign firm over a local enterprise may be in the form of technology, access to capital, differentiated products built on advertising, superior management, or organizational scale. The special asset of the foreign firm must be important enough to more than offset the disadvantages of its alien status and the additional costs of operating at a distance and in a foreign environment. The firm must also find production abroad preferable to any other means of extracting this rent from a foreign market, such as exporting or licensing an established foreign producer.[12]

In addition to explaining "horizontal investments" for foreign production of the same goods produced in the home market, the oligopoly model has been offered as an explanation for "vertical" direct investments to produce abroad a raw material or other input to the production process at home. By controlling input sources, existing firms in an oligopolistic industry may raise barriers to the entry of new competitors and protect their oligopoly position. Cross-investments such as Lever Brothers, the British-Dutch company operating in the United States, and Proctor & Gamble operating in the United Kingdom and the Netherlands are also explained as defensive oligopoly behavior. In an industry with a small number of firms, each company must do as the others to prevent another from getting an unanticipated advantage.

The oligopoly model begins to merge the approaches of economics and management studies. It helps to identify the industries in which

---

[11]Stephen H. Hymer, *The International Operations of National Firms: A Study of Direct Investment* (Cambridge, Mass: M.I.T. Press, 1976).

[12]Richard E. Caves, "International Corporations: The Industrial Economics of Foreign Investment," *Economica* 38 (February 1971): 5–6.

direct investment occurs and to understand patterns of cross investment. The model also leaves many important questions unanswered. Why have firms only recently begun to exploit their quasi-monopolies on such a large scale? Have the quasi-monopolies only recently been achieved? Or have many of the quasi-monopolies existed for some time, but the business enterprise had not yet internationalized its business horizon? Why do some firms within an industry invest abroad and not others?[13] Also, as Cooper has noted, the model can explain continued rapid expansion in foreign investment only to the extent that the special advantages of the investing firm are increasing. Such special advantages may be increasing in certain research-oriented or high-technology fields but are not increasing in other fields that are also expanding.[14] Still other limitations are that the theory is not integrated with alternative ways such as exports or licensing, through which the firm might exploit foreign markets, nor can the theory explain adequately foreign investment through takeovers.[15] In sum, the oligopoly model is a partial analysis of the enterprise's behavior but does not incorporate the full range of issues inherent in the evolution and implementation of global business strategy.

The Product Cycle Model

The product cycle model, associated with the work of Raymond Vernon, has contributed significantly to a better understanding of the evolution of many U.S. multinational enterprises. In explaining direct-investment patterns, the model suggests a sequence of events that are a function of the evolution of a product and emphasizes innovation and oligopoly position as a basis for exports and later direct investment.[16]

In the product cycle model, a firm's international involvement follows sequential stages in the life cycle of the product it innovates. The sequence begins with the *new product stage* in which the product is manufactured in the United States and introduced into foreign markets through exports. In the *mature product stage,* as technology becomes sufficiently routine to be transferred, as a firm's export

---

[13]See Thomas Horst, "Firm and Industry Determinants of the Decision to Invest Abroad: An Empirical Study," *Review of Economics and Statistics,* 54, August 1972, pp. 258-66.

[14]Richard N. Cooper, *The Economics of Interdependence: Economic Policy in the Atlantic Community* (New York: McGraw-Hill Book Co., 1968), p. 89.

[15]Aliber, "Direct Foreign Investment," p. 20.

[16]Raymond Vernon, "International Investment and International Trade in the Product Cycle," *Quarterly Journal of Economics,* May 1966, pp. 190–207; Vernon, *Sovereignty at Bay* (New York: Basic Books, 1971), pp. 65–112.

position becomes threatened, and as foreign demand expands to the point that it can support a production facility of economic size, the enterprise is induced to produce abroad—generally in other advanced countries. In a third stage, the *standardized product stage,* production may shift to low-cost locations in the less developed countries from which goods may be exported back to the home country and other markets.

The home-country location in the first stage is explained by Vernon as the need during the experimental period for having swift communication within the enterprise and with suppliers and customers. Also, when a product is new, profit margins may be high and cost considerations are likely to be less important than at a later stage. The decision to set up foreign manufacturing facilities is explained as a response to a perceived threat to the firm's export position and an effort to retain an oligopolistic advantage. In the final stage, cost considerations become the principal determinant of location.

The product cycle model has been useful for explaining the past history of some U.S.-controlled enterprises, particularly in the manufacturing field.[17] But as Vernon himself has concluded, "Though this may be an efficient way to look at enterprises in the U.S. economy that are on the threshold of developing a foreign business, the model is losing some of its relevance for those enterprises that have long since acquired a global scanning capacity and a global habit of mind."[18]

Another observation that can be made concerning the product cycle model is the limited use it makes of location economies. The sequence of moving from exports to the establishment of decentralized producing facilities has been an evolutionary pattern for market-oriented industries within the United States. The automobile industry was initially centralized in the Detroit area. As demand increased in specific regions of the United States to a point that justified establishing an economic assembly operation, the economics of location (mainly savings in transport costs of components as compared to assembled automobiles) stimulated the enterprise to make direct domestic investments elsewhere. The decentralization of the rubber tire industry from Akron, Ohio, to virtually all regions of the United States is another example of expanding markets and location economics.[19]

---

[17]For example, see L. T. Wells, Jr., "Test of a Product Cycle Model of International Trade," *Quarterly Journal of Economics* 83 (February 1969): 152–62; R. B. Stobaugh. "The Product Cycle, U.S. Exports and International Investment" (D.B.A. thesis, Harvard Business School, June 1968).

[18]Vernon, *Sovereignty at Bay,* p. 107.

[19]Glenn E. McLaughlin and Stefan Robock, *Why Industry Moves South* (Washington, D.C.: National Planning Association, 1949).

A firm "going international" frequently follows a similar sequence from exports to foreign production, motivated by location economics rather than by the maturing of a product or an oligopoly threat. A shift from exports to foreign production can also be stimulated by special international factors such as major currency realignments or import restrictions. For example, the drastic devaluation of the U.S. dollar in the early 1970s in relation to most of the other major world currencies changed dramatically the economics of serving the U.S. market by exports from Europe and Japan as against direct investment in the United States. An increase of almost 50 percent in the value of the deutsche mark in terms of U.S. dollars from 1970 to 1975 was a major factor in the decision of a company like Volkswagen, which had been unusually successful in penetrating the U.S. market through exports, to establish a production facility in the United States.

The location-economics approach complements the emphasis of the product cycle on innovation and oligopoly threat. It also explains why some products such as aircraft and industrial machinery continue to be exported even when they become a "mature" product because of limited potential for savings through a market location, and why an overvalued U.S. dollar which prevailed for many years encouraged U.S. firms to serve foreign markets through foreign production and non-U.S. firms to serve the U.S. market through exports.

International Transmission of Resources

A comprehensive framework for explaining international business patterns has been formulated around the role of the multinational firm in the transmission of economic resources among nations.[20] Extending the basic philosophy of resource transfers embodied in trade theory, Fayerweather enlarges the concept of resources to include technological, managerial, and entrepreneurial skills, as well as natural resources, capital, and labor. He then argues that differentials in the supply-demand relationship of resources among countries generate basic economic pressures for the inter-nation flow of resources and create opportunities open to the multinational firm. Governmental actions or policies distort or reshape these resource-differential relationships as basically determined by free economic forces into the actual patterns of opportunities open to the firm. In responding to these opportunities, the types of resources transmitted, the selection of countries, and the choice of transmission methods depend on the characteristics and

---

[20]John Fayerweather, "International Transmission of Resources," in *International Business Management: A Conceptual Framework* (New York: McGraw-Hill Book Co., 1969), pp. 15–50.

strategy of specific multinational firms. In sum, three groups of factors—resource differentials, governmental actions, and characteristics of the business enterprise—determine the way in which the multinational firm plays a role in the international transmission of resources.

Fayerweather's conceptual framework broadly encompasses economic concepts related to international trade and investment as well as behavioral models of the business enterprise. It recognizes oligopoly elements as a stimulus to foreign investment by including oligopoly advantages within the broad category of skill resources. It assigns a major role to governments in influencing international business patterns through actions that affect resource-differential relationships and the entry conditions for foreign enterprise. It distinguishes the resource transmission role of the multinational firm from that of the strictly national firm in two ways. Having developed a global horizon, the multinational firm is concerned with resource differentials among countries. It is also critically concerned with the institutional constraints of nations which affect the flow of resources among nations.

As a model for explaining and predicting international business patterns in a world where many business enterprises have developed global horizons, the Fayerweather framework makes a significant contribution. It is general enough so that most dimensions of international management can be incorporated within it. It does not, however, address itself to the process by which essentially domestic firms acquire their global horizons, nor does it attempt to provide a general theory of the evolutionary history of international business expansion. Furthermore, it appears to be predominantly concerned with manufacturing activities and the role of markets in motivating international expansion.

THE EVOLUTION OF INTERNATIONAL BUSINESS: AN HISTORICAL MODEL

Practice has clearly run ahead of theory in the international business field. Yet considerable progress has been made in identifying underlying forces and in formulating conceptual frameworks for understanding and predicting international business activities. In summarizing the present state of knowledge, it is helpful to deal separately with two interrelated components of the complex subject, namely, the historical evolution of international business and the normative behavior of the multinational enterprise.

Turning to the historical model, the forces underlying the recent emergence of international business to a dominant role in the world economy can be conveniently grouped into three categories: environmental forces, technological trends, and the growth process of the business enterprise. The purpose of the model is to explain the timing of international business expansion, the industrial patterns, the nationality of multinational enterprises, and the countries into which expansion has occurred. All of the elements, of course, are part of an interdependent system with feedback interrelationships.

Environmental Forces

An Expansionist World Economy. The most pervasive force shaping the timing, size, and structure of international business expansion was the unprecedented and sustained economic growth of the world economy after the early 1950s. The expanding economic environment generated new levels and patterns of demand. It permitted enterprises to mature and grow. And the higher individual incomes that resulted from overall growth meant more than proportionate increases in consumer demand for manufactured and luxury goods of the type that created special opportunities for international enterprises.

Increased demands for natural resources stimulated both public and private investment in resource exploration and development. With improved technology for exploration, many new sources of raw materials have been discovered throughout the world.

International business has both contributed to and benefited from accelerated world-growth trends. Most certainly, a return to the worldwide depression environment of the 1930s or to the historical patterns of frequent business cycles would not have encouraged international trade expansion or the rapid growth of foreign production.

Improved Inter-Nation Framework. Another unique feature of the post-World War II period was the cooperative efforts of the principal nation-states to improve the international financial system so as to facilitate financial transactions between nations. The major nations also supported inter-governmental agreements to reduce trade barriers. The moves to create free trade and common market areas stimulated the expansionist world economy and facilitated the emergence of new patterns of international business activity.

National Economic Environments. National policies can stimulate both inflows and outflows of direct investment, and most home and host countries have been generally favorable toward the growth of international trade and foreign production. Most nations have adopted aggressive and ambitious economic development goals that assigned a high priority to industrial expansion. In many cases, industrialization goals have been easiest to fulfill by attracting foreign enterprise. In other cases, however, for reasons of national security and public policy, governments have limited certain fields of business activity to domestic enterprises and often to government enterprises.

Adverse national economic conditions in their home country can stimulate multinationals to expand abroad. In Japan, for example, domestic investment was hampered during the 1970s by labor shortages, rising labor costs, a scarcity of land, and pollution problems.

National Political Environments. Political goals of national governments have long shaped patterns of international trade and investment. During past periods of colonial expansionist aspirations by many national governments, the phenomenon was referred to as "trade follows the flag." Although colonial relationships have gone out of style, other political goals of nations have fostered the post-World War II expansion of international business. For political reasons, some nations are supporting policies to assist the less developed countries (LDC) by establishing special lending and risk-insurance programs to encourage national firms to undertake business projects in the LDCs. During hot periods in the cold war between the United States and the USSR, the United States provided special incentives for business firms willing to invest in a battleground country like India to meet the Soviet competition of low-interest foreign loans.

Technological Trends

A new era of expanded research and accelerated technological development followed the end of World War II. A deluge of new products and new processes shaped demand patterns and created new business opportunities for technologically dynamic enterprises. New technology, as noted above, stimulated and assisted in the discovery and exploitation of natural resources. Technological developments, particularly in computers, communications, and transportation, spurred and supported the evolution of the business firm from domestic to global horizons.

Trends in technological progress are often associated with national environments. Consequently, they explain a great deal about the nationality of the emerging multinational enterprises. At the end of World War II, the United States enjoyed overwhelming technological superiority (then called the "technology gap") in a vast range of product and process areas. The national defense and space programs of the U.S. government were a major force in creating technological advantages which have been exploited internationally by U.S. business firms. Furthermore, as a result of the disruption of two world wars, Europe had lost its traditional technological lead in such fields as chemicals and pharmaceuticals. In the areas of management and marketing, U.S. firms had also developed advanced capabilities.

New technology tended to alert business firms to foreign market opportunities and new sources of resource inputs as explained in the product cycle thesis. It provided oligopoly elements that gave foreign enterprises a competitive advantage over local firms. It follows that much of the postwar expansion of international business was in science-based or research-intensive industries in rapid-growth sectors and by U.S. enterprises.

Over the past two decades, Western Europe and Japan have been closing the technology gap. These nations borrowed heavily from U.S. technology and created strong research and development capabilities of their own. Furthermore, due to growing resource scarcities and higher prices during the 1970s, many energy-saving and resource-economizing products and processes already being used in Europe and Japan became a technology advantage for foreign direct investment in the United States.[21] This shift in the technology balance partially explains the recent acceleration of foreign direct investment by European and Japanese firms and the increased flow of such investments into the United States.

The Growth Process of the Business Enterprise

The business enterprise, particularly in the industrialized countries, has been accelerating its capabilities greatly in recent years. For many centuries, the gaps among nations in business capability were not sufficiently large to stimulate a rapid growth in multinational business operations. Business firms were generally small in relation to their national markets, and the nature of business operations was relatively simple. But significant advances in transportation, communications, and computer technology have made the world smaller and now place few limits on the geographic area within which the enterprise can operate efficiently. Many firms have grown dramatically in size and resources and are no longer small in relation to their national markets, even in the United States.

At the same time, the complexity of business operations and the resource requirements for an optimal-sized enterprise have escalated manifoldly. Business has become more capital intensive. Research, development, and technology have become more sophisticated and more proprietary. Management functions at many levels are requiring highly advanced skills. With such an acceleration in the capability of the business firm and in the requirements for managers and other business employees, disparities among the managers and firms of different nations have widened. The potential for enterprises to have competitive advantages that are sizable enough to justify taking the additional risks of international operations has increased phenomenally.

As its capability expanded and the opportunities for foreign opera-

---

[21]See Lawrence G. Franko, *The European Multinationals* (Stamford, Conn.: Greylock Publishers, 1976).

tions multiplied, the business enterprise became fertile ground for stimuli that extended the firm's horizon beyond its domestic market. For some firms, an international horizon was only an advanced stage on its learning curve, and the evolution to a global strategy was relatively continuous. For many other enterprises, including relatively large companies in the United States, the move to an international horizon involved an abrupt change in behavior and a major transformation in business thinking.

The study of geographical business horizons involves broad questions of individual and social behavior patterns. The variables are many and complex, yet some order seems to exist. The patterns can be simplified by grouping the motivating forces into two general categories, namely, factors internal to the firm and external forces. The categories are not mutually exclusive because the horizon-extending stimulus may come both from within and from outside of the firm.[22] Some of the principal internal forces for internationalizing horizons have been the influence of a high executive, the development of new technology or products, dependence on foreign sources for raw materials, the desire to find a use for old machinery, the accumulation of excess internally generated investment funds, and the observed need for a larger market. Illustrative of external forces are the influence of customers, the initiative of foreign governments, the pressure and example of competitors, the more general social pressure in business circles that leads to the "bandwagon effect,"[23] the stage of economic development of the home country, the home country's political aspirations, and the occurrence of a dramatic event such as the formation of the European Common Market.

As business enterprises gradually evolved into transnational institutions, their early motivations for establishing foreign production facilities were generally responses to specific opportunities or threats rather than the implementation of a comprehensive global strategy. In some cases, the firm went international as a "market seeker," expanding the production and sale of present products into new markets. In other cases, the firm's move abroad was primarily as a "raw materials seeker," particularly in petroleum and mining. A third group was the "production efficiency seeker," looking for lower costs of production through labor costs but sometimes through lower costs of power or another input. Sometimes a search for knowledge was combined with a search for markets, as in the case of some European firms interested in

---

[22]Yair Aharoni, "The Decision to Look Abroad," in *Foreign Investment Decision Process*, pp. 49–75.

[23]F. T. Knickerbocker, *Oligopolistic Reaction and Multinational Enterprise* (Boston: Division of Research, Harvard Graduate School of Business Administration, 1973).

acquiring marketing and product development experience in U.S. markets that could be fed back into other operations.[24] As the firm developed a global horizon, all of these components became an integral part of a total global strategy.

A RATIONAL MODEL FOR THE GLOBAL BUSINESS FIRM

The key element for explaining and predicting international business patterns is the role of the enterprise and its evolution from a predominantly domestic firm to one with a global orientation. At the present stage of the world economy, the enterprise with a global horizon and strategy is still far from representative of all firms engaging in international business. Yet the tendency for evolving into a global enterprise appears to be inherent in the process of a firm going international. The rational global model, which forms the foundation for Part V—Managing the Multinational Enterprise, should be introduced at this point as being representative of the behavior patterns of a large and ever-increasing number of enterprises conducting business activities across national boundaries. The assumption is that the rational global model will shortly become the representative model.

In the rational model, the business firm evolves to the stage where it has a world horizon and a global strategy. It attempts to maximize the business goals of the firm by operating wherever the best opportunities exist. Typically, the firm will be incorporated and will owe its legal existence to a nation-state or a political subdivision of a nation-state. As an economic or business creature, the firm may even select the best political jurisdiction for its home base in terms of business advantages to the firm. This is similar to domestic firms in the United States choosing to be incorporated in the state of Delaware because of special business advantages inherent in Delaware incorporation. Nation-states, as the current form of political organization in the world, will continue to be extremely important in controlling the business environment. But for the global firm, national political boundaries are a constant rather than an absolute limit for seeking out business opportunities.

On the basis of continuing world reconnaissance of opportunities and threats to its competitive position, the firm selects the markets it wants to be in. These decisions are based upon such factors as differential growth rates of markets, the costs of getting into different markets, and the potentials for securing a satisfactory share of specific

---

[24]W. Dickerson Hogue, "The Foreign Investment Decision-Making Process," mimeographed (Paper presented to the Association for Education in International Business, December 29, 1967).

markets. Working back from its market decisions and following standard location economics criteria, the firm will develop logistic models on a world scale that represent rational patterns for supplying the selected markets. The logistic models will include sources of raw materials, production sites, service and marketing facilities, research activities, and even the supplies of labor, management, and capital. By incorporating the marketing and logistics options into a general programming model, the firm develops its optimal business operations strategy.

On a domestic basis, the rational model is accepted as a normal pattern for doing business within a nation. The global model is basically the same as the more familiar domestic model, except that the global model includes in the decision-making process a new range of variables and risks resulting from crossing national boundaries. To satisfy national interests, nations may exert *fragmentation* pressures on the enterprise—such as to expand local exports—which conflict with a *unification* strategy, which in the case of exports might favor a different unit of the multinational enterprise as a more efficient source of exports. The unification strategy may constitute a substantial portion of the basic rationale for the existence of the multinational firm and the source of a considerable part of its competitive advantage.[25] The optimal location decisions of the multinational enterprise will differ from those made by a group of unrelated national enterprises because the decision to establish a foreign subsidiary depends upon the marginal impact of this subsidiary on the enterprise as a whole and because the existing facilities to which the subsidiary is to be added are located in other countries.[26]

The growth process of the firm might be visualized as following a path along which business enterprises develop from a completely local to a global orientation. To achieve the global enterprise status, a series of necessary conditions underlying the rationale model must be fulfilled. The firm and its management must have an international horizon and access to resources necessary for global operations. It must have competitive advantages that it can exploit. It must be in product or service fields that are not limited economically or legally to local and national markets. For example, the production of common bricks is not a promising field for international business because technology is relatively simple and transportation costs are high in

---

[25]Fayerweather, "The Global Business Strategy," in *International Business Management*, pp. 133–67.

[26]Raymond Vernon, "The Location of Economic Activity," pp. 111–12; David P. Rutenberg, *Stochastic Programming with Recourse for Planning Optimal Flexibility in Multinational Corporations* (Ph.D. diss., University of California, Berkeley, 1967).

relation to the value of the product. Nor is the production of enriched uranium a promising field because it is a business activity legally limited to national markets by national security considerations.

To the extent that these and other necessary conditions are fulfilled, enterprises can be classified across a spectrum into earlier or later stages of internationalization, and their behavior patterns can be explained as predictable variations from the rational model. Thus, no simple pattern presently explains all forms of international business activities. Nor should the establishment of all international operations be considered as *sui generis* or unique to the individual case. Instead, our hypothesis is that a number of behavior patterns exist, that each pattern is a partial or incomplete form of the rational model, that enterprises and types of business activity move in a rational manner from one category of behavior pattern to another, and that the components of international business activity—that is, the movement of goods, services, personnel, financial flows, and capital—can be explained by a finite (and relatively small) number of behavior patterns into which the motivating firms and types of business can be grouped.

SUMMARY

The practice of international business has clearly run ahead of the development of a theoretical framework for explaining and predicting international business patterns. The new and more complex patterns of business transactions across national boundaries cannot be satisfactorily explained by traditional economic theories of international trade and international investment. The principal limitation of such theories is that they have not included the business enterprise and its growing influence on inter-nation business relations.

A series of new approaches, evoked by the international business reality, are beginning to provide a theoretical framework for international business. Among these are the explanations for the emergence of the multinational enterprise as a mechanism for the international transmission of resources, as a consequence of the product cycle, and as a means of exploiting oligopoly advantages in foreign areas. The present state of the knowledge can best be summarized by considering as separate but related issues (1) the historical evolution of international business patterns, and (2) a rational model for the global business firm. The first framework helps to explain how present patterns have evolved. The second framework helps to explain and predict international business patterns as globally oriented firms become increasingly dominant in the world economy.

The recent rapid expansion of international business firms can be explained by a combination of environmental forces, technological trends, and the growth process of the business enterprise. Aided and stimulated by an accelerated capability to extend their operations geographically, business enterprises in the industrialized countries perceived and increasingly responded to foreign business opportunities and threats to their oligopoly positions. Technological trends played a major role in providing enterprises, particularly in the advanced countries, with oligopoly elements that gave them a competitive advantage over local enterprises in a host country. Other sources of competitive advantage were product differentiation built on advertising, access to capital, and management skills. Although the business enterprise has been the active force underlying the recent rapid growth of international business, a pervasive and dominant influence was a favorable world environment. This included an expansionist world economy, an improved inter-national financial and trade framework, and the growth-mindedness of nations that characterized the post–World War II period.

The theoretical framework that is becoming most useful for understanding future patterns is the rational model of the global firm. It has developed a global horizon and continuously scans the world for new opportunities and threats to its position. The global firm has access to adequate financial, human, and organization resources to operate in many countries. It includes in its planning and operations a series of variables and risks that are different in kind and degree from those encountered in operating within a single nation-state. Its operations are heavily influenced by the pressures and policies of diverse national environments.

EXERCISES AND DISCUSSION QUESTIONS

1. As an executive of a predominantly domestic firm that seems unaware of global opportunities or threats, what would you do to expand the horizon of the enterprise and "go international"?

2. Compare the explanatory power of any three theories of international business expansion.

3. Why has the U.S. pharmaceutical industry been internationally minded but the iron and steel industry has not?

4. Which U.S. industries whose production facilities are predominantly in the United States are likely to establish foreign production facilities? See Table 3–1 for information on the extent of foreign operations by the largest U.S. industrial corporations.

5. What answers do the historical and the rational models provide to the questions listed at the beginning of the chapter?

TABLE 3-1

Extent of Foreign Operations by Largest U.S. Industrial Corporations (based on data for the 500 largest industrial corporations as contained in the 1965 *Fortune* summary)

SEC Industry No.	Industry	No. of Companies in Industry Sample*	Median Percentage of Foreign Content of Companies with Foreign Operations†	Median Percentage of Foreign Content of Industry‡ as Represented by Sample
283	Drugs	15	31%	31%
291	Petroleum	29	32	27
352	Farm and construction machinery	14	27	27
301	Tires and inner tubes	6	27	22
357	Office machinery and computer	10	21	21
354	Metalworking machinery	8	20	20
284	Soaps, detergents and cosmetics	7	20	20
355	Special industry machinery	6	20	20
371	Motor vehicle and parts	22	18	18
208X	Soft drinks	3	18	18
342	Cutlery, tools and hardware	3	18	18
356	General industry machinery	8	17	17
383	Optical instruments	7	17	17
366	Communications equipment	12	17	16
211	Cigarettes	5	15	15
333	Nonferrous metals	18	14	13
349	Misc. fabricated metal products	10	18	13
326	Concrete, gypsum, asbestos	9	17	13
281	Chemicals, organic and inorganic	27	13	12
204	Grain mill products	11	15	12
351	Engines and turbines	4	10	10
374	Railroad equipment	4	10	10
285	Paints and varnishes	4	10	10
207	Confectionary products	3	10	10
361	Electrical equipment and apparatus	18	9	9
363	Household appliances	7	9	8
358	Service industry machines	5	8	8
341	Metal cans	3	8	8
321	Glass and glass products	6	10	7
203	Canning fruits and vegetables	15	9	7
202	Dairy products	8	10	7
271	Newspapers and books	10	8	7
372	Aircraft and parts	19	8	6
262	Paper and allied products	21	9	6
208	Alcoholic beverages	8	10	6
365	Radio and television sets	6	6	5
241	Lumber and wood products	5	7	5
331	Steel works and mills	31	6	4
201	Meat products	12	8	4
231	Apparel	6	7	4
221	Textile mill products	18	6	3
314	Footwear, except rubber	5	5	3
205	Bakery products	9	15	2

*Percentages for industries represented by less than 10 companies have a low confidence level. Industry group 25, furniture and fixtures, which was represented by only one company, was omitted.

†These median percentages represent approximations. They are based on either one or a combination of several of the five measurement criteria (sales, earnings, assets, employment, or production abroad). No adjustment was made for differences in the size of the companies in the sample.

‡These percentages were obtained by multiplying the percentages in the preceding column with the percent of companies in each industry having foreign operations.

Source: Nicholas K. Bruck and Francis A. Lees, *Foreign Investment, Capital Controls, and the Balance of Payments* (New York: New York University, Institute of Finance, Graduate School of Business Administration, April 1968), pp. 94–96.

part two

The Framework for International Transactions

A NATURAL STARTING POINT for the study of international business is to examine the framework that has grown up over the centuries for dealing with business transactions across national boundaries. This overall framework is made up of three different though interrelated frameworks:

1. The *international financial framework* deals with the means, the recording, and the control of international transfers of monetary claims.
2. The *international trade framework* deals with the means, the recording, and the control of international transfers of goods and services.
3. The *international regulatory framework* deals with the nature, contents, and limits of arrangements nations have entered into for determining how to treat business rights, obligations, and opportunities that extend across national frontiers.

These three frameworks provide the basic vocabulary for international transactions, and as such introduce many of the terms and concepts necessary for describing international business. They also influence the language of government controls. Controls that governments place on international transactions are largely determined by information collection and reasoning that stems from the conventions of these frameworks. Knowledge of the traditional frameworks is thus important for understanding and predicting the environment within which international business operates.

None of these three frameworks, however, is focused directly on international business. They have been molded by the heritage of international trading between buyers and sellers residing in different countries and acting predominantly as merchants and at arms' length—quite different from the international transactions of large multinational businesses. This has produced a body of knowledge, theories, and controls that concentrates on aggregate flows of goods and finance across a country's boundaries and does not pay direct attention to the objectives and decisions of the businesses that arrange the transactions. The frameworks have limitations given the reality of today's world of multinational firms. Nevertheless, the international businessman must still make international transactions, and these frameworks can provide him with valuable knowledge and perspectives.

An essential similarity in the three frameworks is the absence of a world authority that overrides the jurisdiction of national governments. Each framework is, in effect, a system for relating a particular segment of the economic activities and regulations of different sovereign states. The financial framework is concerned with the way in which the currencies of individual countries are exchanged. With no legal international currency, international transactions must be measured, accounted for, and paid for by converting one currency into another. The trade framework is concerned with the relationship of the productive output of one country to that of another. What one country produces for another's markets is subject to a variety of natural and imposed conditions. Finally, the regulatory framework begins to provide a system whereby governments agree on how they will align their legal constraints and privileges for activities which carry into more than one jurisdiction.

4

The Balance of Payments

IN THE INTERNATIONAL SPHERE a firm's ability to move money across national boundaries is particularly critical. Many factors bear on this prospect. In particular, a country's economic relations with other nations will affect the relative value of its currency and the ability of the country to acquire currencies of other nations. Since international companies depend on foreign exchange for imports, exports, the payment of foreign debts, and dividend remittances, they must assess on a continuing basis the external positions and the currency prospects in the countries in which they operate. This chapter discusses the framework and methodology for such an assessment—namely, a country's balance of payments.

THE BALANCE-OF-PAYMENTS ACCOUNTS

The balance of payments is a system of accounts designed to show how a nation finances its international activities and what role the country plays in the world economy. The focal point of the balance of payments is the nation's external liquidity—the relationship of current assets to current liabilities—which measures the country's ability to meet claims from the outside world and to acquire the goods and services it needs to import. The accounts are set up to summarize all economic transactions between the residents of the reporting country and the residents of other countries during a given period of time, normally a year or a quarter. As such, the balance of payments registers the changes in the nation's financial claims and obligations vis-a-vis the rest of the world. It is a national accounting tabulation comparable

57

to a firm's profit-and-loss statement plus *changes* in its balance sheet. The balance of payments does not measure the total foreign assets or liabilities that a country's citizens may possess at any particular moment, but it does show what changes are taking place and how these changes affect the external liquidity and other financial relations of the nation. The balance of payments' primary purpose is to answer questions pertaining to a country's international financial position, but it also serves as a framework for analyzing and interpreting a wide range of problems dealing with the country's economic and business life.

Transactions

For balance-of-payments purposes, economic transactions include all transfers of property from a resident of one country to that of another which can be valued in monetary terms. This rule is used without qualification. Transactions in kind and in credit are included just as cash transactions. Transactions for which no payments are received or expected, such as shipments of equipment to a foreign branch plant by the parent firm or, conversely, shipments of component parts from the branch to the parent, are included along with sales and purchase transactions. Indeed, the question of quid pro quo is irrelevant in balance-of-payments accounting, as unilateral transfers of value, such as personal gifts, government grants, and philanthropic donations, are also recorded. From a strict accounting standpoint the balance of payments is not a record of international payments but of international transactions. However, its meaning and usefulness derive from the external liquidity changes that the accounts reflect.

Residents

The term *resident* is defined by the International Monetary Fund as all persons and institutions identified with the country concerned. Resident institutions include all business enterprises, government agencies, and nonprofit organizations. International agencies are regarded as a special case and are not treated as resident institutions of the countries in which they are located. Government officials and members of armed forces stationed abroad are treated as residents of the country of citizenship. Foreign branches and subsidiaries of business firms are treated as residents of the countries in which they are located. Transactions with agents are regarded as transactions with the foreign principal for whom they are acting. If a domestic agency of a foreign enterprise acts as a principal for its own account, its transactions with residents do not enter the balance of payments because these transactions take place between residents. Travelers, commuters, temporary residents, and other individuals with dual or multiple residency are classified by the so-called center of interest rule, which assigns them to the country of their principal interest. The residency concept in general refers to normal location rather than to nationality, except for government and military personnel.

The Balance-of-Payments Accounting Process

The tabulation of international transactions in the balance of payments is based upon double-entry accounting. Every entry must have a counter entry. For every debit there must be a corresponding credit, and for every credit a counterbalancing debit. The starting point of double-entry accounting is the identity: assets = liabilities + equity. To preserve this identity, the following accounting rules are followed in making entries:

1. Transactions that increase assets are debits.
2. Transactions that reduce assets are credits.
3. Transactions that increase liabilities or equity are credits.
4. Transactions that reduce liabilities or equity are debits.

Thus debits reflect either increases in assets or reductions in liabilities or equity. Credits designate reductions in assets or increases in liabilities or equity. These are merely accounting rules or conventions for recording transactions; they are not economic truths!

The summary accounts—the assets, liabilities, and equity items—for which changes comprise a country's balance of payments, are listed in Figure 4–1. During a specific time period—say, one year—the changes in these summary accounts are recorded as a country's balance-of-payments result. Thus, the balance of payments is closely analogous to the profit-and-loss and funds-flow statements prepared in corporate accounting.

Referring to Figure 4–1, we can now begin analyzing the various transactions by first identifying their debit and credit components.

The Current Account

In the lower righthand corner of Figure 4–1 are listed a number of items under the account captions Current Account Credits and Current Account Debits. These items for a country are analogous to the revenues and expenses of a business. Hence, when combined, they provide important insights regarding a country's performance in the

FIGURE 4–1
Balance-of-Payments Summary Accounts

Assets	*Liabilities*
Reserves—Monetary Authorities	Official Liabilities
Monetary Gold	
SDR Holdings	
IMF General Account	
Foreign Exchange	
Short-Term Capital	Short-Term Capital
Private Assets:	Private Liabilities:
Banks	Banks
Nonbanks	Nonbanks
Government Short Term	Government Short Term
Long-Term Capital	Long-Term Capital
Private Direct Investment	Private Direct Investment
Portfolio Investment	Portfolio Investment
Government Long Term	Government Long Term
Errors and Omissions	

Equity

SDR Allocations

Current Account Credits:	*Current Account Debits:*
Exports	Imports
Services—invisibles	Services—invisibles
sold	bought
Military sales	Military purchases
Travel and tourism	Travel and tourism
Freight	Freight
Investment income	Investment expense
Transfers (received)	Transfers (granted)

international economic community, just as the profit-and-loss statement of a company conveys important information regarding its achievements.

Merchandise Trade. For most countries, exports and imports of merchandise are the largest single components of total international payments, often accounting for two thirds or more of their overall international transactions. The sale of a product by a country to foreigners is an export and is reflected by a credit in the current account. (Remember that increases in equity items are credits by accounting definition.) The corresponding debit reflects the fact that the exporting country acquires a claim against foreigners for payment; this aspect of the transaction is reflected in a debit to one of the short-term capital accounts, which are divided into private and government subaccounts. The correct item to debit depends on whether a government agency, such as the U.S. Export-Import Bank, or a nongovernment party owns the claim arising from the export. Short-term capital movements are generally confined to commitments with a duration of less than one year and, therefore, if the exporter expects to be paid within that time, a short-term rather than a long-term capital account is debited. If the exporter holds the receivable arising from the foreign sale until maturity, the debit will be to a nonbank capital account. Probably, however, the exporter will sell the receivable to a bank or at least ask a bank to guarantee payment of the money owed by the importer. Such precautions by exporters are customary in international business because of distances, currency problems, and, often, unfamiliarity with foreign buyers. The precautions give rise to instruments called "bankers acceptances" or "bills of exchange" and, in such instances, the appropriate debit is to a bank short-term capital account. Whether an asset or a liability account is debited depends on whether the claim is held within the exporting country (in which case the liability account is debited) or, alternatively, results in the reduction of an existing claim against the exporting country. If the exporter receives a payment outside his home country, the receipt is reflected in a debit to the appropriate asset capital account.

For clarification, an example is provided here with two different means of payment to show the effects each would have on the U.S. balance of payments.

Ford Motor Company sells $100,000 of engine parts to a Volkswagen plant in Germany. VW pays by drawing on its dollar account with a New York bank. This transaction would be shown in the U.S. balance of payments as follows:

Short-Term Capital Private
Bank Liabilities. . . . .$100,000 (dr)[1]
Exports. . . . . $100,000 (cr)

This sale increases the equity of the United States and is reflected in the credit to the current account item, Exports. VW pays for its purchase with dollars, thus reducing the U.S. dollar debt to Germany. This reduction in liabilities is recorded in the U.S. balance of payments by a debit to Short-Term Capital Private Bank Liabilities.

If VW had paid for these parts by drawing on its German bank account, then the entry would be:

Short-Term Capital Private Bank
Assets . . . .$100,000 (dr)
Exports. . . . . $100,000 (cr)

---

[1]The abbreviations dr and cr represent debits and credits.

Here the debit entry reflects the fact that Ford now owns off-shore deposits which previously were foreign owned. The debit to Short-Term Capital Private Bank Assets records Ford's claim against foreigners stemming from the export sale. The balance sheet identity is preserved with the increase in the asset (the debit) matched by a corresponding increase in equity (the export credit).

Services Sold and Bought.   Services, as distinct from merchandise, also contribute to a country's operating performance. These service items, sometimes called invisibles, include tourist expenditures, freight, royalties, rents, consulting and engineering fees, and various administrative and operating expenses of government. If services are bought, they are comparable to imports with debits recorded. Conversely, sales to foreigners of these services contribute to earnings like exports and are, therefore, credits.

As an illustration, the terms of sale in the preceding example are f.o.b. (free on board) destination, and Ford ships the parts by French freighter at a cost of $1,000. Ford pays for this with a check drawn on its New York (dollar) account. This aspect of the Ford-VW sale is recorded in the U.S. balance of payments with the following entry:

Freight. . . . . $1,000 (dr)
    Short-Term Capital Private Bank
    Liabilities. . . . . $1,000 (cr)

Ford has in effect bought a French shipping service—an expense for the United States—so a debit to the current account item, Freight, is recorded. The credit to Short-Term Capital Private Bank Liabilities reflects the increase in U.S. dollar liabilities to foreigners because the French shipping line now owns U.S. dollar deposits.

The investment income service item consists of transfers of dividends and interest. It is important to remember in this connection that dividends, not earnings, are included in the balance-of-payments accounts.

Transfer Accounts.   Included here are international, noncommercial transactions by both private parties and governments. The private transfers consist of personal gifts of all kinds, philanthropic activities, relief organization shipments, and so forth. Government transfers consist of money, goods, and services as aid to other nations—that is, where nothing is received in return.

For example, CARE sends $100,000 worth of food to the Kanpur area in India as part of a drought-relief program. This gift appears in the U.S. balance of payments as:

Transfers (granted). . . . . $100,000 (dr)
    Exports . . . . $100,000 (cr)

The current account item, Transfers (granted), is debited, reflecting the nature of this transaction—i.e., that the United States receives nothing in return. The credit to Exports reflects the "sale" of products by the United States.

The Capital Accounts

Long-Term Capital. This account shows the inflow and outflow of capital commitments that have a maturity of longer than one year. The account is divided into subsections for private and for governmental capital transactions. Private long-term capital items range from the extension of commercial credit to the acquisition of physical properties such as factories, mines, and mills abroad. Where the capital investment involves more than a 10 percent ownership interest, it is categorized as a *direct investment.* Smaller interests are included under the *portfolio investment* subsection.

If ITT, for instance, invests an additional $10 million in one of its foreign subsidiaries, the balance-of-payments entries are as follows:

Long-Term Private
    Direct Investment . . . . $10 million (dr)
        Short-Term Private
        Banks Liabilities . . . . . . $10 million (cr)

The credit in this case reflects the fact that ITT has transferred money outside the country, putting the funds at the disposal of its foreign affiliate. Both the foreign affiliate and its local bank are foreigners for balance-of-payments purposes, and the short-term liquid capital claim *against* the United States is reflected by this credit. If, alternatively, ITT sends equipment to its affiliate, instead of creating a bank account for it, the credit item (offsetting the direct investment debit) is to Exports. This credit reflects the "sale" of products by the United States.

Government long-term capital includes loans to and from other governments, financial support in economic development projects abroad, and, particularly significant for the United States, loans by the Export-Import Bank, subscriptions to various regional development banks, and participation in the financing of other foreign projects either directly or through international institutions.

Credit extended by government agencies for longer than one year requires that the Government Long-Term Capital Assets account be debited, with the counterbalancing credit to a short-term capital account if monies are placed at the disposal of the borrower or, alternatively, to the export merchandise account if the loan derives from an export sale.

To illustrate, the Export-Import Bank grants a $600,000 loan to the Mexican Power and Light Company to finance the purchase of a turbo-electric generator from the General Electric Company. Payment for the generator is made directly by the Export-Import Bank to the General Electric Company. To record this transaction the U.S. balance-of-payments entries would be:

Government Long-Term Capital
Assets . . . . $600,000 (dr)
Exports . . . . $600,000 (cr)

Assuming that the loan extends for longer than one year, the Government Long-Term Capital Asset account would be debited because the U.S. government now has increased its long-term claims on foreigners (Mexico). General Electric's sale to Mexico would be reflected in the credit to Exports.

Long-Term Capital Portfolio Investment. This investment is recorded in an identical fashion. If an individual or institution buys stock in a foreign corporation where the ownership interest is less than 10 percent, the Portfolio Investment Asset account is debited and the corresponding short-term capital account is credited. Conversely, if foreigners buy securities of our government or home-country corporations, the Long-Term Capital Portfolio Investment account is credited with an offsetting amount to the appropriate short-term capital account, reflecting the compensatory money transfer.

Short-Term Capital. In our discussions thus far, changes in the short-term capital accounts have been attributable to current account developments or changes in long-term investment. Stated another way, there have been shifts in the short-term capital accounts due to trade (exports or imports), services, transfers, or investment. Short-term capital movements induced by such transactions are frequently referred to as *compensatory* or *accommodating* adjustments.

By way of contrast, the short-term capital accounts may shift due to factors quite independent of such transactions. Such movements may be caused by differences in interest rates among countries where short-term investors have as their primary objective obtaining the highest possible yield, regardless of country origin. There also may be short-term capital movements due to expectations that foreign exchange rates will change—either temporary fluctuations or permanent movements. These types of short-term capital movements—shifts of an autonomous rather than a compensatory nature—are important to detect, since they may shed important light on a country's currency prospects.

The Reserves and Official Liabilities

A country's reserves are closely analogous to a company's cash and near-cash assets. They provide the liquidity with which to pay for merchandise and services, and for investment. The reserves are official or government-owned assets; only purchases and sales by official monetary authorities, such as the Federal Reserve Bank and the Bank of England, are entered into this account. The *foreign exchange* component of reserves consists of holdings by a government of other countries' currencies, which are freely convertible on the international money market. For most countries, other than the United States, the principal currencies are the U.S. dollar and the British pound, although during recent years other hard currencies, particularly the German mark, the Swiss franc, the Dutch guilder, and the French franc, have become increasingly important as reserve currencies. (Obviously, U.S. dollars are not the reserve currency in the United States, nor are pounds part of the U.K.'s reserves; a country's own currency is not foreign exchange and therefore, by definition, is excluded from the reserve computation.) *Monetary gold* is considered a reserve because it is freely convertible into hard currencies. Special Drawing Rights (SDR's), sometimes called "paper gold," are the assets created by the International Monetary Fund and allocated among the member countries. This reserve asset, in accordance with rules established by members of the Fund, can be exchanged for convertible currencies and used as a means of international payment. When a country receives its SDR allocation, the balance-of-payments entry consists of a debit to the reserve asset with the corresponding credit to the SDR allocation—equity account (refer back to Figure 4–1). A country's IMF general account reflects its contribution to the IMF based on the country's quota within the international organization. A country can withdraw foreign exchange from the IMF without restriction so long as the amounts withdrawn do not exceed the country's contribution against its quota. (Mechanics of the IMF are discussed in Chapter 5.)

A country's *official liabilities* are the counterpart to its reserve assets. This account reflects foreign monetary authorities' holdings of the home-country currency as part of their reserves. For example, the dollar holdings of the Bank of England or the Bank of France are official liabilities in the U.S. balance of payments. From the opposite perspective, these holdings are part of Britain's and France's reserves.

To illustrate a transaction affecting official reserves and liabilities, consider the following: The Bank of France decides that it has accumulated too many dollar deposits and buys $2,000,000 in gold from the Federal Reserve Bank of New York, paying with a check on that bank. The entry in the U.S. balance of payments to record this would be:

Official Liabilities. . . . . $2,000,000 (dr)
    Reserves—Monetary Gold . . . $2,000,000 (cr)

The debit to Official Liabilities indicates the reduction in U.S. dollar debt to France; it is an official liability because these are dollar deposits held by a foreign monetary authority. The corresponding decrease in the U.S. holding of gold is shown with the credit to Reserves—Monetary Gold.

Errors and Omissions

Although in theory the balance of payments should always balance since all debits are offset by credits and vice versa, in reality it rarely does balance because data are incomplete and lend themselves to different interpretation by various people and responsible agencies. The specific reasons for deviations depend on a particular country's data collection and data processing systems and, in general, reflect the fact that information is incomplete or that there have been inaccurate evaluations. The Errors and Omissions account caption is a balancing or "plug" figure, which is derived to keep the accounts in balance.

INTERPRETING THE RESULTS

The preceding material has been primarily concerned with defining terms and outlining the various bookkeeping transactions that are required to record an international transaction or a series of transactions. As we have seen, the balance of payments always balances in the sense that debits are equal to credits. Yet we continuously hear of imbalances—that countries have either deficits or surpluses. The reason for this apparent anomaly has to do with the methods used to interpret balance-of-payments results.

Balance-of-payments statistics are collected by the International Monetary Fund for each of its member countries. This information is presented in a standard format in its *Balance of Payments Yearbook.* In addition to the standard format, a number of other tables are provided to furnish more detail on some balance-of-payments entries. To facilitate interpretation, an analytic presentation table is included, complementing the standard presentation, which attempts to sort out balance-of-payments items according to their true motivation and underlying economic significance.

In order to analyze a firm's position, various ratios are often calculated from its balance sheet and income statement. For example, the current and quick ratios and the average age of receivables are important measures of a company's liquidity. Such items as the debt-equity ratio and "number of times interest earned" provide clues in regard to the firm's ability to service debt. Profitability characteristics are reflected in earnings-per-share calculations, and return-on-investment measures, to name a few.

Similarly, analytical measures are derived from a country's balance of payments and are used for interpretative purposes. These measures focus on certain aspects of a country such as its liquidity, "profitability," or ability to generate foreign exchange. When a country is said to have a surplus or deficit, this interpretative statement is based on one of these analytical measures.

The conventional measures used to interpret a country's position are: the merchandise trade balance, the current account balance and the basic balance. Figure 4–2 shows the components of each and their interrelationships.

FIGURE 4–2
The Measures of a Country's Balance-of-Payments Position

Exports
− Imports
─────────────
= *Merchandise Trade Balance*

± { Military, net
Travel and Tourism, net
Investment, net
Other Income, net
Transfers, net
Freight, net
Other Services, net
─────────────
= *Current Account Balance*

± { Long-term private capital flows, net
Government nonliquid liabilities to other
than foreign official reserve agencies
─────────────
= *Basic Balance*

In essence, analysts focus on those transactions that occur for reasons independent of balancing the accounts. These so-called autonomous transactions include such items as commodity exports, which take place in response to price and supply and demand conditions at home and abroad. The transactions that compensate for these autonomous items (that balance the accounts), such as the receipt of foreign exchange in consideration for the commodity exports, are then disregarded. The arithmetic sum of these autonomous transactions—sometimes also called "above the line" items—is the balance-of-payments surplus or deficit. The balance of payments is in surplus if autonomous receipts exceed autonomous payments during the period in question. By the same token, the balance of payments is in deficit—the international purchasing power of the country is said to have decreased—if autonomous payments exceed autonomous receipts.

It is evident, then, that a country's deficit or surplus will change according to the definition of autonomous transactions. The merchandise trade balance designates only exports and imports as autonomous items; the surplus or deficit depends exclusively on the country's performance as an international trader. The current account balance includes not only merchandise trade items but invisibles and transfers as autonomous items. This performance measure for a country is analogous to the net profit calculation for a business concern. Finally, the basic balance considers long-term capital flows together with the items included in the current account balance to be autonomous. The basic balance yardstick gives recognition to capital movements of a permanaent or quasi-permanent nature which augment a country's operating performance. A developing country may be expected (indeed encouraged) to incur current account deficits so long as long-term capital inflows offset the operating shortfalls. Under such circumstances, the basic balance my be the best indicator of overall country performance.

Keeping in mind these distinctions in the definition of surpluses and deficits, one can examine trends and recent changes in a country's external economic relations, which in turn may provide valuable clues about the future. Consideration of any country's payments situation begins with the determination of whether or not there is a serious problem. One asks several questions about a country experiencing balance-of-payments deficits:

1. Is the payments deficit temporary or does it reflect more permanent, structural difficulties? Just as a firm's loss for the year may either result from an extraordinary loss or be a trend, so a country's deficit may reflect an "extraordinary loss"—temporary rise/fall in imports/exports, natural disaster, labor disruption, etc.—or alternatively be evidence of a permanent condition.

2. What measures are relevant? Which of the interpretative measures discussed earlier is most applicable to the country in question, given its present difficulties?

3. If a country depends heavily on external debt and/or large capital inflows, liquidity questions are important even if the country has good medium- or long-term prospects. Analysts will want to assess

whether the country has the capacity to continue meeting its obligations.

4. Creditors and investors will be concerned with the country's medium- and long-term prospects. Here the questions center around the country's long-term viability or "profitability." The current account balance and the basic balance are likely to be emphasized. Relevant to these prospects are such questions as:
   a. Does the country earn as much foreign exchange as it uses?
   b. Will foreign entities be permitted to "retrieve" their profits or liquidate investments?
   c. What is the composition of trade?
      i. Is it diversified?
      ii. Can imports be contracted without adverse consequences? Are exports dependent on imported items?
      iii. How "elastic" or "inelastic" is foreign demand for the country's exports or domestic demand for imports? A country's ability to expand/contract exports/imports depends on how sensitive demand is to changes in price and income levels.

5. Are the country's present reserves sufficient?
6. What are the country's prospects for additional foreign borrowing from private, official, and international sources?
7. Can the country depend on transfers—aid—or an inflow of monies from private foreign investors?
8. What is the government's commitment to remedying the imbalance?

While there are no ironclad rules to use in obtaining definitive answers to such questions, it is essential to determine the most probable courses of action to be taken by government officials in remedying imbalances. The strategy, or combination of strategies, followed by government officials will have different impacts on the domestic economy and on the exchange market. For example, officials might take any of a number of steps to remedy an imbalance in merchandise trade, such as the imposition of restrictions on imports, export incentives, preferential exchange rates for certain categories of exports or imports, fiscal actions to promote new industries with good potential for either export expansion or import substitution, a change in the overall exchange rate, and so forth.

Determining how a country's position is perceived by "outsiders" is also important. Comparing a given country's difficulties with those of other countries at a similar stage of economic development provides useful insights into foreign perceptions. Deficits for a less developed country (LDC) are often viewed as part of the "development process."

Adjustments made by foreign governments and private lenders are critical, however. For example, an imposition or removal of preferential tariffs or an increase or decrease in the amount of financing available from such organizations as the Export-Import Bank or from private lenders can substantially help or hurt a country's position.

If remedying a trade balance has a high priority in a country, then analysts must focus on the alternative steps that might be taken by policy makers in correcting a deficit (or surplus). The reason for this is that the different moves adopted by a country, such as new or increased tariffs, capital controls, preferential exchange rates, and/or investment incentives will have different effects on different enterprises operating in the country. For example, one corporation may be indifferent to the prospect that the country is likely to impose restrictions on imports, whereas this action might well be disastrous for another concern that relies heavily on imported equipment, materials, etc. Hence, we see the need to conduct balance-of-payments intelligence as a means of devising appropriate business strategies and responses against likely environmental developments.

BRAZIL: AN INTERPRETATIVE EXAMPLE

Balance-of-payments statistics for Brazil for the years 1969–75 are shown in Table 4–1 as presented in *International Financial Statistics* published by the International Monetary Fund. Issued monthly by the fund, it includes the balance-of-payments statistics for all member countries plus other useful information such as a country's interest rates and prices, volume and value of exports (often broken down by major commodities), national accounts, and even population. For many countries, especially the LDCs, it takes a long time to collect the balance of payments and other economic information. Due to this fact, analysts often rely on financial statements of the central bank for more current data.

Referring to Table 4–1, the most conspicuous factor is Brazil's current account deficit (line 77a.*d*), which increased approximately fourfold from earlier levels (−$1,757 million in 1973 to −$7,179 million in 1974 and −$6,751 million in 1975). In an earnings sense, Brazil had been incurring substantial "losses." If we examine more closely the components of this deficit, we see that exports and imports of goods steadily increased during the 1969–72 period but took a big jump in 1973–75. What is critical here is that imports of merchandise had exceeded exports since 1971 and were dramatically larger during both 1974 and 1975 (e.g., $12,555 million of imports against $7,807 million of exports for 1974). A similar problem exists in the services (or invisibles) accounts (77ac*d*, 77ad*d*). While both had steadily increased,

TABLE 4-1
Brazil: Balance-of-Payments Summary

Balance of Payments	Line	1969	1970	1971	1972	1973	1974	1975
Goods, services and transfers	77a.d	-336	-561	-1,317	-1,490	-1,757	-7,179	-6,751
Exports of merchandise, f.o.b.	77aad	2,311	2,739	2,891	3,941	6,084	7,807	8,656
Imports of merchandise, f.o.b.	77abd	-1,993	-2,507	-3,256	-4,193	-6,147	-12,555	-12,169
Exports of services	77acd	290	378	443	567	945	1,558	1,327
Imports of services	77add	-975	-1,192	-1,408	-1,810	-2,667	-3,990	-4,565
Private unrequited transfers, net	77aed	14	13	11	1	23	4	9
Government unrequited transfers, net	77afd	17	8	2	4	5	-2	-9
Long-term capital, nie.	77b.d	546	941	1,347	3,342	3,433	5,851	7,332
Direct investment	77bad	241	131	215	369	940	887	889
Other government	77bbd	185	215	404	532	986	1,562	4,611
Other	77bcd	120	595	728	2,441	1,507	3,403	1,832
Short-term capital, nie.	77c.d	276	97	467	86	242	434	412
Deposit money banks.	77cad	183	-247	-50	199	430	-90	—
Other	77cbd	93	344	518	-113	-188	523	412
Errors and omissions	77d.d	-20	38	-9	438	371	-63	-113
Total (77a through 77d)	78a.d	466	515	488	2,376	2,289	-957	-951
Allocation of SDRs.	78b.d	—	59	47	51	—	—	—
Monetization of gold	78c.d	—	—	—	—	—	—	—
Total (78a through 78c).	78e.d	466	574	536	2,427	2,289	-957	-951
Reserves and related items	79..d	-466	-574	-536	-2,427	-2,289	957	951
Reserves	79a.d	-481	-552	-531	-2,482	-2,341	984	951
Monetary gold	79aad	—	—	-1	—	—	—	—
SDRs.	79abd	—	-62	-48	-51	—	-7	-1
Reserve position in the fund	79acd	—	-105	1	—	—	—	—
Foreign exchange.	79add	-481	-385	-482	-2,431	-2,341	991	953
Other assets.	79b.d	—	—	—	—	—	—	—
Use of fund credit.	79c.d	—	—	-5	—	—	—	—
Other liabilities	79d.d	15	-22	-5	55	52	-27	—

Source: *International Financial Statistics*, The International Monetary Fund, July 1976.

imports of services had increased at a much faster rate than exports, especially during 1973–75.

To better understand Brazil's merchandise trade balance, it would be helpful to examine the composition of exports and imports to see if there is dependency on one item. Such information is provided in *International Financial Statistics.* More detailed information could be obtained from such sources as: the *Balance of Payments Yearbook* and *Survey* by the International Monetary Fund; *Overseas Business Reports* by the U.S. Department of Commerce; and relevant publications of large international banks, other international organizations such as the World Bank, the U.S. Department of State, regional organizations, and private international business consultants. For our particular case, we might look to such publications as *Business Trends, Newsletter Brazil* by Bank of Boston International, and *Brazilian Business* by the American Chamber of Commerce for Brazil.

The more detailed sources would show that approximately 60 percent of Brazilian exports have consisted of commodities, such as sugar, soybeans, iron ore, coffee, cotton, and cacao. In the near term, therefore, a large share of Brazil's export earnings could be expected to depend on the foreign demand and price prospects for such commodities. During recent years Brazil had succeeded in expanding its exports of manufactured products, but as of 1976, continued growth in manufactured exports was awaiting a recovery from recession and unemployment in the industrialized, importing countries. Turning to the import side of the trade balance, Brazil needed to contract imports during this period of sluggish export performance. A nagging problem in this connection was Brazil's dependency on foreign sources of petroleum. With only one fifth of its domestic oil requirements provided internally, Brazil's trade balance would be adversely affected by high oil prices. Thus, we might conclude that Brazil's current account prospects would depend heavily, on the one hand, on world demand conditions for selected commodities and manufactures and, on the other hand, on both internal and external factors affecting the volume and price of imports. There had been current account deficits continuously during the seven years under investigation (1969–75) and there was ample reason to expect the deficits to persist for some time.

At this point the important questions are: How critical is this deficit? and Can the current account deficit continue without becoming problematic? Obviously, as deficits continue and especially if they grow in magnitude, a country's ability to pay for its imports will be called into question more seriously. However, just as a company with sufficient money in the bank can sometimes sustain operating losses without going bankrupt, a country can draw down its reserves, thereby enabling it to import more than it exports. Under such circumstances, the size of the loss in relation to the magnitude of reserves is of critical importance.

The balance of payments shows only changes in the level of reserves. The absolute level of Brazil's reserves can be found elsewhere in *International Financial Statistics* under the caption International Liquidity. Line 1..*d* in Table 4–2 indicates that Brazil's reserves at the end of 1975 were $4,034 million. Reserves are similar to idle balances, which a company holds to meet temporary shortfalls in receipts in relation to disbursements. As a rule of thumb, a country should have reserves that are sufficient to finance two or three months of imports, in case exports should fall. Brazil had sufficient reserves at year-end 1975 to cover four months of imports (based on the 1975 import rate).

One might ask, however, how it was possible for Brazil to have reserves at the end of 1973 of $6,415 million, sustain a "loss" in 1974 of $7,179 million, (Table 4–1) and end 1974 with reserves of $5,272 million. Similarly during 1975 the nearly $7 billion current account loss was associated with a loss of aggregate reserves of only $1.2 billion ($5,272 million less $4,034 million). One might have expected reserves to be wiped out, given the size of the losses.

Further analysis reveals that long-term capital inflows—item 77b.*d* in the balance of payments, Table 4–1—have increased at a substantial rate during the 1973–75 period and that these inflows are the reason Brazil records a balance-of-payments surplus using the basic balance measure (items 77a.*d* + 77b.*d*) every year since 1969, except for 1974. A closer examination reveals that the major sources of the capital inflow are recorded under the account captions—Other Government and Other. Better insights into these items can be gained from Table 4–3 for Brazil, extracted from the IMF's May 1976 *Balance of Payments Yearbook*. (It should be noted here that while there is much more detail for every item, data for 1975 have not yet been recorded.) From Table 4–3 (items 26 and 30), it is evident that much of Brazil's long-term capital inflow has been provided by external lenders. Conversations with IMF Brazil officers or other Brazil watchers would reveal that the same was true during 1975.

It is interesting to note that direct investment, relatively smaller in amount than foreign borrowings, also has been substantial each year, although it has slowed somewhat from a high of $940 million in 1973 to $887 million in 1974 and to $889 million in 1975. Thus, we can conclude that Brazil has financed its current account deficits with long-term capital inflows—external borrowings and direct investment.

The focal question thus becomes: Will external lenders and investors continue to be willing to supply financing to offset the current account deficits? Private lenders may indeed be becoming more

TABLE 4-2

Brazil: International Liquidity, 1969-1975

International Liquidity	Line	1969	1970	1971	1972	1973	1974	1975
International reserves	1..d	656	1,187	1,746	4,183	6,415	5,272	4,034
Gold	1a.d	45	45	50	50	55	56	54
SDRs	1b.d	—	62	120	170	190	199	191
Reserve position in the fund	1c.d	12	117	126	126	140	142	136
Foreign exchange	1d.d	599	962	1,450	3,836	6,030	4,874	3,653
Fund position								
Net draw/Fund sales (–) to date	2dsc	75	-8	-7	-7	-8	-8	-8
Quota	2f.d	350	440	478	478	531	539	515
Monetary Auth. other assets	3..d	333	299	316	476	665	896	1,195
Monetary Auth. liability: Short-term	4e.d	24	2	6	61	54	29	24
Long-term	4f.d	1,183	1,016	923	860	818	780	738
Commercial banks: Assets	7a.d	161	191	335	436	889	1,155	—
Liabilities	7b.d	448	660	958	1,444	2,235	2,824	1,233
U.S. liabilities to Brazil	9a.d	484	371	343	606	862	1,040	1,227
Short-term	9aad	459	346	342	605	861	1,034	1,089
To government and banks	9axd	389	275	267	516	759	878	
Long-term	9abd	25	25	1	1	2	5	5
U.S. claims on Brazil	9b.d	504	576	766	1,233	1,562	2,255	3,363

Source: *International Financial Statistics*, The International Monetary Fund, July 1976.

reluctant, as evidenced by the decline in long-term private loans received (the Other item—77bcd in Table 4–1) from $3,403 million in 1974 to $1,832 million in 1975. Our analysis at this stage of Brazil's credit-worthiness is analogous to the examination of a company's debt capacity. The only difference, and an important one, is that a country can't go bankrupt.

We begin by looking at Brazil's debt-service ratio—the relation of annual interest and principal payments on the external debt to export earnings. Some idea of Brazil's interest payments for 1969–74 can be determined from examining Table 4–3, items 14 and 15, Investment income—other, from the *Yearbook*. Debits exceed credits, reflecting the fact that interest expense exceeds interest income for Brazil. Unfortunately, this published information does not provide us with timely insights regarding debt servicing requirements on debt contracted recently. Again it would be necessary to contact country lending officers in private banks or in such international institutions as the IMF or the World Bank to learn about Brazil's additional borrowing possibilities, the structure of current debt, and so forth. Such conversations would reveal that Brazil's debt servicing will be more difficult in the future given the greater recent borrowings, the harder terms for these financial credits, and by virtue of the fact that financing periods are now five to six years, rather than ten years as in 1973 and 1974.

Lenders' attitudes are important. In the case of Brazil our data suggest that the country relies heavily on the continued willingness of foreign lenders and investors to extend credit, and these creditors in turn are interested in the steps the country will take to assure repayment. This lender/country official interface is important because it sheds light on possible environmental changes affecting enterprises. Reviewing publications such as *Business Week,* the *Financial Times of London, The Wall Street Journal, The New York Times,* the periodic country surveys in the *Economist,* and any special reports prepared by the large international banks, we can learn what country officals are saying about external financial prospects. We discover in the case of Brazil that the official order of priorities is: (1) balancing the country's trade position; (2) containing the rate of inflation; and (3) growth. This might lead us to predict increased import restrictions and tariffs, import substitution programs, possible relaxation in remittance privileges for foreign companies to insure the continual flow of inbound direct investment, and continuation of the crawling peg or mini-devaluations. (Approaches to the exchange-rate adjustment, such as the crawling peg, are discussed in the next chapter.) Business might also expect the government to begin monitoring more closely transfer-pricing arrangements, fees, and royalties in their effort to conserve

TABLE 4-3
Brazil: Balance-of-Payments Standard Presentation (in millions of SDRs)

	1967	1968	1969	1970	1971	1972	1973	1974
A. Goods, Services, and Unrequited Transfers	-276	-526	-336	-561	-1,313	-1,372	-1,475	-5,971
Goods and services	-353	-548	-367	-582	-1,326	-1,377	-1,498	-5,972
Total credit	*1,839*	*2,086*	*2,601*	*3,117*	*3,324*	*4,152*	*5,903*	*7,792*
Total debit	*-2,192*	*-2,634*	*-2,968*	*-3,699*	*-4,650*	*-5,529*	*-7,401*	*-13,764*
1. Merchandise: exports f.o.b.	1,654	1,881	2,311	2,739	2,882	3,630	5,111	6,497
2. Merchandise: imports f.o.b.	-1,441	-1,855	-1,993	-2,507	-3,246	-3,862	-5,162	-10,445
3. Nonmonetary gold	—	—	—	—	—	—	—	—
4. Freight and insurance on merchandise: credit	28	43	66	95	94	110	141	189
5. Freight and insurance on merchandise: debit	-108	-135	-119	-140	-163	-183	-205	-449
6. Other transportation: credit	48	52	65	72	71	58	68	75
7. Other transportation: debit	-23	-31	-151	-209	-258	-287	-519	-703
8. Travel: credit	15	17	28	30	36	35	49	55
9. Travel: debit	-49	-58	-77	-160	-171	-199	-222	-262
10. Undistributed income from direct investment abroad	—	—	—	—	—	—	—	—
11. Undistributed income from direct investment in Brazil	-39	-74	-83	...	...	...	...	—
12. Other direct investment income: credit					2	2		
13. Other direct investment income: debit	-71	-82	-77	-111	-93	-102	-110	-144
14. Other investment income: credit	18	10	22	49	43	121	274	597
15. Other investment income: debit	-204	-156	-206	-291	-373	-501	-762	-1,204
16. Other government: credit	31	26	28	36	41	36	55	78
17. Other government: debit	-99	-89	-92	-105	-127	-146	-159	-174
18. Other private: credit	45	57	81	96	155	160	205	301
19. Other private: debit	-158	-154	-170	-176	-219	-249	-262	-383
Unrequited transfers	77	22	31	21	13	5	23	1
Total credit	*107*	*75*	*83*	*87*	*94*	*96*	*108*	*114*
Total debit	*-30*	*-53*	*-52*	*-66*	*-87*	*-91*	*-85*	*-113*
20. Private: credit	76	55	61	74	88	90	103	110
21. Private: debit	-26	-50	-47	-61	-77	-89	-84	-107
22. Government: credit	31	20	22	13	6	6	5	4
23. Government: debit	-4	-3	-5	-5	-4	-2	-1	-6

B. Capital (excluding reserves and related items)

	85	625	822	1,038	1,809	3,157	3,118	5,224
B. Capital (excluding reserves and related items)..	85	625	822	1,038	1,809	3,157	3,118	5,224
Nonmonetary sectors	138	391	848	883	1,598	2,180	2,799	4,709
24. Direct investment in Brazil	124	150	252	145	215	365	821	786
25. Direct investment abroad	—	-1	-11	-14	-1	-25	-31	-49
26. Other private long-term liabilities	48	65	269	202	486	1,519	1,302	2,360
27. Other private long-term assets	-16	15	23	-1	-21	-48	-37	-82
28. Other private short-term liabilities	-113	186	134	325	595	-65	-250	320
29. Other private short-term assets	-3	-72	-3	11	-79	-56	165	74
30. General government long-term liabilities	100	94	210	218	420	555	886	1,305
31. General government long-term assets	2	-44	-25	-3	-17	-65	-57	-5
32. General government short-term liabilities	-4	-2	-1	—	—	—	—	—
33. General government short-term assets	—	—	—	—	—	—	—	—
Monetary sectors	-53	234	-26	155	211	977	319	515
34. Deposit money banks: long-term	39	228	183	479	335	841	267	632
35. Deposit money banks: short-term	-90	-62	-172	-247	-50	183	94	-75
36. Central institutions: long-term	-2	68	-37	-85	-74	-64	-47	-83
37. Central institutions: short-term	—	—	—	8	—	17	5	41
C. Allocation of SDRs (item 38)	—	—	—	59	47	47	—	—
D. Reserves and Related Items	226	-98	-466	-574	-534	-2,235	-1,940	800
Liabilities	-29	—	15	-22	-5	51	-6	-22
39. Use of IMF credit	-33	-12	—	—	—	—	—	—
40. Other liabilities	4	12	15	-22	-5	51	-6	-22
Assets	255	-98	-481	-552	-529	-2,286	-1,934	822
41. Monetary gold	—	—	—	—	-1	—	—	—
42. SDRs	—	—	—	-62	-48	—	—	—
43. Reserve position in IMF	—	—	—	-105	1	-47	—	-6
44. Foreign exchange and other claims	255	-98	-481	-385	-481	-2,239	-1,934	828
E. Net Errors and Omissions (item 45)	-35	-1	-20	38	-9	403	297	-53

Source: *Balance of Payments Yearbook*, International Monetary Fund, May 1976.

foreign exchange. However, since continued capital inflows are essential, measures that will improve the country's borrowing and inbound investment image are likely to be given emphasis by officials.

Companies will be concerned about three possible aspects of any changes in regulations or administrative procedures. The first is currency availability—foreign exchange for payments and dividends. Is the country likely to ration foreign exchange? Will the firm's ability to move money in and out of the country be hampered? Second, as stated at the end of the last section, firms will be vitally interested in temporary measures taken by government officials to remedy the trade imbalance. For example, new tariffs might seriously affect the profitability of a company that is heavily dependent on imported materials. Finally, a company will be watchful of controls that will hinder its capability to operate freely in the intermediate and long term. Such controls might be at odds with a firm's plans for plant expansion or other new investments. Quite possibly these might force a firm to rely more heavily on local financial markets which may be limited in the amount of funds available.

Further investigation in the case of Brazil would reveal that most observers believe Brazil has the strength to resolve most of the present problems and resume reasonable growth. Brazil is a broad-based economy, and trade is still only about 10 percent of GNP. Furthermore, Brazil produces a wide range of goods and services for both local consumption and exports. There is an enormous untapped wealth of natural resources and vast tracts of unexploited fertile land. These factors together with sound national leadership should keep Brazil solvent.

The preceding analysis was intended to acquaint the student with the sources of information that are available and the fundamental types of questions in analysis of a country's balance of payments. Another example—the United States—provides added insight into the way in which balance-of-payments data might be interpreted for a key-currency country.

THE UNITED STATES' INTERNATIONAL POSITION

Reproduced from the *Survey of Current Business* which is published by the U.S. Commerce Department, Table 4–4 summarizes U.S. balance-of-payments results for the period 1960–75. By examining the most significant figures in this table, we can develop a fairly clear understanding of U.S. performance, problems, and responses over the period.

What are the most conspicuous features of U.S. international economic performance as reflected in the balance-of-payments summary? We might begin our analysis as we did with Brazil, by examining the current account balance (line 7). Described earlier as a measure of operating performance much like the profit measure for a business enterprise, the U.S. current account was in surplus during the early years, growing in magnitude to $5.7 billion in 1964. Thereafter the surpluses declined dramatically, ultimately leading to sizable deficits. The numbers in the table provide important clues regarding the underlying causes for this change in operating performance. Most importantly, the balance on merchandise trade (line 68) began to deteriorate in 1965, with imports eventually exceeding exports by 1971; thus, a major earnings contributor was wiped out. Simultaneously, investment income and other services were insufficient, beginning in 1968, to offset the declining merchandise trade balance, rising outbound transfers, military expenditures, and travel and transportation. The reasons most frequently cited for this change in fortune are more foreign competition in export markets; reduced demand for U.S. products in foreign markets as local sources of supply developed; an overvalued U.S. dollar which persisted under the fixed exchange rate system and made U.S. exports relatively less attractive and imports into the U.S. together with foreign travel by Americans more attractive; excessive military expenditures; and grants in aid. Whether one agrees or disagrees with the various explanatory factors, the important point is that the current account balance deteriorated and that neither government nor businesses took steps until the early 1970s to alter the adverse trend.

Far more important than current account performance during most of the 1960s was the deterioration in U.S. liquidity. Foreigners— official parties (government agencies and central banks) and private institutions—were progressively holding larger dollar balances (line 50) as Americans invested abroad (line 43) and the U.S. government extended credits to foreigners (line 39) which continuously exceeded the amount of current earnings. Foreigners began increasingly to question whether this trend would ever be reversed and whether the U.S. dollar would retain its value, especially as U.S. reserves dwindled. Thus, liquidity of the United States was the central issue—the capacity of the United States to meet its obligations to exchange gold or foreign exchange for dollars on demand. Even though from a balance sheet solvency point of view U.S. assets exceeded liabilities by a substantial margin, foreigners were concerned about the U.S. capacity and willingness to comply with the IMF-Bretton Woods ground rules. The point here is that a key-currency country provides liquidity to the international financial system and that analysts interpreted the U.S. results from this added perspective. It is because of the U.S. role in the international financial system that both U.S. and foreign governments

TABLE 4-4
U.S. International Transactions (millions of dollars)

Line	(Credits +; debits —)	1960	1961	1962	1963	1964	1965	1966	1967
1	**Exports of goods and services**	**27,595**	**28,882**	**30,606**	**32,708**	**37,393**	**39,548**	**42,774**	**45,561**
2	Merchandise, adjusted, excluding military	19,650	20,108	20,781	22,272	25,501	26,461	29,310	30,666
3	Transfers under U.S. military agency sales contracts	335	402	656	657	747	830	829	1,152
4	Travel	919	947	957	1,015	1,207	1,380	1,590	1,646
5	Passenger fares	175	183	191	205	241	271	317	371
6	Other transportation	1,607	1,620	1,764	1,898	2,076	2,175	2,333	2,426
7	Fees and royalties from affiliated foreigners	590	662	800	890	1,013	1,199	1,162	1,354
8	Fees and royalties from unaffiliated foreigners	247	244	256	273	301	335	353	393
9	Other private services	570	607	585	613	651	714	814	951
10	U.S. Government miscellaneous services	153	164	195	236	265	285	326	336
	Receipts of income on U.S. assets abroad:								
11	Direct investments	2,355	2,768	3,044	3,129	3,674	3,963	3,467	3,847
12	Other private receipts	646	793	904	1,022	1,236	1,421	1,669	1,781
13	U.S. Government receipts	349	383	473	499	462	515	604	639
14	**Transfers of goods and services under U.S. military grant programs, net**	**1,695**	**1,465**	**1,537**	**1,562**	**1,340**	**1,636**	**1,892**	**2,039**
15	**Imports of goods and services**	**−23,555**	**−23,353**	**−25,564**	**−26,811**	**−28,895**	**−32,443**	**−38,260**	**−41,220**
16	Merchandise, adjusted, excluding military	−14,758	−14,537	−16,260	−17,048	−18,700	−21,510	−25,493	−26,866
17	Direct defense expenditures	−3,087	−2,998	−3,105	−2,961	−2,880	−2,952	−3,764	−4,378
18	Travel	−1,750	−1,785	−1,939	−2,114	−2,211	−2,438	−2,657	−3,207
19	Passenger fares	−513	−506	−567	−612	−642	−717	−753	−829
20	Other transportation	−1,402	−1,437	−1,558	−1,701	−1,817	−1,951	−2,161	−2,157
21	Fees and royalties to affiliated foreigners	−35	−43	−57	−61	−67	−68	−64	−62
22	Fees and royalties to unaffiliated foreigners	−40	−46	−44	−51	−60	−67	−76	−104
23	Private payments for other services	−593	−588	−528	−493	−527	−461	−506	−565
24	U.S. Government payments for miscellaneous services	−313	−406	−398	−447	−535	−550	−644	−691
	Payments of income on foreign assets in the United States:								
25	Direct investments	−220	−194	−185	−223	−202	−299	−372	−381
26	Other private payments	−511	−535	−586	−701	−802	−942	−1,221	−1,382
27	U.S. Government payments	−332	−278	−339	−401	−453	−489	−549	−598
28	**U.S. military grants of goods and services, net**	**−1,695**	**−1,465**	**−1,537**	**−1,562**	**−1,340**	**−1,636**	**−1,892**	**−2,039**
29	**Unilateral transfers (excluding military grants of goods and services) net**	**−2,308**	**−2,524**	**−2,638**	**−2,754**	**−2,781**	**−2,854**	**−2,932**	**−3,125**
30	U.S. Government grants (excluding military grants of goods and services)	−1,672	−1,855	−1,916	−1,917	−1,888	−1,808	−1,910	−1,805
31	U.S. Government pensions and other transfers	−214	−235	−245	−262	−279	−369	−367	−441
32	Private remittances and other transfers	−423	−434	−477	−575	−614	−677	−655	−879
33	**U.S. assets abroad, net (increase/capital outflow (−))**	**−2,883**	**−4,484**	**−2,979**	**−5,764**	**−8,128**	**−4,176**	**−5,530**	**−8,025**
34	U.S. Official reserve assets, net	2,145	606	1,533	377	171	1,222	568	52
35	Gold	1,703	857	890	461	125	1,665	571	1,170
36	Special drawing rights								
37	Reserve position in the International Monetary Fund	442	−135	626	29	266	−94	537	−94
38			−116	17	113	220	349	−540	−1,024

Line		1	2	3	4	5	6	7	8
39	U.S. Government assets, other than official reserve assets, net	-1,100	-910	-1,085	-1,662	-1,680	-1,605	-1,543	-2,423
40	U.S. loans and other long-term assets	-1,214	-1,928	-2,128	-2,204	-2,382	-2,463	-2,513	-3,638
41	Repayments on U.S. loans	642	1,279	1,288	988	720	874	1,235	1,005
42	U.S. foreign currency holdings and U.S. short-term assets, net	-528	-261	-245	-447	-19	-16	-265	209
43	U.S. private assets, net	-3,878	-4,180	-3,426	-4,479	-6,618	-3,793	-4,554	-5,653
44	Direct investments abroad	-1,674	-1,598	-1,654	-1,976	-2,328	-3,468	-3,625	-3,072
45	Foreign securities	-663	-762	-969	-1,105	-677	-759	-720	-1,308
	U.S. claims on unaffiliated foreigners reported by U.S. nonbanking concerns:								
46	Long-term	-40	-127	-132	162	-485	-88	-112	-281
47	Short-term	-354	-431	-222	-5	-623	429	-330	-498
	U.S. claims reported by U.S. banks, not included elsewhere:								
48	Long-term	-153	-136	-126	-775	-981	-232	317	235
49	Short-term	-995	-1,125	-324	-781	-1,524	325	-84	-730
50	**Foreign assets in the United States, net (increase/capital inflow (+))**	2,120	2,467	1,697	2,981	3,317	382	3,320	6,938
51	Foreign official assets in the United States, net	1,473	765	1,270	1,986	1,661	132	-674	3,450
52	U.S. Government securities	655	233	1,409	816	433	-143	-1,529	2,260
53	U.S. Treasury securities	655	233	1,410	803	435	-136	-1,550	2,221
54	Other			-1	12	-2	-7	21	39
55	Other U.S. Government liabilities								
56	U.S. liabilities reported by U.S. banks, not included elsewhere	215	25	152	429	298	65	113	83
57	Other foreign official assets	603	508	-291	742	930	210	742	1,106
58	Other foreign assets in the United States, net	647	1,701	427	995	1,656	249	3,994	3,488
59	Direct investments in the United States	141	73	132	-5	-5	57	86	258
60	U.S. Treasury securities	-364	151	-66	-149	-146	-131	-356	-135
61	U.S. securities other than U.S. Treasury securities	282	324	134	287	-85	-358	906	1,016
	U.S. liabilities to unaffiliated foreigners reported by U.S. nonbanking concerns:								
62	Long-term	1	50	3	-13	-38	29	180	85
63	Short-term	-91	176	-112	-23	113	149	296	499
	U.S. liabilities reported by U.S. banks not included elsewhere:								
64	Long-term	6	-5	5	53	88	241	188	158
65	Short-term	672	933	331	845	1,730	262	2,694	1,607
66	Allocations of special drawing rights								
67	Statistical discrepancy (sum of above items with sign reversed)	-1,019	-988	-1,122	-360	-907	-457	628	-128
	Memoranda:								
68	Balance on merchandise trade (lines 2 and 16)	4,892	5,571	4,521	5,224	6,801	4,951	3,817	3,800
69	Balance on goods and services (lines 1 and 15)	4,040	5,529	5,042	5,897	8,499	7,105	4,514	4,340
70	Balance on goods, services, and remittances (lines 69, 31, and 32)	3,404	4,860	4,320	5,060	7,605	7,059	3,492	3,020
71	Balance on current account (lines 69 and 29)	1,732	3,005	2,404	3,143	5,718	4,251	1,582	1,215
72	Transactions in U.S. official reserve assets and in foreign official assets in the United States: Increase (-) in U.S. official reserve assets, net (line 34)	2,145	606	1,533	377	171	1,222	568	52
73	Increase (+) in foreign official assets in the United States (line 51 less line 55)	1,258	741	1,118	1,558	1,363	67	-787	3,367

TABLE 4-4 *(concluded)*

Line	(Credits +; debits −)	1968	1969	1970	1971	1972	1973	1974	1975
1	**Exports of goods and services**	**49,933**	**54,699**	**62,483**	**65,614**	**72,664**	**102,154**	**144,773**	**148,410**
2	Merchandise, adjusted, excluding military	33,626	36,414	42,469	43,319	49,381	71,410	98,310	107,133
3	Transfers under U.S. military agency sales contracts	1,392	1,528	1,501	1,926	1,163	2,342	2,952	3,897
4	Travel	1,775	2,043	2,331	2,534	2,817	2,412	4,032	4,876
5	Passenger fares	411	450	544	615	699	975	1,104	1,064
6	Other transportation	2,548	2,652	3,113	3,277	3,555	4,434	5,658	5,727
7	Fees and royalties from affiliated foreigners	1,430	1,533	1,758	1,927	2,115	2,513	3,070	3,526
8	Fees and royalties from unaffiliated foreigners	437	486	573	618	655	712	751	759
9	Other private services	1,024	1,160	1,287	1,539	1,764	1,960	2,250	2,778
10	U.S. Government miscellaneous services	353	343	332	347	354	399	413	432
	Receipts of income on U.S. assets abroad:								
11	Direct investments	4,151	4,819	4,992	5,983	6,416	8,841	17,849	9,456
12	Other private receipts	2,021	2,338	2,671	2,641	2,949	4,330	7,356	7,644
13	U.S. Government receipts	765	933	912	888	796	826	1,028	1,119
14	**Transfers of goods and services under U.S. military grant programs, net**	**2,547**	**2,610**	**2,713**	**3,546**	**4,492**	**2,809**	**1,817**	**2,232**
15	**Imports of goods and services**	**−48,355**	**−53,722**	**−59,545**	**−65,870**	**−78,618**	**−98,249**	**−141,187**	**−132,141**
16	Merchandise, adjusted, excluding military	−32,991	−35,807	−39,866	−45,579	−55,797	−70,499	−103,679	−98,150
17	Direct defense expenditures	−4,535	−4,856	−4,855	−4,819	−4,784	−4,629	−5,035	−4,780
18	Travel	−3,030	−3,373	−3,980	−4,373	−5,042	−5,526	−5,980	−6,417
19	Passenger fares	−885	−1,080	−1,215	−1,290	−1,596	−1,790	−2,095	−2,380
20	Other transportation	−2,367	−2,455	−2,816	−3,078	−3,461	−4,591	−5,826	−5,373
21	Fees and royalties to affiliated foreigners	−80	−101	−118	−118	−155	−209	−212	−241
22	Fees and royalties to unaffiliated foreigners	−106	−120	−114	−123	−139	−176	−186	−192
23	Private payments for other services	−668	−751	−810	−935	−1,017	−1,149	−1,201	−1,351
24	U.S. Government payments for miscellaneous services	−760	−717	−725	−746	−788	−862	−966	−1,045
	Payments of income on foreign assets in the United States:								
25	Direct investments	−388	−417	−441	−621	−687	−955	−5,495	−2,127
26	Other private payments	−1,843	−3,269	−3,591	−2,344	−2,470	−4,028	−6,249	−5,543
27	U.S. Government payments	−702	−777	−1,024	−1,844	−2,684	−3,836	−4,262	−4,542
28	**U.S. military grants of goods and services, net**	**−2,547**	**−2,610**	**−2,713**	**−3,546**	**−4,492**	**−2,809**	**−1,817**	**−2,232**
29	**Unilateral transfers (excluding military grants of goods and services) net**	**−2,951**	**−2,994**	**−3,294**	**−3,701**	**−3,848**	**−3,883**	**−7,184**	**−4,620**
30	U.S. Government grants (excluding military grants of goods and services)	−1,709	−1,649	−1,736	−2,043	−2,173	−1,938	−5,475	−2,893
31	U.S. Government pensions and other transfers	−406	−406	−462	−542	−572	−693	−694	−814
32	Private remittances and other transfers	−836	−939	−1,096	−1,117	−1,103	−1,252	−1,016	−913
33	**U.S. assets abroad, net (increase/capital outflow (−))**	**−8,572**	**−8,823**	**−6,032**	**−9,596**	**−10,245**	**−16,434**	**−33,392**	**−31,131**
34	U.S. official reserve assets, net	−880	−1,187	2,477	2,348	32	209	−1,434	−607
35	Gold	1,173	−967	787	866	547			
36	Special drawing rights			−851	−249	−703	9	−172	−66
37	Reserve position in the International Monetary Fund	−870	−1,034	389	1,350	153	−33	−1,265	−466
38	Foreign currencies								

Line / Item								
39 U.S. Government assets, other than official reserve assets, net	−2,274	−2,200	−1,589	−1,884	−1,568	−2,645	¹4,365	−3,463
40 U.S. loans and other long-term assets	−3,722	−3,489	−3,293	−4,181	−3,819	−4,639	−5,001	−5,936
41 Repayments on U.S. loans	1,386	1,200	1,721	2,115	2,086	2,596	4,826	2,476
42 U.S. foreign currency holdings and U.S. short-term assets, net	62	89	−16	182	165	−602	¹4 541	−3
43 U.S. private assets, net	−5,418	−5,436	−6,920	−10,060	−8,708	−13,998	−32,323	−27,061
44 Direct investments abroad	−2,880	−3,190	−4,281	−4,738	−3,530	−4,968	−7,753	−6,307
45 Foreign securities	−1,569	−1,549	−1,076	−1,113	−618	−671	−1,854	−6,206
U.S. claims on unaffiliated foreigners reported by U.S. nonbanking concerns:								
46 Long-term	−220	−424	−586	−168	−243	−396	−474	−384
47 Short-term	−982	298	−10	−1,061	−811	−1,982	−2,747	−925
U.S. claims reported by U.S. banks, not included elsewhere:								
48 Long-term	338	297	155	−612	−1,307	−933	−1,183	−2,351
49 Short-term	−105	−867	−1,122	−2,368	−2,199	−5,047	−18,311	−10,887
50 Foreign assets in the United States, net (increase/capital inflow (+))	9,439	12,270	5,923	22,445	21,127	18,519	32,433	14,879
51 Foreign official assets in the United States, net	−776	−1,301	6,907	26,895	10,705	6,299	10,981	6,336
52 U.S. Government securities	−771	−2,344	9,437	26,586	8,499	696	4,184	5,203
53 U.S. Treasury securities	−800	−2,269	9,410	26,594	8,243	114	3,282	4,312
54 Other	29	−74	−28	−8	257	582	902	891
55 Other U.S. Government liabilities	−15	251	−456	−510	383	1,153	724	1,732
56 U.S. liabilities reported by U.S. banks, not included elsewhere	10	792	−2,075	819	1,638	4,126	5,818	2,474
57 Other foreign official assets					185	323	254	1,874
58 Other foreign assets in the United States, net	10,215	13,571	−984	−4,450	10,422	12,220	21,452	8,544
59 Direct investments in the United States	319	832	1,030	−175	380	2,656	2,745	2,437
60 U.S. Treasury securities	136	−68	81	−22	−34	−214	697	2,649
61 U.S. securities other than U.S. Treasury securities	4,414	3,130	2,189	2,289	4,507	4,041	378	2,727
U.S. liabilities to unaffiliated foreigners reported by U.S. nonbanking concerns:								
62 Long-term	715	701	1,112	384	594	298	−212	313
63 Short-term	759	91	902	−15	221	737	1,827	−235
U.S. liabilities reported by U.S. banks not included elsewhere:								
64 Long-term	72	160	23	−250	149	227	9	−355
65 Short-term	3,799	8,726	−6,321	−6,661	4,605	4,475	16,008	1,008
66 Allocations of special drawing rights			867	717	710			
67 Statistical discrepancy (sum of above items with sign reversed)	507	−1,430	−402	−9,609	−1,790	−2,107	4,557	4,602
Memoranda:								
68 Balance on merchandise trade (lines 2 and 16)	635	607	2,603	−2,260	−6,416	911	−5,369	8,983
69 Balance on goods and services (lines 1 and 15)	1,578	977	2,938	−256	−5,954	3,405	3,586	16,269
70 Balance on goods, services, and remittances (lines 69, 31, and 32)	335	−368	1,380	−1,915	−7,629	1,960	1,877	14,542
71 Balance on current account (lines 69 and 29)	−1,374	−2,017	−356	−3,957	−9,802	22	−3,598	11,650
Transactions in U.S. official reserve assets and in foreign official assets in the United States:								
72 Increase (−) in U.S. official reserve assets, net (line 34)	−880	−1,187	2,477	2,348	32	209	−1,434	−607
73 Increase (+) in foreign official assets in the United States (line 51 less line 55)	−761	−1,552	7,362	27,405	10,322	5,145	10,257	4,603

Source: *Survey of Current Business*, June 1976.

until recently focused considerable attention on liquidity in appraising U.S. balance-of-payments performance.[2]

A series of steps was taken, beginning in 1963, to improve the liquidity of the U.S. position. In successive steps, capital controls were imposed by the U.S. government to stem the outflow of dollars and to encourage dollar inflows. Efforts were taken to shore up the dwindling supply of U.S. reserves. Dollar convertibility was suspended. Ultimately the dollar was devalued and the entire international financial framework was altered.

During the present era, U.S. authorities and officials from other countries seek to reduce the extent of world dependency on the U.S. dollar as a source of world reserves. In retrospect it is clear that the United States could not pursue its own international economic objectives in an increasingly competitive world economy and simultaneously remain sufficiently liquid to retain the confidence of foreign dollar holders. Cognizant of this fact, U.S. officials are likely to pursue policies in the future which will assure both adequate liquidity and maintenance of confidence in the dollar's longer-term potential. This latter objective is closely related to the U.S. potential to earn foreign exchange.

SUMMARY

The balance-of-payments accounts reflect a country's economic and financial relations with the rest of the world. Using a double-entry bookkeeping system, various transactions involving a country's residents and their counterparts in other countries are collected and disseminated on a regular basis. To interpret the meaning of these data, one must make some judgments regarding which transactions are important—that is, induced by underlying economic and financial forces. Analysis of these transactions, in turn, permits one to assess whether a given country has balance-of-payments problems— difficulties in its external commercial relations. If there is a problem, the country in question must find a solution. By considering various options open to the country, the analyst can develop extremely useful

---

[2]The advent of floating exchange rates with discretionary government intervention, together with the increased accumulation of dollars by oil-producing countries, has limited the usefulness of liquidity measures of balance of payments performance. Prior to 1976, two liquidity measures were reported—the net liquidity balance and the official reserves transaction balance—by the U.S. authorities. In a major revision of data presentation these measures were discontinued during the spring of 1976. The revised presentation format (Table 4–4) is explained together with its rationale in the June 1976 issue of *Survey of Current Business* published by the U.S. Department of Commerce.

insights into the likely strategies that the country will pursue. Fore-knowledge of likely developments can be extremely crucial to the international business enterprise since steps may often be taken to reduce the corporation's vulnerability in advance of a full-blown crisis.

EXERCISES AND DISCUSSION QUESTIONS

Show in double-entry format the entries that would be made in the United States balance-of-payments accounts for the following transactions. Use this sort of format:

Imports . . . . $2 million (dr)
    Private Short-Term
    Capital . . . . $2 million (cr)

1. A Japanese company sells electronic equipment to RCA in the United States for $2 million. Freight ($3,000) and insurance ($2,000) are arranged in the United States and paid for by RCA. Payment to the Japanese company is made by a check drawn on the Bank of America in New York.

2. A U.S. company decides to establish a new plant in Hong Kong to take advantage of cheap labor. The cost of setting up a plant during the year totaled $8.6 million. Half of this was paid out of an account held in Hong Kong, the rest from a U.S. account.

3. A U.S. company exports $400,000 worth of agricultural equipment to New Zealand and accepts $200,000 worth of shares in the local distributor as part payment. The rest is paid in New Zealand dollars.

4. Charles L. Hangover went on a trip to the Pacific Islands. He paid for his airfare of $2,000 in the United States but half the travel was done on Quantas (Australian) and the rest on Pan American. The fare was divided between the airlines accordingly. He spent a further $1,500 in the islands.

5. The U.S. government extends a loan to Israel to purchase military equipment. The loan is for $500 million. It is all spent on fighter aircraft bought from U.S. firms.

6. An investment trust in the United States buys 200,000 £1 shares in Unilever for $9 each and pays for them from its U.S. account.

7. Unilever directors declare a dividend of 6 percent and this is paid into the trust's U.S. account.

8. The United States spends $1.5 million on military exercises in the Pacific. Of this, $.9 million is paid to foreign countries for the use of docking and airport facilities.

9. The United States extends a $10 million loan to Italy to assist the development of its manufacturing industries. However, Italy spends it on equipment purchased from British companies.

5

The International Financial Framework

VARIOUS PARTIES to international business must be able to exchange currencies of one nation for the currencies of another. For the most part, such currency conversions are to facilitate trade and investment transactions. Some currency conversions, however, are of a speculative or protective nature in which participants exchange currencies in anticipation of changes in relative prices either to enhance profits in terms of the home currency or to "lock in" present levels of profitability. The parties to these conversions include individuals, businesses, commercial banks, and governments (especially central banks).

This chapter is concerned with the process of currency conversion. Various rules and practices govern this process, and the first section of the chapter describes the currency exchange system, its antecedents, problems, and prospects. This sets the stage for subsequent discussion of the foreign exchange market, participants in the market, and the relationship between the foreign exchange and other international financial markets.

BACKGROUND

During the 40 years before World War I, the major countries of the world attempted to secure exchange-rate stability by linking their currencies to gold. After the war, they continued with a restructured gold standard into the 1930s. Under the gold standard, exchange rates had fixed par values determined by the gold content of the national monetary units. Each country legally defined its standard monetary unit as consisting of a specified quantity of gold. To keep the national currency equivalent in value to the declared gold content, the government stood ready to buy and sell gold in unlimited quantities at the price implied by its relationship to the standard monetary unit. Thus, for example, in 1930 the U.S. dollar was defined as containing 23.22 grains of fine gold, and the British pound was defined as containing approximately 113 grains of fine gold. The U.S. government freely bought and sold gold at the implied price of $20.67 per fine troy ounce (there are 480 grains in a troy ounce).

Under the gold standard, deficits or surpluses in a country's balance-of-payments situation were expected to provoke internal adjustments that would correct the situation and restore stability. Classical theory placed primary emphasis on domestic price and income changes to restore the equilibrium. In effect, countries were expected to subordinate their national economies to the dictates of external economic and monetary relations.

With the world economic crisis of the 1930s, however, countries became unwilling to undertake domestic policies of price and income deflation or to accept the unemployment that would result from such policies in order to resolve external balance-of-payments problems. Unilateral devaluations, foreign exchange controls, and tariffs began to abound. Beginning with Great Britain in 1931, one country after another abandoned the gold standard, despite the fact that the standard had facilitated a vast expansion in world trade. The 1930s saw complete monetary chaos. Currencies of many of the smaller countries fluctuated wildly in the exchange markets, propelled by underlying economic forces and waves of speculation.

After World War II the United States stood virtually alone as a holder of wealth and producer of goods. Recognizing the need to restructure the international monetary system, free-world representatives met at Bretton Woods, New Hampshire in 1944 and agreed to establish a new systematic monetary order which centered around the International Monetary Fund (IMF) and the International Bank for Reconstruction and Development (World Bank). The object of this system was to facilitate the expansion of world trade and to use the then-powerful dollar as a standard of value to provide liquidity and relatively inflation-free stability with the more traditional use of gold as a standard of value. The dollar, therefore, became the kingpin of this system, which lasted from 1945 to 1971.[1]

International Monetary Fund

The initial objectives of the International Monetary Fund are shown in Figure 5–1. Member governments, of which there were 128 as

---

[1]For a detailed discussion, see Robert Triffin, *Our International Monetary System, Yesterday, Today, and Tomorrow* (New York: Random House, Inc. 1968).

FIGURE 5–1
The Purposes of the International Monetary Fund

1. To promote international monetary cooperation through a permanent institution which provides the machinery for consultation and collaboration on international monetary problems.
2. To facilitate the expansion and balanced growth of international trade, and to contribute thereby to the promotion and maintenance of high levels of employment and real income and to the development of the productive resources of all members as primary objectives of economic policy.
3. To promote exchange stability, to maintain orderly exchange arrangements among members, and to avoid competitive exchange depreciation.
4. To assist in the establishment of a multilateral system of payments in respect of current transactions between members and in the elimination of foreign exchange restrictions which hamper the growth of world trade.
5. To give confidence to members by making the Fund's resources available to them under adequate safeguards, thus providing them with opportunity to correct maladjustments in their balance of payments without resorting to measures destructive of national or international prosperity.
6. In accordance with the above, to shorten the duration and lessen the degree of disequilibrium in the international balances of payments of members.

Source: Articles of Agreement of the IMF, July 22, 1944.

of June, 1976, agreed to establish a fixed exchange ratio (parity) for their currencies, expressed in gold and dollars. Any change in these parities by a country required prior IMF approval and amounted to a formal revaluation (increase in the currency value) or devaluation (decrease in the currency value). The IMF plan fixed the limits for exchange-rate fluctuations to 1 percent above or below the official parity, with each member government committed to pursue policies to keep its own rates within this narrow range. Members also agreed to make their currencies convertible—to dismantle their exchange controls—after a transition period.

Monetary reserves (governments' liquid foreign assets) then consisted of gold, U.S. dollars, and other foreign currencies. The dollar became increasingly important during the postwar period because of its relative availability compared to gold and its stability in relation to many other foreign currencies. Furthermore, the dollar was a desirable reserve asset because dollar investments such as Treasury bills and series E bonds were interest bearing, which was not true of gold. The IMF system, sometimes called the system of the adjustable peg, sought to assure maximum exchange-rate stability, yet facilitated orderly changes when they were needed, and thus avoided competitive devaluations like those of the 1930s.

When joining the IMF, member countries pay a subscription quota, 25 percent of which is due in gold and 75 percent in the member's own currency, based on certain economic criteria related to the size of the country and its national income. This quota also determines a country's voting power in the Fund and the amount of foreign exchange that it may draw. At any time a member can borrow or purchase from the IMF foreign exchange equal to the amount of its subscription that it paid in gold (25 percent). This sum is a country's *gold tranche position* and is included in the calculation of its reserves. In effect, the nation is purchasing foreign currency using its gold on deposit with the IMF. Any borrowing by a member in excess of its *gold tranche position* must have fund approval and only may be used for remedying the country's balance-of-payments difficulties. Such a drawing is made on a country's so-called *credit tranche,* which is limited to 200 percent of the country's quota.

The IMF's leverage over member countries comes from its ability to grant or deny access to the Fund's resources and from the fact that Fund membership is a prerequisite for joining the World Bank. The IMF will approve or deny a member's request to draw primarily on the basis of that country's efforts to reduce exchange restrictions and to establish currency convertibility. Countries that maintain exchange controls must meet with the Fund each year to justify their use of the controls and to discuss the possibilities of removing such restrictions.

The World Bank Group

The representatives who gathered for the Bretton Woods Conference had two objectives in restructuring the international monetary system. These were: (1) to promote international currency stability and the progressive elimination of exchange restrictions and (2) to provide financial assistance for postwar reconstruction and development. The IMF was created in response to the former. The World Bank was established to achieve the latter. Today it is proper to refer to the World Bank Group because the Bank has two affiliates—the International Development Association (IDA) and the International Finance Corporation (IFC). The World Bank Group is presently the major public international institutional source of financing.

The Articles of Agreement of the World Bank proper establish it as an intergovernmental institution, corporate in nature, with its capital stock owned by the member countries. Even though it is an intergovernmental organization, the bank's primary source of funds for its lending operations is the private capital markets. The bank deals mainly in long-term loans to member countries for specific reconstruction or development projects. It also lends for private projects when the government endorses and guarantees the loan. After World War II, much of the lending was to European countries for reconstruction. More recently, virtually all of the lending has been to the less developed countries, mainly for infrastructure projects such as electric power and transportation development. Loans are also made for agriculture, industry, and, lately, education. The World Bank is important to international business more as a general force for stimulating economic development than as a direct source for business financing. However, the bank has begun to expand its industrial lending activities since the late 1960s.

The International Finance Corporation was established in 1956 in response to the need for a specialized international body to stimulate private enterprise and private investment in developing countries. The IFC finances business projects mainly in the manufacturing and processing fields, either through loans or equity participation and without government endorsements or guarantees.[2] The IFC provides a multinational source for financing international enterprise but has not played a broad role in influencing the international business environment.

The International Development Association was created in 1960 for making soft loans—that is, loans with long maturity, relatively low rates of interest, and easy repayment terms—to the less developed countries. Nearly all IDA loans "have been for a term of 50 years, with a 10-year initial grace period and no interest charge, only a service charge of 3/4 of 1 percent per annum."[3] Such loans are made to member governments exclusively for development purposes.

The Bretton Woods System

Within the institutional framework conceived in 1944 and evolving as described above, parity limits assured parties to international trade and investment that countries were prepared to defend the value of their respective currencies. The central banks of the IMF countries undertook to keep the exchange rates of their currencies within a fixed percentage limit to the U.S. dollar. These limits, revised in 1971 to $2^{1}/_{4}$

---

[2]James C. Baker, *The International Finance Corporation* (New York: Praeger Publishers, Inc., 1968).

[3]*Policies and Operations: The World Bank Group* (Washington, D.C.: The World Bank, 1974), p. 7.

percent on either side of parity, were known as "intervention points." In practice, central banks usually intervened in the markets to preserve narrower limits. Under IMF regulations, a "floating" or free exchange rate based on supply and demand conditions in the market was not permitted. Central banks prevented floating through their intervention in the market. Heavy intervention suggested that central banks were having difficulty maintaining the rate and usually preluded a parity change.

The United States had a special status within the system due to the U.S. dollar's peculiar role as a reserve currency. Because of its reserve currency status and free convertibility into gold upon official request, the dollar could be devalued or revalued under IMF rules only by changes in its parity with gold—that is, by increasing or decreasing the price of gold. The United States had no obligation to maintain the dollar within its official limits relative to other currencies in foreign exchange markets, but instead it was formally required under IMF rules to meet all offers from foreign central banks to buy or sell gold for dollars at the official price of $35 per ounce. The resulting system in which currencies were pegged to the dollar and the dollar was pegged to gold worked well for nearly 20 years.

The Crisis of Confidence and Period of Adjustment

With the prolonged and steep deterioration in the U.S. balance of payments during the late 1960s the dollar came under increasing pressure. The growing reluctance of foreigners to hold dollars created a crisis of confidence which led in 1968 to a change in the dollar's historic exchange rate. Excessive demand for gold forced the U.S. to suspend its sale except to official parties during 1968, and a "two-tier" system of official and free gold prices resulted. The private or unofficial price of gold skyrocketed, exceeding $200 per ounce at one point, with the most important result being an almost complete abandonment of gold trading among nations. On August 15, 1971, the United States ceased exchanging gold for dollars even with official parties and, in effect, floated the dollar in a series of measures intended to force both a change in the dollar parity and a review of the entire IMF system. The United States' primary goal was to achieve a more satisfactory relation between the dollar and other currencies under the prevailing international trade conditions.

With the Smithsonian Agreement of December 1971, virtually all of the Paris Bloc countries revalued their currencies against the U.S. dollar,[4] resulting in an effective dollar devaluation of 10.35 percent. As

---

[4]The nine major industrial countries: France, Germany, Italy, the Netherlands, Belgium, England, Sweden, Canada, and Japan.

the United States still refused to sell gold for dollars, however, it was foreseen that the IMF rules regarding the maintenance of adequate international reserves and currency convertibility needed to be shifted to a broader group of countries; such renegotiation, however, was left to the future. The price of gold was reset at $38 per ounce.

The exchange crisis was renewed again during early 1973 with further selling of the dollar against such major currencies as the German mark, the Japanese yen, and French franc. As a consequence, a second 10 percent dollar devaluation was announced in February, 1973, increasing the gold price to $42 per ounce. The impasse in monetary regulations continued since neither the U.S. government (still holder of the largest gold reserves in the world) nor foreign authorities offered to support the dollar through the sale of gold. By March 1973, virtually every major currency was floating without much formal discipline remaining.

The Group of Ten major trading nations originally formed to find acceptable substitutes for the dollar-oriented fixed-exchange IMF system was enlarged to a Group of Twenty (including the major underdeveloped countries),[5,6] but by mid-1973, no common ground for compromise had yet appeared.[7] The dollar slipped to new lows despite increasing signs that the U.S. currency was in fact undervalued and the country's trade deficit was rapidly turning into a surplus.

The two successive 10 percent devaluations of the dollar in fact were the key elements in converting the large 1972 U.S. trade deficit ($8 billion) to a surplus by 1973. With the United States' great strength in agricultural products and relative self-sufficiency in energy, the dollar improved quickly toward the close of 1973 and returned approximately to its position following the Smithsonian Agreement.

While monetary authorities continued to discuss outstanding issues after 1974, they had not reached agreement as of late 1976 on the basis for a new formalized monetary system. Differing goals among the

---

[5]The Group of Ten is composed of the United States, United Kingdom, France, Germany, Japan, Italy, Canada, the Netherlands, Belgium, and Sweden.

[6]The Group of Twenty, currently known as the Interim Committee, consists of the United States, United Kingdom, Germany, France, Japan, plus 15 representatives for all of the other members of the fund.

[7]The Group of Ten during 1968 had orchestrated the creation of a new type of reserve asset called special drawing rights (SDRs). Created by the IMF and distributed proportionately among IMF members, these reserves, along with gold and convertible currencies, have been used as an additional international unit of settlement. SDRs have been issued in successive annual series from 1970–72 and now total $10.719 billion, compared to total official gold holdings of $40.663 billion and foreign exchange holdings of $165.504 billion for all member countries and Switzerland. Like gold, SDRs are non-interest bearing and are not tied to the dollar rate of exchange.

developed and developing countries and among the key-currency countries themselves have forestalled resolution of the monetary issues that surfaced during this period of uncertainty and unrest.[8]

THE MANAGED FLOAT SYSTEM

Despite the upheavals, the present monetary order is remarkably similar to the Bretton Woods system. The exchange rates of most developing countries remain fixed in relation to the currencies of principal trading partners in industrialized countries. For example, the Philippine peso is normally tied to the U.S. dollar. As during the previous era, a country such as the Philippines may be forced to devalue its currency in a crisis, but such an exchange rate correction would be unusual. In general, the developing countries continue to seek a stable rate with their most important economic partner to facilitate desired trade and investment patterns.

There have been important changes in the way exchange rate values are determined among the major industrialized countries—that is, the key-currency countries such as the United States, Germany, France, the United Kingdom, and Japan. These changes are the by-product of both independent actions taken by individual countries and decisions reached through collective discussion at monetary meetings in Ramboullet, France during 1975 and in Jamaica during 1976. While the changes from the earlier Bretton Woods system are significant, what is most important is a continuation of the disciplined interrelationship among the key currencies.

Today, the industrialized countries permit their currencies to float, that is, to fluctuate in price based on supply and demand considerations. Yet these fluctuations are controlled by the monetary authorities of the individual countries. The central banks intervene in the exchange markets, "dirtying" the float to preserve what they construe to be orderly foreign exchange markets and appropriate exchange-rate relationships. This intervention is to counter unwarranted currency speculation and to prevent currency movements that might precipitate competitive currency devaluations among the countries. A system of multilaterally managed float has emerged. While the discipline is less rigid and formal than under the fixed-rate Bretton Woods arrangement, it nonetheless exists.

---

[8]See Tom de Vries, *An Agenda for Monetary Reform,* Essays in International Finance #95 (Princeton, N.J.: Finance Section, Department of Economics, Princeton University, September 1972). Also see Harry G. Johnson, *The Problem of International Monetary Reform* (London: Athlone Press, 1974). Also W. M. Scammel, *International Monetary Policy: Bretton Woods and After* (New York: Halsted Press, 1975).

INTERPRETING MONETARY DEVELOPMENTS

What do these developments mean? Some contend that floating exchange rates mean increased difficulties for exporters and importers in financing their overseas trade. Many observers contend that the situation has been especially hard on capital goods manufacturers— e.g., builders of ships and machinery—in that these producers must contend with high degrees of uncertainty or expensive insurance premiums to protect themselves against currency fluctuation when selling to foreign buyers. To be sure, the increased currency variability makes currency forecasting a more critical management function, with errors in judgment proving to be significantly more costly.

Others argue that floating exchange rates have not impeded world trade and have not imposed undue hardships on national economies. In support of the present arrangement, many cite the success with which the international financial system has coped with the serious problems of external adjustment caused by the oil crisis and the quintupling of petroleum import prices during the mid-1970s. Moreover, international trade has continued to increase.

There is widespread agreement today that the Bretton Woods system, which worked so well during the late 1940s and 1950s, was not well equipped to cope with economic developments during the 1960s. One difficulty of the system was that expansion of international liquidity depended more heavily on foreigners' willingness to hold U.S. dollars than on world needs. By the late 1960s an even greater source of difficulty with the system became apparent. The system did not specify how mutual payments imbalances among countries would be adjusted and by whom, and the role that exchange-rate changes should play in the adjustment process. In these matters, several assumptions made by the designers of the Bretton Woods system turned out over time to become increasingly less appropriate. In particular, many countries refused to adjust their domestic economies to remedy trade imbalances. Price and income deflation policies were considered to be too painful and internally disruptive, and country officials were unwilling to give international payments issues the top priority on which preservation of the system depended.

The designers of the Bretton Woods system wanted to avoid a repetition of the competitive currency depreciations of the 1930s. Viewed from this standpoint, the system was extremely successful. Yet, as often happens, the improvement was made at the cost of moving too far in the opposite direction. The major international monetary problems that emerged during the postwar period resulted from too infrequent, rather than too frequent, exchange-rate changes.

The adjustable peg, as the Bretton Woods system has been called, contained bias against parity changes. At the same time the system permitted only a narrow range of fluctuations of market rates about parity. A bias against parity changes may have been justified in a world in which "beggar my neighbor" exchange-rate adjustments were anticipated, but the international economic climate of the postwar period had changed dramatically from that of the 1930s. Perhaps the most important factor was a better understanding of the proper use of macroeconomic policy management, which considerably reduced the economic incentives for competitive depreciation of currencies as a means of exporting unemployment.

While the bias in the system against exchange-rate changes reduced the frequency of exchange-rate depreciations by deficit countries, it also exacerbated the corresponding problem of the failure of surplus countries to appreciate their currencies when appropriate. Yet maintenance of undervalued exchange rates and balance-of-payments surplus objectives can be just as disruptive to international exchange as attempts to maintain an overvalued rate.

The adverse effects of excessive exchange-rate fixity were further compounded by increased international economic activity in the postwar period, and in particular by the increase in capital mobility. The articles of Bretton Woods did not envision that capital flight would present much of a problem. The mobility of international liquid funds was at that time quite low and was further constrained in most countries by comprehensive systems of exchange controls. By the 1960s, however, the picture had changed dramatically and, in the face of huge increases in the quantities of international mobile funds, the "sure bet" of gains presented by sticky exchange parities generated ever-increasing currency speculation. Governments were left to defend unrealistic rates against crowing speculative and precautionary capital sources. Initial government reactions involved trying to supercede or suspend market forces, with deficit countries attempting to finance their deficits, and surplus countries attempting to sterilize inflows rather than to correct the fundamental disequilibria. Delay in undertaking exchange-rate changes, however, ultimately increased the cost of adjustment once the changes did occur.

By biasing incentives against the use of exchange-rate adjustments, the Bretton Woods system also increased the degree to which policy coordination among member nations was needed for efficient operation of the system. At a time when national economies were becoming increasingly interdependent and with mechanisms for bringing about international policy coordination lacking, this proved to be a fatal deficiency. Acceptance of greater exchange-rate flexibility today has helped eliminate much of the tension that arose between surplus and deficit countries and has permitted a greater degree of autonomy in national policies. Against this backdrop, we can now continue with our examination of the international financial markets themselves.

FOREIGN EXCHANGE MARKETS AND PARTICIPANTS

In a narrow sense, a foreign exchange market provides a mechanism for transferring the money of one country into that of another. In a broader sense, because of its close connections with the money, capital, and other financial markets, a foreign exchange market is also a means of supplying credit for and arranging the financing of international economic transactions.

Foreign exchange markets tend to locate in national financial centers near the related financial markets. The more important exchange markets are therefore found in New York, London, Paris, Frankfurt, Amsterdam, Milan, Zurich, Toronto, and the financial centers of most other developed and industrialized nations. The exchange markets are so well integrated that together they constitute a single world market, despite the distances and time differentials involved. (This closeness exists despite the fact that market participants such as banks, brokers, and traders are not formally linked and do not share common facilities in various cities.) The Euro-currency market is also heavily involved in foreign exchange transactions and may be said to complement the international foreign exchange markets.

Because foreign exchange transactions are closely related to the import and export of goods and capital, many countries, as noted earlier, impose legal restrictions upon the amount and kinds of trading allowed and even upon the rates that may be quoted. Relatively few countries permit free convertibility of their currencies, and it is in these countries that foreign exchange trading is centered.

The foreign exchange markets are governed by an unwritten code of conduct that all participants must follow. Most market transactions are handled in an informal manner by telephone or telex, rather than in written legal form. The apparently casual nature of the market transactions belies the strictness of the unwritten code and the swift punishment of anyone who reneges.

The Role of Central Banks

Central banks are major participants in the foreign exchange markets. The central bank of a country has as its primary obligation the maintenance of an efficient monetary system that encourages domestic growth without inflation. This internal objective is affected by external forces. Balance-of-payments surpluses, if no action is taken, may increase the liquidity of a country to undesirable levels and add to inflationary forces. Balance-of-payments deficits may create pressures that eventually affect the domestic economy or exhaust its foreign exchange reserves. In either case, a central bank, particularly through its exchange control arm, may be forced to intervene actively in the external economic sphere in order to attain domestic goals. In this fashion, central banks often have a pervasive influence on foreign exchange markets.

In simplest terms, central bank dealings in foreign exchange are undertaken to maintain orderly markets for the respective currencies and thereby foster international trade and investment. Actually, a central bank acts in response to the complex interplay of its country's own economic course, balance of payments—trade and capital—and reserve position, domestic and international interest rates, current market psychology, and other factors. Moreover, each central bank acts in its own way. The methods, extent, and frequency of intervention of central banks vary sharply.

In some countries, such as Brazil and Colombia where rates of inflation have been very high, central banks change the exchange rates periodically, perhaps as often as once or twice a month, to avoid intolerable misallocations of productive resources. In these instances, the governments seek to establish exchange rates that preserve desired relations among prices of imports and exports through a policy referred to as "crawling pegs" or "mini-devaluations."

The central banks of other countries—e.g., the United States and Germany—have intervened in the foreign exchange markets to avoid excessive daily changes in exchange rates, but not necessarily to prevent a strong seasonal or cyclical drift upward or downward. These central banks are parties to the prevailing system of a managed float.

In the event of a severe balance-of-payments disequilibrium, a central bank will attempt to neutralize the adverse effect of the disequilibrium on the internal economy through establishing foreign exchange controls. The controls may become a permanent framework within which the exchange markets operate and which may continue even when there is no severe balance-of-payments disequilibrium.

To control the speculative flow to other countries of funds seeking a higher yield, a central bank may change domestic interest levels by adopting a different discount rate or by taking some other action. As an alternative to changing domestic interest levels, the central bank may intervene in the foreign exchange futures market (the forward market) to counteract the undesired money flow. A brief digression into foreign exchange terminology and concepts will help explain this form of central bank intervention.[9]

Currencies can be exchanged either in the *spot market* or in the *forward market.* In the spot market, currencies are traded for immediate delivery. The forward market is where trades are made for future dates, usually less than one year away. Let us assume, for example, that the prevailing quotes to buy or sell pounds sterling in the spot, 3-month, 6-month, and 12-month forward markets are as follows:

Maturity	Buy	Sell
Spot . . . . . . .U.S. $1.7860		U.S. $1.7890
3 months . . .	1.7501	1.7550
6 months . . .	1.7169	1.7280
12 months . . .	1.7009	1.7149

The difference between the bid and the asked prices provides the margin to cover the exchange trader's costs and profit. This refinement is not important for our purposes. Let us assume that U.K. Treasury bills with six-month maturity are selling to yield investors 8 percent per annum, whereas comparable money market instruments denominated in German marks yield only 7 percent. Under the interest parity theory and in normal markets, the forward discount in sterling vis-a-vis German marks would be 1 percent per annum. The reason for this is a phenomenon called *interest rate arbitrage.* Interest arbitrage involves participation in both the British pound and the German mark markets simultaneously to take advantage of any unwarranted differences in rates between the markets. An investor outside the United Kingdom buys pounds in the spot market to invest in pound sterling money market instruments with the higher yield. The investor simultaneously "contracts" to sell pounds in the forward markets for an amount equivalent to the interest and principal obtained at maturity. At maturity the pounds received from the investment are used to settle the forward contract. Thus, an investment in pounds has been made without any risk that the British currency may devalue and reduce the return or erode the principal. Investors selling sterling in the forward market will cause sterling to sell at a discount which, under normal market conditions, will precisely offset the interest rate differential. Interest rate arbitragers will be attracted to markets whenever there is imparity in the various interest rate and forward exchange rate structures. This practice helps explain the earlier comment that interest rates and forward exchange rates are closely interrelated.

---

[9]A glossary of foreign exchange terminology is provided in the appendix to this chapter.

A central bank sometimes intervenes in the forward market through purchases to keep the discount on its own currency from falling to a lower level. Such a step may be considered preferable to adjustments in the domestic money market rates, or may simply disguise indecision or inaction in order to maintain confidence in a currency. From 1964 to 1967, the British government supported the forward pound continually, but it did not couple that tactic with adequate internal measures to protect Britain's trading position. The policy proved to be very expensive and finally ineffective.

Central banks can also offer arbitrage opportunities to their domestic banks at rates not applicable to market conditions. For example, the dollar rate for short-term deposits might be 10 percent per annum when German rates are at 8 percent per annum. If a 2 percent forward premium on the German mark vis-a-vis the dollar exists, German banks would not gain by buying dollars spot, placing them on deposit at 10 percent, and then selling them forward. This is because this swap costs 2 percent (resulting from the simultaneous spot sale of German marks for dollars and the forward purchase of marks), which wipes out the dollar rate advantage. For policy reasons, however, a central bank such as the German Bundesbank might offer swaps at a 1 percent per annum cost to its local banks instead of the 2 percent market cost. In that case, the local banks would be induced to enter into a larger volume of outward interest arbitrage—the spot purchase of dollars for investment, protected by the currency swap arranged with the German Bundesbank. The internal result in Germany would be to reduce bank liquidity and international reserve holdings, although both on a temporary basis. In effect, there would be an artificial reduction of the forward premium on the domestic currency, in this case the German mark.

Although a central bank might be considered a non-profit-seeking entity, both its spot and forward dealings have an inherent profit and loss element. Protection of either a forward rate or a lower spot rate limit may result in severe losses of reserves, which constitute part of the "real wealth" of a country. In that sense, foreign exchange market participation is not riskless, even for a central bank.

To strengthen and defend the international money system, the central banks of various industrialized countries cooperate closely. Central banks on occasion offer large swap facilities to each other on a formal or ad hoc basis; that is, banks agree to lend their currencies to each other with the understanding that the original transactions will be later reversed. In this fashion, one central bank obtains large amounts of another country's currency. This lessens the drain on the second country's reserves and gains time for the country's corrective actions to take effect. During June of 1976, the Bank of England undertook such a transaction, borrowing $5.3 billion from 11 central banks and the Bank for International Settlements (a bank for central banks) to provide the United Kingdom with additional reserves to defend sterling against further speculative attack.

Commercial Banks

The foreign exchange market itself is primarily a market of commercial banks trading directly with each other on a worldwide and instantaneous basis. The banks act both as agents for their customers—corporations, central banks, and individuals—and as active participants for their own account. All trades of currency between banks and between banks and corporations involve transfers of funds on the books of banks in the country whose currency is involved.

The transactions that customers bring to their banks are varied and not entirely predictable. In most cases, spot purchases and sales of the various currencies tend to balance for the international banking system as a whole (a basic requirement of normal market equilibrium), but they may not balance for any individual bank. A single bank may experience demand that is asymmetric to the market, owing to the needs of particular customers or industries it serves. Its spot holdings in any case will not cover, and are not intended to cover, all of the spot requirements over time or even on a single day. Thus, it will be constantly entering the market as an active buyer or seller as much to balance its cash position as to even out its exchange position.

Banks often assume an active principal role on their own behalf. As the volume of international trade and capital transactions has grown in recent years, the exchange markets have also grown in depth and scope. In keeping with these developments, the larger banks are now more likely to take a net exposed position for their own account, whereas formerly banks tended to even out their positions to neutralize the effects of their customers' transactions. Profits can be made by participation in the foreign exchange area, and losses can be sustained as well. Recent history has recorded a number of prominent, even spectacular, losses in bank foreign exchange dealings.

Corporations

Corporations with international operations have many reasons to buy and sell foreign currencies. These transactions account for an important part, perhaps the bulk, of the exchange market turnover. Such dealings may involve an outright exchange based upon the current market ratio (a spot), an exchange to be made in the future at an agreed ratio which may vary substantially from the current price (a forward contract), or a simultaneous purchase and sale involving spot and forward exchange—or two foreign exchanges of different maturities (a swap).

Chapter 21 provides a comprehensive description of the corporate, international financial manager's tasks. It suffices here to suggest that many foreign exchange transactions of corporations are designed to reduce or eliminate foreign exchange risks; these include hedging or covering operations undertaken to protect exposed exchange positions from potential losses due to currency fluctuations, and risk-bearing transactions which involve the assumption of risk for potential profit. Some of the more usual reasons for corporate transactions are as follows:

1. Spot transactions.
   a. To liquidate a current payable or receivable. For example, the American Motors Corp. owes Volkswagen DM100,000 for auto parts shipped on open account cash terms. AMC purchases DM100,000 from its New York bank to make the payment, and the bank debits AMC's account for $40,000 (DM1= $0.40).
   b. To take advantage of higher interest rates or a greater availability of money market instruments.
   c. To speculate on a relative upward valuation of a bought (stronger) currency or a relative downward valuation of a sold (weaker) money. To illustrate, IBM has $500,000 in idle funds and has been told by its foreign exchange consultants that a French franc revaluation will be coming within the next three days. IBM instructs its bank to buy the equivalent of $500,000 in francs to be credited to its Paris account. IBM thus profits when a subsequent 10 percent franc revaluation is announced. Afterwards, the francs can be converted back into dollars with a "profit" of $50,000.
2. Forward purchase or sale.
   a. To hedge against exchange risk losses of a future payable denominated in a stronger currency, or a future receivable denominated in a weaker currency.
      As an example, Texas Instruments must pay 100,000 yens to Sony three months from now for a recent purchase of electronic components. An anticipated revaluation of the Japanese yen would increase the cost of the components. Therefore, TI buys 100,000 yens forward for delivery in three months, paying in all probability a premium, to fix the cost of the components. If the yen revaluation does not occur within three months or is less than the premium paid, then there was a "loss" on this hedge. However, if the revaluation does occur and is of an

amount equal to or greater than the premium, then TI has profited from this forward contract.

b. To cover the exchange risk of the net exposure on an investment in a subsidiary's inventory or working capital.

As an illustration, the Coca-Cola Co. has a net exposed current liability position (liabilities exceeding assets) in France of 1 million francs and has been told that the franc will soon be revalued. Coca-Cola buys 1 million French francs forward which, if delivered after the revaluation occurs, results in a dollar gain to offset the loss from the increased value of the liabilities.

c. To speculate on currency value changes greater than the forward discount or premium.

3. Swaps.

a. To cover interest arbitrage, as discussed in our earlier examples.

b. To cover repayment of foreign borrowings in a stronger currency.

THE INTERNATIONAL MONEY MARKET

The international money market parallels the foreign exchange market. It is located in the same centers as its foreign exchange counterpart. The market has fewer currencies in which to operate, however, because only those currencies for which forward exchange markets exist and which are easily convertible and available in sufficient quantity can be taken as deposits or placed as loans. In the currencies in which it is operative, however, the international money market channels money in and out of domestic markets. Regulations permitting, it acts as a provider and user of funds for a host of concerns that might not naturally be involved in foreign exchange. These include national and local corporations looking for long-term financing, and individual investors whose opportunities are severely constrained in the local national market.

The principal medium of the international financial markets is Euro-currencies, monies traded outside the country of their origin. Euro-dollars are dollar deposits at banks, either non-U.S. banks or foreign branches of U.S. banks, which are located outside the United States; Euro-sterlings are sterling deposits in banks outside the United Kingdom, and so forth. Why do these markets exist? There is a simple answer: government regulations. National governments have imposed a host of restrictions on lenders and borrowers, including interest rate ceilings, reserve requirements, taxes, and the like. These restrictions have caused lenders to seek out opportunities abroad where they could earn higher yields. Borrowers in turn have tapped the Euro-markets because monies in the local markets either were unavailable or could be obtained only on unattractive terms. The Euro-currency market expanded almost twentyfold from 1964 to 1975 (see Table 5–1).

TABLE 5–1
Growth of the Euro-Currency Market*
(in billions of dollars)

End of Period	Estimated Market Size	
	Gross†	Net‡
1964	21	14
1965	24	17
1966	29	21
1967	36	25
1968	50	35
1969	86	50
1970	113	65
1971	155	85
1972	203	110
1973	305	160
1974		
March	339	175
June	366	185
Sept.	354	190
Dec.	373	210
1975		
March	382	220
June	392	230
Mid-Aug.	395	230

*Based on foreign currency liabilities to residents and nonresidents reported by banks in eight European countries covered by BIS data (Belgium-Luxembourg, France, Germany, Italy, the Netherlands, Sweden, Switzerland, and the United Kingdom) and by banks in Canada, Japan, the Bahamas and Cayman Islands, Singapore, and Panama.
†All foreign currency liabilities to residents and nonresidents, banks and nonbanks.
‡Excludes interbank redeposits within the reporting area.
Source: Morgan Guarantee Trust Company.

INTERNATIONAL BANKING

During the past two decades, international banking operations have expanded tremendously. Since the start of this decade, for instance, international earnings for the 13 U.S. banks with the largest overseas operations have risen from $177 million in 1970 to $836 million in 1975, representing compound growth of 36.4 percent per annum. Moreover, international assets of all U.S. banks represented nearly 21 percent of total assets at year-end 1975, compared with only 8.5 percent in 1970.

As multinational business operations have increased in size and number, so bankers have followed them in an effort to better meet their customers' needs. In order to become truly "international," rather than being just in the international loan business, several banks, such as Chase Manhattan, the Bank of America, National Westminster, and Barclays, have formed consortiums as one of their strategies. These consortiums provide the banks with a broader base of operations and the opportunity to diversify international risk and pool expertise and resources.

International banking has also been stimulated by the ever-increasing demands for funds from the developing countries. If private banks had not been there to supply credit, it is unclear how petroleum-dependent countries would have financed their current account deficits, aggregating $35 billion in 1975. "Altogether, about $40 billion, it is estimated, has gone in private loans to these countries, with American banks responsible for well over half that total."[10] Banks, as noted earlier, also lend indirectly to the developing countries through loans to such public institutions as the World Bank and the various regional lenders such as the Asian Development Bank and the Inter-American Development Bank.

In the near future, however, it appears that U.S. multinational banks increasingly may have to change their basic strategies abroad. With risk levels, competitive regulatory constraints, and political opposition intensifying overseas, some economists are projecting that investment prospects will be more favorable in the U.S. than abroad during the next decade. Therefore, future market and product expansion in the international banking field may become highly selective. U.S. bank managements are continuing to assess multiple variables such as international earnings diversification, cross-currency, and political risk considerations. These assessments have and will continue to result in greater geographic and functional dispersion of international assets and funding sources, and refined planning techniques regarding future market penetration (especially in bank-related fields).

SUMMARY

Prior to World War II, the international monetary system was based on the gold standard. For 25 years following World War II, the

---

[10]"Banking on the boom," *Economist*, February 14, 1976.

free-world economies for the most part adhered to the tenets of the Bretton Woods agreement—namely, a system of fixed exchange rates which anticipated that individual countries would make adjustments to imbalances in their external accounts without resorting to exchange-rate depreciations or currency controls. On occasion individual countries were unable to comply with the terms of the agreement. Yet the system remained intact until the late 1960s when the United States, the most important country for the viability of the international financial structure, concluded that the arbitrary discipline of the system was no longer tenable. With the subsequent devaluations of the U.S. dollar and unhinging of the dollar from gold, the free-world economies entered into an era of floating exchange rates. An arrangement has emerged (perhaps it too could be called a system) in which individual countries decide whether to permit their respective currencies to float or to remain pegged to the currency values of some other country. While disagreement abounds regarding the strengths and weaknesses of this new arrangement, most observers agree that a return to the old, fixed-rate system is unlikely during the foreseeable future.

Within this context, the system of closely linked foreign exchange markets throughout the world continues to function. These markets, in turn, are closely related to the international and national money markets and the operations of international banks, all of which can be viewed as a means of supplying credit for and arranging the financing of international economic transactions of various kinds.

APPENDIX: FOREIGN EXCHANGE TERMINOLOGY

Much of the mystery surrounding foreign exchange lies in the specific, trade-related terminology that describes the activities of the exchange traders and their clients. In the interest of brevity, only the most important and commonly used terms and concepts have been included in this glossary.

Arbitrage—Simultaneous buying and selling of foreign exchanges for realizing profits from discrepancies between exchange rates prevailing at the same time in different centers, between forward margins for different maturities, or between interest rates prevailing at the same time in different centers or in different currencies.

Blocked account—Currency that is owned by nonresidents of an exchange control country and cannot be freely transferred.

Broker—A person who arranges for the purchase or sale of foreign exchange between banks but is not a principal to the transaction.

Brokerage—Charges made by a broker for his services in arranging for the purchase or sale of foreign exchange between banks.

Clear, business, or market days—Days on which markets involved in a foreign exchange transaction are open for business and that are used in determining the value dates on which foreign exchange or Euro-dollar transactions must be consummated.

Clearinghouse funds—Funds transferred between banks in New York with good value on the next business day.

Covering—The purchase or sale of forward exchange to parry the risk of fluctuations in a rate of exchange, devaluation, and revaluation when payments are to be made or received in a foreign currency in the future.

Cross rate—The ratio between the exchange rates of two foreign currencies in terms of a third currency.

Euro-currencies—Deposits of foreign currencies, denominated in terms of the foreign currency, in domestic banks. Also, lending and borrowing transactions in those currencies.

Euro-dollars—Deposits of U.S. dollars in foreign banks or foreign branches of U.S. banks located outside the United States.

Euro-dollar market—A group of markets outside the United States, principally in London, that deals in dollar and other currency deposits denominated in dollars and those other currencies as well as in transactions in those currencies.

Exchange controls or exchange restrictions—Limitations of free dealings in foreign exchange or restrictions on the free transfer of domestic currency into foreign currencies and vice versa.

Exchange control risk—The risk of defaulting on a foreign exchange obligation owing to the imposition of exchange controls that prevent the consummation of the transaction.

Exchange rate—The price of one currency in terms of another at a given moment of time. Also, the middle rates for telegraphic transfers of spot exchange between banks.

Exchange rate risk—The risk taken by a party who must make or receive payment in a foreign currency. The risk occurs by reason of fluctuations in the rates of exchange or devaluations or revaluations of the currencies to be received or paid out.

Federal funds—Literally, balances of U.S. commercial banks in the Federal Reserve banks. Used also to designate funds transferred with immediate good (available) value.

Fixed exchanges—A system of relatively fixed parities in which exchange-rate fluctuations are confined to a specified spread above and below par.

Floating exchange rates or floating exchanges—A system in which either there are no parities or the parities are not enforced and the rate of exchange is allowed to fluctuate freely, although subject to occasional government intervention to influence its movement.

Foreign balances—Credit balances in accounts abroad held by domestic residents and denominated in foreign currencies. In a broader sense, all liquid foreign short-term assets.

Forward exchange—The procedures involved in buying or selling foreign exchange for future delivery. Also, foreign currencies bought or sold for future delivery against payment on delivery.

Forward margin, swap margin, or swap rate—The discount or premium on forward exchange with reference to the spot rate.

Hedging—The purchase or sale of exchange, spot, or forward to meet the exchange risks (rates, devaluations, or revaluations) that affect the values of foreign-currency-denominated assets and liabilities. Also, taking an exchange risk to offset a larger risk in the opposite sense.

Interest arbitrage—Transfer of short-term funds between countries to take advantage of interest differentials.

Interest parities—A theory that attempts to explain the differential between spot and forward rates of exchange. It holds that the differential is conditioned by the amount that will equalize the interest rates between any two countries.

Limits—Specifically, the maximum amount that a party, usually a bank, will accept from another party, usually also a bank, for forward or Euro-dollar transactions or for payments arising from foreign exchange transactions on the same day. Generally, any limit placed on foreign exchange transactions.

Marrying foreign exchange transactions—The counterbalancing of exchange commitment or position that arises from a transaction with one client by a transaction for the same amount and maturity and in the same currency but in the opposite sense with another client.

Nostro accounts—The current or deposit accounts of domestic banks with their branches and correspondents abroad. They are denominated in the currencies of those branches and correspondents and are generally used for current requirements.

Open position—The difference between long and short positions in a given foreign currency. Also, the difference between the grand totals of all long and short positions.

Outright forward exchange—Buying or selling of forward exchange without a simultaneous cover in the form of spot exchange.

Position sheet or book—A sheet or book that lists all of a bank's transactions at a given date in all foreign currencies. The transactions are so arranged to enable the traders to ascertain whether they have a long or short position, forward and spot, in any given currency or in all currencies. Also, the bank's position for a given currency, or for all currencies, at various dates.

Spot exchange—The purchase and sale of a foreign currency for immediate delivery (usually for two clear or value days) and paid for upon delivery.

Spread—(1) The difference between the selling and buying rates for a given currency. (2) The difference between the support points, or the arbitrage support points, for a nation's currency. (3) The difference between spot and forward rates for a given currency. (4) In general, any price differential for a given currency.

Swap—(1) The purchase of spot against the sale of exchange forward. (2) The sale of spot against the purchase of exchange forward. (3) The purchase or sale of short against long forward exchange. (4) The exchange between government central banks of deposits to each other's accounts, usually to provide foreign exchange to enable each to protect its rates of exchange.

Value date—The day or date on which foreign exchange transactions are to be settled by delivery and payment, normally two clear days later.

Vostro accounts—The accounts of foreign banks with domestic correspondents or branches denominated in the domestic currency. The vostro account of one bank is the nostro account of the other.

EXERCISES AND DISCUSSION QUESTIONS

1. In economic terms, explain the effects of a devaluation on a country's economy and balance-of-payments situation.

2. Frazer Manufacturing Company established in 1960 a manufacturing and assembling subsidiary in France (as a joint venture with Hooker of the United Kingdom) to supply the European market and for exports to Africa and the Middle East. It is anticipated that the French franc will shortly be revalued by 10 percent in relation to the U.S. dollar. You are the manager of the French subsidiary. The home office in Columbus, Ohio, has asked you to prepare a report advising:
   a. How will the revaluation affect the operations of your subsidiary and its profitability to Frazer?
   b. How should the revaluation influence future expansion plans for serving the growing demand in Europe for flexible couplings?

3. Explain how a move to floating exchange rates might change the way a government manages a country's economy.

4. Would you be in favor of an international currency? Give your reasons for and against.

5. What kind of reform plan for the international monetary system would be most beneficial to multinational business?

6

Trade Theory and Trade Barriers

INTERNATIONAL TRADE THEORY continues to shape much business and government thinking, as was pointed out in Chapter 3, even though it has limited value in explaining the changing pattern of international transactions in today's world. The international manager, therefore, should be reasonably conversant with trade theory. Such knowledge will give a better basis for understanding, analyzing, and predicting government policies with respect to international transactions. It will also help the manager in preparing his or her own submissions to government. When a belief in trade theory underlies a government's actions, arguments couched in terms of the theory are more likely to be effective than those that would appear to be irrelevant to decisions based on the theory.

THE BASIS FOR TRADE

Businessmen do not usually go to the expense of transferring goods from one country to another if they can obtain the goods as cheaply without doing so. Thus trade takes place where the prices of goods, or what their prices would be without trade, normally reflect differences in the costs of the inputs required to make a product. However, the fact that at current exchange rates many things may cost less in one country than in another does not provide an adequate long-term explanation of why trade continues to take place. If one country's costs are lower than the costs ruling in the others, then demand for its cheaper goods would force up the exchange rate. There would be a greater demand for its currency as outsiders sought to buy more of its goods than its own

110

citizens sought to buy overseas. High continued demand for the cheaper products might also lead to an increase in the prices of the resources needed to produce the goods. When the price level and the exchange rate finally settled down, there might still be some trade, but it could no longer be said that at the ruling exchange rates cost levels were lower and hence the cause of the trade. On the other hand, when exchange rates are fixed it may be valid to argue that a country is involved in a lot of trade because at that exchange rate its costs are lower. Such an exchange rate undervalues the country's currency and would probably lead to a surplus in the balance of payments.

Instead of *absolute* cost differences between countries, economists have long placed emphasis on the differences in *relative* costs from country to country as the basis for sustained trade. The idea was first introduced by David Ricardo early in the 19th century and is known as the *doctrine of comparative advantage.* When Ricardo formulated the doctrine, he based his analysis on the prevailing labor theory of value; namely, that costs are determined by the amount of labor time required in production. The labor theory of value was subsequently rejected as invalid on the grounds, among others, that goods are not produced by labor alone but by various combinations of all the factors of production—land, labor, and capital. The doctrine of comparative costs is still widely accepted but it relies on the modern theory of value, which takes into account on the cost side all the factors of production and defines costs in terms of *opportunity costs,* or how much of one commodity must be given up to get more of the other.

If international trade is based on differences in comparative costs, what explains these differences? The question is answered by the Heckscher-Ohlin theorem which attributes differences in comparative costs to differences among countries in factor endowments.[1] Because of the variations in factor endowments, countries will have a comparative advantage in and tend to export those goods whose production requires the factors in greatest supply in that country; countries have a comparative disadvantage in and tend to import those goods whose production requires the factors in relative scarcest supply in that country. *Country A* with large and fertile land resources and few people may produce wheat relatively cheaply compared to *Country B* with little land and an educated urban population. *Country B* in turn may produce advanced technology goods relatively cheaply. *Coun-*

---

[1]See Bertil Ohlin, *Interregional and International Trade* (Cambridge, Mass.: Harvard University Press, 1933). For an overall view of trade theory, see Gottfried Haberler, *A Survey of International Trade Theory* (Princeton, N.J.: International Finance Section, Department of Economics, Princeton University, 1961), and H. Robert Heller, *International Trade, Theory and Empirical Evidence,* 2d ed. (Englewood Cliffs, N.J.: Prentice-Hall Inc., 1973).

try A would then export wheat and import high-technology manufactures, while *Country B* would export high-technology goods and import foods.

The traditional economist would begin to explain the pattern of a country's trade by identifying the resources within the country which were in greatest abundance relative to other countries. In the simplest application of the doctrine of comparative advantage, resources would be classified as land, labor, or capital. For a more advanced analysis, distinctions should be drawn among different types of labor or management skills, the specific production and distribution facilities that have been built up in the past, and the abundance of particular types of natural resources—minerals, rainfall, or agricultural land.

A simple arithmetic example of the production and trade between two countries each making two products illustrates how differences in the relative abundance of resources can lead to trade. Imagine the two countries as Australia and Belgium, each able to produce only wheat and cloth. The output of each product will differ according to the proportion of a country's resources devoted to it and for a range of production alternatives. These outputs are shown in Table 6–1.

TABLE 6–1
Production Alternatives for Australia and Belgium

Percentage of Resources Devoted to		*Production*			
		Australia		*Belgium*	
Wheat (%)	*Cloth (%)*	*Wheat (million bushels)*	*Cloth (million yards)*	*Wheat (million bushels)*	*Cloth (million yards)*
100	—	100	0	40	—
75	25	75	20	30	15
50	50	50	40	20	30
25	75	25	60	10	45
0	100	0	80	0	60

If all the resources of Australia were devoted to the production of wheat, the output would be 100 million bushels. If, instead, these resources were directed to cloth production, the output would be 80 million yards. For combinations of the two products, Australia would have to forego 1.25 bushels of wheat for every yard of cloth produced. Thus, if the Australian population could not trade with the rest of the world and wanted 20 million yards of cloth, it would cost the Australians the alternative of 25 million bushels of wheat. This would be the *opportunity cost,* or price, for obtaining the cloth.

For Belgium, the extreme production alternatives are 40 million bushels of wheat or 60 million yards of cloth. In this case, only 0.67

bushels of wheat would be given up for each yard of cloth, and if the population wished to have 30 million yards of cloth it would cost them the alternative of 20 million bushels of wheat.

So long as the two countries remain isolated and without trade, cloth will be exchanged for wheat at the rate of one yard for 1.25 bushels in Australia and one yard for 0.67 bushels in Belgium. These ratios are easily derived from Table 6–1, which is so constructed that the ratios remain constant for all production combinations of wheat and cloth. If we assume that there is perfect competition in the two countries, then we can argue that the prices of wheat and cloth in each must settle at these rates. If the prices were in any different ratio, businessmen would switch resources so as to get greater revenue from the added output than from the output forgone, and they would keep on doing this until prices changed to bring production back in line with demand. We can also argue that perfect competition will reduce prices to their incremental costs of production. Thus for each country:

$$\frac{\text{Price of 1 yard of cloth}}{\text{Price of 1 bushel of wheat}} = \frac{\text{Resources cost of 1 yard of cloth}}{\text{Resources cost of 1 bushel of wheat}}$$

So prices in Australia and Belgium will differ, given our implifying assumptions, and there will be opportunity and incentive for trade.

Trade under Constant Opportunity Costs

Continuing our example, what happens when trade takes place? The opportunity for trade creates a single market for the two countries, and if we overlook transport costs, a single price for cloth and for wheat will emerge. This new price will probably lie somewhere between the national prices under isolated conditions. It will be less than the Australian price of 1.25 bushels of wheat for a yard of cloth and higher than the Belgian price of 0.67 bushels of wheat for a yard. By producing more wheat, which it then trades for cloth, Australia would receive more cloth than by using the same resources directly for its own cloth production. Conversely, Belgium could obtain more wheat for every further yard of cloth it produced than the 0.67 bushels of wheat it could have produced itself.

Australia will thus tend to specialize in wheat and Belgium in cloth. Together the countries end up with greater production than if they tried to satisfy their individual needs. With trade, they no longer lose output through having to allocate resources to a product that another country could produce comparatively more cheaply.

Note that the emphasis is on the comparative strength of the country in producing an item—not on its absolute strength. In our example, assuming Australia and Belgium have a similar quantity of resources, Australia has an *absolute advantage* in producing both wheat and cloth. It could produce more of either with a given quantity of resources than could Belgium. Australia's *comparative advantage*, however, is in wheat and Belgium's is in cloth.

The gains that result from trade show clearly from a continuation of the example. Let us suppose that Australians and Belgians each demand 30 million yards of cloth for consumption and that the trade price between Australia and Belgium is set at one bushel of wheat for one yard of cloth. This exchange rate lies between the rates at which wheat can be transformed into cloth. Through reallocating resources in either country, the introduction of trade enables wheat production to increase from 82 to 100 while still maintaining the cloth requirements as shown in Table 6–2. Without trade, each country would produce its own requirements of cloth. With trade, Belgium would concentrate on cloth and Australia on wheat, and they would exchange 30 wheat for 30 cloth. Both end up with a larger supply of wheat than before.

TABLE 6–2
Gains from Trade

	Australia		Belgium		Total	
	Wheat (million bushels)	Cloth (million yards)	Wheat (million bushels)	Cloth (million yards)	Wheat (million bushels)	Cloth (million yards)
Without Trade						
Production and consumption	62	30	20	30	82	60
With Trade						
Production.	100	—	—	60	100	60
Exports (−)	−30			−30	−30	−30
Imports (+).		+30	+30		+30	+30
Consumption	70	30	30	30	100	60

Each country does not have to limit itself to only one product. Had the total demand for cloth been 50 million yards and not 60 million, then Belgium would have produced some wheat as well. Nor does it necessarily follow that both countries benefit from trade. If the exchange price for trade settled at one of the prices existing before trade in either country, the other country would gain all the benefits from the trade. The country whose prices were retained would have to produce as much of one product to obtain the other as it had to produce without trade.

FIGURE 6–1
Production Possibilities with Constant Costs

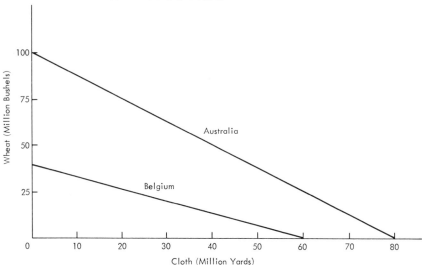

The concept of gains from trade can also be illustrated graphically. Figure 6–1 graphs the production possibilities for Australia and Belgium, with the slope of the curves representing the relative prices of the products in each country and the position of the curves representing the absolute levels of production in the country. When the slopes differ, as they do in this case, there is an opportunity to gain from trade.

In Figure 6–2 the possibility of gains from trade for Belgium is graphed. The rate of product transformation existing in Australia is plotted alongside Belgium's production possibility curve by moving the Australian curve in Figure 6–1 to the left until it coincides with the Belgium curve on the cloth axis. Point *A* indicates Belgian production without trade. Point *B* represents any point lying between the two transformation rates and can always be reached by specializing production and trading with Australia at a rate that would be advantageous to that country. By producing *OQ* cloth, Belgium can export *PQ* in exchange for *PB* wheat. Australia would have had to give up *PC* wheat in order to produce *P* cloth itself, so it gains *BC* in wheat.

Trade with Monetary Costs and Exchange Rates

Up to this point the discussion has been presented with barter prices measured by the opportunity cost of the alternative output possible.

FIGURE 6–2
Gains from Trade under Constant Costs

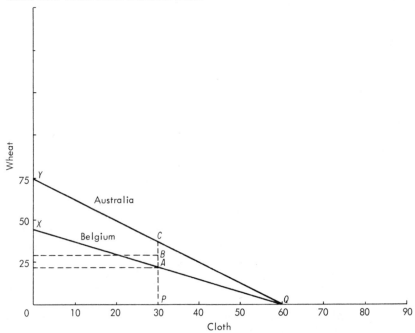

The example becomes more realistic if production is measured in terms of monetary cost, and exchange rates are introduced. Let us suppose that each 1 percent of a country's resources equals 1 million labor hours, that the wage rates are $2 per hour in Australia and 100 francs per hour in Belgium, and that the rate of exchange has been fixed at 50 Belgian francs for 1 Australian dollar.

Before trade, the costs and prices both locally and in their foreign exchange equivalent are as follows:

	Australian Prices		Belgian Prices	
	$	(Fr.)	Fr.	($)
Wheat (cost per bushel)	2.00	(100)	250	(5.00)
Cloth (cost per yard)	2.50	(125)	167	(3.33)

Australia's absolute advantage shows clearly in that its costs, and therefore its prices, in dollars or francs are below the Belgian prices for both wheat and cloth.

Earlier we suggested that with trade the international prices might settle so that a bushel of wheat sold for the same price as a yard of cloth, say, a price of 200 francs. A Belgian importer could buy a bushel of Australian wheat for 200 francs, and an Australian importer spending 200 francs could buy a yard of cloth. It would then pay Australian firms to switch resources from cloth to wheat. For every yard of cloth, they would give up 200 francs revenue to get 250 francs revenue from 1.25 bushels of wheat. It would also pay Belgian firms to switch to cloth because for every bushel of wheat given up, they could get 1.5 yards of cloth, or an additional 100 francs.

In the real world, however, the process by which the international price level is reached is much more complicated. For instance, the Belgian prices before trade in our example are both higher than the Australian prices at the fixed exchange rate. This may mean that once trade is possible, Belgians endeavor to buy only imported goods with consequent unemployment in Belgium. The strain on the Belgian balance of payments and the need to create work might then lead to a devaluation to, say, 75 francs = $1, so that Belgian cloth becomes cheaper than Australian cloth, that is, $2.22. Alternatively, Australian labor could pressure for higher wage rates. Australia's output is certainly higher than Belgium's. If the Australian wage rate rose to $3.50 per hour then international prices of 200 francs would look quite realistic. The cost of Australian wheat would be 175 francs and of Belgian cloth 167 francs.

Whether international prices are reached via changes in wage rates or exchange rates, the effect is to change the relative rewards to Belgian and Australian labor. This illustrates a general theme in international economics that over time and on a global front, factor inputs into production that face international competition tend to be rewarded in proportion to their actual output. If rewards are too high in one country, prices are likely to rise, exports fall, and imports increase. And when prices rise in one country the exchange rate is likely to change, devaluing the currency and bringing rewards back into line with the real international value of the output.

Trade under Increasing Costs

The example used up to this point has assumed constant opportunity costs. For a country as a whole, however, it is more likely that there will be increasing costs. The more that is produced of one product, the greater is the decrease needed in the other in order to obtain a further increment. As land and labor are shifted from wheat to cloth production, for example, it seems reasonable that increasingly those resources better suited for wheat will be used up. Naturally, the initial transfers would be arranged to decrease wheat production as little as possible for any given increment in cloth production. But eventually, increasing quantities of wheat would have to be given up.

The gains from trade with increasing costs are illustrated graphically in Figure 6–3. The production possibilities under increasing costs are now represented by curves *XX'* for Belgium and *YY'* for Australia instead of the straight lines that appeared in Figure 6–2. Point *A* again indicates Belgian production before trade, with a resulting output of *PA* wheat and *OP* cloth. The internal Belgian price is indicated by the slope of the tangent, which touches the *XX'* curve at *A*. The slope of the curve at that point indicates the amount of wheat that would be given up for a given increase in cloth output.

When trade is introduced, the two countries will begin to shift resources toward the product in which they have a comparative advantage in response to traders seeking out the cheaper source. This process will continue until prices in the two countries are equal. In the

FIGURE 6–3
Gains from Trade under Increasing Costs

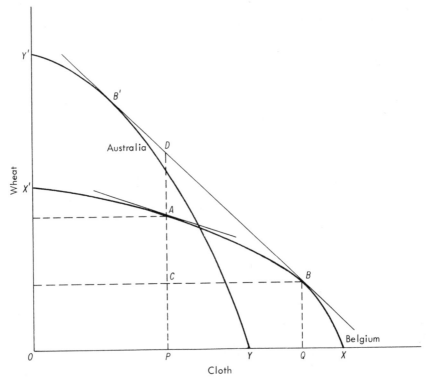

terms of this increasing cost model, this will occur for Belgium at point *B* where the *BB'* price line is tangent to the Australian *YY'* production possibility curve. Belgian production would then move to point *B* with a production of *PC* wheat and *OQ* cloth. If Belgians then want no more cloth than before trade opened up they could trade *PQ* cloth (the same as *CB*) for *CD* wheat, given the international *BB'* exchange rate. This would place them at a higher consumption level (point *D*) than the Belgian production possibility curve would enable them to achieve on their own.

Trade under Decreasing Costs

Even though there are likely to be increasing costs ultimately for a country as a whole, there may well be decreasing costs for individual products or industries. The traditional analysis of cost-volume-profit relationships for an operating firm is usually presented to show economies of scale and hence decreasing unit costs as volume increases. There are also external economies as the size of an industry grows. Specialization may be increased, service facilities sharpened, and risks spread more widely. In industries such as chemicals and electronics, the economies of scale continue up to the largest outputs. Furthermore, for countries in which resources are not fully utilized, the opportunity cost of the other output forgone in order to expand production may be very low and may increase very little, even for considerable expansion of one industry.

When a situation in which a country that is producing under decreasing costs is opened to international trade, it pays the country to move out of the range of production possibilities over which decreasing costs occur. Suppose the *XX'* curve in Figure 6–4 represented Belgium's production possibilities for wheat and man-made fibers for which there are likely to be decreasing costs. Before trade, suppose also that production settles at point *A* and that when trade is opened there is no change in the relative prices of wheat and cloth. It will immediately pay the country to move to point *B* where it could trade *PQ* cloth for *CD* wheat to reach the higher consumption at point *D*.

Comparative Statics and Trade Theory Refinements

The pure or orthodox theory of trade as elaborated above abstracts from many circumstances relevant to world conditions. As mentioned in Chapter 3, it makes many limiting assumptions, such as a competitive market price system; immobile factors of production (land, labor, and capital) between nations; fixed tastes, factor endowments, and

FIGURE 6–4
Gains from Trade under Decreasing Costs

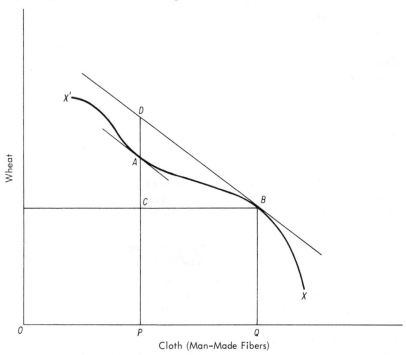

technology; and costless and ubiquitous information. In order to make trade theory more realistic, economic theorists have further refined the pure theory by relaxing some of the key assumptions one at a time, i.e., by comparative statics. Such refinements have taken into account changes in tastes, factor endowments, and technology,[2] and the importance of imperfectly competitive markets.[3]

The modifications that result from these refinements, however, are more important to professional economists than to international managers. In particular, the comparative statics analysis permits theorists to argue that the unreality of the assumptions is not sufficient to justify the discard of trade theory and that "there is enough truth in the basic

[2]See Roger W. Klein, "A Dynamic Theory of Comparative Advantage," *American Economic Review*, March 1973, pp. 173–84; Charles P. Kindleberger, *International Economics*, 5th ed. (Homewood, Ill.: Richard D. Irwin, Inc., 1973), pp. 53–69.

[3]Delbert A. Snider, *Introduction to International Economics*, 6th ed. (Homewood, Ill.: Richard D. Irwin, Inc., 1975), pp. 88–108.

theory, and especially in the corollaries and implications for policy, that it serves as a basis for analysis of interference with trade."[4]

TRADE BARRIERS

Free Trade versus Trade Restrictions

It should now be clear that gains can result from trade under conditions of constant, increasing, or decreasing costs—at least in terms of the simple two-product, two-country model. These gains come about because countries specialize in the products that they can produce at a comparative advantage. With trade, every country can go beyond the limits of its resource endowment to consume a collection of commodities that exceeds any output combination it could produce on its own. With more complicated models involving several countries and several products this general principle still holds.

It is a simple step in any trade model to show that any barrier hampering trade so that an optimum combination of products cannot be reached causes a decrease in the total output and consumption. In other words, free trade maximizes world output.

It may be, however, that an individual country could benefit from restricting trade even though from a global standpoint efficiency in the use of resources and total world output is reduced. By so doing, it might be able to raise employment, bring the country a higher proportion of the gains from trade, or build new industries to a point where they might exist without such protection. In industries where there are decreasing costs, for example, it may be that individual firms do not see the advantages of moving to the higher production levels or are not prepared to bear the risk involved. In order to start the industry moving along the decreasing cost curve, some protection against competition or some form of direct incentive might be considered desirable.

A more detailed analysis of the advantages and disadvantages of trade restriction from the viewpoint of an individual country is left to Chapter 10. When each country independently introduces barriers without anticipating the reactions of others, however, the reduction in trade can be costly to all countries. Thus it is not surprising that on an international level many governments are continually pressing for reductions in trade barriers. First, let us examine the nature of these barriers.

---

[4]Kindleberger, *International Economics,* p. 67.

Tariff Barriers.   The most common method of restricting trade is the tariff. A tariff is a tax, or duty, levied on a commodity when it crosses the boundary of a customs area. Usually a customs area coincides with national political boundaries. Sometimes it includes colonies or territories of the country. A customs area may also include several independent nation-states, as in the case of the European Economic Community. Tariffs may be levied on commodities leaving an area (export duties) or on merchandise entering an area (import duties). As most nations are anxious to increase their foreign exchange earnings through exports, export duties are much less common than import duties.

Nations differ greatly in their tariff systems. When a country offers equal treatment to all commodities of one class, regardless of the country of origin, it is said to have a *unilinear* or *single-column* tariff. Another type of tariff system is the *general-conventional* tariff, in which the general column applies to all countries except those with which tariff treaties or conventions have been made. The lower rates granted by these conventions constitute the conventional column. The principal advantage of the general-conventional system is its flexibility for tariff bargaining. A number of countries have tariff systems that provide maximum and minimum rates for like commodities. The maximum rates apply to all countries except those with which reductions have been negotiated.

An important feature of tariff treaties or agreements is what is known as most-favored-nation (MFN) treatment. This provides that the products of a country that is assured MFN treatment will in each case enter at rates of duty no less favorable than those applied to like products of any third country. A nation that enters into unconditional most-favored-nation tariff treaties is compelled to grant equal treatment to all signatories when it grants tariff concessions to any country. The purpose of such provisions is to simplify tariff bargaining, increasing the likelihood of tariff reductions.

Import duties may be either *specific, ad valorem,* or a combination of the two—*compound* duties. Specific duties are levied on the basis of some physical unit such as dollars per bushel, ton, or yard. Ad valorem duties are calculated on the basis of the value of the goods. The term *drawback* refers to a duty that has been paid on imported goods and is refunded by the government if the goods are reexported.

In the case of ad valorem duties, special problems may arise in selecting the basis for determining the value of the goods. Normally the value is determined by the invoice of sale or by a customs appraiser on the basis of the landed cost in the country—cost plus insurance and freight (CIF). Special provisions may be adopted, however, such as the American Selling Price (ASP) basis of valuation adopted for certain chemical imports into the United States. The ASP law provides that prices prevailing in the U.S. market should be the base for calculating duty rather than the normally lower cost at which foreigners are selling in order to compete in the U.S. market. A number of countries specify the basis of valuation for duty calculation in terms of the wholesale price level in the importing country. This has the effect of raising the height of the tariff and avoiding a duty reduction to the cut-price supplier.

Tariffs have the advantage of a minimum of administrative discretion in their application and they can be selectively levied in terms of products and with differential rates. Thus it is possible to achieve rather precise objectives with tariffs while at the same time increasing government revenues. On the other hand, tariffs usually increase the cost to the consumer and are generally difficult to change because of the political pressures of groups benefited by the tariff. This may limit a nation's flexibility in bargaining with other nations, particularly where the tariffs are established by statute and a change of law would be necessary to implement any change.

Nontariff Barriers. Restrictions on trade in the form of nontariff barriers (NTBs), though not as visible as tariffs, can be extremely effective and important. The principal categories of NTBs are as follows:

1. Government participation in trade—including subsidies, countervailing duties, government procurement, and state trading.
2. Customs and entry procedures—such as valuation, classification, documentation, and health and safety regulations.
3. Standards—for example, product standards, packaging, and labeling and marking.
4. Specific limitations—including quotas, exchange controls, import restraints, and licensing.
5. Import charges—such as prior import deposits, credit restrictions for imports, special duties, and variable levies.

Among the nontariff barriers to trade, quantitative restrictions or quotas are the most widespread form. A quota establishes the maximum quantity of a commodity that might be imported (or exported) during a given period of time. The limits may be set in physical or in value terms. Quotas may be on a country basis or global, with the total limit specified without reference to countries of origin. They may be imposed unilaterally, as in the case of sugar imports into the United States, or they can be negotiated on a so-called voluntary basis, as has occurred in the case of textile imports into the United States. Obviously, exporting countries do not readily agree to limit their sales, so the voluntary label generally means that the quotas have been negotiated with threats that even worse restrictions may be imposed by the importing country if voluntary cooperation is not forthcoming.

To the country desiring to restrict imports, quotas have the advantage of being more certain and precise than tariffs, providing greater flexibility in bargaining, and permitting more flexibility in administration. An import duty that is not so high as to prohibit imports does not set a specific limit on the volume of goods imported. A quota system limits with certainty the extent to which foreign producers can compete in the domestic market.

The administration of quotas usually requires a licensing system and raises the problem of deciding which domestic parties shall receive what share of the quota. If the quotas are relatively small in relation to the domestic market, domestic market prices are likely to be higher than imported prices and the recipients of quotas will receive windfall profits. The government could capture these windfall profits by auctioning off the import licenses to the highest bidders, but the more general case is that the profits go to private parties. Inequities and corruption can occur in the allocation of quotas, and with the greater degree of administrative discretion implicit in the system, business firms may find quotas arbitrary and uncertain. Quotas also encourage firms to manipulate the system. Firms may use all of an allocated quota, for example, to import only one section of the class of commodities included under the quota, hoping to force the issue of a further quota to overcome the scarcity of the remaining items. Perhaps the greatest disadvantage of quotas, however, is that unlike tariffs they exert no pressure to keep the level of domestic prices down.

There is a long list of other restrictions that governments can place on trade. Some are legitimate regulatory functions such as antipollution regulations, which require all automobiles sold in the United States to meet a certain standard for emission of exhaust fumes. It is quite common, however, for regulations ostensibly introduced for other purposes to be applied to restrict trade.

Trade Theory, Terms of Trade, and the Developing Economies

The pure theory of trade and the benefits of free trade, as noted earlier, underlie much business and government thinking, particularly in the advanced nations. The important exception is the developing economies which, as a general rule, reject the free trade approach and make extensive use of trade barriers. The developing countries might agree in principle that free trade maximizes world output *with a given international economic structure,* but their priority concern is with the dynamic issues of accelerating growth and narrowing the economic gap between the less developed and the industrialized nations. In their view, the path for achieving these goals is not through free trade.

The rejection of free trade and the extensive use of trade barriers by the developing nations result in part from their conviction that in the present world environment the terms of trade have been turning systematically against them, and in part from an awareness that internal conditions in their countries do not permit them to transfer resources with facility to adjust to trade opportunities.[5]

The *terms of trade* concept needs further elaboration. In brief, it is the relation between the prices of exports and the prices of imports. The developing nations claim that the prices they receive for their exports, mainly primary commodities, are going down relative to the prices they pay for imports, mainly manufactured goods. The logical support for this belief is Engel's law, which suggests that the income elasticity for exports is less than for imports, and the contention that a high degree of competition exists in the world markets for their exports whereas the markets for their imports involve administered prices and oligopolistic structures. As we shall see in Chapter 7, these views have led the developing nations to press for global trade arrangements that will stimulate structural change and international income redistribution.

EXERCISES AND DISCUSSION QUESTIONS

1. Explain the difference between comparative advantage and absolute advantage.

2. In a recent hearing before a senate committee investigating the need for further trade legislation, a labor union official testified as follows:

   "Free trade policies are based on traditional trade theory which is no longer valid in a world dominated by international investment and multinational companies. When the American business firm is faced with severe foreign competition, it can move abroad and meet this competition by producing in a foreign location for the U.S. market. The capitalists can adjust. The American workers cannot.

   "Furthermore, is it in the United States' interest for American companies to invest abroad as rapidly as they are doing? U.S. advances in technology, often financed by government tax dollars, are being shipped abroad. The production overseas for foreign markets substitutes for U.S. production. We lose the foreign exchange that might be earned by exports. We lose American jobs, tax revenues, and so forth. Does the United States lose or benefit from multinationalism? What's good for international business is not necessarily what is good for the United States.

   "We want protection while the United States works out a program to

---

[5] See Kindleberger, *International Economics,* pp. 70–88 for a fuller discussion in "Trade and Growth in Developing Economies."

control international business. Quotas should be placed on imports into the United States of those goods and product-lines that are displacing significant percentages of U.S. production and employment in order to slow down the disruptive impacts on American society and help to provide an orderly expansion of trade."

You are adviser to a U.S. senator and he has asked you to evaluate this testimony. He would also like your own reasoning as to how the best level of textile quotas, if any, should be determined for the United States.

3. Explain why the protection granted local labor by the imposition of tariffs may not be directly proportional to the heights of the individual tariff rates.

4. "Trade was an engine of growth for the open lands for the 19th century and for the leader in the Industrial Revolution. Today's less developed countries, except for the oil producers, expect little growth from trade." Discuss.

7

The International Trade Framework

THE PERIOD SINCE World War II has been unprecedented as an era of international cooperation in the field of trade and has resulted in the creation of a complicated, piecemeal framework of trading arrangements under various international organizations. These trading arrangements can be grouped into four broad categories: (1) global arrangements directed toward multilateral trade expansion on a nondiscriminatory basis; (2) global arrangements with a principal objective of international income redistribution through the mechanism of trade; (3) regional arrangements that focus on the economic relations of a particular geographic or political area; and (4) commodity-product arrangements that focus on the international terms of trade of a specific product or commodity. Bilateral trading arrangements, although they normally do not involve international agencies, are also part of the international trade framework.

THE GENERAL AGREEMENT ON TARIFFS AND TRADE (GATT)

The General Agreement on Tariffs and Trade, commonly known as GATT, is the principal multilateral arrangement in the first category. It became effective in 1948 with 19 countries as members. Its membership has since expanded to more than 80 nations, including all of the important noncommunist nations and some of the socialist countries of Eastern Europe. GATT was initially designed as a temporary agreement for beginning negotiations on the narrow commercial policy aspects of a much more comprehensive trade agreement that was expected to replace GATT. The comprehensive agreement known as the Havana Charter (1948), which was to be administered by the International Trade Organization (ITO), included detailed provisions on commodity agreements, restrictive business practices, economic development, and employment as well as commercial policy. But the ITO never came into being. The U.S. Congress did not ratify the charter because it was considered too broad and an infringement of national sovereignty. U.S. participation in GATT, however, did not require congressional approval because it was an agreement rather than a treaty. Thus GATT, though originally intended to be a temporary arrangement, developed into an important institution in place of the aborted ITO.[1]

The goal of GATT is to achieve a broad, multilateral, and relatively free system of trading, and it sets down principles and rules of conduct directed to this end. The goal is to be achieved through gradual reduction in tariffs, adoption of the principle of nondiscrimination—equal treatment with respect to customs duties and procedures—and the provision of an organization for settlement of trade disputes. The agreement endeavors also to abolish the use of quantitative restrictions of trade. Preferential tariff systems existing at the time GATT was signed, such as Commonwealth preferences or the Benelux arrangement, were allowed as exceptions. In spite of provisions regarding nondiscrimination, members may form customs unions or free trade areas, provided there is no net overall increase in barriers to outsiders. A wide range of other exceptions are also allowed under which restrictive policies could continue or be adopted temporarily by a country with aggravated trade or financial problems.[2]

In working toward its goal of reducing tariffs, GATT sponsored six major bargaining sessions from 1947 to 1967 which resulted in substantial tariff cuts. The record on trade liberalization negotiations as they affected U.S. tariffs is shown in Table 7–1. The last negotiation, the so-called Kennedy Round (1963–67), reduced tariffs on dutiable nonagricultural products to an average level ranging from 9 to 11 percent for the major trading nations. For the United States, the average tariff level on all dutiable imports dropped from approximately 59 percent in 1932 and 25 percent in 1946 to 9.9 percent after the Kennedy Round. As a result of the GATT negotiations, in most cases tariffs are no longer a major barrier to world trade. However, many nontariff barriers (NTBs) still distort trade and their increased use has made the reduction of NTBs a top priority in the seventh round of multilateral trade negotiations that began in 1975.

---

[1]See Raymond Vernon, *American Foreign Trade Policy and the GATT* (Princeton, N.J.: Princeton University Press, 1954).

[2]For a detailed analysis of the GATT provisions, see Kenneth W. Dam, *The GATT—Law and International Organization* (Chicago: The University of Chicago Press, 1970).

TABLE 7–1
Six GATT Rounds Compared

GATT Round	Scope of U.S. Tariff Cutting*	Depth of U.S. Tariff Cuts†
1947	44%	35%
1949	3	35
1951	9	27
1956	11	15
1962	14	20
1967	64	35

*Value of U.S. dutiable imports on which tariff reductions were made or agreed in the year shown, expressed as a percentage of the value of total U.S. dutiable imports in the same year.

†Average percentage reduction in U.S. duties (considering only items whose duties were reduced), weighted by the value of U.S. imports of those items in the year shown.

Sources: U.S. Tariff Commission; U.S. Department of Commerce; Office of the Special Representative for Trade Negotiations; *First National City Bank Monthly Letter*, September 1967.

The advanced countries have gone a long way toward dismantling their extensive systems of import licensing and quantitative restrictions on nonagricultural products. But GATT's endeavors have been weakened by the exceptions permitted countries (1) in balance-of-payments difficulties, (2) with special domestic agricultural programs, and (3) with temporary domestic shortages of essential goods.

Thus, the vision of a postwar trading system free from the hampering and distorting effects of tariffs, quotas, and discriminatory practices has been only partially achieved. Protectionist sentiment still remains strong when domestic vested interests are threatened. The waivers granted in the field of agriculture leave this area fully planted with restrictions. The exception for countries forming a customs union has encouraged the formation of economic (and political) blocs instead of an integrated world economy. Increased difficulties in the functioning of the international financial system have become an important constraint on trade liberalization. Other new problems have arisen with the increased participation of the communist-bloc countries, which by and large have internal state-controlled systems for international trade.

The developing countries, which now constitute a majority of the membership of GATT, also pose a special challenge to the organization. GATT has always permitted them to use tariffs as protection for infant industries and to use quantitative restrictions on trade to meet balance-of-payments problems associated with development programs. Yet during the first decade and a half of GATT's existence, the developing countries felt that GATT did not adequately represent their trade interests and proceeded in 1964 to organize the United Nations Conference on Trade and Development (UNCTAD). Initially, only a few of the developing countries were members of GATT but over the years many others have joined, apparently in the belief that participation in the detailed GATT negotiations is a useful complement to the UNCTAD focus on major policy issues and structural reform. In fact, immediately after the creation of UNCTAD, GATT made a new and special commitment, referred to as Part IV of the GATT agreement, to assist in the trade and development problems of the less developed countries. Under this new objective, the industrialized countries agreed to work to reduce various trade impediments and not to expect reciprocal concessions from the developing countries. As of 1977, the new GATT commitments were still in an early stage of implementation.

In 1975, after several years of preparation and the signing of the U.S. Trade Act on January 3, 1975, a seventh round of trade negotiations began under the aegis of GATT. The negotiations focused on further reductions in tariffs, nontariff barriers, and special problems of agriculture and tropical products. As three-fourths of the countries taking part in the negotiations were developing countries, the objectives of the exercise included a substantial increase in foreign exchange earnings for developing countries, diversification of their exports, and acceleration of the rate of growth in their trade.

THE UNITED NATIONS CONFERENCE ON TRADE AND DEVELOPMENT (UNCTAD)

The United Nations Conference on Trade and Development (UNCTAD) falls into the second category of global trade arrangements—those with the prime objective of achieving an international redistribution of income through trade.

A dramatic feature of the post–World War II world was the awakened desire of the less developed countries for accelerated growth and economic modernization. The free trade ideology, which assumed a static economic structure of nations, did not fit the needs and aspirations of the less developed countries. They adopted protectionist policies to encourage infant industries. They became convinced that they should not continue to rely so heavily on specialization in traditional agricultural and raw material exports but should diversify into product fields such as manufactures, where world demand was expanding more rapidly. In fact, the development philosophy that emerged, heavily influenced by the Economic Commission of Latin America, had little in common with the trade liberalization goals of

GATT. And the less developed countries, most of whom were not members of GATT, became gradually convinced that GATT did not and could not represent their trade interests.

In response to this sentiment, UNCTAD was convened in 1964 and attended by representatives of 119 nations.[3] The result of the conference was to establish UNCTAD as a permanent United Nations agency which, given its origins and structure, has come to represent the interests of the less developed countries.

Whereas the developed nations have been dominant in the activities of GATT, the less developed countries have been the driving force in UNCTAD. In each of the four UNCTAD conferences held from 1964 to 1976, the developing countries made major demands on the developed nations. At UNCTAD I, the principal demand was for unilateral tariff reductions on imports of manufactures from the developing countries. This was strongly opposed by the United States and others, but after several years of continued UNCTAD pressure the developed countries agreed to what is called a generalized system of preferences with quota limits for manufactured imports from the developing countries. Another successful result of the UNCTAD efforts was the agreement of the International Monetary Fund to make credits available more automatically to countries that suffer a fall in export earnings because of the decline in export prices.

Beginning in the early 1970s, the aspirations of the developing countries were escalated through the United Nations in demands for a New International Economic Order. Under prevailing economic arrangements, the developing countries feel that they have not participated equitably in world prosperity during periods of economic expansions and have had to support a disproportionate burden of adjustment during recessions. Within this context, the principal demands of the developing countries at the UNCTAD IV meetings in Nairobi in 1976 were for an "integrated" program of commodity agreements, including a common fund for buffer stock financing, measures for alleviating the debt problems of the less developed countries, a series of proposals for facilitating the transfer of technology to the developing nations, and new steps to simplify trade relations with the socialist countries of Eastern Europe.

---

[3]The report by Raul Prebisch, Secretary General of UNCTAD, *Towards a New Trade Policy For Development* (New York: United Nations, 1964) presented a set of recommendations for promoting the development of the less developed countries through changes in the trade policies of the developed countries which largely shaped the work of the first conference and subsequent UNCTAD activities. See also Harry G. Johnson, *Economic Policies Toward Less Developed Countries* (Washington, D.C.: The Brookings Institution, 1967).

REGIONAL TRADE ARRANGEMENTS

The third category, regional trade arrangements that focus on the economic relations of a particular geographic or political area, includes the largest number of international organizations. When GATT was created in 1948, it appeared that nations were prepared to move toward global organizations rather than regional trading groups. The general agreement, however, allowed for regional groupings as an exception, with the proviso that such groups should not result in increased discrimination against nonmembers. The desire by neighboring countries to pool political and economic strength against outsiders was a powerful force despite the existence of global trade agreements. And the establishment of regional common markets and free trade areas, referred to under the general label of regional economic integration, began to occur.[4]

The most important regional integration movement has been the European Community. Other significant regional arrangements have been the European Free Trade Association (EFTA) and the Council of Mutual Economic Cooperation (COMECON). In addition, numerous regional trading organizations have been established by the developing countries.

There are various forms and degrees of regional economic integration. The loosest and least intensive form is the free trade area. In a free trade area all artificial restrictions on the movement of goods and services among the participating countries are removed, but each country may retain its own tariffs, quotas, or other restrictions on trade with nonparticipating countries. The customs union is one degree further along the scale. In addition to the complete elimination of tariffs and quotas on internal trade, a common external tariff is established on goods entering the union from outside. A common market represents the next higher degree of economic integration. Besides eliminating internal trade barriers and establishing a common external tariff, a common market also removes national restrictions on the movement of labor and capital among participating countries, and on the right of establishment for business firms.

From an economic standpoint the chief benefit of economic integration is the trade creation effect. With the removal of protective tariffs, lower cost foreign supplies are likely to substitute for higher cost domestic production. The consumer benefits from the lower prices and

---

[4]A clear introduction to the theory of economic integration is in Tibor Scitovsky, *Economic Theory and Western European Integration* (London: Allen & Unwin, 1958); and in Bela Balassa, *The Theory of Economic Integration* (Homewood, Ill.: Richard D. Irwin, Inc., 1961).

domestic resources previously used to produce the newly imported goods can be shifted to more efficient uses.

However, the removal of tariffs on a regional basis, accompanied by the erection of a common external tariff, may lead to trade diversion instead of trade creation.[5] Prior to the formation of the European Economic Community, for example, the lowest cost source of supply of a specific product consumed in France may have been the United States. But after the common market was formed, a higher cost producer in Germany may have substituted for the U.S. source of supply because the tariffs facing the German producer were abolished whereas external tariffs still faced the U.S. producer.

Judgments on the relative magnitudes of trade creation and trade diversion in the case of the European Economic Community vary between a negligible difference to a significant net balance in favor of trade creation, but the effects of regional integration movements extend far beyond trade creation or trade diversion possibilities. One of the less tangible but most pervasive benefits of economic integration is the more efficient market structure that results from the encouragement of increased competition.[6]

Of prime significance to international business is the enlargement of the market area that can be supplied by a producing unit without encountering trade restrictions. This permits the enterprise to take advantage of internal economies of scale and thereby reduce the costs of producing in the market area. An expansion in the size of markets can also provide gains to business firms and the economy by creating new opportunities for external economies of scale. The expansion of one industry may lead to the creation of service industries, manpower training facilities, research institutions, and so forth, which become part of the economy's pool of resources available to be drawn upon by other industries. Also, freeing the movement of labor and capital within a common market area can contribute greatly to more efficient business operations.

The European Community

The most advanced regional integration movement is the European Community. It includes the European Coal and Steel Community (ECSC), set up in 1952 to create a common market in coal, steel, iron ore, and scrap resources; the European Economic Community (EEC),

---

[5]See M. E. Kreinin, "On the Dynamic Effects of a Customs Union," *The Journal of Political Economy*, April 1964, pp. 193–95.

[6]See Charles P. Kindleberger, *International Economics,* 5th ed. (Homewood, Ill.: Richard D. Irwin, Inc., 1973), pp. 174–88.

established in 1958 to remove other trade and economic barriers between member countries and to unify their economic policies; and the European Atomic Energy Community (Euratom), also set up in 1958 as the overseeing authority for nuclear power developments. With the addition in 1973 of the United Kingdom, Denmark, and Ireland to the original six (Belgium, France, Germany, Italy, Luxembourg, and the Netherlands), the community became a major regional trading group with intracommunity trade in 1974 amounting to 13 percent of total world exports. Including external trade, the community's share of world exports was about 21 percent, making it the world's biggest exporter.

The European Community evolved out of a series of post–World War II moves toward economic and political union in Western Europe. The formation of an economic community was expected to reduce costly political and economic rivalries and form the basis for a United States of Europe. But the commitment toward political union by the member countries was more in spirit than in fact and the main accomplishments of the community have been in the economic field.

Under the customs union agreed to in the EEC's Rome Treaty, all customs duties and restrictions on trade in industrial goods within the community were abolished by July 1, 1968 and a common external tariff became fully operational. In the agricultural sector, the community developed a protective common agricultural policy, which consists of a support system designed to promote domestic agricultural production and guarantee farm incomes.

The Rome Treaty contains provisions for steps which could eventually lead to full economic union. Some provisions, such as those concerned with a common antitrust policy, have been implemented. Others, such as those related to a common transport policy, are being worked on. But the goal of complete economic and monetary union is still distant because of periodic economic crises of member countries and other barriers.

Under the Rome Treaty, association with the community is open to all countries. As a result, the community has association agreements with Greece and Turkey and preferential agreements with Spain and a number of other Mediterranean countries. It also has free-trade agreements with the EFTA countries (Austria, Norway, Portugal, Sweden, Switzerland, as well as Iceland and Finland) as a result of which much of Western Europe has become a single industrial free-trade area. Under the Lomé Convention signed in 1975, the community entered into a new program for trade and economic cooperation with 46 African, Caribbean, and Pacific (ACP) countries; see Figure 7–1. The Lomé Convention permits complete duty-free access to the community for all industrial products from the ACP countries and for 96 percent of

FIGURE 7-1

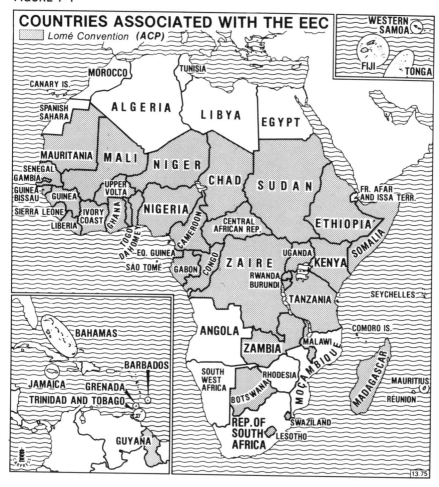

their agricultural production. It also includes an Export Revenue Stabilization Plan (STABEX) financed by the community and other provisions for development assistance.

European Free Trade Association

The European Free Trade Association was inspired by a strong concern about the effects of the European Economic Community on the trade patterns of other Western European countries, who had a variety of reasons for not joining the EEC. The United Kingdom, for instance, had long-standing relationships and tariff arrangements with the rest of the British Commonwealth that presented difficulties. Austria, Sweden, and Switzerland were anxious to avoid any commitment that might be considered to compromise their neutral status.

After prolonged negotiations, the seven countries of Austria, Denmark, Norway, Portugal, Sweden, Switzerland, and the United Kingdom joined in another regional economic integration movement under the Stockholm Convention of 1960. They were later joined by Finland and Iceland. EFTA was less ambitious than the EEC and had no overtones of a political union. The member countries agreed to remove internal tariffs on nonagricultural products in several steps and achieved this goal by the end of 1966, ahead of schedule. Another move was to abolish quantitative import quotas. As a free trade area, there was no provision for a common external tariff for EFTA. Consequently, rules as to origin and location of production were adopted to ensure that only goods that originated in the area benefited from the tariff reductions. The most important rules of origin require that nonarea materials used at any stage of production account for not more than 50 percent of the export price of the goods produced or that the goods be produced by certain specified processes within the area.

EFTA's major achievement was a spectacular increase in intra-EFTA trade. The expansion of external trade was not impressive, mainly because the United Kingdom usually accounted for about half of all EFTA totals, and the United Kingdom experienced difficulties in expanding exports during the 1960s.

The United Kingdom's successful application for entry into the European Community in 1973 brought an end to EFTA's role as a significant trade grouping. Although Austria, Finland, Iceland, Norway, Portugal, Sweden, and Switzerland did not join the EEC, their EFTA membership did bring them free trade area treatment with the EEC.

Council of Mutual Economic Cooperation (COMECON)

The Council of Mutual Economic Cooperation (COMECON) was formed in 1949 to coordinate trade and other forms of economic relations among the centrally planned economies of Eastern Europe. The council includes Bulgaria, Czechoslovakia, East Germany, Hungary, Poland, Romania, and the USSR. COMECON has promoted some product specialization but the centrally planned countries of Eastern Europe secure more of their needs from domestic production than do most capitalist nations. A large share of the availabilities for export or needs for import is determined after decisions have been made on the composition and volume of domestic output. Consequently, foreign trade has often been a means of providing for unplanned shortages or disposing of unplanned surpluses.[7]

In the COMECON countries, trade decisions are normally made by various state trading organizations which have full responsibility for buying and selling a particular product. The state trading companies are separate from the state enterprises that produce or consume the product. Because of this monopoly and the absence of any necessary link between the cost and price of a product, it has been difficult to apply the trading rules of market-oriented organizations such as GATT to bilateral agreements between COMECON countries and nonmember market economies. For example, it is impossible in practice to determine whether exports from a centrally planned economy are subsidized or whether imports are taken on a nondiscriminatory basis.

Regional Trading Arrangements between Developing Countries

One of the most significant trade developments of recent years has been the establishment of numerous trading arrangements between groups of developing countries. Ten major groups and several rather loose trading arrangements existed as of 1975. The major groups, their date of establishment, and their country membership are as follows:[8]

1. Latin American Free Trade Association (LAFTA); 1960; Argentina, Brazil, Chile, Mexico, Paraguay, Peru, Uruguay, Colombia, Ecuador, Venezuela, and Bolivia.

2. Andean Group; formed in 1969 as a subgroup of LAFTA; Bolivia, Chile, Colombia, Ecuador, Peru, and Venezuela.

3. Central American Common Market (CACM); 1960; Costa Rica, El Salvador, Guatemala, Honduras, and Nicaragua.

4. Caribbean Free Trade Association (CARIFTA); 1968; Barbados, Guyana, Jamaica, Trinidad and Tobago, Antigua, Dominica, Grenada, Montserrat, St. Kitts–Nevis–Anguilla, St. Lucia, and St. Vincent.

5. East Caribbean Common Market (a subgroup of CARIFTA); 1968; Antigua, Dominica, Grenada, Montserrat, St. Kitts–Nevis–Anguilla, St. Lucia, and St. Vincent.

6. East African Community (EAC); 1967; Kenya, Uganda, and the United Republic of Tanzania.

---

[7]See Franklin D. Holzman and Robert Legvold, "The Economics and Politics of East-West Relations," in *World Politics and International Economics,* ed. C. Fred Bergsten and Lawrence B. Krause (Washington, D.C.: The Brookings Institution, 1975), pp. 284–87.

[8]Adapted from Robert E. Baldwin and David A. Kay, "International Trade and International Relations," in *World Politics and International Economics,* pp. 107–8.

7. Central African Customs and Economic Union (UDEAC); 1964; Cameroon, Central Africa Republic, Zaire, and Gabon.
8. West African Economic Community (CEAC); 1972; Benim, Ivory Coast, Mali, Mauritania, Niger, Senegal, and Upper Volta.
9. Arab Common Market (ACM); 1964; Egypt, Iraq, Jordan, and the Syrian Arab Republic.
10. Regional Cooperation for Development (RCD); 1964; Iran, Pakistan, and Turkey.

Three loose regional organizations are: (1) the Council of the Entente (Dahomey, Ivory Coast, Niger, Upper Volta, and Togo) formed in 1959 in west Africa; (2) the Maghreb Group (Algeria, Morocco, and Tunisia) formed in 1964 in North Africa; and (3) the Association of South-East Asian Nations, or ASEAN (Malaysia, the Philippines, Thailand, Singapore, and Indonesia) formed in 1967.

In the case of the developing countries, the major objective of the regional arrangements has been to support industrialization efforts through enlarging markets and intra-regional competition. The hope is that an enlarged market and greater internal competition will yield benefits flowing from economies of scale in production and the more efficient use of resources, that these benefits will exceed any costs resulting from trade diversion, and that the net gains could be distributed equitably among the participants.

The Andean Group[9] and the Central American Common Market[10] are examples of regional groupings that involve cooperation in many development areas as well as in trade liberalization. The six participating countries in the Andean Group are aiming at a full-fledged economic community in which free trade will be achieved and in which common development aspirations will be pursed through a concerted effort at regionwide industrial planning and rationalization.

Significance to International Business

Given the success of the EEC, regional economic integration movements are certain to continue as a significant and expanding feature of the international business environment. And regional integration movements can have vital significance for international business operations. Some of the major effects are as follows:

---

[9]Ralph A. Diaz, "The Andean Common Market—Challenge to Foreign Investors, and Harold C. Petersen, "ANCOM: An Andean Paradox," *Columbia Journal of World Business*, July–August 1971.

[10]See Ingo Walter and Hans C. Vitzhum, "The Central American Common Market," *The Bulletin*, no. 44 (New York: Institute of Finance, New York University, May 1967).

1. Competitive conditions are changed as between internal and external producers. Firms previously exporting to the area may find it necessary to jump the trade barrier and establish local producing units. Firms located within the market can become more competitive through larger-scale producing units, if economies of scale are important to the industry.
2. The general attractiveness of markets in countries joining integration movements can increase when growth rates are stimulated by trade creation effects, more vigorous competition, and other related forces.
3. International firms established in common market or free trade areas can become more competitive in third-country markets if the increased level of production secured within the home market permits reduced costs for exported goods.
4. Integration movements generally incorporate measures or policies that favor business enterprises from the area as against international enterprises of other nationalities. The EEC, for example, has promoted mergers of European firms as a defensive measure against the expansion of American companies in the European area.
5. Changes in the rules of competition, such as adopting areawide antitrust policies, can cause problems for multinational firms that have previously given exclusive rights in specific member countries to subsidiaries or licensees.

For these and other business reasons, one of the challenging issues for the international manager is to be able to predict the establishment, the probable success, and future development patterns of specific integration movements. A growing body of research on optimum and necessary conditions for regional integration success can be of assistance in this respect.[11]

INTERNATIONAL COMMODITY AGREEMENTS AND PRODUCER CARTELS

International commodity agreements and producer cartels that focus on the terms of trade of specific commodities constitute a fourth category of trading arrangements. They have been inspired mainly by the developing countries because, from their perspective, commodity trade (excluding petroleum) has traditionally been burdened by two problems. One is the short-term instability of markets for primary products. The second is a conviction that longer-term trends have been

---

[11]For example, see Ardy Stoutjesdijk, "LDC Regional Markets: Do They Work?" *Columbia Journal of World Business,* September–October 1970.

adverse, as reflected in deteriorating terms of trade and sluggish growth in export earnings.[12]

Prices of primary commodities exported by developing countries have been highly unstable, partly as a result of changing supply conditions caused by the vagaries of weather and partly due to fluctuations in the demand for primary commodities in the industrial nations. Consequently, the developing countries have experienced sharp and damaging fluctuations in their export earnings. The industrial nations also suffer from these wide swings in prices and from occasional shortages of imported raw materials.

Two basic approaches have been followed in dealing with the instability of primary commodity markets—compensatory financing arrangements and international commodity agreements.[13] The IMF Compensatory Financing Facility established in 1963 and the Export Revenue Stabilization Plan (STABEX) created in 1975 by the European Community are two significant arrangements for compensatory financing, but neither has been an adequate substitute for stabilizing export earnings. Thus the principal focus continues to be on international commodity agreements in which both importing and exporting countries participate.

No single international organization is responsible for the negotiation of international commodity agreements. UNCTAD has been pressing for more agreements since its formation and it sponsored the conference resulting in an agreement on cocoa. However, GATT was instrumental in concluding several agreements on textiles and wheat. As of 1977, seven major multilateral commodity agreements, which include both producing and consuming countries, were in operation or being renegotiated. They cover textiles, coffee, olive oil, sugar, tin, cocoa, and wheat. Except for the textile agreement, which limits imports into the developed countries from Japan and certain developing countries, the common objective of the other agreements is to prevent excessive price fluctuations.

Export quotas are or have been used to reduce price fluctuations for coffee, sugar, tin, and cocoa. A formal buffer stock system in which a central agency holds a stock and buys and sells to keep the market price within target ranges is also used in the cases of tin and cocoa. Except for short periods of time, however, none of the agreements has been successful in its price stabilization goals. The agreements have encountered three main problems: difficulties in reaching agreement between exporters and importers on an appropriate price range;

---

[12]See Isaiah Frank, "Toward a New Framework for International Commodity Policy," *Finance and Development,* June 1976, pp. 17–20, 37–38.

[13]For general background, see J. Rowe, *Primary Commodities in International Trade* (Cambridge: Cambridge University Press, 1964); and A. D. Law, *International Commodity Agreements* (Lexington, Mass.: D.C. Heath & Co., 1975).

difficulties in reaching agreements among exporters on the basis for sharing export quotas; and difficulties in agreeing on the financial contributions of participants for buffer stock acquisition.

Commodity problems have been of such vital concern to the developing countries that the difficulties encountered in international commodity agreements have been looked upon as a challenge to improve the mechanism rather than as a deterrent to its use. As a new initiative, the Secretariat of UNCTAD proposed in 1976 a so-called integrated program for commodity stabilization that would establish in one agreement a system of international buffer stocks for ten "core" commodities and a common fund for financing the stocks. The core commodities to be included are coffee, cocoa, tea, sugar, cotton, rubber, jute, hard fibers, copper, and tin. The justification for a common fund is that it can be smaller than the sum of separate funds for each commodity because of different patterns and timing of fluctuations in the various commodity markets. Also, as risks would be pooled, the safety of the lenders would be greater and borrowing costs correspondingly smaller. The strategy of negotiating a series of pacts in unison is that participating nations can balance a concession on one commodity against an advantage won on another.

Although the integrated program met a negative reception from the developed countries at the 1976 UNCTAD meeting, the proposal remains a live and important issue. UNCTAD's record of persevering to success on previous "radical" initiatives, such as unilateral tariff reductions on imports of manufactures from developing nations, suggests that new arrangements for international commodity agreements are likely to emerge and that initiatives to stabilize export earnings of primary commodities will persist as a component of the international trade framework.

Trade arrangements to moderate short-term fluctuations in commodity export earnings command a wide degree of international support, but commodity arrangements designed to transfer resources to exporting countries by altering their long-run terms of trade do not. The main reason is that stabilization is perceived by both exporters and importers as being in their mutual interest, whereas changing the terms of trade through price setting by producers is viewed as benefiting the one at the expense of the other. Furthermore, although it could be argued that long-term trends were adverse on the basis of the experience of the 1950s and 1960s, a remarkable upsurge in commodity prices during the early 1970s returned the terms of trade in 1974 between primary commodities and manufactured goods to the 1950 level.[14] As shown in Table 2–3 on page 31, from 1970 to 1974 the

---

[14]United Nations, "Evolution of Basic Commodity Prices Since 1950," Document A/9544, 1974.

price index for agricultural products increased by 120 percent, for minerals and fuels by approximately 370 percent, and for manufactured goods by only 60 percent. Although the 1970–74 upsurge may not represent a new long-term trend, it certainly raises serious doubts about the long-term trend being immutably adverse.

In any event, the spectacular success of the Organization of Petroleum Exporting Countries (OPEC) has encouraged many other producer groups to try to form producer cartels. Since its creation in 1960, OPEC has had two main goals: to raise the taxes and royalties earned from crude oil production and to assume control from the major oil companies over production and exploration. Although well financed and expertly staffed, OPEC was slow to realize its power. Oil revenues per barrel in the Middle East were increased from approximately $0.75 in 1961 to $1.40 in 1972 and then to more than $10 in 1975.[15] A major reason for the OPEC success is that a relatively small group of countries control a large part of world oil reserves. Also, smaller independent companies and government-owned enterprises such as the Italian ENI company have eroded the control over the international market that had been so strongly held by the major international oil companies. In this case, success breeds success and the successes of 1973 and 1974 in increasing revenues, moving toward government ownership, and using oil as a political weapon in the 1973 Middle Eastern war have strongly reinforced the solidarity of the member nations of OPEC.

Aside from its accomplishments in raising the incomes of oil-exporting states, the major impact of OPEC has been the model it provides for other developing nations that export raw materials in pursuing economic and political objectives. The model has already been adopted by the major copper-exporting and the major bauxite-producing nations, and other producer organizations have been formed for phosphate, chromium, and rubber. Although other producer groups are not likely to emulate the success of OPEC, the producer type of international trading arrangement is quite certain to proliferate in the future.[16]

BILATERAL TRADING AGREEMENTS

Despite the restrictions imposed by participation in international trade agreements, there are still numerous instances of countries

---

[15]Zuhayr Mikdashi, "Cooperation Among Oil Exporting Countries with Special Reference to Arab Countries," *International Organization,* Winter 1974, p. 20.

[16]See C. Fred Bergsten, "The Threat From the Third World," *Foreign Policy,* Summer 1973.

making separate bilateral trading agreements for their mutual advantage. Among such bilateral agreements, the U.S.–Canada Automotive Products Agreement concluded in 1965 deserves special mention as a model for creating broader markets to obtain the benefits of specialization and large-scale production for industries in both contracting countries.

The agreement was intended to dismantle tariffs and other barriers in the automotive field and permit the integration of Canadian production of both automotive parts and vehicles with that of the United States. Thus production units in each country could produce at efficient levels and specific products would move between the countries without duty. The selection of products and plants in each country was to be made within a general objective of maintaining an equitable trade balance between the countries in the automotive field.

The agreement, however, has not been a complete success. The United States granted duty-free treatment but Canada's concessions were conditional. For example, Canada still requires that "Canadian value added" be maintained at a certain percentage of Canadian consumption. Nevertheless, automotive trade has increased vigorously between Canada and the United States. Canadian manufacturers to an extent have been able to rationalize their production to take greater advantage of economies of scale. But passenger automobiles sold in Canada continue to be relatively more expensive than in the United States. The restrictions maintained by Canada impede the realization of one of the objectives of the agreement, namely, that of "allowing market forces to determine the most economic pattern of investment, production, and trade."[17]

Bilateral trading agreements are also common among nonmarket or socialist countries and between these and the Western world. The common pattern for the socialist countries, as previously noted, is for the government, through a ministry of trade, to exercise complete control over exports and imports. Foreign traders deal with such a ministry rather than directly with the customer or local vendor of the goods and services. With most economic activities owned by the governments and operated in accordance with national economic plans, foreign trade is also managed according to national plans rather than market-determined commercial opportunities. Political as well as economic considerations can be decisive. Where economic factors prevail, the yardstick is the needs of the total plan rather than the benefits and costs to the individual state enterprise. Under such

---

[17]See *Canadian Automobile Agreement: Ninth Annual Report of the President to the Congress,* U.S. Senate Committee on Finance (Washington, D.C.: U.S. Government Printing Office, January 1976), pp. VI, 29.

conditions, tariffs and subsidies for controlling or stimulating trade are unnecessary and not used. World prices are normally the guide for international transactions, and import or export prices may have no relationship to domestic prices. Nor are the planners necessarily constrained by cost-price relationships.

In addition to this centralized control of trade, there is no arrangement for free convertibility of the currencies of socialist countries, so that trade is frequently arranged on a barter basis or with clearing systems whereby sales are balanced with purchases from another country.[18] This system has led to numerous bilateral trading arrangements with specific trading partners under which attempts are usually made to identify the goods each country will trade and set overall trade limits which the parties will attempt to achieve.

SUMMARY

The large number of organizations and the complexity of the many trading arrangements suggest that a high degree of disarray exists in multinational trading. This is true in the sense that the multinational enterprise must keep informed about and even participate in numerous trade negotiations in many forums. In another sense, however, the picture is rather simple and clear-cut. There are "three worlds" involved and each has its own objectives. The industrialized world favors free trade and specialization and is not vitally concerned about changing the basic structure of the world economy. The developing countries are not in favor of free trade and want to use trade arrangements as one of the means to achieve structural economic changes in their own economies and in their economic relations with the rest of the world. The centrally planned world would like to expand greatly its trading relations with the other two worlds but with a minimum of change in internal economic structures.

The multinational trade agreements "game" is one in which each of the participating groups, and each country within a group, is trying to move a few more steps toward its goals. The game cannot stop because of the growing interdependency of the three worlds. Also there are usually enough mutual benefits involved to warrant the continuing search for new trade arrangements. The results of the negotiations depend, of course, on the respective bargaining power of the participants. The bargaining power keeps changing and involves geopolitical factors as well as economic considerations, such as growing world scarcities of certain natural resources.

---

[18]See Samuel Pisar, *Coexistence and Commerce, Guidelines for Transactions Between East and West* (New York: McGraw-Hill Book Co., 1970).

Institutional arrangements frequently lag behind real needs and deal mainly with the problems of yesterday rather than those of today. This observation is relevant to the international trade framework on two dimensions. One is the relationship of the multinational enterprise and foreign direct investment to trade patterns. The second is the set of terms and conditions for international transfers of technology. Neither of these international dimensions has yet been given proper recognition by the institutional arrangements comprising the international trade framework, with one exception. UNCTAD has been the pioneer by including multinational enterprises and international technology transfers along with trade in its conference deliberations.

EXERCISES AND DISCUSSION QUESTIONS

1. Discuss the following claim: "The longer-run effect of the United Kingdom joining the European Economic Community will be trade diversion, not trade creation."

2. Are the benefits to producer countries from international commodity agreements significant or just an illusion?

3. Would you recommend that advanced industrial countries support moves for further commodity agreements? Why or why not?

4. What difficulties do you foresee for the regional trading arrangements of the developing countries?

5. "The basic problem underlying East-West trade is that the governments in the centrally planned countries make the trade decisions on the basis of national objectives whereas in the market economies the trade decisions are made by private enterprises on the basis of private profit objectives with the governments intervening only in a negative way to control trade that is not considered to be in the national interests." Comment.

8

The International
Regulatory Framework

INTERNATIONAL BUSINESS must function to a considerable degree in a regulatory no-man's land. At the international level, no comprehensive system of laws or controls exists for guiding business transactions across national boundaries. No international regulatory agency or system of international courts is available for controlling multinational enterprises or for resolving conflicts in the international business area between multinational enterprises and host governments or between national governments themselves.

The regulatory and legal environment consists of a multiplicity of national systems and policies which differ significantly in basic philosophy and practice. Each nation-state maintains its own set of courts and regulatory agencies in complete independence of every other nation. And although the effective domain of multinational enterprises exceeds the legal jurisdiction of individual nations, there is no final international authority for handling conflicts of national laws or controls in the way that a supreme judicial body does for a nation-state. As a result, international firms constantly face legal uncertainties and conflicts, and national governments are seriously troubled because of their perception that the transnational enterprise can and does escape from national control policies.

In the traditional fields of international trade and international finance, international businesses do not encounter unusually difficult legal problems. Virtually all nations agree on the desirability of encouraging international trade. As a result, they have cooperated to construct an international framework that facilitates the transfer of

146

goods and money across national boundaries while still reserving the right to impose certain controls over these flows. Nations have also cooperated to create an infrastructure for international communications and travel. But the international framework that serves reasonably well for a world of trade does not adequately serve for the growing sector of the international economy represented by multinational business operations.

A time lag invariably occurs between the identification of a need and the successful negotiation of an international framework to fill the need. As of the 1970s, most nations had become keenly aware of the asymmetry between the operating domain of multinational enterprises and the regulatory domain of individual nation-states and of the consequent need for a comprehensive international regulatory framework. But since negotiations among independent sovereign states are the major vehicle for constructing the framework, agreement is reached only on those policies that all states can accept as being in their own national interests. Given the divergent interests of investor and host nations, of industrialized and developing countries, and of business firms and governments, a comprehensive agreement is a long way off. In the interim, instead of an international regulatory framework, a patchwork system of treaties, codes, and agreements exists. This chapter provides the international manager with some background on this patchwork system. It also identifies some of the principal international legal issues that arise out of this patchwork and discusses possible future international regulatory patterns.

INTERNATIONAL LAW AND INTERNATIONAL BUSINESS

Although contrary to the facts, there is a widely held impression that a rather precise system of international law exists for guiding business transactions across national boundaries. This impression is particularly strong as it relates to the protection of foreign-owned private property. It is common to hear businessmen and government officials declare that the expropriation of foreign property without prompt and adequate compensation is a violation of international law. Such wistful views have long been popular in the economically advanced investor countries, but they are not generally accepted around the world. In order for rules and principles to become international law, nation-states must consider such rules and principles legally binding upon them.

What is normally called international law is more accurately described as *international public law.* It consists of a body of rules and principles which states consider legally binding. It can be enforced through the International Court of Justice, international arbitration, or the internal courts of the nation-states, which lawyers refer to as municipal courts.[1]

Until the late 19th century, international law was mainly concerned with the relationships between states and the delimitation of their jurisdictions. A synonym for international law was the law of nations and control of war was long its primary function. In more recent decades, emphasis has been shifting toward an increased concern with the protection of fundamental human rights of the individual even against his own state. Through the proliferation of treaty law and specialized international organizations, the substance of the law has expanded to include cross-frontier relationships of individuals and corporate bodies.

In order to be operationally meaningful for the multinational enterprise, international law must have a system for adjudication of legal disputes and for enforcement of legal decisions. Here is where the gap exists. The only international court is the International Court of Justice at The Hague. It is the principal judicial organ of the United Nations, and all members of the United Nations are *ipso facto* parties to the statute establishing the court. The function of the court is to pass judgment upon disputes between states, and only states that have submitted to its jurisdiction are parties in cases before the court. Private persons or corporations do not have direct access to the International Court.

In order for private issues to be adjudicated by the International Court, they must be espoused by one of the member states. In some countries, business firms have had reasonable success in securing official government support. In most situations, however, this has not been easy because the political interests of governments must be the guiding rule. Furthermore, the governments representing both sides of a dispute must agree to accept the court's jurisdiction. Even if private issues reach the court and are decided, the problem still remains as to how the legal judgment will be enforced, given the relatively weak form of world government.

In some cases, international law is applied by the municipal courts of a country. For example, the international law providing that foreign sovereigns and their diplomatic representatives enjoy certain immunities from municipal jurisdiction requires the cooperation of municipal courts for its realization. Interestingly enough, where governments trade through state companies incorporated in a foreign country, such as the USSR trading company Amtorg incorporated in New York, an important unsettled issue is whether the state corporation has diplomatic immunity.

---

[1]See Noyes E. Leech, Covey T. Oliver, and Joseph M. Sweeney, *The International Legal System* (Mineola, N.Y.: The Foundation Press, Inc., 1973).

From the standpoint of international business, the nearest approximation to international law is the growing number of treaties and conventions covering commercial and economic matters. According to modern diplomatic usage, the more important international agreements are referred to as *treaties*. Those of lesser importance are called *conventions, agreements, protocols,* and *acts*. All of these forms are agreements between two or more nation-states which normally become legally enforceable through the municipal courts of the participating countries. In some countries like the United States, the constitutions make treaties automatically the law of the land. In certain other countries like the United Kingdom, the legislature must act to give domestic force to the provisions of a treaty. In either case, the path for judicial action becomes the municipal courts and an international court is not essential.

The weakness of the structure of international commitments through treaties, codes, and agreements is its inadequate coverage for many ingredients of business operations that have grown in importance with the internationalization of business. Furthermore, the number of countries participating in particular agreements may be limited in comparison with the global horizon of the multinational enterprise.

In what could be a beginning step toward an international regulatory agency, the Economic and Social Council (ECOSOC) of the United Nations established in 1975 an intergovernmental Commission on Transnational Corporations. The commission is composed of representatives of 48 member countries and has only an advisory function to ECOSOC on the "full range of issues relating to transnational corporations, and in particular the subject of the regulation of and supervision over their activities."[2]

The Right of Establishment

Through bilateral commercial treaties, many governments seek to enlarge the opportunity for their nationals to transact business in foreign countries on a nondiscriminatory basis. Commercial treaties between states encompass an extensive variety of subjects. Specific provisions frequently cover such matters as immigration and emigration, conditions of residence, travel, employment and trade, imposition of taxes, navigation, harbor and quarantine regulations, industrial property rights, and tariffs and customs laws pertinent to import and export trade. In addition, commercial treaties frequently contain a

---

[2]United Nations Economic and Social Council, E/RES/1913 (LVII), 11 December 1974.

most-favored-nation clause, which has great importance in assuring nondiscriminatory treatment in commercial relations.

The privilege of doing business in a foreign country and the conditions under which it is formally granted are the substance of a series of treaties known in the United States as Treaties of Friendship, Commerce, and Navigation. The objective of such commercial treaties is to secure for foreigners the right to trade, invest, or establish and operate a business in a country on a nondiscriminatory basis. The fundamental point underlying commercial treaties is that engaging in business transactions in a country other than one's own is a privilege and not a right. Usually, this privilege and the delineation of its conditions are worked out by negotiation between governments.

The United States had 43 such treaties in force as of January 1, 1975.[3] The signatories include most of the European countries, Japan, and a small selection of less developed countries. The treaties have changed in form and content over the years. Their emphasis is increasingly on investment and the right of establishment, with consular, tariff, and income tax issues being left to other agreements.[4]

Such treaties, of course, are not always observed. In the early 1960s, for example, the French government became greatly concerned because American firms were attempting to take over a number of French companies, including France's largest manufacturer of computers (Machines Bull). The French response was to restrict American direct investment through administrative delays and informal pressures. Although these restrictions violated France's Treaty of Establishment with the United States, the U.S. government never formally protested and apparently was not asked to do so by U.S. firms that were refused. However, the French ban on new direct investment did not last long because other Common Market countries were anxious and willing to receive the U.S. companies.[5]

The Protection of Industrial Property Rights

Most countries of the world protect industrial property rights—a term that includes patents, know-how, and trademarks. But patents are granted and trademarks are registered by national governments and they are valid only within the territorial jurisdiction of the granting government. Consequently, foreign exploitation of a patent or trade-

---

[3]U.S. Department of State, *Treaties in Force* (1975).

[4]Henry Steiner and Detlev F. Vagts, *Transnational Legal Problems* (Mineola, N.Y.: The Foundation Press, 1968), pp. 498–500.

[5]Christopher Layton, *Transatlantic Investments,* (Boulogne-sur-Seine, France: The Atlantic Institute, 1966), pp. 36–44.

mark requires a parallel grant by foreign governments. The burden of having to file a patent application in every country where the patent is to be used is illustrated by this comment: "Of some 62,000 inventions made in this country (the United States) for which patent applications were filed in the U.S. Patent Office during a single year, foreign protection was sought for 23,000 of them by the filing of 115,000 applications in other countries. . . . The president of one large corporation tells us that under the present system the cost of obtaining foreign patents is now running close to $2 million for his company."[6] As another example, 10 percent of the money spent on developing the British Hovercraft, a vehicle for rapid transportation over water, went for securing patents around the world.[7]

The hardship of having to file foreign patent applications is alleviated somewhat by the Convention of Paris, executed in 1883 and periodically revised since that date, which established the International Bureau for the Protection of Industrial Property (BIRPI). Under this convention, once an investor has filed for a patent in one country, he has 12 months' priority in applying for the same patent in all other countries that have signed the Paris Convention. The convention also provides for national treatment in regard to the protection of industrial property; that is, each country belonging to the union grants to nationals of other member countries the same rights it affords to its own nationals. About 80 countries on all continents are members, including the United States and the Soviet Union, which joined in 1965. The United States is also a party to the Inter-American Convention of 1910 on Inventions, Patents, Designs, and Models to which 13 Latin American countries are parties.

A major advance toward simplifying the international framework for patents occurred in 1973 when 16 European countries (the EEC nine plus Austria, Greece, Liechtenstein, Monaco, Norway, Sweden, and Switzerland) signed a convention to establish a European patent office. The office will make one grant for all of the member countries under a single European patent law. It will be located in Munich and is expected to become operational in 1978.[8]

Taxation Treaties

In a world of separate taxing authorities, problems arise because the entity being taxed, or parts of it, may fall under the jurisdiction of more

---

[6]W. O. Quesenberry, Director, Office of International Patent and Trademark Affairs, U.S. Patent Office, in an address before the Joint Symposium of Patent, Trademark and Copyright Section, American Bar Association, Philadelphia, Pa., August 6, 1968.

[7]*Economist,* June 17, 1967.

[8]*Vision Europe,* February 1975, p. 57.

than one taxing authority. An enterprise may have its legal residence in one country, do business in another country, and have headquarters in still another country. How is the enterprise to be taxed and how can it avoid paying taxes on the same base to more than one of the taxing jurisdictions? The solution to this problem must recognize both the right of the enterprise to be free from excessive taxation and the right of the different authorities to tax revenues.

The right to levy and collect taxes is one of the most sacred rights of national sovereignty, but there is no clear or universally accepted theory of tax jurisdiction. Nor is there an international law that specifies who has the right to tax and sets limits to the reach of any country's tax jurisdiction. Business transactions across national boundaries, therefore, can be greatly influenced in both positive and negative ways by the problems or opportunities resulting from varying taxation policies of overlapping national tax jurisdictions.

The tax systems employed by different countries differ significantly in the treatment of who is taxed—that is, in concepts of residence of the firm or individual—and what sources of income are taxed.[9] The most general practice is for nations to tax all income earned within the country, foreign-earned income when remitted, and, in some cases, foreign-earned income on an imputed basis even though not remitted. Credit is normally given for taxes paid to foreign governments. In certain cases, tax credits are allowed for foreign taxes that have been waived, such as through tax-incentive programs of less developed countries trying to attract foreign investment.

The probability that two taxing jurisdictions may claim the right to tax the same property or income has stimulated governments to provide credits for taxes paid abroad and to negotiate bilateral treaties with other countries to share the taxes imposed on business conducted in the territory of one country by nationals of another country.

Treaties for relief from double taxation are common and exist between many of the major countries of the world, especially capital-exporting countries, and between them and certain of the less developed countries. The United States, for example, had tax treaties with 25 countries as of 1976 and others in negotiation or awaiting congressional approval. No multilateral treaties on double taxation have been realized as yet, but a draft convention drawn up by the Organization for Economic Cooperation and Development (OECD) in 1963 has been influential as a guide to countries when they negotiate bilaterally.

The trend in tax treaties appears to be for the host countries of international business firms to impose taxes up to the rates imposed by

---

[9]For example, see *Corporate Taxes in 80 Countries* (New York: Price, Waterhouse & Co., July 1976).

the home countries of the international business firm. Such a policy can maximize the share received by the host country without increasing the total tax burden on a company. Another trend is for nations to use tax exemptions or low taxes as an attraction for international business activities. But the effectiveness of such government policy depends upon the willingness of the home governments of the international business firms to grant "tax sparing," that is, to allow tax credits as if full taxes were paid. The United States, for example, does not grant tax credit for taxes spared abroad and the advantage to U.S. firms of tax inducements in foreign countries may be offset by home-country taxation on the higher foreign profits resulting from the tax concessions.

The Settlement of Investment Disputes

A major area in which the international framework is still deficient is the settlement of investment disputes between parties of different nationalities. As previously noted, the International Court of Justice hears only disputes between nations and is not available to private parties unless their cause is espoused by their respective government. The most recent and promising intergovernmental agreement in this field is the International Center for Settlement of Investment Disputes (ICSID), sponsored by the World Bank. As of June 30, 1975, the ICSID convention had been signed by 71 governments.

The convention was designed to encourage the flow of private foreign investment to the less developed countries by creating the possibility, subject to the consent of both parties, for a contracting state and a foreign investor who is a national of another contracting state to settle any legal dispute that might arise out of such an investment by conciliation and/or arbitration before an impartial, international forum. The center came into being in 1967 but had to wait until January 1972 to receive its first request for assistance in the settlement of an investment dispute.

Despite the large number of signatory nations, ICSID continues to be little used. All the industrialized countries are members, but the membership among the developing nations is predominantly small African and Asian countries, which are not important host countries for foreign investment but which have become members in hopes of improving their attraction to foreign investors. None of the Latin American countries are signatories because all of them view ICSID as an infringement on national sovereignty. Their position is represented by the so-called Calvo doctrine, named after an Argentine jurist. The doctrine asserts that a foreigner doing business in a country is entitled to only nondiscriminatory treatment, and that by entering the country he implicitly consents to be treated as a national.[10] The Mexican Constitution includes a Calvo clause which requires aliens who acquire land or concessions for working mines or for the use of water or mineral fuel to agree "to consider themselves as Mexicans in respect to such property, and bind themselves not to invoke the protection of their governments in matters relating thereto; under penalty, in case of noncompliance, of forfeiture to the nation of property so acquired."

The Calvo doctrine was a response to the unhappy experience of South American countries during the 19th century with diplomatic and military intervention on behalf of foreign investors. Calvo clauses appear not only in statutes and constitutions but also in contracts. The doctrine continues to be used in certain countries but its importance has been diminished by new trends, such as investment guarantee treaties negotiated by investor countries in connection with their investment-guaranty programs. In these cases, investment guarantees such as political risk insurance are provided only for investments in countries that have signed such agreements. The agreements do not, as a rule, provide full and automatic protection against nationalization, but the host country usually agrees to provide fair compensation without undue delay. Agreements can be detailed agreements of substance, as in the case of Germany which has negotiated about 40 agreements dealing with such issues as guarantees, financial transfers, entry permission for foreign personnel, and so forth. Other agreements, such as the almost 90 agreements negotiated by the United States, are limited to more procedural matters in the event that investments should be endangered.

Property Protection in Foreign Jurisdictions

A special category of investment disputes is the expropriation of property and the related issue of adequate compensation. Many governments have attempted to encourage foreign investment by issuing policy statements reassuring investors about the security of their property. Some nations have embodied property protection provisions in domestic legislation and constitutions. The general conclusion of leading legal authorities, however, is that local legislation and constitutional instruments have limited value in the protection of foreign investment and that apparent rights under local laws may in some cases prove largely illusory.[11] Foreign firms may have great difficulty enforcing their rights, because in many countries

---

[10]Steiner and Vagts, *Transnational Legal Problems,* pp. 419–25; Donald R. Shea, *The Calvo Clause* (Minneapolis: University of Minnesota Press, 1955), pp. 269–81.

[11]E. I. Nwogugu, *The Legal Problems of Foreign Investment in Developing Countries* (Dobbs Ferry, N.Y.: Oceana, 1965); Walter S. Surrey and Crawford Shaw, eds., *A*

actions against the state before local courts are allowed only in exceptional cases, under the principle of sovereign immunity. Furthermore, parliamentary sovereignty implies that one parliament cannot bind its successor so far as the legislative functions are concerned. Government policies, local laws, and even constitutional provisions may be altered unilaterally at some future date. No rule of international law makes such changes illegal.

The subject of responsibility by a state for injuries to aliens has been the focus of intensive study and debate in international law. The United States adheres to the position that under customary international law, compensation must be prompt, adequate, and effective when an alien's property is taken by a foreign state. But even where this view is recognized, there is large room for argument over the precise operational meaning of "prompt," "adequate," and "effective" in a concrete situation.

Many of the less developed countries do not recognize the compensation rule as usually asserted. They believe that where the taking is pursuant to a broad program of economic and social reform, the requirement for immediate and full payment would deny to poorer countries the right to undertake reform programs they desire and need. In their view, "social" considerations may be paramount to the rights of the property owner. In the communist nations, expropriation without compensation has been justified as the means of implementing a philosophy opposed in principle to private property.

The international business community and some investor nations, particularly the United States, have been slow to recognize (or accept) this divergence in basic beliefs and have been pressing for a multilateral convention establishing a code for fair treatment and protection of foreign direct investment. Not too surprisingly, the codes proposed by the investors and investor countries focused heavily on the responsibilities of the countries seeking to attract foreign investment. For example, the Guidelines for International Investment proposed in late 1972 by the International Chamber of Commerce, although they also specify a wide range of obligations to be assumed by investors and their governments, require commitments from host countries, such as not to modify agreements other than through negotiation and agreement with investors, not to place restrictions on financial flows, and to make effective payment of "just compensation" in the case of expropriation or nationalization.

Most national governments were slow to join the movement for codes of conduct or principles of international regulation. By the mid-1970s, however, the governments of the industrialized countries

---

Lawyer's Guide to International Business Transactions (Philadelphia, Pa.: American Law Institute, 1963), p. 311.

through the OECD and the developing countries through the UN Commission on Transnational Corporations began to demonstrate considerable enthusiasm for an international code.[12] But the difference between the concerns of multinational firms and those of governments became sharply apparent. To the international business community, international regulation means restraints on governments. To the governments, international regulation means restraints on multinational enterprises. Somewhat ironically, the movement for a code of fair treatment and protection of investors had become transformed into a movement for the fair treatment and protection of countries.

The first product of this new-found concern of governments was a Declaration on International Investment and Multinational Enterprises approved by OECD countries in 1976. The declaration includes rather detailed Guidelines for Multinational Enterprises that "aim at improving the international investment climate," at strengthening "confidence between multinational enterprises and states," and "at encouraging the positive contributions of multinational enterprises to economic and social progress and minimizing or resolving difficulties that may result from their activities. . . . "[13] Although an intergovernmental consultation procedure has been established, the guidelines are voluntary and the parties to the declaration do not include any of the developing countries.

Infrastructure Treaties and Conventions

Most of the infrastructure treaties and conventions of importance to international business have led to organizations currently related to the United Nations. The drafters of the United Nations Charter believed that many areas of economic cooperation, while requiring an intergovernmental approach, could be more effectively covered by relatively autonomous functional organizations. Most of these organizations were to be brought—and have been—into relation with the United Nations as UN Specialized Agencies.

The significance to the international firm of the many infrastructure agencies varies with its fields of business activity. All international business firms are aided through the activities and agreements in the fields of communications and transportation, whereas only those in the pharmaceutical business, for instance, will be directly concerned with the activities of World Health Organization.

The International Civil Aviation Organization (ICAO) fosters the

---

[12]See Commission on Transnational Corporations, *Report on the Second Session (1–12 March 1976)* (New York: United Nations, 1976) E/5782 E/C.10/16.

[13]OECD, *International Investment and Multinational Operations* (Paris, 1976).

development of safe, regular, and efficient international civil aviation through developing international specifications for air traffic, airports, telecommunications, charts, operations, airworthiness, and personnel that are adopted and observed by member countries. The International Telecommunications Union (ITU) controls and allocates radio frequencies and facilitates international telegraph and telephone communications. The Universal Postal Union, initially based on a convention of 1874 and presently a specialized agency of the United Nations, has established compulsory provisions for member countries governing international postal service and operates as a clearinghouse in the settlement of certain accounts. The International Labor Organization (ILO) has adopted conventions on trade union rights and on the protection of the right of workers to organize and bargain collectively. The World Health Organization (WHO) works to improve health conditions and has various international duties relative to the standardization of drugs, epidemic control, and quarantine measures.

As new technologies are developed and new issues become of critical concern to nations, nations are stimulated to create new infrastructure agreements or institutions. Such has been the case with the development of the communications satellite, which led to the formation of the international consortium Intelsat. Intelsat facilitates and regulates the international transmission of television broadcasts and other newly feasible means of international communications. The same has been true in the field of environmental control. In another area of special interest to international business, almost 150 nations have participated since 1973 in periodic Law of the Sea conferences, held under UN auspices, to draft a treaty governing the use of ocean resources and to establish a new international authority to control exploitation of the deep seabed.[14]

NATIONAL LEGAL SYSTEMS

The above review of the international legal situation clearly indicates that the regulatory framework for international business still rests predominantly on a multiplicity of national legal systems, except where there are treaties and conventions or regional laws as are evolving in the EEC. Given the great diversity and complexity of national legal systems, the international manager will undoubtedly rely on specialized assistance for legal matters. He does, however, need a general understanding of the legal systems and the types of problems likely to arise.

---

[14]See special issue of *Columbia Journal of World Business,* Spring 1975, on "Law of the Sea."

Most national legal systems are based on either the common law or the civil law system. The civil law system has traditionally been the legal system for most of continental Europe. From there, it spread to a number of Asian and African countries which decided to westernize their laws: for example, Japan (1890–98), China (1929–31), Thailand (1925), Turkey (1926), and Ethiopia (1958–60). The civil law system, supplemented by religious laws or native customs, also prevails in the former colonies of France, Belgium, the Netherlands, Portugal, and Italy. Supplemented by Islamic law, civil law has come to predominate in the Near Eastern countries.

The common law system, developed in England during the Middle Ages, has been adopted by most of the countries where the English settled or have governed. The United Kingdom, the United States, Canada, Australia, New Zealand, Ghana, Nigeria, India, and other present and former British colonies are all common law countries.

Civil law countries embody their main rules of law in a legislative code. In common law countries, the judge is normally guided not by a code but by principles declared in the reports of previous decisions in similar or analogous cases. In practice, however, the distinction between common and civil law is not clear-cut. Large parts of Anglo-American law are contained in statutes and codes. In civil law countries, large parts of the law have never been reduced to statutes or codes but have been developed by the courts.

The most significant difference between common law and civil law countries is in the role of the judiciary. In common law countries, the responsibility for adapting the law to changing conditions has traditionally been the task of judges. In the United States, the judiciary is the ultimate decision maker in the legal system, and the courts are accepted as the final interpreters of the Constitution and of legislative acts.

In the civil law countries, the judiciary plays a lesser role than in common law countries. In Latin America, it is not the court decision that gives life to the statute, but rather the implementation of the legislative act by government executives through the *reglamento,* which specifies the detailed working rules. Under the French system, the general pattern is to deny law courts the power to pass on executive action and to maintain separate administrative courts. The German system places great emphasis on review of legal questions by government departments. The general result in many civil law countries is that great reliance is placed on the prestige of a career civil service as a counterpart to the judicial power in the Anglo-American system.

Differences in the formal structure of national legal systems are important. Equally crucial can be national differences in the legal process for resolving legal problems and in the infrastructure of attitudes, beliefs, and customs. The gap between the developed legal system and effective administration of justice will vary greatly among nations. In some countries, even the most advanced laws remain dead letters on the books because of a limited capacity to implement the laws or because an underdeveloped judicial system does not have the capability for an expeditious handling of litigation.

The American society probably goes further than any other in translating issues into legal questions and expecting courts and lawyers to resolve them. By way of contrast, Chinese and Japanese societies go to the other extreme: abhorrence of lawyers, laws, and above all, litigation. "It is better to be vexed to death than to bring a lawsuit," says a Chinese proverb. The Chinese and Japanese prefer conciliation and mediation to litigation. The aversion to litigation reflects a fear that legal rules are too impersonal and rigid to accommodate the realities of particular cases and a desire to avoid the disruptions of friendly relations attending a clear-cut victory and defeat in litigation.[15]

The role of lawyers differs greatly from country to country. In the United States, lawyers frequently serve on the boards of directors of corporations. In France, a lawyer (*avocat*) cannot be a member of the board of directors by the rules of his own profession, which reflect a different concept of professional relationship to the business community than is held in the United States. In the United States, one of the attractive areas of legal practice is taxation. In many other countries, tax problems are handled exclusively by the accounting profession.

One important legal practice that is often a surprise to American international managers is the prominent role of the notary public. In the United States, there are many notary publics but they perform only a minor function. In civil law countries, the notary is a key figure. He is trained as a lawyer. By virtue of his office, he gives conclusiveness in a legal sense to contractual instruments. The legal necessity to have virtually all legal instruments notarized requires time and may be considered excessive red tape by the American businessman. But in Latin American, Western European, and other countries, the businessman considers it absolutely essential that a transaction is adequately recorded, preserved, and made firm and certain by being recorded with a notary. The importance of the notary may be illustrated by the case of at least one Latin American country, where the privilege of being a notary is granted only by the president of the republic and is considered to be the most lucrative of all political grants.

---

[15]Steiner and Vagts, *Transnational Legal Problems*, p. 141.

SELECTED LEGAL PROBLEMS IN INTERNATIONAL BUSINESS

Jurisdiction in International Trade

International trade is based chiefly on the use of standardized forms and practices. The standardized instruments contain most of the rules governing the parties. Sales memoranda, brokers' notes, bills of lading, charter parties, marine insurance policies, and letters of credit all embody familiar clauses which shipping clerks and bank tellers are trained to follow. Also, the import or export of goods can be, and usually is, arranged so as to involve the law of a single country. By including a "choice-of-law" clause in the contract, the parties can select the law that will govern their obligations on issues that lie within their contractual capacity—such as sufficiency of performance and excuse for nonperformance. But even with a choice-of-law clause, issues may arise that are outside the contractual capacity of the parties and on which the governing law is uncertain.

Another common legal issue in international trade is whether to include a clause in the contract prescribing the method of arbitration if future disputes arise. If arbitration is to take place in the United States, the normal clause provides that the rules of the American Arbitration Association will be followed.[16] If arbitration is to take place in Europe, the usual pattern is to follow rules developed by the International Chamber of Commerce. Where trade is with Eastern European countries, the agreement may be to submit disputes to the Moscow Foreign Trade Arbitration Commission.

Translation Problems

A unique source of legal difficulties in the international business field is the problem of languages and translation. The problem is present in the drafting of contracts, in the preparation of corporate documents, in negotiation and settlement of disputes by arbitration or court proceedings, and in any reference to foreign laws or concepts. To the businessman, a contract is essentially a set of operating rules to be observed in arranging details of delivery, payment, and similar matters. But as a legal instrument, the contract must also be drafted with a view toward its meaning to a judge or arbitrator when foreign legal elements are involved. The translation problem expands the area of uncertainty not only because of the normal difficulties of translating the meanings of words from one language to another. The translation

---

[16]See American Arbitration Association, *New Strategies For Peaceful Resolution of International Business Disputes* (Dobbs Ferry, N.Y.: Oceana, 1972).

of legal language also involves a transfer of concepts rather than a mechanical matching of words. Furthermore, courts differ in their procedures for accepting documents into evidence. U.S. courts emphasize oral testimony as a means of presenting foreign language documents. In many foreign courts, oral testimony is not allowed and translations are admitted only when made by official translators. The vital issue for the international manager, according to one distinguished legal authority, is to make sure that the matter of translation is properly worked out during the period when the instrument is drafted.[17]

Whose Law Determines "Inc."?

In the present international legal environment, the business enterprise engaged in multinational operations cannot become an international corporation in a legal sense. No international agency has yet been created with the authority to grant international incorporation. Consequently, the multinational business enterprise must content itself with stringing together a series of corporations created by the laws of different nation-states. The legal complexities arising out of such a situation are immense. The presence of the same enterprise in many countries necessarily subjects it to different laws and legal climates, which in many situations may conflict.

In setting up multinational operations, one of the first considerations is to determine which country's laws will be applied to give life and motion to the component parts of the multinational enterprise. This issue has been posed by one legal authority as "Whose Law Determines 'Inc.'?"[18]

The legal test of nationality varies among countries. Like an individual, a corporation can have dual nationality. It can also be "stateless," thereby exposing the members of the corporation to individual liability. The question of nationality may have significant tax consequences. It may also determine whether an enterprise can benefit from government subsidy programs or engage in certain strategic businesses.

In the United States, it is not strictly correct to speak of the nationality of an enterprise. Corporations are created under the laws of the individual states and are identified with the specific state where organized. A Delaware corporation is one organized pursuant to Delaware law even though the activities of the corporation are com-

---

[17]Henry P. deVries, "The Language Barrier," *Columbia Journal of World Business,* July–August, 1969, pp. 79–80.

[18]Henry P. de Vries, "The Problem of Identity: Whose Law Determines 'Inc.'?" *Columbia Journal of World Business,* March–April 1969, pp. 76–78.

pletely outside of the state and the owners are nonresident. Nevertheless, the underlying U.S. view for all corporations is that a corporation secures its life and existence from a grant of the sovereign, and the nationality of the corporation is that of the sovereign power making the grant.

In many other countries, particularly civil law countries, a corporation is considered to be created by the contractual intent of its members rather than by a grant from the sovereign. The nationality of such a corporation is not necessarily that of the country in which it is constituted. In determining the law applicable to a corporation's existence and internal relations, several countries like the United Kingdom and Brazil follow the U.S. pattern and look at the place of incorporation. On the other hand, France, Belgium, and Greece look to the center of management. Italy and Egypt use the test of main business activity. Still others, such as Morocco, look to the place of the registered head office. As a result of these variations, multiple incorporation in various countries may be necessary to protect stockholders from personal liability.

The problems and risks arising from different concepts of nationality can be illustrated by a recent case brought before the German courts. A suit was filed against the U.S. stockholders of a corporation organized in the State of Washington to conduct mining operations in Mexico but with the central management of the corporation meeting in Hamburg. Since the corporation was administered in Germany but not constituted pursuant to German law, the court held that it was an unincorporated association in Germany and that the stockholders were personally liable for corporate liabilities.

Choosing the Form of Business Organization

Another major legal consideration is the form of business organization to be used in different legal jurisdictions. Tax considerations both at home and abroad may play a key role in the choice of legal form. The principal objective, however, normally will be that of insulating the parent organization or the investor from direct liability for obligations incurred in local operations.

In the choice of legal form, a clear distinction exists between common law countries and civil law countries. As noted previously, in common law countries a grant from the public authority gives life to the corporation. In civil law countries, the corporation is created by a contract between two or more persons, and the root concept is that of *société* or *Gesellschaft*. Thus, the one-man corporation is a contradiction in terms, and most civil law countries tend to reject the one-man corporation and the wholly owned subsidiary. In some countries, the acquisition by one individual or legal entity of all the shares of a corporation may lead to its automatic dissolution and to personal liability of the stockholder for the corporation's liabilities.

In most countries, the choice of foreign business organization to operate as a subsidiary or affiliate will be between two forms, both similar to the U.S. corporation. The two forms are a *société anonyme* (S.A.) or a *société à responsibilité limitée* (S.A.R.L.). In German-speaking countries the similar forms are the *Aktiengesellschaft* (A.G.) or the *Gesellschaft mit beschrankter Haftung* (GmbH). The S.A. or A.G. is the most common form of business organization for medium- and large-scale businesses outside of the United States and British Commonwealth countries. However, the S.A.R.L., often referred to as Limitada in Latin American practice, has gained in favor as the form for foreign subsidiaries.[19] Several features of the S.A.R.L. explain its growing attractiveness to international enterprises. As compared to the S.A., it requires fewer formalities for formation and operation. It can afford considerable flexibility through contractual details inserted into the charter, whereas the S.A. must conform to more cumbersome mandatory provision of law. This flexibility is of particular importance for controlled companies, as well as for joint ventures with local interests. The S.A.R.L. can have a simple structure with management often centered in a single person and without a board of directors or other supervisory bodies required of an S.A. In each country, however, the S.A.R.L. will have distinctive features which vary as much as do the laws in different countries relating to the S.A.

The establishment of a joint venture creates special legal problems because the stresses and strains of the normal business operations may result in discord. In the choice of business form for a joint venture, the international enterprise should be alert to the problem of eventual liquidation and dissolution. The divorce may be far more complicated than the marriage, particularly where patents, trademarks, and the use of an internationally known firm name is involved.

Concession Agreements

The right of a multinational enterprise to engage in certain activities in a host country may be based on so-called concession agreements, sometimes referred to as economic development agreements. In its most common form, the concession agreement involves an extractive or public utility enterprise. The provisions of the agreements, which specify a series of rights and obligations for both the enterprise and the

[19]Henry P. de Vries, "Legal Aspects of World Business," in *World Business,* ed. Courtney C. Brown (New York: Macmillan Co., 1970), pp. 289–93.

government, vary widely among countries and industries, generally reflecting the relative bargaining power of the government and the investor.[20]

Unlike traditional examples of contracts between a government and an alien, such as debt instruments or purchase and sale contracts, the concession agreement is apt to be a unique instrument tailored to meet special needs. Furthermore, it may involve mineral rights or other interests controlled by the government and arrangements on matters, such as taxation, which are within a legislature's competence. These agreements often resemble special legislation governing relationships between the country and the international enterprise.

For a variety of reasons, concession agreements are likely to generate disputes between the parties. Problems will turn up for which no solutions or analogies can be found in legislation or in previous legal decisions. When such problems emerge or when governments breach a concession agreement, purely legal considerations have not been of great significance, even though the agreement is a legal instrument. The vast majority of disputes over concession agreements have been settled by direct negotiation between the parties, with the investor's government sometimes involved. The positions taken by the parties have been more influenced by economic, political, and equity considerations than by the wording of legal agreements.

The long-run trends in many concession contracts proceed through several identifiable stages.[21] The first stage begins when a country suspects that it has natural resource possibilities that might attract foreign investors, but the existence of such resources, as in the case of petroleum, or the economic feasibility of production is not known. In this stage, the host government is negotiating from weakness because the risks as seen through the eyes of both parties are high.

A second stage begins when the investments have been made and the projects are successful. As judged by hindsight, the host government reviews the original concession agreement as excessively favorable to the foreign investor and begin to raise its sights regarding its share of the returns from the concession activities. With its bargaining power greatly strengthened, the host government tends to increase its demands in the form of taxation, requirements for foreign enterprise to provide educational and other public facilities, and a number of other ways.

At a third stage, the government presses for greater linkage of the concessionaire's activities with the economic development aspirations

---

[20]See David N. Smith and L. T. Wells, Jr., *Negotiating Third World Mineral Agreements* (Cambridge, Mass.: Ballinger Publishing Co., 1975).

[21]See Raymond Vernon, "Long-Run Trends in Concession Contracts," *Proceedings of the American Society of International Law at its Sixty-First Annual Meeting,* April 27–29, 1967 (Washington, D.C., 1967), pp. 81–89.

for the local economy. For example, the foreign firm may be required to develop local sources of supplies for many types of equipment and services.

At a fourth stage, local governments become interested in sharing in the ownership of the foreign enterprise or in the process of decision making or both. As concession agreements move through these stages, it is the relative bargaining power of the parties, generally economic but sometimes political, that influences the patterns of conflict and resolution rather than conventional legal considerations.

Antitrust: Transnational Reach of Economic Regulation

The transnational reach of enforcement techniques of one government can be interpreted as interference by another government, with the international enterprise in the middle. In many respects, the international enterprise can adjust its global strategy and operating policies to differences in national laws. But the effects of certain business actions or policies are not coterminous with the national boundaries within which such actions are taken or policies decided upon. Certain practices may be legal in one jurisdiction, but the same action may be considered in violation of the laws in another country in which the enterprise is operating. Such a situation raises the difficult problem of extraterritoriality, because legal action in one jurisdiction can have significant effects on activities in another area where the law being applied does not have legal jurisdiction. In this way, the international enterprise can be the vehicle through which conflicts between nations arise.[22] The transnational reach of national laws has presented vexing problems for the international enterprise, particularly in the field of antitrust.

Restrictive business agreements are agreements among enterprises to fix prices, limit production, allocate markets, restrain the application of technology, or engage in similar schemes likely to reduce competition: Such practices have been illegal in the United States for many decades under various antitrust laws, but until World War II they were either permitted or positively encouraged in most countries outside of North America. The situation changed drastically after World War II when many other nations adopted laws designed to curb restrictive business practices and the European Economic Community assumed responsibility for regulating competition in its common market area based on Articles 85 and 86 of the Rome Treaty.

Some significant differences in national laws exist. In its domestic

---

[22]For an assessment of the resentment by other countries to the extraterritorial application of U.S. antitrust laws, see Jack N. Behrman, *National Interests and the Multinational Enterprise* (Englewood Cliffs, N.J.: Prentice-Hall, 1970), pp. 114–27.

application, the U.S. law looks at the *act* of conspiracy, or of monopolizing, whereas the European laws look at the *effects*. The basic philosophy of antitrust laws in the United States is that competition per se is good and that any acts to restrain competition are illegal. The basic philosophy of European antimonopoly law is that some anticompetitive agreements may be harmful but others may be beneficial because they can lead to increased productivity, economic growth, technological advance, and price reductions.[23]

The Sherman Act of 1890 passed by the U.S. Congress at a time when few American firms had foreign subsidiaries holds in Section 1 that: "Every contract, combination in the form of trust or otherwise, or conspiracy, in restraint of trade or commerce among the several states, or with foreign nations, is hereby declared to be illegal." The Sherman Act and subsequent legislation extends the U.S. laws to actions abroad which "substantially affect" the commerce of the United States and competition in the U.S. markets. To do otherwise, it is argued, and to have enforcement depend on nationality or physical events, would open the door to widespread evasion and abuse. The non-U.S. antitrust laws are relatively recent, and the applications are still limited in number. Yet indications are that they will also have a transnational reach.

As a practical matter, a nation must be able to assert jurisdiction over the international enterprise in order to enforce its laws. The legal test of jurisdiction by U.S. courts is whether the foreign corporation is transacting business "of a substantial character," and the test governing service or process is whether the corporation is *found* in the jurisdiction. The wide reach exercised by the U.S. laws is illustrated by the Swiss Watchmakers Case. Two Swiss trade associations headquartered in Switzerland were held subject to U.S. jurisdiction because they had a jointly owned corporation in New York doing advertising and promotional work and acting as a liason agency in servicing the American market with repair parts.[24]

The U.S. courts found the defendants guilty of conspiracy to restrain the commerce of the United States and ordered them to stop all restraints on exports to the United States and to change industry practices developed in Switzerland with the active support and participation of the Swiss government. The decree imposed wide prohibitions on contracts made in Switzerland and on agreements made between the Swiss industry and manufacturers in Great Britain, France, and Germany. It also ordered sweeping changes in certain

---

[23]See *European Competition Policy: Essays of the Leiden Working Groups on Cartel Problems,* ed. The Europa Institute of the University of Leiden (Leiden, The Netherlands: A. W. Sijthoff, 1973).

[24]*United States* v. *Watchmakers of Switzerland Information Center,* 133 F. Supp. 40, SDNY (1955).

bylaws of the Swiss Watch Federation which were considered restrictive of U.S. commerce. After the Swiss government intervened directly with the U.S. government, important changes were made in the final judgment, including the insertion of a provision that nothing in it would limit or circumscribe the sovereign right and power of the Swiss government.

Foreign mergers and acquisitions have been challenged under U.S. antitrust laws. Through the threat of court action, the U.S. Department of Justice delayed and reshaped a merger of two foreign firms: Ciba and Geigy. These two major Swiss pharmaceutical companies postponed a merger and revised their merger plans in 1970 when officially informed that the merger as planned might be in violation of U.S. law. The alleged grounds were that combining the U.S. operations of both companies would reduce competition in the American dyestuff market.

Still another aspect of the transnational reach of antitrust laws has been the concern expressed by foreign firms interested in establishing operations in the United States that U.S. authorities may seek to apply U.S. laws to their activities outside of the United States.[25]

FUTURE TRENDS

Clearly the international regulatory environment is in a transitional stage of adaptation to new international business patterns. The conduct of multinational business has many ingredients in addition to the transfer of goods and money across national boundaries that ideally would be governed and facilitated by an effective world government and international legal system. In the absence of such a system, treaties, codes, and agreements negotiated by nations on a bilateral or multilateral basis have been the principal tool for building a substitute framework. Normally, treaties are obeyed and agreements adhered to. In any event, they serve as an important guide for predicting the behavior of national governments.

Although the multinational enterprise phenomenon is frequently described as a private international government, in the present world of nation-states the key to forecasting future international regulatory trends is a clear recognition that nations make laws or agree to multinational treaties. Consequently, future trends at both the national and international levels are certain to reflect the concerns and aspirations of the individual nations vis-a-vis multinational enterprise.

What are the prospects for nations agreeing on an expanded interna-

[25]J. A. Ellis, "The Legal Aspects of European Direct Investment in the United States," in *The Multinational Corporation in the World Economy,* ed. Sidney E. Rolfe and Walter Damm (New York: Praeger Publishers, Inc., 1970).

tional regulatory framework?[26] The proposals for new measures range in degree of comprehensiveness, including establishment of a forum for discussion of issues concerning private and governmental interests;[27] expanded efforts to harmonize national policies on such matters as taxation and antitrust; the extraterritorial application of national controls such as export restrictions[28] and investment codes and guidelines; and a regional or global international companies law.[29]

The changing ambience for multinationals and the growing assertion by governments of their regulatory powers are realities. As the U.S. representative on the UN Commission on Transnational Corporations has observed, "Whatever may have been the governmental restraints in the past, that period, in comparison with what is likely in the future, may seem to have been a veritable Eden of freedom. Surveillance and restriction are in the air. The multinational finds itself under steady assault from host and home government alike." But he also concludes that "It does not seem likely, however, that the multinational has much to fear from a broad international agreement."[30] As is suggested by another study, the apparent enthusiasm by both governments and some international managers for international codes "masks different conceptions of who is going to be controlled, who is going to do the controlling, and what the purposes of the control will be."[31]

Some internationally agreed measures are likely to emerge from the welter of overlapping proposals. But the forecasts are for only a modest expansion of the international regulatory framework. One authoritative view is that "a modest proposal for a forum may be the most acceptable, and perhaps, at this state, the most useful."[32] A leading Latin American expert concurs in the view that "control" will continue to be exercised nationally rather than internationally. "What can be aimed at internationally," he suggests, "is to 'monitor' investment. We need a monitoring device and information center, a reference bureau

---

[26]See Don Wallace, Jr. and Helga Ruof-Koch, eds., *International Control of Investment* (New York: Praeger Publishers, Inc., 1974).

[27]Seymour J. Rubin, "Developments in the Law and Institutions of International Economic Relations," *The American Journal of International Law* 68:487.

[28]Paul M. Goldberg and Charles P. Kindleberger, "Toward a GATT for Investment: A Proposal for Supervision of the International Corporation," *Law and Policy in International Business* 2, no. 2, (Summer 1970): 295–325; also W. Michael Blumenthal, "Needed: A GATT for Investments," *Business Week,* August 18, 1973.

[29]George W. Ball, "Cosmocorp: The Importance of Being Stateless," *Columbia Journal of World Business,* March–April 1968.

[30]Rubin, "Developments in the Law," p. 487.

[31]C. Fred Bergsten, Thomas Horst, and Theodore H. Moran, *American Multinationals and American Interests* (Washington, D.C.: The Brookings Institution, forthcoming).

[32]Rubin, "Developments in the Law," p. 487.

dealing with all aspects of multinational corporations, a true data bank on the matter. We need, in short, an *international organization* to facilitate the *national control* of foreign investment."[33]

The tension that has stimulated the developing countries in particular to press for international controls comes not so much from bad experience with multinationals, "but from both sides trying to take advantage of, but not be trapped by, dramatically changing asymmetries of bargaining power."[34] The political leaders of the developing countries are searching for ways to limit the price they pay for scarce business skills and technology, which is usually set at the beginning of an operation when both country benefits and business risks are high. On the other hand, the business firms are trying to find means to protect themselves from the ravages of an "obsolescing bargain." The nations want an effective international countervailing power that will represent their interests before they are willing to limit their exercise of national countervailing power. If the recommendations of the Brookings study fall on responsive ears, it may be the United States who will take leadership for improving the international framework.[35]

SUMMARY

Although the paths are uncertain, the prospect is that a sizable number of countries will begin to evolve more comprehensive legal principles to govern the international corporation. There will also be forward movement by groups of countries—either by multilateral international treaties, the adoption of a uniform business law, or by some less formal and more unconventional approach—to evolve codes of legal principles for dealing better with the international business phenomenon. Progress will be uneven and novel approaches will have to be devised. But there are certain to be important changes in the regulatory environment. International business has become such an important component of the world economy that the international regulatory environment will have to adjust to this reality.

EXERCISES AND DISCUSSION QUESTIONS

1. "When a foreign firm does business in our country its local affiliate must legally become a national enterprise," explained the official of a host government. "As a national enterprise the affiliate is entitled to the full legal protection of our laws in case of expropriation, alleged breach of

---

[33]Luis Escobar, "Rules of the Game for MNCs," *Worldview,* February 1974, p. 27.
[34]C. Fred Bergsten et al., *American Multinationals, (forthcoming).*
[35]Ibid.,

concession contract, etc. in the same way as any other national enterprise. Why should the investor countries and the international business firms be insisting on additional legal protection for foreign investment through international investment codes or international organizations to arbitrate what are essentially national legal issues? Such proposals violate our national sovereignty and discriminate against purely national companies." Discuss.

2. The legal doctrine, *rebus sic stantibus,* relates to the presumption in contracts that things will remain in the same condition as they were at the date of agreement. There is a difference of opinion among the authorities as to whether the principle of *rebus sic stantibus* is a recognized rule of international law. To what extent do you think that the principle should be clearly recognized in the settlement of disputes concerning concession contracts?

3. If national laws on antitrust and restrictive business practices were harmonized, as an international manager would you prefer the U.S. version which looks at the act or the European version which looks at the effects? Why?

4. If the United Nations were prepared to establish a new specialized agency with limited powers to improve the international legal environment for multinational business operations, as a representative of the international business sector what specific activities would you recommend that this agency undertake? To what extent would you expect that your recommendations would be acceptable to host countries as well as to investor countries?

5. As the manager of a multinational enterprise, what strategies would you follow to improve the international framework for the transfer of industrial property rights and for expanding the network of tax treaties? Remember that your firm is operating in a number of countries and must appeal to the national interests of all governments.

part three

The Nation-State and International Business

As business enterprises have internationalized and steadily enlarged the geographic span of their operations, the world's governmental structure has not moved along a similar path. Despite some sentiment for creating a world government and some actual progress in regional political integration, the dominant units of government remain sovereign nation-states.

With the decline of colonialism and separatist movements in many parts of the world, the number of sovereign units of government has increased significantly since the end of World War II. Some observers argue that the nation-state is old fashioned and not well adapted to serve the needs of the modern complex world. Yet nation-states persist as the principal governmental unit with which the international enterprise must coexist.

Each sovereign nation-state has its own nationalistic spirit and set of national goals which are often directly competitive with those of other nation-states. The multinational enterprise consisting of many units of diverse nationalities pursues its own business goals on a global basis. In large part, the actions of the multinational enterprise will be in harmony with the goals of some nation-state. But almost inevitably, the same actions will conflict with the goals of other nation-states. Chapter 9 provides an overview of the common interests and potential conflicts between international business and individual national governments. The subject is a central issue that pervades all aspects of international business operations, and governments are becoming increasingly advanced in their measurements of benefits received.

In the traditional fields of international business, nation-states have long recognized the need to control the transfer of goods and money flows across national boundaries in order to harmonize such economic activities with national objectives and to increase national benefits. The patterns of such traditional controls and the underlying national motivations are presented in Chapter 10. As nations have become more aware of the effect that multinational enterprises can have on the achievement of national goals, they have been responding by establishing control programs over the operations of multinational enterprises within their national boundaries. These responses and the objectives that nation-states are attempting to achieve with such controls are the subject of Chapter 11. The multinational enterprise is not without some means of protecting itself against controls that threaten its own objectives and existence. Its countervailing power is considered in Chapter 12. To wait until controls are imposed by nation-states, however, may be too late to escape what too frequently has been a crippling impact. The prudent multinational enterprise will form a view on the likelihood of further controls, even to the extent of assessing the threat from underlying political pressures, and adjust accordingly. The expertise of control forecasting is introduced in the last two chapters in this section.

9

Measuring Benefits to the Nation-State

THE NATION as a sovereign power sets the rules for governing business transactions within and across its national boundaries. Through such controls, it endeavors to increase national welfare and protect the public interest. In dealing with predominantly domestic business enterprises, governments normally feel competent to achieve their goals and do not consider their sovereignty threatened. And as long as international business consisted mainly of arm's-length transactions between independent parties in different countries, nation-states were not particularly sensitive to conflicts of interest with international business. But the rise of the multinational enterprise has tremendously sensitized and dramatically changed business-government relations in international business.

DIVERGENT GOALS OF NATIONS AND FIRMS

The multinational enterprise attempts to direct a corporate family of diverse nationalities under its control toward supranational, or global, goals. The parent and each member of the family have a nationality, having been granted their corporate existence by the authority of a specific sovereign nation. But through bonds of common ownership and common strategy that cut across national boundaries, the family group operates as a transnational system that adjusts its business operations to achieve its global goals. Such goals may be in harmony or in conflict with the goals of one or more nation-states. There is, in fact, likely to be some conflict with *every* nation-state in which it operates, because the actions of the firm are not likely to maximize the goals of any one of those states. These potential conflicts have little to do with good or bad intentions on the part of either international business firms or nation-states. The potential for divergent interests is an ineluctable result of the internationalization of business in a world of sovereign states.

As the inherent differences in goals have become apparent, each of the nation-states has begun to exercise its sovereign power to influence the behavior of the multinational enterprise. One level of national response has been protective or harmonizing—to reduce or reshape perceived threats to national economic, political, and cultural goals. Another level of national response has been not only to reduce conflict but mainly to capture for a specific nation as large a share as possible of the total global benefits generated by the multinational enterprise. In the latter respect, nation-states are competing against other nation-states.

With each nation aiming for a surplus of benefits over costs from the operations of multinational enterprise, it might appear that the international firm is in the middle of an impossible situation. In order for one nation to have net gains, does another nation have to have net losses? Fortunately, two characteristics of the situation help to reduce the stress placed on the multinational enterprise in a world of nation-states. One saving feature is that the cost and benefit items have different values for different nations. A loss of jobs to a full-employment German economy because of the establishment of overseas production facilities by a German multinational enterprise will be valued as a small cost to Germany, whereas the same employment will be valued as a great benefit by a host country with a high degree of unemployment which receives a new subsidiary. The second saving feature is that international business activity is not necessarily a zero-sum game in which one nation has to lose in order for another nation to gain. If international business results in a more efficient use of world resources, all parties can secure increased benefits. Because the pie to be divided is larger, each nation can have a larger slice.

NET NATIONAL BENEFITS: UNDERLYING CONCEPTS

The common interest between business activities and the broader society was cited by Adam Smith more than two centuries ago in support of a laissez faire government policy. He argued that the "annual revenue of the society" will be maximized when the individual (and presumably the business enterprise) is permitted to use his capital to produce what is of greatest value to the individual. Although the degree of regulation exercised by governments is generally greater than that envisaged by Adam Smith, the basic principle—that the interests of the nation can be maximized by permitting individuals and business firms to maximize their own goals—still persists as the guiding philosophy of the market economies of the world vis-á-vis domestic business activities.

For business activities that cross national boundaries, Adam Smith's principle of common interest may not be appropriate. In domestic business, the nation expects to capture somewhere within its boundaries the total net contribution of the enterprise. In the case of international business, however, a specific nation may not receive what it considers to be its legitimate share of the total global benefits. In traditional international trade, most nations accept the free-trade argument that world output from a given set of resources will be increased by international specialization and trade among nations. Yet this acceptance does not remove an active concern for how the gains from trade are distributed among nations and for investigating whether an individual nation might benefit from restricting trade. Likewise, most nations might agree in principle that the free movement of multinational enterprises across national boundaries can stimulate the movement of productive resources from areas of lesser opportunity to areas of greater opportunity and thus improve overall economic efficiency on a world basis. But here again, the priority interest of the nations is in maximizing their own benefits.

At a practical level, the multinational enterprise must thus focus on individual national benefits rather than on world benefits. The measuring stick for calculating national benefits can differ sharply from the gauge used to sum up world benefits. Weighing heavily as world benefits will be greater production efficiency and accelerating economic growth. From the specific nation's point of view, many other aspects are measured, such as the effect on national balance of payments or employment. Also, national benefits from international business must not be confused with national benefits from business per se. Only the net contribution over what might have been available from domestically controlled business activities really counts to the nation. Furthermore, the nation must compare net benefits to net costs. And the surplus of benefits over costs for multinational enterprises must be greater than that for other alternatives available to the nation in order for significant common interests to exist between the enterprise and a specific nation-state.

Simply by focusing on benefits, an enumeration of the potential contributions of international business operations to the goals of specific nations can be made overpoweringly impressive. Multinational enterprises, quite naturally, emphasize these benefits most forcefully as proof of their common interests with nation-states.[1] But a one-sided presentation is fallacious, and multinational business may do its cause more harm than good with such an approach. On the other hand, there are those who overemphasize the effects of multinational business operations that do not coincide with the goals of one particular nation affected by those operations. These, too, give a one-sided view that can be far from academically honest. They tend to depict a direct conflict between firms and nations rather than depict multinational firms as entities that transfer things from one nation to another. The basic fallacy of the view that the multinational firm is in direct opposition to the nation-state becomes rather obvious in those works that make the firm out to be an enemy of every nation or seem to imply that multinationals should always be opposed because they can never fulfill all the desires of all the nations affected by their operations.[2]

It is possible that a single firm could take actions sequentially that produce net disbenefits to every single nation. But over any extended period of time, it takes a great deal of imagination to suggest that the sum total of a firm's activities simultaneously creates a net disbenefit to all nations.[3] This is particularly difficult to imagine given the developmental benefits from transferring technology and know-how across national boundaries and the economies that can result from operating on a scale larger than justified by the size of national markets. Much more likely is that the multinational firm creates overall net benefits. If this is the case, it cannot be possible that across any given period of time the firm causes disbenefit to every nation that its operations affect.

That multinational firms contribute some net benefit, however, does not mean that they must benefit each and every nation. It is possible that some nations benefit by more than the net benefits created by the multinationals. To the extent that this happens it will be at the expense of other nations. A nation's real opponents are thus other nations, as they have always been. It is the same old conflict of nation versus nation, only this time via an intermediary—the multinational firm.

---

[1]Publications of the International Management and Development Institute have this tendency. See, for example, *Corporate Citizenship in the Global Community,* (Washington, D.C.: International Management Development Institute, 1976).

[2]See R. J. Barnet and R. E. Muller, *Global Reach: The Power of the Multinational Corporation* (New York: Simon and Schuster, 1974), chap. 10.

[3]It should be noted that unanimous agreement does not exist on the inevitability of greater global benefits arising from multinational business operations. As Hymer has argued, direct foreign investment "is an instrument which allows business firms to transfer capital, technology, and organizational skill from one country to another. *It is also an instrument for restraining competition between firms of different nations* (emphasis supplied)." If the anticompetitive effect of multinational business offsets positive benefits, it may not contribute to world welfare. See Stephen Hymer, "The Efficiency (Contradictions) of Multinational Corporations," *American Economic Review,* May 1970, pp. 441–48.

The multinational firm is not an opponent. It is an intermediary through which a nation must operate to maximize its own share of those benefits whose location can be influenced by the firm. Although the firm adjusts according to its own objectives whenever any country takes steps to influence or control it, that is not at all the same as being the ultimate opponent to a country's interests.

The case for measuring the net benefits of any international business activity to an individual country is thus very strong. It is not surprising that cost-benefit measures are becoming more common. With the trend toward global operations in business, even home countries who tended to assume that the international actions of their own firms would coincide with national goals have increasingly turned to cost-benefit analyses.[4] In this respect, then, home countries can be viewed as just a particular type of host country.

DIFFICULTIES IN QUANTIFYING BENEFITS AND COSTS

In evaluating national benefits and costs, national authorities may consider political, social, or spiritual effects as well as economic effects. And they may value each effect explicitly or implicitly through the decisions they take. The mix of effects included in any evaluation, however, will vary from nation to nation and reflect differences in national priorities. The same effect will almost certainly be weighted differently by different nations, and the effects considered will change over time as national priorities change.

While these points may be readily grasped at the conceptual level, in practice, the quantification of costs and benefits remains a highly ambiguous subject, even in the economic area. How does a nation measure the value of a transfer of technological and managerial know-how to nationals of that country? What is the value of a foreign enterprise's contribution to national goals of economic and social modernization, or what are the costs of having prized cultural values changed? How much is it worth to have more competition injected into an economy or for indigenous entrepreneurship to be stimulated (or stunted) by the entry into a country of foreign firms? For the home as well as the host country, the quantification problem is equally formidable. Raymond Vernon made the following observation to the President's Commission on International Trade and Investment Policy, which was considering the benefits and costs of U.S. international enterprises to the United States: "There are no economic models as yet

---

[4]A major attempt at overall assessment of benefits accruing to the United States from its own multinationals is presented by: C. Fred Bergsten, Thomas Horst, and Theodore H. Moran, *American Multinationals and American Interests: The Economic and Political Effects and Proposals for a New Policy* (Washington, D.C.: The Brookings Institution, forthcoming).

sufficiently subtle and dynamic to capture the medium-term and long-term consequences of creating an overseas subsidiary. In the end the decision on whether to support or retard this kind of development on the part of U.S. enterprises must be made by what amounts to an intuitive leap."[5] Yet, implicitly more often than explicitly, each nation-state makes such calculations, or intuitive leaps, in establishing and exercising controls over international business. Some of the areas in which the costs and benefits of international business are open to debate are examined below.

THE IMPACT ON NATIONAL SOVEREIGNTY

Ideally speaking, the nation-state has both internal supremacy and external independence. External independence or freedom from outside control, however, is never absolute. In practice, the nation-state must be guided by the impact of its decisions on other sovereign nation-states. The multinational enterprise is subject to the sovereign power of a nation-state over the conduct of its business activities within that state's territory. But, unlike purely domestic firms, the multinational also responds to outside commands emanating from the parent, other family members, or even indirectly from other sovereign states. Furthermore, the local subsidiary can rely for support on the economic power of the entire system and at times on the political power of other sovereigns. The presence within a nation of an appendage of a powerful multinational system may thus generate local tensions and appear to be a threat to national sovereignty.[6] In theory, the "divine right of sovereignty" can always prevail over the "divine right of capital." In practice, however, one nation is limited in its sovereignty by the interests of other nations involved.

Sovereignty is jealously guarded. Some nations have voluntarily accepted limitations to their sovereignty by joining international agencies such as the International Monetary Fund, free-trade areas, or political unions. But the willingness to surrender national sovereignty to wider authority is only limited. Where the international enterprise encounters conflicts, therefore, it can rarely look to a higher world tribunal for harmonizing or resolving differences between sovereign nation-states or between the enterprise and a specific nation-state.

---

[5]Raymond Vernon, as cited in *U.S. International Economic Policy in an Independent Interdependent World* (Washington, D.C.: U.S. Government Printing Office, July 1971), p. 312.

[6]The "threat to sovereignty," however, can also be an "extension of sovereignty" with the host country able to extend its sovereignty into the home country. See Joseph S. Nye, Jr., "Multinational Corporations in World Politics," *Foreign Affairs*, October 1974, p. 158.

Political systems will continue to change and develop, but the international businessman can expect to be facing a world system of sovereign nation-states for some time to come.

Nations' general attitudes toward international business are built from their evaluations of individual business activities. Yet, the threats to sovereignty reflect considerations over and above the sum of the net benefits or costs of individual international business activities. As a result, any specific international business project may become subordinated to the broader issues and may not be evaluated as an independent event. International firms, therefore, should not ignore the more general nationalistic concerns in the cost-benefit analyses.

REDUCTION IN ECONOMIC INDEPENDENCE

In any individual case, the activities of a multinational firm may offer sizable net benefits to a nation in which it is operating. But when a dominant share of the domestic economy comes under foreign ownership and control, the merits of the individual case become subordinated to a nation's broader concern for maintaining its economic independence. Over many decades, the new jobs and other benefits generated by foreign investment in Canada were sufficiently appealing to quiet national fears of foreign economic domination. But when 60 percent of Canada's manufacturing industry, 75 percent of her petroleum and natural gas industry, and 60 percent of her mining industry came under control of foreign corporations by the mid-1960s, national sovereignty tolerance levels were breached. As one Canadian scholar expressed this concern: "Once the most dynamic sectors of our economy have been lost, once most of the savings and investment is taking place in the hands of foreign capitalists, then the best prediction is a steady drift toward foreign control of the Canadian economy with the only certain upper limit being 100 percent."[7]

The Canadian example illustrates a nation's concern because of the total share of the national economy that is foreign owned. Nations also become agitated when foreign enterprises dominate a number of key growth industries. Writing in 1901, a British author observed, "The most serious aspect of the American industrial invasion lies in the fact that these incomers have acquired control of almost every new industry created during the past fifteen years."[8] Referring to the British, he concludes, "We are becoming the hewers of wood and the drawers of

---

[7]Mel Watkins in the preface to Kari Levitt, *Silent Surrender: The American Economic Empire in Canada* (New York: Liveright, 1971), p. xi.

[8]Fred A. McKenzie, *The American Invaders* (New York: Street and Smith, 1901), p. 31.

water, while the most skilled, most profitable, and the easiest trades are becoming American."[9] More than a half century later, a similar manifesto combining nationalistic fears of both sectoral and overall economic domination by foreign enterprise, written by the Frenchman Jean-Jacques Servan-Schreiber, became a best seller throughout much of the world. It warned Europeans that *American industry in Europe* was likely to be the world's third greatest industrial power within 15 years—just after the United States and Russia.[10]

Ironical as it may be, some of the necessary conditions for successful international business expansion are also the sources for creating national tensions. Foreign firms must have something to offer over and above what is available from domestic enterprise in order to have reasonable prospects for success. This means that expansion opportunities are best in nations where indigenous enterprise and management skills are weak and in industries requiring advanced technology or in ones based on new products where the foreign enterprise has an oligopoly advantage. Multinational enterprises have little to offer in the production of low technology and standardized products for local markets. Bricks are an example of such products. But in sophisticated technology and rapid growth areas such as computers, international firms have a competitive-advantage basis for entering foreign areas. Thus arises the national fear of becoming technologically dependent upon foreigners.

The multinational threat to national economic autonomy is perceived in many dimensions. As host nations may complain, the decision centers that control the future of many of their key economic sectors are outside of the country and less subject to national controls. The multinational enterprise can shift resources within the system and thus reduce the effectiveness of national programs to control inflation, improve the balance of payments, or expand employment. The research centers for multinational enterprises are likely to remain in the home country, with the result that a host country becomes technologically dependent on outsiders.[11] Foreign enterprises that command mammoth resources and have a head start in key growth areas are viewed as slowing the emergence of local entrepreneurship in these fields.

The less developed countries, which can benefit most from the transfers of resources, management skills, and technology of the multinational enterprise, are especially sensitive to the economic domination issue. Some of them characterize the issue as economic

---

[9]Ibid., p. 157.

[10]J. J. Servan-Schreiber, *The American Challenge* (New York: Atheneum, 1968).

[11]See *Multinational Corporations in World Development* (New York: United Nations, 1973), p. 49.

neocolonialism, particularly at intermediate stages of development. Foreign investment, as they see it, can change over time from a development stimulant to a retardant. As Hirschman has articulated the case, ". . . foreign investment can be at its creative best by bringing in 'missing' factors of production, complementary to those available locally, in the early stages of development of a poor country. The possibility that it will play a stunting role arises later on, when the poor country has begun to generate . . . its own entrepreneurs, technicians, and savers and could do even more along these lines. . . ." The increased domestic capacity for supplying missing factors may in large part be the contribution of multinational enterprise. But, as Hirschman argues, institutional inertia makes for continued importing of so-called scarce factors even when they become locally available. This line of thinking has resulted in proposals that foreign enterprises should be forced to withdraw, or disinvest, at the stage when the factors brought in by the multinational enterprise are no longer complementary to local factors but become competitive with them and prevent their growth.[12]

THE POLITICAL CHALLENGE

The history of foreign investment during the 19th and early 20th centuries contains many examples of foreign firms, particularly in the extractive industries, exercising their power to influence political events and political decisions in host countries. Probably the best known cases of political intervention are the activities of United Fruit in Central America, ITT in Chile, and the international oil companies in the Middle East.[13] However, direct attempts at political influence by multinational firms have steadily declined. The multinational now tends to face more subtle political problems in which it is unintentionally caught between opposing political interests of different nation-states.[14]

To the host country, the local subsidiary of a multinational enterprise can be perceived as a political arm of the home-country government. Through its control over the parent company, home governments can and have interfered in the political affairs of another, or host country. Over certain periods, for example, the U.S. government has placed partial or complete embargoes on exports of goods and transfers

[12]Albert O. Hirschman, *How to Divest in Latin America, and Why,* Princeton Essays in International Finance, no. 76 (Princeton N.J.: International Finance Section, Department of Economics, Princeton University, November 1969).

[13]See Stacy May and Galo Plaza, *The United Fruit Company in Latin America* (Washington, D.C.: National Planning Association, 1958), pp. 1–23; Robert Engler, *The Politics of Oil* (New York: Macmillan Co., 1961).

[14]Joseph S. Nye, Jr., "Multinational Corporations in World Politics," p. 160.

of technology to certain countries such as mainland China, Cuba, and the Soviet-bloc countries. American subsidiaries in Canada have been criticized for following U.S. policies banning trade with mainland China, even though Canadian policies permit such trade. American subsidiaries in England and in Europe have been coerced into turning away business from Cuba and Soviet-bloc countries, even though the nations in which the subsidiaries are located have different policies.[15]

Other conflicts with host countries have occurred in the area of extraterritorial jurisdiction. The application of domestic laws to the operations of a multinational enterprise in one country can influence operations of the same company in another country. The best known example is the enforcement of U.S. antitrust laws, which has had the effect of banning activities in another country which are not against the law of that country. The transnational reach of one country's domestic laws through international business firms conflicts with the sovereignty and political autonomy of another state.

Still another type of political challenge to a host country occurs when the home country of the multinational parent assumes political responsibility for protecting the foreign interests of its citizens. Although foreign subsidiaries are normally incorporated within the countries in which they are operating and subject to national laws as a national corporation, home-country governments are not always willing to accept the results of expropriation under local law. In 1971, Algeria moved to take over majority ownership in all French oil subsidiaries in that country, one of which was owned by the French government. Among official retaliatory actions taken by the French government was a move to block international loans to Algeria for a natural gas plant.[16] The well-known Hickenlooper Amendment to the Foreign Assistance Act of 1961 legally requires the U.S. government, under specified conditions, to use certain governmental powers to protect the interests of its foreign investors. The interests of the multinational enterprise and those of the home country, however, are not identical, and the use of home-country political power to intervene in the relations between foreign subsidiaries and host governments often becomes a controversial political issue in the home country. Such intervention can be at the expense of other political interests of the home country.[17] For this reason, the Nixon administration failed to apply the Hickenlooper Amendment to Peru in 1969, when the International Petroleum Company was expropriated.

---

[15]See Jack N. Behrman, "Export and Technology Controls," in *National Interests and the Multinational Enterprise* (Englewood Cliffs, N.J.: Prentice-Hall, 1970), pp. 101–13.

[16]*The Wall Street Journal,* March 1, 1971.

[17]The shortcomings of the Hickenlooper Amendment are analyzed in Bergsten, Horst, and Moran, *American Multinationals and American Interests,* chap. 12.

In the continuing formulation and implementation of its foreign policies, the home country may have its options restricted because of the amount and type of foreign private investment by its citizens located in specific countries. The foreign policy options for the United States toward Middle Eastern countries have undoubtedly been narrowed by the existence of massive American oil investments in the region. The large amount of U.S. foreign investment in Cuba most certainly was a crucial constraint in U.S. foreign policy relations with that country. Where host countries closely identify multinational enterprises with home-country governments, the home country may see its political relations complicated by types of behavior on the part of international business enterprises which are resented by host countries.

The general political-conflict problem that has been emerging in home countries is the extent to which the level and allocation of foreign operations by nationally incorporated firms can be left to the dictates of the market *if* the home country must assume political responsibility for the enterprises. Some home governments attempt to guide foreign private investment, through incentives or controls, in ways that might minimize the potential sources of political conflict.

The multinational enterprise faces a complex and ambiguous situation in the political conflict area. It has little, if any, capability for reducing the political challenge it represents to host countries when it is used as a political arm of the home government and in cases involving extraterritoriality. It does not relish its role as a carrier of controls. At best, it can urge the conflicting nation-states to undertake bilateral negotiations or participate in inter-governmental programs to harmonize laws or mediate disputes.

In their relations with home countries, multinational companies have mixed and, at times, ambivalent views. Some companies would like to be independent of the political interests of a home country. Some have even expressed the desire to have an island somewhere in international waters as their home base. Other firms place a high value on having a home-country government that will protect their operations in a foreign country and represent their interests in inter-governmental negotiations on such matters as tariffs and trade policies. In still other cases, multinational enterprises would like to be politically free from their home country on some issues and yet be able to call for its political muscle on other issues.

RESOURCE TRANSFER EFFECTS

A very important component in the calculation of net national benefits is the extent to which the multinational enterprise increases the availability of resources and the supply of productive facilities in the countries where it establishes operations.

In an industrialized country like Canada, where national growth has been constrained by inadequate domestic savings and a shortage of skilled manpower, even nationalistic opponents of foreign enterprise agree that such firms have made net additions to the nation's supply of these factors. In other industrialized countries, the important resource transfers have been identified, with little local disagreement, as the fields of technology, management, and skilled technical manpower.

In the less developed countries, the range of resource transfers has generally been much broader. Outside capital has often been a major contribution. Where foreign exchange is a major constraint on growth, foreign capital can help to break this bottleneck. The transfer of technology and the import of management, marketing, and production skills may be valued even more highly than in the more advanced countries. To the extent that the inflow of resources consists of "missing factors," they may complement and effectively "increase" the supply of local factors heretofore idle or less productively used. Thus, the resource transfer effect may be both the net addition from the outside as well as the net increase in the effective value of domestic resources.

Resource transfers have a cost as well as a benefit side. The multinational enterprise may use local resources that are scarce rather than in excess supply. Although local management skills may be in short supply, the foreign enterprise is frequently under pressure to hire nationals. It is then likely to be charged with the opportunity cost of preempting managers who otherwise would be available to initiate and direct indigenous enterprises. Or enterprises may be required by national policies to form joint ventures by enlisting local capital and may be charged on the cost side with preempting scarce local capital which should be available for local enterprises.

Whether such opportunity costs are valid costs in calculating net national benefits is a complex question. The entrepreneurial function of conceiving, establishing, and taking the risk inherent in a new enterprise is generally recognized as a human skill separate from that required for managers of ongoing businesses. In other words, hiring managers is not the same as employing entrepreneurs. Yet the unique experience a local manager gains by working with a multinational enterprise may give him the additional knowledge, confidence, and resources that transform a manager into an entrepreneur. Similarly, by using local capital foreign enterprises may enlarge rather than reduce the total supply of that resource. In countries that are attempting to strengthen local capital markets, the selling of stock locally by a well-known and presumably financially secure and profitable international firm can provide the confidence essential for developing such institutions and thereby help in attracting more savings to capital markets for equity investment.

The profits earned by foreign enterprises can be considered an offsetting cost by a nation. To the extent that a multinational firm transfers profits out of the country, there is a foreign exchange cost. The foreign exchange question will be considered separately below. If the firm reinvests profits within the country, the cost to the nation may be that a larger amount of the national patrimony comes under foreign ownership. What is frequently overlooked by antagonists to foreign investment is that such profits come out of newly created increments to domestic GNP generated by the multinational enterprise, and that the profits are generally a small share of the total increment. The firm gains profits; the nation gains an even greater increment in GNP and employment.

Turning to a question posed earlier, if the host countries are gaining resources, aren't the home countries losing? This possibility exists, of course. Capital outflows for foreign investment may reduce the supply and/or increase the cost of capital for domestic expansion. They may also reduce the availability of foreign exchange. Sending skilled managers and workers to man foreign subsidiaries will reduce the supply of such skills in the home country. The normal situation seems to be, however, that resources are being transferred from countries in which they are in relatively abundant supply to areas where such factors are in relatively short supply and that the opportunity cost of such resource outflows may be low. Offsetting these home-country costs are a flow of benefits such as repatriated profits, payments to the parent company for royalties and management services, increased exports to overseas subsidiaries, increased exports as an indirect result of expanding world output, and even return flows of technology.

It should be noted, however, that the resource transfer capability of the multinational enterprise extends far beyond that of bilateral transfers between home and host country. Operating with a global strategy, the firm can transfer resources among any of the nations in which it is operating. Where the enterprise does its financing outside the home country, the home country can benefit by repatriated profits and other payments to the parent company without any cost in capital or foreign exchange outflows.

Under most circumstances, in order to welcome international firms a nation must feel that the net value of resource transfers from such operations is positive. There may be some cases where a net cost, rather than a net benefit, is acceptable because of other compensating national gains. One such situation may be where an international business activity generates large indirect or linkage benefits. The establishment of an agricultural processing plant by a foreign firm may not in itself result in a net inflow of resources, but the stimulus of this plant to agricultural employment and farm output may be a more than offsetting benefit. Another type of situation is the interesting case of the French multinational aluminum producer, Pechiney, entering the U.S. market by acquiring a controlling interest in Howmet, an American producer, and by financing this acquisition mainly from U.S. capital sources. Where is the resource transfer? Pechiney would claim that it has transferred advanced technology to the United States. But, even taking the technology transfer into account, with such giant American companies as Alcoa, Reynolds, Kaiser, and others prepared to meet domestic U.S. demand for aluminum, it would appear difficult to demonstrate net resource transfer benefits to the United States.

Resource transfers, of course, have a time dimension. When a direct-investment project is initiated, benefits are greatest and certainly most spectacular. In the initial stages, capital flows in, plants are built, local workers are hired and trained, and local supply contracts are let. After a new project has been started, or a new product or process introduced, a steady decline in benefits is likely to set in. The benefits may never phase out completely. Yet, over time they may lose much of their value to a nation.

The longer the enterprise operates on its original technological, organizational, and other resource transfer base, the smaller is the value placed on the original benefits by the host country. In many, if not most, cases stimulated by opportunity or pushed by local pressures, enterprises have responded by continually adding to or upgrading their initial technological, organizational, or product contributions. Where firms do not continue adding, the question is likely to be raised by the host country as to whether payments to the foreign investor should continue indefinitely since the net contribution to the nation has declined and may even cease over time.[18]

BALANCE-OF-PAYMENTS EFFECTS

The impact of international business on a nation's balance of payments has long been a sensitive and controversial issue. The relative abundance of statistical information on balance-of-payments transactions has led to a growing number of scholarly studies which have attempted to resolve controversy in this area. Still, considerable uncertainty prevails as to the complete and precise impact on either investor or host countries because neither the data nor the measuring

---

[18]Peter P. Gabriel, "The Investment in the LDC: Asset With a Fixed Maturity," *Columbia Journal of World Business*, Summer 1966, pp. 109–19.

techniques have been sufficiently comprehensive to trace through the total effects. Even if the methodological and data difficulties were surmounted, the ultimate conclusions would depend primarily on what assumptions are made as to what would have happened if the foreign investment had not been made.

In many of the less developed countries, the prevailing view is that international business operations result in a net foreign exchange cost to the host country. The factual support for this belief comes from a simple comparison of annual net capital outflows from the investor countries, generally the United States, and net annual inflows of repatriated earnings. For example, over the 10-year period from 1960 through 1969, the net capital outflows from the United States to the less developed countries averaged about $650 million per year. Over the same period, U.S. companies returned to the United States as repatriated earnings an average of about $2,500 million per year. By including the foreign exchange payments of the subsidiaries to the parent company as royalties and fees, the outflow from the host countries would be increased significantly. From these data, the simple conclusion can be drawn that the less developed countries have been suffering a substantial net loss in foreign exchange from the operations of U.S. multinational enterprises in their countries.

This type of calculation, widely used and popularly accepted by opponents of foreign enterprise, is accurate as to the capital accounts but misleading as to the total balance-of-payments effect of multinational enterprises. Inflows in the form of new capital and outflows of repatriated earnings represent some of the impact. Outflows in the form of royalty fees and payments to headquarters for sharing company overhead are also important. But in a quantitative sense, the capital flows are generally overshadowed by the effects on the trade accounts—exports and imports.

A special study sponsored by an organization of American multinational companies dramatically reveals how the opposite conclusion can be supported, namely, that American multinational enterprises make a large and positive foreign exchange contribution to the Latin American countries, by including the trade as well as the capital effects.[19] The study estimates that during the 1965–68 period, U.S. affiliates were responsible for annual foreign exchange earnings by host countries through exports of about $4.5 billion and foreign exchange savings through substitutions for imports averaging at least $4.8 billion, or an average annual total balance-of-payments contribution of $9.3 billion on trade accounts alone. Over the same period, the

---

[19]Herbert K. May, *The Contributions of U.S. Private Investment to Latin America's Growth,* A Report for the Council of the Americas (New York, January 1970).

annual amount of new capital invested in Latin America averaged about $700 million. Repatriated earnings on the accumulated investments were at a level of about $1,410 million annually. Thus, the annual deficit in the capital account of $740 million annually was overshadowed by an annual surplus of $9.3 billion on the trade accounts. The study contains some debatable calculations such as valuing import substitution effects at local prices, whereby imported goods might be available at significantly lower prices. Yet, even with some downward revision in benefits, the net foreign exchange gains to the host countries would be sizable if the assumption is reasonable that the expanded exports or the import savings would not have been achieved without the foreign enterprise.

If host countries are persuaded to give attention to the trade accounts in evaluating foreign exchange benefits and costs, they naturally begin to focus on the prices paid for import substitution production and whether multinational enterprises improve or make more difficult their possibilities for exporting. The automobile industry in Latin America is an example—probably at the extreme end of the spectrum—of the high cost in domestic resources that countries have been paying for the prestige of having nationally produced automobiles and for saving foreign exchange. As a consequence of the uneconomic scale and fragmentation of production facilities, in 1967 a light truck, produced in Mexico with 63 percent local content, cost 1.6 times the imported equivalent. In Argentina, with 83 percent of the value of the finished vehicle produced locally, the same light truck ran 2.5 times import costs.[20] The import substitution example suggests that a complete appraisal of balance-of-payments effects may have to extend even beyond the trade accounts and include costs in local resources incurred in securing foreign exchange gains.

The role of the multinational enterprise in expanding export earnings may be either positive or negative, depending on the particular case. The multinational enterprise following a global strategy will assign its world markets to the various subsidiaries and attempt to supply its export demand from areas of lowest cost, or where excess capacity exists, or where national pressures or incentives for exporting are most effective. Thus, the subsidiary in any specific country may have a better or a worse chance, but not a free chance, of competing for all export markets. As an independent local company, the same operation would have a free, but probably worse, chance of expanding exports. With its ties to other affiliates in the multinational enterprise system, a local subsidiary may bring to a country special export

---

[20]Jack Baranson, *Automotive Industries in Developing Countries* (Baltimore: The Johns Hopkins Press, 1969), pp. 35–42.

advantages because the system provides an easy conduit to sales in other countries. But many different possibilities exist and the conclusion will depend upon the specific case being considered. On the whole, the various studies available suggest that the multinational enterprise has been a means of expanding, rather than constraining, exports.[21]

Most certainly, foreign investments in raw materials industries are a major source of increased exports. But here again the evaluation of net foreign exchange benefits from international enterprises depends on whether these products would be produced and exported in the absence of foreign investment and at what price. Until recent years, it seems reasonably clear that many African, Middle Eastern, and Latin American countries would not have been able to supply the necessary capital, technology, and marketing skills from local sources in order to earn the large amounts of foreign exchange from their sales of petroleum and minerals. For those periods, the assumption that local production would not have taken place without foreign enterprise was most likely a realistic assumption. But more recently, particularly as a result of the technology transfers and the opportunity to accumulate capital that has followed from multinational business operations, a more reasonable assumption for many of these countries is that local production and export can take place without foreign investment. Also, host countries may have alternatives between these two polar positions which change the balance-of-payments effects, such as hiring foreign technology and management on service contracts rather than permitting direct foreign investment. Service contracts will limit the foreign exchange costs in amount and over time. Direct investment requires a continuing outflow of repatriated profits.

Other questions that should be included in a comprehensive evaluation of balance-of-payments effects have to do with the pricing of goods for exports and the longer run effect of foreign investment on productivity and prices within the host country.[22] Will the multinational enterprise reduce a country's foreign exchange earnings by selling its goods to another unit in the multinational system at a price below the fair market value? Will foreign enterprise increase the efficiency of other producers within the host country over time and contribute to increased exports indirectly because export prices can be reduced? Still another effect might be that foreign enterprises indi-

---

[21] *Foreign Ownership and the Structure of Canadian Industry,* Report of the Task Force on the Structure of Canadian Industry (Ottawa: Queen's Printer, 1968), pp. 203–7.

[22] These subjects are explored in greater detail in "Chapter 5—National Economic Consequences," in Raymond Vernon, *Sovereignty at Bay,* (New York: Basic Books, 1971), pp. 151–71.

rectly raise imports as a result of increased incomes in the host country to which the foreign enterprise has contributed.

The most complete and technically sophisticated studies of balance-of-payments effects have been made in response to the controversy in investor countries over the impact of outbound foreign investment. Such studies have attempted to include the trade effects as well as the capital accounts, and they have considered the immediate as well as the long-run effects.[23] As in the case of host-country studies, whether the home countries have foreign exchange benefits or costs from the operations of multinational enterprises based in these countries is overwhelmingly influenced by the assumptions on alternatives. If an enterprise can effectively compete in foreign markets through exports from the home country, the establishment of foreign subsidiaries results in foreign exchange losses from export substitution. In the case of foreign production, the home country receives only that share of total profits that is repatriated. The magnitude of profit remissions is obviously minor compared to total revenues.

If foreign production is for export back to the home country and substitutes for goods previously manufactured in the home country, there is a foreign exchange cost. If domestic producers have been losing the local market to foreign producers anyway, foreign production by a home-country enterprise may result in a net benefit because there is no loss on the current account, and the repatriated profits are likely to more than compensate for the initial investment outflow on the capital account. Furthermore, in many cases the multinational enterprise raises some or all of its capital for foreign investment outside of the home country. When the analyst assumes that products sold in foreign markets will shortly be produced in a foreign location, either because a local or other foreign competitor will find such a market location advantageous or because the country has established formidable quota or tariff barriers to force the establishment of local import substituting industries, the balance-of-payments effects on the investor country will be positive, but paltry, compared to the benefits on trade accounts to the host country.

An unfortunate feature of the controversy over balance-of-payments effects is that even if host and home countries enlarge the scope of their benefit-cost evaluations of the foreign exchange impact of multina-

---

[23]See W. B. Reddaway et al., *Effects of U.K. Direct Investment Overseas: Final Report* (London: Cambridge University Press, 1968); G. C. Hufbauer and F. M. Adler, *Overseas Manufacturing and the Balance of Payments* (Washington, D.C.: U.S. Treasury Department, 1968); Judd Polk, Irene W. Meister, and Lawrence A. Veit, *U.S. Production Abroad and the Balance of Payments* (New York: The Conference Board, 1966); *Implications of Multinational Firms for World Trade and Investment and for U.S. Trade and Labor*, Report to the Committee on Finance of the United States Senate, 93d Congress, 1st sess., (Washington, D.C.: U.S. Government Printing Office, 1973).

tional enterprises, and even if agreement can be reached on the alternatives against which specific projects or business operations should be measured, still another major aspect of the question remains and is only beginning to be considered. As discussed in Chapter 22—International Financial Management—multinational enterprises have become highly skilled in forecasting foreign exchange risk and in protecting their assets against losses when balance-of-payments difficulties cause a country to devalue. They reduce foreign exchange risks by using local borrowing instead of bringing in outside funds, by accelerating payments for goods and services outside the country, by advance repatriation of profits, and by a series of other actions and inactions. In countries where multinational operations are large, financial strategies of such enterprises can easily place a critical amount of pressure on a currency when it appears to be weakening. As the share of international business activity controlled by sophisticated multinational enterprises continues to increase, it is a safe bet that the financial management impact of such enterprises on a nation's balance of payments will begin to overshadow the long-term capital and trade account impacts that receive more attention.

EMPLOYMENT EFFECTS

The mix of national interests which shape a government's actions varies with the changing concerns and influence of different groups within the country. At certain times and on certain issues, a specific region within the nation may be a strong force in determining national interests. At other times and on other issues, the private goals of strong or well-organized business interests or labor unions may be dominant in defining the national interests.

Writing in 1968, on the interest of U.S. labor unions in the overseas expansion of American business, Professor Kindleberger made the following prescient observation: "One must put the limited nature of the reaction of labor against capital exports down as something of a puzzle and in the future keep an eye on this possible source of support for those interests abroad which also oppose direct investment from the United States."[24] The puzzle was solved in 1971, during a year of economic stagnation and increasing levels of unemployment, when the U.S. labor movement launched an attack on multinational enterprises for harming the national interest through exporting jobs.[25]

---

[24]Charles P. Kindleberger, *American Business Abroad* (New Haven: Yale University Press, 1969), p. 70.

[25]Industrial Union Department, AFL–CIO, "New Breed of International Cat," *Viewpoint* (Washington, D.C.: Summer 1971), pp. 10–15.

In response to labor union pressures, the U.S. government commissioned several studies to determine whether the spread of multinational business had reduced U.S. employment. However, a Tariff Commission study undertaken for the U.S. Senate concluded that the question could not be answered definitively because "both the analysis and the answer must depend on crucial assumptions" about the extent to which foreign markets would have been lost if foreign production facilities had not been established. Under a "pessimistic" set of assumptions, a net loss of 1.3 million U.S. jobs in manufacturing was identified. Under a so-called realistic set of assumptions, net employment in manufacturing increased by roughly a half million jobs.[26]

Another study commissioned by the U.S. Department of Commerce examined in depth nine actual foreign investment decisions distributed among nine manufacturing industries.[27] The industry fields of the case studies were food products, paper and allied products, chemicals, petroleum, rubber products, primary and fabricated metals, electrical machinery, nonelectrical machinery, and transportation equipment. Of the nine cases, four were projects in the less developed countries, two were in Canada, two in Europe, and one in Japan.

The study concluded that although American firms have a preference for operating in the United States, in most cases of foreign investment they do not have the alternative of continuing to serve their relevant market from their U.S. plants. In each of the nine cases investigated, the researchers concluded that the companies were forced to invest to preserve their markets. The foreign investments, therefore, did not result in an export of jobs from the United States because the alternative of producing domestically did not exist or would not have existed within a relatively short period of time. On the positive side, the study concluded that "U.S. foreign direct investment provides jobs for production workers manufacturing components for further processing or assembling in foreign plants, goods for resale abroad or for sale on a commission basis that would otherwise not be sold abroad (so-called associated exports), and capital equipment for use in the foreign plants. Further jobs are provided for white-collar workers in the home office providing services for the foreign plants, technical personnel providing engineering and similar services, and research and development activities that could not be justified without the possibility of gaining income from foreign plants."[28]

As the Tariff Commission emphasized, the conclusions as to home-

---

[26]*Implications of Multinational Firms for World Trade*, pp. 6–7.

[27]Robert B. Stobaugh and Associates, *U.S. Multinational Enterprises and the U.S. Economy* (Boston, Mass.: Harvard Business School, January 1972).

[28]Ibid., p. 30.

country employment effects of outbound investment depend on the assumptions about alternatives. In many, if not most, cases of manufacturing operations the enterprise may actually be forced to establish foreign production facilities to defend its markets. But in some cases, the foreign investment may be desirable from the standpoint of increasing profits, rather than necessary for avoiding losses. In such cases, the national interests of the home country might be better served by a tradeoff of more local employment as against greater business profits. Most certainly, nine case studies will not resolve the controversy.

PRACTICAL CALCULATION OF NATIONAL SOCIAL VALUE

Measurement of national social value is not a standard process and it would be risky to attempt to fit all assessments into a standard format. Important effects could be left out completely or effects evaluated in a way inappropriate to the particular use for which the assessment is required. Each case in practice shapes its own format, and the first stage of identifying the significant individual effects is the most crucial in the entire process. Measurements of individual effects, however, have to be reduced to some overall quantitative assessment of the social value of the investment.

An insight into how such an overall assessment is commonly put together should help the international manager to marshal the data needed for a positive evaluation, or to adjust the proposal to match national goals more closely. As an example, an appraisal of a proposal from a multinational firm requesting permission to construct a new plant in a developing nation is presented in some detail below. The expertise in placing quantitative assessments on social value and social cost that is illustrated here falls within the field of project analysis. A considerable literature is available in this field.[29]

Nitrogene: A Worked Example

A European-based multinational firm has requested permission to construct a new plant in Asiatica for the production of Nitrogene, a chemical fertilizer based on a patented process. Although there are

---

[29]See Louis T. Wells, Jr., "Social Cost-Benefit Analysis for MNCs," *Harvard Business Review,* March–April 1975, p. 40ff.; Ian M. D. Little and James A. Mirrlees, *Social Cost-Benefit Analysis: A Manual of Industrial Project Analysis in Developing Countries,* vol. I, II (Paris: OECD, 1969); and by the same authors, *Guidelines on Project Evaluation* (Vienna: UNIDO, 1970); A. K. Sen, *Methods of Evaluating the Economic Effects of Private Foreign Investment,* Report for 5th session of UNCTAD Committee on Invisibles and Financing Related to Trade, United Nations, publication No TD.B.C.3. 94.add. 1.

TABLE 9–1

Calculation of National Social Value for proposed Nitrogene Investment in Asiatica
(in thousands of lira)

	Annual Operating Estimates	Adjustments (numbers refer to written description)	National Social Value (+ = value, – = cost)
Sales (local)	2,000	$\begin{cases} -400 & (1) \\ +320 & (5) \end{cases}$	+1,920
Costs			
Labor (including services)			
Local.	500	−250 (2*a*)	– 250
Foreign	100	+ 20 (5)	– 120
Materials			
Local.	200	—	– 200
Imported	700	$\begin{cases} -140 & (2b) \\ +112 & (5) \end{cases}$	– 672
Taxes			
Local.	100	−100 (2*c*)	
Capital charges			
Local interest.	60	+ 90 (2*d*)	– 150
Depreciation	100	−100 (2*e*)	—
Total costs	1,760		
Net profit.	240		
Taxation on profits	120	−120 (2*c*)	—
Profit after tax (remitted as dividends)	120	$\begin{cases} \text{record} \\ \text{as cost(3)} \\ + \;\; 24 \;\; (5) \end{cases}$	– 144
Social externalities		+ 20 (4)	+ 20
Net social value.			404

other foreign licensees, none shows any interest in submitting competitive proposals. The currency unit in Asiatica is the lira and the proposed investment comprises an equity sum from foreign currency sources of 500,000 lira supported by local long-term financing within Asiatica of a further 500,000 lira at an interest rate of 12 percent per annum.

Annual costs and revenues from operating the proposed plant are estimated as shown in the first column of Table 9–1. The second column records adjustments to the operating estimates to register the social value of the proposal to Asiatica. In this case, there are five major types of adjustment as follows:

1. Adjust the value of output to show its social opportunity cost (i.e., the cost of the lowest cost alternative). Tariff protection, the small scale of production, and the absence of local competition create a

situation in which local prices rise above the world market price by 20 percent. The cost to Asiatica is, in effect, 20 percent above the alternative of buying on the world market and importing. *Reduce the output value by 20 percent.*

2. Adjust the firm's costs to show the social opportunity cost to the country.

   a. *Labor*—Union and statutory hiring rules require that labor be paid going rates although heavy unemployment among unskilled labor means that there is no social cost to Asiatica in providing unskilled labor input. The "shadow price" or "social opportunity cost" of unskilled labor is zero. For the Nitrogene production, unskilled labor represents 50 percent of labor costs. *Reduce local labor cost by 50 percent.*

   b. *Materials*—Imported costs include import duties levied at a tariff of 25 percent. Duties collected by the government are not a cost to the country. *Reduce imported material cost by 20 percent.*

   c. *Taxes*—Local tax payments do not reflect an additional cost to the country. *Eliminate local taxation payments.*

   d. *Interest*—The annual local interest cost of 12 percent to the firm understates the social value of using the local capital for alternative investments. The annual social increment from alternative use of capital is calculated at 30 percent. *Increase interest cost to 30 percent.*

   e. *Depreciation*—If remitted outside the country, depreciation would be a social cost. In this case, depreciation is planned to be retained for plant improvements. There is, therefore, no social cost. *Eliminate depreciation charges.*

3. Adjust the social value to record dividend remittance as a social cost. After-tax profits will be remitted from Asiatica annually as dividends and thus should appear as a social cost to the country. *Include profit after tax as a social cost.*

4. Adjust the social value to record the value or cost of "externalities" not recorded in operating figures. The new operation will train managerial and technical labor and generally extend Asiatica's industrial capability in the chemical processing field. The social value of this training and development is assessed at a national figure of alternative cost of 20,000 lira per annum. *Add external social value of 20,000 lira.*

5. Adjust the social value to record the "real" lira value of entries involving foreign currency. For economic and political purposes, the official exchange rate has been maintained at a level that overvalues the Asiatican lira by about 20 percent. On a free market,

it is estimated that instead of the official rate of 5 Asiatican lira = $1 U.S., the market would clear at 6 Asiatican lira = $1 U.S. *Increase the lira value of all foreign currency items by 20 percent.*

With these adjustments recorded, the project shows an annual net national benefit, or social value, of 404,000 lira. This can be expressed another way as showing a benefit/cost ratio of 1.26 (i.e., $1{,}940/1{,}536$). A third way of expressing the figures is to omit the notional assessment for the opportunity cost of the local resources used (adjustment 2*d*) to arrive at the "social return," which is then expressed as a ratio of the local capital utilized. The local capital in this case is 500,000 lira, with an opportunity cost of 30 percent, or 150,000 lira. The social return is, therefore, 554,000 lira, being the 404,000 shown in Table 9–1 plus the 150,000. The social return ratio is then 111 percent (i.e., $554/500$). By this measurement as well as the other two measurements, the project appears reasonably attractive to Asiatica.

A fourth approach introduces the concept of return on domestic resource costs. The social value, or return, obtained by committing the domestic resources to the project is the net foreign value of the production. This net foreign value is the foreign market value of the output less the cost of foreign inputs. It is measured in foreign currency, and if the local resources would be used effectively, this foreign currency value should translate into the local currency equivalent of the domestic resource costs at an exchange rate that is higher than the "real" exchange rate. On the other hand, if the implicit rate required for the translation is below the real exchange rate, presumably the resources could be used to more account elsewhere. The concept is unnecessarily extenuated, but as it is found frequently in project analysis literature, it is worth following the calculation through for the example. Net foreign value is $244,000 per annum, calculated as follows:

Sales (at world market price).		$400,000
Less foreign costs translated		
at official rate		
Labor.	$ 20,000	
Materials, before import duties	112,000	
Dividends	24,000	156,000
Net foreign value		$244,000

Domestic resource costs at their social cost levels are 580,000 lira:

Labor	250,000 lira
Materials	200,000
Capital charge.	150,000
Externalities	−20,000
Total	580,000 lira

The implicit exchange rate that will translate the foreign value into the domestic resource costs is 2.4 lira = $1 U.S. This is far higher than the estimated real rate of 6 lira = $1 U.S., in the sense that it values the lira more. Again, the project seems worthwhile, this time considerably so.

Finally, any of the four measurements may be extended to allow for the flow of costs and benefits for a longer period than the one year. It is possible to adapt the various methods that have been developed for decision making in private capital investment, such as internal rate of return, payoff period, or discounted present value. The time horizon of the country's decision makers, however, is often a crucial element when time periods are introduced into decisions. The political cost of slow achievement can be very high.

SUMMARY

International business operates across and within the boundaries of many discrete sovereign nation-states. The business firm has its private goals that it pursues within a geographical area of its own choosing, which include the sovereign domains of several or many national governments. Governments have their public purposes, some of which are in harmony with and others that may run counter to the private global goals of international corporations. Where conflicts arise, governments will try to use their sovereign power to direct activities toward their national interests. The multinational enterprise will try to thread its way through the multiple and often conflicting claims of many governments with the minimum sacrifice to its goals.

This matrix of common interests and potential conflicts in goals makes for a love-hate relationship between international corporations and nation-states. The countries love the benefits but hate the costs and the national tensions that accompany the benefits. Furthermore, the benefits may be greatest at the time of the wedding and steadily decline thereafter. On balance, the trade-off to both host and home countries appears to have been generally in favor of the benefits, as evidenced by the continued rapid expansion of international business activities. Nevertheless, national governments have long used controls over traditional international transfers of goods, money flows, and persons to increase their share of national benefits from such international transactions. Such controls are now being extended by nations to increase a nation's share of the global benefits generated by multinational enterprises and to reduce the negative effects, such as the threat of economic domination and challenges to economic and political autonomy.

The need to identify its common interests and potential areas of conflict with many different nation-states is a continuing and never-ending operating requirement for international enterprises. The diversity and dynamic nature of these relations do not permit easy generalizations; nor is a general understanding adequate background for the international manager. He must deal with specific business situations in relation to specific national environments. A specific type of business activity may face one kind of response in *Country A* and a completely different type of response in *Country B* and *Country C.* The only certainties are that the situation will constantly be changing and that, in order to maintain its tenure, the international enterprise must be ever ready to justify to a nation-state not only its entry but its continued presence.

EXERCISES AND DISCUSSION QUESTIONS

1. "It is characteristic of direct-investment projects that their first-order benefits are greatest, certainly most spectacular, in the initial stages of the undertaking. On the other hand, the explicit costs of the foreign investment to the host economy generally behave in an opposite fashion." Explain what the writer meant by this statement and evaluate its validity.

2. Under what circumstances can an acquisition of an existing domestic business operation by a foreign multinational enterprise be justified as contributing national benefits to a country? Under what circumstances would it be difficult to justify an acquisition?

3. As a government official evaluating a proposal for investment by a foreign corporation that could have a 20-year life-span, suggest how the streams of national benefits and national costs should be treated in reaching a decision.

4. "To control the export of American technology, much of which was financed by public funds and the export of American jobs, the government should regulate, supervise, and curb the export of technology and the substantial outflows of American capital for the investments of U.S. companies in foreign operations." Would you agree or disagree with this statement?

10

National Controls over
International Transfers

NATION-STATES have developed a variety of ways to achieve national goals and protect national interests as far as international business transactions are concerned. Traditionally their method was to control the international transfer of goods. They followed with controls covering transfers of money, personnel, technology, and legal rights across national boundaries. More recently, nations have begun to develop ways of directly influencing the operations of multinational businesses within their boundaries. In this chapter, the focus is on understanding how nations attempt to control international transfers. The next chapter looks at controls over the operations of multinational businesses.

The concept of international transfers is broad and comprehensive. It includes the physical transfer of goods through importing and exporting. It includes financial flows in the form of direct-investment capital, portfolio investments, profit repatriation, and other money flows induced by international business operations; the transfer of personnel either in support of business activities or directly as a form of international business, that is, tourism; the transfer of technology across national boundaries through licensing and technical assistance agreements; and the transfer of legal rights such as patent protection or governmental concessions to exploit certain natural resources.

NATIONAL MOTIVATIONS FOR CONTROLLING
INTERNATIONAL TRANSFERS

In their attempts to control international transfers, nation-states exhibit complex and changing patterns of goals. An understanding of the range of goals that can shape controls, and of the arguments that are used to justify particular controls in terms of those goals, is essential for comprehending the changing maze of controls.

Revenue Goals. Some nations rely on international transfers as a major source of government revenue. Many tariffs were originally imposed primarily to raise revenue. The administration involved in collecting tariff levies is much less than that needed for income or sales taxes because the import and export of goods are usually concentrated in a relatively small number of locations, such as ports. A tariff imposed entirely for revenue purposes, however, would be applied to different products and be at a lower rate than would a protective tariff. A tariff level that is too high may keep goods from entering or leaving a country or may encourage smuggling and evasion and yield no revenue.

Governments also use international transfers as a source of revenue through exchange controls. In Brazil, for example, the government appropriates part of the foreign exchange earned from coffee exports. The coffee exporter is required to turn over his foreign exchange to the government and receives payment in local currency at a special rate below the free-market rate. Revenue goals also lie behind controls preventing the transfer of operations or profit outside a country into another tax domicile.

Job Protection. Strong domestic pressures for protection against foreign competition arise when established economic activities become threatened by foreign competitive forces. Protective controls are notable in the textile field in both the United States and the United Kingdom. The industry employs a large number of workers and is a major contributor to national output. As imports have threatened the position of the local industries in their home markets, both employers and labor have pressed for tariff increases and quota restrictions to protect domestic industry against "low-wage" foreign producers. The desire to protect domestic workers from foreign competition can also be a reason for restrictive immigration policies. A major U.S. objective for many years has been to protect American workers from the undercutting influence of uncontrolled influxes of workers from less prosperous areas who might be willing to work for less money.

Development Goals. Tariffs, quotas, and other nontariff barriers may be adopted to implement economic development goals and to encourage the establishment of new economic activities. Here we have the venerable "infant industry" argument which is directed toward changing the structure of a nation's economy and accelerating economic growth. The argument is that late-comer countries must provide a period of protection to infant industries for the time-consuming learning process and for expanding to an efficient scale of production.

It assumes that new industries have a potential for becoming economically viable without protection after the learning period and after reaching a feasible scale of operations. To encourage such infant industries, nations ban or restrict imports through tariffs, foreign exchange controls, import quotas, and similar measures. It is interesting to note that in his Report on Manufactures submitted in 1791 to the U.S. House of Representatives, Alexander Hamilton elaborated most persuasively the infant industry argument as the central justification for U.S. policies to encourage manufacturing.[1]

Development goals may be the justification for governmental actions that provide special incentives for foreign direct investment and special tax or foreign exchange incentives to encourage exports. In other situations and during different time periods, development goals may also be the reason for removing tariffs and moving toward free-trade policies which are expected to stimulate greater efficiency and higher levels of output from domestic industry.

Balance-of-Payments Goals. Nations are constantly under pressure to achieve equilibrium in their international transactions and to maintain relatively stable exchange rates. Controls over financial flows and international transfers of goods and services are frequently adopted on a temporary or indefinite basis to assist in the resolution of balance-of-payments problems.

Domestic Economic Adjustment. Even domestic economic adjustment may require controls over international transfers. For example, the U.S. government felt it necessary to restrain Euro-dollar inflows in 1969 in order to implement its domestic anti-inflation policy. Inflationary pressures were high, but commercial banks were avoiding monetary restraints by borrowing abroad to increase their loanable funds.

Health and Safety Protection. Nations frequently restrict the import of certain commodities, generally agricultural or animal products, to protect the health of their citizens. Such restrictions, which attempt to keep out agricultural pests and diseases, may be temporary or permanent and generally are applied to commodities from specific infected areas. From time to time, beef products from Argentina could not be imported into the United States because of the danger of spreading hoof-and-mouth disease.

International Political Goals. National policies over international transfers have long been used to reward political friends and to oppose political enemies. The Arab countries have imposed transfer constraints on foreign firms that do business with Israel. Mainland China

---

[1]See Alexander Hamilton, *Papers on Public Credit, Commerce and Finance,* ed. Samuel McKee, Jr. (New York: Columbia University Press, 1934), pp. 204–5.

has barred international trade with companies that deal with Taiwan. The United States created special trading preferences for the Philippines after that country emerged from 50 years of colonial status to become an independent nation. France maintained special relationships with its former colonies after the colonies secured independence. The United States imposes controls over East-West trade, that is, trade with the Soviet-bloc countries. Trade was completely forbidden with countries like Cuba and mainland China, with whom the United States was not enjoying friendly relations, on the grounds that trade helps potential enemies to be stronger and eventually works to the political disadvantage of the United States.

National Security Goals.   The more traditional manifestations of national security goals have been in protecting high-cost domestic industries such as those in minerals and petroleum, so that supplies of critical materials are more likely to be domestically available in the case of war. National policies have also emerged for controlling international transfers of nuclear raw materials and technology. The fact that nuclear technology has peaceful as well as military uses and that a vast commercial industry in nuclear electric power plants has developed means that special national-security constraints and government participation in the sale of nuclear power equipment have become part of the civilian business scene.[2]

Special-interest groups in a country have used national-security arguments to limit competition rather than to achieve sound national-security goals. Often there is no general agreement in a country as to what are valid national-security considerations, and at times bitter controversies arise between different interest groups in a nation as to what kind of protection is justified on national-security grounds and as to the best way of achieving national security. For example, the United States established quota restrictions on foreign petroleum imports with the justification that the high-cost domestic petroleum industry should be kept operating in the event of a national emergency.

Opponents of controls over international transfers argue that the national-security policies on which these controls are based assume an obsolete type of warfare. In a nuclear war, they say, victories or defeats will be decided quickly, and the availability of materials after the initiation of such warfare will no longer be of critical importance. Furthermore, by allowing more imports, domestic resources will be conserved for national defense emergencies rather than rapidly consumed.

---

[2]See Lee C. Nehrt, *International Marketing of Nuclear Power Plants* (Bloomington: Indiana University Press, 1966).

CONTROLLING TRANSFERS OF GOODS

The Pros and Cons of Protectionism

Protectionism is a mildly pejorative label attached to national policies that shelter certain domestic activities from foreign competition by preventing imports in these fields or making them excessively expensive. Protection directly benefits the domestic producers engaged in such activities who generally attempt to identify their private gains as contributing to the national interests. Such national interests may be infant-industry protection, national security, the need to maintain domestic employment and income and reduce foreign exchange outflows by controlling import competition from goods produced by low-wage labor in foreign countries, and the desirability of diversifying the domestic economy to improve economic stability and stimulate growth. Normally, domestic pressures for protection are resolved by political considerations and in favor of the domestic parties with the most political muscle. Yet, the political debate invariably revolves around economic arguments, some of which have qualified validity while others are highly questionable from the standpoint of national interests.

Protectionist measures generally favor one group in a country and have a negative impact on other sectors of the economy. Therefore, nations have to evaluate the trade-offs involved in protectionist policies and determine the net benefits or costs to the country. If the American steel industry, for example, is given protection against foreign steel imports and domestic prices remain higher than they might otherwise be, the steel companies and the workers in the industry may directly benefit. The first-round effects may result in foreign exchange savings to the United States. On the cost side, other U.S. industries that use steel to produce machinery for export are certain to become less competitive in foreign markets. Their profits, their workers, and their foreign exchange earnings for the country are likely to suffer. Domestic consumers of steel products will have to pay higher prices and, in effect, subsidize the protected industry. Furthermore, foreign countries are likely to retaliate with their own protectionist measures, which could reduce exports, profits, and employment in other U.S. industries. Both the positive and negative effects will have different weights depending upon the economic situation of the country. Even where the net economic impact is negative, a nation may be willing to pay this price to satisfy long-run or noneconomic goals.

The infant-industry argument for protection can be a valid argument if the industry being protected has realistic possibilities of maturing into an adult that no longer requires protection. This justification has been used, however, for initiating types of business activities that are more likely to remain infants and require what amounts to a permanent subsidy. National security can also be a reasonable justification for protection and worth the cost to a country if the national-security goals to be served are consistent with a sound, modern security strategy. Likewise, protectionist measures that encourage the diversification of the domestic economy may provide substantial long-term gains to a country that more than offset short-term costs.

Most of the other arguments for protection are questionable or invalid from an economic standpoint, even though they may have great emotional appeal that garners strong political support. Most common among these is the highly plausible but generally fallacious cheap-labor argument, which both industry and labor use to demand protection against "unfair" competition from low-wage workers in foreign countries. The fundamental shortcoming of the argument is the confusion between wage rates and unit labor costs. Labor costs depend on labor productivity as well as wage rates. Productivity depends in turn on the other factors of production such as capital, management, and technology that are combined with labor in the process of producing goods and services. Assuming that all other factors are constant, low wages will mean lower labor costs. But in reality all other factors, including the skills of the workers themselves, are not constant, and high-wage industries in one country can, in fact, produce goods with lower labor costs per unit of output than competing industries in countries where wage costs are low.

The low-wage argument for protection also assumes that the only important cost involved in the ability of businesses to be competitive is the cost of labor. Labor costs vary greatly from industry to industry as a share of total costs per unit of output. Therefore, even if labor costs (irrespective of wage rates) are lower in some countries, the competitive advantage may be minor compared with variations in other production or distribution costs. The cost of electric power, for example, is much more significant in the production of aluminum than are labor costs. One nation may have comparative advantages in large supplies of low-cost labor. Other nations may have their comparative advantages in low costs of raw materials, transportation, borrowing of money, or electric power. The relative importance of the cost components depends on an industry's production function. Labor costs are neither the only, nor the most important, competitive consideration.

Some proponents of protection broaden the low-wage argument to a general plea for equalizing all production costs between foreign and domestic producers on the grounds of "fair competition." Such a policy would violate whatever validity there is in the argument that a country should specialize in those fields in which it has a comparative advantage due to differences in resource endowments and trade with others. It would be just as valid or invalid for Japanese steel manufacturers to ask for protection against the lower prices that U.S. firms are able to pay for coking coal because the United States happens to have favorable resource endowments in these fields. In fact, if the arguments for protection to equalize differences in costs of production were accepted, there would be no basis whatever for trade taking place.

Current Levels of Protection

In evaluating a country's degree of tariff protection, average tariff levels are not very informative. Tariff levels vary tremendously from product to product. Furthermore, nominal tariffs as they appear in government tariff schedules, that is, the rate of duty expressed as a percentage of the total value of the imported product, are not really a measure of the full effect of the tariff. If import protection on the raw material is zero, but 10 percent on a processed form of the product, the effective protection against imports of the product in processed form is much higher than the apparent, or nominal, rate of 10 percent.

The distinction between *nominal* and *effective* rates can be illustrated by the case of textiles. Fabric may enter at a duty of 20 percent and yarn at 10 percent. Suppose that $250 of yarn is required to produce $500 of fabric. The duty on $250 of yarn will be $25. The value added to the yarn by weaving would be $250. If the fabric were imported at 20 percent duty, the total duty on $500 worth of fabric would be $100. Thus, the difference in the duty between the yarn and the fabric, or the duty on the value added by weaving ($250), is $75. The net duty difference as a percentage of value added is the effective, as opposed to the nominal, tariff rate. This gives an effective rate of 30 percent, as compared with the nominal rate of 20 percent. Since tariffs normally escalate with each stage of manufacture, the effective rate on value added often exceeds the nominal rate by a substantial amount.

Generalizations about tariff patterns must necessarily be subject to many exceptions. Nevertheless, the general pattern seems to be as follows:

1. Low tariffs on raw materials that a country does not produce—to encourage domestic processing industries; high tariffs on semi-finished products easily produced in many countries—to protect local demand.
2. High tariffs on agricultural products and minerals where local production is noncompetitive with imports and does not completely fill local demand.

3. Low tariffs on products of advanced technology where producing nations have been successful in reciprocal bargaining and where local production may not be feasible. Average tariffs on manufactured and semi-manufactured goods are now less than 10 percent for the major developed countries.

With tariff rates reduced to quite low levels, much attention has switched to nontariff barriers to the international transfer of goods, as outlined in Chapter 7. Some international firms believe these barriers have reached levels at which they are more burdensome than tariffs. Identifying that NTBs exist and that they do significantly distort trade, however, is a major problem. For example, many governments follow policies of local preference in awarding government contracts, yet few particulars of such policies are published. One attempt by the U.S. government to highlight foreign government purchasing policies was incorporated by the Department of the Interior in invitations to bid to supply turbine generators for the Grand Coulee Dam. Foreign bidders were required to furnish a statement with their bid disclosing their country's policy for government purchasing of heavy electrical equipment. While most trade restrictions may eventually be detected and matched by other countries, the detection is slow and by no means certain. There is clearly a range of NTBs that can be adopted by individual countries with little chance of immediate retaliation. This being so, governments come under internal pressure to adopt them.

In current and future GATT negotiations (see Chapter 7), U.S. negotiators are likely to push hard for removal of NTBs applied against U.S. agricultural products and restrictive practices in foreign government procurement. Barriers established by packaging, labeling, or product specification requirements are likely to be viewed as less important distortions. Of course, the United States will have to reciprocate by reducing its own NTBs. Removal of agricultural product barriers would eliminate one of the major distortions in trade between the developed nations. The EEC Common Agricultural Policy protects European farmers against significant competition from the United States, which holds a comparative advantage in the agricultural field. Japan, too, protects itself with quotas on a wide range of agricultural items.

Export Promotion

Nations adopt programs for promoting exports as well as for restricting imports. The less developed countries in particular have become greatly concerned about the need to earn foreign exchange through expanding exports. And the United States itself, with a steadily disappearing balance-of-trade surplus in the late 1960s, established programs for export promotion.

Governmental action to promote exports may even include assuming responsibility for normal business functions, such as sponsoring market research on foreign sales opportunities and establishing trade promotion offices in foreign countries. At the more traditional level, governments offer tax incentives such as exemption from certain domestic taxes if goods are exported, direct bonus payments or subsidies through administration of exchange controls, special credit for exporters, and insurance programs under which the government assumes varying degrees of political and commercial risk.

The United States has its Export-Import Bank, which promotes U.S. exports by providing medium- and long-term financing to foreign buyers. Under the Webb-Pomerene Act of 1918, American companies are exempted from the prohibitions of the Sherman Antitrust Act when they join with other companies, who might be competitors, in an export trade association. Another means of promoting exports is the special tax arrangement offered since 1942 of a 14-point reduction in the U.S. tax due by companies that can qualify as a Western Hemisphere Trade Corporation. To qualify for this benefit, an American company must do all of its business in the Western Hemisphere, derive 95 percent of its gross income from the active conduct of trade or a business, and receive 95 percent of its gross income from sources outside of the United States.

Since 1962, export credit insurance has been offered to U.S. exporters by the private Foreign Credit Insurance Association, in partnership with the Export-Import Bank. As incentives for expanding exports, the association offers low-cost blanket insurance policies covering both commercial and political risks in selling abroad on credit. Most big exporting countries have a similar institution which provides exporters with cover against risk. Britain, for example, has its Export Credit Guarantee Department which performs this function. A recent innovation in this field by the United States was the Domestic International Sales Corporation (DISC), permitted under the Revenue Act of 1971, which grants unlimited deferral on export profits to this new type of corporation. To qualify as a DISC, a domestic corporation must derive 95 percent or more of its gross receipts from exports and related income and 95 percent or more of its assets must be used in export activities.

The issue of unfair competition frequently arises in connection with incentive programs for encouraging exports. Importing countries may interpret these incentives as encouraging dumping (i.e., selling at lower prices in foreign than in home markets) or unfair competition. From the standpoint of international business, such incentive programs may be significant, but they may also create potentials for conflicts with importing countries. One example of retaliation occurred when Michelin Tire Company established a plant in Nova Scotia, receiving the benefit of Canadian tax incentives designed to spur regional growth. With lower costs Michelin was able to cut prices on the U.S. market. This led to complaints from U.S. tire firms, who argued that Canada was subsidizing the exports, and as a result the U.S. imposed a countervailing duty on tires from this source.

Export Restrictions

While restrictions on imports have traditionally been the main controls over transfers of goods, restrictions on exports have been increasing in recent years. More and more nations have been adopting such controls to achieve goals that vary from increasing world prices to restraining local prices, and from national defense to economic warfare.

The United States has statutorily specified the circumstances under which it will apply export controls in the Export Administration Act of 1969, as amended in 1974. The act authorizes control for three purposes: security, foreign policy, and protection against scarcity or inflation. Under the act, the Department of Commerce has established general licenses that permit most goods to be exported without specific approval being needed to all but embargoed destinations (i.e., Cuba, Vietnam, North Korea, and Southern Rhodesia). Specific licenses are required for three broad types of commodity. The first type includes products with a high-technology content that have significant strategic uses. The second type covers nuclear weapons and crime control and detection apparatus that are controlled for foreign policy reasons. Lastly, petroleum and related products are controlled for short-supply reasons.

The United States holds considerable economic leverage through its ability to control agricultural and food exports. The administration has generally opposed the use of this leverage, maintaining that new restrictions might lead to escalating controls from a variety of nations that would be detrimental to global welfare. The action to embargo grain exports to the USSR in 1973–74 was taken only following strong public pressure to avoid any further increase in domestic inflation.

Other nations have not taken the same view as the United States, and the success of the OPEC cartel in raising world oil prices through restricting output has set an example for all natural resource exporters. Further cartels may become common, with a resulting shift in the share of oligopoly rents flowing to countries owning resources. To offset the effects of such policies, importing countries may be led to restrict the access to their markets.

CONTROLLING TRANSFERS OF MONEY

Nations influence international transfers of money through foreign exchange controls, capital controls, policies of tied aid, supervision of the foreign operations of domestic banks and other financial institutions, and taxation. Many economists and some businessmen argue against any kind of national control over money transfers. They prefer freely fluctuating exchange rates determined by the market forces, which will provide automatic adjustments for balance-of-payments disequilibrium and allocate resources with market efficiency. But even for nations that have adopted fluctuating exchange rates, the normal policy has been to make frequent and extensive use of controls over financial transfers.[3]

Foreign Exchange Controls

Among their adjustment measures for payments imbalances, nations frequently resort to direct controls over all foreign exchange transactions. With such controls a nation's currency becomes inconvertible; that is, it is not freely transferable into other currencies. There can be degrees of inconvertibility depending on the nature and extent of the exchange controls. The government normally requires that all receipts of foreign exchange be turned over to the central bank or some other designated government agency. Exchange can be bought only for specified purposes and in amounts determined by the government. A license is therefore required for the purchase of foreign exchange. Exchange controls can be limited to import and export transactions, or they can also cover transfer payments such as profit remittances and capital flows.

Once exchange controls are established, it becomes the role of the government to determine the priorities and quotas for the allocation of foreign exchange, and the choice is often rather arbitrary. The system can vary from the simplest allocation of available foreign exchange among domestic individuals or firms to a complex licensing system discriminating between many different categories of goods. In some exchange-control systems, quotas of foreign exchange have been allocated to the different categories of goods and then auctioned off to the highest bidders. Others establish multiple exchange rates, varying by category of goods, which permit the import of high-priority goods at

---

[3]The International Monetary Fund's *Annual Report on Exchange Restrictions* describes current policies and practices of each member country of IMF and is a valuable reference for international managers.

the lower rates and nonessential or luxury goods at the higher rates. Some systems also require importers to make substantial deposits in order to obtain an import license. The deposit requirement ties up funds that might otherwise be earning a return and thereby increases the cost of importing.

Effective functioning of an exchange-control system requires not only that all foreign exchange purchases be regulated but that all foreign exchange receipts by individuals, businesses, and government agencies be captured and directed into a central pool. Consequently, an export licensing and policing system is generally designed to assure that foreign exchange receipts are turned over to the government in exchange for local currency at fixed rates. At times, a so-called free market is allowed to operate alongside exchange controls, but only limited types of transactions are legal in the free market. Exporters may be allowed to keep a share of their export earnings, which they can sell at the higher rates prevailing in the free market, and generally the free market is also used by tourists for securing local currency.

One of the major problems constantly confronting exchange-control authorities is the black market, where exchange is bought and sold in disregard of official regulations. Depending upon the severity of the exchange controls and the administrative capacity of government agencies, black-market activities in foreign exchange and import licenses can be extensive. In the case of one less developed country, the black market became so highly developed that future sales of import licenses were even being quoted. When the official rates are far below what would be a free rate, the opportunities for earning illicit profits are great, and extensive graft and corruption are almost certain to emerge.

Exchange controls may have great advantages in buying time while basic adjustments are undertaken to secure balance-of-payments equilibria or to implement development programs. However, the more serious the imbalance between supply and demand for local currency, the more difficult such a system is to administer effectively. Under all circumstances a government needs a high degree of knowledge concerning a nation's economy and its future prospects along with an honest and highly skilled administrative capacity. If exchange controls are substituted for policies to correct underlying imbalances and are maintained over long periods of time, illicit operations are inevitable, with their detrimental influence on business morality and the effectiveness of the controls. Yet while controls are at best a temporary measure, they frequently are retained as permanent fixtures. The United Kingdom, for example, established exchange controls after World War II and has retained them ever since, with no clear restatement of the purpose served by the controls. A generation has grown up inclined to believe that the holding of foreign currency is immoral. At one stage in the late 1960s, while retaining strict limits over the amount of funds residents could export, the U.K. government added controls to limit the inflow of foreign exchange from foreigners. Control seemed to have become the end in itself, and not just a means of rationing scarce foreign exchange.

From the standpoint of the international businessman, exchange controls will complicate and burden international money transfers by adding to costs. They can be beneficial, however, to certain types of operations when used to encourage investment inflows or exports of particular goods. The financial management problem is increased in some ways but may be reduced in other ways if, for example, such controls avoid major devaluations.

Capital Controls

Flows of short-term and long-term capital can be influenced by traditional exchange-control programs, but it is more common for nations to adopt special capital controls. Like foreign exchange controls, capital controls normally require licensing by governmental authorities for international transfers of funds. The motivation for capital controls has most frequently been to attain balance-of-payments equilibrium at desired exchange-rate levels. But they have also been used to implement national development priorities, to influence the patterns and size of international business operations in a country, and to support varied foreign policy objectives.

Normally the United States has had no controls over outward or inward flow of capital, except to selected enemy countries. Unlike the majority of countries, it offered a free capital market, and this was extended even to foreign governments. In the mid-1960s, however, the country became concerned about its persistent balance-of-payments deficit and initiated statutory and voluntary controls. An interest equalization tax was established in 1964 of up to 15 percent payable by American purchasers of foreign securities issued in the United States by most borrowers from developed countries in order to reduce the outflow of U.S. capital. Later, voluntary and then statutory restraints on outflows of direct private investment were adopted, and additional restrictions were placed on the foreign financial activities of U.S. banks. But there was considerable objection to the controls and they were dismantled in 1974, as mentioned in Chapter 5.[4]

---

[4]For an example of the domestic debate over U.S. controls, see F. Michael Adler and G. C. Hufbauer, "Foreign Investment Controls: Objective-Removal," *Columbia Journal of World Business*, May–June 1969, pp. 29–37.

The importance of capital controls will vary from country to country depending upon the size of capital movements in relation to the country's balance of payments. Administration may be simpler than a full-fledged exchange-controls program, with fewer parties involved in either capital inflows or outflows. Furthermore, such controls generally allow governmental authorities a great deal of discretion to meet changing circumstances. The disadvantage of capital controls, however, may be that short-term benefits in improving the balance-of-payments situation are secured at the expense of even greater long-term gains. Profitable direct investment, for example, can generate a continuing stream of return flows in the form of repatriated profits.

Other Controls

A number of new types of national controls over financial transfers are emerging in response to the growing importance of international commercial banking and the international securities industry. The home governments of multinational banking firms, particularly the United States, are showing increased interest in foreign banking activities as they affect domestic policies. An example already cited was the expansion of loanable funds in the United States through Euro-dollar borrowings abroad. The growth outside the United States of mutual investment funds, which were selling shares to local citizens in many countries and investing in foreign security markets, was so dramatic in the late 1960s that countries in which the mutual funds were operating began to establish regulations over such activities. The regulations are motivated by the desire both to control international transfers of funds and to provide protection to local investors.

Taxation laws are used in many ways to influence international financial transfers. Taxation levied on remittances of profits, for example, encourages reinvestment and discourages remittance back into the tax jurisdiction. In both the United States and the United Kingdom the policy is moving away from taxation on remittances and toward taxation when the income arises, whether or not remitted. Taxation laws are also being created to discourage tax deferral through transfer of funds to corporations owned but registered in other tax jurisdictions.

Control over funds granted for foreign aid has at times been attempted through tied aid or tied loans. The granting country requires that funds be utilized in purchasing goods or services from the granting country, hoping to avoid balance-of-payments problems from the outflow of funds. However, the country receiving aid may be able simply to replace purchases it would otherwise have made; moreover to force a country to buy other than from the lowest cost source could defeat the objectives of the aid.

CONTROLLING TRANSFERS OF PERSONS

Nations have numerous policies affecting the movement of persons across national boundaries which are important to international business. The temporary movement of persons, as tourism, has itself become a major international business activity and a major source of foreign exchange earnings for many nations. International trade depends to a large extent on the ability of businessmen to move from nation to nation. The identification and exploitation of direct-investment business opportunities require even more that business executives be free to travel internationally. International business operations may be dependent upon the ability of management personnel or production workers to move across national boundaries. The transfer of technology through the transfer of persons can be significantly influenced by national policies toward the international movement of persons.

National policies for controlling the entry and exit of persons from a country generally are not motivated primarily by international business considerations. Broader political, economic, and social considerations invariably underlie such policies, which generally distinguish between persons entering a country for a temporary stay such as tourists or, at the other end of the spectrum, persons who want to enter a country on a permanent basis. Between are persons who want to stay in a country for a reasonably long period without intending to seek employment in the country, such as students. Still another intermediate category would be foreigners who enter for a period of employment but do not intend to become permanent residents of the country.

Passports and visas are the basic means for controlling the international movement of persons. Passports are issued to persons by the country of which they are a citizen or permanent resident. The issuing country can restrict movements by not authorizing passport holders to enter specified countries, as the United States forbade its citizens to travel in Cuba. Visas are issued by the country into which persons desire to travel. Political considerations can be grounds either for refusing citizens a passport or for denying visas.

Generally speaking, however, restrictions on exit are regarded as morally less defensible than restrictions on entry. Apart from the Communist bloc, only a few countries make it very difficult to depart. Few make any attempt to charge departing individuals with the cost of their education, but limitations on the right to export capital other than this human capital are very common. From the United Kingdom, an emigrant may take no more than about $10,000 in funds until four years after departure. It is considered that without this provision, "temporary emigration" could become a major loophole for exporting funds of any type.

Most countries, anxious to expand their tourist industry, impose minimum restrictions on the entry of persons on temporary visits. The most restrictive policies are applied to persons who wish to seek employment in a foreign country or become permanent residents. During certain periods of history, such as the late 19th and early 20th centuries, countries like the United States encouraged immigration. Up until 1940, the United States received millions of immigrants from Europe. Australia and Canada aggressively encouraged and even promoted immigration during periods when they were trying to develop their vast countries. Argentina and Brazil have also had periods of relatively open immigration. But the general world pattern, except for internal movement in Western Europe and the Arab states, has become one of selective and limited immigration. The United States has become one of the toughest on matters of immigration, even making it difficult, until recently, for foreign companies established in the United States to bring in their own management personnel to work in the United States.

For most countries the basis for admitting immigrants has increasingly favored those professionally trained or highly skilled, with resources, and of a workable age so that they do not create a drain on social welfare systems. For the underprivileged of any country, the opportunity to gain admission to another country is steadily decreasing. Projecting ahead a few decades, we may see bilateral negotiations on immigrant quotas between pairs of countries, with balanced transfers taking the place of net migration in one direction.

In Western Europe since about 1955, there has been a greatly increased movement of workers across national borders. A basic feature in the European Economic Community treaty was to permit the free movement of labor within the community. The major movements have been northward, especially to Switzerland, Belgium, France, and Germany, first by Italians and then by Greeks, Spaniards, Portuguese, and Turks. The mobility of workers in Europe has tended to limit wage-rate variations and has greatly improved the functioning of the European labor market. With unemployment in the mid-1970s, however, the morality of forcing those without jobs to return to their home countries simply by not renewing visas became a controversial issue within the EEC for workers from those nonmember countries and proved to be more permanent than temporary. Having levied taxes on the workers there was a moral obligation to continue both unemployment benefits and residence.

From the standpoint of international business, the complex and even discriminatory national regulation of the international movement of persons is likely to be more burdensome than prohibitive. Yet, there may be specific cases where persons important to the international operations of an enterprise may be restricted from entering a country in which the enterprise would like to have the person work. It is certainly true that if the nationalities of a firm's executive strength are to match its global needs for those nationalities, then recruitment must look a long way ahead in forecasting the geographic growth of the firm.

CONTROLLING TRANSFERS OF TECHNOLOGY

The concept of technology encompasses technical and managerial know-how which is embodied in physical and human capital and in published documents and which is transmitted across national boundaries in various ways. Traditional trade theory, by limiting its horizons to land, labor, and capital, did not direct the attention of economists and government officials to technology as a key production factor. But the situation has been changing rapidly, and governments have become keenly concerned about encouraging inflows of technology as a major means of achieving national goals for economic and social development. At the same time, nations have become active in trying to minimize foreign exchange costs to a country and maximize national benefits through policies for influencing the amount, type, and conditions for transfer of technology.

Technology may be transferred in many ways including (1) flows of books, journals, and other scientific and technical publications; (2) the movement of people including the inflow of technical, scientific, and management personnel, and the outflow of nationals on foreign educational, training, and observation assignments; (3) the direct importation of machinery and equipment; (4) direct foreign investment accompanied by equipment and personnel; (5) licensing, patents, and know-how agreements; and (6) technical assistance programs of governments, on either a bilateral or a multilateral basis. The means of transfer are not mutually exclusive. At this stage, we will confine attention to the controls aimed at direct transfers of established technology for business use.

In the industrially advanced countries, technological progress is encouraged through a patent system that gives the owner of new technology ownership rights during a fixed number of years—17 years in the case of the United States. In most cases, these countries have applied no controls over the international transfer of technology or even over the price received for transfers.[5] This is so even when the international sale of technology can produce major social costs in the shape of unemployment and redundant production facilities. Even

---

[5]For a summary of U.S. policy see *Foreign Direct Investment in the United States*, vol. 1 (Washington, D.C.: U.S. Government Printing Office 1976).

taxation authorities have little say in transfer prices as long as they are determined at arm's length. One notable exception, however, is the U.S. restriction on "trading with the enemy" which places statutory prohibition on technology transfer, either directly as "naked technology" or embodied in products.

Attitudes in the less advanced countries differ markedly. They are predominantly buyers rather than sellers of technology. To them the question is whether the adoption of a patent system will help or hinder the country's access to foreign technology on acceptable terms. Consequently, national patent systems for protection of rights over technology do not exist universally, and where they do exist, the rights of foreigners to use the protection vary greatly. On the other hand, less developed countries are making more and more attempts to control the transfer of technology across their borders.

The objectives of the LDCs are ambitious. They want to ensure that imported technology is appropriate to their needs, which generally means smaller-scale and labor-intensive technology, and that it will actually be transferred to local nationals. They particularly want to ensure that charges for technology, either explicit or concealed, are not excessive. And excessive is usually defined as any price above the lowest possible cost for obtaining the technology any other way. Another common objective is to minimize the restraints in technology transfer agreements, such as limiting the markets in which the licensee can sell or the quantity that can be produced. Such restrictions have been common in order to protect the licensor from competition from his licensee or to ensure that the licensed subsidiary fits into a global strategy. Finally, and inconsistently, many countries also want to retain for their own country all rights arising from local development of technology.

Attempts to achieve these objectives commonly take the form of a technology transfer law, requiring the registration of all documents and agreements to do with payments to foreigners for patent rights, trademark authorization, technical knowledge, engineering, technical assistance, and so on. Agreements that are not registered are by statute neither valid nor enforceable. Moreover, the act usually states grounds on which registration can be refused, such as those listed in the 1972 Mexican law, set out in Figure 10–1.

The prima facie evidence is that such controls are effective from the country's standpoint. Firms can be thrown into a negotiating position with government as their applications for registration are first rejected and then accepted after amendment. Reported royalty levels for Mexico registered in the first two years following the 1972 act were mainly below 3 percent, as against prior rates of 5–15 percent.[6] Such

---

[6]*Business Week,* July 14, 1975, p. 69.

FIGURE 10-1

Grounds for Refusing to Register Contracts in the Mexican National Register of Technology Transfer

---

I. When their purpose is the transfer of technology available in the country free of charge or under more advantageous conditions than those governing its acquisition abroad, provided the same technology is concerned.

II. When the price or the compensation is not related to the technology acquired, or it constitutes an unfair or excessive levy on the national economy.

III. When clauses are included whereby the supplier is permitted to control or intervene, directly or indirectly, in the administration of the party acquiring the technology.

IV. When the obligation is established to transfer, onerously or gratuitously, to the party providing the technology, the patents, trademarks, innovations, or improvements which may be obtained in the country.

V. When limitations are imposed on the research or technological development of the party acquiring the technology.

VI. When the obligations are established to acquire equipment, tools, parts, or raw materials of an exclusively determined origin.

VII. When the total prohibition is established on exportation or the possibilities of the party acquiring the technology are limited with regard to exporting, in a manner contrary to the interests of the country.

VIII. When the use of supplementary technologies is prohibited.

IX. When the obligations are established to sell on an exclusive basis to the supplier of the technology the goods produced by the party acquiring the technology.

X. When the party acquiring the technology is obliged to permanently utilize the personnel indicated by the supplier of the technology.

XI. When production volumes are limited or sales or resale prices are imposed for domestic production or for the exports of the party acquiring the technology.

XII. When the party acquiring the technology is obliged to enter into selling contracts or exclusive representation agreements with the supplier in Mexico.

XIII. When excessive validity periods are established. In no case can said periods exceed ten years and be obligatory for the party acquiring the technology.

XIV. When presentation is made to foreign courts-of-law of the facts or resolution of the judgments which may derive from the interpretation or compliance with the aforementioned memoranda, contracts, or agreements.

Source: Government of Mexico, *Diario Oficial*, December 30, 1972, Article 7.

levels, however, can be deceptive. The really important indicators of success are much more difficult to assess. Does the law perhaps reduce the priority that firms place on the country as a site for more advanced development? Do restrictions on the multinationals' rights to locally developed technology discourage local research and development? Does the control of royalty rates lead to reduction in the quality of available technology or limit the terms of the agreement? With limited investment to meet worldwide demands, the answers to these questions are very likely in the affirmative.[7]

Joint attempts by developing countries to forge a common approach for improving the terms for transfer of technology have been made by the Andean Group and by UNCTAD.[8] In fact, a major issue at the UNCTAD IV meetings in 1976 was a proposed code of conduct covering international technology transfers. Whether or not the effect of widespread adoption of the proposed code would be to reduce the cost of technology to individual countries is open to debate.

Many countries will continue to negotiate individually the terms and quantity of international investment with multinational firms, and firms will tend to favor the more attractive opportunities. While identifiable payments for technology may be decreased, firms may be rewarded in other ways.

CONTROLLING TRANSFERS OF RIGHTS

Governments can also regulate the international transfer of rights. Rights of nonnationals to own, hold concessions, or operate a business, for example, may be restricted either absolutely or for certain areas of the economy. Such restrictions are common for natural resources and land. A few countries expressly prohibit all foreign ownership of land, others extend the prohibition to only agricultural land or forestry rights. Concessions for mining radioactive materials, such as uranium or thorium, are restricted in some cases to domestic enterprises. Other areas in which restrictions apply are those with a strong national cultural and political impact, such as newspapers, magazines, and broadcasting; those that form an integral part of any national security network, such as telecommunications operation or military manufac-

---

[7]See *The Acquisition of Technology from Multinational Corporations by Developing Countries,* United Nations Publication No. E.74.II.A.7, p. 43.

[8]See "Andean Commission. Decision 24. 31 December 1970. Standard régime for treatment of foreign capital and for treatment of marks, patents, licenses and royalties," *International Legal Materials,* X: 152. Also, *Guidelines for the Acquisition of Foreign Technology in Developing Countries: With Special Reference to Technology License Agreements,* United Nations Publication No. E.73.II.B.1.

turing; and those that are essentially part of the economic regulatory mechanism, such as major banks.[9]

The motivations behind limitation of foreigners' access to local rights are partly xenophobic and partly reasoned economic, political, or security precautions. Where foreigners' rights are removed, the method used is quite likely to be public nationalization of the activity in question. Local private rights are removed at the same time so the action appears less like expropriation of foreign property. In fact, the underlying motivation may have little to do with a belief in state ownership of the particular field.

Restrictions on owning foreign rights are less common but there has been a marked trend toward limitation of the right to hold foreign assets that might enable individuals to circumvent the intentions behind local taxation laws or exchange controls. The United Kingdom, for example, requires full disclosure of foreign assets to the Bank of England, which has the power to withdraw permission for the holding of the asset. The adoption of exchange controls can have the effect of removing completely an individual's power to acquire foreign rights that the government does not approve for allocations of funds.

SUMMARY

The transformation of the world economy from a dominance of trade to a flourishing of international business will gradually move governmental and business thinking out of the traditional framework of national controls over trade and international payments. International business depends upon a much wider range of international transfers than those of goods and money. Even within the field of money and goods transfers, the concern of nations for influencing these flows has broadened considerably from the traditional patterns designed for a world of trade.

In principle, international business firms prefer a minimum of national interference over transfers of goods, money, persons, technology, and rights across national boundaries. They support their position by traditional free-trade theory, which argues that economic output for the world as a whole can be maximized under conditions of free international flows. In practice, international enterprises can be benefited as well as hindered by restrictive national policies.

The nation-states give lip service to the venerable concepts of the virtues of free trade, but in practice they have chosen not to let

---

[9]Policies and regulations of the United States and major industrial nations are summarized in *Foreign Direct Investment in The United States*, (Washington, D.C.: U.S. Government Printing Office 1976), chaps. 8, 10.

free-market forces prevail. One of the most basic reasons, generally more implicit than explicit, motivating nations to influence international transfers is the fact that maximizing output for the world as a whole does not necessarily mean that each country will share these benefits in a satisfactory proportion. Thus, many controls and incentives to influence transfers have been designed by nations to attempt to increase their shares of the benefits.

EXERCISES AND DISCUSSION QUESTIONS

1. What policies do you think the United States should follow with regard to East-West trade? To what extent should the United States use pressure to influence policies of other Western nations in regard to trade with the socialist countries? Should most-favored-nation treatment be extended by the United States to other socialist countries as has been done for Yugoslavia?

2. "Export promotion activities can produce just as much distortion to free trade as do tariffs, therefore no nation should actively stimulate exports." If you disagree with this statement, compile a list of export promotion activities the United States should undertake and suggest how the limit should be determined for each activity.

3. Suggest a set of guidelines for the negotiators of a major trading country to use in bargaining for reductions in nontariff barriers at a GATT meeting. What reductions should they try to achieve and what reductions should they offer in return? What countries should they approach?

4. What are the principal objectives of exchange-control systems and how do exchange controls serve these objectives?

5. "To prevent the outflow of direct private investment is to kill the goose that lays the golden eggs." Discuss.

6. "There is no cost in making available technology that has already been developed for other purposes, therefore an acquiring nation will maximize its benefits by strictly limiting the amount that can be charged for existing technology. The return permitted on investment associated with any technology transfer, however, should be set in a much different way." Comment on these statements and draw up a set of practical rules for a developing nation to use in controlling the returns going to foreigners for technology and investment.

11

National Controls over Multinational Operations

AS NATIONS have become increasingly aware of the nature and growing importance of multinational enterprises with global horizons, they have been responding with new national policies to deal with this modern phenomenon. One response has been an extension of traditional transfer controls to influence the activities of foreign-owned subsidiaries in host countries and parent companies in home countries. Capital controls, for example, previously used mainly in support of balance-of-payments goals, have been broadened to regulate entry conditions for foreign enterprise. But with a growing conviction that something more is needed, most nations have adopted additional piecemeal measures specifically directed toward multinational business. Slowly, but inevitably, nations have been moving from piecemeal measures toward a general and coordinated national policy in this area.

The responses of host and home countries have not been uniform, either in timing or in substance. The levels of sensitivity to multinational enterprises have varied greatly among countries. Even where levels are similar, responses have differed depending upon country characteristics and national goals.[1] But the underlying rationale for

---

[1]Useful reference sources are the information guides published periodically by accounting firms such as Price, Waterhouse & Co. and Arthur Anderson & Co.; *Investment Laws of the World* (Dobbs Ferry, N.Y.: Oceana) a loose-leaf service prepared by the International Centre for Settlement of Investment Disputes. See also, *Obstacles and Incentives to Private Foreign Investment, 1967–1968*, Studies in Business Policy, no. 130, 2 vols. (New York: The Conference Board, 1969); J. J. Boddewyn, *Western European Policies Toward U.S. Investors*, The Bulletin, nos. 93–95 (New York: New York University, Graduate School of Business Administration, Institute of Finance,

controls is frequently similar, and an understanding of the evolving pattern of controls can prepare the international manager for anticipating where the operations of an international enterprise are likely to be affected.

The term *controls* is used here in a particular sense to cover anything done by a government directly or indirectly to influence or regulate international business, whether through its operations, ownership, or existence. Controls in this sense may be negative curbs or restraints. They may also be direct incentives. In many cases what are usually referred to as *incentives* are relaxations of restrictions with corresponding savings to business enterprises. Tax concessions, tariff reductions, remittance guarantees, and increased depreciation allowances are examples. Nevertheless, the chapter looks separately at incentives aimed at encouraging international business, and restraints aimed at regulating international business.

The chapter also deals separately with home-country and host-country controls. Investor, or home, countries, however, will invariably be host countries as well and their control policies as both investor and host will be interrelated. Restraints on foreign business within their boundaries are likely to be constrained by the likelihood of retaliation against their own businesses operating abroad. For example, if the United States broadens its controls over the domestic operations of non-U.S. companies or the foreign operations of U.S. companies, other countries are likely to react by creating similar or more burdensome controls over the foreign operations of U.S. companies.[2]

INVESTOR OR HOME-BASE COUNTRIES: INCENTIVE CONTROLS

Over many decades, for political as well as economic reasons, the colonial powers in the world encouraged their business firms to expand in the colonies. This trend became outdated after World War II with the rapid move of the colonies toward independence and with the shift in national priorities by former colonial powers toward domestic

March 1974); Henry King "Foreign Restrictions on U.S. Investment," *San Diego Law Review* II, no. 1 (November 1973); Commission on Transnational Corporations, UN Economic and Social Council, *National Legislation and Regulations Relating to Transnational Corporations* (New York: United Nations, January 26, 1976).

[2]Donald T. Brash, "Australia as Host to the International Corporation," in *The International Corporation,* ed. Charles P. Kindleberger (Cambridge, Mass.: The M.I.T. Press, 1970), p. 304. As Brash reports, "the decisive factor" in the 1968 decision of the Australian government to restrict the freedom of foreign enterprises to borrow on the Australian market "was the introduction of the U.S. 'guidelines' policy" restricting the export of capital from the United States by U.S. companies.

recuperation from the ravages of war. Of the principal home-base countries for international firms, only the United States encouraged the foreign expansion of its international firms during most of the post– World War II period. This situation began to change in the late 1960s. The United States introduced some restrictive controls at about the same time West Germany and Japan began to encourage the foreign expansion of international enterprises based in their countries. Both countries had highly favorable balance-of-payments situations and both encouraged private investment outflows as an alternative to revaluation.

Home-country inducements vary in detail among the countries. But the general types of inducements are as follows:

Foreign Risk Insurance.   All major investor nations now have insurance programs to cover major types of foreign investment risks. The key features of each country's investment guaranty programs are presented in Table 11–1. The geographic coverage varies from worldwide to investments in 11 selected countries in the case of Sweden. The types of risks generally insurable are those of expropriation, war losses, and inability to transfer profits. Some countries extend the insurance to exports of home-country goods, and Japan also insures investments in non-Japanese companies engaged in developing mineral resources for import into Japan.

The U.S. program warrants special attention as the earliest, the largest, and in some ways a model that others have followed. The program got started as part of the Marshall Plan to provide an incentive for U.S. firms to invest in Europe. Later, it became attached to the development assistance section of the Agency for International Development. In recent years, as the public commitment to development assistance has declined, the purpose and actuarial soundness of the program have come under critical review. It is likely that the program will be shifted completely into the private sector and when that happens any subsidy in lower than soundly based commercial rates will disappear. The only element of incentive remaining will be the ease with which insurance can be obtained against the specified risks.

Associated with the insurance of investment risks, a number of countries have negotiated bilateral investment agreements with the governments of host countries. By the end of 1974 the German government had concluded bilateral agreements with 44 developing countries for the protection and promotion of German direct investment, and the United States had signed investment-guarantee agreements with 44 countries. The German experience has been that the developing countries have been careful to avoid even minor breaches of the agreements. The German agreements provide for an arbitration procedure. If a country is condemned under the arbitration procedure,

TABLE 11–1
Investment Guaranty Schemes (generally covering expropriation, war, and transfer risks)

Country	Date Established	Geographic Coverage	Investment Coverage	Premium Rate per Year (in percent)	Amou Out stand (end 197 in millio
Australia.......	1966	Worldwide	All types	0.75	$ 24.
Belgium	1971	Worldwide	Equity and loan	0.75	4.
Canada........	1969	Less developed countries	All types	0.3–0.9	44.
Denmark.......	1966	Less developed countries	All types	0.5	14.
France	1971	Selected less developed countries and countries with bilateral agreements	Mainly loans	0.8	17
Germany.......	1960	Countries having signed bilateral agreements (44)	All types	0.5	406
Japan.........	1956/57	Worldwide	All types	0.55–0.70	1,075
Netherlands.....	1969	Less developed countries	All types	0.8	21
Norway........	1964	Worldwide	Equity plus loans, if equity present	0.5	24
Sweden........	1968	11 selected countries	Equity and loan if controlling interest	0.7	n.a
Switzerland.....	1970	Less developed countries	All types	†	42
United Kingdom..	1972	Worldwide	All types	1.0	3
United States	1948	Countries having signed bilateral agreements (114)	All types	0.3–1.50	2,98

*As of end of 1973.
†Normal rates: principal—1.25 percent, profits—4 percent of expected profits.
‡n.a. = not available.
Source: *Investing in Developing Countries,* 3d ed. (Paris: OECD, 1975), pp. 12–14.

it may lose international standing, which may lead to a loss of credit-worthiness. Thus, in a not so subtle sense, insured investments carry with them an implicit hint that investor countries will be concerned about the imposition of controls and the adoption of policies that will require insurance payments.

Capital Assistance.   Special loan programs to industry through government banks such as the Japan Development Bank, loans by the United States of local currency available in certain countries from the sale of agricultural "surpluses" under Public Law 480, and even equity participation by governments (West Germany) in specific projects in developing countries have been advanced to induce firms to invest as governments would wish.

Development Assistance.   The United Kingdom, for example, will provide aid to developing countries for basic infrastructure projects, such as a road or power facilities essential to a British private investment project.

Investment Promotion.   Subsidies or cost sharing for conducting investment feasibility studies, and programs to collect and disseminate data on foreign markets, economic trends, and investment opportunities are commonly extended to help foreign operation of multinational firms as well as local production for export.

Tax Incentives.   Steps to eliminate double taxation of foreign income, mainly through bilateral tax treaties, have been motivated to maintain a degree of equity rather than to encourage foreign operations. Some nations, however, do maintain lower tax rates, exemptions, or special deductions for income earned abroad. Two common provisions which may act as incentives to foreign investment are the tax deferral and tax credit provisions. Deferral provides that taxes will not be levied by the home country until profits are repatriated, and tax credit provides that direct taxes paid to a foreign government will be credited against the tax liability to the home country. These two provisions have been part of U.S. legislation for over 50 years but have come under considerable recent criticism for their purported subsidy of foreign investment. Deferral has been circumscribed by minor regulatory changes in recent tax acts, such as removal of the provision for profits left in tax havens and requirements for full allocation of common overheads between chargeable and deferred income.[3]

Political Representation.   Investor countries have used their political influence to persuade host countries to relax their restrictions over inbound foreign business investment. For example, in recent years the United States has pressured Japan directly and through the OECD to liberalize its stringent limitations on foreign investment.[4]

---

[3]Removal of deferral provisions would probably lead to greater use of foreign financing as well as to more U.S. tax revenue. See Thomas Horst, "American Multinationals and the U.S. Economy," *American Economics Review*, May 1976, p. 151.

[4]M. Y. Yoshino, "Japan as Host to the International Corporation," in *The International Corporation*, ed. Charles P. Kindleberg (Cambridge, Mass: The M.I.T. Press, 1970), p. 371.

Under the Hickenlooper amendment to the 1962 Foreign Assistance Act, the United States is also committed to economic retaliation by ceasing all bilateral aid to any country that expropriates private U.S. property without prompt action to provide fair compensation. The principle has also been extended to U.S. support for loans from the Inter-American Development Bank and the allocation of U.S. import quotas for sugar.

In general, investor countries have provided more extensive inducements for international business expansion in the less developed countries than in industrialized countries. The effectiveness of such programs, however, has not been clearly measured. As might be expected, international enterprises generally favor such inducements and frequently urge the expansion and improvement of incentive programs. A greater recognition of the possible divergence between the interests of the international enterprise and its home country, however, is likely to produce reductions in incentive controls of investor countries. In some cases the incentives may be changed to restraints.

INVESTOR OR HOME-BASE COUNTRIES: RESTRAINING CONTROLS

Most investor countries have some degree of control over capital outflows, although West Germany, Canada, and the United States are virtually free in this respect. Such controls are generally inspired by balance-of-payments considerations rather than by a motivation to mold international business to meet particular national objectives as to foreign business activity. In the period from 1965 to 1974 when the United States extended controls over the ways in which foreign investment could be financed, the balance-of-payments deficit with an overvalued dollar was the major concern.

But balance of payments is not always the motivation. Until recently, the Japanese Ministry for International Trade and Industry (MITI) exercised a great deal of influence over the direction of external investment through its system of review and licensing. Although detailed criteria for approval were not clearly published, investments to increase exports or develop raw material supplies were favored, and later policies seemed to favor investments that would help stabilize world prices for basic materials such as steel and paper or further the competitive position of certain leading Japanese industries. MITI's power of review extended to reinvestment of funds from earnings and capital realizations; and with no requirement to publish criteria for approval, MITI had virtually complete control over Japan's external investment.

Sweden also has extensive powers of control over outward investment. Legislation passed in 1974 empowers the government to prohibit any foreign direct investment by a Swedish-based firm if the
prohibition will help achieve Swedish economic policy. Prior to this
legislation, authorization was needed only for foreign exchange purposes. Proposals are now submitted to a government committee that
includes representatives of both blue-collar and white-collar labor
organizations. With high wage rates in Sweden, unions have been
concerned about the possible export of jobs and they will now have
power to veto any investment in which this concern arises.

In the United States, efforts to establish controls over foreign
investment by U.S. firms in order to prevent export of employment
have largely failed. Labor unions have unsuccessfully urged the
government to regulate, supervise, and control the export of U.S.
technology.[5] The Burke-Hartke bill introduced in the U.S. Congress in
1971, but never passed, provided that foreign licensing of patents
should be prohibited when in the judgment of the President of the
United States "such prohibition will contribute to increased employment in the United States."[6] Nevertheless, there has been some
recognition of the pressures. In the Trade Act of 1974 provision is
made to give support to communities where layoffs have followed
relocation of jobs to other countries, and the law also asks for at least 60
days' advance notice to employees to be laid off as a result of relocation
in foreign countries, as well as efforts to find them new jobs.

Another emerging control issue stems from the impact of the
multinational corporation on its home country's foreign policy. The
United States has assumed a great deal of responsibility for using its
governmental influence to protect the interests of international business firms with U.S. nationality, and the question of imposing controls
that might reduce the foreign policy impact on the United States of
overseas operations by American multinational companies came to the
fore in the late 1960s and early 1970s. In 1969 the government of Peru
expropriated the assets and operations of the International Petroleum
Company, a Canadian company whose shares were almost completely
owned by Standard Oil of New Jersey.[7] In 1971 a new Marxist
government in Chile expropriated the local subsidiaries of major U.S.
copper companies. In both cases, for reasons of foreign policy and
political relations with Latin America, the United States backed away

---

[5]Testimony of AFL–CIO President George Meany before the Subcommittee on
International Trade of the U.S. Senate Finance Committee, May 18, 1971.

[6]S. 2592, 92d Congress, 1st session, September 28, 1971, Sec. 602(a).
&See Richard N. Goodwin, "Letter from Peru," *The New Yorker,* May 1969, pp. 41–46.

[7]See Richard N. Goodwin, "Letter from Peru," *The New Yorker,* May 1969, pp.
41–46.

from a hard-line position and did not impose the retaliatory actions called for by law.

The question raised by these cases is whether an investor country that assumes responsibility for representing the interests of its international business firms in foreign areas should also assume responsibility for screening the expansion plans of international firms so as to minimize the potential damage that controversies over international business interests can have on the foreign policy interests of the investor country. The political problem was bluntly raised as far back as 1962 by Secretary of State Dean Rusk, in testimony before the Foreign Relations Committee on the hearings of the Foreign Assistance Act of 1962:

> I don't believe that the U.S. can afford to stake its interests in other countries on a particular private investment in a particular situation, because someone has to live with the results anyhow . . . I do think that such a provision would create very severe complications in our relations with other governments . . . If we are to tie American policy by law to the private investor overseas, then I think that we, of necessity, must reassure ourselves as to the operations, the conduct, the financial structure, and other aspects of those private investors . . . [8]

As the absolute and relative importance of international business increases, the potential for conflicts with the foreign policy of the major investor countries seems to increase almost geometrically. One alternative for investor countries is a comprehensive screening program as was used by Japan. In the early 1970s, when Japan became concerned about rising resentment toward its business expansion, which was being viewed as neocolonialism in some Southeast Asian countries, it added a review of political impact to its examination of proposed outbound investments.

Another alternative is to screen only those projects that apply for government risk insurance. Still another alternative is for the home country to be neutral and require international business firms of its nationality to assume all of the risks of dealing with foreign governments. The latter alternative may be feasible if the foreign interests of national firms are small. But for countries like the United States, international firms are powerful domestic political forces. Many of them expect their government to give them protection. Furthermore, the activities of international firms may have significant repercussions for an investor country, even though such a nation is not anxious to assume responsibility for its international firms. Disputes may cause difficulties for the home country whether it likes it or not.

---

[8]*Foreign Assistance Act of 1962, Hearings Before the Committee on Foreign Relations,* U.S. Senate, 87th Congress, 2nd Session (Washington, D.C.: U.S. Government Printing Office, 1962), p. 31.

It is not always the firm that activates foreign policy concern. The United States has in the past taken the initiative in attempting to hold the foreign subsidiaries of U.S.-based multinationals to its national prohibition on trading with communist countries. These initiatives were clearly attempts to control the operations of firms within other jurisdictions and as such have been strongly opposed by other countries. So too have been attempts to extend U.S. antitrust regulations to cover the activities of foreign subsidiaries, as discussed in Chapter 8.

Because attempts to restrain the foreign operations of units already established in foreign countries necessarily lead to a conflict of sovereignty, home-base countries have tended to focus their major attention on the point at which transfer out of the nation of jobs, technology, or finance might take place. But even these controls are not extensive. There is considerable range for home-base countries to devise controls that would limit the actions of their multinationals to what are deemed to be national objectives. In fact, the burgeoning controls of host countries, which we outline in the next section, are likely to create the need for investor countries to protect themselves against their own enterprises as they react to meet the demands of other nations.

HOST COUNTRIES: INCENTIVE CONTROLS

For obvious reasons, the less developed countries and the less developed regions within an economically advanced country are most likely to be offering incentives to encourage the establishment and expansion of business enterprises. But a country may offer attractive incentives at an early stage of development, and later reduce its incentives and even impose restraints. Or it may have a mixture of inducements for some fields and restraints in others. Normally, the incentives are available to either domestic or foreign firms—such as Italy's long-standing effort to accelerate development of its poorer southern region. But in the case of many of the newly industrializing nations, where indigenous enterprise is weak or nonexistent, incentive programs are intended primarily to attract foreign business firms.

Incentives offered reflect a nation's stage of economic development, its specific development priorities, and its need to compensate for such business limitations as small local markets in order to attract new industries. Many small, newly independent countries with little local industry may offer a broad range of incentives that are not selective as to type of business activity. On the other hand, the semi-industrialized or even industrialized countries may direct their incentives to specific types of new activities. For example, Brazil decided in the middle 1950s to develop a domestic automobile industry and established a series of attractive incentives specially designed to persuade new investors to enter this field.[9] Japan has made special concessions in selected cases where the expansion of specific types of international business activity was given a high national priority.

Great ingenuity has been shown in developing incentives to fit the particular goals of individual countries, or individual states or provinces as in the cases of the United States and Canada. Flexibility is increased, moreover, by a common practice of wording the enabling laws so as to leave considerable bargaining discretion for government administrators. As a result, incentives within one particular country might vary according to the location of the investment, the size of the investment, the industry, the employment created, or even, as in the case of India, according to the number of shifts worked. In some cases, usually through administrative discretion rather than published regulations, countries try to encourage a mix of nationalities for inbound investment so as to reduce the appearance or reality of foreign economic domination by one country.

Incentives offered generally fall into the following categories:

Tariff Protection.   Potential import competition is reduced or eliminated by special high tariffs or through import controls.

Duty-Free Imports.   Equipment and sometimes future supplies of raw materials or components are allowed to enter the country duty-free or on special concessionary terms.

Financial Assistance.   Short- and long-term loans, generally from government agencies, may be available at special low-interest rates.

Tax Concessions.   Tax reductions, deferrals and even 10-year tax holidays are being offered in certain countries.

Foreign Exchange Guarantees.   Specific governmental guarantees that foreign exchange will be granted for profit remittances and capital repatriation.

Other Governmental Assistance.   The government may assist in assembling parcels of land or agree to build roads or other public facilities needed to complement a project, or even provide subsidies for training personnel.

An important force in shaping incentive programs has been the competition among host countries, states, or provinces as potential locations for the international enterprise. This has been particularly important in relation to regional integration movements. With the elimination of internal tariff walls within the European Economic Community, a foreign firm locating in any of the member countries gained free access to the markets of the others. Consequently, competition developed among the countries in attracting foreign investment.

[9]Lincoln Gordon and Englebert Grommers, *United States Manufacturing Investment in Brazil* (Boston: Harvard Business School, 1962), pp. 46–64.

Some of the smaller member countries, in particular, have offered strong inducements to foreign industry interested in the community.[10] A similar pattern has developed within the United States in recent years. Competition among the states to attract the Volkswagen plant investment resulted in an extremely attractive package of inducements.

The establishment of a free port or a border industry program can effectively attract foreign investment by using a combination of incentives. In both types of programs, the industry is permitted to import materials and components duty-free, employ local labor to assemble them, and export the products paying a duty on only the value added. Mexico's National Frontier Program, adopted in 1966, attracted within six years 280 U.S. plants employing an estimated 40,000 Mexican workers in a 12-mile zone along Mexico's border with the United States.[11] The sites are generally leased in order to circumvent Mexico's prohibition against foreign ownership of land along the border.

Investment promotion efforts are not limited to the nonsocialist countries. Several Eastern European socialist countries have taken special steps to permit and encourage foreign private companies to make direct investments in their countries. The investment promotion measures being used illustrate the reciprocal nature of inducements and restrictions because reductions in restrictions have operated as incentives. An early technique was to permit coproduction agreements whereby a Western private company provides technology and machinery to build or reequip a plant in a communist country and takes part of the production in payment.[12] In 1967 Yugoslavia went further and passed new foreign investment legislation which reinterpreted its concept of *social ownership* to permit joint industrial ventures with foreign capitalist companies under a *pooling-of-funds contract*.[13] Still another technique has been to encourage arrangements whereby a Western company and a communist state enterprise incorporate a fifty-fifty joint venture in a third country-capitalist. The new entity then engages in business in both the East and West and splits the profits.[14]

The effectiveness of incentives in implementing host country poli-

---

[10]Boddewyn, *Western European Policies Toward U.S. Investors,* p. 52.

[11]See Donald W. Baerresen, *The Border Industrialization Program of Mexico* (Lexington, Mass.: D.C. Heath & Co., 1971).

[12]Emile Benoit, "Business Partnerships With Communist Enterprises," *Worldwide P & I Planning,* November–December 1967, pp. 18–24.

[13]Miodrag Sukijasovic, "Foreign Investment in Yugoslavia," in *Foreign Investment: The Experience of Host Countries,* ed. Isaiah A. Litvak and Christopher J. Maule (New York: Praeger Publishers, Inc., 1970), pp. 385–406.

[14]*Business Week,* January 16, 1971, p. 41.

cies and aspirations varies greatly. In countries where the ingredients necessary for making an international business project viable and profitable are not present, even the most attractive incentives will not yield the desired results. On the other hand, in a case such as Brazil's effort to develop quickly a major automobile industry, the special incentives almost certainly were a major factor in the decisions of the foreign firms to establish automobile assembly and components plants. The size of the market was large, and many other conditions appeared to be favorable. The incentives provided a significant reduction in risk.

HOST COUNTRIES: RESTRAINING CONTROLS

Host countries are at many different stages in devising policies and programs for restraining multinational business. A small but growing number of nations, having addressed themselves directly to the issue, have formulated a comprehensive set of policies and devised a coordinated set of control instruments. The more usual situation has been for countries to follow an evolutionary case-by-case approach in responding to the novel and complex multinational business phenomenon.

Given the variations in national goals, national control programs differ in the aspects of multinational business on which they focus and the tools used. Tax measures, foreign exchange controls, and legal restrictions are used in varying proportions. A growing tendency has been to supplement restrictive measures over multinational firms with affirmative policies to strengthen domestic industries—through mergers, financial assistance for research and development, and other means. Where these incentives discriminate against foreign-owned firms, those firms are in effect penalized to the extent of the advantage accorded their competition.

Some control policies are established by specific laws or as provisions of the nation's constitution. Other policies may be periodically formulated as part of national economic planning. The various Indian Five-Year Plans, for example, have specified which fields are to be open to foreign enterprises over the plan period. In addition to, and sometimes instead of, specific laws and plans relating to foreign enterprise, host countries may have one or more government agencies with responsibility for screening, coordinating, and bargaining with foreign direct investors, and granting government permission for entry.

Many governments have encountered difficulties in designing coordinated control programs for international business because several government agencies with varying time perspectives and different government responsibilities are involved. For example, in countries where the treasury, the ministry of finance, and the central bank have been the government agencies most concerned with foreign capital, policies have often been excessively molded from a foreign exchange perspective with a short-run horizon.[15] Also, policy makers have tended to focus upon new foreign enterprises and projects, thereby neglecting established international business activities which may be having an even greater impact on host-country goals. Since the early 1970s, however, there has been a marked trend toward establishment of central agencies for monitoring multinational business operations. Such agencies are advocated for host countries in a recent United Nations publication.[16] In the United States, an Office of Foreign Investment in the United States has been established within the Department of Commerce, and there is also an interagency Committee on Foreign Investment. The establishment of such agencies invariably leads to more substantial data collection as the basis for monitoring the multinationals. The comprehensive report on foreign investment within the United States, prepared under the Foreign Investment Study Act of 1974, recommends more regular collection of data not solely tied to balance of payments.[17]

Entry and Takeover Controls

Many nations now require approval for new investment or takeovers of existing local firms. Any firm wishing to invest in France must apply to the Ministry of Finance for permission. In Japan, the Foreign Investment Council makes the final decision on whether an inflow of investment or technology (licensing agreements) should be allowed after receiving the recommendations of a subcommittee on which various ministries are members. India has a Foreign Investment Board that is responsible for coordinating and expediting all matters related to foreign private investments and collaborations, but decision-making authority on separate features of a foreign investment project is decentralized. Where government authority is widely dispersed, where guidelines are vague, where strict ethical standards do not prevail, the process of controlling the entry of foreign projects may involve crude or highly sophisticated forms of bribery and corruption.

With the ease of regulating new investment simply by requiring

---

[15]This has been true even in the United Kingdom; see Michael Hodges, *Multinational Corporations and National Government: A case study of the United Kingdom's Experience 1964–1970* (Westmead, Farnborough, England: Saxon House, D.C. Heath Ltd., 1974).

[16]*Multinational Corporations in World Development* (New York: United Nations, 1973), p. 83.

[17]*Foreign Direct Investment in the United States*, vol. 1: Report of the Secretary of Commerce to the Congress (Washington, D.C.: U.S. Government Printing Office, April 1976), p. 238.

approval from some statutory authority, few criteria for indicating approval need be specified by statute. Canada's Foreign Investment Review Act passed in 1974 calls simply for the establishment of "significant benefit" to Canada.

By requiring a potential investor to gain approval, the host country throws onto the would-be investor a responsibility to describe operational, financial, and expansion plans in some detail and to justify the anticipated contributions to national goals. The reviewing authority is automatically placed in a position of power to open negotiations on adjustment of particular aspects of the proposal. If the host nation has signed a treaty of friendship, commerce, and navigation with the home country of the investor (see Chapter 8), it might technically be a breach of the treaty for the reviewing authority to withhold approval. The would-be investor should be accorded "national treatment" identical to the treatment of local firms. Delay in approval, however, is not a breach and most investors would think it very dangerous to establish a business against a host government's wishes.

Prohibition of Foreign Ownership

In numerous countries, foreigners are excluded from specific business fields. They are excluded from the tobacco and mining industries in Sweden; from development of certain natural resources in Brazil, Finland, and Morocco; from retail trade in the Philippines; from Norway's textile and shipping industries; from holding mining rights in Italy; and from oil exploration and development in Brazil and Chile. Mexican exclusions are particularly sweeping. Mexico prohibits foreign ownership of land within 31 miles of the coastlines or 62 miles of the borders with other countries, and Mexican companies permitting foreign shareholders are not allowed to own land in the restricted zones. In accordance with the constitution, the petroleum industry, the generation and distribution of electric power, railroads, and telegraphic communications are legally reserved for the government. Private enterprise, whether domestic or foreign, is therefore restricted from these fields. Foreigners, except as minority investors, are not permitted to invest in Mexican banks or other credit institutions, or in insurance companies. Recent administrations have also required, but not retroactively, either 100 percent ownership or a majority of Mexican ownership in a wide range of industries, including radio and television broadcasting; production, distribution, and exhibition of motion pictures; all phases of the soft-drink industry; advertising and publishing; and fishing and packing of marine products.

Public-utility fields are widely restricted, either because of ideological preferences for public enterprise or because the activities are considered indispensable for national development. Governments generally restrict the communication fields such as television, radio, and news publications to domestic firms or the government for protection of vital national interests. As a Canadian government report explains, "Communications media lie at the heart of the technostructure of modern societies. Canadian ownership and control facilitate the expression of Canadian points of view."[18] Protecting national interests is also the rationale for prohibiting foreign ownership in the banking, insurance, and other financial fields. To quote the Canadian report again, "Financial institutions, because of their pervasiveness and their potential as bases for influence and control, constitute the commanding heights of the economy. Canadian ownership and control facilitate the exercise of Canadian economic policies."[19]

Controls over Natural Resource Extraction

Host-country policies controlling international business activity in natural resource fields have a special ideological and even emotional flavor. In most countries of the world, subsurface mineral rights and often forestry resources are reserved by law as the *property of the Crown*, or of the nation as a whole. This legal pattern results from the belief that resources provided by nature should be used for public benefit rather than private profit. Thus, the international business firm operating in the natural resource field is frequently dealing directly with government officials rather than with private owners of property, and with an issue that is of public rather than private concern. The situation is further complicated when the natural resource being exploited is exhaustible, and the nation cannot expect the project to continue indefinitely making its contribution to the national economy and public welfare.

The issue of controls over foreign firms does not arise, obviously, where countries restrict the exploitation of certain natural resources to government or domestic enterprises. But where foreign firms are allowed to operate, special controls or policies are generally imposed.[20] The standard arrangement has been for a foreign company to purchase a concession giving it exclusive rights to explore in a particular area and to develop and produce the minerals or the petroleum found in

---

[18]"Foreign Ownership and Structure of Canadian Industry," *Report of the Task Force on the Structure of Canadian Industry* (Ottawa: Queen's Printer, 1968), p. 389.

[19]Ibid., p. 389.

[20]See R. F. Mikesell, ed., *Foreign Investment in the Petroleum and Mineral Industries: Case Studies on Investor-Host Relations* (Baltimore: The Johns Hopkins Press, 1971); Raymond Vernon, "The Raw Material Ventures," in *Sovereignty at Bay* (New York: Basic Books, 1971), pp. 26–59.

that area for a stated number of years. The host government receives royalties on the materials extracted and income taxes on the net earnings of the concessionaire. The production of petroleum and minerals is generally for export, frequently to other foreign affiliates of the producing companies. The bulk of international business activity in resource exploitation is located in the less developed countries, and in these countries the resource industries are likely to be major sources of foreign exchange earnings, domestic employment, and economic growth. Consequently, host countries are especially anxious to secure a maximum share of the benefits by extending national controls over production, pricing, and marketing.

Specially negotiated concession agreements are intended to spell out the conditions under which foreign enterprises can operate. But in many of the countries, governments have changed with great frequency, and the new government may endeavor to alter or renegotiate the agreements. In fact, the renegotiation of concession agreements is almost certain when foreign enterprises have secured unusually favorable arrangements and when the respective bargaining power of the two parties changes.

New control measures may be invoked when a nation feels that the foreign firm has not made sufficiently vigorous efforts to find new reserves in its concession areas. In April 1965, the Mexican government suspended all sulphur shipments by the Pan-American Sulphur Company, a U.S. firm which produced the bulk of Mexico's sulphur. The government charged that the company had made little effort to discover and develop new reserves of sulphur and that reserves were being depleted at too rapid a rate. Export quotas were then established with provision for upward adjustment as new reserves were discovered.

Over time, the degree of ownership and control by foreign firms is likely to decline because the unique contributions that the foreign firm makes to the domestic resource industries are also likely to decline. The bargaining power of the foreign firm is ultimately based on the degree to which its capital, technical skills, managerial ability, and marketing knowledge are needed by a foreign country. As the foreign enterprise earns profits for the country and trains local technical and operating personnel, it undercuts its own bargaining power by making less scarce the unique contributions that it had to offer initially.

Expropriation

Strictly used, the term *expropriation* refers to governmental action to dispossess someone of property, but with compensation. Government takeover without compensation is referred to as *confiscation,* as occurred with the takeover of foreign investment in Cuba in 1960. Distinction should also be made between expropriation and nationalization. Expropriation normally refers to the taking of a single property or business activity by the state. Nationalization usually means the taking of all activities or properties in a certain field—such as the nationalization of the steel industry in Great Britain, of the banks in Tanzania, and of petroleum distribution in Ceylon. Nationalization may involve a number of expropriations. Nationalization and expropriation are, however, frequently used interchangeably or even replaced with such terms as *indigenization* or *domestication.*

Expropriation is in many ways the ultimate control of the host country over multinational business. Not only does the firm lose assets and profitable operations for which it has risked capital, but a reduction in the sales base may also lead to a situation where the remaining sales cannot support the overhead structure that has been built up. On some occasions, too, the loss of a subsidiary may mean the creation of a competitor.

The investor countries have generally taken the position that international law mandates a minimum treatment of foreign investors, requiring that any taking of foreign-owned property be for a public purpose, neither arbitrary nor discriminatory, and accompanied by payment of prompt, adequate, and effective compensation.[21] When these conditions are met, however, the host country may gain little. Compensation that represents the discounted present value of future cash flows, or "going concern" value, would save a country nothing at all. To pay compensation, moreover, requires the diversion of resources of the host country from other uses, and the very fact of expropriation may discourage investment that would otherwise have been attracted to the country.

Nevertheless, the number of expropriations and nationalizations since World War II has been significant, although only a relatively small share of international business activity has been affected. And this form of control continues to be important in selected areas and fields of business activity. The techniques for achieving the goals of expropriation and nationalization have become more varied and ingenious, but as one scholar has recently observed, "the straightforward, standard form of expropriation and nationalization is not yet extinct

---

[21]For an examination of the law and practice of expropriation in Argentina, Brazil, Chile, Mexico, Peru, Venezuela, and the United States, see Andreas F. Lowenfeld, ed., *Expropriation in the Americas: A Comparative Law Study* (New York: The Dunellen Co., 1971).

and not really significantly diminishing in frequency or magnitude—it is alive and well in South America, Africa, and the Middle East."[22] A recent example of a sweeping indigenization program has been unveiled in Nigeria.[23] By 1978, 100 percent Nigerian ownership will be required in 17 categories of business, ranging from wholesale distribution of local goods to travel and estate agencies. A further 19 categories will require 60 percent Nigerian ownership.

Some selected cases of major expropriations of U.S. and British private foreign investment are shown in Figure 11-1. Geographically, British losses were concentrated in former colonies. For U.S. firms, the bulk of the expropriations were concentrated in Latin America. As measured by the number of individual firms deprived, insurance was the most vulnerable British foreign investment, with export-import trade, commercial banking, and petroleum product distribution next in order of popularity. In contrast, expropriations of U.S. firms were concentrated in petroleum, especially distribution, followed by public utilities and manufacturing. The manufacturing cases involved the production and distribution of detergents in Iraq and Algeria and a textile manufacturing joint venture with the government in Nigeria.

A study by the U.S. government identified 70 examples over a ten-year period in noncommunist countries of nationalizations, expropriations, negotiated sales, or contract disputes involving property in which U.S. corporations have a majority or minority interest.[24] Of the total situations, 16 were in Chile alone. The large majority of the cases were resource industries and banking and insurance operations. Aside from several situations in Chile, virtually no manufacturing industries were affected.

Not surprisingly, the compensation following expropriation has usually been lower than the lost value to the international enterprise— book value of the net assets or even less, say, invested capital less repatriations. But companies can gain as well as lose by expropriation, even though the international enterprise may be more interested in the right to continue to do business than in the payment for assets. In 1970, the government of Peru took over the 51 percent interest that Chase Manhattan Bank held in the Peruvian Banco Continental. The government reportedly paid Chase more than twice the price Chase originally paid for its stock in 1964, and roughly three times the quoted market value of the shares.

---

[22]J. F. Truitt, "Expropriation of Foreign Investment: Summary of the Post–World War II Experience of American and British Investors in the Less Developed Countries," *Journal of International Business Studies,* Fall 1970, pp. 21–34.

[23]*Financial Times,* July 2, 1976.

[24]*Nationalization, Expropriation, and Other Takings of United States and Certain Foreign Property Since 1960* (Washington, D.C.: Bureau of Intelligence and Research, U.S. Department of State, November 30, 1971).

FIGURE 11-1
Expropriations of U.S. and British Private Foreign
Investment: Selected Cases

U.S. Direct Private Foreign Investment

Bolivia, 1952, tin and petroleum
Guatemala, 1953, land
Argentina, 1958, utilities
Brazil, 1959–60, utilities
Indonesia, 1960–65, petroleum and rubber
   plantations
Ceylon, 1962, petroleum distribution
Iraq, 1965, bank facilities
Algeria, 1966–67, insurance and detergent
   manufacture
Chile, 1967, utilities

British Direct Private Foreign Investment

Burma, 1948, collectivization of agriculture,
   forestry, river transport, and petroleum
Ceylon, 1948, rubber plantations and tea
   estates
Iran, 1951, petroleum
India, 1955, banking
Egypt, 1956–64, Suez Maritime Canal
   Company, banking, agriculture, commerce,
   and manufacturing
Burma, 1963, banking and commerce
Tanzania, 1967, banking, manufacturing, and
   trade

Source: J. F. Truitt, "Expropriation of Private Foreign
Investment" (Ph.D. diss., Indiana University, 1969).

Limitation of Foreign Control

Policies to minimize the effects of foreign ownership are two-pronged. They can be designed to strengthen domestic enterprise or weaken the power of foreign firms. Sometimes, both objectives are accomplished in single actions. The Japanese government has long had a policy of encouraging licensing rather than direct foreign investment. Such a policy can be effective if a country is extremely attractive to international business firms, and if the domestic industry sector is strong and has potential and resources for fully utilizing the technology part of the foreign business package without the accompanying investment and management resources.

Governments also attempt to minimize foreign domination by opposing or prohibiting the acquisition of domestic firms by international enterprises. Even though Machines Bull, France's largest manufacturer of computers, was in financial difficulties in 1963, and General Electric was willing to provide urgently needed additional capital in exchange for minority participation, the French government agreed to the GE-Bull partnership only after trying to keep Bull viable with French capital and other assistance. With the same objective of favoring domestic firms, the French government has limited the import quotas of foreign oil companies operating in France more severely than those of French companies. France has also followed the strategy of promoting and encouraging mergers on the assumption that larger and presumably more competitive domestic firms will reduce the competitive advantages of foreign firms and restrict the inflow of foreign investment. For example, two of France's biggest companies—steelmaker Pont-a-Mousson and glassmaker Saint-Gobain—joined in 1969 to create the country's biggest industrial corporation, in line with governmental policies to make French firms more competitive in domestic and foreign markets.

Other policies aimed at reducing foreign control are generally directed toward having nationals share in the ownership and control of foreign business projects. Most countries favor joint ventures, that is, a partnership between the foreign firm and a local business firm or group, or preferably the sharing of the ownership with nationals through public sale of equity within the country. Japan followed a policy for many years of limiting foreigners to 49 percent ownership in joint ventures, although exceptions were made when highly desired industries could not be secured on these terms.[25] Mexico, which along with Japan has been an attractive area for foreign investment, has also taken a hard line on having Mexicans share in the ownership of Mexican affiliates or subsidiaries of international business firms. Its so-called Mexicanization policy is promoted through bargaining when permission is granted for foreign firms to establish businesses in the country and through policies that limit certain tax exemptions or export permits to companies at least 51 percent owned by Mexican nationals. In other cases, countries may discriminate in taxes, granting import permits, and government purchasing in favor of firms that have a large or majority share owned by nationals. Some countries such as Sweden require that the directors of a Swedish joint stock company be resident Swedish subjects. However, the Swedish Board of Commerce can grant exemptions allowing up to one third of the board to consist of foreign nationals.

---

[25]See Noritake Kobayashi, "Foreign Investment in Japan" in *Foreign Investment,* ed. Litvak and Maule, p. 150. In 1967, 58 companies in Japan were owned 100 percent by foreign investors.

Controls over Local Content, Employment, and Production

Some governments have developed what are called *local-content* policies. Prospective investors are asked to commit themselves to a schedule of increasing the locally produced content of the final product over a stated period of time. Such local-content policies have been widely applied to automobile manufacturers who have expanded in Latin America, with the hope that the development impetus of new types of activity will continue over time and be extended into other related areas of activity. But countries may have to pay a high price for having local content when local markets are not large enough to permit economic scale production for many parts and components.

Another way of increasing local benefits is through employment policies imposed on international enterprises. The labor law of Mexico provides that at least 90 percent of a foreign company's employees must be Mexican citizens. Executives are generally excluded in calculating this percentage. The immigration of foreigners for managerial and other positions is permitted only if qualified Mexicans are not available. Some countries, such as the Central American nations, also establish limits in relation to the total payroll. Interestingly, each firm may exclude two administrators from the above computation.

Export strategies of multinational enterprises have become the focus of another set of controls. Countries have realized that the global strategies of multinational firms may not allow or encourage subsidiaries and affiliates to compete freely for export markets. Some countries thus make it a requirement for approval of all new operations that the units are completely free to export and earn foreign exchange. Some will even force divestiture if a specified proportion of output is not exported. And there are many pressures exerted for further processing of local materials before export.

Financial and Fiscal Controls

Balance-of-payments objectives are increasingly obvious in the development of controls over financing. Many host countries require external financing for new foreign investments and some limit the access of foreign firms to local sources of capital. Some of these policies emerged in reaction to the U.S. attempt at capital controls from 1965 to 1974. Other common policies are to set limits or establish continuing control over remission of profits, repatriation of capital, and royalty payments to the home office of the foreign enterprise. To back these controls, however, more and more countries are realizing that they need additional controls to regulate transfer pricing for goods and services moving among units of the international enterprise.

Yet another way of increasing national benefits is to adjust ta policies. Because international enterprises are subject to taxation in th home country for profits earned abroad and generally receive credit fc foreign taxes, many countries have raised their tax rates to a leve comparable to that in the United States, the principal home country c the international enterprises. The business firm does not have to pa extra taxes, but the host government rather than the home governmer gets the revenue.

MULTINATIONAL ALIGNMENT OF CONTROLS

There have been many moves in the last ten years for groups c countries to sign agreements on standard controls over multinationa corporations. The outstanding example of cooperation to reduce com petition among host countries in the natural resource field has been th Organization of Petroleum Exporting Countries (OPEC). Created i 1960, it includes most of the principal oil-producing countries an through a variety of moves has considerably strengthened the hand c the selling nations. The Andean Pact is another example of a commo approach to controls over inward foreign investment. Negotiated i 1971 by Bolivia, Chile, Colombia, Ecuador, and Peru and joined late by Venezuela, the pact took a hard line toward foreign investments. I limited the degree of foreign ownership and generally required tha foreign firms divest their ownership into national hands over a fixe period of time. While the common policy certainly reduced competi tion among the Andean countries, the net result has been to discourag foreign investment. OPEC includes almost all the principal countrie available as sources of supply for the multinational oil companies, bu the Andean countries have no such strength. Not surprisingly, ther have been recent suggestions among the pact countries to relax th common restrictions.[26] Bolivia has even relaxed its restrictions in th controversial mining sector.[27]

While groups of countries may easily agree on the adoption o standard controls because they can all see individual benefits fron doing so, global agreement on standard controls is not so simple. I many countries benefit significantly, others are likely to perceive costs As the vast majority of countries are host countries only, their majorit pressure for standard controls has been against the interests of investo countries. This pressure has surfaced in several forms within th United Nations organization. Over the abstention of the major investo countries, the second general conference of UNIDO in 1975 approve

---

[26] *The Wall Street Journal,* May 24, 1976.
[27] *Business Week,* May 4, 1974.

a declaration that every state has an inalienable, permanent right to exercise its sovereignty freely over its own natural resources including their nationalization. At the same conference the Group of 77 (the developing nations) also advanced a proposal for a new mechanism for redeploying specific industries from developed to developing countries. Both these moves are dominated by the developing host countries, as is a proposed code of terms and conditions for the transfer of technology prepared by the Committee on Transfer of Technology of UNCTAD.

The United States and the European Community in particular have opposed one-sided guidelines that would appear to penalize investor countries.[28] While accepting that multinational corporations should adhere to binding codes of good conduct, they affirm that governments as well as enterprises must respect contractual obligations undertaken by them. The developed nations would generally have preferred a binding code of conduct, possibly within GATT, and have been active in shaping the recent OECD guidelines. These guidelines are directed solely at the actions of multinational enterprises, but along with their adoption by the OECD council in June 1976, the member countries agreed to extend national treatment to all foreign-controlled enterprises once admitted to their country. While neither the guidelines nor the agreement to national treatment is legally binding, a clause has also been adopted that member countries will establish "consultation procedures" on their application. Such procedures will very likely hasten the standardization of controls among the member nations.[29]

EXERCISES AND DISCUSSION QUESTIONS

1. "Investment-guaranty insurance merely encourages both investing companies and host governments to behave more irresponsibly, knowing that the investing company's government would bail the company out. Safeguards should be written into such schemes that would prevent a company claiming on the guarantee scheme if it had somehow provoked the host government into nationalization, for instance by bad labor practices or disguised political activity locally." Discuss.

2. What are the advantages and disadvantages of varying the cost and availability of investment-guaranty insurance for different types of business activities and for different host countries as against charging a standard risk premium for all projects and all areas?

3. The United States has a vital national-security interest in acquiring

---

[28]"Multinational Undertakings and the Community," *Bulletin of the European Communities,* supplement 15/73 (Luxembourg: Office for Official Publications of the European Communities, 7 November 1973).

[29]See Chapter 8.

dependable foreign sources of critical minerals at a reasonable cost. Therefore, it should give maximum support and protection to the foreign direct investments of U.S. international resource industries in such fields as petroleum and copper, where U.S. domestic production is insufficient for U.S. needs. Discuss.

4. You have been retained by an industrialized country, such as France, to recommend strategy and policies for regulating the entry and continuing operations of foreign multinational companies in that country. What are the two or three most important issues that you would have to resolve? What information would you need to complete your assignment? In what ways would the key problems and the nature of your recommendations be different if you were working for a less developed country, namely, a small, newly independent country in Africa?

5. Host-country policies that require multinational companies to share ownership with nationals are frequently used to minimize the economic power of foreign interests. But such policies will also reduce the amount of foreign capital transfers to the host country and reduce the supply of local capital for domestic entrepreneurs. Why do you think so many host countries are insisting that foreign firms share ownership with locals?

6. Under what circumstances would you as a host country prohibit foreign companies from acquiring domestic companies?

7. In formulating an investment promotion program to attract foreign direct investment to a less developed country, which incentives do you think would be most effective and why?

12

The Countervailing Power of
International Business

INTERNATIONAL BUSINESS is not without its own power for countering the impact of national controls. There is a landmark English legal case in which Lord Justice Tomlin ruled that every man is entitled to order his affairs so as to minimize the tax for which he would be liable (*Inland Revenue Commissioners* v. *Duke of Westminster*—1936). A similar concept applies to the international enterprise. It is under no obligation not to use the legal means available to it to avoid controls that may hinder attainment of its legitimate global business objectives.

The experienced international enterprise goes even further. It will plan to avoid future controls. It will examine the existing strategies of relevant countries toward multinational business and international transfers, project the likely pattern of change, and adapt its own strategy accordingly. The firm is not an unprotected, misused pawn of omnipotent nations; it is a powerful player in the international business game.

This chapter introduces some of the means at the command of international firms for adjusting to controls and for exerting countervailing power. The focus is on the ways in which the business enterprise can act to mitigate the effects of national controls. The decision-making procedures by which businessmen choose an appropriate mix of these adjustments are the subject of Part V of the book.

REFUSAL TO PARTICIPATE

The simplest and most direct form of countervailing power available to the international enterprise is to refuse to make new investments, or even to discontinue existing operations, in countries where national controls have made the business environment unattractive. From a nation's point of view, its optimum strategy is to set each of its controls at a level that maximizes net national benefits. This control optimum must recognize the opportunity loss of benefits from investments not made and business activities that would have come or remained if such controls had not been imposed. With nationalistic enthusiasm, nations have frequently exceeded the control optimum and been forced to relax or abandon controls when they became aware of what they were losing in potential new investments and expansions, or even in terminated operations.

In both developed and less developed countries, the loss of future foreign investments has operated as a constraint on national control policies. In the case of France, for example, during the period between 1963 and 1968 when strong de Gaullist policies restricted foreign investment inflows, U.S. investment increased by 141 percent in Holland, 113 percent in West Germany, 175 percent in Belgium, and only 55 percent in France. The trend did not coincide with President Pompidou's view of France's national interests. Shortly after he was elected in mid-1969, national control policies were sharply altered, even to the point where the ministry of industry opened an office in New York to stimulate U.S. investment.[1] In contrast to France's previous refusal to allow General Motors to build a major plant in the Strasbourg area, French officials in 1970 began aggressively to solicit another major American automobile manufacturer, the Ford Motor Company, to invest in France.[2]

Argentina offers a similar example. In 1973 the Peronist-controlled congress approved a highly restrictive foreign-investment law and foreign investment came to a virtual halt. Within three years, the regime that overthrew President Isabel Peron drafted a new law, eliminating among other restrictions a 12.5 percent limit on profit remittances after a five-year waiting period and a requirement for mandatory contracts with the government for any new investment.[3]

A change in national controls may alter the optimum locational pattern for the operations of an international firm and the ranking of its alternatives on its investment schedule, as will be discussed in Chapter 13. In some cases, the firm will choose an alternative country in which to expand. In other situations, a prospective expansion may be deferred or abandoned because expected profits no longer fall within the investment limits of the firm. In fewer cases, the firm may withhold

---

[1]*Business Week,* September 5, 1970.

[2]*Economist,* February 28, 1970.

[3]*The Wall Street Journal,* June 29, 1976.

operating funds or shut down existing operations. In late 1975, a number of U.S. firms denied further funds to Portuguese subsidiaries when nationalized banks refused to grant advances, and at least one withdrew completely.[4]

HOME-COUNTRY SUPPORT

Although investor countries vary in their willingness to lend official support to assist the foreign operations of their international enterprises, the possibility of support merits inclusion in an examination of the countervailing power of international business. In some cases, home countries have been enticed to support the purely private interests of its citizens in foreign situations. The more common situation in recent years is for the investor country to undertake certain actions because it sees that its national interests are at stake.

By having foreign projects covered by home-country investment-guarantee schemes, the international enterprise may secure home-country support as well as risk insurance. Such programs, however, do not explicitly guarantee that the home country will intervene on behalf of the international enterprise.

In 1963, the United States threatened to withhold government economic assistance from Indonesia in order to get Indonesia to improve its settlement terms for the takeover of U.S. oil-company properties. The U.S. Export-Import Bank has refused to make loans to Chile for the purchase of American jet aircraft after Chile's expropriation of U.S. copper companies, and the U.S. government has used its influence in international agencies such as the World Bank and the Inter-American Bank to deny financing to countries that have taken undesirable action against U.S. companies.

But the United States is not alone in lending its official support to counter host-country measures against multinational enterprises. In a countermove following Algeria's seizure in 1971 of 51 percent of French oil interests, the French government officially requested the U.S. Export-Import Bank to deny a $150 million loan that Algeria was seeking for a natural gas plant. France also threatened to discontinue the sizable financial and technical assistance it was giving to Algeria in order to negotiate a better settlement on the oil expropriations. When Libya expropriated the oil assets of British Petroleum in 1971, the British foreign office is reported to have approached other oil-importing nations, "expressing concern for BP's rights."[5]

In some situations, home-country support can be more direct. The

---

[4] *The Washington Post*, September 11, 1975.
[5] *The Wall Street Journal*, December 31, 1971.

United States and other countries have pressured the Japanese to reduce their restrictions on the entry of foreign investment. The United States in particular has mentioned the possibility of retaliation through increased restrictions on Japanese business access to the U.S. market. As a result of these official efforts, in 1971 U.S. automobile manufacturers were allowed to make their first direct-investment entry into the Japanese market through minority joint-venture arrangements with Japanese companies.

Still another way in which the home country can give support to its multinational enterprises is through legal actions in the World Court, as discussed in Chapter 8. But such support through World Court litigation has not been an effective source of countervailing power.

MEASURES TO DETER HOST-COUNTRY CONTROLS OVER FOREIGN INVESTMENT

Stimulating Local Enterprise

If the international firm accepts the hypothesis that a host country's receptivity varies inversely with the share of the total economy or of key sectors controlled by foreign interests, it can take steps to increase receptivity and deter controls by stimulating the growth of indigenous enterprise. It can, for example, plan and implement aggressive programs for encouraging independent local firms to become suppliers, processors, further manufacturers, and sellers of the product of the foreign-financed venture. The linkage benefits are much heralded by proponents of foreign investment but, too frequently, the linkage opportunities are left to slow natural forces or are realized not by domestic business but by other foreign investors.

More by necessity than by design, Sears Roebuck de Mexico demonstrated two decades ago the effectiveness of policies to stimulate local enterprise in increasing host-country receptivity without prohibitive costs. In establishing its first large, modern department store in Mexico, Sears had assumed that it would import about 70 percent of its merchandise from the United States. But in late 1947, less than a year after opening its first store, the company had to face a drastic change in the Mexican economic situation. Due to foreign exchange difficulties, Mexico placed an embargo on a wide range of consumer imports. To meet this unexpected challenge, Sears responded by a mammoth program of encouraging new local enterprises as sources of supply. Within six years, and through cooperation with 1,300 local firms, Sears was able to buy in Mexico 80 percent of the merchandise it sold there.[6]

---

[6]Richardson Wood and Virginia Keyser, *Sears Roebuck de Mexico, S.A.* (Washington, D.C.: National Planning Association, 1953).

Developing Local Allies

Another interesting example of measures to deter national controls is the case of Firestone's rubber-growing operations in Liberia. As a planned rather than an unanticipated program, Firestone initiated a rubber-growers assistance program designed to help Liberians grow rubber on their own farms. As reported in another NPA study,

> Firestone provides not only free trees but also free technical services. It will survey the planter's farm and draw up a planting program for him. When the trees reach tapping age, the Company will prepare a complete management plan, which includes a detailed map of the tree stands, their division into tasks and the marking of each tree with its task designation, and a tapping schedule best suited to the needs and capabilities of the farm. At the farmer's request, the Company will periodically inspect his rubber trees and advise him on improved care, cultivation, and tapping. It will set up his bookkeeping and records systems and teach him how to keep them current. It will provide free biological services in the event of tree disease, storm damage, or other difficulties, Firestone will sell him at cost and on interest-free credit terms all of the plantation equipment and supplies he needs both initially and subsequently.
>
> Finally, the Company will market his production and will transport it to the Harbel and Cavalla plantations if the farmer has no suitable vehicle of his own.[7]

Through assisting local enterprises, a number of which happen to be owned by political leaders and government officials, Firestone increased its supply of rubber while reducing its relative share of the local rubber-growing industry. It was also protecting itself against adverse governmental controls by helping many nationals secure a vested interest in favorable governmental actions toward rubber growing.

Sharing Ownership through Joint Ventures

Probably the best-known deterrent to host-country controls is the sharing of ownership in local subsidiaries with nationals. Although the decision to engage in joint ventures involves many considerations other than a defensive move against national controls, this strategy can have the multiple effect of reducing the apparent threat of foreign domination, securing local allies, and enlarging the role of indigenous enterprise in the local economy.[8] Complete ownership of local subsidi-

---

[7]Wayne Chatfield Taylor, *The Firestone Operations in Liberia* (Washington, D.C.: National Planning Association, 1956), p. 94.

[8]For example, see Lawrence G. Franko, "Joint Venture Divorce in the Multinational Company," *Columbia Journal of World Business*, May–June 1971, pp. 13–22.

aries gives the multinational enterprise greatest flexibility in such areas as organization, intercompany pricing, and dividend policy. Yet, many firms find that divestment of some of the equity can provide more than offsetting benefits through protection against controls. The greater the proportion of ownership that is divested, the greater the gain in protection and the greater the loss of parent-company control. The distribution as well as the share of the local ownership can be important. The advantage of having local ownership in the hands of a small number of local partners with significant holdings is that such partners are likely to take an active interest in protecting the profitability of their investment from erosion by government controls. The advantage of a wide dispersion of local ownership is that the international firm may be able to retain a degree of control greatly in excess of its ownership share.

Under the pressure of necessity, the predominantly negative attitudes of most multinational enterprises toward local sharing of ownership have been changing. A common objection expressed by many companies has been that host-country security markets are not sufficiently developed to absorb any significant amounts of stocks. This argument probably has limited validity and may not have held true even in the past. In 1968, for example, when General Electric made a public offering of 10 percent of the total stock in its Mexican subsidiary, the issue was quickly oversubscribed.[9] In the mid-1960s a joint venture of the Cummins Engine Company in India offered $24\frac{1}{2}$ percent of its shares to the public through the Bombay stock exchange and the purchase orders received totaled more than 50 times the number of shares being offered.[10]

At one time partnership with national governments was almost completely avoided by international corporations. It was regarded by many American executives as next door to communism. Realization of some of the advantages, however, has made this sort of arrangement more common. In 1970, as one example, U.S. Steel entered into a joint venture with the government of Brazil whereby it had a 49 percent interest in a new iron ore mining project estimated to cost $300 million to $400 million. With the local government as a partner, there is a negative incentive for controls or harassment—and in some cases an incentive for positive advantages. Moreover, a government usually has ample funds for desirable expansion, is less interested in profit distribution than in growth, and is generally uninterested in taking over the business itself or undertaking day-to-day management. Private partners frequently produce problems on each of these counts.

---

[9]*The Wall Street Journal,* July 5, 1968.
[10]Personal interview with Cummins' officials, 1965.

Selective Ownership Divestment

Another ownership strategy is to separate the parts of the activity requiring physical assets from the commercial or technical sides and to arrange heavy local ownership in the physical side. Less can be expropriated if it is already owned locally, and the local investors may find it entirely in their interests to retain the pattern and not to become involved in a wider range of activity with which they are unfamiliar. United Fruit, a favorite leftist target in Latin America for many years, finally divested itself of the majority of its Latin American landholdings and focused more heavily on its marketing and transportation activities in the banana business.[11]

Conversely, some international businesses may find that retention of commercial activity by local entrepreneurs is advantageous. In many countries, for example, the importer-distributor is a powerful political force. Working through such an outlet may ensure continued access to the market, even though the international company would be able to carry out much more effective distribution on its own account.

Multiple Nationality for International Business Projects

In some countries, the domination of the foreign business sector by firms of a single nationality may be an important stimulus for stronger national controls. One response to this fear of economic domination is for multinational enterprises to acquire multiple nationality or to undertake projects with firms of other nations. Both Royal Dutch Shell and Unilever have carefully nurtured the dual Dutch-British nationality of the parents because they have found the ambiguity to be useful. When Indonesia's Sukarno was unfriendly to the Dutch, these enterprises emphasized their British identity. Where antagonism emerges against the British, it is the Dutch identity that comes to the fore.

Consortia of international business firms of different nationalities, such as the Iranian consortium of Western companies, have been common in the field of petroleum. A similar pattern has been followed more recently in mining. Some examples are the Fria bauxite project in Guinea, the Freeport nickel project in Indonesia, and iron ore mining projects in Australia.

Some have argued that ownership should be spread multinationally, including multinational institutions such as the World Bank, international financial centers such as Zurich or London, and business partners from many nations. The theory is that the host country would act more circumspectly if tempted to repudiate the terms of an

---

[11] *Business Week,* November 22, 1969.

agreement when faced with the multinational "establishment."[12] A somewhat similar strategy practiced by firms in natural resource fields is to sell output forward to buyers in a number of countries in order to increase the problems that the host country would face if it attempted to expropriate.[13] Kennecott Copper worked out such a defense prior to Chilean nationalization in order to protect its compensation position.[14]

Changing Nationality

A multinational enterprise may find that its greatest countervailing power lies in its ability to change its nationality, either to avoid home-country controls or to be better received by host countries. A number of firms have switched domicile in recent years from the United Kingdom to Australia, Canada, and elsewhere. Several have left Canada. Even Massey-Ferguson, one of Canada's largest, threatened to leave Canada following a change in the law that would have led to taxation of nonremitted foreign profits not earned from its primary business.[15] With the threat of the Burke-Hartke legislation in the early 1970s, many U.S. firms had laid plans to establish binational structures in order to place their foreign activities with a non-U.S. corporate entity.

Corporate emigration is not, however, a procedure that receives automatic blessing from the home country. Such a move out of the United Kingdom, for example, would require exchange control approval from the Bank of England, taxation approval from the Treasury, and industrial policy approval from the Department of Trade and Industry.

ENTRY AND OPERATING STRATEGIES

A wide range of defensive measures for avoiding national controls can be grouped under the rubric of entry and operating strategies. These defenses make use of the inherent flexibility and total enterprise capability of the multinational firm. They permit a company to adjust or rearrange its patterns of location, its logistics, and its operating policies to have activities take place where the costly effects of national

---

[12]Joseph S. Nye, Jr., "Multinational Corporations in World Politics," *Foreign Affairs*, October 1974, p. 157.

[13]Theodore H. Moran "Transnational Strategies of Protection and Defense by Multinational Corporations: Spreading the Risk and Raising the Cost for Nationalization in Natural Resources," *International Organization* 27, no. 2 (Spring 1973).

[14]Charles T. Goodsell, *American Corporations and Peruvian Politics* (Cambridge: Harvard University Press, 1974).

[15]"Canada: A Tax Law May Go Too Far," *Business Week*, March 17, 1973.

controls are minimized. Some of the options, as discussed below, are the choice of business activity, selection of products, location of production sites, location of intangible assets, sourcing and movement of funds and profits, ownership divestment of certain assets, and control of distribution and markets.

The Choice of Business Activity

One of the most obvious ways for a firm to avoid controls is to change its type of activity. Gone are the days when a maker of buggy whips limited his activity to making and trading in nothing but buggy whips. Confronted with restrictions concerning one area of business, the firm can quickly move to others. For many international corporations this is particularly easy. Most have many facets to their business and can develop those in which controls do not hamper achievement of the firm's objectives. When ITT's telephone company was bought out by the government of Peru in the late 1960s, the company shifted its Peruvian activities into more acceptable company lines, such as the construction of a Sheraton hotel (ITT subsidiary) and the manufacturing of electrical equipment. Union Miniere, S.A.—the Belgian company described as "a mining company without any mines" after its vast copper mines were expropriated in the Congo in 1967—began investing in chemical and industrial concerns and became active in data processing, nuclear research, engineering, and metallurgy.[16]

Where the compensation terms for the sale or expropriation of a company's assets require reinvestment for a period of time in the same country, such as in the case of ITT, the choice of new business activity will be influenced by the locational restriction. In other situations, such as the Union Miniere case, the company can scan the global environment for opportunities, thus placing all interested nations that might receive the investment in competition with each other.

The prime criteria in the search and selection of expansion opportunities will almost certainly be growth, risk, and return on capital. Whatever the emphasis in any individual case, these criteria will favor expansion where capital and profits look least vulnerable to erosion by government controls or by political risk. Variations in the vulnerability of different types of business activities will be discussed in Chapter 14 on political risk. A few decades ago, foreign investments in public utilities were politically and economically popular with both host countries and investors. But styles have changed and public utilities presently have the highest degree of vulnerability to expropriation and national controls and are generally avoided for new investments. The

---

[16]*The Wall Street Journal,* December 28, 1970.

extractive industries, particularly petroleum and mining, also have a high degree of risk. By using a high-risk factor in evaluating such investments, international firms weigh them less favorably as attractive choices for business activity.

Lower vulnerability is likely to occur in intermediate production which buys from and sells to local entrepreneurs. Both supplier and customer can act as buffers against imposition of controls. In many cases the intermediate type of production is likely to be essential to the customer's output, and to require technological expertise that neither supplier nor customer could or would want to provide for itself.

Location of Operations

Some national controls are directed toward increasing production levels of local subsidiaries by forcing such foreign resident firms to export, or at least to maximize, the proportion of local production in their local sales. Firms, however, have objectives other than maximizing production in any one location, and these may lead them to locate their production so as to gain economies of scale or lower transportation and tariff costs. The extent to which a firm can adopt a cost-minimizing plant location plan can be limited by the actions of competing firms. Nevertheless, a firm normally has sufficient locational flexibility for many countries to be restrained in their imposition of controls. As soon as a nation's controls are raised above those of alternative locations, the country becomes a less likely location for new investments or expansions of existing facilities by international firms. Conversely, when it reduces its control level, as did France after General Motors built its major plant in Antwerp, Belgium, rather than in Strasbourg, France, a country is more likely to be a recipient of future investment.

An interesting case of using location to avoid what the company considered unacceptable pollution controls was the decision of Hoechst AG to locate a new steel plant in Dortmund, West Germany, when Dutch authorities raised antipollution objections to a planned Hoechst plant near Rotterdam. The Rotterdam plant was to be a joint project with the Hoogovens of Holland.[17]

In some industries, firms have been known to maintain reserve production potential in several countries as a deterrent to individual nations imposing added controls. In the 1950s, for example, United Fruit kept large amounts of improved land prepared for banana planting but unplanted. The stated company objective was to have land reserves in case its plantations were exposed to diseases or other

---

[17]*The Wall Street Journal,* July 6, 1971.

natural hazards. Another obvious advantage was the possibility of shifting the location of production as a defense against national controls. The international oil companies were accused of stockpiling oil reserves in some countries as an implicit threat to oil-producing countries that there were limits to the extent to which national demands could be met and output still maintained.

Strength can be built against both home and host countries by setting up directly competing units within the same organization but located in different countries. Such an arrangement can be particularly effective in limiting national controls if the subsidiaries directly compete with each other for the same export markets. Any restraining controls applied locally might give the competing subsidiary an export advantage.

Yet another defense available to the multinational enterprise lies in adoption of a truly international production network in which each plant specializes in some part of the total process. This means that most subsidiaries will contribute export income to the country of residence. Any insistence by the local government on further local production could be demonstrated by the international corporation as likely to jeopardize exports to units elsewhere in the network.

The location of management can be changed as well as the location of production. The U.S. business community in Britain made strong representations to the British government in 1974 that the proposed imposition of high U.K. taxes on the unremitted foreign income of U.S. nationals in Britain would force them to leave. Some relaxation of the proposals was gained, but there was subsequently a significant transfer of multinationals' offices to Paris and other locations.[18]

Location of Intangible Assets

A powerful source of strength for international firms in combating national controls is their ability to control the location of intangible business assets. These include research and development ability, technical, marketing, and management know-how. When the firm controls essential technical know-how, the extent to which any host country can move against it is severely circumscribed. If the activity requires continual injections of updated research output, expropriation of purely production facilities could be self-defeating. More gradual attempts at creeping controls, such as limitation of profit remittances or permission to expand, could be offset by the firm through withholding new developments as a bargaining gambit. The same situation prevails when the international firm retains the production, marketing, and

---

[18]*Business Week,* March 10, 1975.

management expertise through the use of expatriate personnel rather than training nationals. This suggests, unfortunately, that countries perceived to be high-risk control areas are less likely to maximize the technology-transfer benefits from multinational enterprises.

Control of Distribution and Markets

When production or extraction is located in one country and the consumer in another, the international firm can build a strong position through control of access to the market. If the firm owns the channels of distribution or has built an unassailable market position, controls imposed over production must not take the costs beyond those the marketing organization could obtain elsewhere. So long as no supplying country is in a monopoly position and supplying countries do not act in unison, any action by one will be checked by the failure of the others to act likewise. In some cases, international corporations have built themselves into virtually single-buyer positions from competing suppliers.

But just as a nation's bargaining position can be undercut by the availability of other sources of supply, so can the bargaining strength of an international enterprise be sapped when other companies are willing to do the marketing. In 1971 Guyana nationalized its bauxite mines owned by Alcan. Given a world oversupply of bauxite, Alcan was unlikely to have trouble finding other sources of supply. In the closely knit world of a small number of aluminum producers, it appeared that Guyana was going to have serious difficulty in selling its bauxite. But to Guyana's rescue (and Alcan's dismay) came a London metal brokerage company that apparently saw market possibilities in Eastern Europe and Japan. As the *Economist* observed, the brokerage firm "has been rather rude to the world's major aluminum companies, which will not make its task easier."[19] To be sure, the London firm encountered marketing difficulties. Shortly thereafter, Alcan was able to arrive at a mutually acceptable settlement, which included acting as the marketing agent for Guyana.

Even within one country, an international business firm likely to be hampered by creeping controls may build a stronger position by retaining dominance of the market. Some of the U.S. manufacturers of branded consumer goods in Japan, for example, seem to have adopted a policy of purchasing supplies from a range of local suppliers while retaining all the marketing in their own hands. This limits the amount of investment required, and at the same time builds added protection against controls. Small producers without experience in marketing

---

[19]*Economist,* July 3, 1971.

branded consumer products should act as a buffer against Japanese government interference, being in a position to make growing production profits and not at all keen to take over the marketing themselves. There would be no incentive to expropriate locally owned operations and a great deal of difficulty in expropriating marketing know-how.

Sourcing and Movement of Funds and Profits

When governments place controls on financial remittance or the use of local funds for balance-of-payments reasons, to implement domestic economic policies, or to avoid excessive profit taking, the multinational firm is in a particularly strong position to avoid much of the intent behind these controls. Using a variety of legal forms of incorporation, it can generally arrange to allocate the ownership control of its assets and activities to a preferred pattern of jurisdictions. It can use assets in one nation to support borrowing in another, obtain funds from outside a nation for inward remittances at a time when local firms would find great difficulty obtaining further capital, or adopt a range of other financial management policies discussed in Chapter 21. This strength has been used frequently in both home and host countries in times of inflation and tight monetary controls to build up a larger market share at a lower cost than would be the case were local competitors on the same footing.

The international movement of funds can also be carried out through a range of internal transactions that are difficult to police. Charges for royalties, interest, travel, training, research and development, corporate overheads, machinery, advice, use of overseas facilities, and so on endlessly, can be arranged in such a way that few governments could prevent significant transfers of funds without stopping all business transactions. Then there are the more controllable, but still quite effective, possibilities of altering the transfer prices for components, raw materials, part assemblies, or finished goods.

All these actions affect the location of profit. They may thus equally be used for arranging the place at which profit is taken so that taxation is minimized. In some cases, however, the arrangement that would minimize taxation is not that which would locate the funds in the way the business would find optimal. In such cases, the avoidance of taxation may dominate the other motives.

TRADE-OFF DEALS

The use of trade-offs and bargaining as a countervailing power to national control policies can be illustrated by the case of Merck Sharp & Dome in India. During the 1950s, Merck had developed a solid market in India for drugs through exporting and some local packaging. In 1955 and 1956, the Indian government made it clear that it was moving in the direction of producing more antibiotics in its fully owned company, Hindustan Antibiotics (Private) Limited. In support of this plan, India received technical assistance from the USSR in developing a master plan for expanding government production in the pharmaceutical field and an offer of a large loan at extremely low rates of interest.

At the time these plans became known, representatives of MSD International were in India negotiating to establish a plant on quite different terms. Because of the preeminence of MSD's technological know-how, the Indian government suggested a partnership with a government corporation. It also suggested as an alternative that MSD provide technical assistance and train personnel to help Hindustan Antibiotics establish a plant for manufacturing streptomycin. After a period of bargaining, agreement was reached on a compromise plan. MSD was permitted to join forces with a privately owned Indian firm to manufacture a wide range of products in return for providing technical assistance to the state-owned company for the production of streptomycin. MSD agreed to prepare the plans for the government plant, train Indian personnel, and make its know-how in this field available for a modest fee.

As a key official of MSD explained, "We ended up not on our initial terms but not on theirs either. It was a period of often tough bargaining, but never chiseling. A basic understanding was reached by the willingness to appreciate each other's philosophy, motivation, objectives, and problems. Should we have adopted the attitude that she would do business with us on our terms or not at all? Should we have surrendered the field to Russia by default? I hardly think anyone would seriously advocate that course."[20]

The key source of MSD's bargaining power was its superior technical know-how. With this as a starting point and a willingness to bargain and consider trade-offs, it was able to bend a government policy that was rapidly moving in the direction of precluding private and foreign enterprise from an important business field.

LEGAL AND OTHER DEFENSES

The local subsidiaries of multinational firms generally have the option of contesting national control actions in the local courts. When

---

[20]Dr. Antonie Knoppers in a speech to the Pharmaceutical Manufacturers Association, New York, December 8, 1958.

Venezuela passed a new law in 1971 which appeared to give the government reversion rights at the end of a concession period to oil company investments not directly connected with oil production, the major oil producers in Venezuela contested the constitutionality of the law before the Venezuela supreme court. Two American copper companies, whose properties were nationalized by Chile in 1971, appealed the terms of settlement offered by the government to a special tribunal created by the constitutional reform that permitted the nationalization of these properties. Although such appeals may take a long time to be decided and although the international companies are uncertain about success, in the judgment of the companies such resort to legal defense in local courts appears to warrant the effort.

Another related strategy has been to undertake legal action in the courts of nations other than the host country. One of the American copper companies expropriated in Chile brought suit in a U.S. federal court in New York to block Chile's use of assets in the United States pending resolution of the copper company's claim for compensation. Subsequently, Chile agreed to pay the copper company for a loan it made to its Chilean subsidiary for developing a copper mine in Chile. As reported by an American newspaper, "There was some speculation that President Allende cleared payment to unfreeze the government's assets in the U.S."[21] Indeed, after Chile consented to make the payments, the copper company agreed before the New York court to give 36 hours notice before trying to attach the assets of LAN-Chile Airlines, the Chilean national carrier, which had temporarily suspended flights to the United States.

Where the output of multinational firms is exported from the host countries, international firms have used boycotts as an effective means of countervailing power. When Libya nationalized the local assets of British Petroleum in 1971, BP advertised in more than 100 newspapers around the world advising potential purchasers that the company reserves its rights with regard to Libyan oil. Although both BP and the British government denied that they had organized a formal boycott of Libyan oil, other petroleum companies and oil-importing nations began to shun the purchase of crude oil from the expropriated properties. In 1951, when foreign oil properties were nationalized by Iran, BP and other oil companies successfully used the boycott technique to block oil sales by Iran for three years. Iran eventually invited BP back as a 40 percent interest holder in a Western consortium.

---

[21] *The Wall Street Journal,* February 28, 1972.

DIRECT INFLUENCE OVER GOVERNMENTS

A review of the countervailing power of international companies must include the possibility of influencing governmental authorities through direct action and lobbying.[22] In a political world it would be unusual if the business firm could not find some basis for exerting influence. For an international enterprise there may always be some local interest that would identify with it and be prepared to lobby accordingly. The larger the involvement, the stronger the incentive for those interests locally identifying with it. In some countries it is usual for particular interest groups to exercise influence disproportionate to the importance of their claims. It would not be too much to claim that international firms have found direct influence so effective that on many occasions they have decided not to use it simply because they know that the arrangement they would be able to make would be so inequitable in their favor that a later backlash would be very likely.

COMPETITION BETWEEN COUNTRIES

The encouragement of competition between different countries is also an option open to the international firm if the nature of its business permits a number of alternative locations. Auction markets for internationally traded commodities ensure this competition, for example. For the international investor, it is just as feasible to move from requesting permission to carry on business in a particular country to a solicitation of what amounts to bids from competing countries. In some cases, the weakest countries will be adding taxation holidays, dividend-remittance guarantees, and many other incentives in order to attract investment away from countries in which location is initially more attractive to the international investor.

Whenever a business has something of value that can be offered to several nations, the power to control can be eroded by competition between countries. And the limits on the exercise of this power are set by the weakest of the nations concerned. No other nation can impose on a firm a higher cost in terms of controls unless that cost is offset in some other way by higher profitability.

SUMMARY

This chapter has shown that indeed the international enterprise is not without protection against the nation-state. In fact, its countervail-

---

[22]See Jack N. Behrman, J. J. Boddewyn, and Ashok Kapoor, *International Business-Government Communications* (Lexington, Mass.: D.C. Heath & Co., 1975), chap. 4.

ing power is much greater than the picture of sovereign nations and their control programs and policies would indicate.

EXERCISES AND DISCUSSION QUESTIONS

1. "The management of a multinational firm should in no way take it upon itself to decide what different contributions the firm will make to the various societies in which it operates. Within the external pressures and constraints surrounding the firm, management's first task is to ensure the firm's survival, and beyond that to pursue the balanced interests of its owners, employees, and customers." If you do not agree with this statement, what guidelines would you give to the management of multinational firms?

2. Discuss the following proposals: The chief executive of a multinational corporation *should not:*

   a. Accept any politically motivated direction from the government of the corporation's home country that would limit the performance of a foreign subsidiary.

   b. Seek partnership with a foreign government in order to gain privilege or protection for its operations.

   c. Use power stemming from its domestic operation to lobby the home government to intercede on the firm's behalf with foreign governments under whose jurisdiction the firm's subsidiaries operate.

   d. Select expatriates for the top management of foreign subsidiaries because they can be trusted to place the firm's interests ahead of the local environment.

3. "In order to protect their traditional international business operations some multinational firms monopolize distribution channels and effectively deny small producers in developing countries reasonable access to international markets. Such action is against the principles underlying U.S. commercial law and should not be permitted under U.S. law simply because those harmed fall outside its jurisdiction." Comment on this statement. Can you identify any firms to which you think this statement might apply?

4. It has been argued that one way a multinational firm should use its strength is to ensure that countries know they are really in direct competition for its new investment. If you agree, how would you suggest the firm go about ensuring this awareness and what risks do you see?

5. What are the distinguishing characteristics of product areas that will in general have low vulnerability to government controls in less developed countries and what reasons do you have for your expectations?

13

National Control Forecasting

NATION-STATES are generally in an early stage of formulating national policies toward international business operations—in large part because of the newness of the phenomenon. But the situation is highly dynamic because international business activity has grown at a rapid rate, both absolutely and in relation to the total size of national economies. The actions of home-base countries and host countries can modify investment returns and the attractiveness of global opportunities being considered by the multinational firm. Thus, international enterprises are finding it increasingly justified to devote major attention to a careful prediction of the controls to which their activities will become subject within different countries.

To make predictions of the changing pattern of controls requires an underlying theory. Classification of countries as more or less risky solely on the basis of a general review of their individual situation is not adequate. Without a sound underlying theory, predictions are almost certain to be excessively influenced by immediate past conditions. Important determinants of change may be given inadequate weight, and predictions are likely to be inconsistent between countries. Many businessmen, for example, relate the risk of controls to the economic and political stability of a country and completely ignore signs pointing to additional major controls from such stable countries as Canada or Australia.

The different classes of controls that governments have used were described in Chapters 10 and 11. This chapter presents one attempt to develop a predictive theory of controls. Working from objectives and decision rules of representative firms and countries, predictions are made of the overall pattern of controls over international business and of control strategies for countries in similar strategic positions with respect to international business. Readers should regard this as only one example of possible theories and use it as a datum against which to test and refine their own theories. The field of control prediction is not yet well developed, but that does not mean that the international businessman can ignore the need to base his decisions on some prediction of how controls will affect the various alternatives open to him.

INTERNATIONAL BUSINESS AS A GAME

The imposition of controls over international business can be depicted as a vast international game. There are players, moves, strategies, and payoffs. The players are firms and countries. The moves are changes in location of business investment and location of operations on the side of firms, while countries may change the nature and level of controls. The moves of the players interact to determine the payoff to each. For purposes of this theory the players are depicted as representative firms and representative countries acting to achieve payoffs of return on investment for firms and national benefits for countries.

Although multinational firms in the real world aim for return to the firm rather than return to the economies in which they operate, neither firms nor countries are motivated solely by rational economic calculation. The limitations to rationality in firms have been shown clearly in many studies.[1] Few people would attempt to argue that countries act rationally. Pressure groups, coalitions, selective perception, and a range of other behavioral phenomena better explain particular decisions. Real-world objectives, however, would produce descriptions so complicated that any simple prediction would be impossible. Nor is it necessary for a theory to be based on completely realistic assumptions. Assumptions need only be sufficiently good approximations of reality for the purpose in hand in order to yield sufficiently accurate predictions. A useful theory should be simple and efficient, explaining a lot with a little.[2] The success of simplifications must then be judged by the success of the predictions and not by the theory's correspondence with reality.

---

[1]Yair Aharoni, *The Foreign Investment Decision Process* (Boston, Mass.: Division of Research, Harvard Graduate School of Business Administration, 1966); Richard M. Cyert and James G. March. *A Behavioral Theory of the Firm* (Englewood Cliffs, N.J.: Prentice-Hall, 1963).

[2]Milton J. Friedman, *Essays in Positive Economics* (Chicago: University of Chicago Press, 1953), pt. I.

An assumption of rationality seems to provide an efficient basis for predictions when applied to an aggregation of countries and firms over time. It can predict an unfolding pattern of controls over international business very similar to what has actually been emerging, as evidenced with footnotes throughout the chapter. For any individual firm, however, the investment pattern may not approximate a profit-maximizing one, and for any individual country, the pressures influencing its policies at any point in time may produce controls quite contrary to the maximization of national benefits.

The international business game proposed here is a non-zero-sum game. Rewards to any one of the players do not necessarily reduce total rewards to the opposing players by the same amount. But there is definite conflict between the objectives of the different players. A control that increases the benefits to one country will usually reduce the payoff to firms in some way. The same control may also decrease the benefits to some other country. For example, the main effect might be to switch the firm's productive activity from one country to another, with a secondary effect of decreasing the firm's profits. The players are thus not arranged simply with countries on one side and firms on the other. Countries also compete with countries, and firms compete with firms. It is the competition among countries for shares of a virtually independent total of business activity globally that plays the major role in determining the pattern of controls. As discussed in Chapter 9, this idea moves well away from a common assumption in international business that controls may be explained from an examination of the conflict between firms and individual countries independent of other countries.[3]

The game is sequential and dynamic with continually evolving action and reaction. Players do not all disclose their hands at the same time before knowing their opponents' moves. With a large number of players competing under these conditions it is not feasible to extend the formal presentation of the game to the point of proving optimum strategies. The prediction of strategies is based instead on the following simplified sequence of play:

1. International firms locate business activity for a "practical maximization" of expected return on capital subject to allowances for the risk of potential controls.
2. Countries alter controls to maximize national benefits, bearing in mind the likely reactions of firms and ultimate reactions of other countries.

---

[3]See Charles P. Kindleberger, *American Business Abroad* (New Haven: Yale University Press, 1969), p. 150ff.; Raymond Vernon, "Conflict and Resolution Between Foreign Direct Investors and Less Developed Countries," *Public Policy,* Fall 1968, pp. 333–51.

3. Firms realign existing operations and redirect new investment in the light of the changed controls.
4. Other countries feel indirect effects of the changed controls and move to alter their own controls.

The prime focus of this chapter is the prediction of step 2 in the sequence—the strategies of countries. Step 4, of course, will be covered by the same prediction. This prediction is itself made against the backdrop prediction of where firms locate their activity with an existing set of controls and how they react to changes in controls. Firms' objectives are therefore the starting point for the analysis.

OBJECTIVES AND DECISION RULES OF THE REPRESENTATIVE FIRM

The representative international firm is defined as motivated toward a "practical maximization" of the present value of expected net cash flows from its activities. While it would be theoretically possible for the representative firm to calculate for any point in time the location of further investment and the relocation of production activity that would maximize the present value of future profits, the practical difficulties in making such a calculation are legion. Not the least would be the impossibility of collecting adequate data on costs and demand to choose between a large number of alternatives. Instead of representing the decision process of the representative firm by the impracticable programming calculation that would be needed, it is replaced by a 12-step approximation to maximization. This is summarized in Figure 13–1. Many of the steps incorporated in this decision process coincide with what is widely regarded as good practice in international business decision making. Only the salient points are outlined at this stage, however, as the individual steps will be examined in more detail in Chapter 18, which covers the building of a global strategy.

The horizon year is the target year that the firm chooses as the basis for setting sales targets and building an optimum location of production activity to meet those targets. A four- or five-year horizon is common in the real world.[4] An earlier horizon may produce a pattern of investment location that is far from optimum for the subsequent pattern of market demand, whereas a later horizon may produce a pattern in which the profits are well below what they might be for some time.

The dominant role of marketing in the modern firm is emphasized

[4]George A. Steiner and Warren M. Cannon, *Multinational Corporate Planning* (New York: Macmillan Co., 1966), pp. 85, 97, 107.

FIGURE 13-1
The Representative Firm's Decision Process for Practical Maximization

1. Select a horizon year.
2. Predict country demands for products supplied by firm, annually up to the horizon year.
3. Decide marketing emphasis to be placed on each country, for example, full development, distributorship, agency.
4. Set annual target sales for each country to horizon year.
5. List countries where operations *must* be located to meet targets in horizon year.
6. List countries where operation in horizon year is not required but probably economic.
7. Estimate costs of investment and operation for the set of alternative sites, and the transport and tariff costs from these into alternative markets.
8. Calculate an optimum location and logistics pattern for horizon year.
9. Prepare schedules of annual additions to investment that meet the annual targets and the horizon patterns.
10. Calculate the expected cash flow and return on proposed investments.
11. Calculate limits to available investment.
12. Align investment plans and sales targets.

by the next three steps. Market potential is taken as the basis for allocating the firm's effort.[5] From a prediction of country demands the representative firm decides the marketing emphasis to be placed on each country and sets annual sales targets to the horizon year. These decisions will usually be based on broad indicators of the profit potential from supplying a market and the competitive vulnerability from not doing so.

With market targets established, the next stage is the calculation of the investment in additional capacity required to meet the targets. There will be some countries where controls make it imperative to locate production if the targets for their markets are to be met. A set of alternative production investments to meet the remaining capacity needed for the total horizon target can then be generated. These alternatives will again be based on broad indicators of what are likely to be the most economic sites; for example, low resource cost, low outward transport, and low entry barriers to other markets. From these,

---

[5]Judd Polk, Irene W. Meister, and Lawrence A. Veit, *U.S. Production Abroad and the Balance of Payments* (New York: National Industrial Conference Board, 1966), pp. 59–61.

the alternative with the lowest cost of meeting the sales targets in the horizon year is calculated.[6]

This horizon investment alternative is next translated into annual investment schedules over the intervening years. A practical decision rule would be to invest each year in those additions needed to achieve the horizon objective that would give the lowest cost of meeting the next year's targets. The procedure next moves to return-on-investment calculation. For each proposed addition the calculation would be based on the incremental net cash flow accruing from it, estimated as far into the future as practicable and reduced by the expected effects of controls and other risks. Any limit the firm's resources may place on investment is now calculated and projects accepted in decreasing order of return on capital, so long as the return is above the return from other alternatives open to the firm. Finally, if the investment limit is operative, the whole process will be repeated with lowered sales targets. If there is surplus investment capacity then sales targets will have to be raised.

FIRM'S INITIAL STRATEGIES

What is the likely pattern to emerge from the strategies of representative international firms? The starting point for the prediction is the schedule of the firm's market targets. For many products it is the markets of the developed countries in which the demand will build up first. Higher levels of disposable income generally lead to faster adoption of new consumer goods and higher wage rates lead to faster adoption of labor-saving industrial goods.[7] The firms that supply these more advanced markets gain the advantage of the earliest experience and hence a higher position on the learning curve and also the earliest economies of scale.[8] It follows then that a rational global strategy would be to move into these markets early and from these to successively less attractive markets for the products in which the firm has established a lead.

Using this schedule of market targets, the representative firm will locate production through the process already described. For new products this is likely to mean location of as much production as possible close to the more advanced markets where the managers of the international enterprise are already located. At this stage, speedy

---

[6]Robert E. McGarrah, "Logistics for the International Manufacturer," *Harvard Business Review,* March–April 1966.

[7]Raymond Vernon, "International Investment and International Trade in the Product Cycle," *Quarterly Journal of Economics,* May 1966, pp. 190–207.

[8]Louis T. Wells, "A Product Life Cycle for International Trade," *Journal of Marketing,* July 1968, pp. 1–16.

adjustment of the marketing mix carries greater weight for profits than siting for minimum production cost.[9] But as the product matures, design tends to become less flexible and production costs more important. In step with this, the demand in other markets will grow to justify production on an economic scale and transport and tariff costs add a further incentive to relocate production away from the initial base. Production will then tend to move to the lowest cost sites taking into account the cost of transport, tariffs, and other controls—actual and expected. This trend, though, will be conditioned by the sequence in which markets develop. Established plants, because they represent sunk costs, may be retained when later market expansion might suggest relocation at otherwise lower cost sites.

Relocation may also be hindered by internal management rules of the firm. Exports to other countries are frequently discouraged or prohibited for subsidiaries as a matter of policy.[10] It is not difficult to show that a profit-maximizing production and distribution pattern for an international corporation as a whole would not allow free competition between units of the same firm. Subsidiaries developing in the same field as a strong international parent can be confronted with an established network of foreign activity by the parent and its other subsidiaries in what could otherwise be potential export markets for an independent firm.

There are exceptions, of course, to the general pattern suggested by the "product cycle" approach. One exception relates to investments in raw materials extraction and certain stages of raw materials processing which can only be located economically near the source of raw materials. Other exceptions occur when new products are developed to meet culturally conditioned demands specific to one market.

The firm's organizational evolution as it expands internationally will influence the location of top management functions. A likely pattern is a "hen-and-chickens" approach with a large home base in a developed market on which strategic decisions are centralized, while subsidiaries are established elsewhere and local management is expected to introduce products and experience from the parent rather than initiate new areas of activity.[11] Such a pattern can foster a caretaker type of subsidiary management not required to use great

---

[9]Vernon, "International Investment and International Trade in the Product Cycle," p. 193.

[10]Donald T. Brash, *American Investment in Australian Industry* (Canberra: Australian National University Press, 1966), p. 228; A. E. Safarian, *Foreign Ownership of Canadian Industry* (Toronto: McGraw-Hill Book Co., 1966), p. 133.

[11]Gilbert H. Clee and Alfred di Scipio, "Creating a World Enterprise," *Harvard Business Review,* November–December 1959.

entrepreneurial skill in forming and shaping the firm.[12] Promotion to headquarters would be needed to exercise such skill, and this would further remove expertise from the country in which the subsidiary is located.

Following the same sequence of development, a rational business strategy with regard to research and development would be to concentrate on producing innovations first for the markets of developed countries. The worldwide expansion of the international corporation would provide a bigger market against which to justify expenditure and reinforce research activity in the developed countries with little incentive to duplicate research facilities elsewhere.[13] The establishment of research facilities in many less developed countries would be limited—perhaps only adaptation centers. This would mean little support and feedback from industry for universities and advanced research institutions in such countries and fewer opportunities locally for top graduates—all of which would reinforce a brain drain.[14]

It also follows from the profit objectives of representative firms that they will arrange their investment so that it is protected against a future control when the cost of protection is less than the resulting reduction in the expected cost of the control. The expected cost of a control is the loss of profits that would result from its imposition, multiplied by the probability that the control will be imposed. In the real world, firms may seek local associates or raise debt finance. There is an incentive to those providing local finance or productive services to act as a buffer against local pressures for increases in controls. The retention of marketing, management, or research expertise in the hands of expatriates can also limit the risk of expropriation.[15]

Where the international firm supplies market demand in one country with raw materials or products produced in another country, reduction of risk may take the additional form of developing alternative sources of supply. Alternative sources would lower the level of controls of maximum benefit to the current supplier country because of the increased likelihood of business being transferred to other sources.

---

[12]Kenneth Simmonds, "Multinational? Well, Not Quite," *Columbia Journal of World Business,* Fall 1966.

[13]Brash, *American Investment in Australian Industry,* p. 150; Safarian, *Foreign Ownership of Canadian Industry,* p. 174.

[14]Committee on Government Operations, House of Representatives, *The Brain Drain into the United States of Scientists, Engineers, and Physicians* (Washington, D.C.: U.S. Government Printing Office, July 1967).

[15]Richard D. Robinson, "Conflicting Interest in International Business," *Business Review,* Boston University, Spring 1960, pp. 3–13.

International corporations in the oil, mineral, rubber, and produce fields have resorted to such strategies in the past.[16]

FIRM'S REACTIONS TO CHANGES IN CONTROLS

A change in any control may alter the optimum location pattern for a firm's existing operations and possibly the ranking of alternatives on its investment schedule. For every control change that increases profitability of local production in a particular country, there are likely to be some representative firms for which the change leads to an investment being made in that country that would otherwise fall outside their investment limits. Conversely, a change in controls that reduces profitability is likely to shift some existing operations to other countries and lower some alternatives on investment schedules so that they no longer fall within the investment limits. As a general rule, then, at the margin, foreign business activity and investment will be discouraged when controls that decrease profitability are extended and encouraged when such controls are reduced.

But this is not the full story. There are classes of controls with other effects. Tariffs and local component requirements, for example, discriminate among the production sites open to a firm for supplying a market. Their imposition will usually increase the cost of supplying a market from outside sources and, even though the cost of local production is also likely to be increased, lead to the transfer of more production activity into the local market. Another class of controls places restrictions on the transferability of resources. This class includes capital controls, inward or outward pricing rules, royalty, and dividend-remittance restraints. These may also reduce the firm's after-tax profitability, which would discourage investment, yet the desire to make use of locally retained resources may induce more firms to expand local production.

OBJECTIVES AND DECISION RULES OF
REPRESENTATIVE COUNTRIES

We now turn to the objectives of countries. A representative country for this theory is motivated toward maximization of net national benefits. And national benefits embrace all those tangible and intangible objectives, already discussed in Chapter 9, which countries consider as a basis for governmental action, such as contribution to devel-

---

[16]For example, see S. May and G. Plaza, "The United Fruit Company in Latin America" (Washington, D.C.: National Planning Association, 1959).

opment, expanded foreign exchange earnings, monetary stability, defense, economic independence, and national prestige. To specify a national benefit function in full, together with measures for the achievement of each objective, would require a study of its own. For the purposes of this chapter, however, the general notion of national benefit is sufficient. Others have introduced similar omnibus concepts in referring to maximization of "net social benefits,"[17] "a social-welfare function,"[18] or adjusted "social yields."[19] In Chapter 9 it was explained that costs to the country must be balanced against the gains to calculate net benefits. Moreover, only the incremental benefits over domestic or international alternatives open to the country should be included. It is also assumed here that controls are independent and their individual benefits additive. Country control strategies can then be expressed in terms of a collection of separate controls.

The representative country acting rationally to maximize national benefit will set each individual control at its *control optimum,* which is defined as the level at which the control brings maximum net national benefit. The national benefit from adjustment of any control is the incremental benefit accruing as a result of the adjustment. An increased control, for example, may increase the national benefit from investment and business activity that remains in the country as well as from activity that comes on the new terms. But there may be an opportunity loss of the benefit from lost investment and business activity that would otherwise have come or remained. If a control is increased beyond its control optimum the loss of national benefit from discouraged international investment or business activity outweighs the gain from imposing the control.

Implicit in this definition of the control optimum for any control is an allowance for reactions by other countries, and reaction may be expected when alteration in controls will alter the control optimum of another country. The greater and the more immediate the effects on another country's business activity, the more likely the other country is to take matching action. For example, with a fixed supply of international business investment, the lowering of controls by a less developed nation might siphon off a large proportion of the investment that another marginal recipient of such investment would have received. This second country might then move very quickly to offer the same or greater incentives. In many cases, however, countries will be unable to

---

[17]John H. Dunning, "The Multinational Enterprise," *Lloyd's Bank Review,* July 1970, p. 29.

[18]Kindleberger, *American Business Abroad,* p. 192.

[19]Vernon, "Conflict and Resolution Between Foreign Direct Investors and Less Developed Countries," p. 334.

predict what reactions their actions will produce from individual competitor countries. There are too many countries, too many investors, and too many controls for individual effects to be assessed very accurately. The reaction of many other countries to change by one country is, moreover, likely to be a gradual process over time and best predicted as a decay in the benefit gained from a control as a function of time. Where it is clearly apparent that competition among countries can weaken each country's bargaining position and the number of such competing countries is relatively small, as in the case of the oil-producing countries, a possible strategy is to form a cartel and bargain as a group. This possibility, however, is limited to countries in an oligopoly situation as suppliers of raw materials.

GENERAL FEATURES OF COUNTRY STRATEGIES

The theory has now reached a stage where it is possible to derive some general features of country control strategies from the juxtaposition of country objectives and decision rules against the prediction of strategies for representative firms.

Controls for which the control optima are likely to be high are those for which a given gain in national benefit would come with the smallest reduction in expected profits of investors or, what amounts to the same thing, where a given reduction in expected profits would be accompanied by large increments in national benefit. This may occur when a control:

1. Results in a contribution to the country that is crucial to continued development.
2. Was anticipated by firms and its imposition does not therefore alter the expected cash flow to firms or its position on the firms' investment schedules.
3. Takes effect a considerable time in the future.
4. Is not reflected in return-on-investment calculations.
5. Restricts access to the local market to gain power over location of production.

An example of a control that might produce a major contribution to development with a small cost to firms is the requirement to use local nationals in the management of local activity. While it may impose some immediate costs, it can bring offsetting benefits.[20] A local top executive reduces the foreign image, cuts the cost of expatriate staff, introduces someone attuned to the local culture and influence network,

---

[20]John C. Shearer, *High-Level Manpower in Overseas Subsidiaries* (Princeton, N.J.: Industrial Relations Section, Princeton University, 1960), chap. 3.

and adds a local ally. For the country, the move contributes to the pool of trained management, which is essential for continuing development.[21]

The controls anticipated by firms will depend very much on the firm's forecasting assumptions and on the messages countries have themselves relayed about future controls or the implications of their ideology. Cash flows will be heavily discounted for opportunities in countries with an image of opposition to capitalist ownership if it seems likely to lead to costly controls or expropriation.[22] The situation can be created where there is nothing to be lost from increased controls because they have already been discounted.

The further in the future that increases in controls begin to take effect, the less the current discouragement. The effect is discounted by the rates used in the investment calculations of the investing firms. Any control affecting an investor's cash flow after the first 10 years is likely to carry little weight in the investment decision, because its discounted cost would be infinitesimal given the discounting rates commonly used for assessing international opportunities. A country that guaranteed income for the first 10 years, but required a renewal of license after that time, might actually increase its attraction to investors.

Regulations that do not affect cash-flow calculations and do not show up in return-on-capital calculations are also potentially very significant. The right to expand into further areas of business within a country, for example, is unlikely to be highly weighted in a return-on-investment calculation for any investment that by itself is worth undertaking. Yet by removing this right, a country can retain opportunities for national firms, and it can protect itself against the international corporation expanding without bargaining separately for further access to the market. Controls that limit the share of foreign ownership also reduce foreign participation in a country's markets without reducing the return on investment to investing firms. If such controls are coupled with restricted access to local loan capital, then the investment inflow to the country may be unaffected yet obtained on reduced ownership terms. Finally, controls on transferring funds out of a country are also likely to create minimal discouragement to further

---

[21]Peter P. Gabriel, *The International Transfer of Corporate Skills* (Boston: Graduate School of Business Administration, Harvard University, 1967); Harry G. Johnson, "The Multinational Corporation as a Development Agent," *Columbia Journal of World Business,* May–June 1970, pp. 25–30; Frederick Harbison and Charles A. Myers, *Industrialism and Industrial Man: The Problems of Labor and Management in Industrial Growth* (Cambridge, Mass.; Harvard University Press, 1960).

[22]National Industrial Conference Board, *Obstacles and Incentives to Private Foreign Investment 1967–1968,* pp. 9–10.

initial investments if return on investment remains high and there are opportunities for profitable reinvestment locally.

Controls that restrict access to the local market to gain power over the location of production are also likely to have high control optima. Production for the home markets of many countries will not be located locally in the absence of controls, and production that has been located locally will tend for some to move to lower cost locations. Controls such as tariffs, import licensing, or local component requirements that would change firms' location decisions are thus likely to bring high national benefits, particularly for countries with large, advanced markets. While many economic studies have investigated the conditions under which reaction by other countries will eliminate any gains, the imperfections of the multilateral international business game are likely to mean that for individual countries the national benefits are not always eliminated.[23] And on the firms' side of the game it may well be that investment required to supply the market from within the restricted areas remains profitable, further supporting the argument that the optimum level for these controls will be high for some countries.

Some statements can also be made about the sort of controls with low optimum control levels. First, anything than threatens assets is likely to produce much greater reaction than other equally effective controls aimed at operations. To those identified with a firm's performance, the removal of the right to capital which is clearly recorded in the firm's books is more drastic than an equivalent reduction in potential earning capacity.[24] The crude concept of expropriation gives way then to more refined actions to restrict the profits taken from the market, for example, compulsory selling through a government marketing organization.

Nor will controls be common that can be avoided through an international firm's foreign ramifications. Attempts by the United States to prevent foreign subsidiaries of U.S. firms from trading with the communist bloc were not very successful. Countries have also been generally unsuccessful at enforcing retention of export markets when a local production base has been taken over by the subsidiary of an international corporation. French attempts to prevent the expansion of U.S. ownership in some industries have similarly been thwarted by the ease with which the same firms can locate in other EEC countries and then export to France.

---

[23]Harry G. Johnson, "Optimum Tariffs and Retaliation," *Review of Economic Studies* 21, no. 55 (1953–54): 142–53.

[24]National Industrial Conference Board, *Obstacles and Incentives to Private Foreign Investment 1967–1968*, p. 9: "An act of expropriation lingers long in the minds of potential foreign investors, swaying investment decisions for many years after the event."

COUNTRY STRATEGIES OVER TIME

It can be argued that optimum control levels, and hence controls, will rise with the level of development of a country relative to other countries. This happens because the national benefit from business operations or investment lost as a result of increased controls is likely to be lower and because the growth of the country's market is likely to raise the country's position on firms' investment schedules. The reduction in potential national benefit occurs for two main reasons. First, with development there will be lower incremental benefits from additional international business because the country can do more from its own resources. Its local alternatives will have increased because it will be better able to provide skills in management, production or technology, and necessary capital. Second, rising incomes and wage rates will make other countries with lower labor costs increasingly attractive for some types of manufacturing, and controls will not so much discourage new investment and activity as they will prevent investment and business activity from leaving. As a corollary, then, the more advanced a country's market is relative to other countries, the more likely that certain important types of production will move elsewhere and the more it will pay to use controls to retain production locally. Exceptions will occur, though, where the increasing demand brings economies of scale from local production that outweigh the cost advantages of other locations when transport costs are included.

For any given set of conditions for supply from outside, a country's bargaining power in setting the conditions on which it is supplied increases with the size of its local demand. One reason is that with bigger volume it is less costly to produce locally. Ultimately, control of the market demand dominates ownership of resources—because value of resources stems from their use in the market. Suppose the country with a market increases controls over business to the extent that at the previous cost of supplying the market it becomes no longer economic to supply. Yet suppose in addition the previous cost included the cost of controls, say, local taxation, imposed by the resource-owning countries. Then these latter controls could be forced down, particularly if resource-owning countries competed among themselves.

With optimum control levels changing over time, besides the fact that they are difficult to identify without information about firms' other investment opportunities, countries will be reduced to experimentation and adjustment as results are fed back. Over time, countries' control strategies should come nearer to their control optima—by definition, their best strategies.

There may come a time for some countries when the strategies of international firms would lead to extraction of earnings and little further investment. Markets important to an expansion strategy at one point can become saturated and no longer included on investment schedules. In such situations, control optima could become infinite and economically justify controls up to and including expropriation. But this would be a special case for a country with very little growth.

This process of adjustment over time raises the question as to whether initial strategies will undervalue or overvalue the optimum control levels. One likely hypothesis is that the greater the gap between a given country and the most advanced country, the higher are its unfilled aspirations and the greater is the likelihood it will increase controls beyond the control optima.[25] Since national benefits from additional business investment are high for relatively backward countries, there will be a tendency to add controls to achieve the maximum from international firms—only to produce the opposite effect. Conversely, more highly developed countries are likely to underestimate their control optima in the absence of a major lag in their development, particularly when their own international firms dominate the market.

It seems generally clear that the stronger hand in the international business game lies with the more developed country. The weaker a country's attraction to firms, the less it will find it worthwhile to impose controls to increase national benefits. While countries' strategic positions with respect to international business will vary markedly with such factors as population, business capabilities, agreements with other countries, ownership of international business, and level of gross national product, the strategies of countries in similar positions under these headings should have major similarities. Drawing on the elements of our outline theory, the strategies of five broad classes of country are projected in sketch form in the remainder of this chapter. They are (1) less developed countries, (2) smaller, more advanced countries, (3) countries with their own foreign investment as well as foreign-owned local activity, (4) minority partner countries, and (5) centrally controlled countries.

Less Developed Countries

This grouping covers the great number of countries for which foreign investment is deemed to be of outstanding national benefit because of the contribution it can make to further development.[26] Foreign investment contributes to development by providing capital

---

[25]Ragnar Nurske, *Problems of Capital Formation in Underdeveloped Countries* (Oxford: Basil Blackwell, 1953), p. 61; Hadley Cantril, "A Study of Aspirations," *Scientific American,* February 1963, pp. 41–45.

[26]See *Multinational Corporations in World Development* (New York: United Nations, Department of Economic and Social Affairs, 1973).

and know-how to mobilize local resources that would otherwise not be mobilized—or, at least releases foreign exchange available to a country to do the same thing. Foreign investment that develops production for the local market contributes to the circular flow of demand and supply and also saves foreign exchange through import substitution. Foreign investment that provides local production or resource extraction to meet foreign market demands adds to export revenue.

Not only are the national benefits and hence the opportunity cost of foreign investment high for these countries, but elasticity of investment in response to controls is likely to be high. Except for investments in extractive resources, there will be many other countries almost as attractive to international investors and ready to replace those countries in which profitability is impaired in any way.

Countries in this situation are likely to avoid high controls because there will always be some other country not invoking equivalent restriction which would gain the investment. A good initial strategy for the least developed countries would be to present an environment as attractive as possible to international business with no hints of national animosity. On the other hand, nationalistic pressures against foreign ownership will frequently build up to produce controls in excess of these very low control levels. When this happens, the inflow of investment will slacken, and if the controls are high enough, or the nationalistic pressures seem likely to produce such controls, the inflow may dry up altogether. Interests from within the country that realize that investment is being forgone are then likely to begin advocating policies that will bring the country back toward its control optima, pointing out the national benefits from doing so.

Indonesia, India, and the Andean Pact countries are examples of countries that exceeded their control optima in this way. In Indonesia's case, an increasing antipathy toward foreign business under the Sukarno regime discouraged investment, and confiscation of properties completed the process. This extract comes from a statement by the government of Indonesia made at the time.

> At present, foreign investment in the traditional classic form is not acceptable. Indonesia does not deem it compatible with its economic philosophy if foreigners establish enterprise in Indonesia, owned and run by them, and then claim the right to transfer profits for an indefinite period and insist as well on the transfer of depreciation and salaries.[27]

The inevitable result was a complete cessation of foreign investment. The new regime after 1966, however, reversed the policies, handed back expropriated property, and took active steps to encourage

---

[27]National Industrial Conference Board, *Obstacles and Incentives to Private Foreign Investment, 1962–1964,* Studies in Business Policy, no. 115 (New York, 1965), p. 83.

foreign investment. The reversal seems to have brought Indonesia back below its optimum control levels, as illustrated by the growing investment figures and this statement from a U.S. company three years later:

> Events in Indonesia make it necessary to revise our 1964 remarks to the point where they are nearly reversed. Indonesia has done a great deal in the intervening years to restore confidence in Indonesia both as a market and as a place to invest. The Indonesian Government seems to be making genuine efforts towards curtailing rapid inflation, stabilizing their currency, and (by means of worthwhile incentives) making Indonesia generally a market worthy of investigation. We plan a detailed survey of that market with the ultimate aim of manufacturing there in the reasonably near future.[28]

Statements by firms also indicate that controls eliminated much activity that would otherwise locate in India, leaving it with a negligible share of private foreign investment.[29] Unlike Indonesia the relaxation of controls in recent years has been minor, for example, some relaxation of local component requirements and loosening of import controls over materials. Given its great need for foreign exchange to spur its development, India has almost certainly retained many controls above the control optima.

The gradual raising of control optima as a country develops and an accompanying policy of creeping controls have already been mentioned. The more developed a country, the more likely it is to avoid drastically exceeding its control optima. In striking contrast to the experience of Indonesia and India and its own expropriations of past eras has been Mexico's ability to increase controls and yet successfully maintain capital inflow. Rapid and sustained growth, political and monetary stability, greater infrastructure to support local production activity, and less open hostility to foreign investment have all contributed to higher sanction limits. Moreover, the high controls on foreign ownership, foreign personnel, and local content which Mexico imposed may have discouraged less investment than would controls over capital and profit repatriation, which have been largely avoided.

There may be exceptions to the general pattern of strategy predicted here when foreign capital is not a major limiting factor to development. In Libya, for example, high petroleum revenues and an abundance of foreign exchange altered the strategy to one of resource conservation.

[28]National Industrial Conference Board, *Obstacles and Incentives to Private Foreign Investment, 1969,* p. 76.

[29]Ibid., pp. 66–73; and Commission on Transnational Corporations, UN Economic and Social Council, *National Legislation and Regulations Relating to Transnational Corporations* (New York: United Nations, 1976).

Smaller, More Advanced Countries

Quite different strategies can be predicted for the smaller, more developed countries which have not developed much international activity of their own. Countries in this group include Australia, New Zealand, South Africa, Finland, Austria, and Norway. These countries have sustained reasonable growth and can normally expect to have a fairly high ranking as market targets for international firms, with their small size offset by high incomes and high purchase rates. They also tend to have policies of encouraging local industry through tariffs and subsidies and, in addition to their ranking as market targets, appear well up on international firms' investment schedules.

It is unusual, on the other hand, for these markets to attract investment that will engage in worldwide exporting, or support much development of new products. With high income levels these are not low labor-cost locations, and the scale of local production is generally limited. International business, therefore, is likely to develop only subsidiary activities in these countries aimed solely at the local market. It is also likely that as one international competitor makes a move into one of these markets it will be matched by others also feeling that the market is ready for increased attention and not wishing a competitor to gain an advantage. For a particular industry the result may well be a collection of small subsidiaries with none undertaking much international business. From the viewpoint of international businesses these countries become permanent subsidiary countries.

Another effect of this pattern of expansion by international firms is for existing local firms to be circumscribed by international competitors either with a cost advantage or with newer products or techniques. Firms operating on a global scale with a larger sales base can afford more rapid product innovation and support a wider range of development. This extends to service industries as well as manufacturers. Banks, stockbrokers, equipment lessors, insurance firms, and business consultants, for example, have all been following the international expansion of their customers into this group of countries. They bring little capital with them, yet operate with a competitive advantage because they have developed to serve the international corporation. Moreover, with an international network behind them they facilitate centralized management from New York or London, reinforcing the advantages a multinational firm may have over local firms.

Countries in this grouping, then, have a high attraction for international firms but also strong reasons for controlling international operations. Yet until recently they had few protective controls against international business, and little international business of their own against which others might retaliate if controls were extended. These conditions produced high control optima relative to the controls of the 1960s. While some of the potential has been realized through increased controls, realization that they can play the international business game to still greater advantage may be expected of these countries. Turning this around to the viewpoint of international business, the expected cost of controls may be much higher for these countries than for more aggressively nationalistic underdeveloped countries.

The strategy likely to emerge is one of increasing selectivity for further foreign investment that uses home markets as a lever to extend the international activity centered on these countries. Permission for entry will become harder to obtain where the investment might threaten local firms who are not so much inefficient as behind in global market percentage. For international units that are permitted, efforts will be directed at increasing their local autonomy and their incentive to export. Controls likely to emerge will be limitation of foreign ownership percentages, pressure to offer equity on local stock markets, and official approvals that favor foreign-debt capital over equity capital.

A range of new control combinations can also be expected. These countries just beginning to realize the potential in controls have the capability to design and to administer quite sophisticated strategies. For example, it might be fruitful to couple tariff protection with a selection policy for incoming investment that gave preference to investment that would develop exports. Differentiation between investment according to the country ultimately controlling the activity might also be attempted. This would dilute the influence of any one country. Furthermore, investment from smaller investing countries can bring with it a greater possibility of expansion from the local base to supply leading markets not covered by the parent organization. With such policies, for example, Australia might have developed a strong research and even export center in the chemical field. As it is, the Australian market is sliced between half a dozen or more subsidiaries of established giants in the chemical field.

These countries are also likely to develop a range of positive encouragements to expand outwards across their borders, for both their own firms and local international subsidiaries, as the awareness grows of what is necessary to avoid permanent subsidiary status. The external growth of any local unit will become strongly identified with national benefit. In the long run, these efforts should produce international operations of a significant size and this very success should begin to modify control strategies in a way similar to that for countries already having substantial international businesses, which make our next grouping.

Countries with Their Own Foreign Investment as well as
Foreign-Owned Local Activity

For countries with significant foreign investment of their own, either direct or portfolio, their dual capacity as investor as well as recipient of foreign investment will influence their decisions concerning controls. The perception of national benefits by such countries as the United States, United Kingdom, Germany, France, Canada, and Switzerland is likely to embrace benefits from foreign investments by firms with their home base in the country as well as those from foreign investments of firms based in other countries. To the extent that this is so, investor countries will avoid controls on inbound investment for which the national benefits might be offset by further controls over their own foreign investments—imposed in direct retaliation or because their own action provides an example for other countries of what can be achieved. The potential cost of retaliation can be very high if other countries were prepared to escalate their response, and even a small amount of investment in another country will give that country scope for escalation.[30]

To avoid specific retaliation, then, controls in this grouping of countries are more likely to be proposed as positive encouragement of desired characteristics and of local ownership than as negative restrictions on foreign ownership. Canada, for example, has a reduced taxation rate for companies with at least 25 percent local ownership and in the 1960s, published a set of 12 guiding principles for foreign companies, designed to minimize the disbenefits of foreign control. There is also likely to be more informal administration of controls than formal published regulation. Foreign-owned operations are required to obtain permission before they can be set up in France, although published rules that discriminate against foreign investment have been generally avoided.

A natural extension of these elements of strategy is the development of positive steps to strengthen a country's own international business operations. Simply to protect the home market for local producers is inadequate when the local market base is too small to provide research, production, and management economies to match the largest international operations. And if indigenous international corporations of the

[30]"Insofar as multinational companies played a part in the formulation of taxation policy, the Treasury's objective was to encourage inward investment and prevent the most blatant forms of tax evasion, without taking stern measures which might provoke retaliation against the overseas subsidiaries of British companies," Michael Hodges, *Multinational Corporations and National Government* (Westmead, Farnborough, England: Saxon House–D.C. Heath Ltd., 1974), p. 97.

strength needed fail to emerge on their own, governments will increasingly give them a hand through forced merger, government aid, and protected home markets. The idea is not new. The United Kingdom successfully created the Imperial Tobacco Company in 1902 to oppose the American Tobacco Company and between the wars created ICI to meet German and U.S. competition. Methods of using attack as a means of defense grew in popularity in Europe and Japan in the late 1960s. Perhaps it owed something to Servan-Schreiber's advocacy of this means of countering what he diagnosed as an American challenge.[31]

A further stage of this sort of strategy is to develop controls that will strengthen a country's multinational firms in their foreign operations. The United States went farthest in this direction. For example, under the Cooley Loan amendment to Public Law 480, U.S. government holdings of foreign currencies received in payment of agricultural surpluses were permitted to be lent to U.S. firms for trade expansion in the foreign country, but under no condition were the funds to be used for production that would be exported to the United States in competition with U.S.-made products or marketed to compete with U.S. agricultural exports.

The Foreign Assistance Act of 1961 also followed this pattern by limiting loan guarantees and insurance to what it euphemistically called "friendly" countries. A friendly country was one that would sign guarantees not to expropriate. This statement recorded in 1965 illustrates the strength of the U.S. legislation:

> It has generally been a policy of the Government of India to insist that in the case of all new industrial companies in the private sector, at least 51 percent of equity capital is held by Indians. The American Mission that was visiting India a few months ago informed the Finance Minister quite definitely that unless he was prepared to allow American control, there would be no further private American investment in India. The reason for this is that the United States Government appears to have introduced an insurance scheme for overseas investment in developing countries, but projects will only qualify for cover provided American control is assured.[32]

The strategy of countries with their own foreign investment, however, is not likely to continue along a straight progression of increasing influence over foreign operations of locally based firms. What is good

---

[31]J. J. Servan-Schreiber, *The American Challenge* (New York: Atheneum, 1968); Stephen Hymer and Robert Rowthorn, "Multinational Corporations and International Oligopoly: The Non-American Challenge," in *The International Corporation,* ed. Charles B. Kindleberger (Cambridge, Mass.: The M.I.T. Press, 1970).

[32]National Industrial Conference Board, *Obstacles and Incentives to Private Foreign Investment, 1965,* p. 81.

for the foreign performance of local corporations is not necessarily good for the home country. The possibilities for divergence between maximum performance of firms and what is seen as maximizing national benefit are very many indeed.

While investor countries will embrace the idea that poorer countries should be helped to develop and be generally opposed to multinational firms hindering development, with traditional ambivalence they will also be preoccupied with the need to retain their own international position. Retention of central head office functions, maintenance of financial centers, retention of technical leadership, and high spending in research and development will be advocated.[33] Controls will be steadily oriented towards these "leadership" ends, quietly, positively, and not competitively—yet definitely using the multinational enterprise as an intermediary in the competition to stay ahead.

The strategy for this class of countries then might be summarized as cautious unpublicized discouragement of others' international activities coupled with positive encouragement of desirable locally owned activities. Initially there will be an active stimulation of international expansion by local firms. Ultimately, though, the identification with locally based multinational firms will decrease as their interests diverge.

Minority Partner Countries

These are countries that are partners to trade agreements for which permitted tariffs plus transport costs do not deter imports from partners, yet which, by reason of their size, will be less preferred for major investment than their larger partners. The outstanding examples are the smaller EEC partners, Belgium and Holland. Controls leading foreign investment to locate outside a minority partner's boundaries would in these circumstances hinder export opportunities for any local plant that could be developed and might instead produce imports into the local market. Conversely, foreign investment that does come in is likely to lead to exports to the partner countries.

When there are a number of such countries competing against themselves, or when the advantages of their larger partners appear large to foreign investors, competition to de-escalate controls is likely, even to the extent of positive encouragements. Such a strategy has emerged in Belgium, somewhat to the detriment of France. Low-cost sites, capital and interest subsidies, and various types of taxation

---

[33]Both the United Kingdom and the United States have carried through government-financed studies that evidence major concern for technical leadership. For example, see Chapter 3 in M. D. Steuer et al., *The Impact of Foreign Direct Investment on the United Kingdom* (London: Department of Trade and Industry, 1973).

remission have been offered.[34] An EEC study that circulated but was not published reportedly argued for EEC countries to eliminate competition on these fronts and increase the optimum control levels for the community as a whole.[35] Agreement to avoid competition through controls is not a foregone conclusion, though, with such divergent interests. A similar tendency to weaken controls also happens within countries where states, provinces, regions, or cities have significant power to offer incentives or reduce costs.

Centrally Controlled Countries

A fifth type of strategy is appropriate for the communist-bloc countries and Japan—countries that achieved a significant measure of development while virtually excluding capital that placed majority ownership in foreign hands. These countries have strong central control which emerged in equally strong approaches toward foreign investment. They evolved strategies of attracting technological gains while retaining control of their own markets and preserving access to export markets. While limitations on foreign ownership may have delayed the inflow of the latest technological advances from international corporations, the multinational firm is still likely to protect its technological supremacy by withholding the latest advances even when it fully owns a subsidiary.

Once international corporations accept that they cannot gain majority ownership and that the direct threat to their own operations is not immediate, they have shown that they will settle for whatever participation they can get on the principle that something is better than nothing. U.S. national policy for a long time restrained U.S. firms in deals with communist countries, but the speed with which the Firestone-Goodyear competition built up for the Romanian market in 1964 following relaxation of the U.S. embargo was a good example of how competing capitalist units react when faced with limited access and centralized purchasing.[36]

A corollary to this sort of strategy is that these countries develop their own strong local operations able to move into international attack. In the initial stages this attack is likely to aim at building export markets and outgoing investment should be largely to acquire outlets

---

[34]National Industrial Conference Board, *Obstacles and Incentives to Private Foreign Investment, 1967–1968*, pp. 10–12.

[35]*Economist*, June 27, 1970, p. 73.

[36]See Frances Sheridan and R. W. Bareness, *Firestone and Trade with Rumania (A) and (B)*, Northwestern University, School of Business (Boston, Mass.: Intercollegiate Case Clearing House), no. 10G73, 10G74.

and market position. As the international attack meets with success, however, the strategy is likely to change into something very like the global planning of our representative international firm.

Pressure to relax the restrictions placed on international investment capital in the home markets of these countries is unlikely to make much of an impression until reverse investments and exports can be used as a lever. But when a significant lever does develop, the countries affected are more likely to be concerned with protection from the attack than relaxation of controls in the home market of the attackers.

Yielding to repeated pressure, particularly from OECD countries, Japan began in the late 1960s to reduce controls on inward investment.[37] The relaxations have continued, and the 1973 round of liberalizations enabled foreign companies, in theory, to establish fully owned subsidiaries after routine approval by the Japanese government in most industries. In 1975, direct entry into retailing was permitted. As our theory would predict, however, entry by foreign multinationals has since been very slow, mainly because the Japanese industries have built up to international strength and are not easy to beat on their home ground, but partly because obstacles are still placed in the way by the government authorities.[38]

In comparison to Japan, the communist countries are behind in their international expansion, but as they move outward they, too, begin to play the international game to maximize benefits. They have recorded notable success in pitting Western suppliers against one another to obtain technological expertise at the lowest competitive rates. In a number of cases, Russia and other bloc countries have obtained as much as 12 years' credit from international firms competing on narrow margins to supply what amounts to pure technological input, while unskilled labor and materials are supplied largely from local sources. On the export side their producing units show evidence of rational strategies, with products such as Polish hams aiming for strong positions in the leading markets.

In summary, the pattern of strategy of this class of countries is predicted as limitation of foreign ownership with maximum acquisition of technological know-how, followed by international expansion that shapes them as investing countries.

---

[37]Herbert Glazer, "Japan Unbars a Door," *Columbia Journal of World Business*, July–August 1967.

[38]See Charles Smith, "Foreigners' Stake," *Financial Times*, November 12, 1975; also *Foreign Direct Investment in the United States*, vol. I: Report of the Secretary of Commerce to the Congress (Washington, D.C.: U.S. Government Printing Office, April 1976), p. 240.

SUMMARY

The emphasis of this chapter has been entirely away from the popular concern for the decaying power of the nation-state in the face of the rise of multinational firms. The emphasis has been on prediction of the pattern of controls that will emerge as countries adjust to competition through these changed intermediaries. Countries have been taken as the ultimate competing powers, endeavoring via their controls over international business to alter the allocation of activities for their national benefit.

Several conclusions stand out. Countries are not in equal strategic positions with respect to international business and the poorer nations have the weaker hands. Moreover, they cannot find an easy way out through unilateral nationalistic action. Such action is a quick way to decrease the national payoff from the international game. Their best strategy lies with gradually creeping controls. On the other hand, the most costly controls from the viewpoint of international business are likely to be imposed by the smaller, more developed countries who have less to lose and are likely to lose less from strict control policies. There will also be major differences in the effectiveness of controls because of the way they affect the performance of multinational firms. Tariffs will remain strong because they tie the attraction of the local market to local activity, and controls not reflected in return-on-investment calculations or taking effect some time in the future will be widely used. In particular, limitation of foreign equity ownership will be more widespread.

Given the concept of the international business game and an embryo terminology for approaching its analysis, the international businessman should be able to develop cost and benefit calculations as the basis for his decisions. Such calculations will be limited by the assumptions made about the various interacting strategies, but control risk will be quantifiable. For any investment the cash flow can be reduced by the cost of controls multiplied by the expectation (probability) that they will occur.

EXERCISES AND DISCUSSION QUESTIONS

1. Numerous writers have observed an "inevitable tension" between multinational companies and nation-states and proposed ways for governments to control the operations of these firms. Is the conflict really between firms and countries, or simply between countries just as it has always been? What are the implications of this distinction for the sort of controls that might be recommended?
2. In recent years the Canadian government has been introducing more and

more controls over the Canadian operations of foreign firms. What would you expect will be the characteristics of further controls to be imposed in the forseeable future, and why?

3. Do you think managements of tomorrow's multinational corporations will generally act to minimize the effects of controls on their firms' performance? Should they? If not, what exceptions would you wish to see?

4. Select one country and, as a consultant to its current government, prepare an overall strategy for control of international business activities that fall within its jurisdiction.

5. What types of controls will be most likely to affect the performance of international firms as against simply being passed on by the firm to its customers? Does it make any difference?

6. Criticize the assumptions of the model that has been proposed in this chapter for forecasting controls.

14

Forecasting Political Risk

GENERAL FORECASTING of national controls provides one level of insight into risks associated with international operations. Another level can be attained by developing methods of forecasting political actions that will have an impact on a firm's operations. Political risk has long been a familiar term in the lexicon of international business, yet until recently few companies undertook systematic evaluation of political risks, "involving their identification, their likely incidence, and their specific consequences for company operations."[1] One of the challenges facing the international manager is to develop techniques for evaluating and forecasting political risk so that political-risk elements can be included in decision making on a more objective basis.

The mention of political risk is most likely to bring to mind the business environment characteristic of the newly independent and less developed nations. But political risk is a much more pervasive issue for the multinational enterprise. It can be encountered by investors in industrialized countries such as France and Canada, as well as in the LDCs, and even in the home countries of investors like Sweden and the United States.

U.S. companies doing business in South Africa have experienced political boycotts and harassment in the United States from groups opposed to the racial policies of South Africa. In 1965, the Firestone Tire and Rubber Company terminated negotiations for a contract to

---

[1]Franklin R. Root, "U.S. Business Abroad and the Political Risks," *MSU Business Topics*, Winter 1968.

design and equip a synthetic rubber plant in Romania because of unanticipated political pressure from a conservative youth organization vigorously opposed to expanded U.S. business relations with Soviet-bloc countries.

In Sweden the big electrical firm, ASEA, became the target for intense leftist criticism for its proposed participation in an international power-plant project in the Portuguese colony of Mozambique. The political opposition in Sweden argued that the project would serve the objectionable Portuguese colonial power and weaken opposition movements.[2]

Political risk usually connotes the possibility of losses. Yet, as in the case of other types of risk, political risk can result in gains as well as losses. Political considerations were responsible for the 1962 restrictions by Brazil on profit remittances, but opposing political forces caused a change in the government in 1964, and one result was a liberalization of profit remittances and other policies relating to foreign private investment. Similarly, drastic political changes in Indonesia in 1966 and in Argentina during the same year had the effect of improving the international business environment.

DEFINING POLITICAL RISK

To assess and forecast the likely influence of political risk in international business decisions, one must start with an operational definition—political risk in international business exists (1) when discontinuities occur in the business environment, (2) when they are difficult to anticipate, and (3) when they result from political change. To constitute a "risk" these changes in the business environment must have a potential for significantly affecting the profit or other goals of a particular enterprise.

It follows, therefore, that political fluctuations that do not change the business environment significantly do not represent political risk for international business. It follows, also, that what is political risk for one firm may not be political risk for another. Abrupt changes in concession agreements are political risk for petroleum companies but not for soft-drink producers.

Political considerations are continually modifying the business environment at home and abroad, but not all such changes can properly be considered as political risk. Where change is gradual and progressive, and when it reflects continuity in government policies and political forces, future trends are neither unexpected nor difficult to

[2]Sven Ersman and Torsten Gardlund, "In Sweden, Investment Abroad Is a Moral Issue," *Columbia Journal of World Business,* January–February 1970.

anticipate. In such "normal" circumstances, the decision maker's task is to recognize the evolutionary path along which change is occurring, identify the principal motivating forces behind the change, and make judgments as to timing. For example, tax laws and tax burdens are constantly changing, but much, if not most, of the change does not represent a radical departure from past trends and it is not difficult to anticipate.

It would be convenient if the international manager could look to the political scientists for an understanding of the sources of political risk for international business operations. Political scientists have done considerable research on the subject of "political instability" in the form of revolutions. But they still disagree significantly on how to define political stability or instability, on how to measure the phenomenon, and on the causal forces. Furthermore, the political scientists' principal focus of interest is not likely to produce the answers needed for international business. For one thing, the discontinuities that might affect international business do not necessarily require a revolution.[3] Another consideration is that political instability, depending on how it is defined, is a separate, although related, phenomenon from that of political risk.

A conceptual framework is presented in Figure 14–1 showing the sources of political risk, the political groups through which political risk can be generated, and the types of influences that political-risk elements can have on international business activities. It should be noted that several of the specific effects shown in the far right column are not exclusively associated with political risk. Taxation policies, transfer freedom, market restrictions, and pressures for local sharing of ownership can change in relatively stable political situations and as a result of reasonably predictable nonpolitical forces. In such cases the difference between normal business risk and political risk is a matter of degree. It becomes difficult to draw the line between continuity and discontinuity, between certainty and uncertainty, and to determine that political forces are in fact dominant.

A particularly difficult problem at times may be to separate political and economic risk. Although government decisions are always political—by definition—the forces dictating the decisions may be purely economic. For example, the political-risk insurance offered by the U.S. government to domestic firms investing abroad includes inconvertibility of currency as a political risk. Yet currency inconverti-

[3]Anthony Leeds, *Latin American Research Review,* Spring 1968, p. 83. Leeds defines "revolution" as a "systemwide disturbance characterized by organized fighting flowing out of conflict in a social situation where one or more major *classes* is fundamentally unrepresented in the decision-making and reward-allocating operations of the state."

FIGURE 14–1
Political Risk: A Conceptual Framework

Sources of Political Risk	Groups through Which Political Risk Can Be Generated	Political Risk Effects: Types of Influence on International Business Operations
Competing political philosophies (nationalism, socialism, communism)	Government in power and its operating agencies Parliamentary opposition groups	Confiscation: loss of assets without compensation
Social unrest and disorder	Nonparliamentary opposition groups (e.g., anarchist or guerrilla movements working from within or outside of country)	Expropriation with compensation: loss of freedom to operate
Vested interests of local business groups	Nonorganized common interest groups: students, workers, peasants, minorities, and so forth	Operational restrictions: market shares, product characteristics, employment policies, locally shared ownership, and so forth
Recent and impending political independence	Foreign governments or intergovernmental agencies such as the EEC	Loss of transfer freedom: financial (for example, dividends, interest payments), goods, personnel, or ownership rights
Armed conflicts and internal rebellions for political power	Foreign governments willing to enter into armed conflict or to support internal rebellion	Breaches or unilateral revisions in contracts and agreements
New international alliances		Discrimination such as taxes, compulsory subcontracting
		Damage to property or personnel from riots, insurrections, revolutions, and wars

bility can occur for predominantly economic reasons in politically stable nations and at times when political systems and political leadership are not changing.

In some situations, political forces may be the dominant factor in inconvertibility. Political uncertainties in some nations have stimulated large outflows of flight capital, which in turn caused a balance-of-payments crisis. Or internal political forces in opposition to foreign enterprise have compelled governments to limit the repatriation of profits and other financial transfers by foreign firms. For example, the restrictive Brazilian Capital Remittance Law, adopted in 1962 by the Goulart regime, was motivated primarily by antagonism to foreign enterprise and a conviction by powerful political forces that foreign firms were draining too much foreign exchange from the country.

The international manager must be aware of the potential intermingling of political and economic motivations. Even where considerable intermingling of motivations exists, the decision maker may get useful results by trying to separate the political factors from the others.

Macro Political Risk

The international business enterprise may encounter both macro and micro types of political risk. The risk is of a macro nature when politically motivated environmental changes affect all foreign enterprise. The risk is of a micro nature when the environmental changes are intended to affect only selected fields of business activity or foreign enterprises with specific characteristics.

Macro political risk can be indirect and spasmodic. At times of political turmoil, foreign companies are tempting targets for political factions of just about every stripe. Harassment or physical damage can occur to embarrass the political regime in power. An example of this indirect type of political risk occurred in 1969, when a large number of U.S.-owned supermarkets in Argentina were bombed on the occasion of Governor Nelson Rockefeller's visit to Buenos Aires as a special envoy of President Richard Nixon. The supermarkets were owned by the International Basic Economy Corporation, which Nelson Rockefeller had founded.

Direct and relatively permanent macro risk can be illustrated by the takeover of private enterprise in 1959–60 by the Castro government in Cuba. Foreign enterprises were seized along with domestic firms. In part, the broad-sweep confiscation of foreign investment has been explained by a basic change in political philosophy brought about by the Cuban revolution—a shift from a private enterprise to a socialist or communist system. And in part, the large size and the specific composition of foreign investment in Cuba may have played a significant role in shaping the policies to expropriate all foreign private investment.[4]

The Cuban experience deserves special attention. It suggests that specific business projects may be subjected to political risk because the overall size of the foreign-owned business sector is large relative to the total size of a country's business sector; or because foreign firms dominate several strategic and politically sensitive fields of activity. In such situations, revolutionary political changes are likely to be accompanied or even supported by political pressures to end the "economic colonial" status of a country by reducing or eliminating the influence of all types of foreign business.

The Cuban case is not an isolated example of macro risk. In recent years, international enterprises have felt the impact of broadside actions—frequently along with domestic private enterprise—in Algeria, Burma, Chile, Egypt, Ghana, Indonesia, Uganda, and Libya. These are in addition to the communist expropriations in Eastern Europe and China following World War II.

Macro-risk situations can also occur where broad action is taken against foreign enterprise as a political boycott. In the Middle East, various Arab countries began in 1955 to boycott any companies that had branches in Israel or allowed the use of their trade name there. The Arabs ignored direct trade with Israel, but any permanent investment in that country, or any long-term agreements, such as licensing arrangements or technical assistance, earned the company a place on the blacklist. The implementation of such policies has been sporadic, but after the 1967 war with Israel, the boycott was tightened.

An even more comprehensive boycott was announced in 1970 by mainland China. The Chinese prime minister told visiting Japanese traders that China would not do business with Japanese companies that gave credits to or invested in Taiwan and South Korea or with firms that entered joint ventures with U.S. companies or otherwise assisted in the Vietnam war. In retaliation, Nationalist China (Taiwan) announced its own list of Japanese companies which it was banning for doing business with mainland China.

Micro Risks and Product Vulnerability

Macro political risk is dramatic. Micro political risk is more prevalent. With considerable frequency, the international manager is likely to encounter abrupt and politically motivated changes in the business

---

[4]See Leland L. Johnson, *U.S. Private Investment in Latin America: Some Questions of National Policy*, Memorandum RM-4092 ISA (Santa Monica, Calif.: The Rand Corporation, July 1964).

environment that are selectively directed toward specific fields of business activity. But the types of business operations with a high vulnerability to micro risk will vary from nation to nation and over time in the same nation.

At a particular point of time and for a specific country, it should be possible to rank types of business activities according to their degree of political-risk vulnerability. However, such rankings constantly change. The forecaster of political risk must do more than look at a snapshot to identify and assess the sources of political risk for specific business activities and to understand the rationale for radical shifts. He must analyze a continually evolving situation over time.

In a current ranking of industries, public utilities have the highest degree of political-risk vulnerability. A few decades ago, public-utility investments by foreigners were politically and economically popular with both host countries and investors. But styles change, and recent worldwide trends have been toward domestic, usually government, ownership of public-utility enterprises because of national-security and developmental goals. As a result, international enterprises have not been expanding in these fields, and the high political-risk ranking is relevant only to such operations as still exist, mainly in less developed countries, as holdovers from a previous era.

The extractive industries, particularly petroleum and mining, also have a high degree of political risk because of growing nationalistic feelings and a conviction that natural resource endowments should be exploited for the welfare of all people in a nation rather than for private profit. As the Gordon Report in Canada explained, financial institutions are also vulnerable because of "their pervasiveness and their potential as bases for influence and control."[5]

Two factors can change the political-risk vulnerability of an industry over time. One is the dominance of foreign enterprise in a major industry sector. If the share of the automobile industry controlled by foreign countries is relatively low, as in the case of West Germany, political risk also tends to be low. If foreign companies completely dominate the industry, as was the case in Peru during the early 1970s, political risk is likely to be high.

A second factor that may affect or compound the risk is the capacity of nationals to operate a business successfully. At an early stage in a nation's development, foreign enterprises may be welcomed because they provide scarce capital, management know-how, and technical skills not locally available. Over time, countries manage to accumulate

---

[5]*Foreign Ownership and the Structure of Canadian Industry: Report of the Task Force on the Structure of Canadian Industry* (Ottawa, Canada: Information Canada, 1970), p. 389.

capital and nationals who have learned the techniques of management and become skilled in the technology of the foreign enterprise. To the extent that local personnel have been trained for copper mining, running a tea plantation, or managing some other type of business initiated by foreign firms, the political pressures for curtailing or eliminating foreign enterprises are likely to increase. To the extent that an enterprise is dependent upon a continuing import of new technology in a technologically dynamic industry, local political-risk elements are likely to be weak.

If one were to judge by the fee schedule for political-risk insurance offered by many governments, one would have to conclude that the degree of political risk is similar for all types of business activities and for investments in all countries. Insurance fees are at the same rate for all projects. Yet the implication of the fee schedule is not consistent with historical experience.[6]

Sources of Political Risk

From the standpoint of international business, the six general sources of political risk shown in Figure 14–1 are of particular importance. The most comprehensive is the existence of political forces hostile toward foreign enterprise in general, or toward foreign participation in selected business fields, for philosophical reasons that diverge sharply from prevailing government policies. Others are social unrest and disorder, the private vested interests of local business groups, recent or impending independence, new international alliances, and armed conflicts. Less predictable, and political only in the sense that it is a tool of politicians, is the exposure of corruption or scandal. It is often linked to a government official who might well have provided influence for a foreign firm.

Latent Hostility. Some latent hostility to foreign enterprises is present in most nations, including the United States. The potential strength of such hostile forces affects the degree of political risk. The avenues available for making such political strength effective in changing government policies are numerous. The basic form of government can be changed, as happened in Cuba. The leadership of government can change but the political system remains the same, as happened when Pompidou succeeded de Gaulle in France. Or concessions can be exacted from the political parties and leaders in power without changes in the form or leadership of the existing government.

A drastic change in policy without a change in political leadership

---

[6]See Dan Haendel, Gerald T. West, and Robert G. Meadow, *Overseas Investment and Political Risk* (Philadelphia: Foreign Policy Research Institute, 1975), chap. 1.

can be illustrated by events in Zambia and in Trinidad. The Zambian case was described by the *Economist* in its August 30, 1969, issue: "For some time internal strife in Unip, the ruling party, has threatened to bring down the whole government. It was partly to prevent this happening that President Kaunda announced at the Unip national council meeting earlier this month the 51 percent nationalization of the copper mines." The Trinidad case followed a similar pattern. According to the *Economist* in its August 29, 1970 issue: "Trinidad's Dr. Eric Williams has pulled off a major coup to regain the confidence of his electorate and to disprove his critics who maintain that he is a mere puppet of foreign capitalists. At the beginning of this month he announced that the government will buy 51 percent of the island's largest sugar producer, Caroni, a subsidiary of the British Tate & Lyle group."

The hostility of strong internal factions of a country to foreign enterprise may arise out of adherence to socialist or nationalist philosophies. They may also spring from attempts to achieve specific national goals, whether of security, welfare, or development.

Socialism commonly means government rather than private owner-ship of the means of production. Yet political labels can be misleading. "Socialism" as a label has been extremely popular in many parts of the world in recent decades. But the specific goals of political forces banded together under the socialism label vary greatly. For example, government leaders in India have declared that India's guiding politi-cal philosophy is socialism. Although the public-enterprise sector is large in India, a substantial share of the business activity has been reserved for private enterprise, much of which is foreign. Likewise, Yugoslavia calls itself a communist or socialist country, yet numerous joint ventures with foreign private enterprise have been negotiated in recent years. Thus, the international enterprise must look behind labels for the specific goals of political groups in different countries.

The nationalistic philosophy generally asserts that control over a nation's economic destiny should be in the hands of nationals and that nationals should have preference over foreigners in benefiting from economic and business opportunities in the country. Both of these views can generate political risk for international business enterprises.

An example of national-welfare goals that can create political risk is the persistent pressure in many countries of the world for land reform. If land-reform measures are suddenly accelerated, as occurred in 1969 when a military junta took control of the government in Peru, foreign as well as domestic business firms with landholdings are likely to be expropriated.

National aspirations for economic development can create political risk for international business when the nation believes that the ultimate goal of development is to enlarge the domestic capacity for *self-generating* growth. This view implies that a country does not want to increase its dependence on outside forces any more than is necessary. This philosophy underlies the stated policy of the government of India that private foreign investment is not allowed in industries where indigenous capital, talent, and know-how are available.[7]

Other Sources of Risk. Social unrest and disorder may create political risk, not because of specific hostility to foreign enterprise, but because of general disruption of business activities. The causes of social unrest may range from the existence of extreme economic hardships to racial disorders as experienced in the United States and religious disputes such as have occurred in India, and even student riots.

Ineffective law enforcement can also be included in this category. It can result in risk to property and to persons and can greatly influence the costs of doing business and the efficiency of production, transportation, and communications.

The risk that can result from the political influence of local business interests that consider themselves threatened by foreign enterprises should never be underestimated. In Japan, local business interests have been extremely active and successful in influencing government policies or decisions that have restricted the activities of foreign enterprise. It was an open secret in Brazil that conservative indigenous business interests allied themselves with radical left-wing political groups in 1962 to influence President Goulart and the congress to adopt highly restrictive policies on the remittances of profits by foreign firms.

Nations recently attaining independence, or about to do so, are likely to face great political uncertainty. In many cases, a nation secures widespread political cohesion on the issue of gaining independence but not on what policies should be followed after independence. In addition, new nations frequently lack experienced political leadership and undergo considerable turmoil while experience is gained and the policies and political power of various groups are tested. The role to be played by private enterprise and the attitudes toward foreign investment are not always clarified in the early stages of organizing a new nation.

Internal rebellion may be an extreme stage of social unrest and disorder. The situation in the late 1960s between the central government of Nigeria and Biafra illustrates the kind of political risk that can occur. The effects on foreign business may be similar to those on

---

[7]Indian Investment Center, *Seminar on International Investment in India* (New Delhi, 1968).

domestic business or they may be accentuated because of the leverage that the opposing groups think they have in gaining support by putting pressure on foreign firms.

Armed conflicts between nations such as the ones that have occurred between India and Pakistan and Israel and the Arab states can greatly affect the feasibility and profitability of foreign business operations.

An extreme case of political risk arising out of new alliances by a nation would be a situation in which a previously noncommunist nation establishes close relations with a communist country. Such was the case in Indonesia during the early 1960s. New pressures were placed on foreign enterprise, and the alliance offered Indonesia the possibility of alternatives to foreign enterprise.

New international alliances would also include the case where a country joins a common market or free-trade area and in the process agrees to give preference in certain ways to business activities of common market nationality. Or, as in the case of the Andean Common Market in Latin America, the member countries agree to harmonize their policies toward foreign private investment. When such inter-governmental agreements are concluded, some national policies under which international enterprises are operating may drastically change. Still another example is the action taken in 1970 by the European Economic Commission to reconsider its association agreement with Greece because the commission disapproved of the political behavior of the Greek military regime.

Political Risk Effects

The principal ways that political risk are likely to influence international business operations were shown in Figure 14–1. They fall into two general categories. New operational restrictions, loss of transfer freedom, contract breaches and revisions, tax policies, damage to property and personnel will change the operating environment for the international enterprise, usually in a negative way. Confiscation, expropriation, and, in some cases, contract breaches eliminate completely the feasibility of foreign operations.

To the sophisticated international enterprise, expropriation risk is not a bar to investment but an element to be weighed against prospective gains. Over time, the risk may increase. Nevertheless, the international enterprise may conclude that the profit possibilities up to the time when the risk of expropriation is high are sufficiently attractive to make the project of interest. Such an approach has been characteristic of the international petroleum industry.

The prevailing philosophy in many countries, particularly the newly independent nations, is that concessions or agreements can be revoked or revised at the discretion of the host country if the national interests are no longer being adequately served. In practice such revisions are likely to occur when the goals of national governments change, when a new political regime feels that contract revisions will strengthen its domestic political support, and when key circumstances surrounding an agreement change.

In September 1969, for example, a group of young military officers seized control of Libya, sweeping aside the monarchy of King Idris I, and established a "socialist republic." The announced goal of the new regime was to reduce foreign influences in the country. Shortly after the 1969 change in government, Libya began to revise its agreements with the international oil companies. One of the reported motivations was the need felt by the new regime to prove its toughness to the people by standing up to the oil companies, and the oil companies were blamed for corrupting the previous government with bribes.

Concessions negotiated with colonial governments or with newly independent regimes when the bargaining power of the governments was weak, and when few foreign investors were attracted, have been vulnerable to revocation and renegotiation after a change in government. This is especially so when the success of the pioneering foreign investors has stimulated other investors to come forward with more attractive offers. Many new governments feel that they are not obliged to suffer under the terms of the original agreement. In the absence of international legal constraints, such governments are likely to invoke their maximum degree of bargaining power for unilateral revision of concession contracts.

Political Instability and Political Risk

To what extent are perceptions of "political instability" a reliable guide to political risk? The question deserves special attention because political instability is so frequently cited as an obstacle to flows of private foreign investment.

In a broad study of investors from the 12 major capital-exporting countries—Belgium, Canada, Denmark, France, Germany, Italy, Japan, the Netherlands, Sweden, Switzerland, United Kingdom, and United States—many investors reported that they had eliminated countries and even whole geographical regions from their investment considerations for political reasons. By far the most frequently cited political obstacle was political uncertainty or political instability.[8]

With such a high sensitivity to political instability, it is quite

---

[8]National Industrial Conference Board, *Obstacles and Incentives to Private Foreign Investment, 1967–1968*, 1 (New York, 1969).

possible that inexperienced international enterprises have missed business opportunities because they perceived more political risk than actually existed. When international managers with limited background and experience perceive political risk, it often means that they are not familiar with the political patterns and styles of a foreign country and would feel insecure trying to operate in a strange environment. In such cases, the problem is to come to terms with an unfamiliar rather than a hostile situation.

Another possibility is that international managers are applying ethnocentric standards, based on political systems with which they are familiar, which are not appropriate to the country being considered. As one study of international business experience notes, "Governments reject many charges of political instability as due to lack of knowledge or unfounded fears on the part of the foreign businessman. There is evidence, they say, that political differences that would pass at home as 'natural discord' become 'disturbing imbalances' when viewed by investors in a distant country. 'The political struggles that take place within a parliamentary regime,' says one government spokesman, 'should not be mistaken for political instability.'"[9] In other words, the criteria for political instability are different for each political system.

An approach to political instability that can be highly misleading is to interpret frequent changes in the leadership of governments as political instability. France, after World War II, had many different heads of government until the return of de Gaulle. Yet continuity in governmental policies was maintained by a strong professional civil service with considerable stability and strong institutional norms, characteristics of the French political system.

From 1947 to 1970, Brazil had 11 presidents of the republic. It is not surprising that the flamboyant political style of that country was widely interpreted by international managers as presenting a high degree of political instability. But an analysis of the links between political events and two principal indexes of the business environment, namely economic growth trends and rates of inflation, suggests that such links were not strong except for the three-year period from 1961 to 1964 of the Goulart administration. The growth rate of Brazil fluctuated during a few of the years, but the declines can be explained by the effect of a serious drought in one period and the collapse of the international coffee market in another period. Inflation has been generally high, but the sharpest rise in inflation prior to the Goulart regime occurred in 1959 during the Kubitschek regime, one of Brazil's most stable political periods. President Kubitschek was determined to

---

[9]National Industrial Conference Board, *Obstacles and Incentives to Private Foreign Investment, 1962–1964* (New York, 1965).

push the construction of a new capital city at Brasilia to the "point of no return" so that the project could not be abandoned after his term of office. And to accomplish this big push, measures were taken that resulted in a major increase in inflation.

A reasonable presumption for international business operations may be that frequent and unexpected changes in government leadership should not be interpreted per se as political instability. The more fundamental question is whether strong factions are present with divergent views from those of the government on policies toward foreign business. Furthermore, the potential for political instability and political risk in countries with centralized political control, sometimes headed by a military dictator, can also be great. One-man governments can often behave erratically and generate underlying tensions. Considerable uncertainty may exist as to how an orderly transition to a successor will be possible.

A considerable amount of work has gone into the development of overall political instability indices for individual countries. The Business Environment Risk Index (BERI) and the Business International Index of Environmental Risk (BI) have been available to business firms for some years. Both are based on predictions by panels of experts, updated from time to time. A third method, the Political System Stability Index (PSSI), has been developed using hard quantitative measurements of a range of indicators over a four-year period.[10] Whether a firm arrives at its assessment of a country's political instability through internal subjective analysis or external indices, however, will be only one factor in forecasting the political risk associated with a specific investment, particularly if the life of the investment is long and conditions can change radically over the period.

FORECASTING POLITICAL RISK

As international corporations are becoming more experienced and more widely involved, they are beginning to establish political forecasting staffs on more or less the same level as economic forecasting staffs.

The task of political forecasting involves four basic steps: First, an understanding of the type of government presently in power, its patterns of political behavior, and its norms for stability; second, an analysis of the multinational enterprise's own product or operations to

---

[10]A comparison of the three approaches is contained in Dan Haendel et al., *Overseas Investment and Political Risk,* chap 3; see also Harald Knudsen, "Explaining the National Propensity to Expropriate: An Ecological Approach," *Journal of International Business Studies,* Spring 1974, pp. 51–71.

identify the kind of political risk likely to be involved in particular areas, for example, is the problem one of macro or micro risk; third, a determination of the source of the potential risk. If the risk is expropriation, is the source that of socialistic or nationalistic philosophy? If the risk is on operational restrictions, is the source that of local businessmen? Having developed a familiarity with the political system of a country, having identified the kinds of political risk to which the business operation can be vulnerable, and having determined the political force or group that may be the source of that risk, the fourth step is to project into the future the possibility of political risk in terms of probability and time horizons.

Throughout the process, the emphasis must be on political forces that can cause abrupt changes in the environment for the business firm. To repeat, changes in governments, in parties, and in leaders may or may not involve political risk.

The necessary background information on the political environment of a country goes far beyond a knowledge of the attitudes and policies of the present administration to foreign private enterprise. The need is to understand within a nation's historical context its type of government, its political parties and forces, and their philosophies.[11] The challenge is to understand the path along which all policies and attitudes have been traveling, particularly those of the political groups that are not shaping the policies of the present administration but are likely to do so.

The second step in evaluating the vulnerability of a company to political risk is to analyze its operations, with the following questions in mind:

1. Are periodic external inputs of new technology required?
2. Will the project be competing strongly with local nationals who are in, or trying to enter, the same field?
3. Is the operation dependent on natural resources, particularly minerals or oil?
4. Does the investment put pressure on balance of payments?
5. Does the enterprise have a strong monopoly position in the local market?
6. Is the product socially essential and acceptable?

In general, projects or products that contribute strongly to national goals are likely to receive favorable political attention when first initiated. But as the projects become taken for granted over time and a

---

[11]See Lee C. Nehrt, *The Political Climate For Foreign Private Investment* (New York: Praeger Publishers, Inc., 1970) for an excellent analysis of political risk in North Africa. Nehrt suggests a model for political analysis and applies it to Tunisia, Algeria, and Morocco.

local capacity is developed to operate such projects, political favoritism may shift to new fields.

The third step is the most difficult. Once the types of risk to which a company is especially vulnerable have been analyzed, how can the sources of these risks and their strength be identified and evaluated? The easiest situation is that of a parliamentary democracy where the opposition views can be determined from parliamentary debates or political platforms. At the other extreme is the difficult task of determining views and weighing the political strength of antagonistic opposition forces in a dictatorship where considerable censorship occurs. In such cases, the task of political forecasting should include an examination of the views of political exiles. This final step of forecasting the specific environmental risks may result in a considerable amount of error and uncertainty. But over time, skill can be developed to accomplish this task within limits of probability. In retrospect, it appears quite certain that many expropriations of minerals and petroleum operations could have been forecast with reasonable certainty. The same is true with changes in contract conditions and the nationalization of the various public utility companies.

How One Company Forecasts

Political risk forecasting as practiced by one major international company calls first for two projections: one on the chances of a particular political group being in power during discrete forecast periods, and another on the types of government interference to be expected from each of the political groups. From these data, probability estimates of the political risks likely to arise during specific time periods can be calculated. Finally, the present value of expected cash flows, or the internal rate of return from the investment project under consideration can be adjusted to reflect the timing and magnitude of the risk probabilities.[12]

The following oversimplified example shows how the first projection can be arrived at. It assumes that there are only two political parties concerned—the Conservatives and the Radicals. The Conservatives are in power in 1975. The next election will come in 1976, and the following one in 1981. It assumes that the elected party will stay in power for a five-year period.

The consensus of the political analysts, shown in Figure 14–2, is that the probability of being elected in 1976 is 70 percent for the Conservatives and 30 percent for the Radicals. If elected in 1976, the

---

[12]This section is based on unpublished research carried out by a major international company. The procedure follows the general outline suggested by Robert B. Stobaugh, Jr., "How to Analyze Foreign Investment Climates," *Harvard Business Review*, September–October 1969.

FIGURE 14-2
Quantitative Political Forecast for a Hypothetical Country, 1976–1985

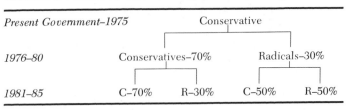

| *Present Government–1975* | Conservative | | | |

| *1976–80* | Conservatives–70% | | Radicals–30% | |

| *1981–85* | C–70% | R–30% | C–50% | R–50% |

Conservatives are estimated to have a 70 percent probability of being reelected in 1981. Thus, following only the left half of the probability tree, the probability of a Conservative government from 1981 through 1985 is 49 percent (70 percent of 70 percent).

Now turning to the right half of the probability tree in Figure 14–2, if the Radicals are elected in 1976, for which there is a 30 percent chance, the probability of the Conservatives regaining power in 1981 has been estimated at 50 percent. Thus the weighted probability through this chain of future events is an additional 15 percent probability in 1981 for the Conservatives (50 percent of 30 percent). By joining the political chances of the Conservatives through both of the possible paths, the combined probability of the Conservatives coming to power in 1981 is 64 percent–the 49 percent chance of staying in power throughout the period plus the 15 percent chance of regaining power following a Radical victory. This leaves a 36 percent probability of a Radical government coming to power in 1981.

The next step is to assess the probabilities of risk associated with each political group. To simplify the illustration, only one type of risk is dealt with—confiscation. In this case the consensus of political analysts is that the Conservatives present virtually no risk of confiscation in either period. But if the Radicals come to power, there will be a 50 percent probability of confiscation in the first period, and a 60 percent probability in the second.

Finally, the probabilities of being in power, and the propensity to confiscation of each political group are weighted to give an average risk of confiscation during each time period. In the case of the example, the results in Table 14–1 show a 15 percent probability of confiscation in 1976–80 and a 22 percent probability in 1981–85.

Confiscation is, of course, only one of many types of risk likely to be encountered. Additional types of risk can be incorporated into the overall forecast by the same method.

Using only three types of possible interference: no interference, confiscation, and expropriation, the hypothetical example could have

TABLE 14–1
Probability of Confiscation

	1976–80	*1981–85*
Conservative Party		
a. Probability of being in power 70%		64%
b. Risk of confiscation 0		0
Radical Party		
c. Probability of being in power 30		36
d. Risk of confiscation. 50		60
Weighted average risk of confiscation		
(b × a) + (d × c). 15		22

10 different possible outcomes over a 15-year period, ranging from early confiscation at one extreme (a 15 percent probability) to no interference over the entire period (a 10.7 percent probability).

The final step is to adjust the anticipated cash flow pattern according to each of the possible 10 outcomes and calculate the present values of the adjusted cash flows. If three of the possible outcomes, for example, show negative values and their combined probability totals 33.3 percent, the project has one chance in three of a loss due to political risk. Also the adjusted present values of all the outcomes can be averaged after weighting each outcome by its probability of occurrence. If the result is negative, the political risk analysis favors a negative decision on the project even though there is only one chance in three of a losing outcome.

If different political assumptions appear to be reasonable possibilities, additional political risk appraisals can be made on the basis of the new assumptions. Or the analysis can be extended to consider the effect of changes in the timing and form of the project.

MINIMIZING POLITICAL RISK

It is obvious that political risk forecasting can be crucial to the international enterprise in reaching a "go" or "no go" decision on a particular project. It may be less obvious that risk identification and evaluation can guide the firm in reshaping a project so that a "no go" can become a modified "go." The international enterprise is not helpless in the face of political risk. To the contrary, it has a significant range of options for minimizing the magnitude and effects of such risks.[13] Some of the possibilities have been discussed in Chapter 12.

[13]See Jean Boddewyn and Etienne F. Cracco, "The Political Game in World Business," *Columbia Journal of World Business,* January–February 1972, pp. 45–56.

SUMMARY

The international manager operates in many sovereign political units whose systems differ radically in form and philosophy from those of his own country. Lack of familiarity with foreign political environments and lack of a process for systematic evaluation of political risks increase the probability that the multinational enterprise will invest in countries when it should not or refrain from investing when it should.

Some sophisticated international enterprises are beginning to establish forecasting staff units to improve the techniques for assessing, forecasting, and minimizing political risk; and to make more objective the political-risk elements included in decision making. Such enterprises will be in a far better position to deal successfully with the uncertainties and challenges of the international business environment.

EXERCISES AND DISCUSSION QUESTIONS

1. How would you define political risk? Would you consider a political risk the "inability to convert into dollars foreign currency representing earnings on, or return of, the investment or compensation for sale or disposition of the investment," one of the items included as political risk in the U.S. risk-guaranty program?
2. "Political stability is equated with democracy, with elections, with modernization, with a broad income distribution, with consensus, with participation, and so forth. This conception is derived from an ideologized model of what the American type of democracy is supposed to be like, projected on to other societies." Evaluate and discuss.
3. "When Castro came to power in Cuba, the total book value of U.S. business enterprise in Cuba was greater than in any other Latin American country except Venezuela. On a per capita basis, U.S. investment in Cuba was over three times the average for the rest of Latin America. One third of the U.S. investment in 1959 was in public utilities. Another large share was in agriculture, particularly sugar production. Seven of the ten largest latifundios (agricultural estates) were owned by U.S. interests." How would you have assessed the macro political risk in Cuba prior to the revolution?
4. How would you rank types of business activities as to their political risk vulnerability? What is the basis for your ranking?
5. What is the relationship between political instability and political risk for international business? What criteria would you use to identify political instability?
6. What steps are required for political risk forecasting? Why is the time dimension important?
7. How can a business project be modified to reduce political risk?

part four

Assessing National Environments

MANY DIMENSIONS of the business environment that can be taken as constants in domestic business become significant variables in multinational business. This part of the text focuses on the assessment of these dimensions.

Assessment involves two stages—identification and forecasting. First, the business manager must identify the environmental factors that are both significant to the particular enterprise and likely to vary among the countries in which it is involved. Second, changes must be forecasted. Environments are dynamic and constantly changing and the multinational enterprise is continually required to make decisions in which future conditions may be far more important than the existing situation.

The facets of national environments examined in this part of the book are those most closely linked with the revenue and cost performance of the corporation—the culture, the economy, and the demand environment. These three subjects are interrelated, but it is customary to apply separate approaches in assessing the differences within each, largely stemming from the underlying disciplines of cultural anthropology, macroeconomics, and marketing.

The multinational enterprise will have several levels of concern within each facet. At one extreme falls the need for a "macro-scanning" of differences as a basis for selecting broad global opportunities. At the other end of the spectrum, the firm may require a detailed analysis of some aspects of the environment, particularly when the assessment may indicate the probable outcome of a specific course of action.

15

Cultural Differences and Culture Change

CROSSING NATIONAL BOUNDARIES involves a step into different social and cultural environments. The problems faced by the enterprise that does business in one language and one culture are quite different from those that arise when dealing with two, three, four, or perhaps fifty, languages and cultures. Groups of people, or societies, differ in their values and beliefs, in their aspirations and motivations, and in the ways they satisfy their desires. Such cultural differences pervasively influence all dimensions of international business activity.

THE MEANING OF CULTURE

By culture we mean the whole set of social norms and responses that condition a population's behavior. It is these that make one social environment different from another and give each a shape of its own. The basic discipline that is most relevant here is cultural anthropology. Cultural anthropologists have devoted a great deal of time and effort to definitions of culture, arguing what should or should not be included.[1]

Basic to all is the idea that culture is acquired and inculcated. It is the set of rules and behavior patterns that an individual learns but does not inherit at birth. For every society these norms and behavioral responses develop into a different cultural pattern which gets passed down through the generations with continual embellishment and

---

[1]See A. L. Kroeber and Clyde Kluckhohn, "Culture: A Critical Review of Concepts and Definitions," (Papers of the Peabody Museum of American Archaeology and Ethnology, Harvard University, Cambridge, Mass., 47. no. 1, 1952), pp. 1–223.

adaptation; but with its own focus on aspects that are most highly developed.

For much cultural conditioning, the individual is unaware of the learning. The subtle process of inculcating culture through example and reward or punishment is generally much more powerful than direct instruction, and the individual unwittingly adopts the cultural norm. This process of learning a cultural pattern, called *enculturation,* conditions the individual so that a large proportion of his behavior fits the requirements of his culture and yet is determined below his level of conscious thought.[2] To the individual his cultural conditioning is like an iceberg—he is unaware of nine tenths of it.

The concept of culture is so broad that it gives little guidance to anyone wishing to study or compare cultures. Some classification of the elements of a culture is needed as a basic framework for grasping the cultural pattern. One such approach was proposed by George P. Murdock in the form of an elaborate list of more than 70 cultural universals which he argued occur in every culture known to history or ethnography. Arranged in alphabetical order to emphasize their variety, these are listed in Figure 15–1. While a one-dimensional checklist such as this has major limitations, it can nevertheless be of considerable value. The international manager of a firm selling razors and razor blades, for example, must be aware that he is dealing with the puberty customs of different cultures. Moreover, as most razors are given as gifts he is also dealing with gift giving, courtship, and family patterns. An examination of cultural patterns under each of these headings will certainly suggest differences in marketing strategy from country to country.

A sensitivity to the elements of culture and the ways in which they differ brings with it an ability to analyze any happening from its cultural perspective. What on the surface may look like a similar happening in different cultures may well be composed of many different cultural elements. The apparently simple phenomenon of a family meal, for instance, could be viewed as an extensive set of different rules concerning the time the meal is eaten, the seating arrangements, the roles played by each in initiating or ending conversation and in interrupting or changing the subject, the comments regarded as humorous, the facial expressions used, the values placed on different foods, the attitudes toward age, and so on. Moreover, the shape and size of the table will differ, as will the utensils, the way they are used, and how the people eat.

---

[2]Melville J. Herskovits, *Cultural Anthropology* (New York: Alfred A. Knopf, Inc., 1963), p. 326.

FIGURE 15–1
Cultural Universals

age grading	food taboos	music
athletic sports	funeral rites	mythology
bodily adornment	games	numerals
calendar	gestures	obstetrics
cleanliness training	gift giving	penal sanctions
community organization	government	personal names
cooking	greetings	population policy
cooperative labor	hairstyles	postnatal care
cosmology	hospitality	pregnancy usages
courtship	housing hygiene	property rights
dancing	incest taboos	propitiation of
decorative art	inheritance rules	supernatural beings
divination	joking	puberty customs
division of labor	kingroups	religious rituals
dream interpretation	kinship nomenclature	residence rules
education	language	sexual restrictions
eschatology	law	soul concepts
ethics	luck superstitions	status differentiation
ethnobotany	magic	surgery
etiquette	marriage	tool making
faith healing	mealtimes	trade
family	medicine	visiting
feasting	modesty concerning	weaning
fire making	natural functions	weather control
folklore	mourning	

Source: George P. Murdock, "The Common Denominator of Cultures" in *The Science of Man in the World Crises*, ed. Ralph Linton (New York: Columbia University Press, 1945), pp. 123–42.

CULTURE AND COMMUNICATION

A language is inextricably linked with all aspects of a culture, and each culture reflects in its language what is of value to the people. Culture is largely inculcated through language—spoken or written. Very little of what man learns is actually learned from his individual experience. Language, then, becomes the embodiment of culture. It may even condition what we look for and therefore see. One anthropologist comparing the structure of languages pointed out that Eskimo languages have several different words for types of snow, while the English language has one, and Aztec uses the same basic word stem for snow, ice, and cold. With only one word for snow we tend to identify only the broad classification.[3]

When communication involves translation from one language into

---

[3]Paul Henle, *Language, Thought, and Culture* (Ann Arbor: University of Michigan Press, 1958).

another, the problems of ascertaining meaning that arise within one culture are multiplied many times. Translation is not simply a matching of words with identical meanings. It involves interpretation of the cultural patterns and concepts of one country in terms of the patterns and concepts of another. Awareness of the difficulties of translation is particularly important for legal agreements. As a distinguished international lawyer has noted, "When contracts cross national borders, they may alter in character as well as language."[4]

Communication does not always take the form of language. All behavior communicates and, as Edward Hall has so clearly pointed out, each culture may be different in the way it experiences and uses time, space, relationships, and a variety of other aspects of culture.[5] The use of time in one culture may convey a set of meanings quite different from the meanings for a similar use of time in another culture. To be 30 minutes late for an appointment with a business associate may be the height of rudeness in *Culture A* but in *Culture B* it may be early and unexpectedly reliable. Different messages may be conveyed by the amount of notice given for a meeting, the time of departure, invitations to future commitments, or the way in which a party agrees to the order of discussion at the meeting. In some cultures a delay in answering a communication is interpreted by the other party as a lack of interest. In other cultures the more important a matter the more time is taken to respond. Operating difficulties can arise when workers from an agrarian peasant society are required to accept the kind of scheduling of time and routine essential for efficient industrial operations. In most agrarian societies, work is not equated with time and is not regularly and precisely scheduled. Instead, work is geared to seasonal emergencies, climatic threats, or sporadic exhaustion of supplies or resources.[6] Thus, setting time schedules or deadlines will evoke a positive response in certain cultures and a negative response in others.

In a similar way, the use of space conveys different meanings. The distance one person stands away from another indicates the degree of relationship or interest and can dramatically influence what is said. Different cultures have different norms for the appropriate distance for a given type of interaction. Middle Easterners and Latin Americans, for example, stand much closer than Western Europeans. The size of an office in relation to other offices conveys a great deal about the status of an American executive. In the Arab world, the size and location of

[4]Henry P. deVries, "The Language Barriers," *Columbia Journal of World Business,* July–August 1969, p. 79.

[5]Edward T. Hall, *The Silent Language* (New York: Doubleday & Company, 1959).

[6]Conrad M. Arensberg and Arthur M. Niehoff, *Introducing Social Change: A Manual for Americans Overseas* (Chicago: Aldine Publishing Co., 1964), p. 164.

an office are poor indicators of the importance of the person who occupies it.

IMPACT OF CULTURAL DIFFERENCES ON THE INTERNATIONAL FIRM

Any business operating within a single country must adjust to the culture within which it operates, but the need for cultural sensitivity and adjustment is much greater for the international firm. The local firm may introduce an innovation in the form of a new product or new business practice only infrequently. For the international firm, in comparison, cross-national transfer of any one of its old products or conventional practices may represent an innovation. When a firm has an existence outside a culture, many of its actions will introduce something new. There are many ways in which a firm may be an unwitting agent for transplanting aspects of one culture into another.

Cultural differences that can affect international business operations arise in all aspects of business activity and have their impact within each of the traditional functions. Differences in the behavior of customers must be taken into account in product policies and market-ing strategies. The German housewife values convenience and can be rather easily persuaded to buy packaged soup. The French housewife prefers homemade soup because it fulfills her image of herself as the mother.

Differences in behavior and values of employees can have a major impact on the effectiveness of production-management policies. The African factory worker, for example, may find paternalism a desirable practice because it helps replace security feelings that are lost when the worker leaves the tribal group. The American factory worker, on the other hand, tends to feel that paternalistic management is outdated because it restricts a current need to express individuality.

The external relations of the international firm can also be strongly influenced by cultural variables. In dealing with local business firms in a specific national environment, the international enterprise may have to recognize that agreements and accommodations among poten-tial competitors, rather than aggressive competition, are the accepted norm. In raising money from local banks or security markets, personal reputation may be the key requirement in one environment whereas a high degree of financial disclosure may be the more important element in another.

For the multinational enterprise the impact of cultural variables affects management at two levels—the national and the multinational. The issues at the national level might be characterized as bicultural. The distinction is essentially the same as that made in Chapter 1 between foreign operations and international business. At the national level, the situation is largely of a "we and they" type. The manager of a subsidiary must be aware of possible conflicts between local conditions and the cultural assumptions underlying the business practices being imported. Essentially these problems are two-sided, and management personnel of subsidiaries must be the bridge between the local situation and the international enterprise.

At the multinational level, or more specifically at the global or regional headquarters of the international enterprise, the task is to coordinate and integrate business activities that are operating in many different cultural environments. Managers must deal with many languages and across many cultures. The problems are both horizontal— across many cultures—and vertical—between each subsidiary and headquarters. And the organizational structure and policies of the global enterprise must facilitate communications and the implementation of policies across many cultures in order to achieve global goals.

CULTURAL ASSESSMENT FOR INTERNATIONAL BUSINESS

The extent of the impact of cultural differences on international business makes quite clear the need for skills in cultural assessment on the part of the international manager. The manager may never become an expert anthropologist, sociologist, and social psychologist in addition to his prime role as a management specialist, but he should at least develop skills in assessing the key cultural elements that will have a direct bearing on his effectiveness as a manager.

There is no one method to adopt in making cultural assessments as a basis for specific business decisions. Business problems cover such a wide range that the methods used may extend from a narrow-depth study of receptivity to a new management practice, through to broad assessment of a society's attitudes to spending. In this section the characteristics of various approaches that the business manager might adopt are outlined. The remainder of the chapter then concentrates on the basic content of cultural assessment.

Approaches for Assessing Cultural Differences

The most common approach to cultural assessment is a partial approach confined to studying particular aspects of a culture. Partial approaches are less powerful than comprehensive approaches that endeavor to identify and classify an entire range of cultural differences. The immense number of elements that can vary between cultures, however, makes overall approaches extremely unwieldy and costly to use. A compromise, often used by social anthropologists, is to compose a word picture of some constrained slice of behavior in the culture being examined, emphasizing, as would an artist, the more significant elements in the subject. Examples of such word pictures would be a description of a day in the life of a typical consumer,[7] or the motivation and thinking leading an employee to instigate a major confrontation with another worker.

In examining cultural patterns the manager should be aware of similarities as well as differences. Cross-cultural analysis for international business tends to emphasize differences because they are likely to create business problems. But to err by perceiving more differences than actually exist can also cause serious difficulties. Take the matter of managerial preferences for risk taking. The American executive may see the Japanese as different, whereas recent cross-cultural studies suggest that they are alike.[8] An American might find himself needlessly overexplaining his position, trying to convince the Japanese to be more adventuresome.

Another general caveat is that observed cultural patterns may be representative of a national group yet not applicable to everyone in the group. What is usually being discussed is a modal pattern, and considerable variation from the mode will exist within a group or a subset of the group. In fact, for some cultural characteristics there may be a wider range within a given society than between societies. The businessman should be careful always to define the limits of the group he is interested in and still be prepared to allow for individual differences.

Approaches for Assessing Cultural Change

Whatever the scope of the variables included in a cultural assessment, the assessment may be either static or dynamic. A static assessment serves only to identify the differences in variables between cultures. A dynamic assessment seeks to indicate which variables will change and perhaps in what order and with what speed. For the international manager engaged in cross-cultural transfers of products, practices, and ideas, the identification of what changes will be readily accepted and what will be rejected can mean the difference between success and failure.

Two approaches that may be helpful in mapping cultural change as

---

[7]Oscar Lewis, *Five Families: Mexican Case Studies in the Culture of Poverty* (New York: Basic Books, Inc., 1959).

[8]Bernard M. Bass, *The American Adviser Abroad,* Technical Report 27, Management Research Center of the College of Business Administration (Rochester, N.Y.: University of Rochester, August 1969), p. 12.

a basis for business decisions have begun to develop in business literature. The first is a mapping of the way any change is expected to diffuse through the culture. The second is a mapping of the decision-making and influence process for the key individuals to be affected by the change at each stage. Such mappings make quite explicit the assumptions that are held about the change process and frequently provide a necessary framework against which to specify actual research questions. Without some mapping of these two processes, any quantification on which to base a decision to introduce the change could hardly be soundly based.

An interesting summary of research, which finally resulted in a verbal presentation of these two processes after tortuous study, has been used as a case study in many business schools over the last decade.[9] Failing to gain adequate penetration of the French market for its packaged soups, an international company commissioned a motivational research study into the attitudes of French housewives toward soup. After research involving 60 nonguided interviews, 4 group discussions, 200 localized semi-guided interviews, 2,000 general interviews, and 400 supplementary interviews, the research group identifies the characteristics of housewives with different attitudes toward the purchase of packaged soup. The reader is then left to discuss the problems of measuring the numbers of housewives in each category and building an appropriate promotional campaign.

Research into the pattern and speed of adoption, diffusion, or negative diffusion (i.e., elimination) of products or practices within cultures has received a great deal of attention in recent years. An increasing tendency is to examine the process of change quantitatively over time.[10] The accumulated curve for numbers adopting a particular change has been widely shown to be S shaped. This basic shape holds for social changes in, for example, education, divorce, and career patterns, as well as for technological advances and changes in business practices. Moreover, a general logistic equation fits these diffusion curves almost as well whether the adopting units of the social system are individuals, families, firms, or governments.

The generality of these accumulated findings on diffusion suggests that quantitative analysis of change will be a valuable line of approach for the international manager. To date, most attention has been confined to demand forecasting of the direct adoption of products, but

---

[9] *The Chardon Company*, a case prepared by L'Institute pour l'Etude des Methodes de Direction de l'Enterprise (IMEDE), Lausanne, Switzerland, 1960.

[10] Robert L. Homblin, R. Brooke Jacobsen, and Jerry L. L. Miller, *A Mathematical Theory of Social Change* (New York: John Wiley & Sons, Inc., 1973).

forecasting of social changes that influence the demand for a product should prove equally useful. Attempts to project ahead the rate of adoption of a new product, based on the rate of adoption at very early stages, have so far proved of only limited value, but accuracy increases as the degree of penetration expands.[11]

Adjusting for Cultural Bias

In all cases requiring cross-cultural assessment the problem of cultural bias will be present. Everyone tends unwittingly to bias their view of other cultures by unconscious acceptance of their own cultural conditioning. It takes a great deal of discipline to force the mind to see things that one's own culture ignores or places in low value. Then again, the closer the observer is to the culture, the more difficult it is to see accurately the changes that are taking place in it.

Cultural bias can be reduced by using researchers from the culture to be studied, and through the development of culturally sensitive management (see Chapter 23). Specific attempts to eliminate what Lee has called the "self-reference criterion" (SRC), however, can be built into the research approach.[12] Lee suggests that problems be first defined in terms of the cultural traits, habits, or norms of the home society, and then redefined, without value judgments, in terms of the foreign cultural traits, habits, and norms. The difference between these two specifications indicates the likely cultural bias, or SRC effect, which can then be isolated and carefully examined to see how it influences the concept of the problem. Following this examination, the problem is redefined with the bias removed. Lee has illustrated how such an approach can be used for a wide variety of business problems. Its value lies in forcing the researcher or manager posing the problem to make very specific his assumptions about the cultural elements affecting the problem and to question whether they hold for another culture.

PARTIAL CULTURAL ASSESSMENT: SOME KEY ASPECTS

It would be impossible to list and evaluate any significant propor-
tion of the variables that could have a major impact on international business. This section, therefore, is limited to a brief introduction to

---

[11]Frank M. Bass and Charles W. King, "The Theory of First Purchase of New Products," in *A New Measure of Responsibility for Marketing*, ed. Keith Cox and Ben M. Enis (Chicago: American Marketing Association, 1968).

[12]James A. Lee, "Cultural Analysis in Overseas Operations," *Harvard Business Review*, March–April 1966, pp. 106–14.

some key aspects that are fundamental to the way in which business is managed and yet vary greatly among cultures.

Attitudes toward Work and Achievement

The dominant view in a society toward wealth and material gain can have a significant bearing on the types, qualities, and numbers of individuals who pursue entrepreneurial and management careers as well as on the way workers respond to material incentives.[13] In most countries in the world, wealth tends to be considered desirable and the prospect of material gain operates as a significant motivation. But there are societies where a worker will be on the job until he earns a certain amount of money and then be absent until these earnings are exhausted. In some affluent societies, moreover, young people are becoming more interested in job satisfaction per se, or the opportunities in a prospective job for involvement in public welfare activities, than in straight financial rewards.

Variations among cultures in the dominant views toward achievement and work, which can be a vital determinant of management performance and productive efficiency, have been the subject of considerable research by David McClelland and his associates under the rubric of "achievement motivation."[14] The achievement motivation of an individual refers to a basic attitude toward life, namely, the willingness to commit oneself to the accomplishment of tasks considered by the person to be worthwhile and difficult. An achievement-motivated person makes accomplishment an end it itself. He does not reject tangible rewards, but they are not essential.

Measures of achievement motivation have been devised, and desires for achievement within different countries compared. Attitudes toward achievement in a country appear to be closely associated with rates of economic development. Countries where individuals show a high achievement motivation tend to have rapid rates of growth. McClelland maintains that achievement motivation is the prime factor in managerial success. He suggests that the best place to recruit managers in a number of countries is from the middle and lower classes because these people are more apt to have a high achievement need than if they come from either upper- or lower-class background. Most recently, experiments have been undertaken in various countries on the effectiveness of techniques in changing achievement motivations.

[13]Richard N. Farmer and Barry M. Richman, *Comparative Management and Economic Progress* (Homewood, Ill.: Richard D. Irwin, Inc., 1965), pp. 177–89.

[14]David C. McClelland, *The Achieving Society* (Princeton, N.J.: D. Van Nostrand Co., 1961).

Attitudes toward the Future

Some of the principal differences among cultures lie in assumptions and attitudes relating to man's ability to influence the future. For example, an assumption that people can substantially influence the future underlies much of U.S. management philosophy. This belief in self-determination contrasts sharply with a fatalistic viewpoint in some Moslem cultures that the future is not in man's hands. It differs also from a mystical view that events are likely to be determined by the capricious influence of spirits that must be appeased.[15] Whatever the explanation for varying attitudes, the critical issue for business operations is whether a person believes that events will occur regardless of what he does or whether he believes that he can help shape future events.

The self-determination or "master of destiny" attitude is generally qualified by the accompanying view that future aspirations must be realistic and that hard work is necessary to achieve future goals. With these qualifications, the self-determination assumption has profoundly shaped U.S. management practices. As only one illustration, long-range planning becomes a worthwhile investment because of confidence that planning can influence what is to happen. Obviously, in cultures where the fatalistic or mystical attitudes prevail, management practices based on other assumptions are not likely to be effective.

Patterns of Decision Making

The extent to which objective analysis is used for decision making varies greatly among cultures. There is a strong cultural goal underlying U.S. management practices that decisions should be based on objective analyses of facts and that all persons who can contribute relevant information should do so. Such a norm leads to large collections of data and the development of impersonal decision-making techniques.

Decision making on a factual and rational basis is not the standard pattern in some societies. The personal judgment of a senior executive may be the accepted basis for a decision, and a request that the executive explain or give the rationale for his decision would be interpreted as a lack of confidence in the executive's judgment. Furthermore, it may be considered inappropriate for a senior executive to seek facts and consult others—especially his juniors—on matters on which he is already presumed to be wise. In such cultures, hierarchi-

---

[15]William H. Newman, "Is Management Exportable?" *Columbia Journal of World Business,* January–February 1970, pp. 7–8.

cal, emotional, and mystical considerations, rather than objective analyses, may dominate.

Attitudes toward Authority

The dominant view of authority in a society may range from an autocratic system at one extreme to a democratic-participative system at the other extreme. If authority is looked upon as an absolute natural right of management or of other types of formal leaders, the effect on managerial behavior would typically be a high degree of centralization and little delegation of authority. At the other extreme, managerial authority would be shared with subordinates and workers, and considerable decentralization in decision making would be typical of business enterprises.

It is not possible to say which forms of managerial authority along the continuum are best in terms of efficiency or in achieving other business goals. The forms vary greatly from Japan to West Germany and from the United States to Yugoslavia. Yet each of these countries has had impressive records of business performance and economic growth in recent years. Whatever authority system prevails in a given country, the international enterprise will have to relate its management patterns to the expectations and traditions of local employees.

Authority systems are highly relevant to aspects of business operations other than management. In marketing, it is important to know whether decision making within customer organizations with respect to purchases is typically decentralized or reserved for the top-echelon executives. In negotiating with governments, the international businessman will have to know whether decision authority resides with low-level bureaucrats or must be handled at the highest levels of government bureaucracy.

Expression of Disagreement

Another cultural element that affects interpersonal relations is the difference among societies in frankness of expression and tolerance for personal differences. In Far Eastern cultures it is traditional to value politeness over blunt truth. The Japanese businessman finds it inappropriate to say no in many situations. In dealing with an American, the Japanese may make all kinds of barely favorable noises and then maybe say that he'll think about the matter. He has actually told the American no, but it is entirely possible that the American thinks he has said yes, and the American later imagines that he has somehow been deceived.

In many Latin American countries, frankly expressed differences in views do not easily fit the culture. If a person expresses criticisms of a policy in order to improve the quality of decision making, such statements are likely to be interpreted as personal attacks. If a subordinate disagrees with his boss, the boss will most certainly feel insulted. Persons in subordinate positions are expected to either present information or judgments that support the ideas of senior officials or be silent.

Responsibility to Family

Some version of the extended family still prevails in many countries. Under this pattern large numbers of near as well as quite distant relatives are encompassed in a system of shared rights and obligations. All members of this group are interdependent, and it is the responsibility of the leaders to see that economic resources are available to satisfy the needs of each member of the group. The extended family pattern is still strong in a country like India. In contrast, the more limited nuclear family, which only includes the mother, father, and children, is the significant unit in many of the advanced countries.

Strong and extended family ties can result in what has been characterized as patrimonial management.[16] Ownership and key positions in a business enterprise are held by family members. Nepotism is generally dominant in the full range of employment decisions, and business goals are oriented toward family interests and aspirations. Such patrimonial management has the advantages of encouraging teamwork, loyalty, and mutual interest. Family codes can enforce morality in financial and other matters, and family loyalty attracts and holds managers in situations where the supply of qualified managers is limited. But the extended family situation also has drawbacks. It emphasizes nepotism rather than competence. It can vitiate the will to work by limiting personal incentives. Family business may be run like an authoritarian household with little concern for considerations other than family goals. And family enterprises may suffer from a lack of invigorating ideas and innovations which can come from outsiders.

Family patterns can be extremely important from the standpoint of marketing as well as general management. In Western societies, the husband and wife typically share decision making on family purchases, with children and other members of the family having a secondary vote. In the extended family, the family patriarch holds the key decision-making position, although this is declining with the monetization of the economy, the demise of family enterprises, and an

---

[16]Frederick Harbison and Charles A. Myers, *Management in the Industrial World* (New York: McGraw-Hill Book Co., 1959), pp. 69–73.

increase in geographic and social mobility. Notwithstanding these changes, the international manager must understand the different family patterns that prevail.

Social Structure

A final category of cultural elements can be grouped under the general heading of social structure. It includes such variables as interclass mobility, determinants of status, and patterns of education.

Few societies in the world assume that all men are equal. Instead, societies have traditional systems of ranking individuals and groups. Relative positions in the social hierarchy are based on ethnic, cultural, educational, and linguistic differences, as well as on economic position. Sometimes traditional social structures are fairly rigid such as the caste system of India. Sometimes the distinctions are more fluid and considerable interclass mobility is the rule. In most countries of the world there is a distinction between the elite, who have political and economic control of the country, and the relatively underprivileged peasant groups.[17]

Two aspects of social structure are of special concern to the international enterprise—interclass mobility and the status assigned by a society to individuals who engage in business occupations. If a rigid social structure prevents a substantial number of individuals from moving into the ranks of management or other responsible business positions, managerial effectiveness is likely to be constrained in many, if not most, business activities. If the status assigned to business pursuits is low in the social structure, it will be difficult to attract adequate numbers of competent persons to business positions.

Even the United States, which is widely regarded as a rather open society with few class distinctions, has extensive class barriers to individual mobility. Many business firms have excluded from executive positions virtually all minority groups, including blacks, Jews, Mexicans, Orientals, American Indians, and many others. Such barriers have been breaking down, yet it is still true that social barriers may be serious obstacles for many highly qualified and competent persons in the United States. In most other countries, social barriers are likely to be even greater hindrances to individual mobility. The British social system, although much more flexible than it was a few decades ago, still assigns great importance to family and university background when individuals are being considered for high-level positions in government and business.[18]

---

[17]Arensberg and Niehoff, *Introducing Social Change*, p. 41.

[18]For example, see David J. Hall and Gilles Amado-Fischgrund, "Chief Executives in Britain," *European Business,* January 1969; David Granick, *The European Executive* (London: Weidenfeld and Nicolson, 1962), chap. 7.

In many countries of the world much higher status tends to be associated with land ownership or government positions, or professional or intellectual activity than is enjoyed by the businessman, engineer, mechanic, agronomist, or some other person concerned directly with production.[19] There is probably no country in the world where businessmen have the highest status. Even in the United States such occupations as supreme court justice, medical doctor, professor, and physical scientist have outranked corporation executives in surveys of high school students. Yet in many countries such as the United States, Japan, and even the USSR, managers of business enterprises have sufficiently high social status to enable business enterprises to attract large quantities of capable recruits.

Educational patterns generally reflect and reinforce patterns of class mobility and status. Where class mobility is high and status depends upon merit rather than family or caste, the educational system is likely to be open to students on the basis of their performance, and training in technical and management fields is available. Most commonly throughout the world, higher education has been restricted to the elite and upper classes and the patterns of education have emphasized the liberal arts and preparation for living the good life. Thus, the supply of trained people may be relatively small and the kinds of training available not closely related to business.

OVERALL APPROACHES TO CULTURAL ASSESSMENT

The international businessman may never have the time nor the need to build a comprehensive picture of a particular culture. He will usually be concerned with individual elements of culture that have a direct bearing on his managerial decision making. On the other hand, a familiarity with one or two ways in which an overall culture can be conceptualized will give him a framework on which to draw. At least it will provide him with a mental checklist of elements that may be important to his particular problem. Two such overall approaches which have been utilized in the international business literature, both two-dimensional, will be briefly outlined here. The first is that developed by Edward T. Hall and the second is an attempt by Richard N. Farmer and Barry M. Richman to develop a cultural framework specifically related to business decision making.[20,21]

Hall presents his map of culture as a two-dimensional matrix composed of 10 aspects of human activity which he calls Primary Message Systems. These are shown in Figure 15–2. While each aspect

---

[19]UNESCO, *Report of the World Social Situation* (Paris: March 9, 1961), p. 79.
[20]Hall, *The Silent Language,* especially Chapter 3.
[21]Farmer and Richman, *Comparative Management.*

FIGURE 15–2

Primary Message Systems of Edward Hall's *The Silent Language*

Primary Message System	*Depicts Attitudes and Cultural Rules for:*
1. Interaction	The ordering of man's interaction with those around him, through language, touch, noise, gesture, and so forth
2. Association	The organization (grouping) and structuring of society and its components
3. Subsistence	The ordering of man's activities in feeding, working, and making a living
4. Bisexuality	The differentiation of roles, activities, and function along sex lines
5. Territoriality	The possession, use, and defense of space and territory
6. Temporality	The use, allocation, and division of time
7. Learning	The adaptive process of learning and instruction
8. Play	Relaxation, humor, recreation, and enjoyment
9. Defense	Protection against man's environment, including medicine, warfare, and law
10. Exploitation	Turning the environment to man's use through technology, construction, and extraction of materials

Source: Adapted from Edward K. Hall, *The Silent Language* (Garden City, N.Y.: Doubleday & Company, Inc., 1959), pp. 61–81.

can be examined alone, Hall shows how a grasp of the complex interrelationships of a culture can be obtained by commencing with any of the 10 aspects and studying its intersection with each of the others. In a matrix there will be two intersections of each pair of aspects. If we were to start examination of a culture through the learning aspect, it would first intersect with the interaction aspect to raise questions about interaction in learning and the learning of interaction. We might want to examine the pattern that teachers and learners adopt for communicating with each other or what rules and knowledge get passed on within the culture concerning the ways people should interact. Again, the matrix provides two intersections of bisexuality and learning. Under these we could study the differences in how and what the sexes are taught and, on the other hand, what is taught about sexual roles in society. Both aspects will differ from culture to culture.

For a more direct application of Hall's matrix to international business, take the example of a large manufacturer of toys and games assessing opportunities in a new country. The firm will be directly engaged in the play aspect of the new culture, and it is certain that the cultural patterns with respect to play will differ from those the firm is currently dealing with. Use of Hall's matrix would raise 18 categories of questions about play patterns in the new culture. Stemming from the intersection of play with the remaining primary message systems, the first two categories would ask about interaction in play and about play in interaction, the second two would ask about the associations—that is, organizations involved in play and games involving associations, and so on. Questions raised within the 18 categories are illustrated in Figure 15–3 but it must be clear that the map does not magically produce the right answers or even the right questions. This is simply one structured approach to investigating how a new culture may differ. The reader who rejects a structured approach, however, should be sure in his own mind that his ad hoc alternative does develop an adequate sensitivity to the important cultural differences.

Farmer and Richman also use a matrix approach. They propose a list of critical environmental constraints, or cultural elements, from which the 15 shown in Figure 15–4 are taken. Against this, they set another list of 77 critical elements in the managerial process. The general categories for the critical elements are planning and innovation, control, organization, staffing, direction, leadership and motivation, marketing policies, production and procurement, research and development, finance, and public and external relations. Farmer and Richman contend that managerial effectiveness is largely determined by the pattern of external constraints. As the environment changes, so too must the pattern of management. What might be effective in producing results in one culture may be completely ineffectual in another. By examining the managerial alternatives against the background of external constraints, managers will move toward a pattern of business practice most appropriate to the situation and away from absolute rules imposed without regard for the situation. In a very simple application, for example, the internal procedures and organization structure should change radically where the bulk of the workers do not accept the idea of cause and effect, that is, the scientific method. Fewer rational requests and guiding principles will be called for and more direct rules and internal checking procedures will be required.

This type of matrix approach can be readily adapted to any business situation. On the vertical axis would appear relevant cultural variables and along the horizontal axis the dependent variables of interest to management. The body of the matrix would show the nature of the

FIGURE 15–3
A Business Application of Edward Hall's Map of Culture

Intersections of Play and Other Primary Message Systems	*Sample Questions Concerning Cultural Patterns Significant for Marketing Toys and Games*
1. Interaction/play	How do people interact during play as regards competitiveness, instigation, or leadership?
2. Play/interaction	What games are played involving acting, role playing, or other aspects of real-world interaction?
3. Association/play	Who organizes play and how do the organization patterns differ?
4. Play/association	What games are played about organization; for example, team competitions and games involving kings, judges, or leader-developed rules and penalties?
5. Subsistence/play	What are the significant factors regarding people such as distributors, teachers, coaches, or publishers who make their livelihood from games?
6. Play/subsistence	What games are played about work roles in society such as doctors, nurses, firemen?
7. Bisexuality/play	What are the significant differences between the sexes in the sports, games, and toys enjoyed?
8. Play/bisexuality	What games and toys involve bisexuality; for example, dolls, dressing up, dancing?
9. Territoriality/play	Where are games played and what are the limits observed in houses, parks, streets, schools, and so forth?
10. Play/territoriality	What games are played about space and ownership, for example, Monopoly?
11. Temporality/play	At what ages and what times of the day and year are different games played?
12. Play/temporality	What games are played about and involving time, for example, clocks, speed tests?
13. Learning/play	What patterns of coaching, tuition, and training exist for learning games?
14. Play/learning	What games are played about and involving learning and knowledge, for examples, quizzes?
15. Defense/play	What are the safety rules for games, equipment, and toys?
16. Play/defense	What war and defense games and toys are utilized?
17. Exploitation/play	What resources and technology are permitted or utilized for games and sport, for example, hunting and fishing rules, use of parks, cameras, vehicles, and so forth?
18. Play/exploitation	What games and toys about technology or exploitation are used, for example, scouting, chemical sets, microscopes?

FIGURE 15–4
Critical Environmental Constraints

Educational-Cultural Variables

1. *Literacy level:* The percentage of the total population and those presently employed in industry who can read, write, and do simple arithmetic calculations, and the average years of schooling of adults.
2. *Specialized vocational and technical training and general secondary education:* Extent, types, and quality of education and training of this kind not directly under the control or direction of industrial enterprises; the type, quantity, and quality of persons obtaining such education or training and the proportion of those employed in industry who have such education and training.
3. *Higher education:* The percentage of the total population and those employed in industry with post-high school education, plus the types and quality of such education; the types of persons obtaining higher education.
4. *Special management-development programs:* The extent and quality of management-development programs which are not run internally by productive enterprises and which are aimed at improving the skills and abilities of managers and/or potential managers of different types and levels attending or having completed such programs.
5. *Attitude toward education:* The general or dominant cultural attitude toward education and the acquisition of knowledge in terms of their presumed desirability; the general attitude toward different types of education.
6. *Educational match with requirements:* The extent and degree to which the types of formal education and training available in a given country fit the needs of productive enterprises on all levels of skill and achievement. This is essentially a summary category; depending on the type of job involved, different educational constraints indicated above would be more important.

Sociological-Cultural Variables

1. *Attitude toward industrial managers and management:* The general or dominant social attitude toward industrial and business managers of all sorts, and the way that such managers tend to view their managerial jobs.
2. *View of authority and subordinates:* The general or dominant cultural attitude toward authority and persons in subordinate positions, and the way that industrial managers tend to view their authority and their subordinates.
3. *Interorganizational cooperation:* Extent and degree to which business enterprises, government agencies, labor unions, educational institutions, and other relevant organizations cooperate with one another in ways conducive to industrial efficiency and general economic progress.
4. *Attitude toward achievement and work:* The general or dominant cultural attitude toward individual or collective achievement and productive work in industry.
5. *Class structure and individual mobility:* The extent of opportunities for social class and individual mobility, both vertical and horizontal, in a given country, and the means by which it can be achieved.
6. *Attitude toward wealth and material gain:* Whether or not the acquisition of wealth from different sources is generally considered socially desirable and the way that persons employed in industry tend to view material gain.
7. *Attitude toward scientific method:* The general social and dominant individual attitude toward the use of rational, predictive techniques in solving various types of business, technical, economic, and social problems.
8. *Attitude toward risk taking:* Whether or not the taking of various types of personal, collective, or national risks is generally considered acceptable, as well as the dominant view toward specific types of risk taking in business and industry; the degree and extent to which risk taking tends to be a rational process in a particular country.

FIGURE 15-4 *(concluded)*

9. *Attitude toward change:* The general cultural attitude toward social changes of all types which bears directly on industrial performance in a given country, and the dominant attitude among persons employed in industry toward all types of significant changes in enterprise operations.

Source: Richard N. Farmer and Barry M. Richman, *Comparative Management and Economic Progress* (Homewood, Ill.: Richard D. Irwin, Inc., 1965), p. 29.

relationship between cultural variables and each management variable.

CULTURE CHANGE AND RESISTANCE TO CHANGE

A characteristic of human culture is that change does occur. Attitudes, values, beliefs, and behavior are constantly changing, although change may not be occurring rapidly or without resistance. The manager and the enterprise operating cross culturally, therefore, cannot rely upon a static understanding of cultural elements. Business performance can be very sensitive to changes in cultural patterns through their effects on both customer demand and the internal operations of the firm. Furthermore, successful marketing is very largely a matter of correct timing and strategy in the development of innovations, the adoption of which imply a receptive culture. Of greatest interest to the international businessman will be an understanding of what aspects of a culture will resist change and how those will differ among cultures, how the process of change takes place in different cultures, and what the speed of change will be.

There are two seemingly contradictory forces within cultures. On the one hand, people attempt to protect and preserve their culture with an elaborate set of sanctions and laws invoked against those who deviate from their norms. On the other hand, the environment within which a culture exists is continually changing, and a culture must change in order to ensure its own continuity.[22] Where a culture comes into contact with other cultures, this same dichotomy exists. There is, on the one hand, an ingrained belief, called *ethnocentrism,* that the ways of one's own culture are superior to those of other cultures, and on the other hand, a realization that a culture must be competitive if it is to retain its own identity.

These conflicting forces operate to make some elements of culture highly resistant to change, while others immediately fall to innovations. Yet other elements may give an impression that they are

---

[22]Arensberg and Niehoff, *Introducing Social Change,* p. 99.

immutable but then change suddenly. How can these elements be differentiated?

Edward Hall's classification of cultural aspects into formal, informal, and technical provides a valuable insight here. The distinction between these classes is based primarily on differences in the way the cultural norm is learned, the culture's level of awareness of the norm, and the response to a deviation from the norm.

Formal rules are at the core of the culture and really determine its essence. They are taught through example and admonition as rules for which there is either right or wrong, with clear indication of when a mistake has been made. There is a formal awareness of what the norm is and a great deal of emotion if the norm is violated. In most societies it has been a formal rule, for example, that there should be no enjoyment from hurting others physically or from seeing them hurt. The rule is that hurting people is not fun, and from early childhood this will be made very clear, with penalties for breaking it.

Informal rules are not taught so directly. Usually the learner picks them up by imitation and is unaware of learning them. The society is generally unconscious of the rules, and if one is violated, there would be only an expression of anxiety or some informally learned reaction. The average child does not receive direct instruction in how to play. He is left to observe others and to do likewise. If the child attempts to dominate his playmates, for example, they will very likely develop ways of excluding him, but it would be unlikely for him to receive direct instruction on how to behave in groups.

Technical rules are usually taught in an instructional sense with logical and coherent reasoning attached to them. These are at the highest level of awareness as they are verbalized, reasoned, and explicit. There are few emotions attached to the violation of a technical rule. Breaking a rule by adopting a different training approach for an athletic sport, for example, would occasion intellectual interest but little emotion.

The aspects falling into each category differ from culture to culture. If we continue with a sporting example, for instance, we might find that the English regard acceptance of the referee's rulings as a fundamental principle of sportsmanship—a formal rule that would produce an emotional response from most of the population if they were confronted with a direct violation. On the other hand, the Germans may have a clear set of technical rules for when and how to object to rulings, while Americans adopt an informal approach that objections should be made as and when justified. Any aspect of culture could be compared between cultures in this way, and it is possible on an overall comparison probably incorporating a great deal of selective perception to argue that England has a formal culture, Germany a

330 International Business and Multinational Enterprises

technical culture, and the United States an informal culture. The reason for introducing the distinction, however, is not to produce comparisons but rather to produce a first classification of cultural aspects that indicates the likelihood of resistance to change.

Attitudes towards change clearly differ for each of the three classes. Formal rules would be held with great tenacity, change very slowly, and be particularly resistant to any attempt to force change from outside. Informal rules can change more easily. There is room for more deviation by individuals and imitation can be selective in one direction or another. Change comes most easily with technical rules, because they are readily observed, talked about, transmitted, and accepted at a more or less rational level.

While early conditioning in the rules of a culture gives it stability, later enculturation gives it the opportunity to change. Such changes are most likely to take the form of learning from real experience or from conscious comparison of alternatives on the technical level, with discussions among mature individuals as to the advantages of change and eventual consensus.[23] Thus, the key to culture change seems to lie in the informal system. In a complex and changing environment, imitation of others will not be perfect. When some of the variants that emerge seem to work better than others, they are copied and eventually develop as technical rules. As such, they are brought up to the conscious level and communicated as worthwhile.

Technical changes are most likely to deal with details of an activity—for example, the use of a new fertilizer or the introduction of a new type of motor. But the piling up of many minor variations that are initially consonant with the existing formal system can open the way for more fundamental changes in the formal and informal systems. A series of technical changes in this way creates a "cultural drift."[24] Technical and informal rules seem to surround each part of the formal system, and when these supports are removed, formal rules may eventually give way. This may explain why some parts of a culture reject change persistently only to collapse later on. Hall illustrates this sort of phenomena with the change in attitude towards premarital chastity in the United States.[25] Changes in women's social life, education, career patterns, and dress habits, and the widespread use of the private car removed many technical supports to the formal rule. After resisting change for many years, the rule eventually changed very rapidly.

The interrelationship of the elements of culture fuels the change process. Each change may affect others with which it is in association.

---

[23]Herskovits, *Cultural Anthropology*, p. 453.

[24]Ibid., p. 506.

[25]Hall, *Silent Language*, p. 113.

An extreme variant introduced at the technical level may produce a dynamic reaction throughout the entire culture. The introduction of the motor vehicle would be an example here.

Not all the new elements that evolve from within a culture, or are introduced from outside, are adopted by the culture. They have to fall on fertile ground in the sense that there is a perception of the need for the change and a broad acceptance of it. The social structure of the society and those who introduce the change or are aware of it will thus be important factors in its acceptance. These are examined more fully in the next section. Anthropologists, however, have noted that cultures tend to develop a particular interest in some parts of their system—called a *cultural focus.* One culture may build up a very elaborate set of rules concerned with family life, another may focus on agriculture, technology, or religion, and so on. Where this happens the culture is more likely to develop and adopt changes in those areas on which it places this emphasis. Conversely, less important areas will change less and there will be lower tolerance for change in them. The Arabs, for example, have regarded the "fellahin" engaged in agriculture as of very low status and have adopted few agricultural innovations in comparison with the Israelis who accord agriculture high status and reward successful agricultural innovation with almost national fame.

The international manager, then, would probably have the most success in introducing change into those parts of the culture that are treated technically and that are considered important. The greatest opportunities for business, though, may lie in identifying those areas where informal adaptations seem to be most successful and then acting as the agent in making a broader section of the population aware of them.

SOCIAL DYNAMICS OF CULTURAL CHANGE

It is as important for the international businessman to identify the roles different people will play in the change process as it is to identify what cultural aspects will resist change. When we talk of cultural change, we are really talking of changes in the pattern of behavior of the individuals adhering to that culture. The order in which persons with different characteristics adopt an innovation and the influences that affect their decision are thus of particular importance. The field of diffusion studies has a great deal to say about these.

Adopters of any innovation are conventionally classified into five groups according to the order in which they adopt the innovation, as follows:[26]

---

[26]Everett M. Rogers, *Diffusion of Innovations* (New York: The Free Press of Glencoe, 1962). Chapter 6 provides the references for most of the research generalizations that follow in this section.

Adopter Category

Innovators	First 2.5%
Early Adopters	Next 13.5%
Early majority	Next 34%
Late majority	Next 34%
Laggards	Remaining 16%

The idea behind this classification is that common characteristics may be identified for the adopters of each stage. It has been observed that adopter distributions for a wide range of innovations follow a bell-shaped curve over time that tends towards normality. Hence, the standard adopter classification divides innovations into those within one, two, or three standard deviations of the mean on a time basis. The rate of adoption refers to the time scale for the diffusion through the relevant population. A great deal of research has gone into identifying the characteristics of an innovation that will determine its rate. For example, the more advantageous an innovation, the faster its rate of adoption. Similarly, the faster the rate, the more compatible the new idea is with the culture and the greater is its communicability.

An individual's innovativeness has been shown to vary directly with the norms of his social system, but there are fairly general findings that innovators are regarded by themselves and by others as deviants from the norms of their culture or subculture. They tend to have a characteristic venturesomeness and to have seen more of other cultures than later adopters. One study of firms commencing export activity showed almost all the innovators to have international backgrounds.[27]

Early adopters tend to have a higher position in the social hierarchy than innovators and to rate high as opinion leaders. They may have a considerable influence on later adopters. The dominant characteristic of the people who make up the early majority seems to be their capacity for deliberation. They do not adopt until other respected persons have done so, seldom emerging as leaders. Contrasted with this, the dominant value of the people who make up the late majority is skepticism. They tend to wait until the weight of public opinion strongly favors the innovation before they proceed. Laggards tend to be older, to be suspicious of innovations, and to take the past and tradition as their point of reference.

Associated with the study of diffusion, and particularly relevant for cultural change, is the concept of an adoption process. This is conceived as a set of five mental stages through which an individual passes from first hearing about an innovation until he finally adopts it. These are (1) awareness, (2) interest, (3) evaluation, (4) trial, and (5)

---

[27]Kenneth Simmonds and Helen Smith, "The First Export Order: A Marketing Innovation," *British Journal of Marketing*, Summer 1968.

adoption. Studies of each of these stages and the information and influence sources important at each stage have provided some signficant generalizations about adoptions. It has been found that impersonal sources of information tend to be most influential at the awareness stage, and personal sources tend to be most influential at the evaluation stage. Commercial change agents, that is, advertising and selling, seem to be more important at the trial stage than at any other stage. In the earlier stages of the process nonlocal sources of information tend to be most important. But in the later stages local sources take the command position. These findings may be very significant for firms planning the introduction of products into new cultural environments.

It has been found that the period from awareness to trial is shorter for earlier adopters than for later adopters. Thus, awareness spreads faster than the adoption of an innovation. It is not surprising, therefore, that over the diffusion cycle, commercial change agents tend to become less important and personal influence tends to become more important.

In the marketing field it has been shown many times that when buying new or important products, buyers consult or copy other users.[28] These are frequently called reference groups,[29] but may be reference individuals.[30] They may be groups to which the customer aspires or belongs, or possibly to which he wants to avoid belonging. In some cases these reference groups will be the ones who have already adopted the innovation and in other cases merely the ones whose opinion is sought.

Opinion leaders can play an important part in the introduction of an innovation and many studies have examined the "two-step flow of communication" in which opinions are sought, weighted, and discussed and then finally a decision made.[31] Early adopters are most likely to be opinion leaders and, as against their followers, have a higher social status and financial position, have more social participation, and use more impersonal and technically accurate sources of information, with a wider geographical spread.[32]

Social-class identification by groups within a culture can also affect

---

[28]For example, see Eva Mueller, "The Sample Survey," in *Consumer Behavior,* vol. 1, *The Dynamics of Consumer Reaction,* ed. Lincoln H. Clark (New York: New York University Press, 1954), p. 45.

[29]Tamotsu Shibutani, "Reference Groups and Social Controls," in *Human Behavior and Social Processes,* ed. Arnold M. Rose (Boston: Houghton Mifflin Co., 1962), p. 128–47.

[30]Herbert Hyman, "Reflections on Reference Groups," *Public Opinion Quarterly,* Fall 1960.

[31]Elihu Katz and Paul Lazarsfeld, *Personal Influence* (Glencoe: Illinois Press, 1955).

[32]Rogers, *Diffusion of Innovations,* chap. 8.

334 International Business and Multinational Enterprises

the diffusion of an innovation. A social class, however defined, is likely to exhibit some common variants of the overall national culture, particularly if its members are grouped in the same living environment. One landmark study suggests that the cultural norms of a social class at the particular time were a significant factor in the acceptance or rejection of a particular innovation.[33] The pattern of interaction and influence that leads to adoption or rejection may also be largely carried on within one social class.[34] Changes may thus not trickle down the social scale with each class striving to copy classes above it. The international businessman must be prepared, therefore, to observe what happens within social groups as well as across a society as a whole.

ADJUSTING TO CULTURAL DIFFERENCES

To the extent possible, the experienced international enterprise will try to accept the values of local culture patterns and seek to work within the limits of the accepted behavior patterns and customary goals that underly these beliefs. In all circumstances, local traditions and habits are given respect and, as often as is possible in foreign operations, local concepts are permitted to continue in preference to substituting those of another culture pattern. As a general rule, foreign firms find it wise to adjust to local standards with less deviation than is permitted native companies because of nationalistic sensitivity to foreign influences.

Lee suggests that three general classes of business adaptation are important—product, individual, and institutional—and that the degree of necessary adjustment ranges from none, or token, to comprehensive.[35] Adaptation is defined as the achievement of business goals with a minimum of problems and setbacks due to the various manifestations of cultural conflict.

Adaptation in product policies, which includes marketing strategies, can be illustrated by the experience of the Singer Sewing Machine Company in meeting different requirements of cultural patterns in the various markets it sells.[36] In Moslem countries, the

---

33Graham Saxon, "Class and Conservatism in the Adoption of Innovations," *Human Relations* 9, no. 1 (1956): 91–100.

34Charles W. King, "Fashion Adoption: A Rebuttal of the 'Trickle Down Theory'," in *Toward Scientific Marketing,* ed. Stephen A. Greyser (Chicago: American Marketing Association, 1963), pp. 108–25.

35Lee, "Cultural Analysis," p. 107.

36"How to Attract the Ladies Without Starting a Riot," *Forbes,* October 15, 1964, p. 22.

women's position had been a secluded and protected one, particularly with strangers. The practice of purdah, or wearing a veil so as to be screened from the sight of strangers, reflected this cultural pattern. The success of sewing machine sales had been through sewing classes which Moslem women would not ordinarily be permitted to attend. In fact, at least one sewing machine salesman was sent to jail in Sudan for trying to encourage the wives to attend sewing classes. Singer was able to overcome this problem by selling the husbands first on how much additional work the women could do with sewing machines after taking sewing lessons. This was accomplished by having demonstration classes for the men who became convinced of the advantages and then ordered the wives to attend.

Individual adjustment is required of managers, and in the case of overseas personnel, the wives and families are also faced with the need to adjust to cultural differences. An expatriate manager who wishes to motivate natives in a host nation, not merely order them around, must first make some changes in himself. He may have to make adjustments in his personal manner of dealing with people. He should learn the local language. He should understand different attitudes toward time and adapt his behavior to local norms where such adaptation does not prejudice the achievement of business goals. Individual adjustments may be required to deal with other businessmen and government officials, as well as with employees and colleagues.

Institutional adaptation relates to changes in organizational structure and organizational policies to fit cultural differences. Institutional adaptation may be required at either the national or international level, or more commonly at both levels. The Syntex Corporation, with headquarters in Mexico City, its research center in California, and operations in at least 10 countries other than Mexico and the United States, chose to approach its adaptation problems through emphasis on organizational change. The company's philosophy was that the organization's culture must be changed in order for employees to change and develop most effectively. As a result, considerable attention was devoted to an organization model and the establishment of guidelines for creating the projected type of organization.[37]

International enterprises will have to face adaptation issues related to the home environment as well as to the cultural patterns of foreign countries. Adaptation may be required in governmental relations policies, in patterns of dealing with other business enterprises, and in internal operating policies. Hiring practices used in the United States may overlook class distinctions and assume that people from different

---

[37]Harold M. Rush, *Behavioral Science: Concepts and Management Applications* (New York: National Industrial Conference Board, 1969), pp. 130–38.

areas and factions will work well together. A company operating in Bangladesh may encounter serious difficulties by hiring Bihari refugees from India to work side by side with native Bengalis.

The general approach for cultural adaptation is to become explicitly aware of the cultural traits, habits, or norms of both the international enterprise and the foreign environment as they affect particular business problems. Then it is possible to examine how the culture bias of the enterprise complicates or prejudices an optimum solution of the problem. Where the effect of the culture bias is significant, adaptations of a product, institutional, or individual nature may be required by the enterprise. In many cases, as we will discuss below, part or all of the solution may be to try to change local cultural patterns.

PROMOTING CULTURAL CHANGE

Promoting change in the buying patterns of consumers and in the working behavior of employees is a common challenge facing the business enterprise, whether domestically or internationally oriented. And guidelines developed for inducing change are generally applicable to both domestic and international business operations. Additional complications at the international level are the significantly larger number of cultural variables, unfamiliarity and lack of experience with many new situations, and the limitations of culture conditioning on the manager or the enterprise trying to induce change.

Some of the guidelines for promoting change that have been developed by the anthropologists for cross-cultural situations are as follows:

The New and the Old. Unless they produce dramatic benefits, the easiest way to have innovations accepted is to have them present no open conflict with traditional values and customs and to graft on to them. Medicine is one field in which this problem has often occurred. In societies that have continued to rely on folk-medical practices, it has frequently been effective to relate new Western medical products to irrational traditional beliefs.

Prestige. Individuals may change because of a desire for prestige, in emulation of people with more status than themselves. The acceptance of a foreign-made product over a domestic one frequently occurs because of such a status motivation for change.

Timing and Introduction. A well-conceived project can fail because the right time was not chosen to initiate it. For many years the principal department stores in Mexico City were of an elegant type, catering to the upper classes. By the time Sears, Roebuck opened their first store in Mexico City in 1947, a growing middle class was emerging which demanded different goods and service. The timing for Sears entry into Mexico was most certainly a major factor in the company's success.[38]

The examples cited from the anthropological literature have been related primarily to the marketing side of international operations. There are also many ways of introducing the change essential for achieving managerial goals. Most frequently, change is introduced through formal authority. Another important way is to expose employees to new experiences through expertly designed training programs. Also, rational arguments and theoretical explanations have been used to convince others. Incentives can be developed that reward changed behavior such as increased output. Participation and group discussions may also stimulate persons to recognize the need for change and initiate it.

The success of induced change in other cultures will invariably depend upon success in closing a communications gap between the innovators and the people to be motivated. Another major need is to set up various measures to protect employees from economic loss or from decreases in status and personal dignity. Furthermore, where a great deal of change is desired, people should not be worn out with trivial changes. The willingness to accept change in a given cultural setting should be saved for only large and crucial issues.

The international enterprise may promote change, but it is the members of the foreign culture who have to accept change. The general strategy, therefore, must be to discover the ways and incentives characteristic of the culture that are likely to result in acceptance. The comparative business literature is replete with examples of unsuccessful attempts to induce cultural change. Yet, the success stories are numerous also and provide considerable encouragement for the likely success of well-designed and well-informed efforts to promote cultural change.

INTERNATIONAL BUSINESS AS A CHANGE AGENT

A final topic related to the cultural components of the international business environment is the role of international business as a change agent. Here we are referring to the cultural fallout as well as the deliberately promoted cultural changes. The concept of international business as a change agent usually has a favorable connotation in business circles and refers to such benefits as the transfer of tech-

---

[38]Richardson Wood and Virginia Keyser, *Sears, Roebuck de Mexico, S.A.* (Washington, D.C.: National Planning Association, 1953).

nology and management skills,[39] the training of workers, and the social and economic modernization effects in the host country. All of these features of international business are generally assumed to be positive and desirable contributions to the countries in which international business activity takes place. But as the social scientists have observed, cultural change can have both positive and negative aspects for the members of a given society.

A case study of the International Basic Economy Corporation (IBEC) provides some interesting examples of cultural change being pushed too fast with resulting negative backlash. IBEC was founded shortly after World War II by Nelson Rockefeller and other members of his family as a pioneering business venture to demonstrate the beneficial role that private enterprise could play in the less developed countries. The early operations of the company were primarily in Brazil and Venezuela. In appraising this early experience, Broehl concludes:

> Cultural difference and resistance to change were greater than had been anticipated in both countries. . . . The laborers on the IBEC farms were expected quickly to adopt new methods, the Venezuelan fishermen were to be taught better methods by the U.S. fishermen. The consumer was counted on to accept a new concept of food marketing in the supermarket. Some of these concepts were proved not as sound as the ostensibly outmoded ways, but even those that were manifestly "better"—in the sense of being more efficient and less costly—were often not quickly adopted. . . .
>
> Early attacks in Venezuela against "the Rockefeller interests" can, in part, be explained by this resistance to change. For such resistance is bred of fear of the change, and brings an almost conditioned reflex of retaliation.[40]

Some of the cultural changes for which the international enterprise can claim credit are consistent with the goals of national leaders who are anxious to modernize and industrialize their society. The nature or the pace of other changes, such as in the case of IBEC, can provoke negative reactions to the international enterprise by government leaders or groups in the society. Because it is an agent of change, whether or not the change is intentional, the international enterprise should attempt to anticipate the changes for which it might be held responsible and the full chain of results from changes it is promoting.

---

[39]See Karl P. Sauvant, "The Potential of Multinational Enterprises as Vehicles for the Transmission of Business Culture," in Karl P. Sauvant and Farid G. Lavipour, eds., *Controlling Multinational Enterprises: Problems, Strategies, Counterstrategies* (Boulder, Colorado: Westview Press, 1976).

[40]Wayne G. Broehl, Jr., *The International Basic Economy Corporation* (Washington, D.C.: National Planning Association, 1968), p. 79.

Where the changes are perceived as beneficial by local interests, the bargaining position of the enterprise is strengthened. Where the expected changes are likely to appear dysfunctional and be negatively received, the international enterprise may want to modify its operational patterns or prepare to meet local antagonism, for a while at least.

SUMMARY

When the business firm crosses national boundaries and begins to operate in a number of countries, it is faced with a wide range of cultural differences that can significantly affect the achievement of business objectives. The problem of identifying cultural differences is difficult because of the natural tendency for people to observe and evaluate behavior of others in terms of the cultural conditioning of their own country. Furthermore, cultural patterns are not static but constantly changing. The problems faced in the cultural field involve much more than an intellectual appreciation that differences exist. International managers must develop cultural sensitivity, frequently through living experience in different cultures. With cultural sensitivity, the enterprise will be aware of the need to identify cultural variables and to adjust its organization and its operations to cultural differences. In many situations, the enterprise will have to promote cultural change in order to achieve its business goals. In a broader sense, the international enterprise itself is a powerful change agent. It must anticipate the changes that it causes and the reception that such changes will receive in host countries.

EXERCISES AND DISCUSSION QUESTIONS

1. "Cultural anthropology has certainly spawned a lot of empirical research, but as far as theory is concerned it is barren. The few tested theories that are available, moreover, have to be stretched a long way to reach anything of value to inter-cultural business." Discuss.

2. Give your own definition of culture.

3. Some multinational firms issue a standard corporate manual for international use containing set organizational definitions and rules, personnel policies, and budget and accounting instructions. What limits on the types of standardized instructions would you recommend that a firm with operations in many countries adopt?

4. From whatever sources are available to you, build a comparison of the family decision-making process for a major consumer purchase in two different cultures. Specify the roles played by the different family members, the pattern over time of interaction among the family with respect to the purchase, the weighting placed upon different product characteristics

by each family member, and the rules by which a consensus is finally reached.

5. Select one of the aspects of a culture—(1) the status ranking of different occupations, (2) the roles of the sexes, (3) the times of life with which different activities are associated, (4) the exercise of organizational authority, or (5) courtship patterns—in which you are aware of a change in the cultural norms and carry out the following activities:
   a. Describe the nature of the change.
   b. Give your opinion as to whether the culture regarded it formally, informally, or techinically.
   c. Identify some distinguishing characteristics of the innovators and early adopters.
   d. Describe any role you think business played in stimulating the change.
   e. Describe the business significance of the changes for any foreign firm operating within the culture.

6. "The prime function of most executive development courses is not knowledge transmissions but rather the transfer of a set of norms which conform with organizational objectives." Do you think it is acceptable for a U.S. top executive of a multinational firm to use executive-development courses to transfer to the management of foreign subsidiaries the norms that he has chosen?

16

The National Economy

MODERN BUSINESS ENTERPRISES have long recognized the continuing need for assessing and forecasting the economic environment within which they operate. It has become standard operating practice for the business manager to keep informed, either through in-house staffs or outside sources, on trends in the overall economy, in specific sectors, and in consumer-buying patterns. Thus, assessing and forecasting the economic environment, unlike the parallel task for the cultural environment, will not require the international firm to initiate a new type of activity. Instead, its task will normally be one of extending the scope of on-going programs.

As the firm moves from domestic to international forecasting of the economic environment, changes are needed. First, it must evaluate a number of national economies instead of just one. It must develop an understanding of widely varying economic patterns and institutional settings, particularly in the less developed countries. It must forecast the balance-of-payments outlook for specific countries. It must be prepared to handle special problems which arise when cross-national comparisons are needed or when national data must be consolidated on a regional or international level. Furthermore, it must incorporate into its assessments and forecasts of national economies likely changes in the international framework for international transfers—the subject of Part II—as well as the economic impact of anticipated expansions in a country by the international enterprise itself.

ECONOMIC ASSESSMENT WITHIN THE INTERNATIONAL ENTERPRISE

For the business firm newly venturing into international activities, the task of analyzing the economic environment in many nations of widely varying characteristics will appear formidable. Nevertheless, even at its early stage of internationalization, the firm can reduce the task to manageable proportions. First, it must be selective and focus on those aspects of the environment that are of special importance to its field of business activity and its specific interest in a country as a market seeker, resource seeker, or production-efficiency seeker. Second, the firm can obtain much of the needed information from data and reports published by national and international agencies. And third, short-cut techniques are available for a preliminary scanning of the economic environment in many countries to reduce the number of situations where in-depth analysis is required.

As the enterprise becomes multinational, the task of assessing and forecasting the economic environment will be decentralized and shared among the various units of the system. The foreign subsidiaries will assume primary responsibility for economic and market studies in their areas of operations. Headquarters staff can then limit its responsibilities to making cross-national comparisons, integrating national forecasts into an enterprise-wide forecast against which global policy decisions can be made, and assessing the international financial framework and trends in inter-nation relationships.

Much of the environmental-forecasting activity of the subsidiaries will be to guide local operating decisions. But as part of a multinational system, the subsidiary will have to fulfill two additional requirements. First, it will have to follow a sufficiently standardized approach so that headquarters can make cross-country comparisons and combine individual country results into a broader mosaic. Second, each subsidiary will have to include sufficient information in its assessment and forecast of the country's international economic relations, such as balance-of-payments forecasts, so that the links can be made between the economic environment of the subsidiary and the rest of the multinational system.

At the headquarters level, the assessments of national economic environments and the international framework for inter-nation transfers are needed as inputs for capital-budgeting decisions, for guiding operating decisions, for formulating systemwide policies, and for exercising a review function. When the firm expands into new countries where there is no subsidiary, headquarters will have to assume full responsibility for economic environmental analysis.

The technical responsibility for assessing and forecasting will usually be handled by specialists. But in order to use such forecasts, the international manager will need to have considerable familiarity with techniques and limitations. He or she must be aware of statistical perils, inaccurate perceptions, and the risks inherent in making cross-national comparisons or in joining economic information based on different data bases into broader mosaics. A manager should be generally familiar with the process of appraising overall growth prospects of different countries, and should comprehend the need for and the limitations of balance-of-payments forecasting. In dealing with the less developed countries, the manager should have an understanding of the development process, international development-assistance programs, and the importance of national development priorities. In dealing with host and home governments, he or she will need to understand the conceptual and measurement difficulties involved in the economic analyses of the impact of the enterprise.

International managers may have to adjust to new and unfamiliar patterns in economic institutions and policies. For example, when undertaking international responsibilities, a manager from the United States may have the first contact with national economic planning and government enterprises as major features of a foreign nation's economic environment. In such a situation, the manager's background will have to be enlarged to understand why such patterns exist and what role they are expected to play.

As a business firm moves toward becoming a global enterprise, one of its forward planning activities will be to scan the world horizon continuously for expansion opportunities. In particular, it will want to identify promising market areas and develop a reconnaissance system that will survey all countries for attractive market opportunities. But in a world of almost 200 separate countries, it may not be feasible for any but the international giants to undertake such a continuing and comprehensive global search.

Fortunately, by following a sequential process and by making use of general economic data available from international agencies, even a small firm can keep globally informed.

ECONOMIC SCANNING

Economic scanning makes use of standard economic measurements to provide a general comparison of the potentials of different countries from the viewpoint of an international business. The indicators are primarily macroeconomic measures of economic size, income level, and growth trends, but can also extend to indicators of sectoral growth and economic dependence.

Economic Size

The economic size of a nation is measured by its total gross national product (GNP) or by a very similar measurement, gross domes-

TABLE 16-1
Comparative Estimates of Gross National Product, Population, GNP per Capita, and Eight-Year Growth Rates

	1974			*1965–1973* Average Annual Growth Rate in:	
	Gross National Product at Market Prices (U.S. $ millions)	Population (millions)	GNP per Capita (U.S. $)	Population (%)	GNP per Capita (%)
United States	1,406,610	211.9	6,640	1.0	2.5
USSR	580,750	252.1	2,300	1.0	3.5
Japan	425,880	109.7	3,880	1.2	9.6
Germany, Fed. Rep. of.	365,220	62.0	5,890	0.6	4.0
France.	272,410	52.5	5,190	0.8	5.0
China, People's Rep. of.	245,840	825.0	300	1.7	4.6
United Kingdom	188,630	56.2	3,360	0.4	2.3
Italy.	153,570	55.4	2,770	0.7	4.2
Canada	136,570	22.5	6,080	1.4	3.5
Brazil	93,180	104.0	900	2.9	6.0
Poland.	82,440	33.7	2,450	0.8	4.2
India.	78,990	595.6	130	2.3	1.5
Spain	68,650	35.1	1,960	1.1	5.3
Netherlands	66,060	13.5	4,880	1.1	4.3
Australia	63,450	13.3	4,760	1.9	3.0
German Dem. Rep.	58,880	17.2	3,430	0.0	2.9
Mexico	58,130	58.0	1,000	3.5	2.8
Sweden	54,850	8.2	6,720	0.7	2.4
Belgium.	51,080	9.8	5,210	0.3	4.6
Czechoslovakia	47,270	14.7	3,220	0.3	2.6
Argentina.	46,900	24.6	1,900	1.5	2.9
Switzerland	43,110	6.5	6,650	1.2	3.0
Iran	35,120	33.1	1,060	3.2	7.4
Austria	30,480	7.5	4,050	0.5	5.1
Denmark	29,390	5.1	5,820	0.7	3.8
South Africa.	29,210	24.3	1,200	3.2	2.0

Hungary	22,410	10.5	2,140	0.3	2.7
Norway	21,070	4.0	5,280	0.8	3.8
Venezuela	19,830	11.6	1,710	3.3	1.3
Finland	19,350	4.7	4,130	0.2	5.2
Indonesia	18,600	127.0	150	2.1	4.5
Nigeria	17,830	73.0	240	2.5	8.3
Greece	17,680	9.0	1,970	0.5	7.6
Saudi Arabia	16,690	8.0	2,080	1.7	10.1
Korea, Rep. of	15,800	33.5	470	1.9	8.7
Bulgaria	15,390	8.7	1,770	0.6	3.6
Portugal	13,930	9.0	1,540	-0.1	8.0
Philippines	13,030	41.4	310	3.0	2.6
New Zealand	12,440	3.0	4,100	1.4	2.0
Thailand	12,140	41.0	300	3.0	4.5
Colombia	11,630	22.8	510	2.8	3.1
China, Rep. of	11,370	15.7	720	2.8	7.3
Israel	11,150	3.3	3,380	2.8	6.7
Kuwait	10,830	0.9	11,640	n.a.†	n.a.
Peru	10,670	15.0	710	2.9	1.8
Iraq	10,400	10.8	970	3.3	2.9
Egypt, Arab Rep. of	10,090	36.4	280	2.5	0.8
Algeria	9,840	15.2	650	3.4	4.3
Pakistan	8,770	68.2	130	2.9	2.5
Chile	8,490	10.4	820	2.0	1.4
Malaysia	7,610	11.6	660	2.5	3.7
Libyan Arab Rep.	7,530	2.2	3,360	3.7	5.7
Ireland	7,330	3.1	2,370	0.7	3.9
Puerto Rico	7,260	3.0	2,400	1.6	5.2
Bangladesh	7,260	76.2	100	2.4	-1.6
Morocco	6,940	16.3	430	2.4	2.5
Hong Kong	6,550	4.2	1,540	1.9	5.8
Korea, Dem. Rep. of	5,960	15.4	390	2.8	2.7
Cuba	5,780	9.1	640	1.8	-0.7
Singapore	4,700	2.2	2,120	1.8	9.4
United Arab Emirates	4,590	0.3	13,500	n.a.	n.a.
Zaire	3,650	24.1	150	2.7	2.9
Mozambique	3,590	8.5	420	2.1	4.1

TABLE 16-1 (continued)

Syrian Arab Rep.	3,480	7.2	490	3.3	3.6
South Vietnam	3,440	20.4	170	2.6	-0.7
Angola	3,370	5.8	580	1.3	3.2
Ghana	3,310	9.6	350	2.6	0.8
Lebanon	3,300	3.1	1,080	2.7	3.5
Uruguay	3,210	3.0	1,060	1.2	0.0
Ecuador	3,200	7.0	460	3.5	2.8
Tunisia	3,080	5.6	550	2.1	4.9
Guatemala	3,010	5.3	570	2.1	3.8
Vietnam, Dem. Rep. of	3,000	23.8	130	2.5	-0.5
Rhodesia	2,930	6.1	480	3.5	3.5
Dominican Rep.	2,710	4.6	590	2.9	5.1
Burma	2,710	30.2	90	2.2	0.7
Kenya	2,580	12.9	200	3.3	3.3
Ivory Coast	2,570	6.1	420	4.0	3.0
Sudan	2,560	17.5	150	2.8	-0.6
Ethiopia	2,550	27.2	90	2.4	1.6
Zambia	2,310	4.8	480	2.9	-0.2
Jamaica	2,270	2.0	1,140	1.4	4.8
Tanzania	2,060	14.4	140	2.8	2.6
Luxembourg	1,990	0.4	5,690	n.a.	n.a.
Sri Lanka	1,790	13.4	130	2.1	2.0
Uganda	1,780	11.2	160	3.0	1.2
Cameroon	1,650	6.3	260	2.0	4.9
Panama	1,640	1.6	1,010	3.1	4.3
Afghanistan, Rep. of	1,620	17.0	100	2.2	0.9
Trinidad and Tobago	1,590	1.1	1,490	0.9	2.2
El Salvador	1,540	3.9	390	3.4	0.8

Costa Rica	1,520	1.9	790	2.9	3.5
Malagasy Rep.	1,440	8.6	170	2.8	0.9
Bolivia	1,390	5.5	250	2.6	2.2
Nicaragua	1,310	2.0	650	2.5	1.6
Nepal	1,310	12.3	110	2.1	−0.1
Senegal	1,310	4.2	320	2.2	−2.8
Albania	1,260	2.4	530	2.7	5.1
Iceland	1,220	0.2	5,550	n.a.	n.a.
Paraguay	1,200	2.5	480	2.6	2.2
Papua New Guinea	1,150	2.7	440	2.5	5.0
Qatar	1,110	0.2	5,830	n.a.	n.a.
Jordan	1,040	2.6	400	3.4	−2.6
Honduras	990	2.9	340	3.0	1.1
Oman	930	0.8	1,250	n.a.	n.a.
Mongolia	860	1.4	620	2.8	1.6
Cyprus	850	0.6	1,310	n.a.	n.a.
Gabon	820	0.5	1,560	n.a.	n.a.
Yemen Arab Rep.	740	6.4	120	2.4	n.a.
Guinea	660	5.4	120	2.8	0.1
Haiti	640	4.5	140	1.6	0.7
Malawi	630	5.0	130	2.6	3.7
Cambodia	570	7.7	70	2.6	−5.2
Bahrain	550	0.2	2,250	n.a.	n.a.
Sierra Leone	520	2.9	180	2.2	1.5
Liberia	500	1.5	330	3.3	4.7
Bahamas	490	0.2	2,460	n.a.	n.a.
Upper Volta	470	5.8	80	2.1	−1.1
Congo, People's Rep. of	470	1.2	390	2.8	1.9
Niger	470	4.5	100	2.7	−4.6
Togo	460	2.2	210	2.7	2.5
Mauritius	420	0.9	480	n.a.	n.a.
Mali	410	5.5	70	2.0	0.5

TABLE 16-1 (concluded)

Fiji	410	0.6	720	n.a.	n.a.
Guyana	370	0.8	470	n.a.	n.a.
Benin, People's Rep. of	370	3.0	120	2.7	1.5
Chad	360	4.0	90	2.0	-3.3
Central African Rep.	350	1.7	200	2.2	1.0
Rwanda	330	4.1	80	3.0	3.2
Burundi	300	3.7	80	2.0	1.4
Mauritania	290	1.3	230	2.5	1.2
Barbados	270	0.2	1,110	n.a.	n.a.
Somalia	260	3.1	80	2.5	1.6
Laos	220	3.3	70	2.4	2.5
Yemen, People's Dem. Rep. of	200	1.6	120	2.9	n.a.
Swaziland	190	0.5	400	n.a.	n.a.
Botswana	180	0.7	270	n.a.	n.a.
Lesotho	150	1.2	120	2.2	2.6
Gambia, The	80	0.5	170	n.a.	n.a.
Equatorial Guinea	80	0.3	260	n.a.	n.a.
Bhutan	80	1.2	70	2.3	-0.2
Western Samoa	40	0.2	280	n.a.	n.a.
Grenada	30	0.1	300	n.a.	n.a.

*The 145 countries comprise World Bank member countries and countries with mid-1973 populations of 1 million, excluding Romania

†n.a. = not available.

Source: *World Bank Atlas*, 1975.

tic product (GDP). GDP measures the value of goods and services produced in a country without taking account of the nationality of those supplying the labor or the capital. When factor income received from abroad is added and factor income paid abroad is deducted, the resultant figure is GNP. Recent estimates by the World Bank of the GNP for 145 countries are shown in the first column of Table 16–1.

At the top of the economic ladder is the United States with a GNP of more than $1,400 billion (expressed in 1974 dollars). At the bottom of the scale are small countries with total GNPs of $200 million or less, such as Botswana, Lesotho, and Bhutan.

The attraction of the developed countries on the basis of economic size is highlighted by several comparisons. France's GNP is greater than that of mainland China, even though China has 16 times France's population. Canada has very nearly double the GNP of India, although India has 26 times as many people. Finland's total GNP is greater than that of Indonesia, even though Indonesia's population is 27 times as large.

Income Levels

GNP per capita—total GNP divided by total population—can be used as a rough guide to the purchasing power of a country. It does have many limitations, however, including its failure to allow for different patterns of income distribution.[1] From the third column of Table 16–1 it can be seen that the countries with the top-ranking GNP per capita are the United Arab Emirates with $13,500 per person and Kuwait with $11,640. There is then a drop to Sweden with $6,720, Switzerland with $6,650, and the United States with $6,640. At the bottom come countries with GNP per capita of under $100, such as Ethiopia, Cambodia, Mali, and Bhutan.

Countries are often classified as developed or developing countries based on average per capita GNP. Developing countries are also referred to as LDCs (less developed countries). Although there is no general agreement as to where the dividing line should be, one representation of the gap between the LDCs and the economically advanced countries of the world is shown in Table 16–2. From this table it can be quickly calculated that 75 percent of world population receives less than 25 percent of world GNP.

The development gap is both a cause and an effect of the more rapid expansion of international enterprise in the advanced countries of

---

[1] For example, see Everett E. Hagen, *The Economics of Development*, rev. ed. (Homewood, Ill.: Richard D. Irwin, Inc., 1975), pp. 10–14.

TABLE 16–2
Countries Grouped by 1973 GNP per Capita*

Income Groups	Number of Countries	Population (millions)	GNP (US$000 millions)	Average GNP per capita (US$)
Less than $200	43	1,151	136	120
$200 to $499	52	1,184	332	280
$500 to $1,999	53	531	530	1,000
$2,000 to $4,999	28	654	1,871	2,860
$5,000 and over	12	316	1,886	5,970
Total.	188	3,836	4,755	1,240

*Countries with per capita income of: less than $200: Afghanistan, Bangladesh, Benin (People's Rep. of), Bhutan, Burma, Burundi, Cambodia, Central African Rep., Chad, Comoro Islands, Ethiopia, Gambia (The), Guinea, Haiti, India, Indonesia, Kenya, Laos, Lesotho, Malagasy Rep., Malawi, Maldive Islands, Mali, Nepal, Niger, Pakistan, Portuguese Timor, Rwanda, Sierra Leone, Sikkim, Somalia, South Viet-Nam, Sri Lanka, Sudan, Tanzania, Togo, Uganda, Upper Volta, Viet-Nam (Dem. Rep. of), Yemen Arab Rep., Yemen (People's Dem. Rep. of), Zaire.

$200 to $499: Albania, Angola, Antigua, Bolivia, Botswana, British Solomon Islands, Cameroon, Cape Verde Islands, China (People's Rep. of), Colombia, Congo (People's Rep. of), Dominica, Ecuador, Egypt (Arab Rep. of), El Salvador, Equatorial Guinea, Ghana, Gilbert and Ellice Islands, Grenada, Guinea-Bissau, Guyana, Honduras, Ivory Coast, Jordan, Korea (Dem. Rep. of), Korea (Rep. of), Liberia, Macao, Mauritania, Mauritius, Morocco, Mozambique, New Hebrides, Nigeria, Papua New Guinea, Paraguay, Philippines, Rhodesia, Sao Tome and Principe, Senegal, Seychelles Islands, St. Kitts-Nevis Anguilla, St. Lucia, St. Vincent, Swaziland, Syrian Arab Rep., Thailand, Tonga, Trust Ter. of the Pacific Islands, Tunisia, Western Samoa, Zambia.

$500 to $1,999: Algeria, American Samoa, Argentina, Bahrain, Barbados, Belize, Brazil, Brunei, Bulgaria, Ceuta and Melilla, Chile, China (Rep. of), Costa Rica, Cuba, Cyprus, Dominican Rep., Fiji, French Guiana, French Ter. of Afars and Isaas, Gabon, Gibraltar, Greece, Guadeloupe, Guatemala, Hong Kong, Hungary, Iran, Iraq, Isle of Man, Jamaica, Lebanon, Malaysia, Malta, Martinique, Mexico, Mongolia, Netherlands Antilles, Nicaragua, Oman, Panama, Peru, Portugal, Reunion, Romania, Saudi Arabia, Singapore, South Africa, Spain, Surinam, Trinidad and Tobago, Turkey, Uruguay, Venezuela, Yugoslavia.

$2,000 to $4,999: Australia, Austria, Bahamas, Belgium, Bermuda, Canal Zone, Channel Islands, Czechoslovakia, Faeroe Islands, Finland, France, French Polynesia, German Dem. Rep., Greenland, Guam, Ireland, Israel, Italy, Japan, Libyan Arab Rep., Luxembourg, Netherlands, New Zealand, Norway, Poland, Puerto Rico, United Kingdom, USSR.

$5,000 and over: Canada, Denmark, Germany (Fed. Rep. of), Iceland, Kuwait, New Caledonia, Qatar, United Arab Emirates, United States, Sweden, Switzerland, Virgin Islands (U.S.).

Source: *World Bank Atlas,* 1975.

North America, Western Europe, and Japan. It explains the aspirations of the less developed countries for a greatly accelerated rate of economic progress, toward which international enterprise can make valuable contributions. At the same time, though, the development gap nourishes nationalistic feelings and defensive controls, which often make the LDCs unattractive to the international enterprise. Yet much of the world's population is in LDCs and many are making remarkable economic progress, so they should receive careful consideration in the economic scanning of the globally oriented business enterprise.

Recent Growth Trends

Data on economic size and income levels must be supplemented by recent trend data in order to secure a more dynamic picture of a country's economic attractiveness. *Country A* may have high income levels but be relatively stagnant. *Country B* may have lower levels of income but have more attraction to the international enterprise because the country is growing rapidly. Such trend data for population and GNP per capita are also shown in Table 16–1.

High growth rates in GNP per capita are usually associated with fairly low rates of population growth—approximately 1 percent per annum. Examples are Japan, Germany, and France with average annual growth in GNP per capita for an eight-year period of 9.6, 4.0, and 5.0 percent, respectively. In contrast, countries with population growth of around 3 percent find it difficult to achieve even higher rates of growth in total GNP than would be needed to keep GNP per capita increasing. A host of underdeveloped countries show high rates of population growth and low rates of GNP per capita growth, including India, Pakistan, Mexico, Venezuela, and Colombia. But there are exceptions. Brazil, Israel, the Republic of China (Taiwan), the oil-rich countries of the Middle East, and Nigeria have all managed to achieve significant growth in GNP per capita along with high population growth.

Historically, as a nation's income levels rise and urbanization increases, the rate of population increase slows down. Population control as an affirmative development measure is being adopted to some degree in the less developed countries, but whether or not rapid population increases burden economic development efforts is still a controversial question in many countries. Yet the arithmetic is clear. The faster population expands, the larger is the overall rate of growth required to achieve per capita increases. Countries with rapid population growth normally have a large share of their population in the lower age groups. As a result, the potential labor force will be a relatively small share of total population. Expenditures required for education will be disproportionately large, and the heavy educational costs have to be borne by the relatively small share of the population that is productively employed.

Sectoral Trends

The international business may need to extend its scanning of the economic environment into individual sectors of an economy. A firm whose markets lie in the agriculture sector, for example, may need to compare the size and trends of that sector in different countries. Sectoral data can also provide indications as to the overall potential for growth of individual countries. Growth potentials are generally less for countries where agriculture comprises a large share of national output. More than in other sectors, growth in agriculture is constrained by low-income elasticities in the demand for foodstuffs and by the rate at which new production techniques can be adopted. As industry approaches agriculture in size, countries become capable of more rapid growth, particularly during the period in which domestic manufacturing is substituting for imported goods. Empirical studies have shown a regular pattern of change in economic structure associated with rising levels of income. As income increases, the shares spent by consumers for necessities decrease, while the shares for luxury goods, service, recreation, and other goods produced by the manufacturing (secondary) sector and the trade and services (tertiary) sectors increase. As shown in Table 16–3, the average pattern, based on a study of about 100 countries, is for industry (including mining) to account for only 7 percent of total output in countries with $50 per capita GNP. Industry's share rises to 39 percent of total output for countries with $2,000 per capita GNP. Agriculture follows a reverse trend of a declining share in total output as income rises.

Structural changes within sectors generally accompany the changes in the relative importance of the sectors and again follow a regular

TABLE 16–3
Normal Variations in Economic Structure with Level of Development

	Output Composition (percentage share of total)				
Level of GNP per Capita (in 1964 U.S. $)	Primary (agriculture, fishing, and forestry)	Industry (manufacturing and mining)	Services	Utilities	Total*
$ 50	58.1	7.3	29.9	4.6	100
100	46.4	13.5	34.6	5.7	100
200	36.0	19.6	37.9	7.0	100
300	30.4	23.1	39.2	7.7	100
400	26.7	25.5	39.9	8.3	100
600	21.8	29.0	40.4	9.1	100
800	18.6	31.4	40.5	9.7	100
1,000	16.3	33.2	40.4	10.2	100
2,000	9.8	38.9	39.3	11.7	100

*May not total 100 percent because of rounding off.
Source: Hollis B. Chenery, "Targets for Development," in *The Widening Gap*, ed. Barbara Ward et al. (New York: Columbia University Press, 1971), table 1, pp. 30–31. All values are computed from multiple regressions for a sample of about 100 countries over the period 1950–65. The values shown apply to a country of 10 million population in the year 1960.

pattern. For example, the manufacturing sector of low-income countries is likely to have a predominance of textile and food processing industries, whereas high-income countries have a heavy concentration in the manufacture of machinery and other technologically sophisticated products. Although the development pattern of a specific country will deviate in varying degrees from the normal pattern deduced from the growing number of empirical studies, the normal patterns are still extremely useful in forecasting the growth prospects for industries or products closely related to the sectoral structure of a country.[2]

External Dependence and Economic Integration

The degree to which a country's economy is dependent upon external forces can be another important indicator of the economic environment. The ratio of foreign trade to GNP indicates a national economy's vulnerability to fluctuations in international trade. Thus the Netherlands, with foreign trade representing the equivalent of more than 30 percent of GNP, depends to a high degree on economic expansion trends in the countries to which it is exporting. At the other extreme, a nation that has a closed or relatively self-sufficient economy has maximum control over its economic future, and the forces influencing such trends will be predominantly domestic. The United States, with 1975 exports representing only 7 percent of GNP, is less affected by fluctuations in other countries. Both the USSR and mainland China also have very low external dependence.

Another form of external dependence is a country's obligations to service and repay foreign loans. External debt and interest obligations can be compared to foreign exchange earnings as a measure of the capacity to repay. For many less developed countries, annual public debt service and investment-income payments have risen to a level of more than 10 percent, and, in a few cases, more than 25 percent of foreign exchange earnings. But a high ratio of debt service to foreign exchange earnings is not necessarily an indication of crisis. The capital inflow may have been invested so as to increase future capacity to repay through increased exports or import substitution.

External dependence is not good or bad per se, but high external dependency means that a careful analysis of external forces must be included in assessing and forecasting a country's future prospects. A high degree of external dependence may mean a high foreign exchange earning capacity and an ability to secure a great deal of external stimulation to internal growth.

---

[2]See *Sectoral Aspects of Projections for the World Economy,* 3 vols. Papers delivered at Elsinore, Denmark, August 14–27, 1966 (New York: United Nations, 1969).

For a growing number of nations, an important type of external dependence comes from participation in a regional economic-integration movement. If a high degree of coordination is achieved by such groups as the European Economic Community and the Andean subregional integration movement in Latin America, the task of assessing national economic environments may become easier for the international enterprise. An assessment or forecast for a regional grouping may be substituted for similar studies of a number of separate countries.

Sources of Economic Data

National economic statistics are published regularly by international agencies such as the United Nations, the World Bank, the International Monetary Fund, and the Organization for Economic Cooperation and Development (OECD). Of particular significance for economic scanning is the monthly OECD publication "Main Economic Indicators," which is designed to provide a picture of recent changes in the economies of member countries. Every two years, the monthly statistics over the last decade are published as a companion volume. These sources also include data on the performance within individual sectors of economies.[3]

CROSS-NATIONAL COMPARISON

Pitfalls in Translation Rates

Special problems arise when the multinational enterprise has to make inter-country comparisons and when a composite picture of several national economies must be constructed. Not only are national differences involved, but financial data expressed in national currencies must be converted to a common unit for inter-country comparisons. Most commonly, current exchange rates are used to translate measures in local currencies to a common currency unit such as the U.S. dollar or the currency of the enterprise's home country.

Ideally, for purposes of inter-country comparisons, translations to a common currency should be derived from national currency figures on the basis of purchasing power parities or through direct real-product comparisons. However, such comparative data are available for only a limited number of countries and generally relate to different periods.

---

[3]For example, see the table for each country in "Gross Domestic Product by kind of Economic Activity," in *United Nations Yearbook of National Account Statistics 1974* (New York, 1975); also *National Accounts of OECD Countries 1962–1973* (Paris: OECD, August 1975).

Those concerned with economic development have long recognized the deficiencies inherent in the exchange-rate approach to comparative income analysis and have been searching for better ways to compare countries' economic progress. The most ambitious effort undertaken in this area is the UN International Comparison Project (ICP),[4] a study begun in 1968 jointly by the United Nations Statistical Office and the University of Pennsylvania with the support of the World Bank and a number of other international, national, and private institutions. The ICP, which is now entering its third and final research phase, has developed a highly sophisticated method for measuring total expenditure, which can be used to derive more reliable and directly comparable estimates of per capita income on an international scale than previously possible. The published ICP findings represent detailed comparisons for 10 countries and will be extended to cover 35 to 40 countries, including 20 to 25 developing countries.

The figures produced by this study illustrate the considerable overstatement of economic differences between countries that can arise using current exchange rates, especially those in the highest and lowest income categories. When the comparison is based on exchange rates, for example, the U.S. GNP per capita in 1970 exceeded that in India by a ratio of 45:1. But based on a purchasing power parity calculation, this ratio was reduced to 14:1.[5]

The reason for such different results lies primarily in the divergent price and product structures of different countries. Exchange rates, even when they approximate balance-of-payments equilibrium rates, equate at best the prices of only internationally traded goods and services. They may bear little relationship to the prices of goods and services not internationally traded, which in most countries form the large bulk of the total national product. Specifically, the prices of farm products and of services in less developed countries are in most cases considerably lower relative to industrial prices than in the more developed countries. Moreover, agricultural output generally accounts for the major part of overall national output in the LDCs, whereas the opposite is true in developed countries. As a result, the internal purchasing power of the currency of a low-income country will generally be greater than indicated by the exchange rate.

The use of exchange rates for converting national currency data into a common currency is further complicated by the fact that official or

---

[4]The results of the first phase of the ICP have recently been published in Irving B. Kravis et al. *A System of International Comparisons of Gross Product and Purchasing Power* (Baltimore and London: The Johns Hopkins University Press, 1975).

[5]See "Technical Note" in *World Bank Atlas* (Washington, D.C.: International Bank for Reconstruction and Development, 1975).

par value rates do not always constitute equilibrium rates. Economic history provides countless instances where a given exchange rate has been maintained for a lengthy period of time, even though the internal price level has long since fallen out of line with prices in other parts of the world. A straight conversion on the basis of the overvalued rates would overstate both absolute levels and changes over time. An additional problem arises when no single or unique rate of exchange exists. The international enterprise wishing to express national data in a selected currency is given the choice of free rates, controlled rates, preferential, basic, auction, nonpreferential rates, and so forth, depending on prevailing national policies.

No easy solution exists for the problem of inter-country comparisons. To the extent that nations follow flexible exchange-rate policies, the problems of multiple and nonequilibrium rates are reduced. A partial solution is to rely on the statistical reports of international agencies, such as the *International Financial Statistics* publication of the International Monetary Fund (IMF), which attempt, so far as possible, to present comparable data from the various countries. Where comparable data are not available, the business firm will have to make its own judgments, keeping in mind the consistent downward bias in converting the figures from the less developed countries into a common currency.

Pitfalls in Comparability of Statistics

The likelihood of inaccurate perceptions of economic environments is always high because of variations in the concepts, coverage, and quality of national statistics, and because of statistical biases correlated with a country's stage of economic development. Biases frequently exist in GNP per capita. Although most nations use the same general concept,[6] the extent to which statistical estimates reflect the actual situation in different countries can vary significantly.[7]

In less developed countries there is a bias toward understating levels of economic activity. Statistical coverage becomes increasingly comprehensive as economic levels rise and the availability and quality of data improve as a country becomes more affluent and develops more

---

[6]This is not true for centrally planned economies. See M. A. Jansen, "Problems of International Comparisons of National Accounting Aggregates Between Countries with Different Economic Systems," *The Review of Income and Wealth* (March 1973): 69–77.

[7]See T. P. Hill, *The Measurement of Real Product* (Paris: OECD, February 1971). This study examines growth rates of gross domestic product for all OECD member countries and for many individual industries from the standpoint of the different types of measurement used and the margin of error attached to each.

complex institutions and improved record keeping. Moreover, as an economy develops, an increasing share of economic activity passes through the marketplace and is counted as national output. For example, housewives purchase bread instead of baking it themselves.

Another statistical peril involves variations in official definitions from country to country. The label "manufacturing activity" is an example. French statistics, unlike those of most other nations, include fishing and the quarrying of building materials as manufacturing, whereas wine production is classified as agriculture. Iran includes the extraction of crude petroleum as manufacturing, whereas most countries report petroleum production as mining activity.[8] Another example arises with differences in the measurement of the labor force. United States data use 16 years of age as a lower limit as compared to 14 years for many other countries.

Even where definitions and statistical coverage are similar, statistics can vary greatly in quality or in margins of error. Statistical quality varies among nations, among different items in the same country, and among different statistical observations for the same item in a country. Statistics of LDCs are likely to have large gaps and wide margins of error.

Variations in statistical quality among economic sectors result in large part from the greater difficulty of collecting data in one area as against another. For example, data on imports and exports are usually the best, while data on agricultural production are the weakest. The high quality of foreign trade statistics results from the fact that imports and exports generally flow through a limited number of ports of entry and involve some government surveillance for tax or control purposes. Contrast this situation with the problem of collecting agricultural data from hundreds of thousands (or millions) of reporting units widely separated geographically and from an agrarian social group which frequently has low levels of education and record-keeping experience.

For the international manager, the degree of error that can be tolerated depends upon the decision being made. In many situations, a wide margin of error would not seriously affect a decision. For example, national product estimates for a country may understate the economic reality. Yet, if the statistical bias is rather consistent from year to year, the business firm can draw a reasonable conclusion as to whether a country is expanding and even as to the rate of expansion. Likewise, cost-of-living data for a given country may be based on observations in only one or two principal cities but they may provide a reasonable indicator over time of general trends in price levels.

---

[8]United Nations, *Statistical Yearbook 1970* (New York, 1971), pp. 221–31.

MACROECONOMIC FORECASTING

For many reasons the international enterprise may require a deeper assessment of a country's economic prospects than is involved in economic scanning.

Basic Economic Forecasts

Comprehensive long-range planning studies and economic forecasts are available for most countries. Such planning studies vary immensely in quality and in validity. Still, many are highly useful and reasonable guides to future prospects and future growth patterns.[9] Such planning studies may be for the nation as a whole, for regions, and for sectors of the economy. For the less developed countries, extensive planning studies are frequently available from national agencies and from international organizations. The World Bank, in particular, has sent economic survey missions to most of the less developed countries, and many of the mission reports are publicly available. For the industrialized countries, future outlook studies may be available from the OECD and from government and nongovernment sources within the country. The government of Sweden publishes once every five years a long-term forecast prepared by the Secretariat for Economic Planning. The study published in 1970, for example, covers in detail the development outlook through 1975 and examines prospective trends up to 1990 in a more general way.[10]

A survey undertaken a decade ago of the extent to which large econometric models were being used for national-economic planning and forecasting identified more than 30 countries with such work underway by either governmental or private groups. Most of the models were for the national economy as a whole, but a few also had regional subdivisions. This work has become increasingly refined and efforts were underway in the mid-1970s to link national models together.[11]

When acceptable economic forecasts are not available for a country, the international firm will have to build its own. There is comprehensive literature and advanced expertise in macroeconomic forecasting;

---

[9]The OECD publication, *Techniques of Economic Forecasting* (Paris, March 1965), describes the methods of short-term economic forecasting used by the governments of Canada, France, the Netherlands, Sweden, the United Kingdom, and the United States.

[10]Secretariat for Economic Planning, Ministry of Finance, *The Swedish Economy 1971–1975 and the General Outlook up to 1990* (Stockholm, 1971).

[11]Richard Stone and Colin Leicester, "The Methodology of Planning Models," in *National Economic Planning*, ed. Max F. Millikan (New York: National Bureau of Economic Research, 1967), pp. 15–38; R. J. Ball, ed., *The International Linkage of National Economic Models* (New York: Humanities Press, 1972).

for a detailed treatment the reader should refer to one of the standard texts.[12] Seldom, though, will the international firm require a comprehensive forecast of an entire economy. Beyond the general trends of economic growth,[13] the usual need will be for specific forecasts of price-level changes (i.e., inflation), changes in the country's external accounts with the rest of the world, and changes in the international exchange rate for its currency. The following sections provide a brief introduction to practical forecasting of these three aspects. It must be remembered, however, that macroeconomic variables are not independent of each other. The price level, the balance of payments, and the exchange rate are closely interrelated. While it is possible to forecast each separately, forecasts obtained by examining a complete economic system are more soundly based.

Price-Level Forecasts

Inflationary pressures are of particular significance to the international enterprise because inflation may be the prelude to devaluation of the country's currency in the foreign exchange market. Furthermore, an inflationary environment requires special business strategies. There has been a widespread, though invalid, belief that high rates of inflation are unattractive for business operations and cannot be accompanied by economic growth.[14] It is true, however, that management will have to change its policies ahead of the full impact of inflation in order to benefit. Moreover, when a country experiences wide fluctuations in the rate of inflation it is not easy to predict the fluctuations and adjust accordingly.

A standard source for data on past price levels is the monthly *International Financial Statistics* of the International Monetary Fund. For forecasts of future price-level changes, the analyst should also look to changes in monetary and fiscal policy, probable rates of change in labor costs and productivity, as well as any inflationary pressure particular to the country under consideration. Countries dependent on export earnings from raw materials or primary products can experience major inflationary pressures following increases in world prices for their exports.

The forecasting of monetary and fiscal policies is an art in itself. For

---

[12]See John P. Lewis and Robert C. Turner, *Business Conditions Analysis,* 2d ed. (New York: McGraw-Hill Book Co., 1967), pp. 363–91.

[13]For an excellent development of methods of estimating GNP, see Alan Heston, "A Comparison of Some Short-Cut Methods of Estimating Real Product Per Capita," *The Review of Income and Wealth* (March 1973): 79–104.

[14]For a wide-ranging examination of the issues, see Werner-Baer and Isaac Kerstenetzky, *Inflation and Growth in Latin America* (Homewood, Ill.: Richard D. Irwin, Inc., 1964).

short-term forecast of price levels, however, it is possible to gain an indication of whether the quantity of money that the authorities have permitted will have further inflationary impact. Money supply was generally allowed to expand excessively during 1972, as shown in Table 16–4, with the result that price levels increased markedly over the succeeding 18 months. The correlation between percentage increase in money supply over 1972 and percentage increase in consumer prices from mid-1973 to mid-1974 is remarkable.

Wage increases that outstrip productivity increases can also have a major impact. In developed countries particularly, the processes of wage negotiation have gained a momentum that can carry wages upward even with no increase in productivity either before or after the increased wages. Britain has been an outstanding example here. With strong trade unions cutting across industries and firms so that one firm may face 20 or 30 separate unions, there were few brakes on the power of individual unions to demand higher wages before government instituted a wages policy. No one firm could argue that wage settlements would give local competition an advantage, nor usually that an increase to one union would bankrupt the firm. Table 16–4 illustrates clearly the British wages-led inflation of 1974–75. Even with a return to a national policy of wage restraint, however, prices continued to be pushed upward by wage demands.

Finally, it is necessary in price-level forecasting to examine the measures used to minimize or neutralize the effects of inflation. In many countries, both developed and less developed, policies and techniques have been adopted to offset the effects of inflation in selected areas of economic activity or even across the board. Loans, savings accounts, pensions, or other fixed obligations, as well as wages and salaries, can include provisions for cost-of-living adjustments.

TABLE 16–4
Percentage Rises in Money Supply and Consumer Prices

Country	End 1972 over End 1971 (percent)		Mid-1974 over Mid-1973 (percent)		Mid-1975 over Mid-1974 (percent)	
	Money Supply	Consumer Prices	Money Supply	Consumer Prices	Money Supply	Consumer Prices
United States	11	3.5	5	11	5.5	9.5
Japan	25	5.75	16	22	8.5	14
Germany	14	6.5	5.5	7	13.5	6
Britain	14	7.75	5	16.5	14.5	26
Industrial countries average	12.5	4.5	7	12.5	8.5	11

*Source: Adapted from "Seesaw, Monetary Daw," *The Economist*, September 13, 1975, pp. 13–14.

Brazil has probably the most comprehensive policies where fiscal correction is applied to virtually all incomes, long-term debt obligations—both private and government—and even delinquent taxes. With such a policy Brazil was able to achieve real growth from 1968–74 averaging 10 percent annually, despite the persistence of a 20 percent rate of inflation.

Balance-of-Payments Forecasts

The most practical way to proceed in balance-of-payments forecasting is to take a view on the future level of each item in the balance-of-payments accounts.

Foreign Exchange Earnings Prospects. Future supplies of foreign exchange will depend upon exports of goods, sale of services (including tourism), unilateral transfers, and both short- and long-term capital inflows. Forecasting future export prospects involves conventional supply and demand analysis of a country's principal export products and prospective new exports. In the case of traditional exports, an examination of recent trends in both quantity and price of specific exports and growth trends in the principal buyer countries can provide considerable insight into future prospects. Additional considerations will be a country's capacity for increasing the supply of export goods, possible variations in supply conditions due to weather and related conditions, the price and income elasticity of demand for specific products, the competitive position of countries that are alternative sources of supply, and the possibilities for changes in tariff and quota regulations imposed by buyer countries.

Fortunately for the international businessman, many official agencies, both national and international, undertake and publish on a continuing basis studies of the future international trade prospects for a wide range of products. FAO undertakes many studies in the agricultural area. In the field of manufactured goods, the U.N. Conference on Trade and Development (UNCTAD) has been studying many products to identify new export possibilities for the less developed countries. In the field of minerals, the U.S. Bureau of Mines is an important source for research on future world demand and supply conditions.

Many countries, particularly the less developed countries, have been trying to change the composition of their exports from heavy reliance on primary products from agriculture and mining to increased exports of manufactured and semi-manufactured goods. In support of this effort, UNCTAD has been pressing the advanced countries to grant unilateral tariff concessions for manufactured exports from the LDCs. In addition, individual countries have established trade-promotion programs and special incentives for the export of manufactured goods and, in a number of cases, achieved significant results. The forecast of future export prospects of many LDCs will have to include an evaluation of the possibility of achieving success in such trade-diversification programs.

Unilateral transfers can be either from foreign governments or from individuals. Foreign exchange inflows as development-assistance grants can be sizable in the case of certain countries, and the prospects of future flows will depend heavily on political and security policies of donor governments and the availability of resources for international development agencies. Private unilateral transfers are significant for some countries such as Israel, which has received sizable foreign donations; the Philippines, where many Filipinos receive veterans payments after serving in the U.S. armed forces; or some southern European countries, where nationals have migrated to work in other countries and are sending regular remittances to families remaining at home.

Capital inflows will depend on the interest of foreign firms in making direct investments and on the policies of the country toward encouraging or controlling foreign investment. Future prospects for inflows of portfolio investment, loan funds, and short-term deposits attracted by high-inerest rates must also be analyzed.

Foreign Exchange Needs.   Set off against the forecast of future foreign exchange availability will be an estimate of foreign exchange needs for imports, for purchases of foreign services, and for servicing foreign debt and the capital accounts. The forecast of import requirements can begin with an analysis and a projection of recent trends in both quantities and prices of principal import items. The projections should then be modified to reflect significant future changes likely to occur. Such a change might be the discovery of new resources that will substitute for imports, for example, petroleum, or a one-time need for large imports of capital goods to initiate a major industrialization project, or a high demand for kinds of goods not being produced within the country stimulated by rapidly rising consumer incomes.

Forecasting the foreign exchange requirements of the capital accounts involves mainly government debt service, private dividend outflows and foreign debt service, profit remittances by foreign business firms, and related business outflows such as licensing and royalty payments. Data on government and private debt obligations are normally published by the central bank or some other financial agency of a country. Such data are frequently incomplete and should be supplemented by information from international financial agencies or multinational banks. Information on past private remittances will have to be supplemented by data on inflow trends of direct private investment and by prospective changes in remittance patterns. For example, when local expansion prospects for foreign firms become less promising, as in the case of countries that have discontinued granting new exploration concessions to oil companies, profit remittances are likely to be as high as permitted by local authorities.

Exchange-Rate Forecasts

The purchasing power parity theory of international currency adjustment goes to the extreme in its proposition that exchange rates adjust to maintain purchasing power parity between the currencies of related countries.[15] On this premise, a forecast of comparative inflation rates would be all that is needed to forecast exchange-rate changes.

A change in purchasing power relative to partner countries, however, may be offset by other factors. The availability of adequate international reserves, for example, may permit a country to tolerate balance-of-payments deficits without having to devalue its currency. Thus, price-level forecasting should be complemented by a forecast of future changes in the country's balance of payments and an examination of its external assets and obligations. Without reserves, the country may be forced to borrow from external sources that will usually require the adoption of an acceptable economic policy as a condition for a loan. And such a policy will be likely to include devaluation. On the other hand, if reserves are available, the political decision maker has a string of temporizing alternatives to devaluation. He can use import controls, exchange controls, foreign short-term borrowings from abroad, export incentives, selective taxes, and so forth. A similar range of alternatives to avoid or postpone revaluations are available.

Another strong guide in exchange-rate forecasting is to examine the difference in interest rates that would be received over a specified period on assets involving similar risk in the two countries for which the exchange rate is expected to change. Based on a proposition advanced by Irving Fisher in his classic economic work *The Theory of Interest,* the difference in interest between the two markets represents the expected cost (or gain) from exchange variation over the period. In other words, the effective rate of return from foreign investment after allowing for exchange risk is seen by investors as equal to the rate from local investment. If this were not so, the argument goes, then sums would flow to the more attractive market and away from the other, until the changed supply of investment altered interest rates sufficient to bring the effective rates into equilibrium.

---

[15]Bela Balassa "The Purchasing-Power Parity Doctrine: A Reappraisal," *The Journal of Political Economy,* December 1964, p. 584–96.

While there is as much merit in this "Fisher effect" approach as in the purchasing power parity approach,[16] any simple formula is doomed to failure in an imperfect and changing world. The forecaster in international business cannot avoid the multiplicity of factors that might determine exchange-rate changes.[17] While economic analysis can suggest what an exchange rate should be at any point of time, few governments allow their exchange rates to fluctuate freely. In most cases the ultimate decision to let the exchange rate fluctuate will be influenced by a variety of local political, bureaucratic, and social pressures. Consequently, for short-term forecasting, the analyst must become familiar with the background, education, training, and past behavior of those with power to influence the decision if he is to anticipate whether they will lean toward controls or toward free-market solutions for balance-of-payments problems. And the analyst must observe the way in which the authorities progress through the temporizing alternatives in order to delay an exchange-rate change that may be inevitable. Such surveillance is essential for forecasting the timing. And timing is extremely important because the cost of hedging against foreign exchange risk is high and increases with the time for which the cover is sought.

FORECASTING NATIONAL INSTITUTIONAL ENVIRONMENTS

The international firm may want to extend its investigation into aspects of the institutional environment that are of special importance for the activity being considered. The firm may need to know about local banking and other financial institutions, as well as the extent to which local capital markets operate effectively. Other significant factors may be the role of labor unions and patterns of labor-management relations, the importance of government enterprises and the business fields in which they are operating, the influence of economic planning agencies, the types of business regulation that will be encountered, and patterns of social-welfare programs.

In some situations, an assessment of the institutional environment may heavily influence the firm's decision to invest or initiate opera-

---

[16]See Robert Z. Aliber and Clyde P. Stickney, "Accounting Measures of Foreign Exchange Exposure: The Long and Short of it," *The Accounting Review* January 1975, p. 44–57.

[17]For more detailed discussions of exchange-rate forecasting techniques, see David B. Zenoff and Jack Zwick, *International Financial Management* (Englewood Cliffs, N.J.: Prentice-Hall, 1969), p. 68–88; R. B. Shulman, "Are Foreign Exchange Risks Measurable?" *Columbia Journal of World Business,* May–June 1970, pp. 55–60.

tions. For example, the prospective business opportunity may be in a field where government enterprises are likely to extend their activities and where future expansion possibilities for a private foreign company may be restricted by institutional patterns rather than by economic growth prospects. In other situations, assessing the institutional environment may not be critical for the investment decision but of primary importance in shaping the business project and in providing guidance for future operations. For example, if local capital markets are poorly developed and promise to remain so, the firm that would prefer to do local financing through a public offering of shares in the subsidiary might still proceed with its project but change its financing plans in favor of other strategies.

In securing the information it needs on current patterns, the firm is not likely to encounter serious problems. But where rapidly changing dimensions of the institutional environment have to be projected into the future, the forecasting task can be difficult. The need for forecasting the institutional environment has not yet become well recognized and techniques are still in an incipient stage. Furthermore, unlike the situation in economic forecasting, the international firm cannot yet look to international and national governmental and research organizations for a large flow of institutional forecasting studies.

Yet the situation is far from hopeless. In some cases, such as antitrust laws, many countries appear to be moving toward a harmonization of substantive laws,[18] and separate forecasting for specific nations may become part of a broader forecast of the legal environment. In other areas, forecasting can be done by an analogy technique whereby patterns in one country can be projected on the bases of patterns in another country at a higher stage of development. For example, if the less developed capital markets in Western Europe appear to be evolving toward the more developed patterns in the United Kingdom or the United States, the U.K. or U.S. patterns can provide important clues as to future trends in Western European countries. The analogy approach assumes that the economic structure of low-income countries will generally follow the path already traveled by more advanced countries.

But where institutional patterns are clearly following different evolutionary paths in different countries, forecasting will have to be based on more speculative techniques. For example, the role played by labor unions and patterns of labor-management relations appears to be

---

[18]Seymour J. Rubin, "The International Firm and the National Jurisdiction," in *The International Corporation,* ed. Charles P. Kindelberger (Cambridge, Mass.: The M.I.T. Press, 1970), p. 193.

following independent patterns in Italy, Japan, and the United States.[19] Consequently, it is unlikely that the role of labor unions in Italy will eventually become similar to present U.S. patterns. In such situations, the forecasting approach will have to identify in each country the particular factors that have been shaping institutional patterns and then attempt to forecast trends in the underlying factors. Italian labor unions generally have a political affiliation and play an important, direct political role in the country. Furthermore, many of the issues that are normally resolved in the United States through collective bargaining, such as vacations and pensions, are resolved in Italy through governmental legislation. Consequently, a forecast of labor union patterns in Italy would require that considerable attention be given to the political situation and political trends.

Many dimensions of the institutional environment will be considered in subsequent chapters. At this stage, however, two general features of the institutional environment can be examined to illustrate in greater detail the importance of institutional dimensions and how judgments might be made in those areas as to future trends. Government enterprises and national economic planning have been selected because these are likely to be unfamiliar features of the institutional environment for business managers and enterprises of American nationality.

Government Enterprise

Most governments, including those of the so-called capitalistic countries, influence the national economic environment through direct participation in business activities.[20] Enterprises may be completely owned and operated by the government, or may be organized as mixed corporations with the government as the major stockholder and in effective management control. Increasingly, governments have been forming joint ventures with foreign enterprise. Government enterprises have been of major importance in most of the advanced industrial countries, as well as in the less developed countries. In Italy, for example, through such holding companies as National Hydrocarbon Agency (ENI) and the Institute for Industrial Reconstruction (IRI), the government is a significant and frequently majority stockholder in enterprises producing motor vehicles, machinery, iron and steel, shipbuilding, and chemicals. In 1974, the IRI group controlled over

---

[19]See Paul T. Hartman and Arthur M. Ross, *Changing Patterns of Industrial Conflict* (New York: Wiley, 1960); Everett M. Kassalow, *Trade Unions and Industrial Relations: An International Comparison* (New York: Random House, 1969).

[20]See A. H. Hanson, *Public Enterprise and Economic Development*, 2d ed. (London: Routledge and K. Paul, 1965); W. Friedmann and J. F. Garner, eds., *Government Enterprise: A Comparative Study* (New York: Columbia University Press, 1970).

100 companies with annual sales of more than 8,000 milliards (thousand of millions) of Italian lira and over 500,000 employees. A similar development was introduced by the British Labour government in 1975 with the formation of the National Enterprise Board. Controlling shareholdings in many industrial firms, including Leyland and Rolls Royce, are vested in this board.

Aside from preempting fields of business activity, government enterprises can exert a wide range of influences on the economic environment. Any attempt to forecast economic growth in Argentina during the middle 1960s would have had to take into account the extraordinary deficit of the government-owned railways. To meet the deficit, the government diverted resources from programs designed to stimulate economic expansion and contributed greatly to inflationary forces by increasing the supply of money in circulation. Government enterprises can exert an inhibiting influence on the development of capital markets. Government enterprises frequently secure new capital directly from governmental financial institutions or taxes, thereby reducing the potential size of private capital markets for business financing. Where government enterprise is strong, labor costs and labor-management relations can be strongly influenced by the patterns of public enterprises, which can be subjected directly to political pressures. And finally, the costs of certain materials and services may be determined by social policies implemented by government enterprises in the fields of transportation and electric power rather than on the basis of normal business criteria.

In order to assess and forecast the role of government enterprises in the business environment, the forces that have stimulated the establishment and expansion of government enterprise can be identified and grouped into eight categories.

1. *National attitudes toward natural resources.* As previously discussed, where natural resources are the legal property of the state, one way of trying to share the benefits of these resources with all of the people in a country is through government enterprise.

2. *Social-welfare goals.* Where public aims are considered to prevail over private-profit goals, government enterprise is one of the ways to achieve such aims. In public-utility fields, such as transportation, public-welfare possibilities are important and some government enterprises are actually run at a loss in order to achieve social goals.

3. *Absence of private enterprise as a feasible alternative for achieving priority development goals.* The establishment of government steel plants in many LDCs has been justified by the felt national need for a steel industry and by the absence of private business interest in such projects because of large capital requirements or other considerations.

4. *Involuntary nationalizations.* The nationalization of the coal-

mining industry in Britain and passenger railways in the United States are examples of situations where private industries were operating with great difficulties. The government took over to rationalize operation and to save businesses considered vital to the national interest.

5. *Revenue purposes.* Governments have assumed monopolies of such business activities as tobacco and liquor (state governments in the United States) simply for the purpose of capturing profits for public revenue.

6. *Competition.* Government enterprises have been established to operate as competitive yardsticks in fields in which private enterprises also exist, such as the electric power operations of the Tennessee Valley Authority in the United States.

7. *Historical accidents.* A prime case in this category is the Renault automobile company of France. During World War II, the private owners of Renault collaborated with the enemy. In retaliation, the French government expropriated the company immediately after the war.

8. *Ideological forces.* Government ownership has sometimes had its origins in a moral crusade to wrest the commanding heights of the economy from self-seeking capitalists or, in its more modern version, from foreign interests. Ideological forces have been important in both advanced and less developed countries. In the less developed countries, indigenous private enterprise may be extremely weak and, where nationalistic forces want to reduce the role of foreign enterprise, government enterprises are created to substitute for foreign business.

For any specific country, the total public enterprise sector may have evolved as a consequence of a mix of the various underlying forces. In order to speculate about future trends, the several types of business activities will have to be analyzed separately. In the natural resource fields, for example, where the motivation for public enterprises comes from a philosophy that the benefits of these resources should be public rather than private, future trends are likely to be in the direction of more public enterprise, particularly in the less developed countries where local private capital and entrepreneurship are not feasible alternatives. The main determinant of momentum will be the speed with which nationals acquire the skills and experience to operate such enterprises. Similar trends should be expected in the fields of public utilities, such as electric power, telephones, and railroads, because of the underlying social-welfare motivation.

Although private enterprisers may feel that there is a strong and immutable trend toward an increasing role for government enterprises, numerous instances exist where enterprises once owned and operated by the government have moved into the private sector. In the Philippines, the government established textile plants as pioneering projects to demonstrate the viability of a type of manufacturing activity that had been given priority in development planning and had been neglected by private enterprise. Although the government projects were not outstanding commercial successes, they were sufficiently successful to attract private enterprise to the field, and the government withdrew. A similar strategy was followed by Puerto Rico in its "Operation Bootstrap" development program. Still another example of denationalization when certain government goals were achieved is the case of Volkswagen in Germany. The company was government owned after World War II because the private sector was in disarray. But as reconstruction progressed, Germany reverted to its ideological preference for private enterprise and sold shares in the company.[21]

National Economic Planning

In recent years, with the notable exception of the United States, economic plans and national economic planning have become a common feature of country environments. For non-U.S. multinational enterprises, economic planning is a familiar environmental factor but the same is not likely to be true for most enterprises of U.S. nationality.

Economic planning is a difficult term to define since it has been applied in so many different ways. Certainly the type of comprehensive economic-planning practices in the USSR, sometimes referred to as imperative planning, or planning with controls, differs sharply from the kinds used in Western Europe. The best known of the European planning styles is the indicative planning of France in which discriminatory taxation and financing facilities, rather than direct controls, are used to persuade private firms to accept the plan targets. The less developed countries have chosen forms of economic planning which lie somewhere in between.[22]

Across the spectrum, economic planning rejects the efficiency of laissez faire as the guiding force. Goals and priorities are established through governmental planning and controls or incentives are used for allocating scarce resources to projects or activities considered to be priority goals for the economy.

Among the Western European countries, France, the Netherlands, Norway, and Sweden have practiced economic planning the longest.

---

[21]Volkswagenwerk, GmbH was transformed in July 1960 into Volkswagenwerk, A.G. whereby the Federal Republic of Germany and the state of Lower Saxony each retained 20 percent of the share capital. The remaining 60 percent was sold to qualified residents of Germany. See *Moody's Industrial Manual: 1972* (New York: Moody's Investor Services, 1972). p. 3814.

[22]Albert Waterson, *Development Planning: Lessons of Experience* (Baltimore: The Johns Hopkins Press, 1965).

Norway has sought to rationalize and coordinate investment and economic policy through a system of annual and intermediate-range national budgets which represent the action program of the government. The Netherlands prepares long-term development plans, but the plans do not carry official sanction. In Sweden, economic planning is closer to economic forecasts than to plans for action. The Dutch and Swedish plans are drawn up with the help of the private sector, while in Norway there are no such consultations.

French indicative planning embraces the entire economy but operates through indirect rather than direct controls. The effectiveness of French planning is furthered by a close degree of cooperation between leading industrialists and their counterparts in the nationalized industries.[23] Discriminatory treatment in taxation and financing is applied to those firms that conform to planning guides and carry out specific targets. The chief financial institutions are under government control and tend to discriminate in favor of firms and industries adhering to the plan.

Planning is quite different in the less developed countries. Many of them have adopted plans which are much more extensive than in the developed countries of Western Europe and Japan. But their plans have often been much less successful in terms of what they hoped to accomplish. This unfavorable situation reflects problems characteristic of less developed countries—inadequate administrative and technical skills, overambitious demands for development, lack of statistical data, high degree of sensitivity to agricultural changes, and often unstable political conditions. Although considerable disillusionment has set in for national economic planning as a development panacea, forms of planning are likely to continue as part of the international business environment.

Foreign private enterprise has generally been subjected to more restrictive attention than national business firms. In India, for example, national plans have established overall limits for the total participation of foreign enterprise and have delineated the specific areas in which foreign investment would be permitted.

National planning attempts to establish priorities for sectors and for specific targets in sectors, and international enterprises will have to fit their plans within these priorities in order to be well received. Even when projects fall within priority sectors, projects are likely to be evaluated by detailed criteria as a means of determining the contribu-

---

[23]For two contrasting views on the impact of French planning on business decision making, see Hans Schollhammer, "National Economic Planning and Business Decision Making: The French Experience," *California Management Review.* Winter 1969, pp. 74–88; John McArthur and Bruce R. Scott, *Industrial Planning in France* (Boston: Harvard University, Graduate School of Business Administration, 1969).

tion and the cost in relation to scarce resources being allocated or goals being sought. For example, the foreign exchange earning (or saving in case of import substitution projects) and the foreign exchange costs will be closely scrutinized where foreign exchange constraints are significant. Criteria may exist with regard to choice of technology and the amount of employment that will be created. And where the geographical distribution of new projects is given high importance, the proposed location of the new project will be important. Expansions that can be located in the depressed regions of countries are generally given special preference.

In assessing and forecasting the economic environment, the international enterprise will have to become familiar with the planning activities and the plans. It will also have to appraise the degree of commitment to planning and plans that actually exists. It is easier to prepare plans than to implement them. In many countries, for a variety of reasons, government actions may not follow published plans. In some cases, international enterprise will be able to participate in the planning process and make important contributions. In all cases, the planning dimension of the environment is dynamic.

ASSESSING THE DEVELOPMENT PROCESS

Some business firms have long been active in the less developed countries (LDCs) as resource seekers for supplies of petroleum, minerals, and tropical agricultural products such as tea, cane sugar, and bananas. More recently, some production-efficiency seekers have been establishing feeder plants in the LDCs to produce textiles and electronic components for export to the advanced countries. But as market seekers, international enterprises have been showing only modest interest in the LDCs because of their small markets, low income levels, and perceived political risk. Yet, a large share of the world's population is in the LDCs, and many of the LDCs are achieving relatively high growth rates. As incomes rise, effective demand rises even faster for the kinds of advanced products that can be supplied by international firms. It is a reasonably safe forecast that the LDCs will have a much greater business attraction for the multinational enterprise in the future than they have had in the recent past.

Since most international managers have acquired their international experience in dealing with economic environment issues in the advanced countries, it is quite likely that the reservoir of experience and knowledge may be inadequate for assessing and forecasting the significantly different economic environments of the LDCs. A few brief comments should suffice to demonstrate the complexity of the development process and the need for considerable expertise on the part of the international enterprise in forecasting the economic conditions.

The LDCs have almost universally given top priority to the achievement of rapid economic and social development. The challenge of trying to raise economic levels for such a large share of the world's population has stimulated considerable research on the development process. The growing body of knowledge is being widely applied in the LDCs to accelerate development. Economic policy in the LDCs has been much influenced by evolving theories of the development process. Many different theories have been advanced to account for the low levels of economic activity in certain countries, ranging from climate and natural resources endowment to cultural and social factors.[24] The principal differences among the many development theories stem from different assumptions as to the facts and from questions of emphasis. The various theories, however, are more complementary than contradictory and are gradually evolving toward a complex explanation that recognizes the need to move on many fronts in order to accelerate economic growth.

In terms of general strategy, the early approach of most nations was to emphasize capital as the prime mover. Increasing savings and stimulating capital formation through domestic or foreign means were seen as the principal needs for accelerating economic growth. As experience and understanding increased, development strategies became broader and more complex. Capital continues to be recognized as a crucial bottleneck but not necessarily the only one. Other issues are emphasized such as increasing the absorptive capacity of a country for capital flows, the elimination of institutional blocks, investment in human resources, and the importance of encouraging technology transfers from more advanced countries. Foreign exchange as a constraint has also received considerable attention, leading to an emphasis in many nations on expanding exports and attracting more public and private transfers of capital. In virtually all cases, heavy reliance has been placed on national economic planning and on government enterprise as a source of entrepreneurship.

The development process requires much more than preparing economic blueprints or injecting more capital into a system. Many preconditions for investment must be established in order to secure significant results. Such preconditions may be a mixture of increasing the skills of people, improving the administrative capacity of private

---

[24]The theoretical literature on economic development is vast. For a survey and synthesis, see Gerald M. Meier, *Leading Issues in Economic Development,* 3d ed. (New York: Oxford University Press, 1976); Everett E. Hagen, *The Economics of Development,* rev. ed. (Homewood, Ill.: Richard D. Irwin, Inc., 1975).

and public institutions, creating new technologies, and securing greater efficiency in the operations of political institutions and political decision making in a country. The detailed requirements for a specific country will vary, depending upon resources, the present state of the economic infrastructure such as transportation and communications facilities, soundness of economic policies, and so forth.

In most cases, development-minded countries give great emphasis to industrialization as a means of expanding national productivity and creating new employment. Industrialization strategies vary greatly. In many countries, industrialization policies are first directed toward opportunities for further processing of raw materials normally exported from the country. Import substitution industries will also be encouraged as an easy means of stimulating the industrialization process, because a domestic market will already be available, and because such industries hold the promise of saving foreign exchange. More recently, attention has shifted to encouraging export industries because the growth possibilities for import substitution industries appear to decline after an initial period.[25]

The agricultural sector traditionally receives a great deal of development attention because it is generally the largest sector in the LDCs and because productivity is generally low. Land-reform proposals to increase output generally face major opposition in this sector.

Conflicts among economic, political, and social goals is a general phenomenon. Most countries have less developed regions such as the south of Italy or the northeast of Brazil where, for political reasons, development will have to receive special incentives. Geographic distribution to satisfy political goals may conflict with achieving rapid growth rates. From the social-welfare viewpoint, the issue invariably arises as to how increased economic gains should be distributed between increased consumption and increased investment. On the one hand, there is widespread desire for economic growth to be reflected quickly in improved living conditions. On the other hand, increased consumption generally means the reduced availability of savings for new investment in further growth.

Within many sectoral programs, particularly industry and agriculture, conflicts frequently arise concerning the use of capital-intensive rather than labor-intensive technologies. Most of the less developed countries have serious problems of unemployment and underemploy-

---

[25]See Albert O. Hirschman, "The Political Economy of Import-Substituting Industrialization in Latin America," *Quarterly Journal of Economics*, February 1968, pp. 1–12; Stefan H. Robock, "Industrialization Through Import-Substitution or Export Industries: A False Dichotomy," in *Industrial Organization and Development*, ed. J. W. Markham and G. F. Papanek (Boston: Houghton Mifflin Co., 1970), pp. 350–65.

ment. Thus the preference is for adopting new technologies that will create maximum employment.[26] But in many situations, the only technology options available are capital-intensive ones developed in the advanced countries to fit the needs in such countries. In other cases where the labor-intensive technology option is available, its adoption may make the enterprise less competitive than if capital-intensive technology is used.[27]

The advanced countries and the international agencies have recognized the development gap between the LDCs and the advanced countries as a critical world problem and have established a wide range of governmental programs to transfer financial and technological resources to the LDCs. A major share of the activities of the United Nations is concentrated on development assistance. The International Bank of Reconstruction and Development has become a major multilateral source of development assistance. Many regional development banks such as the Asian Development Bank and the Inter-American Development Bank have also been created as multilateral agencies to support the development efforts of the poor countries.

The specific content and the size of bilateral and multilateral development-assistance programs change as a result of political forces and experience. Yet their importance to the international enterprise should continue. Development-assistance programs can play a key role in determining future economic trends in specific countries and must be taken into account in environmental forecasting. They can also be a source of financial resources and other types of support for a wide range of international business projects. The development role that can be played by international enterprise has been well recognized by development-assistance agencies, both bilateral and multilateral. Thus many development-assistance programs have included specific incentives to encourage the expansion of international business activities, and considerable attention has been devoted to finding ways to expand the flow of foreign private investment that are acceptable to the host countries.

SUMMARY

Modern business enterprises, whether domestic or international in their orientation, have developed considerable sophistication for analyzing and forecasting economic trends. Through in-house staffs or outside consulting services, the domestic manager keeps abreast of

[26]Guy Pfeffermann, "Men and Machines in Africa," in *Finance and Development,* March 1974, p. 16–19.

[27]R. Hal Mason, "Some Observations on the Choice of Technology by Multinational Firms in Developing Countries," *Review of Economics and Statistics,* August 1973, p. 349–55.

national economic trends and future prospects in gross national product, in specific sectors of the economy, and in product fields of special interest.

All the conventional limitations of forecasting the future that exist in domestic economic forecasting carry over to the task of forecasting the economic dimensions of the international business environment. In addition, the great variations in national patterns and crucial domestic variables plus the influence of the inter-nation economic framework make the international task more complex and difficult.

For countries that engage in national economic planning, the international enterprise can use national-planning studies as a principal source for its forecasts. Such studies will have to be evaluated in terms of their possible real impact on governmental policies and actions. They should also be examined to identify crucial development bottlenecks and constraints.

The forecasting of structural changes, which can be of major significance for a specific type of international business activity, is also frequently a part of the national-planning exercises. Input-output matrices which incorporate the interrelationships of different sectors of the economy are sometimes used as a tool in forecasting future structural patterns. Analogies with other countries at a higher stage of development are another basis for structural forecasting. As the economic structure of national economics is certain to change with economic growth, an extrapolation of past trends would be almost certain to give misleading forecasts for the future.

To the extent that a national economy is dependent upon external economic considerations such as foreign markets or inflows of private investment of external development assistance, the economic forecasts will have to examine carefully such external forces and external future prospects.

Forecasting the economic environment must also include estimates and projections of institutional features of national economics such as the role of economic planning and of government enterprise.

EXERCISES AND DISCUSSION QUESTIONS

1. As an exercise in macroeconomic scanning, rank the first five African nations with a population of 1 million or more in terms of the total size of their economy. In terms of growth rates in per capita GNP, what are the five fastest growing Asian economies with a population of 1 million or more?

2. According to the normal pattern, what would you expect industry's contribution to total GNP to be in France, Malaysia, and Brazil? How do these expected patterns compare with the actual structure?

3. Would you consider establishing operations in a country like Brazil that

has been experiencing annual rates of inflation of about 20 percent per year from 1967 to 1974? Why or why not? (Note: Over the 1967–74 period, Brazil's GNP expanded at an average rate of 10 percent annually, in real terms.)

4. "International executives of big pharmaceutical companies with a stake in Italy are so concerned about the outlook for the country's enticing but volatile $1 billion drug market that they are ready to reach for their tranquilizers. The immediate cause of their jitters is a combination of rising labor costs and the government's desire to hold down drug prices. Way in the distance, like a creeping Excedrin headache, is the specter of a state-owned pharmaceutical company to manufacture and sell drugs on the open market" (*Business Week*, May 15, 1971, p. 62). As an official of an international pharmaceutical company, how would you assess this speculation that government enterprise might become a competitor of yours in Italy?

5. Under what circumstances, if any, would you be in favor of comprehensive national economic planning in India? the United Kingdom? Mexico? the United States?

6. "A country may have a trade surplus, but still have an increasingly serious balance-of-payments deficit because of capital outflows or rising remittances. Careful assessment must be made of short-term v. long-term outflows." Discuss.

7. "Whatever the causes, rapid increases in prices mean a currency is depreciating internally—and an external depreciation may become necessary." Discuss. Under what circumstances would domestic inflation *not* lead to devaluation?

17

Market-Demand Forecasting

How does the global firm assess the market demand for the type of product or services it can supply in a large number of foreign markets? Even after the search has been narrowed to countries that are potentially attractive because of their economic size and growth trends, the number of promising opportunities is still likely to be too large. But is the principal difference between domestic and international market-demand forecasting mainly one of a greatly increased number of market areas to be assessed?

In large part, market-demand forecasting is the same activity and requires the same skills and techniques whether it is directed to domestic markets or foreign markets.[1] But there are differences.

The environments in which the tools and techniques are applied are different, and the variations among countries in the availability and quality of the needed data may also require less familiar and less sophisticated techniques than are customary for domestic market research. The multinational enterprise with a global strategy will want the market-demand studies for different countries to be sufficiently standardized so that cross-country comparisons can be made. From the standpoint of cost, relatively inexpensive techniques may be needed so that a large number of potentially interesting market opportunities can be appraised. A final difference may be in the time period used for domestic as against international market-demand forecasts. Where foreign opportunities involve initiating new operations, require a large

---

[1]For a standard reference on market research, see Harper W. Boyd, Jr. and Ralph Westfall, *Marketing Research,* 3d ed. (Homewood, Ill.: Richard D. Irwin, Inc., 1972).

commitment of resources, and where a high degree of risk is perceived because of limited familiarity with operations in a new country, the firm may want to have a longer-range forecast than would normally be required for guiding domestic decisions.

The American firm "going international" will have to make an especially large adjustment in its market-demand forecasting activity. Not only is the United States outstanding in the availability of data from government, trade associations, and other sources, but it has also accumulated an impressive stock of market research studies, market research organizations, and skilled personnel. Furthermore, the flowering of market research in the United States has been aided by a cultural variable that favors considerable openness concerning economic and business information as contrasted to the attitudes of secrecy prevailing in many other countries.

In Western Europe and Japan, local interest in market research has grown rapidly in recent years. National and international efforts have markedly improved the availability and the quality of data that can be used for market research. Thus in a growing number of foreign countries, techniques used in the United States can be applied with relatively few modifications.[2] The main requirements will be knowledge of a foreign language and some awareness of statistical perils resulting in different definitions. In one important respect, the task may be even easier than in the United States because many national economic-planning studies are available in foreign countries, whereas national economic planning has not been part of the recent U.S. environment. Furthermore, research data may even be provided by the government. The U.S. Department of Commerce makes available a wide range of market surveys prepared on a contract basis by private research organizations or by Commerce Department market research officers abroad.[3] Such studies ranged from the market for graphic art equipment in Argentina to the market for electronics production equipment in West Germany. Other governments also aid their firms in a similar way, but the emphasis in such studies is likely to be on products for export rather than for foreign production.

The special international activity to which this chapter is addressed is market-demand forecasting for countries where the availability of data and planning studies is limited and where different and relatively inexpensive techniques may have to be used. In particular, when analyzing the small and fragmented markets of the numerous less

---

[2]See Feliksas Palubinskas, *Guidebook to Worldwide Marketing* (Westport, Conn.: Technomic Publishing Co., 1975).

[3]U.S. Department of Commerce, *Publications for American Business* (Washington, D.C.: U.S. Government Printing Office, 1975).

developed countries, techniques are needed that provide useful demand estimates from a minimum of data and at a modest expense. The resulting market-demand forecasts may be less authoritative than desired but still of reasonable quality for business decision making.

THE GENERAL APPROACH

Market-demand forecasting can be based either on past experience in the country being studied or on analogous experience in another country. Forecasts can be made directly by extending actual sales data into the future, or indirectly on the basis of an established relationship between demand for the product or service and independent variables such as economic or demographic characteristics of the country. All market-demand forecasting represents some blend of these approaches.

In many countries, particularly the less developed nations, the data problems limiting market-demand forecasting are likely to be threefold. First, actual sales data may not be available. Second, data may not be available on some of the important variables that influence future demand, with the consequence that forecasts will have to be based on fewer variables than would be desired. Third, some or all of the bare minimum of data required are not available for the country being studied, that data and relationships used for forecasting will have to be based on the experience in other countries.

A number of techniques have been used successfully for analyzing country markets where data sources are limited. Historical demand patterns can be extrapolated by using trade and production data as a substitute for actual sales information. The relationship between demand and an independent variable can be analyzed through the use of income elasticities or regression analysis. In some cases, more complex econometric models and input-output studies can be used.[4] These techniques are discussed separately below, but all of them are different versions of the general approach of forecasting on the basis of relationships.

EXTRAPOLATING PAST DEMAND PATTERNS

Where sales rates are not available for a country, the most common approach is to use trade and production data as a proxy for market-demand patterns. These data are relatively easy to secure from national and international publications. Through the adoption of a uniform

---

[4]Most of these techniques are discussed in greater detail in Reed Moyer, "International Market Analysis," *Journal of Marketing Research* 5 (November 1968): 353–60.

tariff classification by many countries, the comparability of trade data among countries has been improved. The United Nations now publishes import-export data in great detail for most countries.[5] Market demand, also called *apparent consumption,* is estimated by combining local production and imports, and then making adjustments for exports and fluctuations in inventory levels.

A major problem in relying on published statistics is the time lag before publication. Another complication is that inventory data generally are not available in countries with underdeveloped statistical systems. One way to compensate for short-term inventory and other fluctuations is to use longer time periods and calculate an annual average or a moving average. The disadvantage of this adjustment is that the estimate may not indicate current sales rates.

Forecasts of future market demand can be made by extrapolating historical patterns of apparent consumption. Where imports supply a large share of local market demand, an extrapolation of historical trends may understate future demand if imports have been controlled. Furthermore, when local production replaces imports, domestic demand may increase faster than suggested by import trends, assuming that domestic prices remain constant, merely because local facilities can provide quicker and more flexible service to customers. Characteristically, too, import substitution industries expand rapidly during an early stage when an established market already exists and domestic production is substituting for previously imported goods. After the substitution stage, the growth rate in production tends to slow down to the normal pace of growth in domestic demand.

Having developed an historical series on apparent consumption, the crucial question becomes the appropriate pattern for projection. A straight extrapolation is most valid for a short time period and for a relatively mature economy. But it assumes that future trends will follow the patterns of the historical past. This assumption is precarious for a low-income country that is expanding rapidly and undergoing structural changes.

One basis for modifying extrapolations may be the. industrial growth patterns already experienced by other countries of the world. The typical patterns of growth in manufacturing industries based on trends in seven to ten countries are shown in Figure 17–1. Within the manufacturing sector, the chart relates the percentage of total manufacturing production accounted for by major industrial groups to gross domestic product per capita. Although the typical pattern does not necessarily describe the actual development pattern to be followed by any given country, it suggests that the share of income spent on

---

[5]United Nations, *Yearbook of International Trade Statistics.*

FIGURE 17-1

Typical Patterns of Growth in Manufacturing Industries*

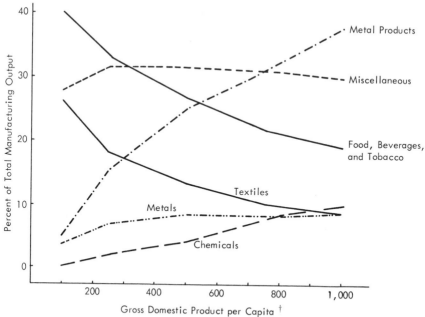

*Based on time-series analysis for selected years, 1899–1957.
†Dollars at 1955 prices.
Source: Alfred Maizels, *Industrial Growth and World Trade* (Cambridge, England: Cambridge University Press, 1963), p. 55.

textiles, as one example, should be extrapolated at a declining rather than a constant rate, whereas the demand for metal products can be expected to increase at a rate faster than gains in per capita GDP.[6]

Extrapolation of apparent consumption can be based on per capita as well as total consumption. For example, a straight-line extrapolation of per capita aluminum consumption in Latin America over the period from 1950 to 1963 shows a gain from 0.44 kilograms per capita in 1963 to 1.85 in 1975. The per capita projection when joined with population forecasts translates into an increase in total market demand from 93,000 metric tons in 1963 to 580,000 metric tons in 1975. In the case of aluminum, after experimenting with several types of projection techniques, the straight-line extrapolation with some slight adjustments was evaluated as the best forecast.[7]

---

[6]For further details, see Alfred Maizels, *Industrial Growth and World Trade* (Cambridge, England: Cambridge University Press, 1963); H. B. Chenery, "Patterns of Industrial Growth," *American Economic Review,* September 1960.

[7]Joseph L. Fisher, "Global Projections for the Mining Sector," *Sectoral Aspects of Projections for the World Economy* 2 (New York: United Nations, 1969), pp. 54, 113.

FORECASTING WITH INCOME ELASTICITIES

In many situations, market-demand forecasting can be partially or wholly based on income elasticities. The concept of income elasticity measures the relationship between the change in demand for a product and changes in income.

Symbolically the formula below measures the income elasticity for commodity A where Q represents the quantity demanded, Y is the income, and Δ refers to quantity changes.

$$\frac{\dfrac{\Delta QA}{QA}}{\dfrac{\Delta Y}{Y}}$$

If demand increases at the same rate as income, a product would have an income elasticity of one. If demand increases only half as fast as income, the income elasticity of a product would be 0.5. Goods with values of more than one are income elastic. Goods with values of less than one are income inelastic. Income elasticities have been calculated for individual or family incomes and separately for various levels of income. Where detailed data on family and personal income distribution are not available, as in many LDCs, income elasticities have been calculated for a country as a whole in relation to average per capita income for the country. In the absence of better market information, the latter form of income elasticities can be a reasonably satisfactory approach to market-demand forecasting.

Market-demand forecasting by the income-elasticities method requires four steps. First, current levels of demand are determined. Second, average per capita income is forecast for the selected future period. Third, income elasticities are determined either from a country's own historical experience or from the experience of other countries. Finally, future market demand is estimated as current demand times a factor derived by multiplying the projected increase in per capita income and the income elasticity for the commodity. If per capita income is expected to increase by 50 percent in the forecast period and the income elasticity of the product is 1.5, total demand should increase by 75 percent.

Income elasticities are widely used by economic planners for establishing development targets for a country. Consequently, a considerable amount of information has been developed on income elasticities.[8] In general, the empirical information follows the patterns

---

[8]See United Nations, *Industrialization and Productivity, Bulletin 9,* "Analysis and Projections of Consumption Demand: Methodological Notes" (New York, 1965), pp. 49–81.

suggested by Engel's law. The income elasticities for food and other necessities are generally less than one and for luxury goods more than one. The results of several income-elasticity studies that cover both consumer and industrial products and some services are shown in Table 17–1. The data are averages and may not apply equally to all income groups. Also note the differences that can result by calculating the elasticities through cross-sectional analysis—comparing a number of countries at different levels of income for the same time period, and through times series—comparing patterns over time for the same country.

The Agricultural Commodities Projections study of the FAO was heavily based on income-elasticity data for food and other agricultural commodities.[9] The coefficients used in the study were determined from a collection and analysis of more than 100 household surveys undertaken in the FAO member countries. Based on these and other studies, income-elasticity coefficients and demand functions were selected for each of the numerous products covered by the study.

TABLE 17–1
Income Elasticity Measurements

Commodity	Cross Section	Time Series
Food and beverage, excluding alcoholic beverages	0.54,† 0.53‡	0.8*
Alcoholic beverages	0.77†	—
Tobacco.	0.88†	—
Clothing	0.8,* 0.9,* 0.84,† 0.89*	0.7,* 0.8*
Textiles	0.5*	0.8*
Household and personal services.	1.19†	—
Communication services	2.03†	—
Recreation	1.15†	—
Health.	1.80†	—
Durable consumer goods.	—	2.7*
Furniture.	1.61‡	—
Appliances.	1.40‡	—
Metals.	1.52‡	—
Chemicals	—	2.1*
Machinery and transportation equipment, except passenger cars	—	2.1*

*Source is Meritt L. Kastens, "Organizing, Planning, and Staffing Market Research Activities in an International Operations," *Market Research in International Operations,* Management Report no. 53 (New York: American Management Association, 1960), p. 42.
†Source is Milton Gilbert and Associates, *Comparative National Products and Price Levels* (Paris: OECD, 1958), p. 66.
‡From author's calculations.
Source: Reed Moyer, "International Market Analysis," *Journal of Marketing Research,* table 2, 5 (November 1968): 356.

[9]*Agricultural Commodity Projections, 1970–1980,* 2 (Rome: Food and Agricultural Organization of the United Nations, 1971) presents a comprehensive statement on the scope and methodology of the study. Research Working Paper No. 1 on "Income Elasticities of Demand for Agricultural Products" is available as a separate release from the official report.

Several cautions in the use of income elasticities should be noted. A high income elasticity for a product does not necessarily mean a high-volume market. It merely indicates that demand will increase rapidly as incomes rise. In terms of volume, the large markets for some time to come in most countries will be in necessities, even though the growth in these markets may be relatively slow. Furthermore, income elasticities indicate a constant relationship between demand changes and income changes. For specific products, it is likely that after income reaches a certain level, the demand will increase at an increasing rate. This is particularly noticeable for consumer durables. Prices also affect the elasticities in several ways. If prices in a country for the products of a new industry are relatively high, and if such prices fall as the industries become more mature, demand for such products will increase from a combination of price and income factors. As between countries, prices can vary greatly because of taxes, subsidies, and other factors. Such differences must be taken into account in using income elasticities. Thus, income elasticities are useful guides but no perfect substitutes for specific market research.

ESTIMATING BY ANALOGY

Prevailing patterns of demand in more advanced countries can be used to estimate future market demand in a late-developing economy as incomes rise. This approach assumes that product usage moves along a similar path as a country's stage of development advances. The use of cross-sectional income elasticities to forecast demand is an example of estimation by analogy in this way. The typical extrapolation of patterns of growth in manufacturing industries is another.

An example of using the analogy method for estimating a country's future demand for copper is shown in Figure 17-2. Per capita consumption of copper over the 1959–63 period was calculated for 24 countries and 6 regions and plotted on a double logarithmic chart in relation to average per capita GDP for each of the countries and regions. For example, Mexico with per capita GDP of about $350 (1960 dollars) consumed about 0.6 kilograms of copper per capita. If we assume that Mexico is following a development pattern similar to that of Argentina, we can estimate that copper use will approximate 0.9 kilograms as per capita GDP approaches $600. If the South African pattern is more analogous, Mexican copper use will rise more sharply to about 1.4 kilograms when per capita GDP rises to $480.

The analogy method can also be used for verifying the reasonableness of market-demand forecasts based on other techniques. Figure 17–3 was actually used in this way for testing forecasts of the demand

FIGURE 17–2

Per Capita Copper Use and GDP (1959–63)

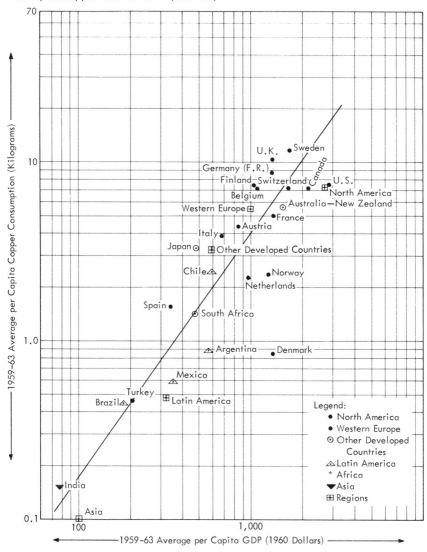

Source: *Sectoral Aspects of Projections for the World Economy,* vol. 2. Papers delivered at Elsinore, Denmark, August 14–27, 1966 (New York: United Nations, 1969), p. 87.

for electricity in South Central Brazil based on a wide range of separate studies and varied techniques.[10] The average per capita consumption and per capita GDP were calculated for a four-year period for 55 countries and then plotted on a double logarithmic chart. A regression line (see below) was then calculated for all the observations and plotted. The forecasts for South Central Brazil for 1970, 1975, and 1980 all fell above the line, implying a higher than average per capita use of electricity in relation to per capita GDP. This result was consistent with the actual patterns in the past and could be explained by a number of special characteristics of the area for which the forecast was made.

Careful grouping of countries by similar characteristics can provide a basis for more refined comparison than simply grading countries by stage of development as indicated by their GNP per capita. Groupings can be arrived at easily by classifying countries that are reasonably similar over a range of specific characteristics, for example dependence on agriculture, degree of urbanization, or level of education. Alternatively the groupings could be arrived at more formally using cluster analysis.[11]

Blind reliance on analogy, however, can result in erroneous estimates. Differences in culture, tastes, and habits that dictate consumption patterns may limit the validity of analogies. Technical advances such as new inventions or substitute products may cause future patterns of consumption in late-developing countries to change sharply from the patterns of presently advanced countries. Price differences among countries, because of import tariffs for example, or over time, can also cause errors. Nevertheless, used with caution, the method can be extremely useful where data are limited.

REGRESSION ANALYSIS

Regression analysis can be a powerful tool in forecasting market demand, especially for countries where data on current demand are scarce. Also, where estimates are made by income elasticities or by analogy, regression analysis provides a basis for checking the reasonableness of estimates.

Regression analysis is simply a statistical technique for determining

[10]Antonio Dias Leite, Stefan H. Robock, and Leonid Hassiley, *Methodology for Long-Term Forecasting and Application to South Central Brazil,* (Paper delivered at the World Power Conference, Tokyo, Japan, 1966. no. 75).

[11]See, for example, S. Prakash Sethi, "Comparative Cluster Analysis for World Markets," *Journal of Marketing Research,* August 1971, p. 348–54; and S. Prakash Sethi and Richard H. Holton, "Country Typologies for the Multinational Corporation: A New Basic Approach," *California Management Review,* Spring 1973, p. 105–18.

the relationship between two or more variables. A regression equation can express the quantitative relationship between the demand for a specific product and a gross economic indicator. In a technical sense, demand would be called the dependent variable and the indicator (or

FIGURE 17-3
Per Capita Consumption of Electricity and per Capita GDP

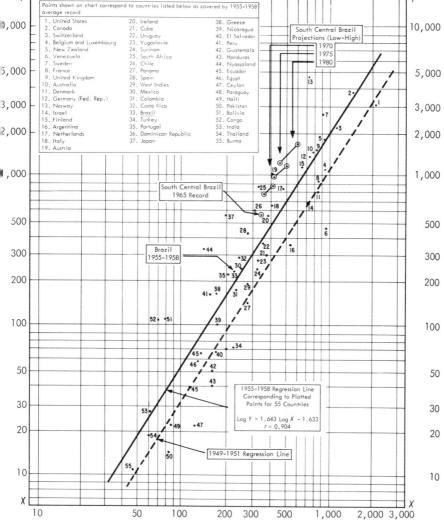

*Y—Per capita net consumption of total electricity (kilowatt-hours).
†X—Per capita gross domestic product (dollars at 1950 prices).
Source: *NACIONES UNIDAS—Estudios Sobre la Electricided en America Latina,* 1 (Mexico, D. F., October 1962): 75.

several indicators) would be the independent variable. This relation-ship can be determined for *Country B,* or a number of countries, and then applied to *Country A* in which the firm is interested, even though information is not available in *Country A* on current market demand for the product. In such a case, the market-demand estimate is based on both regression analysis and analogy, as the relationship discovered for other countries is assumed to be applicable for the country in which the business firm is interested. Regression analysis can also be used when data on current consumption are available for *Country A* to compare market-demand patterns in *Country A* with the experience in other countries so that future forecasts can be verified or modified.

Some regression results that relate the consumption of various commodities to a gross economic indicator are summarized in Table 17–2. A linear regression model $(y = a + bx)$ was used with y as the amount of a product in use per thousand of population and x as per capita GNP. The equations explain from 50 to 78 percent of the variation in the dependent variable as shown by R^2. Actually these regression results are an example of using a proxy for demand data, because they are actually based on the amount of each product in use per capita rather than on sales.

The regression results in Table 17–2 show that an increase of $100 in per capita GNP will result, on the average, in an increase of 10 automobiles, 10 refrigerators, 9 washing machines, 7 television sets, and 27 radio sets per 1,000 population. This, however, is a very simple way of predicting demand for consumer durables. More advanced techniques that allow for saturation of the market, life of the product, and replacement rates are common.[12]

Another example of regression analysis was shown in Figure 17–3, which analyzes the demand for electric power in relation to per capita

TABLE 17–2
Regression of Consumption on Gross National Product (various products)

Product	Number of Observations	Regression Equation	Unadjusted R^2
Autos	37	$-21.071 + 0.101x$	0.759
Radio sets	42	$8.325 + 0.275x$	0.784
TV sets	31	$-16.501 + 0.074x$	0.503
Refrigerators	24	$-21.330 + 0.102x$	0.743
Washing machines	22	$-15.623 + 0.094x$	0.736

Source: Reed Moyer, "International Marketing Analysis," *Journal of Marketing Research,* tables 4, 5 (November 1968): 358, based on United Nations, *Statistical Yearbook,* 1962; Alfred Maizels, *Industrial Growth and World Trade* (Cambridge, England: Cambridge University Press, 1963), pp.. 308–9.

[12]For example, see Erwin E. Nemmers, *Managerial Economics,* part 2 (New York: John Wiley and Sons, Inc., 1962).

GDP. The relationship for all the 55 countries is expressed in the regression line, and the positive r of 0.9 indicates that there is a very high positive correlation between GDP per capita and the demand for electric power.

Regression analysis may not give reliable results for some products where the relationship of demand to other variables is highly complex and data are not available on all the essential variables. For example, demand forecasts may require data on many variables other than income (or GNP), such as prices, government expenditures, availability of consumer credit, advertising and promotion for a new product, and so forth. Fortunately, however, the consumption of many products can be estimated reasonably accurately by knowing only the per capita income (or GNP) in the countries being studied.

MORE ADVANCED MODELS

More complex and more costly multiple regression models are used by major multinational firms to obtain projections for a variety of indicators that will affect sales. The expertise involved in developing these models falls within the field of econometrics and will not be compressed into this chapter. Instead, we will simply illustrate the field through one example—the use of an econometric model to measure the sales for still cameras, as developed by Armstrong.[13] His econometric model was based on the following conceptual model:

$$S_{i,t} = f(M_{i,t}; A_{i,t}; N_{i,t})$$

where

S = camera sales per year by country
M = market size (i.e. number of potential buyers)
A = ability to buy
N = consumer needs and
    i refers to the country and t to the year.

Trade and production data were used to estimate sales by country for 30 countries. The model assumes that camera sales depend in each country on some relationship to market size, ability to buy, and consumer needs. In turn, market size was estimated on the basis of total population, literacy rates, proportion of the population aged 15 to 64, and the share of the population in nonagricultural employment.

Ability to buy was estimated on the basis of an index of living standard, an estimate of rate of change in the ability to buy, and

---

[13]J. Scott Armstrong, "An Application of Econometric Methods to International Marketing," *Journal of Marketing Research* 7 (May 1970): 190–98.

information on camera prices. Various measures were used for consumer needs, such as households per adult, rainfall, and proportion of children in the population.

On the basis of this conceptual model and subsequent analysis, a predictive model was developed. The forecasting model was tested by backcasting, that is, estimating camera sales for an earlier period, from 1960–65. The results were reasonably good.

As is apparent from even this brief description, the data-collection task for developing and for using more complex regression models is substantial. The selection of the minimum number of variables to include in the model requires considerable testing and judgment. If the necessary investment in time and resources can be justified, market-demand forecasting with an econometric model can have the additional benefit of producing a substantial amount of information that can be used for guiding marketing and other operations once a project is established in the country being studied. For firms such as Xerox, Kodak, and Singer, a solidly developed quantitative estimate of the potential in each market can form the basis for controlling subsidiary performance and for longer-range commitments to production facilities.

INPUT-OUTPUT ANALYSIS

Input-output or inter-industry analysis has been used for a number of years to describe the economic structure of a country and as a basis for national economic planning.[14] More recently, market researchers have recognized the value of input-output tables, where available, for market-demand forecasting, particularly for industrial products where much of the demand will be derived from the growth of other industries.[15] Input-output tables have been published for many of the developed countries, such as the United States, Japan, and the Netherlands, and for a large number of underdeveloped countries. An inter-industry model used for Japanese sectoral planning divided the total economy into 60 productive sectors, resulting in what is called a 60 by 60 matrix. However, many of the tables break down the entire economy into only a small number of broad industry groups and cannot provide much detail on specific products.

---

[14]United Nations Statistical Office, *Problems of Input-Output Tables and Analysis* (New York, 1966); U.S. Department of Commerce, *Input-Output Structure of the U.S. Economy: 1967* (Washington, D.C.: U.S. Government Printing Office, 1974).

[15]Jack G. Faucett, "Input-Output Analysis as a Tool of International Market Research," *Market Research in International Operations,* Management Report no. 53 (New York: American Management Association, 1960), pp. 41–59; Roger K. Chisholm and Gilbert R. Whitaker, Jr., *Forecasting Methods* (Homewood, Ill.: Richard D. Irwin, Inc., 1971), pp. 62–95

Conceptually, input-output tables recognize the interrelationships of each sector in an economy to all others (see Table 17–3). The total output of one sector reading across the rows in the transaction table, for example agriculture, becomes the input of all sectors (including the agricultural sector itself). At the same time, reading down each column, each sector receives its inputs from the other sectors. The input and output relationships of each sector, including households and foreign trade, to all the others are quantitatively expressed by coefficients.

Where input-output tables are sufficiently detailed, one can trace the direct and indirect impact on the demand for one product of changes in demand for the products of other industries. The tables can show the extent to which sales are made to final users or consumed as inter-mediate goods. Also, input-output tables can provide information on the number of sectors that are users of the products from another sector.

Input-output tables were used as a tool for the sectoral planning phase of Japan's Medium-Term Economic Plan covering the period from 1964 to 1968.[16] By applying known input-output relationships to projections of the general magnitude and direction of the economy's growth, as one example, gross output of pulp, paper, and related products was estimated to increase over the period at an annual rate of 16.1 percent. The plan also revealed the projected increases in the various components of gross output such as intermediate demand, final demand, exports, and government purchases.[17]

Input-output analysis has its limitations. A tremendous amount of data and analysis is required to construct tables that can provide detailed industry or product information. Data limitations and the lack of resources have often resulted in tables that are too general or too incomplete to be of great value for specific market-demand forecasting. Also, input-output tables normally use fixed technical coefficients. This means that the effects of changes in production processes or in production levels are not taken into account by forecasts based on the tables. There could be a variety of other dynamic changes, too.

Despite these limitations, input-output analyses can be useful. Many countries have been devoting sizable resources to the improve-ment of input-output tables for their countries, and considerable effort is being made by technicians to resolve the problems of fixed coeffi-cients and inadequate data. The principal motivation and justification

---

[16]Economic Planning Agency, *Medium-Term Economic Plan, 1964–1968* (Tokyo, 1965).

[17]Shuntaro Shishido, "A Multisectoral Projection Model for a Developed Economy—An Experience with Japanese Sectoral Planning," *Sectoral Aspects of Projections for the World Economy* 3 (New York: United Nations, 1969), p. 184–85.

TABLE 17-3
Input-Output Tables: A Simplified Illustration

COUNTRY A—TRANSACTIONS, 1960

	Agriculture	Food Processing	Coal	Electric Energy	Plastic Products	Apparel	Final Demand					Total Output
							Consumer Expenditures	Government Operations	Exports	Investment	Total Final Demand	
Agriculture	—	50	—	—	—	—	100	—	50	—	150	200
Food processing	25	—	—	—	—	—	150	—	25	—	175	200
Coal	—	10	—	50	10	5	15	5	—	5	25	100
Electric energy	10	30	5	—	25	5	35	10	—	30	75	150
Plastic products	—	10	—	5	—	5	10	—	220	—	230	250
Apparel	—	—	—	—	—	—	50	—	150	—	200	200
Wages and salaries . . .	80	50	40	30	100	70	—	20	—	100	120	490
Imports (total)	35	20	15	25	40	75	150	10	—	175	335	545
Agricultural chemicals . .	20	—	—	—	10	—	—	—	—	15	—	—
Paint and varnishes . .	5	—	—	5	10	60	5	—	—	—	—	—
Textiles	5	—	5	5	—	—	15	—	—	10	—	—
Iron castings	5	—	10	15	30	15	—	—	—	150	—	—
Other	—	20	—	—	—	—	130	10	—	—	—	—
Profits, interest, depreciation, taxes	50	30	40	40	75	40	—	—	—	50	50	325
Total output	200	200	100	150	250	200	510	45	445	360	1,360	1,360

COUNTRY A—PRODUCTION COEFFICIENTS, 1960

	Agriculture	Food Processing	Coal	Electric Energy	Plastic Products	Apparel
Agriculture	—	0.250	—	—	—	—
Food processing	0.125	—	—	—	—	—
Coal	—	0.050	—	0.333	—	—
Electric energy	0.050	0.150	0.050	—	0.040	0.025
Plastic products	—	0.050	—	0.033	0.100	0.025
Apparel	—	—	—	—	—	0.025
Wages and salaries	0.400	0.250	0.400	0.200	0.400	0.350
Imports (total)	0.175	0.100	0.150	0.167	0.160	0.375
Agricultural chemicals	0.100	—	—	—	—	—
Paints and varnishes	0.025	—	—	0.033	0.040	—
Textiles	0.025	—	0.050	—	—	0.300
Iron castings	0.025	—	0.100	0.033	—	—
Other	—	0.100	—	0.100	0.120	0.075
Profits, interest, depreciation taxes	0.250	0.150	0.400	0.267	0.300	0.200
Total output	1.000	1.000	1.000	1.000	1.000	1.000

Source: Reprinted by permission of the publishers from AMA Management Report no. 53, *Market Research in International Operations*, © 1960 by the American Management Association, Inc.

for such efforts are the value of input-output tables for governmental planning and policy making.

INFRASTRUCTURE REQUIREMENTS AND SERVICES

The market demand for many products and services that can be supplied by international enterprises results directly or indirectly from governmental programs to expand infrastructure facilities and services such as transportation, electricity, education, housing, and health. Because of the government's direct responsibility for infrastructure and its need to provide financing, wholly or in part, for such facilities, a considerable amount of governmental planning work is likely to be available. From these data the business firm can obtain excellent guidelines to future market demand. Where the less developed countries are soliciting international financing from agencies like the World Bank, market studies must normally be prepared as a component of the project proposal submitted for financing.

The types of planning studies usually undertaken for planning future infrastructure needs vary greatly among the particular fields.[18] In the case of electric power, future needs are derived from growth targets for the total economy and the planned expansion of specific types of industrial and other productive activity. Such planning studies have a high probability of being implemented. Electric-power projects are revenue producing and thus can provide some of their financing. Electric power must also be available in order that other growth targets can be reached. In the case of housing, education, and health, the implementation of official plans is likely to be more uncertain because social-welfare plans are generally limited by the future availability of government revenues. For political and welfare reasons, it is common for governments to establish ambitious targets in these fields which may not be realistic.

SUMMARY

After screening the global horizon and making a preliminary identification of countries that appear to have attractive economic situations, the globally oriented firm will want to examine the market-demand prospects for its products in countries that appear promising. In a growing number of countries, government planning reports or available market research studies can supply the international firm with

---

[18]See Richard Cibotti, "Projections of Infrastructure Requirements and Services," *Sectoral Aspects of Projections for the World Economy* 2 (New York: United Nations, 1969), pp. 148–205.

sufficient information on which it can decide whether or not it will undertake a detailed business opportunity analysis for the country. In other situations, particularly in the less developed countries, the firm will need to make its own market-demand studies, using techniques that are not too costly and that can produce reasonable results where the availability of data is limited. A number of such techniques have been suggested. In general, they make use of analogies and methods that relate the market demand for a product to one or more general economic or demographic indicators. As a subsequent step, in-depth field surveys will be required to examine the competitive and operating environment that the international firm will encounter in the promising markets.

EXERCISES AND DISCUSSION QUESTIONS

1. Compile a list of sources of economic and market data for a specified African nation other than South Africa.

2. *Country A's* GNP rose from $6 billion by a further $550 million during 1976 and its steel consumption, all imported, rose by 400,000 tons to 3.8 million tons. Population also increased from 10 million to 10.4 million. What is the income elasticity of demand for steel? Do you think this would provide a very accurate indicator for predicting steel usage over the ensuing five years?

3. Select a less developed country and for either textiles or metal manufactures determine the forecasting methods you think would have been most appropriate for forecasting demand at each of two dates within the last 20 years, separated by at least five years.

4. "It may be true that all European countries are travelling the same road towards what has been called 'salvation through industrialization' and it may be possible, therefore, to forecast some of the probable changes in living habits as the process continues. Even so, there are still great differences between one place and another, between one nation and another, and in the rates at which they change. These differences reveal themselves in a great diversity of what people will buy. Economic development is certainly affecting culture and customs, habits and attitudes, traditions and mentality; but these, in turn, are reacting on what is going on in the economy—in production, consumption, and distribution. You may detect the general trend; but look around Western Europe and you will discover all sorts of subtle variations in the speed and character of the change. Here the emancipation of women may be moving more slowly. There peasant and aristocratic attitudes may persist."
In the light of this extract, what types of products would you expect to follow dissimilar demand patterns over time in European countries? Of these, would you expect a country's past demand to provide a better basis for predicting demand than analogies with other countries at a more advanced stage?

5. Give your own definition of the market saturation point for a consumer durable, such as washing machines, and explain why the level may vary from country to country.

6. "Comparison of either total demand or per capita demand for different countries may be misleading for the purposes of formulating a global strategy, particularly if major variations occur within countries." Elaborate on this statement and suggest how the problem might be overcome.

7. You would expect to find some relationship between a country's demand for medical drugs and the numbers of doctors and hospital beds in the country. What other indicators might be used for forecasting the level of drug purchases? As the basis for a global marketing plan how would you go about predicting a country's spending on drugs five years hence?

8. Explain how demand for the output of a primary industry might be forecast using an input-output table. What are the limitations in the input-output method?

part five

Managing the Multinational Enterprise

THIS SECTION OF THE BOOK concentrates on international business from the viewpoint of the decision maker within the firm and is prescriptive rather than descriptive. Only those managerial issues that bear a uniquely international slant and require new and different approaches by decision makers will be dealt with at any length here. They are legion, however, and the analytical and decision-making approaches can be only introduced rather than exhaustively treated in the chapters that follow.

The first chapter in this part of the book sets out a framework for the overall planning of a firm's international activities. Subsequent chapters then fit into this framework, examining particular aspects in more detail. Global strategy deals with the planning, timing, and location of a firm's expansions as well as the strategies for entry, ownership, and management of a global operation. Organizational patterns for the multinational enterprise constitute an area of managerial responsibility where a growing amount of analysis is beginning to define the principal options and the criteria for choice. Managing the international product mix deals with the question of choice of products, distribution channels, and marketing strategies, while financial management involves some of the more complex new variables resulting from crossing national boundaries into a number of currency areas and financial environments. The information and control process is also complicated by special international factors. The final topic covered is managing human resources, both managerial and work force.

Throughout the managerial function, conventional analytical and decision-making approaches may require considerable modification to allow for varying national interests. Decisions concerning internal pricing, location of research, production, and financial resources can be of critical importance to the individual nations in which the firm operates. Also differences in the objectives of different nationalities represented within firms can be a significant constraint.

The earlier parts of the book are an essential background for understanding the management task in the multinational enterprise dealt with in these final chapters. Successful performance of the managerial decision-making role in the multinational firm requires an understanding of the framework for international transactions, the goals of national governments and the controls they may adopt, and the changing cultural and economic environment.

18

Building a Global Strategy

MOST BUSINESS FIRMS become international by a process of creeping "incrementalism" rather than by strategy choice. Some firms are first attracted to foreign markets by unsolicited export orders and, after discovering new opportunities, move through a series of stages to the establishment of foreign production facilities. Other firms initiate international activities in response to threats to an oligopoly position. Still others respond to specific opportunities for developing supplies of resources or achieving greater production efficiency through foreign operations. But rarely are these early moves part of a comprehensive global strategy. And in some stage of becoming a global enterprise, the international activities of many firms could be best characterized as a portfolio of diverse and separate country companies tied together by a network of ad hoc relationships.

In fact, a survey of several major American and European international companies reveals that in many enterprises, "the strategy (if it can be called that) has been to put an operation wherever it was feasible . . . and then let things shake out later."[1] Even in the late 1960s formalized global strategic and long-range planning were still in a stage of infancy in most companies.

Increased competition, growing environmental pressures, and a keener awareness of the synergistic benefits of a multinational enterprise are, however, more and more forcing international companies to adopt global strategies and global planning.

---

[1] John S. Schwendiman, "International Strategic Planning: Still in Its Infancy?" *Worldwide P & I Planning*, September–October 1971, p. 52.

WHAT IS A GLOBAL STRATEGY?

A global strategy is simply a plan whereby an enterprise makes its major business decisions of allocating limited resources by taking into account global opportunities, global alternatives, and future global consequences. A global strategy means that the decision maker frees himself of any national blinders and considers world markets and world resource locations and not simply the markets or resources of a particular country in isolation. A global strategy aims to maximize results on a multinational basis rather than treat international activities as a portfolio of diverse and separate country companies. And a global strategy generally requires that the enterprise engage in a formal process of strategic and long-range planning.

Consider the large U.S. chemical company with plants in over 20 countries whose chief executive proudly asserts: "I don't like to be too explicit in telling my division managers what I think we should be doing around the globe. They just might take me too literally—and then they might not do enough of their own thinking. . . ."[2] Such a management philosophy, where the president does not assume a leadership role in developing global goals and strategy, runs the risk that the enterprise will go in so many directions that it will miss the advantages of being a multinational enterprise.

A firm does not need to reach the point of outrunning its national market before global planning becomes desirable. Most businesses have potential for achieving economies of scale extending beyond the size of national markets, even if these economies are only in marketing or management expertise. If its domestic competitors extend their horizons to include a broader sales base, the firm could find itself less able to maintain the same pace of research or product development given its smaller sales base. Even where domestic competition is not moving rapidly to other markets, foreign firms may be developing strategies that pose a threat. European firms that disregarded the higher growth rates of U.S. or Japanese firms in a number of industries were largely unprepared for the competitive challenge when the foreign firms broke into their own national markets. An excellent example of how the U.S. pursuit of international economies provoked havoc among provincial foreign competitors is given by Anthony Sampson in an article discussing the giant multinational, ITT:

> ITT's telecommunications companies at present have the best of two worlds: their own research and production have the advantages of cross-fertilisation between laboratories and factories all over Europe.

---

[2]Ibid., p. 25.

Thus, even though each European government has a different telephone system, ITT's experience in one country can be very helpful in another. Its competitors, on the other hand, based on a single country, lack its resources and have not yet been able to build up a genuinely European industry."[3]

Other firms have been left behind in the competitive race because they failed to go to the cheapest sources of supply.

On a strictly rational basis, no firm should automatically limit its horizon to its home market. For example, with its large population, high-wage rates, high discretionary spending power, and high propensity to innovate, the U.S. market has been the leader in adoption and growth rates for many products. This has placed U.S. firms at an advantage. They did not need to think globally in the early stages of a product's life, because the strategy coincided with achievement in the U.S. market. But many firms outside the United States needed to plan globally from the beginning. A United Kingdom firm introducing a technological advance was likely to find that after the very early stages the U.S. market took off more rapidly. If U.S. demand was left to U.S. competitors, the sales and experience of U.S. competitors soon outpaced that of the U.K. firm.[4]

Without some form of global strategy, the timing and location of a firm's expansion would become merely a reaction to perceived opportunities and threats with no basis for evaluating their enterprise-wide significance. Thus, thinking globally would help avoid present actions which might create future obstacles to a firm's expansion. If a global strategy indicated that there would be future advantages in separating production activity from marketing activity, then an arrangement that sets up a combined production and marketing unit with outside ownership interests in one country would clearly be undesirable.

The nature and necessity of a global strategy have been well expressed in a study of Massey-Ferguson, a leading Canadian multinational farm machinery company, as follows:

> It seems that the essence of a sophisticated international industrial corporation is that it, at all times, is prepared and in a position to develop markets for its products wherever on earth such opportunities exist and seeks to deploy its manufacturing and engineering facilities internationally in a way that will minimize its global production and development costs and will assist in the development of particular markets. Arbitrary rules guiding asset deployment can only do harm to such a corporation. Rational judgments relating to prospective rates of return, based on

---

[3]Anthony Sampson, "ITT in Europe," *Vision,* July/August 1973, p. 53.
[4]For a discussion of European strategic planning, see Renato Mazzolini, "European Corporate Strategies," *Columbia Journal of World Business,* Spring 1975, pp. 98–107.

detailed knowledge of local social, political, and economic conditions must lie at the heart of its international asset deployment decisions. Emotional attachments to the "home base" and misconceptions about conditions and opportunities abroad have no place.[5]

INTERNATIONAL STRATEGIC AND LONG-RANGE PLANNING

Corporate planning is an essential task in virtually every enterprise, but in no other organization is it of more vital importance than in a multinational firm that follows a global business approach.[6] The broadest planning level with the longest horizon can be identified as strategic planning. Strategic planning is the determination, for a particular point in the future, of (1) what a firm can and wants to be and (2) what the societies in both the home and host countries want this corporation to be. It involves the selection of policies and strategies, which become the guiding framework for determining resource commitment, based on the company's long-range objectives. The core of strategic planning is a realistic evaluation of the firm's present strengths and weaknesses and a thorough analysis of the effects of possible changes that are, or might be, occurring in the firm's environment over the long run.

The analysis of anticipated internal and external operating conditions provides a foundation for the realistic determination of long-range objectives, such as, what markets to serve with what products; sales, profits, and return-on-investment targets; and social commitments. A clear set of objectives leads to a consideration of alternative courses of action that might be used to accomplish them and to the adoption of a specific set of strategic programs. These options include the choice of countries for expansion, the location of supply and production, and coordinated long-range plans for each of the major management areas.[7] Strategic planning provides a framework into which each functional plan can be integrated, resulting in a global plan for the entire company.

The "ideal" international corporate planning process shown in Figure 18–1 indicates the four major elements in the formal planning

---

[5]E. P. Neufeld, *A Global Corporation: A History of the International Development of Massey-Ferguson Limited* (Toronto, Canada: University of Toronto Press, 1969), p. 385.

[6]See George A. Steiner and Warren M. Cannon, *Multinational Corporate Planning* (New York: Macmillan Co., 1966).

[7]Richard D. Robinson, *International Management* (New York: Holt, Rinehart & Winston, 1967), p. 6. Robinson has divided the total international management field into eight subsets of strategies: marketing, supply, labor, management personnel, ownership, financial, legal, and control.

FIGURE 18-1
An Ideal International Corporate Planning Process

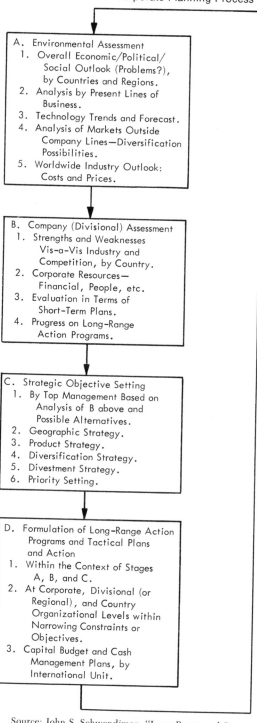

Source: John S. Schwendiman, "Long-Range and Strategic Planning in the International Firm" (Ph.D. diss. Alfred P. Sloan School of Management, Massachusetts Institute of Management, Cambridge, Mass., 1974).

of global strategies: (1) environmental assessment, (2) internal company assessment, (3) the strategic objective setting, and (4) formulation of long-range action programs.[8] International planning, as indicated, should be a multilevel activity, with integration both in a "top-down" and "bottom-up" context. But global strategies must be thought out at the top, not arrived at by simply totaling plans from individual countries where local bias may conceal important data needed for global planning. Furthermore, decisions for expansion into new areas must necessarily be made at the top.

An Example of an International Strategic Planning System

After examining the planning system of 22 major American and European multinational companies, Schwendiman selected *Company W*, a European chemical company, as having the best system.[9] In *Company W*, the executive committee of the management board takes the lead in plotting corporate strategy. It is primarily concerned with how to allocate corporate resources and how to influence company growth and responsibility. The company has six phases in its planning process.

1. The executive committee decides on corporate policies, objectives, and worldwide strategies, making substantial use of inputs by product division managers.

2. Concurrently, a "planning data base" is prepared throughout the company. Major components are environmental assessments around the world and analyses of the company's strengths and weaknesses vis-a-vis competitors. The competitive evaluation covers the current situation and a five-year future period. It includes R & D capabilities and manufacturing capacities for the company and its competitors. The planning data base is updated each year. After the data base is analyzed, tentative conclusions are reached for possible strategies.

3. Five-year plans are prepared by the different "planning units," generally country subsidiaries. As guidelines for this planning step, management distributes to all divisions and subsidiaries a statement of corporate objectives and policies and suggestions as to how the subsidiary should plan in order to integrate well into total corporate strategies. Fitting the strategies of the subsidiaries into the total corporate plan receives a lot of attention in the dialogue between different planning levels, and alternative strategies are thoroughly

---

[8]For a related approach, see Hans Schollhammer, "Long-Range Planning in Multinational Corporations," *Columbia Journal of World Business,* September–October 1971, pp. 79–86.

[9]Schwendiman, "International Strategic Planning," p. 61.

FIGURE 18-2
Company W's Written Plan Format (prepared by each "planning unit")

Chapter 1	Introduction (1–2 pages)
Chapter 2	Assumptions (1–2 pages)
Chapter 3	Opportunities and problems, with objectives and strategies (10–15 pages)
Chapter 4	Time schedule for strategies (1–2 pages)
Chapter 5	Personnel and resource requirements (3–5 pages)
Chapter 6	Five-year budget (3–5 pages)
Chapter 7	Problems for higher management attention (1 page)

Source: John S. Schwediman, "International Strategic Planning: Still in Its Infancy?" *Worldwide P & I Planning,* September–October 1971, p. 61.

considered. As plans are developed and written up, they generally follow the format shown in Figure 18–2.

4. As a fourth phase, the written plans are integrated into a corporate framework and presented to top management for decision on final plans. Generally, conflicts between planning units or among the divisions are arbitrated before the final integration. The plans are reviewed carefully by top management with particular attention to assumptions, possible inconsistent objectives, and action plans. The final product of this phase is a planning letter approved by top management that contains (*a*) top management's decisions and priorities, (*b*) emphasis on actions in the next year, and (*c*) details on corporate decisions that will affect the longer-range planning horizon.

5 and 6. The fifth and sixth phases are the preparation of one-year plans, budgets, and the financial integration of all budgets.

Keeping the Planning System on Target

As Figure 18–1 shows, after the environmental and company assessments are made and the strategic objectives are set, long-range plans are formulated and adopted. The critical nature of having plans that take the firm directly to its objective—to that point in the future where it becomes what the firm and society wanted it to be—is evident from this process. The following points will help to insure that the planning department stays exactly on target.[10]

1. Set goals for the planners. Gather only that information which is necessary and avoid wasting time on nonessentials.
2. Stay flexible. Contingency planning is of utmost necessity in any multinational corporation. Be able to respond quickly to environmental changes.

[10]Taken from "Corporate Planning: Piercing Future Fog in the Executive Suite," *Business Week,* April 28, 1975, p. 52.

3. Keep a balanced outlook. Do not overact. Keep in mind the stage of the business cycle you are in and the possible cultural differences which may exist in doing business.
4. Involve top management. Their positive support is essential if the planning department is to be effective.
5. Beware of future spending plans. Managers always underestimate.
6. Test the assumptions behind forecasts.
7. Reward those who dispel illusions (or bring the bad news). The sooner a firm learns of a problem, the better off it is.
8. Don't focus on only today's problems. Be alert to changes in host- and home-country sentiments toward the multinational firm.
9. Establish goals before you plan. Do not allow short-term thinking, such as short-term profit maximization, to take over.
10. Let managers do their own planning. Have the subsidiary/branch managers or operators—the "doers" of the company—formulate the plans or be actively involved in the planning process. In Sweden, this idea has even become law, with the recent passage of the Law on Codetermination in Working Life. Briefly, the new law sets the legal framework for increased worker participation in the management of both Swedish and multinational companies. Resolving the practical details is left to individual companies and their unions.[11]

A PRESCRIPTIVE APPROACH TO GLOBAL PLANNING

In practice, many firms expand and operate without a global strategy, and do so profitably. Others plan only part of their operations or build decision rules for measuring opportunities when they arise, without making any effort to search for opportunities or bring them about. But the purpose of studying international business is not to describe what firms do. It is to decide what they could do to improve decisions. The better the underlying model against which decisions are made, the better the decisions might be.

Specific decisions and actions, of course, must be largely determined by environmental factors, internal considerations such as the history and structure of the organization, and the objectives of the individuals and groups of which it is composed. Disruptions in the world monetary markets, fluctuating home- and host-country attitudes and policies toward multinational firms, and inflation have all combined to make the planning of activities difficult for the multinational manager. Some managers have decided that the use of decision models

---

[11]See *Business Week*, June 21, 1976, p. 42.

is unproductive, given the environmental uncertainty, and have abandoned the development of planning models, relying instead upon defensive strategies.

There are other limits to rational decision models. It might be theoretically possible to calculate for any firm a global profit-maximizing allocation of investment, production, and marketing activity over a specified period. But there are many practical difficulties in making such a calculation. Invariably, many approximations must be made in collecting data and the number of possible alternatives for comparison must be kept to a manageable number.

This is not to say that formal planning should be disregarded. On the contrary, planning is now even more important precisely because the future is so uncertain. As the president of RCA has stated: "The businessman in the current climate has to be very agile. He's confronted with unexpected, unanticipated things. This makes long-range planning more critical, absolutely."[12] Noted management philosopher Peter F. Drucker believes that "strategic planning is necessary precisely because we cannot forecast."[13] Likewise, George A. Steiner, professor of management at UCLA, contends that "planning has become intimately associated with the whole management process."[14]

The entire planning process is currently in a transitional stage. Methods that have worked before will not work in the future, and a firm's continued existence may very well hinge on its ability to read the future. Planning alerts management to potential markets and/or desirable locations for foreign manufacture and possible environmental changes affecting present operations. The organization that is able to identify new opportunities and probable changes, and make preparations and adaptations for them now, clearly will have a competitive edge.

Today, major changes are occurring in corporate planning in the areas of speed and flexibility.[15] In comparison to previous years, corporations are now more often reviewing and updating their plans according to changing environmental conditions. A good example of this is the Xerox Corporation, which presently makes and revises its plans almost continually, something that is unusual for them.[16] One beneficial aspect of this development is that now the firm is in the position to constantly monitor new production, marketing, finance,

---

[12]"Corporate Planning: Piercing Future Fog in the Executive Suite," p. 54.
[13]Ibid., p. 49.
[14]Ibid., p. 46.
[15]Ibid.
[16]Ibid., p. 48.

and personnel possibilities. Planners are also coming up with multiple contingency plans and alternate scenarios, rather than one plan for the corporation. The planning director for E. I. du Pont de Nemours & Co. says that "we shoot for alternative plans that can deal with either/or eventualities."[17]

The value of any prescriptive model offered here must lie in producing a framework that gives those within a firm a basis for explicating their thoughts and intuitions and guiding their organizational participation. A corporate planning officer for Exxon Corp. states: "They're [decision models] a framework for analysis even if you can't put much faith in them."[18]

With all of these considerations, the decision model presented here for developing and implementing a global strategy has been prepared to meet four major objectives.

1. It should be a general model that can be adapted to different types of activity and organizational settings.
2. It should make specific provision for considering variables known to have a significant effect on international business performance.
3. It should specify how the variables should be weighted and decisions arrived at. It should be a model with decision rules, not merely a list of considerations.
4. It should be as simple as possible, adding complexity only when the additional value in improved decision making outweighs its cost.

The decision model follows the 12-step procedure shown in Chapter 13 as Figure 13–1.

Market Assessment as the Starting Point

The formulation of a global strategy starts from global markets and works backward toward the location of activity and investment to achieve the best performance in these markets. Although the prime objective may be to obtain the greatest return on invested capital, the way to reach it is not to take country after country and calculate what rate of return would be obtained from investing in a plant in that country. This would be a replication of national thinking many times over. It is not global strategy. Global strategy requires that the investment location be decided against the global pattern of market targets.

This in turn requires some prediction of demand and competition in

---

[17]Ibid., p. 46.
[18]Ibid., p. 50.

the different markets. With different rates and patterns of growth in each market, any simple extrapolation of the current situation would be inappropriate. A more refined prediction of market growth is needed. In making such predictions, a whole range of forecasting methods can be used as discussed in Chapter 17. The international businessman should be well prepared to use the best methods available.

Whatever the methodology, the basic data required will involve past measurements of actual demand, indicators or determinants of demand, and then estimates of how indicators or determinants will behave in the future. In the initial stages of building a global strategy, the fastest and most effective approach for analyzing market potentials may be to centralize this responsibility in headquarters staff and rely on data sources centrally available, such as from international agencies. As the firm develops an international planning system, it can begin to rely on its foreign subsidiaries for much of this information. But in the initial stages, the decentralized approach will be extremely slow because of the time required to receive information from around the world. Also, the communication problem of specifying what figures and estimates are required will be extremely difficult if at the time of the request the subsidiaries have had no experience with the practical aspects of the planning process for which the data are required. Finally, consistent forecasts are probably more important than accurate forecasts when they are to be used for allocating emphasis among markets. To call for estimates from a wide range of sources is to invite major inconsistencies. Different individuals will have different biases in assessing future market growth for their areas.

The analysis of market potentials provides part of the information needed for building a global strategy, but management's investigation of foreign business opportunities should go beyond judgments of market growth if it is to recognize the opportunities before they become obvious to the world at large. For promising markets, it will want to appraise the competitive situation by making a financial, economic, and operational analysis of competing companies. This broader type of evaluation has been labeled "opportunity analysis."[19]

How far into the future should market opportunities be predicted? This will depend on the time horizon of the decision maker. Given the inflexibility of an investment once it has been committed, an early horizon may produce a supply pattern that is far from optimum for the subsequent market pattern. On the other hand, if the horizon is set far in the future, intermediate profits will be more likely to suffer, the

---

[19]Raphael W. Hodgson and Hugo E. R. Uyterhoeven, "Analyzing Foreign Opportunities," *Harvard Business Review,* March–April 1962, pp. 60–72.

market pattern more likely to vary from the prediction, and current management less likely to see the full fruits of its decisions. In practice, a four- or five-year horizon is common.[20]

Allocation Rules

Once these market opportunities have been established, the next and most important step in building a global strategy is to select a set of decision rules against which the firm should allocate its efforts to different markets. These rules are chosen with a view to producing the highest present value of profits from the allocation. Any rules used are essentially a compromise on a mathematical optimization model which is not workable in practice. Such a model contains too many alternatives and will collapse under its own weight. Therefore, some set of rules for reducing the alternatives is unavoidable.

Such rules might be conceived as simple choices between participation or nonparticipation in a market, but they are more likely to emerge as guidelines for determining the emphasis to be placed on achievement; in other words, what the sales budgets should be. The sort of rules that are commonly found in policy documents are as follows:

1. Enter all markets for which the absolute size is over a certain level and competitive entry conditions are favorable.
2. Expand as fast as possible without losses in all markets above a certain size for which the growth rates exceed a given figure.
3. Reduce margins where competitor market shares are high, the company's market shares low, and margins are above a specified figure.
4. Enter new markets only if necessary to match a competitor who would otherwise build up a strong position unchallenged.

These rules will depend on the products involved. As for all business decisions, actions must be reasoned back from the characteristics of the marketplace in which their effectiveness will ultimately be tested. The way in which potential customers make their purchasing decisions will determine the speed and manner in which activities can be built up in individual countries. Suppose, for example, the product range covers industrial capital goods sold largely to industrial organizations who purchase against bids from competing suppliers. Involvement in individual countries might then require only local agents to obtain enquiries for bids and maintain a continuing local base for customer service of one sort or another. In contrast, a branded food manufacturer might decide on local production, warehousing, mer-

---

[20]Steiner and Cannon, *Multinational Corporate Planning*, I.

chandising to retail outlets, and heavy consumer advertising, based on knowledge of how customer decisions to purchase a particular type of food are made.

Some writers on global strategy recommend that instead of setting targets directly for individual markets, the markets be first classified according to some definition of importance which, in turn, would indicate the appropriate entry strategy. Such a classification might be:

1. Markets requiring immediate, direct, and full-scale development by the firm.
2. Markets for major development in the next five years, or immediately if entered by significant competitors. Develop distribution outlets and build image through promotion.
3. Markets to be covered through resident distributors.
4. Markets to be covered through export agents or periodic sales trips.
5. Markets warranting no particular attention.

Other groupings have been suggested frequently, in particular that based on Rostow's classification of stages of development.[21] Whatever the intermediate steps introduced, however, the ultimate result must be the selection of targets for individual markets.

Location of Supply and Production

While alternative sources of supply may have been loosely considered in setting the market targets, detailed planning of the sources of supplies must wait until after targets and market-entry strategies have been set. It is then possible to design a supply system from raw material to final delivery to the customer that would minimize costs of achieving the targets. Few firms can determine supply independently for each market without throwing away significant economies from coordinating supply.

While it is theoretically possible to calculate a profit-maximizing pattern of supply and the consequent investment needed to meet market targets up to the horizon year, such calculations would invariably be too complicated for practical application. The number of alternative supply patterns is infinite. The ownership strategy options are many and will influence the investment required. And the introduction of a sequence of changing targets for each market further complicates the issue. Here again it is necessary to simplify the calculation by adopting a set of rules that limit the alternatives considered without moving the result too far away from a best

---

[21]W. W. Rostow, *The Stages of Economic Growth* (Cambridge, England: Cambridge University Press, 1960).

solution.[22] Where, for example, there is no major impediment to separating out the decision as to the best location of manufacturing activity, the decision rules that might be used would be:

1. Retention of existing locations as against new locations where fixed costs are high and an experienced labor force is a valuable asset.
2. Consideration of new sites when the local market is above a certain size, resource costs are below a certain figure, or tariffs exceed a certain level.

In some cases, too, the adoption of targets for particular markets will require local production because of the local regulations concerning access to the market.

With the reduced number of required and potential siting alternatives determined, the next step is to estimate the costs of investment and operation at alternative sites and from each the transport and tariff costs into alternative markets. For each possible alternative the lowest cost of supplying the market targets in the horizon year might then be calculated. The alternative with the overall lowest cost would then be selected. The methodology involved in such calculations can become very advanced, but it is possible to reduce it to a linear-programming calculation.

Subject to the accuracy of the assumptions, estimates, and decision rules, the lowest cost combination should approach that which maximizes the firm's cash flow in the horizon year. But it does not follow that the firm immediately extends to the locations indicated. The horizon objective must be translated into annual investment schedules over the period up to the horizon year, and each year's schedule submitted to return-on-investment analysis and limited to the firm's resource availability. A practical decision rule for deriving the annual schedules would be to invest each year in the additions needed to achieve the horizon objective that would minimize the cost of meeting the next year's targets—although it would be possible to calculate an optimum over the full period. The return-on-investment calculation for each item would then be based on the incremental net cash flow accruing from the expansion, estimated as far into the future as practical and reduced by the expected effects of changes in controls and other risks that might affect the flow.

Finally, each year's investment schedule will be subject to a cutoff

[22]Robert E. McGarrah, "Logistics for the International Manufacturer," *Harvard Business Review*, March–April 1966; David P. Rutenberg, *Stochastic Programming with Recourse for Planning Optimal Flexibility in Multinational Corporations* (Ph.D. diss., University of California, Berkeley, 1967); Richard H. Ballon, "Dynamic Warehouse Location Analysis," *Journal of Marketing Research*, August 1968, pp. 271–76.

limit determined by the firm's capacity to expand. The representative firm can be assumed to operate under capital rationing with a specified expansion capacity determined by management's ability to cope with expansion. This capacity might be expressed as a maximum investment sum for any year which together with reinvestment funds is available to meet the schedule of investment opportunities. The firm then accepts these opportunities in decreasing order of return on capital until the investment sum is fully committed. It is assumed that this sum is committed to projects for which the least profitable would show an expected return well above the cost of raising capital, hence the firm's capacity to handle expansion is what limits investment and not the cost of capital. Finally, if the available investment is not used up, then the firm will raise its market targets and repeat the process. Conversely, targets that cannot be met will have to be lowered.

Thus, the prescriptive approach to global planning would follow the process described above. To make the approach more concrete, an illustrative example is presented in Table 18–1.

ENTRY STRATEGIES

The entry strategies adopted by a firm are an important consideration in building the total global strategy and warrant more attention at this point. The firm has a choice of alternative approaches for penetrating new markets and for establishing new sources of supply. These alternatives imply different levels of commitment for the resources of the firm. They also have a time dimension and can operate as a building block or an obstacle to the achievement of long-term goals.

Moving from a minimum to a maximum commitment of company resources, entry strategies can be grouped into the following five categories:[23] (1)licensing, (2) exporting, (3) local warehousing with direct sales staff, (4) local packaging and/or assembling operations, or (5) full-scale local production and marketing.

Within these categories, several options exist.[24] Direct export and sales through a local company sales organization, for example, can be done by setting up regional distribution centers or warehouses. Or the firm can create a regional sales branch office and/or subsidiary. Or it can organize an overseas franchise system with independent, or a combination of company and independent, franchises.

A similar set of entry strategies is available for initiating projects

---

[23]Business International Corporation, "Alternative Ways to Penetrate a Foreign Market," in *100 Checklists: Decision Making in International Operations,* Reprint Report, 1970, pp. 6–8.

[24]Ibid.

TABLE 18-1
A Simplified Application of the Prescriptive Model for Global Planning (given: demand, sales, and cost data)

			Seven Country Markets					
	A	B	C	D	E	F	G	Total
Market projection and sales targets in 00s units:								
Year 1 Market	260	400	320	800	250	470	510	3,010
(Target)	(60)	(90)	(80)	(160)	(100)	(80)	(110)	680
Year 2 Market	280	420	350	840	260	480	510	3,140
(Target)	(65)	(95)	(90)	(165)	(100)	(80)	(105)	700
Year 3 Market	310	420	390	880	270	490	480	3,240
(Target)	(70)	(100)	(110)	(175)	(100)	(90)	(105)	750
Year 4 Market	360	420	430	930	280	510	460	3,390
(Target)	(90)	(105)	(130)	(185)	(100)	(100)	(100)	810
Year 5 Market	410	440	470	930	290	560	460	3,560
(Target)	(110)	(105)	(150)	(195)	(100)	(110)	(100)	870
Market price per unit	$85	$100	$100	$90	$90	$95	$85	
Current annual production in 00s units	—	90	—	300	200	—	140	730
Production cost per unit with existing plant	—	$ 70	—	$65	$60	—	$60	
Cost of standard plant extension of 5,000 units annual capacity $250,000.								
Production cost per unit from a new extension	—	$ 65	$ 75	$65	$55	$70	$55	
Transfer cost per unit (including transport and duty, in dollars)								
From A to:								
B	15	—	20	10	15	15	20	
C	20	25	—	10	15	15	5	
D	25	25	10	—	15	10	5	
E	20	25	15	20	—	10	5	
F	20	25	15	20	15	—	5	
G	25	25	15	15	15	15	—	

Simplifying Assumptions

1. Five-year horizon with plant extensions possible for year 3.
2. No change expected in sales prices.
3. Production cost per unit excludes plant cost and is taken as directly variable.
4. All transfer costs directly variable and no possibility of customs duty saving through manipulation of transfer prices.
5. Production strategy to be determined independently of corporation tax considerations.

Decision Analysis

Inspection of the following table shows that all expansion should be located at E to supply A's requirements and the balance of F. (Where one alternative is not so dominant a linear-program calculation would be needed to establish profits of the alternatives.) Extensions should be completed to increase capacity by a further 5,000 units in each of years 3, 4, and 5.

Return on capital can be based on the profit that would be forgone if the extension were not available. If this meant simply the elimination of sales to the least profitable market given the reduced supply system, it would be solely sales to A in years 3 and 4, but in year 5 production would be reallocated and 1,500 sales forgone in B, 1,000 in C, and 500 in F for a total revenue lost of $262,500.

Profits per Unit from Alternative Location of Plant Extensions (in dollars)

Source	Destination						
	A	B	C	D	E	F	G
A.	—	—	—	—	—	—	—
B.	5	35	15	15	10	15	—
C.	-5	5	25	10	5	10	10
D.	-5	20	25	25	10	20	15
E.	10	20	30	15	35	30	25
F.	-5	5	15	—	5	25	10
G.	5	20	30	25	10	25	30

that are primarily a source of supply for the multinational enterprise. A minimum commitment of resources would be involved in establishing only a buying office in a foreign location. A maximum commitment of resources would be needed to invest in company-operated production facilities and in supporting infrastructure such as transportation, electric power, or housing, health, and educational facilities for employees. Many alternatives are available between these two extremes.

Given these many alternative entry strategies, what are the variables that determine the best choice for a company? Returning to the case of a market seeker, the decision variables will be both external and internal to the firm. Most of the decision variables apply also to the entry decision for supply projects.

External factors
    Host-country policies and controls
    Size and attractiveness of markets
    Competitive conditions in the foreign market
    Availability of local supply sources in the country
Internal factors
    Characteristics of technology and products
    Enterprise-wide availability of productive capacity
    Minimum economic size for producing units
    Locational characteristics of production
    Availability of capital and managerial resources
    Company's willingness to assume risk
    Long-term corporate goals

In many cases, one or a few of the decision variables will dominate the decision on entry strategy and, in effect, sharply reduce the available options. Until recently, Japan followed severely restrictive policies regarding foreign investment. This is reflected in the fact that from the end of World War II through 1971, foreign investment in Japan totaled approximately $18.4 billion, with only 4.6 percent of this being direct foreign investment.[25] Thus, in several cases, the only options available to an international company for entering the Japanese market were licensing, exporting, and holding a minority position in a joint venture. In some instances, quota or tariff restrictions further reduced the options to only licensing. Or a less developed country attempting to encourage foreign direct investment may have such prohibitive import restrictions that the only realistic option for enter-

---

[25]See Wilbur F. Monroe, *Japan: Financial Markets and the World Economy* (New York: Praeger Publishers, Inc., 1973), p. 143.

ing its market is to establish a foreign production subsidiary. Or the size of the market may be so small in relation to the minimum economic size required for efficient production that exporting is the only sensible initial entry strategy.

During the 1960s, Japanese firms made extensive use of loan-purchase agreements whereby they assisted in the establishment of foreign supply sources by making loans and by agreeing to buy a given share of the output from the new project. In this way, Japanese companies expanded the availability of needed resources without taking an equity position and without assuming any managerial responsibility for new projects. Another interesting strategy used by some textile companies operating in Southeast Asia has been to establish local warehouses for raw materials and finished goods but to subcontract the manufacturing function to independent local companies. The international firm does the purchasing of supplies, the design and fashion work, and the international marketing, but not the actual manufacturing. Other strategies are to establish producing facilities in free port or border industry areas, primarily to make use of lower labor costs in a foreign country.

For each project, the feasible alternatives will have to be sorted out and compared as to profitability and consequences for achieving the firm's long-term goals. In all cases, the firm should make sure that its initial entry strategy will not create future obstacles for achieving long-run objectives. An essential characteristic of global planning is that interim moves should be designed to achieve long-term goals. A licensing arrangement may have immediate attractiveness to a neophyte international company because it is an inexpensive and profitable way of becoming educated on foreign markets and international business operations. But when the company later matures and wants to become a multinational enterprise, it may discover that the once-attractive licensing arrangement has become a barrier to the establishment of the company's own production facilities in a promising foreign market. Licensing is a relatively low-risk and low-cost entry strategy, available to both large and small firms that have something to sell. It is an option that allows a company to spread out the cost of its research and development and has the potential benefit of technology feedback. Furthermore, it enables a firm to move into markets where there are strict import or investment laws. Frequently, however, licensing is not an optimum way to maximize the gains from a company's competitive advantage.[26]

---

[26]See David B. Zenoff, "Licensing As a Means of Penetrating Foreign Markets," *IDEA*, Summer 1970, pp. 292–308.

OWNERSHIP STRATEGIES

Ownership strategies are another important component of overall global strategy. Should foreign subsidiaries be wholly owned by the multinational enterprise? Or should the firm follow the joint-venture approach of sharing ownership in its foreign subsidiaries with local interests, either private or government? If the joint-venture approach is adopted, should the international firm seek a majority or minority participation? Ownership policies change investment requirements and other resource commitments for new projects and can significantly affect the extent to which individual subsidiaries participate in an enterprise-wide global strategy.

In several countries, ownership policies for foreign firms are prescribed by national-control policies or laws. Mexico and India are examples of countries that require joint ventures, generally on a minority participation basis. Some bargaining has been possible in such countries, and a few firms which control a product or technology keenly desired by the host country have been able to get permission for establishing a wholly owned subsidiary or securing majority participation. But in general the ownership strategy alternatives are limited in these countries. For a wide range of other countries, however, the multinational firm has considerable choice.

Of the 170 major U.S. international enterprises, less than 25 have never entered into a joint venture. The remaining companies have been involved in roughly 1,100 joint ventures in countries where they could have legally chosen wholly owned operations.[27] There has been a widely held view, particularly in Europe, that preference for wholly owned or majority-owned subsidiaries is a peculiarly American trait. Yet, one recent investigation concludes that any great difference in ownership policies between U.S. and European companies, either in attitude or in fact, has been difficult to substantiate on the basis of available information.[28]

The benefits to be gained by joint ventures fall into three areas: technical resources, financial advantage, and political considerations. Where competitive conditions make speed an important factor in entering a foreign market, a joint venture with an established local enterprise may be the means of acquiring local marketing know-how or other managerial skills at substantial savings in time and expense as compared to the alternative of creating an entirely new organization.

[27]Lawrence G. Franko, "Joint-Venture Divorce in the Multinational Company," *Columbia Journal of World Business*, May–June 1971, p. 14; Lawrence G. Franko, *Joint-Venture Survival in Multinational Corporations* (New York: Praeger Publishers, Inc., 1971).

[28]Michael Z. Brooke and H. Lee Remmers, *The Strategy of Multinational Enterprise* (New York: American Elsevier Publishing Co., 1970), p. 262.

Moreover, by participating with a strong local firm that has access to or controls supplies and resources necessary to the company's operations, such as one of the large trading companies in Japan, the company will insure a supply of such items, perhaps even on a more favorable basis. Frequently, the small firm trying to expand internationally at a rapid pace to keep up with its larger competitors may have little choice because of its limited resources. But actual benefits will depend upon whether the local partner in fact has the complementary abilities needed for the kind of local operations desired by the international enterprise.

The joint venture that Xerox Corporation entered into with the Rank Organization of the United Kingdom to produce and market its copying machines outside the United States has been explained by the rapid growth in the U.S. market for Xerox machines.[29] Domestic business expanded at such a rate that all available managerial resources of Xerox were being absorbed at home. Rather than lose out on the vast potential that foreign markets promised, Xerox opted for a partner and a joint venture.

The financial advantages of joint ventures may also permit an international enterprise to enter into more foreign projects when its financial resources are limited or its home country is imposing restrictions on the export of capital. In some cases, local partners will accept the technological know-how, patent rights, or even the trade name of the international enterprise as a substitute for capital in payment for a share of the subsidiary's equity. Economizing capital as a motivation for entering into joint ventures has been more important for Japanese and European than for American firms.[30] Joint ventures also provide a hedge against political risks and lessen the risk of foreign exchange losses by reducing the amount of investment at stake.

Political considerations have probably been the most important motivation for joint ventures in many countries. Sharing ownership with nationals can encourage national identification and reduce the appearance of foreignness and thus the risk of expropriation. Furthermore, local partners may in some cases be able to contribute political influence and protection against the possibility of increasingly severe national controls. The maximum local protection could be achieved by a joint venture with the national government, although where governments change with frequency, even this strategy cannot be a complete defense. In terms of public-relations benefits, a wide distribution of shares among the investing public may be the best strategy.

---

[29] Ibid., p. 362.

[30] W. G. Friedmann and G. Kalmanoff, eds., *Joint International Business Ventures* (New York: Columbia University Press, 1961).

Studies of the joint-venture experience of the principal U.S. multi-national firms suggest that a company's long-run tolerance for joint ventures is closely related to its product strategy.[31] Firms following a strategy of foreign product diversification aimed at continually enlarging their range of products and services and their coverage of foreign markets have found joint ventures positively useful in both the short and long run. In such firms, marketing and production decisions are largely taken at the subsidiary level, and marketing policies are relatively unstandardized across a number of countries. Joint ventures also appeal to companies involved solely in raw material extraction. These firms rely on a foreign partner to provide a market for their "products." They are not concerned with controlling the market just as long as they can supply it.[32]

Conversely, product-concentrating firms, specializing in providing few products or services to their customers, find it most difficult to succeed with joint ventures.[33] In such firms, marketing and production-output decisions need to be relatively centralized on a supranational or regional level. Marketing policies tend to be standardized across borders and expenditures on product differentiation tend to be high. A coordinated export strategy is required so that the firm avoids meeting itself in many export markets. Under these circumstances, a high potential exists for conflicts between the parent company and the local partners over market decision making. As an example, the Coca-Cola Co. uses a marketing approach that relies heavily on advertising. This has worked well in the United States and they want to use the same strategy worldwide. Often, however, their local subsidiaries protest the large advertising budget. So, when the Coca-Cola Co. does enter a joint venture it tries to control the marketing operations.[34]

The disadvantages of joint ventures revolve largely around the desire and need of the multinational enterprise to retain control over the decisions of foreign subsidiaries. This control issue can be the source of many conflicts between the international firm and its local partners. Where the special advantages of the multinational enterprise lie in a unification of markets and the rationalization of production, finance, and other functions on a regional or global basis, the interests of any subunit and the local partners owning shares in that subunit are likely to conflict with global objectives and opportunities. As one

---

[31]Franko, "Joint-Venture Divorce in the Multinational Company," pp. 20–21; John M. Stopford and Louis T. Wells, Jr., *Managing the Multinational Enterprise* (New York: Basic Books, 1972), pp. 99–168.

[32]See Louis T. Wells, Jr., "Joint Ventures—Successful Handshake or Painful Headache?" *European Business,* Summer 1973.

[33]Franko, *Joint-Venture Survival,* pp. 15–16.

[34]Wells, "Joint Ventures—Successful Handshake or Painful Headache?"

example, for tax reasons the firm may prefer to show its profits in one subsidiary rather than in another and adopt transfer-pricing policies to implement this goal. Or local partners may prefer dividends rather than retaining earnings as a source of financing expansion. In such cases, conflicts with local partners may be inevitable.

In the past, many international enterprises have followed strongly fixed attitudes which insisted on having 100 percent ownership at all times and under all circumstances.[35] Such policies have been justified in terms of the need for complete control or by the attitude expressed by one executive, who said, "We do all the work and take all the risk; if it's a success why should we let the locals in on it? If it's a flop, they won't be interested. Either way, I can't see the point."[36] Other strong opponents of sharing ownership locally have argued that nationals can share in the operations of a subsidiary by purchasing shares in the parent company, either in the home-base country or when listed on local exchanges.

But with a growing body of experience and greatly increased pressures for control by host countries in the developed as well as in the less developed countries, multinational enterprises have moved toward more flexible and pragmatic views on joint ventures. Indeed, with increased government regulation and control, the joint venture is sometimes the only available entry strategy. For U.S. firms, the dollar devaluations have been another factor influencing their increased willingness to participate in joint ventures. When the U.S. dollar was overvalued, full ownership was relatively less expensive and therefore easier to acquire. To illustrate this new receptiveness, during the third quarter of fiscal 1975, the Overseas Private Investment Corporation (OPIC) insured 34 new U.S. investment projects for a total of $106 million. In 23 of these 34 projects host-country capital was involved, in four there was third-country participation, and in two the International Finance Corporation was a participant.

Recently, a new style in joint ventures has been flourishing in Europe.[37] While coming under the general category of partnerships, these new ventures are more aptly described as flexible cooperatives over a wide spectrum. European motor manufacturers provide excellent examples of this new approach. Saviem, Van Doorne's Automobielfabrieken (DAF) and Volvo have flexible cooperation agreements covering production, but each firm is still allowed to compete freely in any other aspect of their operations. Volvo has also joined

---

[35]See Richard D. Robinson, *International Business Policy* (New York: Holt, Rinehart & Winston, 1964), pp. 147–74 for results of a 1956–59 study of 172 American firms.

[36]Brooke & Remmers, *Strategy of Multinational Enterprise*, p. 269.

[37]See Claude Riviere, "Joint Venturing Towards the Next Decade," *Vision*, November 1973, pp. 59–62.

Renault and Peugeot in setting up a plant to manufacture a common engine, has signed an agreement with Klockner-Humboldt-Deutz (KHD) and two U.S. firms to develop a 500-horsepower gas turbine, and is working with DAF, Saviem, and KHD to build some commonality into the development, production, and purchasing of components for a range of medium-weight industrial vehicles. More common are step-by-step agreements with definite terms, which permit the firms involved to seize a particular market opportunity without surrendering any freedom of action. Whether this new approach results in the sharing of distribution networks or production facilities, or in achieving economies of scale, the problems often accompanying mergers or direct investment in companies beyond one's own borders are avoided. The future of this novel approach is still uncertain. While some believe it will be short-lived, others feel this is the start of reshaping corporate structure. Whatever the outcome, this is nevertheless a step toward meeting the disadvantages of joint ventures.

As in the case of entry strategies, the decision criteria that should influence ownership strategies will be a mixture of factors internal and external to the firm. The internal factors will be the product strategy of the firm, the availability of adequate financial and other managerial resources, the degree of operating experience it can command for new and different situations, and the speed with which it desires to initiate new projects for competitive or other reasons. The external factors will be the control policies of the host countries,[38] the availability of local partners or of adequate financial markets where widely shared local ownership is desired, and the local competitive situation, which may require that entry be made through acquiring a local firm that desires to retain an ownership interest.

Home-country policies may be another important external factor. U.S. tax policies, for example, limit foreign tax credits for the parent company to situations where a specified minimum of ownership is held. Or antitrust liability may arise where agreements exist between the parent company and jointly owned subsidiaries, whereas the same arrangements with a wholly owned subsidiary would not be challenged. Or home-country investment-guarantee programs may be unavailable for foreign projects with less than a certain minimum ownership.

---

[38]It is significant that the United Nations in 1971 published a *Manual on the Establishment of Industrial Joint-Venture Agreements in Developing Countries* (New York: United Nations, 1971) in response to the growing desire of LDCs to secure joint ventures.

STRATEGY REVIEW AND UPDATING

As the planning process dictates, it is also important for the firm to make regular reviews of the particular business techniques being used in its different markets. Factors such as inter-regional shifts, urbanization and suburbanization, technology, transportation, competition, social pressures, local expertise, changing buying patterns and selling outlets, and government policies and regulations make periodic examinations essential if the company is to stay abreast of changing conditions.[39] A firm that does not modify its style of operation according to changes in local conditions and laws, e.g., "choosing to invest in a market only as a majority owner or selling only through its own sales force, may be passing up opportunities for great profits. None of the many possible routes to market penetration should be overlooked in a company's periodic review of its approaches."[40]

The issue of ownership strategy has a time dimension. The point has been made that the stream of benefits of the foreign investment to the host country may decrease over time. Such a maturing of benefits and an increase in the alternatives open to a country can reduce the bargaining power of the foreign enterprise for maintaining 100 percent or even majority ownership.[41] And in a number of countries, the international firm may encounter national policies that require gradual divestment of foreign ownership over time, or what has been called a fade-out policy.[42] Or the enterprise itself may want to change ownership patterns over time. A joint venture may have served the purpose of helping a firm acquire local experience in the initial entry stage but no longer serves this need at a later stage. The reverse can also be true; firms may develop preferences for joint ventures during mature stages of foreign market penetration. For example, certain international banks with extensive overseas branch networks have begun to form joint-venture banks in the same countries where they currently operate branches. The reason for the tactical shift is to provide protection against possible policy moves by local governments to evict or substantially curtail foreign banks. The point is simple. Conditions change and firms must routinely review and adjust their plans,

---

[39]Business International Corporation, "Alternative Ways to Penetrate a Foreign Market," p. 6.

[40]Ibid.

[41]Peter Gabriel, "The Investment in the LDC: Assets With a Fixed Maturity," *Columbia Journal of World Business,* Summer 1966, pp. 109–19.

[42]Albert O. Hirschman, *How to Divest in Latin America, and Why* (Princeton, N.J.: International Finance Section, Princeton University, November 1969).

operating strategies, and ownership arrangements to compete most successfully in international markets.

A GLOBAL HABIT OF MIND

In the last analysis, developing a global strategy depends upon the way executives think about doing business around the world. The design and implementation of a global strategy require that managers in both headquarters and subsidiaries follow a worldwide approach which considers subsidiaries as neither satellites nor independent city-states but as parts of a whole, the focus of which is on worldwide as well as local objectives. And each part of the system makes its unique contribution with its unique competence. This approach, which Perlmutter has popularized as "geocentrism," involves collaboration between subsidiaries and headquarters to establish universal standards and permissible local variations on the basis of which key decisions are made.[43] However, geocentrism requires a reward system for subsidiary managers which motivates them to work for worldwide goals and not just to defend country objectives.

Three general types of headquarters orientation toward subsidiaries in international enterprise have been described by Perlmutter. While they never appear in pure form, and there is some degree of each philosophy in most firms, they are clearly distinguishable as ethnocentric (home-country oriented), polycentric (or host-country oriented), and geocentric (world oriented).[44]

The ethnocentric attitude can be characterized as: "We, the home-country nationals, are superior to, more trustworthy than, and more reliable than any foreigners in headquarters or the subsidiaries." In such firms, performance criteria and decision rules are generally based on home-country standards. Ethnocentrism works against a global strategy because of a lack of good feedback and because the experience and views of managers familiar with local conditions in the areas of operation do not carry appropriate weight in decision making.

Polycentric firms go to the other extreme by assuming that local people always know what is best for them and that the unit of the multinational enterprise located in a host-country should be as local in identity and behavior as possible. A polycentric firm is more akin to a confederation of quasi-independent subsidiaries. A polycentric management philosophy is likely to sacrifice most of the unification

[43]Howard V. Perlmutter, "The Tortuous Evolution of the Multinational Corporation," *Columbia Journal of World Business*, January–February 1969, pp. 9–18.

[44]For the interested reader, the relevance of this framework to international marketing strategies and decisions is discussed in Yoram Wind, Susan P. Douglas, and Howard V. Perlmutter, "Guidelines for Developing International Marketing Strategies," *Journal of Marketing*, 37 (April 1973): 14–23.

and synergistic benefits of multinational operation. The costs of polycentrism are the waste due to duplication of effort and inefficient use of home-country experience. The approach has the advantage of making intensive use of local resources and personnel but at the cost of global growth and efficiency.

Geocentrism also has costs, largely related to communication and travel expense, time spent in decision making because of the desire to educate personnel about global objectives and to secure consensus, and the expense of a relatively large headquarters bureaucracy. But the payoffs are a more objective total enterprise performance, worldwide utilization of resources, improvement of local company management, a greater sense of commitment to worldwide goals, and, last but not least, more profit. A globally oriented enterprise, of course, depends on having an adequate supply of managers who are globally oriented.

SUMMARY

Few, if any, companies are born with a global philosophy or a worldwide view. They normally become international by a process of creeping incrementalism, adding a series of international units to the parent company as isolated reactions to perceived opportunities or competitive threats. But at some stage of internationalization, either as a result of growing experience or competitive pressures, the firm becomes aware of the need for a global strategy and a global decision model in order to benefit from the synergy potential of multinational operations and to maximize results on a worldwide basis. At this stage, if not before, the truly multinational enterprise engages in a system of international strategic and long-range planning. A case study of an actual international planning system has been briefly described.

The formulation of global strategy starts from the identification of global markets and works back to determine the location of supply and production activities and investments to achieve optimum performance in these markets. It requires decisions as to the best entry strategies for securing access to markets and foreign locations of resources or production. Another component of a global strategy is a company's decisions concerning ownership. Above all, the formulation and implementation of a global strategy require managers with a global, or geocentric, habit of mind.

EXERCISES AND DISCUSSION QUESTIONS

1. If a global strategy is required to maximize the special advantages and synergistic benefits of multinational operations, why have so many firms

been successful in their international operations by responding to perceived opportunities and competitive threats without international strategic planning and global decision models?

2. How can an enterprise simplify the complexities of international possibilities and reduce to management proportions the variables it includes in its decision making?

3. Under what circumstances would global planning be desirable, even if the firm's international involvement is minor?

4. What decision rules other than those mentioned in the chapter might be used for choosing among alternative sources of supply?

5. Global planning based on a sales horizon of four or five years and annual return on investment from those sales is in direct conflict with the normal return-on-investment calculations of financial management. But the top executive of the multinational firm will be measured on his five-year profit achievement before anything else." Comment.

6. "Entering a new market through licensing is generally the best strategy because market potentials can be tested with little or no investment." Comment.

7. "A multinational firm needs to have complete control over its subsidiaries in order to make optimum use of its resources and compete most effectively. This generally means 100 percent ownership." Comment.

19

Organization for Multinational Operations

THE ORGANIZATION STRUCTURE of a firm doing business internationally is a vital determinant of success. The appropriate structure is a reflection of many factors: the scope and breadth of international business activities, the firm's objectives and strategy, the relation of products to markets and buyer behavior, and the degree of international management experience and competence. As the foregoing suggests, organization structures should probably change over time.

Perhaps the most important function of the organization structure is to provide for an effective decision-making process and a smooth flow of communications between various parts of the organization. An enterprise that begins operating in more than one national market normally finds that this leads to new organizational problems that require changes in its organizational structure. The multinational firm must cope with geographically dispersed operations, personnel from many cultures, diverse political and economic environments, and divergent trends in different countries. A firm operating in a single market does not have these challenges. Usually, an organizational structure designed for purely domestic business is unsuitable for multinational operations.

The array of different organization structures used by international firms is as diverse as the strategies they have been following in achieving growth abroad.[1] Few, if any, are identical and no simple

---

[1]For example, see Harold Stieglitz, *Organization Structures of International Companies* (New York: National Industrial Conference Board, 1965); Business International, *Organizing the Worldwide Corporation* (New York, 1970); and John M. Stopford and Louis T. Wells, Jr., *Managing the Multinational Enterprise* (New York: Basic Books, 1972), pp. 13–18.

criteria exist for selecting the best organizational form. Despite the diversity within the broad organizational categories, a number of useful guidelines exist for resolving the organization problems as a firm develops from a domestic to a multinational enterprise.

STATUTORY AND MANAGERIAL ORGANIZATIONS

The international enterprise encompasses two distinct but interwoven component structures: the statutory, or legal, organization, and the managerial organization.[2] The statutory organization exists on paper only. It is designed to conform to legal requirements while best meeting the objectives of the firm, for example, minimization of commercial restrictions or taxation. The managerial organization may cut right across the statutory structure and is concerned with the authority and responsibility of each executive and the lines of communication among these executives. It is also concerned with the information that flows along these lines of communication and the procedures for channeling and processing the information.

The statutory organization defines the legal and ownership structure that links the parent company with its various units. Each unit may have a different statutory status—branch, subsidiary, holding company, and so forth—depending in part on the legal requirements of the jurisdiction in which it is established. Holding companies in low-tax areas have often been used for the statutory organization, with the statutory center rarely serving as the operating center. In fact, some statutory centers may consist of only a part-time local lawyer and a mail clerk. Thus, the statutory and managerial structures must be considered as separate entities. The lawyers and tax experts will be primarily responsible for designing the statutory structure. The international manager will be involved mainly in the design and function of the managerial structure—the subject of the rest of this chapter.

EVOLUTIONARY STAGES OF ORGANIZATION

The evolution of the organizational structure of an enterprise can be viewed as a series of stages, with each stage a modification or adaptation of the structure in the previous stage. A description of the detailed organization structure at any specific stage is something like a snapshot, or still picture from a film, that shows isolated but typical moments in a continuing process of organizational change. The speed of the process varies from company to company. Some tread cautiously

---

[2]John G. McDonald, "New Organizational Concept of the World Enterprise," *Management International* 1, no. 5/6, 1961.

and take one step at a time, whereas others rush through certain stages and bypass others. In general, the evolutionary process of U.S. firms going international has closely paralleled the structural developments that accompanied growth and diversification at home.[3] As yet, less research is available on the evolutionary process of non-U.S. firms.

In the early stages of entering foreign markets through exports, a company may assign the export responsibility to an independent trading company. As foreign sales increase in importance, the typical organizational response of the large enterprise is to establish an export department with some medium-level company official as export manager. Still concentrating on exports, the firm may go further and set up its own sales, service, and warehousing facilities abroad.[4] In the early stages, the basic organizational structure of the firm is left undisturbed.

An example of a statutory organizational response for U.S. companies at this stage is to assign responsibility for Western Hemisphere exports to a Western Hemisphere Trade Corporation (WHTC) to reap the tax advantages given to such units. More recently, many U.S. companies have organized a Domestic International Sales Corporation (DISC) for exports in order to gain tax benefits authorized by the Revenue Act of 1971 intended to encourage export expansion.[5] Again, however, the WHTC and DISC are generally statutory organizations and are unlikely to affect the managerial organization structure.

The Japanese firm typically follows a different pattern in entering foreign markets through exports because they have been able to rely on the services available from the giant Japanese trading companies instead of forming their own export departments. The Japanese general trading firms have no comparable counterpart in other countries. Their basic business is foreign trade and they handle many of the international business functions that U.S. and European companies normally perform for themselves. While there are several thousand trading companies, the ten largest handled 50 percent of Japan's exports and 60 percent of its imports in 1974.[6] As another indicator of their great size, the six giants, Mitsubishi, Mitsui, Marubeni-Ida, C. Itoh, Nissho-Iwai, and Sumitomo, own shares in 1,848 companies quoted on the Japanese stock exchange.[7] Some Japanese firms, such as the major automobile and consumer electronics companies, have followed an

---

[3] Stopford and Wells, *Managing the Multinational Enterprise*, p. 11.

[4] See James Greene, *Organizing For Exporting* (New York: National Industrial Conference Board, 1968); Endel J. Kolde, *International Business Enterprise* (Englewood Cliffs, N.J.: Prentice-Hall, 1968), pp. 242–45.

[5] See Chapter 10.

[6] See *Economist*, March 9, 1974, p. 91; Yoshi Tsurumi, *The Japanese Are Coming* (Cambridge, Mass.: Ballinger Publishing Co., 1976), Chap. 5.

[7] Ibid.

evolutionary pattern similar to that of U.S. companies in order to secure more specialized attention for their export business than the giant trading companies could provide.

As the nature of international operations changes from exporting to a mix of exporting, licensing, and foreign production, and as the scale of international sales becomes of more than incidental importance to the firm, conflicts of interest arise between internal units of the firm that are not easily handled by an export department type of organization. Where a need has emerged to fortify the firm's foreign market position by establishing production facilities in areas served by its export department, an export department structure is particularly inadequate. The export department may fail to recognize the need or may prefer to continue with exports because foreign production facilities may mean a loss of export sales attributed to the department. The usual organizational response by U.S. companies to such conflicting interests has been to create a full international division, which includes the previously independent unit for handling exports.[8]

Before moving to an international division structure, some companies pass through an intermediate stage where the firm acts only as a holding company for largely autonomous foreign subsidiaries. The autonomous foreign subsidiary pattern can be adopted without making any significant changes in the organizational structure of the remainder of the company. It occurs where foreign ventures are first established, not as a result of planning but in response to a specific threat or opportunity. Because such first ventures are small and not critical to the success of the organization, and because the parent firm has insufficient international experience to make much of a contribution to the new foreign ventures, foreign managers are allowed virtually unlimited powers of decision and action. As one study explains, "The need for learning exceeds the desire for control."[9] The subsidiary will have rather loose financial ties to the senior financial officer of the parent company, but its operating freedom will be great so long as the financial results of the venture are satisfactory.

For U.S. companies, the autonomous subsidiary phase may have a short life. If the foreign units grow rapidly and accumulate significant resources, pressures will arise within the parent company to introduce management controls. The success of the foreign venture makes it significant to the total enterprise. The international experience that ownership of the subsidiary has brought to the parent firm enables it to approach the design and implementation of controls with more assur-

[8]Cedric L. Suzman, "Whatever Happened to the Export Manager?" *Worldwide P & I Planning,* Nov.–Dec. 1968, pp. 16–25.

[9]Stopford and Wells, *Managing the Multinational Enterprise,* p. 20.

ance. The possibility of economic gain from coordinating its foreign subsidiaries will generate pressures for organizational change to permit a greater degree of central control over the subisdiaries' decision making.

The establishment of an international division, generally of equal status to other major divisions, normally results from four factors. First is the matter of size. The international commitment of the firm has reached an absolute size and a relative importance within the enterprise to justify an organizational unit headed by a manager with a senior level of authority. Second, the complexity of international operations requires a single organizational unit that can resolve within it such conflicts as the best means for entering foreign areas on the basis of a broad view of the firm's international opportunities. Third, the firm has recognized the need for a group of specialists within the enterprise who can deal with the special features of international operations. And finally, the enterprise wants to develop an affirmative capability for scanning the global horizon for opportunities or competitive threats rather than simply responding to situations that are presented to the company.

By the early 1960s, the international division organizational approach was the most common type of structure in large U.S. enterprises with foreign operations. However, the continued growth of these divisions sowed the seeds of their destruction by enlarging the interest of top management in the international opportunities. By the mid-1960s, a growing number of firms had abandoned their international divisions in favor of a global organizational structure.[10] As Clee and Sachtjen have observed, "The really decisive point in the transition to world enterprise is top management recognition that, to function effectively, the ultimate control of strategic planning and policy decisions must shift from decentralized subsidiaries or division locations to corporate headquarters, where a worldwide perspective can be brought to bear on the interests of the total enterprise."[11]

At the global stage, responsibility for both foreign and domestic business is moved to the top echelons and new subdivisions are specified on either a functional, geographic, or product basis. The choice among the functional, geographic, or product division structures depends primarily on the business strategy of the enterprise.

The global structure, however, is not the final stage in the development of organizational structures capable of providing effective administration for a multinational enterprise. Most global structures are

---

[10]Ibid., p. 25.
[11]Gilbert H. Clee and Wilbur M. Sachtjen, "Organizing a Worldwide Enterprise," *Harvard Business Review,* November–December 1964, p. 67.

based on the management principle of unity of command: one man having sole responsibility for a specified part of the business, either subdivided by function, product, or geographic areas, and accountable to a single superior officer. But the conflicting need for coordinating all three dimensions can still remain a serious problem. Some firms have attempted to build new structures where managers have dual or multiple reporting relationships and where area, function, and product responsibilities overlap. Experimentation is underway with various types of grid structures, and evolution to organizational forms beyond the global structure is already underway.

European multinational firms appear to follow a somewhat different evolutionary pattern from that of U.S. companies. Unencumbered by huge domestic markets, European firms tend to move directly to a global form of organization without passing through the international division stage.[12] A company based in a small country knows from the beginning that it can never grow large without expanding into foreign markets. Its export-marketing operations may be placed in a special export unit. But its domestic and foreign operations develop together under a top management that is committed to international business. This integrated approach does not necessarily mean that the foreign company has become a global firm in the sense that it has a global strategy and attempts to maximize the potential gains from worldwide operations. It simply accepts the need to do business across national boundaries as a normal condition of growth and structures its organization accordingly. By necessity, the greater dependence of European firms on exports and foreign production has emphasized worldwide organizational forms rather than a separation between foreign and domestic activities through the creation of an international division.

THE INTERNATIONAL DIVISION

For the firm extending its activities internationally from a large domestic market like the United States that has dominated the company's attention, the international division provides an organizational umbrella for all the foreign activities of the enterprise and a focus for learning about the management of international operations. It permits centralized direction of a company's foreign operations, particularly during the developmental and expansion stages of the international

[12]See Hans Schollhammer, "Organizational Structures of Multinational Corporations," *Academy of Management Journal*, September 1971, pp. 345–65; Andrew J. Lombard, Jr., "How European Companies Organize Their International Operations," *European Business*, July 1969, p. 37; Lawrence G. Franko, "Strategy + Structure − Frustration = The Experience of European Firms in America," *European Business*, Autumn 1971, pp. 29–42.

program. It concentrates international know-how and skills in a separate unit detached from domestic responsibilities and makes possible a concentrated drive on market expansion and investment overseas. It places a champion of foreign activities and a strong voice in the top-management echelons for allocating the necessary resources to new foreign activities.

The international division is usually headed by a vice president who reports directly to the president or chief executive of the company. Some enterprises form an international company headed by a president that plays essentially the same role as an international division. In most cases, the international division is responsibile for policy and global strategic planning for international operations. But in some situations, this responsibility has shifted to executives at the corporate level without significant change in the formal structure. And there is considerable variation in the administrative practices for maintaining links between the international activities and the domestic side of the enterprise.

A representative organization diagram for a firm using an international division structure is shown in Figure 19–1. At an early stage, the corporate staff groups, except for finance and control, are likely to continue to be domestically oriented. The international division will rely mainly on its own divisional staff. As policy and strategic planning shifts to the corporate level, the marketing, manufacturing, research, personnel, and other staff will become internationally oriented. As mentioned previously, both patterns can occur while maintaining the international division or international company structure.

The international division usually has direct responsibility for all export and licensing activities of the parent company and is accountable, directly or indirectly, for the operations of overseas manufacturing and sales units. Its task is to coordinate all the international activities so as to raise the level of performance above that likely where subsidiaries are autonomous and other international functions, such as exporting and licensing, are dispersed within the firm. The division may be able to reduce the cost of capital for a subsidiary by borrowing in some other area or in international capital markets. It can be the channel for the transfer of experience among subsidiaries. It may be able to reduce tax liability through transfer-pricing policies. In brief, it has responsibility for improving total performance through the unification or synergy potentials of multinational operations.

The international division has constraints on its ability to assist the foreign subsidiaries. As a division, it normally does not have the resources to develop detailed knowledge about the environments and characteristics of large numbers of local areas and must heavily delegate direct operating responsibilities to the foreign subsidiaries. It

FIGURE 19–1
An International Division Structure

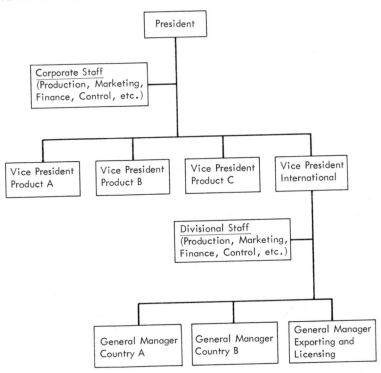

cannot centralize many decisions because the competitive position of the subsidiary may be reduced by the time lag involved in securing decisions from the international division. In general, the amount of decentralization will vary with the particular functions involved, product characteristics, the degree of expertise accumulated at the divisional level, and the time taken to refer matters to the division. Firms engaged in the production and sale of a narrow line of mature goods with relatively stable technologies and markets, for example, tend to move farther in the direction of centralization than firms expanding into many different markets with diversified lines of new products involving rapidly changing technologies.

Where the products manufactured or sold abroad are the products developed at home, as is normally the case, the international division is heavily dependent on the domestic product divisions. In this respect the international division has less autonomy than the product divisions and depends upon their assistance more than they depend on each other. The international division normally does not have its own product development, engineering, and research and development staff, and the domestic divisions controlling these important components of the overseas operations are frequently reluctant to give priority to foreign needs because they are measured solely by their domestic performance. Thus the international division depends heavily on the communication and cooperation procedures that are worked out with the domestic product divisions for making the specialized skills of the domestic units available to the international operations. As product divisions become more familiar with international needs, the effectiveness of the communication and cooperation devices can improve. But the inherent conflict between the goals of the domestic and international divisions is never completely eliminated.

The fact that the international division structure remains dominant in the majority of U.S. multinational companies, despite a strong move toward global structures and grid arrangements, suggests that many firms have been able to work out informal arrangements or formal devices for resolving the problems inherent in dividing the international unit from the rest of the company. One authority cites the example of a giant U.S. automobile manufacturer with plants in 20 countries, its own sales operations in 18 others, and more than 100,000 workers overseas that was able to continue to operate successfully with an international division structure by making adjustments within the structure for altering patterns of management decision making.[13] Another example is the International Business Machines Corporation, which continues to handle its extensive and rapidly growing international operations through its separate IBM World Trade Corporation while integrating basic research, product development, and manufacturing activities on a world wide basis.[14]

GLOBAL STRUCTURES

As the international division increases in size relative to the total enterprise, the same forces that led to its creation begin to work toward its dissolution. Top management becomes aware that there are gains to be realized by coordinating production, for example, on a worldwide scale by taking advantage of economies of scale. Unless all components of the enterprise are judged on their performance worldwide, they will not be motivated to act in accordance with the worldwide interests of the enterprise.

The alternative to the international division structure is the global

---

[13]Clee and Sachtjen, "Organizing a Worldwide Enterprise," pp. 57–59.
[14]Business International, *Organizing the Worldwide Corporation,* January 1970, pp. 12–13; and *Business Week,* March 24, 1975, p. 122.

structure, which eliminates the domestic-international dichotomy and pays no more attention to national boundaries than the realities of time and place require. No single national market draws greater interest or attention than its contribution to overall corporate objectives. The global company may be structured along functional, product, or regional lines, and if a functional or product basis is used, divisional managers have worldwide responsibilities. The global or world corporation concept, of course, requires a global management philosophy and an integrated management team at the top level that thinks in terms of the worldwide commitments of the firm.

The Functional Structure

The functional organization structure for international operations has been the dominant form used by European companies. The division of responsibility at headquarters is organized by functions such as marketing, manufacturing, and finance; and the heads of these divisions have worldwide responsibilities as line executives (see Figure 19–2). The marketing or sales division, for example, has worldwide marketing responsibility, with direct control over all sales companies and distributors, wherever located. In addition, the division normally has staff responsibility for coordinating the marketing of manufacturing subsidiaries, which usually control sales of the goods they produce, except for exports that are handled directly by the marketing division. The manufacturing division usually has line control over domestic plants, staff responsibility for worldwide product standardization, product development, quality control, and research and development, and a mixture of line and staff responsibility over the foreign manufacturing subsidiaries.

FIGURE 19–2
Functional Organization Structure

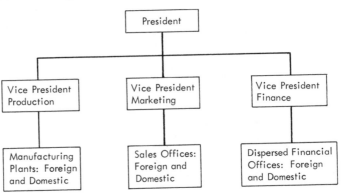

As long as companies remain comparatively small and have a fairly narrow range of products, the functional structure usually works rather well. Even in large international companies like SKF of Sweden, with a limited product line—ball bearings—that is not heavily dependent on the vagaries of regional markets, the functional structure is used with great effectiveness.[15] Some European firms that have grown rapidly, however, have experienced difficulties with the somewhat hazy responsibility assignments of this organizational form and with breakdowns in the informal lines of communication and reporting.[16]

The functional structure has the advantage of tight control over specific functions such as production, marketing, and finance.[17] It allows a relatively small group of officers to maintain line control over operations without much duplication. But the functional approach also has three basic weaknesses. Sales and production tend to become separated in their operations and objectives. Managers of subsidiaries normally have to report to more than one person. Finally, the structure results in tremendous duplication with regard to environmental inputs. Each of the functional divisions may need its own regional specialists and could be making different assumptions about future trends in the various areas of operations.

The Geographic Structure

Under a geographic structure, the primary operational responsibility is assigned to area managers, each being responsible for a specific geographic area of the world, as shown in Figure 19–3. Corporate headquarters retains responsibility for worldwide strategic planning and control. Where the geographic form of organization has replaced the international division in U.S. companies, the United States becomes simply one of a number of world markets. Each area division has responsibility for all functions within its area and is able to coordinate marketing, production, finance, and so forth, within its region.

Companies successfully using the geographic structure are ones with a narrow range of products whose end-use markets, local marketing requirements, technological base, and methods of manufacture

---

[15]Business International, *Organizing The Worldwide Corporation,* pp. 45–46.

[16]Lombard, "How European Companies Organize Their International Operations," p. 38.

[17]See Michael Z. Brooke and H. Lee Remmers, *The Strategy of Multinational Enterprise* (New York: American Elsevier Publishing Co., 1970). Brooke and Remmers call this a *Type A* company. For an example of the decision-making process in an actual *Type A* company, see Figure 2.2, p. 30. By their designation, *Type B* has a geographical structure, *Type C* is organized worldwide by product groups, and *Type D* is a complicated mixture which has also been called a grid structure.

FIGURE 19–3
Geographic Structure

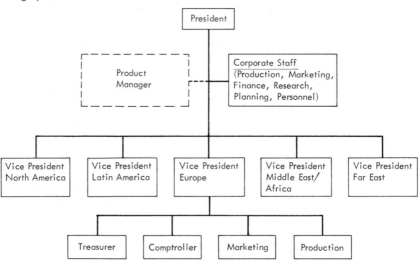

tend to be similar, if not identical. The major oil companies generally use a variant of the geographic structure. Key decisions on concessions, refinery scheduling, and tanker-fleet management are logically made on a centralized basis. Within this framework, the area manager exercises true line responsibility or functions as a coordinator for all operations in his particular geographic area. The geographic form permits handling variations from market to market which require modest levels of technological skills. It works well also where the product is highly standardized, but techniques for penetrating markets differ, as in the case of soft-drink companies.

The principal difficulties of the geographic organization arise when the firm has a diverse product range. The structure does not easily handle the tasks of coordinating product variations, transferring new product ideas and production techniques from one country to another, and optimizing the flow of product from source to worldwide markets. One organizational response has been to create a global product manager at the corporate level who is assigned worldwide responsibilities for particular products or product lines. His principal tasks are to mold a global product strategy and to facilitate the transfer of experience from one area to another. But his operating relationships with the area managers who have line responsibility are likely to be ambiguous.

A geographic structure usually requires a large number of internationally experienced executives to staff the various regional headquarters. It may result in too much information being screened from corporate headquarters and undue focus placed on the performance of the specific regions as opposed to the company's worldwide interest. It may also require considerable duplication of product specialists within the enterprise.

Product Structure

The product structure organization assigns worldwide product responsibility to product-groups executives as the primary line managers, and coordinates activity for all products in a given geographic area by having area specialists at the corporate staff level (see Figure 19–4). Overall goals and strategies for the company are set at corporate headquarters and within these corporate guidelines, the plans of each product group are reviewed and approved by top management. Each product group, however, has primary responsibility for planning and controlling all activities for its products on a worldwide basis.

The product structure works best when a company's product line is widely diversified, when products go into a variety of end-use markets, and when a relatively high technological capability is required. It is also advantageous when high shipping costs, tariffs, or other considerations dictate local manufacture of the product.

The most important problem with the product structure is that worldwide responsibility is frequently assigned to managers with great product expertise whose experience has been largely domestic. Similar problems can arise at all levels when the personnel assigned are selected because of their product expertise and may have little

FIGURE 19–4
Product Structure

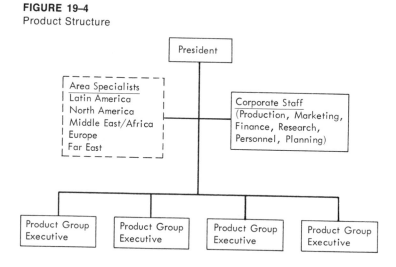

experience and capability for dealing with the new kinds of problems that arise out of international operations.

Another problem inherent in the product structure is the difficulty of coordinating the activity of different product divisions in any given area. Suppose, for example, that *Product Division A* wanted to license a European company to manufacture *Product A,* while *Product B's* European plant was operating below capacity and could avoid a loss only by taking on an additional product. Without someone on the local scene responsible for the success of the enterprise as a whole, the two divisions might be unaware of each other's needs. *Product Division A* would incur the unnecessary expense of licensing the European plant. *Product Division B* would take a loss. The company as a whole would suffer.

The Grid or Matrix Structure

More recently some companies have moved to the matrix or grid form of organization. This structure is an effort to gain the benefits of more than one of the global structures and requires a move away from the traditional hierarchy of power and unity of command management principles to more of a balance of power and the sharing of responsibility. Most multinational firms that have adopted this form of organization have developed a dual reporting structure along product and area lines. The grid structure, however, has still not been widely embraced. Forsaking traditional management principles for a new system, which does not yet have definite ways of working effectively, has been difficult for managers to accept.

The General Electric Company provides an excellent example of the matrix form of organization. The firm centered its foreign activities for many years in an international division that was organized as a separate company—International General Electric Company. Under pressure from changing internal and external forces, the company gradually moved to a structure that assigned worldwide responsibility to its domestic product groups. A reorganized International Group, however, continued to operate along with the product groups, as one company executive explained, "to provide a mechanism that would avoid the risk that 50 to 60 general managers might start at a furious pace reinventing the wheel, competing with each other in committing the same blunders instead of learning from each other's experience."[18] The International Group has four overseas area managers who are responsible for governmental and business relations in their areas, and

---

[18]W. D. Dance, "An Evolving Structure For Multinational Operations," *Columbia Journal of World Business,* November–December 1969, p. 29.

whose staff experts assist operating departments on entry strategy and environmental assessment.

Through a form of grid arrangement, G.E. has assigned heavy international responsibility to units that contain product expertise while still trying to achieve coordination on a geographic area basis. The difficulties of finding a perfect organizational structure are demonstrated by the fact that a product organizational structure adopted by G.E. in 1964 was restructured within only five years by creating a strong International Group to review and coordinate all international operations of the company. Probably G.E.'s costly experience in assigning managers with product expertise but with little international experience to head its computer operations in France, after the acquisition of Machines Bull, had much to do with the reorganization move to dilute the responsibility of product divisions. The G.E.-Machines Bull project caused a loss to the company of many millions of dollars over the period.[19]

CHOOSING AMONG ALTERNATIVE ORGANIZATIONAL STRUCTURES

The basic organization problem common to all firms operating internationally can be summed up in three questions:

1. Should the corporation be divided into domestic and international divisions?
2. Should line responsibility be subdivided for management purposes according to major functions, major product lines, or major geographic areas?
3. What is the best way to provide for needed specialization and coordination according to the other two variables, or how should the three necessary inputs—functional, product, and geographic—be meshed?

Clearly, there is no one right way to organize, no perfect organizational structure, and no organization form that can remain static when once adopted. Successful companies are using various organizational patterns to manage their international business operations effectively.

Although there are no standard requirements, the choice of organizational pattern has generally been determined by a relatively small number of variables. The variables that help to choose an organizational form that best fits the needs of a given firm in a given set of circumstances are the following:

---

[19]Gregory H. Wierzynski, "G.E.'s $200 Million Ticket to France," *Fortune*, June 1, 1967, pp. 92–5, 159–62.

1. The relative importance in the present and future of foreign and domestic markets as perceived by top management.
2. The historical background of a firm and its evolutionary stage in international operations.
3. The nature of a firm's business and its product strategy.
4. The management traits and management philosophy of the firm.
5. The availability of and willingness to invest in internationally experienced management personnel.
6. The capacity of an enterprise to adjust to major organizational changes.

The absolute size of international sales will determine the desirability of moving from an export-manager form of organization to an international division for most U.S. companies. The choice between an international division and a global structure will be influenced by the relative importance of international and domestic markets as perceived by top management. The benefits of having all senior managers experienced in the diversities of international business may be great. But when a company's future is likely to be dominated by a large domestic market like the United States, the investment needed to man a global organization with internationally experienced personnel may not be warranted. Also, so long as domestic activities promise to continue to be much larger than international operations, separate attention may continue to be required for international activities so that they do not become subordinated to domestic considerations. At the other extreme, European companies have quickly adopted global structures because foreign markets are invariably of major importance relative to domestic markets.

The choice of organizational structure is inevitably influenced by a company's history and past experience. A company that has operated internationally for decades and possesses a top management experienced in dealing with worldwide problems will approach organizational change differently from a company that is a comparative neophyte on the international scene. During a firm's early stages of growth abroad, its organizational decisions are likely to be influenced by the need to encourage a concentrated drive on international opportunity by separating foreign from domestic activities. At a more advanced stage, organizational decisions will be increasingly motivated by the potential gains to be realized by coordinating all components of the enterprise on a worldwide scale.

As a firm's international activities become large relative to domestic business, the choice of organizational structure is closely related to the nature of the company's business and its product strategy. Where there is little product diversity, and where the success of the firm is not heavily dependent on diverse trends in different geographic markets, a functional structure can be effective. Where there is a limited product line and great similarity in end-user markets and in marketing techniques and distribution channels, but where area expertise plays a major role, a regional or geographic structure operates well. In such cases, it is less costly to duplicate product and functional expertise than area expertise. Where product lines are diverse, have a high-technology component, serve different end-user markets, and where production and sourcing can be advantageously rationalized on a worldwide basis, the product structure for organization has major advantages. The product structure facilitates the transfer of technology and sales support from producing divisions to international operations and can accelerate growth by forcing domestic divisions to become more aware of the markets and potentials of foreign areas.

Management traits and philosophies can be other key variables determining the organizational structure of a firm. Some managements are bold and willing to make frequent organizational changes. Others are cautious and make changes only when absolutely necessary. The management philosophies and heritage of executive experience of European-based multinational companies favor structures that facilitate a potentially more centralized control over the totality of corporate operations by a few key executives, thus giving preference to functionally oriented organization structures. The management philosophy of U.S. firms is more likely to favor structures that provide greater opportunities for decentralized decision making, but with formal control devices like the profit center concept which allow for a more strict supervision, control, and coordination within the product-oriented or regionally oriented divisional activities.[20]

Another dimension of a firm's management philosophy is its orientation toward foreign people, ideas, and resources in headquarters and subsidiaries, and in host and home environments, which Perlmutter has described as ethnocentric (home-country oriented), polycentric (host-country oriented), and geocentric (world oriented).[21] A polycentric firm would have something akin to a holding company structure with loose connections to quasi-independent subsidiaries. A geocentric philosophy leads to a global structure that permits a worldwide approach in both headquarters and subsidiaries.

But, even if a firm can determine the merits of one organizational form over another, the question arises of finding qualified managers. All global structures require an increase in the number of internation-

---

[20]Schollhammer, "Organizational Structures of Multinational Corporations," pp. 352–53.

[21]See Chapter 18.

ally experienced managers, and a shortage of such managers can be a serious barrier to adopting a global structure. As noted previously, the investment required to expand the international experience of the numerous managers needed for a global structure would have to be justified in terms of the future relative importance of international activities as compared to domestic business.

A final variable, related in part to management traits, is the capacity and willingness of an enterprise to adjust to organizational changes. Major organizational realignments are likely to disrupt delicate working relationships. Executives of domestic divisions may be unwilling to accept new managerial roles until there is overwhelming evidence of the need for change. Or a forceful manager of a successful international division is likely to use his record of success to resist reorganization pressures that would dilute his responsibility and authority over international activities. Where the capacity and willingness of an enterprise to adjust to organizational change are limited, informal arrangements and devices other than a major organizational change may have to be adopted to secure some of the prospective benefits of a major change.

Organizational structures normally cannot be changed and operated effectively when they are imposed unilaterally by top management. The choice of structure must emerge out of a political process of group bargaining in which decisions are frequently reached by coalitions of groups. As one study of the process of structural change in multinational corporations emphasizes, "Although the choice of structure is ultimately the responsibility of top managers, they have the role of identifying a workable solution, persuading each group of its logic, and implementing the reorganization."[22]

RELATIONSHIPS BETWEEN CORPORATE HEADQUARTERS AND FOREIGN SUBSIDIARIES

One of the crucial issues facing multinational corporations is the organizational relationship between corporate headquarters and operating units. The ideal relationship for implementing a global strategy is for corporate management to determine overall corporate objectives, to specify organization-wide strategies and policy guidelines, to decide on the allocation of corporate resources to the various operating divisions, and to institute effective systems of communications, coordination, and control. Within this framework, managers of individual units are supposed to be free to determine a specific course of action for achieving the expected contribution to corporate objectives.

---

[22]Stopford and Wells, *Managing the Multinational Enterprise*, p. 75.

As one example, the policy of Massey-Ferguson Limited of Canada, a large, multinational farm machinery company, is to give maximum responsibility and authority to its local operating units for achieving the defined objectives of the parent company. Its philosophy stresses the maximum separation of corporate or parent-company executives from line responsibilities in local operations, even to the extent of avoiding the temptation of sending executives from the "home base" to manage operations abroad.[23]

On the other hand, Philips Lamp Co. of Holland, a giant multinational radio, television, and appliance manufacturer with plants in more than 40 countries, sales companies in 60, and more than 360,000 employees worldwide, is moving away from a highly decentralized structure to one with more centralized control.[24] Even though Philips has a broad geographic spread of operations, it had been unable to take advantage of economies of scale or the benefits of the EEC, as autonomy on the local level was the rule. This resulted in factories producing for only their domestic markets. With centralized control, major plants now specialize in a single product line for the entire company. Centralization has helped Philips reduce its inventory and cut financing costs. Thus, Philips' profit margins, which had been declining steadily through the 1960s before the change in organizational structure, turned upward in 1972.

But whatever the stated ideology and intentions of the company, complicated and contradictory pressures cause relationships to oscillate between varying levels of centralization. Among factors that determine the degree of centralization or decentralization are the age, size, and profitability of a specific subsidiary. Large, long-established, and profitable subsidiaries are likely to have a maximum degree of autonomy.[25] Another important factor is the amount of confidence placed in subsidiary management. Still another force that can press for local autonomy is an environment with strong national governmental controls which requires frequent and unique local decisions. Factors that work toward centralization are an increasing integration of multinational operations, an increasing speed of technological change, and the rapid development of global techniques, strategies, and communications. Brooke and Remmers, after studying in depth the organization of subsidiaries and the power and control systems operating between the head office and foreign subsidiaries of a large number of multina-

---

[23]E. P. Neufeld, *A Global Corporation* (Toronto, Canada: University of Toronto Press, 1969), pp. 389–90.

[24]This example is taken from *Business Week,* January 13, 1973, pp. 64–69.

[25]For extended discussion and case studies of the "Relationships With Foreign Subsidiaries and Affiliates," see Enid Baird Lovell, *The Changing Role of the International Executive* (New York: National Industrial Conference Board, 1966), pp. 140–48.

tional companies of nine different nationalities, concluded "that a decentralizing ideology masks a centralizing reality."[26]

In virtually all cases, however, the relationship will vary by function. Corporate control will be strongest in those functional areas in which the suboptimization problem is likely to arise and where important economies of scale can be achieved by the joint utilization of high-cost specialized personnel.[27] Depending, of course, on a firm's product strategy, the opportunities to optimize for the entire system may be in a regional or worldwide rationalization of production, in the field of purchasing, or in research and development activities. Such functions tend to be centralized, whereas the marketing function tends to be most decentralized.

An important form of geographic organization that some companies have developed between corporate headquarters and the subsidiary is a regional office. This is designed to coordinate the activities of local companies in a group of countries and is normally regarded as a part of the corporate headquarters that has been moved physically nearer to the operations it controls. The number of companies actually having regional offices has been increasing, particularly among U.S. firms. The advantage of a regional office is that it brings some part of the head office into closer contact with local operations. It meets the lack of local knowledge at headquarters and the lack of expertise in the subsidiary. The disadvantage of the regional unit is that it lengthens the lines of communication and tends to reduce the autonomy of the national operation.[28]

An Illustration: The International Financial Function

A recent study of U.S. practices in organizing and managing the international financial function illustrates how organizational patterns and the allocation of responsibility between headquarters and the subsidiaries vary over time with the possibilities for optimization and with the relative capabilities of staff at headquarters and in the subsidiaries.

In the early stages of foreign operations, the domestic financial staff at headquarters generally copes with the new problems, ignoring at times some of the more sophisticated approaches to foreign financing and planning. At later stages, many companies decide to employ full-time specialists in international financial management or to desig-

---

[26]Brooke and Remmers, *The Strategy of Multinational Enterprise,* p. 285.

[27]Richard D. Robinson, *International Management* (New York: Holt, Rinehart & Winston, 1967), pp. 151–53.

[28]Brooke and Remmers, *The Strategy of Multinational Enterprise,* pp. 43–47.

nate one of their financial staff for handling foreign financial matters. A few companies feel that their extensive international operations are best served when every senior financial executive develops equal expertise in both the international and domestic aspects of their particular function.

The principal U.S. international companies follow no single master plan in organizing the management of the international financial function. In broad terms, however, three basic patterns exist.[29] The international functions of both policy making and performance of financial services may be:

1. Centralized at corporate headquarters.
2. Centralized at the headquarters of the international management unit with only overall guidance from corporate headquarters.
3. Split between corporate headquarters and some subordinate headquarters (that is, central international unit, regional headquarters, product division headquarters, and so forth.

The important determinants of organizational patterns and the resulting financial behavior have been the size of an international company and its degree of international involvement. The small firms, defined as having foreign sales of about $50 million, typically run a decentralized operation with an "every tub on its own bottom" policy. Headquarters provides little direction and few decision rules, and makes little effort to move toward optimum financing for the entire system. Medium-sized firms, with foreign sales of about $200 million, typically run a centralized operation with strong direction from headquarters and substantial concern for the net cost of an action to the total system. Large firms, with foreign sales of about $1 billion, often run a decentralized operation but with guidelines issued from the headquarters staff, which also performs a coordination function.[30]

The large multinational enterprises strongly favor systemwide optimization but are too large and too complex to attempt an overall system approach. A computer optimization model of a multinational enterprise with subsidiaries operating in as many as 100 countries and with numerous interconnecting flows of goods and money, would be well beyond the capabilities of today's most advanced high-speed computer system. As a result of this complexity, headquarter's management uses a variety of rules of thumb to assist them in decision making, for example, setting equity equal to fixed assets in forming a new subsidi-

---

[29]Irene W. Meister, *Managing the International Financial Function* (New York: National Industrial Conference Board, 1970), p. 5.

[30]This section is a summary of Robert B. Stobaugh, Jr., "Financing Foreign Subsidiaries of U.S.-Controlled Multinational Enterprises," *Journal of International Business Studies,* Summer 1970, pp. 43–64.

ary. Even if the large multinational enterprise were capable of calculating some crude overall systems optimum, it could not take actions that might jeopardize its position in a foreign country.

The medium-sized firms have a greater tendency than other enterprises to attempt an overall systems optimization and more nearly approach the economists' concept of one "economic man" running the enterprise from headquarters. Small firms, on the other hand, typically lack international experience and tend to have decentralized operations without close control from headquarters or coordination among subsidiaries. In fact, each subsidiary may be viewed as an independent operation, and little attempt is made to take the overall system into account in financing one subsidiary.

The different patterns of organization and of financial policy behavior that prevail among U.S. international firms undoubtedly represent different stages of evolution along the path toward following global strategies and integrated management policies. They also reflect the state of knowledge in optimizing complex systems and the likely constraints on such optimization because of potential conflicts between optimization on a world basis and the interests of nation-states. As increasingly sophisticated organization and management techniques emerge, organizational patterns for the international financial function will continue to change.

Control over the financial function is a key element in achieving global corporate goals, and pressure usually builds up for strong central guidance from corporate headquarters and systemwide optimization. Ideally, the financial management function of a multinational enterprise would have three goals. One would be to take advantage of the potentials in multinational operations for reducing financial costs and increasing efficiency. A second would be to adapt to environmental constraints at the national and regional levels. A third would be to protect the value of assets and revenues so that the benefits of multinational operations are not eroded through financial risks. The efficiency contribution can occur through the ability of the multinational enterprise to secure capital at a lower cost since it has access to many different sources and can achieve economies of scale and skills in financing. The adaptation responsibility is one of meeting national constraints on remittances of funds across national boundaries in both home and host countries. The protective function is to avoid losses through foreign exchange devaluations or revaluations, or through differential rates of inflation.

SUMMARY

An international commitment by a business enterprise normally requires significant changes in a firm's organizational structure. There is no one organizational structure that is ideal for multinational operations, and any structure once adopted must be continually reviewed and revised as internal and external factors keep changing. At the senior management level, the broad types of organization options for assigning responsibility and authority are relatively limited. But within the broad patterns, considerable diversity is possible.

The organizational structure of most international enterprises evolves over time in a series of stages. American companies have typically moved from an export unit structure to a separate international division or international company as operations are extended to foreign areas. As top management becomes increasingly interested in international opportunities, a global organization structure may be adopted. International companies based in Europe and Canada tend to skip the international division stage and move directly to a global structure because domestic markets are smaller and less important to their overall success. Global structures can be organized with primary emphasis on function, product, or geography. Some firms have attempted to build complex grid structures where managers have multiple reporting relationships, and function, product, and area responsibilities overlap.

The choice among alternative structures depends on a small number of variables. The key problem is the inherent conflict between three dimensions of a firm's activities—functional, product, and geographic. A functional structure has the benefits of integrating marketing, finance, and production, but at the cost of area coordination and difficulties in transferring product and technological expertise from the parent company to the subsidiaries and among foreign operations. The product structure reduces problems of transferring technology and new products among locations, but it incurs the costs of duplication in functional tasks and of coordinating all the interests of an enterprise in a foreign area. The area structure gives good coordination geographically but at the cost of product coordination among areas and duplication in functional expertise. In the final analysis, the choice of organization structure will reflect management's choice between sets of problems.

The relationships between corporate headquarters and the foreign subsidiaries present another difficult organizational problem—namely, centralization versus decentralization. In general, the preference is for headquarters to be responsible for strategy and the final decisions on long-range goals, and for the subsidiaries to have maximum responsibility and authority for operations. Here again, a firm's product strategy becomes a key determinant. Where the product strategy may result in suboptimization by not taking advantage of enterprise-wide unification possibilities, such functions as manufacturing, research and development, and financial management are likely to be closely controlled or coordinated at the center. At the other extreme, where great diversity in products and in end-use markets exists, marketing is particularly likely to be decentralized.

EXERCISES AND DISCUSSION QUESTIONS

1. What are the principal considerations that make organizational structures that work well for domestic operations less suitable for multinational operations?

2. "There is no single best structure for all international companies. Each company's operations are different, and each company has an almost unique set of needs to be served by its organizational structure." Discuss.

3. Why do you think one of the major U.S. automobile companies retains an international division structure whereas a company like General Electric has a global structure that emphasizes product groups?

4. "Within a tendency toward greater centralization of decision making, there is yet a discernible trend to greater individual independence for managers in multinational enterprises. Increased independence can accompany a reduction in the area of decision making by subsidiary managers." Discuss.

5. One of the major advantages of multinational operations is the possibility of optimizing the financial function on a worldwide basis. Why do many large and small companies fail to do so?

20

Managing the International
Product Mix

HOW DOES INTERNATIONAL MARKETING differ from domestic marketing? The objectives and methods of the marketing process both
domestically and internationally are the same and so are the marketing
functions required. The difference is that international marketing
activities are conducted across national boundaries and simultaneously in a number of different national markets. This means that the
international firm is serving markets that differ widely from country to
country, reflecting variations in cultural and social circumstances. This
means also that many governments with varied national interests—
rather than a single government—are shaping the environment in
which marketers operate. There is generally no equivalent to these
factors within the domestic economy.[1]

The international elements affect both marketing strategy decisions
and marketing management. At the strategy level, the global setting
makes the product mix decision substantially more complex, but it also
enlarges greatly the potential opportunities for the firm. At the marketing management level, the global setting expands manyfold the task of
adjusting the individual elements of the product mix to the needs of
the identified markets.

STRATEGIC MARKETING DECISIONS

In its global planning at the corporate level, the multinational firm
must make several strategic marketing decisions. As discussed in

---

[1]See Robert Bartels, "Are Domestic and International Marketing Dissimilar?" *Journal of Marketing* 32, (July 1968): 56–61.

Chapter 18, it must decide what markets to serve with what products. In making these decisions, the firm does not limit its product possibilities to existing products or its geographic horizon to its home market. Instead, it seeks to identify demand areas where its capability for performance against competitors is greatest, even though the specific customer needs to be filled are different from those the firm has been filling in the past.[2]

Since there are so many countries in the world, the multinational firm must establish priorities for selecting those markets against which it will make its strategic evaluation and choice. It must decide whether strategic evaluation is carried out against one major single market, many single markets, or some segments of many markets. It must also decide how it is going to organize the responsibility for carrying through this strategic assessment. Will it be done by central headquarters, by multinational committees, or by national units?

In the major single market, or central market, approach, the firm selects its mission based on one national market, establishes a marketing mix, and later expands to other national markets. The central market approach reduces decision problems and can bring high profits when expansion into other markets becomes opportune because of the low marginal cost of geographic extensions. But which central market should the firm choose? Normally the firm begins with its home market, but this may not be the best choice.[3] Some Japanese and European firms have selected the high-income, sophisticated U.S. market for selected product lines. The size of the U.S. market has both advantages and disadvantages. Many Europeans see the cost of communications and coordination efforts in such a large market as a deterrent to producing products first in the United States as part of their world product strategy.[4]

The multiple market approach implies a high degree of decentralization. It may be the best strategy in situations where special local conditions require particular products, such as fertilizers and pesticides, where economies of large-scale production are not important, and where the firm's competitive advantage depends upon capabilities other than advanced product design. In the case of an industrial product such as aluminum ingots, for example, the market characteristics such as product usage patterns, customer attitudes, and target con-

---

[2]Kenneth Simmonds, "Removing the Chains From Product Strategy," *Journal of Management Studies,* February 1968; see also James Leontiades, "Patterns in International Markets and Market Strategy" (Paper presented at European International Business Association Conference, Joueny-en-Josas, France, December 15–16, 1975).

[3]See Chapter 18, pp. 401, 408–11.

[4]Business International, *European Business Strategies in the United States* (Geneva, Switzerland, 1971), p. 24.

sumer groups may be quite similar for many countries, and the best product strategy may be to focus on developing a more economical production process so that the competitive advantage is price.

In the market segment approach, the firm identifies segments of national markets which could profitably be given separate treatment across national boundaries. Small market segments in individual countries may be insufficient for any one country unit to justify development of an appropriate product or to make the necessary investment in market development. Worldwide or for a number of countries, however, such a segment may readily justify the expense. The Japanese auto companies, for example, began their invasion of the European market in the early 1970s by entering smaller European countries where there was little local production rather than the larger countries where they would encounter much stronger competition from the major European auto producers who were located in the large markets. The small segments of several markets as a group comprised a large enough demand area to justify the added distribution and marketing effort. But, as we shall see, the choice among alternative strategies involves the central issue of international standardization versus product differentiation.

INTERNATIONAL STANDARDIZATION
VERSUS DIFFERENTIATION

Having made its choice as to general market focus, the multinational firm must still be concerned with identifying which segments should be treated differently. The advantages of product differentiation to meet the special needs of smaller segments of the market conflict with the advantages of reducing unit costs through standardization.[5] Standardization can bring great savings from production economies and from spreading such expenditures as research and development, advertising, promotion, and general management over a greatly expanded sales base. Consequently, an international firm's best strategy, if the local environment is not excessively unreceptive, could be to avoid detailed adjustment of its product to local markets and to act as a change agent transplanting its culture around the world.

The pressures toward differentiation, however, are great. The international firm usually considers individual countries as the basic building blocks for its organization and it prefers to identify with each country. One way to achieve this identification is to adjust products to fit country markets. In fact, the orthodox emphasis in marketing is to

---

[5]See Robert D. Buzzell, "Can You Standardize Multinational Marketing?" *Harvard Business Review,* November–December 1968, pp. 102–13.

adjust the marketing mix against an assessment of each market's characteristics. The difficulty confronting the firm is to decide when market differences are sufficient to justify the loss of standardization.

The case for standardization or differentiation of products and marketing practices rests on a number of decision elements including consumer characteristics and the impact on total revenues and costs of the alternative strategies. Differentiation is easiest when the necessary adjustments to individual markets are not costly and when the initial design of a product has taken important market differences into account.

The most costly elements to adjust in a product already designed are its physical characteristics. If agricultural equipment, for example, is designed to be marketed in many countries, it must be tested to withstand extremes in temperature and not simply for performance in one particular climate. Also, the design should recognize variations in attitudes regarding repair and maintenance of machinery and variations in the availability of technicians and repair facilities, or else a design for the market of a developed country might produce equipment that is unusable in less developed areas.

Building a potential for a high degree of differentiation into the initial design of a product is not an easy task because detailed rather than general knowledge of culture patterns is needed. In designing products for international performance, a large number of different cultural settings should be examined for ways in which a product is purchased and used to develop a list of important design criteria. Even better guidance can be obtained if test samples can be made available to those concerned with selling in different countries and shown to outlets and users.

Despite the potential costs of failing to consider the global suitability of different product features at the design stage, the product design strategy of even globally oriented firms has generally been to focus heavily on establishing a product in just one market. And although this practice may result in major impediments to later expansion in other country markets, a marketing success in the initial market can unwisely reinforce the practice of not considering international performance criteria in the initial design work.

As compared to changing physical features, the product title is more easily changed. But a name change can be costly if the spillover from advertising into other areas is lost and brand loyalty must be established anew. Coca-Cola stands out as an example here. While the flavor can be easily adjusted to local palates, a change of name in any market would mean a great loss in an established market value. It becomes important, therefore, that the product title initially selected does not have any unfortunate meaning in any of the major languages.

ALTERNATIVE PRODUCT STRATEGIES

The product strategy of an international firm generally falls somewhere between the extremes of central market focus and decentralized development and between the extremes of product-mix standardization or diversification. The choices available can be illustrated by the five alternative strategies summarized in Table 20–1.[6]

TABLE 20–1

Multinational Product-Communications Mix: Strategic Alternatives

Strategy	Product Function or Need Satisfied	Conditions of Product Use	Ability to Buy Product	Recommended Product Strategy	Recommended Communications Strategy	Relative Cost of Adjustments	Product Examples
1	Same	Same	Yes	Extension	Extension	1	Soft drinks
2	Different	Same	Yes	Extension	Adaptation	2	Bicycles, motor-scooters
3	Same	Different	Yes	Adaptation	Extension	3	Gasoline, detergents
4	Different	Different	Yes	Adaptation	Adaptation	4	Clothing, greeting cards
5	Same	—	No	Invention	Develop new communications	5	Motor vehicles

Source: Warren J. Keegan, "Multinational Product Planning, Strategic Alternatives," *Journal of Marketing,* January 1969, p. 59.

Strategy One: One Product, One Message—Worldwide

The easiest and most profitable strategy is that of product and communications extension. The same product is sold worldwide using the same sales message. International cosmetics firms sell the same products worldwide and use the same advertising and promotional appeals that are used in their central markets. They find little variation from country to country in target consumer groups, product usage patterns, and consumer attitudes. As one executive explained[7]

A woman is a woman is a woman,
irrespective of where she lives . . .
Even in Japan we use the same copy,
with American models and English words.

[6]This section is based largely on Warren J. Keegan, "Multinational Product Planning: Strategic Alternatives," *Journal of Marketing,* January 1969, pp. 58–62.
[7]Ulrich Wiechmann, "Integrating Multinational Marketing Activities," *Columbia Journal of World Business,* Winter 1974, p. 12.

The product communications extension strategy has great appeal to most international companies because of the enormous cost savings associated with this approach. Important among these are the substantial economies resulting from the standardization of marketing communications. For a company with worldwide operations, the cost of preparing separate print and TV-cinema films for each market would be extremely high.

This strategy is widely used in marketing advanced-technology producer goods. As Holton has noted, "The world of advanced technology is more nearly a single world than is the world of consumer goods."[8] A firm selling equipment to commercial television stations, for example, normally does not find specifications varying as much across markets as is likely to occur in the case of consumer goods. Even in the less developed countries, the technological specifications for producers' goods generally follow those developed in the advanced countries.

Unfortunately, the product communications extension strategy does not work for all products. When Campbell soup tried to sell its U.S. tomato soup formulation to the British, it discovered after considerable losses that the English prefer a more bitter taste. Numerous other examples can be cited of cases where consumer preferences in new markets do not favor a product developed for the central market, and where an adjustment or innovation rather than an extension strategy is required.

Strategy Two: Product Extension— Communications Adaptation

When a product fills a different need or serves a different function under use conditions identical with or similar to those in the central market, the only adjustment required is in marketing communications. Bicycles, for example, satisfy needs mainly for recreation in the United States but provide basic transportation in countries like India. The appeal of the product extension communications adaptation strategy is that savings in manufacturing, research and development, and inventory costs can still result. The only additional costs are in identifying the different product functions the product will service in foreign markets and in reformulating advertising, sales promotion, and other dimensions of market communications around the newly identified function.

---

[8]Richard H. Holton, "Marketing Policies in Multinational Corporations," *Journal of International Business Studies,* Summer 1970, p. 18.

Strategy Three: Product Adaptation—
Communications Extension

A third international product strategy is to extend without change the basic communications strategy developed for the central market but to adapt the product to different use conditions. The product adaptation communications extension strategy assumes that the product will serve the same function in foreign markets under different use conditions. Esso followed this approach when it adapted the physical characteristics of its gasoline to the different climatic and user conditions of different countries while continuing to use on a worldwide basis the invitation to "Put a tiger in your tank." International companies in the soap and detergent fields have adjusted their product formulation to meet local water conditions and the characteristics of local washing machines, with no change in the companies' basic communications approach.

Strategy Four: Dual Adaptation

Strategy four is to adapt both the product and the communications approach when differences exist in environmental conditions of use and in the function that a product serves. In essence, this is a combination of strategies two and three. U.S. greeting-card companies have faced these circumstances in Europe, where the occasions for using greeting cards differ from those in the United States. Also, in Europe the function of a greeting card has been to provide a space for the sender to write his own message, in contrast to the U.S. situation where cards contain prepared messages.

Strategy Five: Product Invention

A final strategy is that of product invention. When potential customers cannot afford one of the firm's products, an opportunity may exist to invent or design an entirely new product that satisfies the identified need or function at a price that the consumer can afford. If product-development costs are not excessive, this may be a potentially rewarding product strategy for the mass markets in the less developed countries.

As an example of this approach, both Ford and General Motors developed entirely new motor vehicles designed specifically for markets in the underdeveloped countries, including, it was hoped, markets in mainland China. The vehicles are small, inexpensive, easily assembled, and designed with emphasis on utility and durability rather than on style and comfort. The Ford vehicle is built in the Philippines for sale throughout Asia. The GM vehicle is designed to be assembled by company-owned or independent distributors in the developing countries. GM supplies essential components from its subsidiary in England but up to 50 percent of the components, those not requiring heavy tooling expense, can be manufactured locally. The product strategy not only attempts to meet the low price requirements of the less developed countries but is also designed to satisfy the pressure of the countries for a high degree of local content. The engineering requirements are relatively unsophisticated so that with blueprints and instructions supplied by the multinational company, "any sheet-metal shop in any country can be used to build this car," according to a GM executive.[9] The companies see their product as a replacement for the animal cart, bicycle, motor scooter, and even three-wheel vehicles in the developing countries.

The best product strategy—the one that optimizes company profits over the long term—will depend upon the specific product-market-company mix. Some products demand adaptation, others lend themselves to adaptations, and still others are best left unchanged. The same is true of markets. Also, companies differ not only in their manufacturing costs but also in their capability to identify and produce profitable product adaptations. *Thus the choice of product and communications strategy in international marketing is a function of three key factors:*

1. The need to define the product itself in terms of the function or need it serves.
2. The definition of the market in terms of the conditions under which the product is used, including customer preferences and their ability to buy the product in question.
3. The costs of adaptation and manufacture to the company.

Only after analyzing the product-market fit, the company's capabilities, and costs can managers choose the most profitable international product strategy.

INTERNATIONAL MARKETING AND ORGANIZATION

Marketing more so than any other function has been viewed in the past as a local problem and was conspicuous by its absence from the functions planned at the corporate headquarters. This view reflected a conviction that a multinational approach was not realistic because of the great differences that existed among nations. The limited role of

---

[9]*Business Week,* May 27, 1972, p. 15.

headquarters has been characteristic of both extremes of product strategies. Where products and marketing approaches have been extended from the center market to foreign areas with little or no adaptation, a major contribution to the marketing function from headquarters was considered unnecessary. At the other extreme, where market differences were so great that major adaptations were required, the prevailing view was that the strategies and the implementation had to be handled at the local level.[10]

More recently the trend has been toward designing marketing strategies with a multinational perspective and toward an increased role by headquarters.[11] The trend has been called "interactive market planning," a strategy which recognizes similarities as well as differences in national markets, and is based on the belief that although there are many obstacles to the application of common marketing policies in different countries, the tangible benefits from doing so can be substantial.[12] The degree of headquarters participation will, of course, vary by marketing function, by industry, by company, and over time.[13] The normal pattern, however, is for headquarters to play a significant role in standardizing some parts of the marketing strategy, while leaving the subsidiaries with principal responsibility for handling the differences and unique factors.

This pattern is illustrated in a recent sample study of major U.S. and European companies in four consumer industries.[14] Product policy decisions (physical characteristics of the product, brand name, packaging, product line) involved the greatest degree of headquarters control. Headquarters participation was far less pronounced in pricing, distribution, and advertising and promotion decisions.[15] By industry, centralized decision making was comparatively stronger for nonfood than for food products, the latter generally perceived to be more "culture bound."

What guidelines are appropriate for defining the role of headquarters and for organizing the marketing-management function? Finding the right balance between local autonomy and central coordination is

---

[10]Warren J. Keegan, "Multinational Marketing: The Headquarters Role," *Columbia Journal of World Business,* January–February 1971.

[11]Buzzell, "Can You Standardize Multinational Marketing?" p. 112.

[12]Keegan, "Multinational Marketing, pp. 26–27.

[13]R. J. Aylmer, "Who Makes Marketing Decisions in the Multinational Firm?" *Journal of Marketing,* October 1970, pp. 26–27.

[14]Wiechmann, "Integrating Multinational Marketing Activities," pp. 7–16.

[15]Similar conclusions were reached in a study of Japanese, European, and American multinational subsidiaries in Brazil. See William K. Brandt and James M. Hulbert, "Marketing Strategy in the Multinational Subsidiary: The Role of Headquarters," in *Making Advertising Relevant,* Proceedings of the American Academy of Advertising, 1975.

not an easy task, any more than is balancing the gains of standardized marketing strategy against the needs of heterogeneous national markets. First, headquarters must be adequately informed concerning markets to carry out its responsibility for strategic planning. Market research is an important source of information and, therefore, should be monitored by headquarters. Second, headquarters should be able to make international comparisons on marketing performance and coun-try potentials, and certain market measures can be standardized so that such comparisons can be made. Third, headquarters involvement should insure that no country or area unknowingly duplicates market research or marketing experimentation that has already been undertaken somewhere in the international system. Fourth, the benefits from headquarters involvement must be related to the cost of such involvement in terms of personnel, information flows, and standardization of the research formats.

The principal justification for headquarters participation in the marketing function along the lines just considered is that headquarters can better fulfill its roles of strategic planning and controlling performance. But to make the process interactive, headquarters must be alert and aggressive in making affirmative contributions in the marketing field to the local subsidiaries. Such contributions can be in the form of making experience from one country available to other countries where comparable conditions prevail. If good ideas are scarce, and if some of them have universal appeal, they should be used as widely as possible. It can supervise experimentation in marketing and make the results of different experiments available to all units in the system. If a manager questions the relative effectiveness of advertising versus personal selling, instead of splitting the communications budget between these two activities, he could run 75 percent advertising and 25 percent personal selling in *Country A* and reverse these proportions in *Country B*, where both countries were preselected as most nearly comparable in other marketing dimensions.

Headquarters can also perform certain functions that cannot be easily accomplished at the subsidiary level. For example, as previously mentioned, it may discover opportunities that consist of a number of small market segments in different countries which country subsidiaries might regard as too small to warrant development. Other arguments favoring central market control stem from the need to allocate limited resources according to a global strategy. Development of individual markets must be started in ways that fit the total development pattern laid out for the enterprise and arranged so that individual markets can fit without problems into later stages of the plan. It may be necessary, for example, to choose outlets or sign distribution agreements not initially the best for a smaller range of products selling in lower volumes than will be the case later on. The brand image might also be important for carrying future lines and require special attention when products are first introduced. In pricing, too, central guidance is frequently necessary if the advantages of an international scale are to be realized.

One of the more common ways of placing responsibility at the level of those closest to the customer, yet still retaining overall control over the marketing diagnosis, is through the use of a standard annual plan and review routine. Plans are requested in a standard format working from an assessment of the market environment toward specific action proposals and budgeted profit performance and resource requirements. These are then subjected to careful scrutiny and related to the overall plan for global performance. Any clashes or omissions discovered can then be raised before actions are taken.

This method of central control also acts as a major implement in educating the international organization in the use of marketing. A good grasp of marketing cannot be assumed to exist throughout any international organization. The ideas are alien to many cultures and frequently opposed to the message of the programs under which many international executives have been educated. The discipline of the marketplace, however, is clearly demanded in any planning system that works from an assessment of the market through to recommendations for action in that market. When the central executives are seen to check for consistency and completeness in both the analysis and the planned actions and each year to raise the quality of market assessment and analysis they expect, the message of marketing control is carried much more concretely than it would be through a less direct educational program.

The decisive question is not where ultimate control of strategic planning should lie, for this inevitably must rest with top management. The real question is the extent to which headquarters executives should be involved in the strategic planning process. In the absence of headquarters involvement in the individual subsidiary planning processes, it is difficult, indeed impossible, for headquarters to impose global considerations in the strategic planning process effectively. In the absence of subsidiary involvement, on the other hand, the local adaptation requirements of a market may be overlooked.

As a general rule, headquarters should be involved in subsidiary planning processes to the extent necessary to keep informed of the nature of basic opportunities and threats globally. Also, headquarters involvement should be measured against the degree to which it stimulates or contributes to subsidiary planning efforts. Alternatively, a check should be kept on the extent to which it may detract from initiative and enterprise on the part of subsidiary managers. The organizational form must facilitate the task of international marketing, particularly where marketing skills are important as a key element in the competitive advantage of the international company. As Terpstra has pointed out, marketing skills and orientation were critical components of the competitive advantage on which many U.S. companies based their expansion into European markets.[16]

INTERNATIONAL PRICING

From the marketing standpoint, price is only one of the variables of the marketing mix to be considered, along with many other variables. But from the standpoint of the total enterprise, prices determine the total revenue available for all functions and to a large degree the profitability of the enterprise. Thus, pricing decisions must take into account the interests of many groups within the enterprise and frequently conflicting price objectives.[17]

The director of international marketing and the managers of foreign subsidiaries seek prices that will be competitive in the marketplace. But where product divisions of the parent firm supply products or components to overseas units, the product managers seek transfer prices that maximize the profits of their division. The tax manager is concerned with the implications of pricing decisions on the total tax liability of the corporation, tax deferral opportunities, and government regulations on transfer pricing. With these and other sectors of the enterprise crucially dependent on pricing decisions, top management invariably assumes substantial responsibility for formulating pricing policies and strategies. The implementation of these policies, however, may be widely diffused throughout the organization.[18]

The role of pricing differs considerably for different types of goods and from market to market. In the case of standardized or relatively undifferentiated products, the market sets the price and the seller has little control over the level of prices. The same will be true of situations where government price controls prevail or prices are fixed through patent-licensing agreements. But for differentiated products selling in nonregulated markets, the producer has genuine alternatives in setting

---

[16]Vern Terpstra, *American Marketing in the Common Market* (New York: Praeger Publishers, Inc., 1967).

[17]This section draws heavily from *Solving International Pricing Problems* (New York: Business International, 1965).

[18]For an example of how the responsibility for pricing is distributed among the various units of an international company in the pharmaceuticals and chemicals field, see Enid Baird Lovell, *The Changing Role of the International Executive* (New York: National Industrial Conference Board, 1966), p. 52.

prices. And much of the international business activity is based on differentiated products and oligopoly elements.

In setting its pricing policies, two basic choices are available to a company. Prices may be used as an active instrument for accomplishing market objectives. Or prices may be considered as a static element in business decisions. American companies generally regard price as an important variable in their marketing decisions. Japanese companies are probably even more aggressive in pricing. Newly established foreign subsidiaries generally have sales growth as their prime target, assuming that profits will come in due course, and use low-price strategies to achieve their sales goals.[19] In other countries, a more passive attitude toward the strategic role of pricing is likely to exist. For example, a study of marketing practices in the European Economic Community reached the conclusion that "among those manufacturers who had reasonable latitude in setting their prices, there was generally a tendency to disregard pricing as an important element in the marketing strategy."[20]

In setting prices for any single market, both cost and market considerations are important. Costs set the price floor, and competitive prices for comparable products set the price ceiling. Between the floor and the ceiling there is an optimum price which is a function of the demand for the product and the cost of sourcing the product. The international company that uses pricing as part of the strategic product mix will develop a pricing system and pricing policies that recognize the diversity of national markets in three basic dimensions—cost, competition, and demand. In addition, pricing policies will have to be consistent with a number of international constraints such as tax policies, dumping legislation, resale price-maintenance legislation, and governmental price controls where they exist. Another constraint may be multinational accounts that demand equal price treatment regardless of location.

The cost considerations that set the lower limit for prices may not be easy to define. Firms must decide whether they are going to use variable costs or full costs in their pricing decisions. In variable cost pricing, the company is concerned only with the marginal or incremental cost of producing the goods sold in foreign markets. The logic for using variable costs may be that foreign sales are incidental to a company's main operations and any returns over the marginal costs are

---

[19]William K. Brandt and James M. Hulbert, "Marketing Strategies of American, European and Japanese Multinational Subsidiaries" (Paper presented at the Academy of International Business Meetings, Fontainebleau, France, July 7–9, 1975).

[20]Bertil Liander, *Marketing Development in the European Economic Community* (New York: McGraw-Hill Book Co., 1964), p. 49.

a bonus contribution to net profit, or that the firm has to price more competitively to enter a foreign market or to meet local competition. But companies selling products in foreign markets at lower prices than in domestic markets are subject to charges of "dumping," which may subject the company to antidumping tariffs or penalties.

The firm that regards itself as a global enterprise is more likely to think in terms of full-cost pricing for all markets.[21] Full costs do not have to be covered in every market, and occasions may arise where the firm should price below full cost. But as previously mentioned, the determination of full costs may not be an easy matter. How much of general administrative, research and development costs, and other overhead items should be included in intracorporate transfer prices? What share of marketing, sales, and advertising costs incurred in the domestic market but which generate marketing approaches that can be extended abroad should be included in the cost to foreign subsidiaries? Where capital is tied up for longer periods because of the time lags inherent in international transactions, and where foreign exchange risks are involved, how should these financing and risk costs be incorporated into the pricing decisions? And innumerable other cost uncertainties exist, depending on the market, the product, and the situation.

The cost-plus pricing strategy results in relatively uniform prices worldwide, except for variations in such costs as freight and import duties. It has the advantage of simplicity since information on competitive or market conditions is not required for its implementation. It is widely used for export pricing and can be designed with some flexibility for adjusting the markup over costs to fit different market conditions. But it has the serious disadvantage that it is not directed toward maximizing the company's sales and revenues or profits in each national market.

Without ignoring the realities of cost, a market-pricing strategy gives principal emphasis to the demand and supply conditions of each market and the state of competition. The example in the appendix to this chapter shows how different demand elasticities in different markets can result in advantages from different price policies for subsidiaries in each market. Through the separate adjustment of prices for each market, a greater profit can be achieved for the total system than by any choice of a common price for both markets. It should be noted, however, that in situations where national markets are not separated from each other, a common, final price policy may be

---

[21]Philip R. Cateora and John M. Hess, *International Marketing*, 3rd ed. (Homewood, Ill.: Richard D. Irwin, Inc., 1975), p. 431.

necessary in order to minimize country-to-country arbitrage through companies other than those controlled by the international firm.

INTRACOMPANY TRANSFER PRICING

When a company is engaged solely in exporting, its pricing task is limited to setting export prices and terms for goods sold to customers outside the firm. Once the company establishes foreign subsidiaries, intracompany transfer prices—i.e., prices for goods and services exchanged within the corporate family—become an important dimension of pricing strategies. When transactions between units of the same enterprise take place across national frontiers and the units are subject to different environmental factors such as custom duties, tax rates, and currency risks, adjustments in transfer prices can be used to advance various enterprise goals and increase overall enterprise profits.[22]

Through a transfer-pricing policy that charges high prices for intracompany sales to an affiliate and low prices for intracompany purchases from the affiliate, a multinational enterprise can shift earnings from a high-tax to a low-tax country, circumvent dividend repatriation restrictions, reduce the affiliate's exposure to currency devaluation and expropriation risks, lower apparent profits in situations where high profits might encourage customers or local authorities to ask for price reductions or labor unions to press for wage increases, and allocate markets by making the exports of an affiliate noncompetitive.

Through the reverse policy of low-import and high-export prices for intracompany transactions, the multinational enterprise can provide financing to a new subsidiary or help it show a profit during a start-up period and thereby improve its ability to get local credit. Low transfer prices on imports will also reduce duty costs and import deposit requirements where the latter exist.

As is generally true for pricing decisions, numerous internal and external pressures exist that push the firm toward different transfer-pricing policies. Executives in home-country producing units want to push up transfer prices and service charges to foreign affiliates. Buying units abroad want to reduce them. Outside the company, home-country tax authorities and custom officials abroad press for high transfer prices; foreign tax officials pressure the local company to buy cheap. From an enterprise-wide perspective, optimum transfer-pricing decisions would be based on where and when it is most advantageous

---

[22]See *Solving International Pricing Problems* (New York: Business International, 1966).

to take the profit on a transaction without regard to national boundaries, and on the real role of intercompany transactions in improving the corporation's total profitability over a time horizon that usually extends beyond the current accounting period.

Given the opportunities to shift funds and profits by the transfer-pricing mechanism, how extensively is the instrument used by multinational companies? Because of its attractiveness as a subject for applying operation research techniques, transfer pricing has attracted considerable academic attention.[23] But despite the intriguing theoretical possibilities developed by model builders, several recent studies suggest that transfer pricing, particularly as a means of avoiding taxes, is no longer widely used by U.S. companies for operations in Europe and North America.[24] In practice, most American firms claim that they apply arm's length standards to their transactions with overseas controlled subsidiaries.[25] Among British companies, few executives admitted that they used transfer pricing to shift profits between various units of the group.[26]

The developing countries, however, have been reluctant to accept these declarations of "innocence" and have made transfer pricing a major issue in their proposals for a code of conduct for the multinationals. They are aware that the controls prevailing in most developing countries make the rewards to the enterprise from manipulating transfer prices extremely attractive. And they fear that transfer-pricing policies will undercut the national objectives they are trying to achieve through controls.[27] But there is more suspicion than factual documentation about the actual practices of the multinationals in the developing countries. In support of their concerned view, however, the developing countries frequently cite a case study conducted in Colombia, which concluded that in 1968 the multinational pharmaceutical companies were "overpricing" sales to their Colombia affiliates by an

---

[23]For example see David P. Rutenberg, "Maneuvering Liquid Assets in a Multinational Company: Formulation and Deterministic Solution Procedures," *Management Science,* June 1970, pp. B-671 to B-674. As an interesting sidelight, this research project funded by a government agency was publicly attacked by an American legislator as an improper use of government funds to assist multinational companies in evading U.S. taxes.

[24]Michael Z. Brooke and H. Lee Remmers, *The Strategy of Multinational Enterprise* (New York: American Elsevier Publishing Company, 1970), p. 176; Jeffrey S. Arpan, *International Intracorporate Pricing: Non-American Systems and Views* (New York: Praeger Publishers, Inc., 1972).

[25]James Greene and Michael G. Duerr, *Intercompany Transactions in the Multinational Company* (New York: National Industrial Conference Board, 1970), pp. 22–23.

[26]Brooke and Remmers, *Strategy of Multinational Enterprise,* p. 176.

[27]*The Impact of Multinational Corporations on Development and International Relations* (New York: United Nations, 1974), pp. 88–90.

average of 155 percent more than prices quoted in different markets around the world. Lesser rates of "overpricing" were documented for the rubber, chemical, and electronics industries.[28]

In discussing transfer pricing, it should be noted that firms using the highly popular profit-center concept may not be able to manipulate transfer prices. If foreign units are made profit centers for purposes of monitoring their performance and financially rewarding their managers, goods must be transferred at competitive and relatively uniform prices between units in the system whose performance is being compared. However, several techniques can be used to maximize total system profits through manipulating transfer prices while still retaining the profit-center concept. One method is to share the total realized profits of the company between the parent and foreign subsidiary on the basis of assets used, costs incurred, or on a more subjective basis of equitable treatment.[29] Another way is to keep two sets of accounts—official accounts for tax and other local purposes and another set for management control purposes. Still another is to take account of transfer-price manipulations in the budget and measure performance against planned results, even if a loss were intended. But each of these techniques has drawbacks and the critical question becomes one of whether the gains from manipulating transfer prices more than offset the resulting cost and complexity of judging performance.

Another major constraint on transfer-pricing policies has been the rapidly expanding surveillance of tax and custom authorities.[30] The transfer-price review program of the U.S. Treasury is perhaps the most advanced in the world today. It includes not only the sale of tangible property but also the pricing of money, services, the use of tangible property, and the transfer of intangible property such as patents and trademarks. From the viewpoint of the U.S. Treasury, Section 482 of the Internal Revenue Code (1954) and the regulations promulgated by the Treasury in 1968 to govern international pricing practices are intended to insure that the U.S. government gets its fair share of the taxes on income earned by the multinational corporate system.[31] The

[28]Constantine V. Vaitsos, *Transfer of Resources and Preservation of Monopoly Rents,* Economic Development Report No. 168, Development Advisory Service (Cambridge, Mass.: Harvard University, June 1970); see also, Constantine Vaitsos, *Intercountry Income Distribution and Transnational Enterprises* (London: Oxford University Press, 1974).

[29]Greene and Duerr, *Intercompany Transactions in the Multinational Company,* p. 10.

[30]Brooke and Remmers, *Strategy of Multinational Enterprise,* p. 175, report that international companies have experienced many disputes with customs authorities even though avoidance of duties is one of the lesser reasons for manipulating prices.

[31]See Warren J. Keegan, "Multinational Pricing: How Far is Arm's Length?" *Columbia Journal of World Business,* May–June 1969, pp. 57–66.

general rule of the Treasury governing the pricing of controlled intracompany transactions is that transfer prices should be set at a level comparable to prices where the two parties are relatively independent and "bargaining at arm's length."

Although more and more limits are being imposed on transfer-pricing policies by governmental tax and customs regulations in home and host countries, within these limits there is frequently latitude for pricing to meet market and competitive factors. Even the U.S. regulations appear to leave an opening for a company to lower its transfer price for the purposes of entering a new market or meeting competition in an existing market. Consequently, for most companies the opportunity to support marketing goals and to increase systemwide profits by alternative transfer-pricing strategies should not be disregarded.

With all of these counterbalancing and conflicting forces to be considered, how does a multinational enterprise establish its international pricing policies? The international complications, added to those that always arise, whether or not national boundaries are crossed, clearly point to the impossibility of having fixed rules for pricing in the multinational corporation. They equally point to the need for central monitoring of price strategy and an open-minded approach to the possibility of significant gains from central action to alter patterns that otherwise emerge. Naive calculations of the profit in individual units should not be accepted without measurement of the ultimate effect on the system, and the effects on the enterprise as a whole can be complex. Nor should pricing decisions be imposed without a realization of offsetting costs. In sum, getting the most out of pricing decisions within a multinational corporation requires a mapping of the entire system and a calculation for any potential change of the net effects across all units.[32]

INTERNATIONAL CHANNEL MANAGEMENT

In the marketing literature dealing with the choice of distribution channels, the message is clear that the product mix reaching the consumer must be carefully matched against the channels that are available or can be built.[33] Channels cannot be changed frequently and moves are usually not reversible. Alternatives forgone may not remain open and outlets that have been dropped in the past may not be again willing to carry the line.

---

[32]See Thomas Horst, "The Theory of the Multinational Firm: Optimal Behavior Under Different Tariff and Tax Rates," *Journal of Political Economy*, September–October 1971, pp. 1059–72.

[33]John A. Howard, *Marketing Management*, rev. ed. (Homewood, Ill.: Richard D. Irwin, Inc., 1963).

At the international level the same approach applies. The firm will have to decide on the best channel pattern for each of a number of countries, not only for immediate marketing goals but for future development. A newly formed domestic firm in the early stages may not have a sufficient reputation or adequate resources to mold the channel structure it would like to have. But when an established firm moves into global expansion, it generally has much greater flexibility in choosing its channel structure in new markets.

International channel management is intimately related to many other dimensions of marketing management and global strategy. If the best strategy for entering a given market appears to be through licensing, the primary responsibility for developing and managing distribution channels becomes that of the licensee. Likewise, if the indicated strategy is to serve a market through exports, the channel decision may be a choice among exporting indirectly through export merchants or middlemen, exporting directly to an importer in the market area, or establishing overseas sales branches, subsidiaries, or foreign warehouse facilities.[34] If the entry strategy is through foreign production as a joint venture or wholly owned subsidiary, then the channel management problem is largely a domestic business question.

No matter what the initial entry strategy, the choice of channels must be evaluated against the longer-range goals of the company in the specific market. Will the channels be sufficiently effective to develop the scale of sales in the country that will permit the company to move at a later stage to local production? Or will the channels be a barrier to the expansion of direct selling activities in the area when such a channel strategy becomes economic and desirable? Or will the channels be an efficient transmitter of information to the producer that will help it to match its product policies to changing consumer demands?

As a first step after identifying attractive markets and their potentials, the marketing manager should specify the functions that the channel system is expected to accomplish.[35] These functions will be determined both by the nature of the product mix and by the environmental characteristics of the markets. As producers of automobiles exporting to the U.S. market or producers of construction machinery exporting to less developed markets have discovered, a necessary function that must be performed by the channels of distribution is the

---

[34]See Franklin R. Root, *Strategic Planning For Export Marketing* (Scranton, Pa.: International Textbook Co., 1964), pp. 72–88.

[35]For more detailed discussions of international channel management, see Gordon E. Miracle and Gerald S. Albaum, *International Marketing Management* (Homewood, Ill.: Richard D. Irwin, Inc., 1970), pp. 313–416; Philip R. Cateora and John M. Hess, *International Marketing*, 3d ed. (Homewood, Ill.: Richard D. Irwin, Inc., 1975), pp. 479–533.

provision of after-sales service and repairs. Or in other types of products, an essential function may be the carrying of an adequate inventory in order to stimulate sales or the provision of consumer financing.

The next step is to understand the channel alternatives available and the environmental characteristics of the institutions. In this respect, much detailed information on many countries has become available through comparative market research that can help the enterprise to develop its distribution strategy and select its channels,[36] In most areas the structure of the distribution system is in process of change, and the formulation of a strategy and the selection of channels must take into account the process of change. Retailers and wholesalers are middlemen, not only in the flow of goods, but also in the whole process of satisfying the material needs and desires of a society. Their effectiveness is largely determined, therefore, by the changing environment in which they stand.

The key elements in decisions as to a distribution system are (1) the availability of middlemen, (2) the ability and effectiveness of the alternatives in performing the necessary functions, (3) the cost of their services, and (4) the extent of control which the multinational enterprise can exert over the middlemen's activities. The preferred system is the one that will provide the optimum patterns of function, cost, and control. However, variations among nations may indicate different solutions to channel distribution needs for various market areas.

The alternatives available for exporting, as previously noted, are agent middlemen, merchant middlemen, or a company's own sales and distribution system. In many instances, the enterprise will use more than one of these methods at the same time. The principal differences between the agent and the merchant is that merchant middlemen purchase for their own account and bear the majority of the trading risks for the products handled. Agents do not take title to the merchandise but work on a commission basis. In general, the firm has more control over prices and other aspects of the distribution function through agents. It has even more control by establishing its own distribution system, but the prospective scale of operations in a given market may not justify in terms of cost the establishment of a company's own system.

The wholesale distribution function can be handled by foreign

---

[36]For studies in comparative marketing, see Jean Boddewyn, *Comparative Management and Marketing* (Glenview, Ill.: Scott, Foresman and Co., 1969); David Carson, *International Marketing: A Comparative Systems Approach* (New York: John Wiley and Sons, 1967); Montrose S. Sommers and Jerome B. Kernan, eds., *Comparative Marketing Systems* (New York: Appleton-Century-Crofts, 1968).

importers, by the companies own overseas facilities, or by independent wholesalers.[37] A wholesaler is a middleman who sells to retailers or industrial users. His chief functions are negotiating for the buyer,[38] buying, selling, and storing. He may also offer a host of other services such as financing or servicing. The distribution system for industrial goods in advanced countries is generally quite similar. In the less developed countries, because a large share of industrial goods is imported and the volume of any one item may be small, the distribution of industrial goods is generally handled by importers who deal in a wide range of products in order to generate enough sales to support their operations. The smaller the market, the wider the range of products the wholesaler must carry. This feature reduces the choice of alternatives and frequently means that a distributor handles goods of several competing firms in the same field.

The retail distribution systems vary greatly among countries in the size of distribution units, in the services they perform, and in the assortment of goods they handle. In the Middle East, for example, "retail distribution is characterized by large numbers of little shops with small capital investments, much imitation, low turnovers, high margins, and high mortality."[39] In parts of the Middle East, however, the oil boom of the 1970s radically changed retailing patterns.

Generally, as we go up the economic scale, the sizes of retail units increase, the amount of personal attention given to customers decreases—moving toward self-service—and the assortment of goods handled changes from a high degree of specialization to a wide variety of goods in one retail unit. Again, many comparative studies of retailing patterns are available for the marketing manager to secure essential information for deciding on his channel choices for a specific country.

In summary, international channel management requires the design of a structure of distribution units that will perform the physical distribution task, provide service and other functions, and provide an effective transmission system for returning necessary market informa-

---

[37]See Robert Bartels, ed., *Comparative Marketing: Wholesaling in Fifteen Countries* (Homewood, Illinois: Richard D. Irwin, Inc., 1963); Sommers and Kernan, eds., *Comparative Marketing Systems.*

[38]See John Fayerweather, *International Marketing*, 2d ed. (Englewood Cliffs, N.J.: Prentice-Hall, 1970), pp. 73–74. "Negotiation for the buyer" refers to investigating sources of supply, checking the quality of products offered, and working out reasonable prices. Much of the negotiation on behalf of the buyer is performed by the channels of distribution.

[39]Charles F. Stewart, "The Changing Middle-East Market," *Journal of Marketing,* January 1961, p. 50.

tion to the company. The alternatives vary tremendously with the environment and are in a process of change around the world. Starting from its market targets and an understanding of the functions that the distribution system must perform for each product or group of products, the marketing manager must design a system that not only serves present needs but also has the flexibility to permit changes in the channel structure over time.

How is the international channel-management responsibility shared between headquarters and the subsidiaries in a multinational company? Obviously, in the case of foreign production, the responsibility must be highly decentralized. But headquarters has a need, under all circumstances, for keeping informed and for appraising the effectiveness of distribution channel experience. Some of the experience might be profitably transferred from one area to another. Some of the experience may indicate changes that should be made in the product mix in order to permit distribution channels to be more effective. Where distribution channels are having great difficulty in providing postsales service, for example, product redesigns that reduce or simplify the service requirement add to the effectiveness of the available channels.

The need to develop working relationships with outside channels in a different cultural background presents further problems in the international firm. The firm faces problems not only in seeking to transmit its past experience to these channels but also in communicating with them about current questions. Particular concepts will often not be directly translatable, and the approach to market assessment is likely to have many cultural biases.

One way of overcoming some of the problems is to develop representatives with preparation in both liaison with channels and the peculiarities of particular cultures. Caterpillar, for example, developed a range of international representatives with language and area courses and special training for aiding distributors in solving inventory, financial, and merchandising problems.

INTERNATIONAL ADVERTISING

International standardization versus differentiation has long been debated in the advertising field around the question of whether advertising themes and advertisements should be uniform internationally or developed specifically for individual national markets. Increasingly, advertising experts have been accepting the view that the advertising task is essentially the same in most markets—namely, to communicate information and persuasive appeals effectively. Therefore, the same approach to communication can be used in every country but the specific advertising messages and media strategy sometimes must be changed from country to country.[40]

Any component in the set of components making up an advertisement—the words used, the symbols, the illustrations, and so on—might be changed to produce an improved impact when the culture of the audience changes. The age of a product user depicted in an illustration might appear just right to one culture yet young and immature to another. The overall message that an advertisement conveys might also be changed for different cultures. The product image that would most influence purchasing will differ in many ways from country to country. Finally, media characteristics vary from country to country.

For these reasons there is an initial bias in favor of separate advertising in each country. Good advertising campaigns, however, are expensive to produce. When they have proven effective in one culture, it seems worthwhile testing them in others before starting at the beginning again to develop separate campaigns for each culture. As the head of a Swedish advertising agency has said, "Why should three artists in three different countries sit drawing the same electric iron and three copywriters write about what after all is largely the same copy for the same iron."[41] The economic arguments for using a standard appeal in international media are great, particularly in new markets that do not warrant the cost involved in developing entirely new material.

Advertising strategy will depend, of course, on the product strategy. When a product fits a different need or serves a different function in a foreign market than in the central market, adjustments are required in the market communications. The same is true for a product strategy based on developing new products designed specifically for foreign markets.

There can be no doubt that good advertising built specifically for one culture will be superior to that built for another. One comparison of the relative effectiveness of American and British television commercials within the British market concluded as follows:

> From this particular study, there emerges the conclusion that current or fairly recent American commercials, even of the highest creative caliber, are less likely than current British commercials to be effective in the British market and that the reasons for this are either (a) that despite a common language, the social, cultural, and marketing differences be-

---

[40]See Gordon E. Miracle, "International Advertising Principles and Strategies," *MSU Business Topics,* Autumn 1968, pp. 29–36.

[41]Eric Elinder, "International Advertisers Must Devise Universal Ads; Dump Separate National Ones, Swedish Adman Avers," *Advertising Age,* November 27, 1961, p. 91.

tween the two countries are so great that a commercial which is successful in one country is unlikely to be very successful in the other, or (*b*) that in marketing and advertising terms, Britain is five years behind the United States, exemplified possibly by the fact that the successful British commercials for Coca-Cola and Excedrin were, perhaps, similar in style to American commercials for those same products of a few years ago. It may be that both of these factors apply in some measure.[42]

While the nature and motives of men are more or less universal, the way in which men satisfy their needs are not. Cultural and socioeconomic environmental differences play an important part in shaping the demand for specific types of goods and services and in determining what promotional appeals are best. Thus the appeals, illustrations, and other advertising features used to sell them often must differ from market to market. But this may be only a matter of changing specific advertising messages rather than the basic advertising approach. Esso was able to use its advertising theme "Put a tiger in your tank" with considerable success in most countries in the world. In French, however, the word tank is *reservoir* which in the context of the phrase could be highly suggestive, so the word *moteur* was substituted. And in Thailand, where the tiger is not a symbol of strength, the campaign was not understood.[43] In England, an American-designed advertising campaign built on the slogan "Don't spend a penny until you've tried . . ." had to be modified because the phrase "spend a penny" in Britain is the equivalent of "got to see a man about a dog" in the United States.[44]

Because of cultural differences, the advertiser must choose with care the symbols used in advertisement for a market. Colors as one form of visual symbol may have a different significance in one culture as compared to another. In China, yellow has always been the imperial color and is not used extensively except for religious purposes. Advertising symbols must be in harmony with the prevailing mentality of a market. In some countries, the use of a certain brand of lipstick by a well-known fashion model may enhance the appeal of the product to working girls. But, "In Belgium (for example) it doesn't. Models are scarce and their trade is hardly considered honorable."[45] Illustrations for the same product may have to differ from country to country. In

---

[42]John Caffyn and Nigel Rogers, "British Reactions to T.V. Commercials," *Journal of Advertising Research* 10, no. 3, (June 1970): p. 27.

[43]"Put a Tiger in Your Tank," *Marketing Insights,* November 28, 1966, p. v.

[44]*Business Week,* September 12, 1970, p. 49.

[45]Dan E. G. Rosseals, "Consumer Habits and Consumer Advertising in the Benelux Countries," *Export Trade and Shipper,* January 28, 1957, p. 17.

Germany an advertisement for cheese might show a large, foaming glass of beer, but in France the advertisement would substitute a glass of red wine.

In the area of media selection, considerable deviation from home-country patterns may be required, particularly for American companies. In many countries, ownership of radio and television media is in the hands of the government and no commercials are allowed. The barring of radio to advertisers in much of Europe has been evaded to some extent by using commercial stations in locations such as Luxembourg and Monte Carlo to reach European audiences. Several imaginative entrepreneurs even established "pirate ships" as broadcasting stations outside the three-mile limit to bypass the laws against commercial radio in the Scandinavian countries. Except for these media restrictions, the availability and capability of media in foreign countries are similar to the United States. But the coverage and relative economic cost of foreign media are different and require adaptation.[46]

One special feature of international advertising deserves to be mentioned. Most of the principal American advertising firms have gone international. They are particularly well represented in Europe. With many U.S. domestic advertisers expanding overseas, U.S. advertising agencies have expanded internationally as a defensive measure, required in some cases in order to keep the domestic business. This trend has increased the capability of advertising agencies that work with headquarters of multinational firms to develop advertising programs that have international appeal from the beginning.

In summary, the principles underlying communication by advertising are the same in all nations. It is only the specific methods, techniques, and symbols which sometimes must be varied to take account of diverse environmental conditions. Uniform advertising for various market segments, whether national or international, have tremendous economic advantages for the firm. The critical questions for the multinational firm are *when* and *when not* to make adjustments. The best strategy is to try to take into account the international differences when preparing an advertising campaign and to export the same advertising approach to as many different markets as possible. But final decisions on copy or media should be handled by personnel who have intimate knowledge of foreign markets.

---

[46]C. D. Philips, "Radio Broadcasting in the Sudan," *NAEB Journal* 23 (July–August 1964): 59. In Sudan, radio ownership was found to be out of proportion to the incomes of people. A radio is a status symbol and even the lowest paid laborer has a personal portable transistor.

EXPORT MARKETING AND EAST-WEST TRADE

Export marketing deserves separate mention even though most aspects of reaching foreign markets through exports have already been touched upon.[47] Where production is restricted to the home country for reasons of company strategy or the economics of location, the principal issue in export marketing is whether the firm should engage in indirect exporting where no special activity is carried on in the firm, or in direct international marketing. In most of the indirect approaches, foreign sales are handled in essentially the same way as domestic sales, and a minimum of international marketing know-how is required by the firm. For U.S. firms, the indirect approach generally means that the enterprise is small and that its international commitment and potential is limited. For a Japanese company, on the other hand, the use of the indirect approach may be explained by the availability of large and experienced international trading firms which have a significant comparative advantage in foreign selling even over direct operations by large enterprises.

In direct exporting, the responsibility for identifying markets, physical distribution, export documentation, pricing, and so on all become the responsibility of the export department or the export manager. Where exporting is only part of the activities of a multinational firm, and sales are mainly to foreign subsidiaries as components or inputs to foreign production or to sales subsidiaries of the enterprise itself, many of the marketing functions such as market research, promotion, and pricing are assumed in whole or in part by the subsidiary. But where export sales are directed primarily to independent foreign buyers, export pricing in particular becomes a critical issue. Decisions have to be made as to whether exports should be at full-cost or marginal-cost pricing, whether prices should be quoted as f.o.b. (free on board) or c.i.f. (cost, insurance, freight) to foreign ports and in home-country currencies or in the currency of the market being served, and on how to use export credit.

Exporting has received intense attention by the less developed countries because of the need to earn foreign exchange for financing their development efforts.[48] More recently, the United States has also given emphasis to the encouragement of exporting. As a result, an extensive amount of literature has emerged on the how-to-do-it of

---

[47]For a specialized study on export marketing, see Franklin R. Root, *Strategic Planning for Export Marketing* (Scranton, Pa.: International Textbook Co., 1966).

[48]For example, see Amicus Most, *Expanding Exports: A Case Study of the Korean Experience* (Washington, D.C.: Agency for International Development, June 1969).

export promotion, and governments have adopted incentive programs and developed facilities for offering technical assistance to exporters with which international managers need to become familiar.

A specialized area of export marketing is that of selling to centrally planned economies of the Soviet Union, mainland China, and Eastern Europe. Over the last decade, these markets have begun to open up to international companies of Western nationality. But unlike the usual business experience of selling directly to consumers or users, sales to the centrally planned countries are arranged through government trade ministries.[49] Imports are planned along with domestic production in both annual and five-year plans, but these requirements are never published. The currencies of these countries are not freely convertible. Barter or special financial arrangements are generally required. Because of long-standing U.S. restrictions on East-West trade, U.S. multinational companies have developed much less experience in trading with the Sino-Soviet-bloc countries than have international companies of European and Japanese nationality. However, some U.S. companies have gained expertise by doing business through their European subsidiaries. Also, a number of U.S. trading companies now specialize in trading with the Soviet Union, Eastern Europe, and mainland China because of the unique features of this type of exporting.

SUMMARY

The basic functions involved in managing the product mix and the marketing activity are the same for both domestic and international markets, but the implementation can be quite different because of environmental differences. Consequently, the international firm faces many special problems in selecting its marketing mission and in adjusting its mix of marketing actions. Throughout most dimensions of the marketing function, there is a conflict between differentiation to meet the needs of market segments and international standardization to reduce costs. The conflict relates to product strategies, pricing, advertising, and the way in which the marketing activity is organized. Unfortunately, there are no general or fixed rules for resolving this conflict. The international marketing manager must therefore be constantly alert to the impact of decisions for any unit in the multinational system on the corporation as a whole.

---

[49]For example, see Lyman E. Ostlund and Kjell M. Halversen, "The Russian Decision Process Governing Trade," *Journal of Marketing* 36, no. 2 (April 1972): 3–11.

APPENDIX

Table 20A–1 illustrates how different price elasticities will lead to different price policies for subsidiaries in different markets where each obtains its supplies at the same unit cost and acts to maximize its profit. At a transfer price of £50 from the supplying unit, *Country A* would sell at £75 and *Country B* at £90. An increased transfer price, however, would lead to increased prices in both countries.

Given that the selling subsidiaries are motivated to maximize their profits, they will price so that their marginal revenue just equals the marginal cost to them. The greatest system profit will then emerge if a unit is charged a transfer price equal to the cost of supplying a unit which in most cases can be taken to be the variable cost of production and distribution. The nearer the transfer price is to this variable cost, the closer a subsidiary's pricing policy will bring the firm to maximizing its contribution over and above this variable cost. Table 20A–2 illustrates how the system profits increase as the transfer price is brought down to variable cost in this way.

Suppose now that the firm were to fix the final market price in order to maintain uniform world prices. Inevitably this would lead to a decreased system contribution because, in this case, one subsidiary or both would be forced away from an optimal adjustment to the particular situation ruling in its market. Comparing Table 20A–3 with

TABLE 20A–1

	Price (in £)							
	100	*95*	*90*	*85*	*80*	*75*	*70*	*65*
Sales volume that would result								
Country A (units). . . .	900	1,400	2,000	2,600	3,300	4,000	4,500	5,000
Country B (units). . . .	1,200	1,400	1,600	1,800	2,000	2,200	2,400	2,600
Total revenue								
Country A (£000s). . .	90	133	180	221	264	300	315	325
Country B (£000s). . .	120	133	144	153	160	165	168	169
Contribution when transfer price = £50								
Country A (£000s)	45	63	80	91	99	100*	90	75
Country B (£000s)	60	63	64*	63	60	55	48	39
£60								
Country A (£000s)	36	49	60	65	66*	60	45	25
Country B (£000s)	48	49*	48	45	40	33	24	13
£70								
Country A (£000s)	27	35	40*	39	33	20	—	—
Country B (£000s)	36*	35	32	27	20	11	—	—

*Indicates greatest contribution for a given transfer price.

Table 20A–2, it can be seen that no choice of a common price level for the two markets would produce a contribution for any given variable cost that is as high as that possible when the prices are adjusted separately.

TABLE 20A–2

	Sales Volume to Maximize Contributions				System Contribution When Variable Cost =		
Transfer Price	Country A (units)	Country B (units)	Total Units	Total Revenue (£000s)	£40 (£000s)	£50 (£000s)	£60 (£000s)
£40	4,000	1,800	5,800	453	221*	—	—
£50	4,000	1,600	5,600	444	220	164*	—
£60	3,300	1,400	4,700	397	209	162	115*
£70	2,000	1,200	3,200	300	172	140	108

*Indicates transfer price bringing greatest contribution for a given variable cost.

TABLE 20A–3

Common Market Price (£S)	Combined Volume Country A + B (units)	Contribution When Variable Cost =		
		£40 (£000s)	£50 (£000s)	£60 (£000s)
100. 2,100		126	105	84
95. 2,800		154	126	98
90. 3,600		180	144	108
85. 4,400		198	154	110*
80. 5,300		212	159*	106
75. 6,200		217*	154	93
70. 6,900		207	138	69
65. 7,600		190	114	38

*Indicates price bringing greatest contribution for a given variable cost.

EXERCISES AND DISCUSSION QUESTIONS

1. In what ways does a strategy of joint ventures rather than wholly owned subsidiaries place constraints on the task of managing the international product mix?

2. "There is a movement on the part of European companies for greater standardization and guidance of marketing policies in U.S. operations, particularly in relatively low-technology, high-market-saturation product areas such as petroleum, paper, and various sorts of consumer goods." In what ways do you think the type of product influences the degree of centralization and standardization?

3. Examine Tables 20A–2 and 20A–3 and explain why no choice of a common

price level for the two markets will contribute as much to profits as is possible when prices are adjusted separately.

4. What are the main advantages and disadvantages of manipulating intra-company transfer prices?

5. "Until we achieve One World, there is no such thing as international marketing—only local marketing around the world." Do you agree or disagree and why?

6. Why do national differences in distribution channels frequently result in gaps in market coverage?

7. Do products sold primarily on the basis of objective physical characteristics such as razor blades and automobile tires, lend themselves to uniform international advertising strategies more than products such as foods or dress clothing? If so, why?

21

International Financial Management

WHAT NEW DIMENSIONS are added to the financial management function as an enterprise expands its international commitment? At a minimum level of international business involvement such as incidental importing and exporting activities, the financial manager has to deal with only a few international elements such as multiple currencies and alternative sources and techniques of import-export credit. But as a firm becomes a global enterprise, the new complexities not encountered domestically increase dramatically.

In the multinational enterprise, the financial manager must deal with many different currencies. He or she must work with units in the system that are organized and operating under different legal and tax systems and must take into account variations in inflation trends, interest rates, tax burdens, and the availability and costs of capital in the domestic environments in which units of the system operate. In addition, the manager must recognize the impact of national controls on financial flows across national boundaries.

In brief, international as compared to domestic financial management involves new environmental considerations, new sources of risk, and new opportunities for economies and efficiencies from an integrated global financial system. To deal with the environmental differences, the international financial manager must be familiar with the international financial framework and many national situations and have an effective global intelligence system that keeps such information current. The new risks such as foreign exchange risk and changes in tax liability that arise because of movements of funds across national borders require a considerable forecasting input into international

481

financial management. The new opportunities arising out of access to many capital markets and the potentials for achieving indirect benefits in one part of the system from activities in another part require the development of complex management tools for optimizing financial goals on a systemwide basis. By taking a systems approach, the criterion for any particular financial decision should be the potential contribution of this decision to the entire system at the margin.

The international financial elements have already been introduced in Part II as components of the environmental framework. In this chapter, the same elements will be recast into a managerial framework and related to capital-budgeting decisions, continuing financial operations, and the control function. As information flows are the basic material for performing the financial management function, the subject of accounting in international business will be considered first. It should be noted, however, that this chapter is limited to the international financial function in industrial and commercial firms. Financial intermediaries, such as banks and insurance companies, have their own financial problems, which will not be considered here.

REPORTING FOR INTERNATIONAL FINANCIAL MANAGEMENT

Effective financial management requires a continuing flow of meaningful reports. These reports must provide financial data for decision purposes that are understandable both in the country in which a particular unit of the enterprise is operating and in the regional headquarters and home country where decisions involving more than one country have to be made. To prepare such reports on an accurate and timely basis requires a determined effort to overcome several obstacles. These include the multiple currency problem, major variations in the accounting systems that must be used by various units in the system, and time lags due to competing demands for staff time and geographic distances. Fortunately, the technology for solving many of these problems is readily available. Time delays can be minimized by accessing computer networks which link most parts of the industrialized world and permit rapid storage, processing, and dissemination of data among business units. The express letter and telex have long been available throughout the world. Much has been learned during recent years about how to refine and interpret financial data prepared in various countries, which are subject to different accounting systems and affected by varying degrees of internal inflation and exchange-rate change. The international financial manager must seek to obtain enough information about the current and future financial status of various units to evaluate and analyze financing alternatives. The financial manager will be forced to evaluate risks and make decisions regardless of whether adequate data on which to base the decisions have been synthesized. Obviously, the likelihood of making costly mistakes can be reduced by accumulating as much relevant information about the factors involved as is practicable. What information is needed?

The Exposure Report[1]

To manage the financial positions of geographically dispersed business units, the international financial manager requires a foreign exchange exposure report and a flow-of-funds schedule. These financials, together with balance sheets and income statements for the various units, provide sufficient information on which to base informed decisions.

Foreign exchange gains and losses affect the overall earnings of the enterprise. Consequently, the financial manager must be aware of foreign exchange exposure as well as various units' cash positions. A foreign exchange exposure report is similar to a balance sheet with the exception that several items considered to be protected from foreign exchange risk are omitted. Under recently adopted accounting rules, which are discussed below, the items not considered exposed include inventory, fixed assets, intangible assets, long-term investments, and owners equity. Off-balance sheet items, such as foreign exchange contracts and future commitments to sell or purchase and to make lease or rental payments, must be included in the exposure report as well. Another major difference between a foreign exchange exposure report and a balance sheet is that the exposure report states the assets and liabilities in the currencies in which they are denominated. Whereas the balance sheet for a Brazilian affiliate will list all items in local currency (cruzeiros), the exposure report will distinguish between the cruzeiro and noncruzeiro denominated transactions and commitments of the affiliate. The reason for the distinction is that cruzeiro receivables derived from local sales are likely to have a different value when collected than that of export sales resulting in French franc receivables, even though both receivables may have had the same value at the time of sale.

An example will help to clarify this distinction. A British-based company, Winfield Products Ltd., has a subsidiary in the Philippines which manufactures solid-wood products for sale in the local, Japanese, and U.S. markets. The Philippine subsidiary's balance sheet is

---

[1]This section draws heavily from *Corporate Foreign Exposure Management* (New York: First National City Bank, 1975).

shown in Figure 21–1. The balance sheet conceals important information from the international financial manager. It appears as though the subsidiary has more liabilities denominated in pesos than current assets—32,500 versus 19,520 of pound sterling equivalents. In reality, there are more peso assets, as revealed in the foreign exchange exposure report (Figure 21–2), because most of the liabilities are denominated in foreign currencies. The balance sheet also hides important exposure elements—the 1,000 pounds of yen-equivalent futures sales commitments, 6,000 pounds of yen-equivalent purchase commitments, and 5,000 pounds of German mark-equivalent purchase contracts. These off–balance sheet items are picked up in the exposure report and provide crucial added information on which to assess the impact of a Philippine peso devaluation or revaluation on Winfield Products operations.

The international financial manager can now calculate the exact impact of currency change on profitability once applicable tax regulations and accounting treatment are incorporated in the analysis. With respect to the subsidiary profiled in Figure 21–2, the firm has 1,900 pounds of Philippine peso-equivalent net asset exposure; 18,980 pounds of U.S. dollar-equivalent net liability exposure; and 3,100 pounds of Japanese yen-equivalent net liability exposure. When predicted exchange-rate changes are applied to these exposures, the magnitudes of loss or gain can be derived after making the necessary adjustments for taxes.

FIGURE 21–1

Winfield Products Ltd. Balance Sheet for Winfield Philippines (pounds sterling at £/peso spot rate on December 31, 1976; in 000s)

Assets			*Liabilities*	
Cash		1,760	Accounts payable.	4,000
Short-term investments.		—	Taxes payable	500
Accounts receivables		10,445	Other payable	—
Intercompany advances		—	Intercompany payable . . .	8,000
Inventory		7,200	Total current	
Finished goods	3,200		liabilities.	12,500
Work in process.	2,450			
Raw materials	1,550		Long-term debt.	20,000
Other current assets.		115		
			Total liabilities	32,500
Total current assets . . .		19,520		
			Capital stock	5,000
Plant and equipment		18,900	Earned surplus.	2,920
Gross.	21,000			
Less depreciation	2,100			
Land		2,000	Total equity	7,920
Total assets		40,420		40,420

FIGURE 21–2
Winfield Products Ltd. Foreign Exchange Exposure Report for Winfield Philippines (pounds sterling at £/peso spot rate on December 31, 1976; in 000s)

Assets and Liabilities	Philippine Pesos	U.S. Dollars	Japanese Yen	German Mark	Consolidated Figures
Cash/short-term investments	1,760	—	—	—	1,760
Accounts receivables	3,625	4,420	2,400	—	10,445
Intercompany advances and receivables	—	—	—	—	—
Other exposed assets	115	—	—	—	115
Foreign exchange purchase contracts	—	—	—	5,000	5,000
Future signed sales commitments	—	—	1,000	—	1,000
Exposed assets	5,500	4,420	3,400	5,000	18,320
Accounts, taxes, other payables	3,600	400	500	—	4,500
Intercompany advances and payables	—	8,000	—	—	8,000
Long-term debt	—	15,000	—	5,000	20,000
Foreign exchange sales contracts	—	—	—	—	—
Future signed purchase commitments and leases	—	—	6,000	—	6,000
Exposed liabilities	3,600	23,400	6,500	5,000	38,500
Net position	1,900	(18,980)	(3,100)	—	n.a.*

*n.a. = not available.

The Flow-of-Funds Report

Although the exposure report has provided additional insights regarding the Philippine subsidiary's financial condition, the information base is still incomplete. The deficiency relates to the static nature of both the balance sheet and the foreign exchange exposure report. These financial reports pinpoint conditions as of December 31, 1976—a single point in time. For example, the exposure report suggests that the 5,000 German mark debt is offset by 5,000 mark purchase contracts at year end, and that, therefore, no mark exposure exists. Yet the German mark debt may be repaid at some future date, say, 5 years hence, which does not coincide with the maturity date of the purchase contract, say, 6 months. The mark debt and purchase contract, therefore, are not truly offsetting.

Accounting regulations, as outlined in the next section, place great emphasis on this static aspect of managing foreign exchange exposures. These regulations sometimes provoke international financial managers into making decisions that are suboptimal from an economic point of view. To illustrate, the financial manager may be persuaded to "roll over," i.e., renew the 5,000 German mark purchase contract when it matures in 6 months in order to offset the mark debt, even though no money is needed to repay the principal on the debt for 5 years. The reason is to offset the mark debt on the balance sheet with mark purchase contracts at all times, thereby avoiding the need to report any accounting loss resulting from revaluation of the mark.

Yet the mark purchase contracts, rolled over every six months, have little nonspeculative value. At each rollover date the firm must sell the marks from the preceding purchase contract at the prevailing spot exchange rate, since it does not need the marks to repay the debt for many years. (It simultaneously purchases the marks forward six months to achieve the desired balance sheet offset.) The sale of marks every six months at undetermined exchange rates causes unknown cash gains or losses, and these cash-flow effects can be far more important than accounting implications.

The funds-flow report supplies data about the future flow of currencies. By profiling business transactions on an ongoing basis, it provides the necessary dynamic elements for incorporating cash-flow considerations into exposure management decisions. A funds-flow report for the Winfield Philippines subsidiary is shown as Figure 21–3. This statement is based on information supplied by the affiliate

FIGURE 21–3
Winfield Products, Ltd. Flow-of-Funds Report for Winfield Philippines (pounds sterling at spot rate on December 31, 1976; in 000s)

Maturity	Net Assets and Liabilities				
	Philippine Pesos	U.S. Dollars	Japanese Yen	German Mark	Consolidated Figures
Cash and net receivables.	1,900	4,020	1,900	0	7,820
Month 1.	(3,500)	2,400	1,500	—	400
Month 2.	(3,500)	2,400	1,500	(200)	200
Month 3.	(3,500)	2,400	1,500	—	400
Month 4.	(3,500)	2,400	1,500	—	400
Month 5.	(3,500)	2,400	1,500	—	400
Month 6.	(3,500)	(2,700)	1,500	5,000	300
Months 7–9.	(10,500)	7,200	4,500	(200)	1,000
Months 10–12	(10,500)	7,200	4,500	—	1,200
More than 12 months	—	(23,000)	(5,000)	(5,000)	(33,000)
Total.	(40,100)	4,720	14,900	(400)	(20,880)

concerning such factors as estimated sales during the forthcoming year, currency of receivables denomination, and assumptions about receivables collection. The funds-flow report illustrates that exposures in the different currencies vary dramatically over time and that the static balance sheet exposure is often insignificant in comparison to the exposure generated by the flows of an ongoing business. With the added information in the funds-flow report the international financial manager can evaluate how various means of protection against foreign exchange risk affect exposure to accounting and cash-flow losses over time. If the reporting system does not provide this added dimension, decisions will be based on incomplete information.

Accounting for International Operations

The accounting system for an international company must satisfy several requirements simultaneously. It must provide the kinds the information described above on which managerial decisions can be based. In addition, the accounting system must provide financial statements that can be consolidated on an enterprise-wide basis. To fulfill the consolidation requirements, the labeling and content of accounts must be uniform throughout the system and major difficulties inherent in translating values from one currency to another must be resolved.

The process of restating financial accounts from one currency to another is referred to as *translation.* The actual sale of one currency for another is called *conversion.* When foreign currency financial reports are transmitted for combination or consolidation at headquarters, the typical sequence would be to adjust them for home-country accounting principles and procedures. After such adjustments, local currencies are translated into home-country currency amounts. While many companies disagree vehemently regarding the prescribed translation method, at least there is now a single set of guidelines to which all U.S. public corporations and foreign corporations that issue securities in the United States must now conform. Prior to 1976, companies were permitted by independent auditors to choose among alternative translation procedures.

These principles are embodied in Bulletin #8 of the Financial Accounting Standards Board (FASB) which was released during 1975. In essence, this pronouncement requires companies to translate results of foreign operations into the currency of the home company (for U.S. companies into U.S. dollars) using the "temporal method." In the application of this method all financial assets and liabilities—cash, receivables, marketable securities, payables, and debt—are translated from local currency into the currency of the home country at current, or ending, exchange rates, that is, the rates of exchange prevailing at the date when the financial statements are prepared. The translation of these "revaluable" financial assets and liabilities gives rise to gains or losses to the extent that exchange rates have fluctuated during the accounting period vis-a-vis the currency of the home country. If local currencies have depreciated relative to the home currency, revaluable local currency assets will result in losses, and revaluable local currency liabilities will result in gains; appreciation of local currencies relative to the home currency produce the opposite result. According to FASB #8, these gains and losses are to be included in reported income as incurred, rather than deferred or amortized over several accounting periods.

To illustrate how the translation process works, the financial statements of the German subsidiary of a U.S. company are shown in Figure 21–4. According to FASB #8 guidelines, the German subsidiary has 2,800,000 of U.S. dollar-equivalent revaluable assets—that is, the cash and receivables; and 7,000,000 of dollar-equivalent revaluable liabilities. Its net liability exposure is thus, 4,200,000 of U.S. dollar equivalents—the difference between exposed assets and exposed liabilities. Assuming that the mark revalues 10 percent against the dollar during the accounting period—from $0.40 to $0.44—the dollar equivalent of these net mark liabilities will increase by $420,000 (10 percent of $4,200,000). This increase in the dollar equivalent of the mark liabilities must be recorded in the consolidated financials as a foreign exchange loss. Moreover, this loss of $420,000 (4.2 percent of total assets) must be reflected in the current period's financials. It cannot, as was permitted in the past, be amortized over the maturity pattern of the liabilities.

This example highlights one of the troublesome dimensions of the prescribed translation rule for international financial managers. What does the foreign exchange loss mean? Perhaps the operating prospects of the German subsidiary will suffer due to the mark revaluation. If the

FIGURE 21–4

German Subsidiary Balance Sheet as of a Specific Date (U.S. $000s; translated from deutsche marks)

Assets		*Liabilities*	
Cash	600	Accounts payable	1,000
Receivables	2,200	Short-term debt	1,500
Inventory	2,200	Current liabilities	2,500
Current assets	5,000	Long-term debt	4,500
Net plant	5,000	Equity	3,000
Total assets	10,000	Total liabilities and equity	10,000

subsidiary exports to countries whose currencies have devalued, it may encounter difficulties in maintaining its market share. In all likelihood, however, the reported exchange loss will overstate the future operating losses caused by increased competition in export markets. If the subsidiary sells only within Germany, the loss will be overstated further.

How can the international financial manager avoid or reduce the company's vulnerability to accounting losses? The answer is obvious—simply denominate the subsidiary's debt in dollars instead of marks. By repaying the mark debt with $4,500,000 of dollar borrowings, the financial manager can reduce the accounting vulnerability to $300,000 of net asset exposure. Then if the mark revalues by 10 percent, there will be a foreign exchange gain of $30,000 instead of the $420,000 loss. Additionally, with only $300,000 of exposure, even significant exchange-rate changes will have only minor impact on consolidated profits. From an operating viewpoint, however, this shift in denomination of debt could have disastrous consequences. The German subsidiary generates deutsche mark cash flows, with only a minor percentage of its sales going to the United States. A funds-flow report, as shown in Figure 21–3, would reveal that the German subsidiary would now have a large overhang of dollar debt payments with no offsetting dollar inflows. In effect, the exchange risk has been shifted from the balance sheet that FASB #8 emphasizes to operations. The operating risk is real in the sense that the dollar debt obligation might conceivably bankrupt the Germany subsidiary. The affiliate might be unable to generate sufficient marks which, when converted to dollars, are sufficient to repay the external dollar debt. Without dollar cash inflows, the German subsidiary lacks a natural hedge or offset for the borrowing, and the short-term accounting "solution" should not be selected. As a consequence of the accounting translation guidelines, international financial managers are sometimes confronted with the dilemma just illustrated. They must choose between protecting the consolidated balance sheet from foreign exchange losses and selecting financial structures for affiliates that maximize long-term economic prospects.

Another major accounting issue is whether reports should be consolidated. A parent corporation can treat its investments in foreign subsidiaries as it would treat portfolio investments. Such investments are carried at cost, and income is shown only when actually received in the form of dividends, interest, or service charges. Consolidated statements that include the foreign subsidiaries give much more information about the operations over time and the situation at a balance sheet date. For companies with a substantial fraction of their activities conducted through foreign subsidiaries, consolidation seems desirable for informing both management and the public about the true state of affairs.

Yet, the process of consolidating accounts for multinational operations has many technical hazards. The financial statements to be consolidated have a domicile in terms of an underlying set of accounting principles, and such domicile orientation cannot be easily changed through restatements or adjustments of the financial statements themselves. For example, financial statements prepared according to good accounting practices in Argentina and then restated somehow to a Canadian basis would differ markedly from those resulting if the Argentine operation had taken place in Canada and been accounted for originally in terms of Canadian practices. Consolidation raises such problems as the treatment of reserves for future taxes on repatriated profits. A conservative accounting approach that includes such reserves in a consolidation, even though it is unlikely that the taxes will be paid, can be misleading as to the profitability of a foreign operation. A similar problem can arise in the treatment of depreciation expenses. To secure comparability among subsidiaries, a uniform rate of depreciation may be used. But to reduce current taxes and increase cash flows, the most rapid rate of depreciation allowed for local tax purposes should be taken. Faster depreciation for a subsidiary in a country where tax laws permit it will increase cash flows but decrease net income in the short run. To consolidate the accounts of foreign subsidiaries, the financial manager may thus face a two-stage exercise: first, restatement according to home-country accounting and then translation of accounts into the home-currency conventions. This two-stage process is illustrated in Figure 21–5.

Other accounting problems arise with transfer pricing, service charges of various sorts, and the allocation of headquarters and research expenses to the subsidiaries. Generally, the parent-company management reserves final authority in such decisions and attempts to make them in terms of systemwide optimization. Thus, financial comparisons and evaluations of local operating companies may be determined as much by parent-company decisions as by the actual operating results of the subsidiaries. In many cases, therefore, it is extremely difficult to make the necessary adjustments for a fair evaluation of the profitability of individual units of the enterprise.

Given the multiple purposes that must be served simultaneously by financial reporting and the variations in accounting principles, multinational enterprises are finding it necessary to use three or four different sets of financial statements. National financial statements are prepared on the basis of nationally accepted accounting principles. A second set of financial statements is prepared by each unit of the system which complies with the accounting principles and the translation methods that are accepted in the country of the home office. Still

FIGURE 21–5

Restatement and Translation of a Subsidiary's Accounts for Consolidation Purposes

	Subsidiary's Accounts before Adjustment (000 pesos)	Adjustments (000 pesos)	Restatement (000 pesos)	Translation into U.S. Dollars Using "Temporal Method" ($000)
Revenue account				
Sales	3,600	—	3,600	180
Less cost of sales	2,400	−120	2,280	114
Gross margin.	1,200	+120	1,320	66
Less expenses	1,075	− 80	995	50
Profit before tax	125	+200	325	16
Taxation provision	25	+137	162	8
Net profit	100	+ 63	163	8
Assets and liabilities				
Cash	50		50	3
Accounts receivables.	850		850	42
Inventories	700		700	47
Current assets	1,600		1,600	92
Current liabilities	1,100	+137	1,237	62
Working capital	500	−137	363	30
Fixed assets.	600	+ 80	680	45
	1,100	− 57	1,043	75
Long-term liabilities	300	—	300	15
Net worth	800	− 57	743	48
Capital	600	—	600	40

Adjustments are required as follows:

Reduce cost of sales by 120,000 pesos representing parent-company margin eliminated from last year's consolidation.

Reduce depreciation by 80,000 pesos to express it at standard rates used by parent company.

Increase taxation provision from 20 percent to 50 percent to allow for tax on future profit remittances.

another set may be prepared to comply with the regulations of the various tax authorities involved. And finally, separate financial statements may be prepared which present a picture for management of the enterprise. In such a statement, for example, uniform valuation methods for assets of all subsidiaries might be used, regardless of the different legal regulations or locally accepted accounting practices.

MANAGING FOREIGN EXCHANGE RISK

For many multinationals, managing foreign exchange exposures—that is, responding to anticipated changes in exchange rates—is the most important international financial challenge. Changes in the value of currencies, generally devaluations but sometimes revaluations, have been frequent and significant in amount. But statistics on the number and extent of changes understate the frequency with which the financial manager must be concerned with foreign exchange risk. The number of devaluations or revaluations has been much fewer than the number of false alarms, which must be considered and dealt with.

The risk of foreign exchange loss is run not only by companies with foreign operations, but also by any company with a receivable or payable to be collected or paid in a foreign currency. The problem can be illustrated most simply in the case of importing and exporting. The trader is exposed to the risk of a loss from the depreciation in value of a foreign currency he has contracted to receive in the future, or a loss from the appreciation in value of a foreign currency he has contracted to deliver in the future. If a U.S. exporter had sold merchandise to a British buyer and agreed to accept payment in pounds, and if the U.K. devaluation in 1975 from $2.35 to $2.05 occurred between the time of the sale and the time the exporter collects for the sale, the exporter would receive 9 percent less in U.S. dollars than he had expected. He would suffer an exchange loss of 9 percent of the sale.

The exposure of the trader is limited to foreign currency receivable or payable. The exposure of the multinational enterprise is far more complex. The firm has a range of assets and liabilities that are exposed in the sense that a currency fluctuation will change their value in the yardstick currency of the company. For U.S. companies, the U.S. dollar has normally been the yardstick because it is U.S. dollars that are to be maximized, not foreign currency profits. A truly multinational company, however, might logically consider the strongest world currency, such as the Swiss franc, as its yardstick and try to manage foreign exchange risk so as to protect values in that currency.

There are five components to managing foreign exchange risk. First, the enterprise must collect timely information regarding all aspects of its operations that have foreign exchange implications. As noted earlier, this information pertaining to current financial conditions and future prospects should be summarized in exposure reports and funds-flow reports for each entity. These data regarding currency exposures must be supplemented by the latest information regarding taxes, currency restrictions, and hedging (protective) options which apply in each country.

The second component of exposure management is the series of accounting rules affecting translation with which various units of the enterprise must comply. These rules, and ultimately FASB #8 for U.S. companies, govern the magnitude of accounting exposure with which the enterprise must contend. The presence of exposure and the possibility of losses usually cannot be permanently avoided without changing the operations of the firm, because the net exposure is created by the normal operations of the enterprise. Despite the importance of protecting the profit statement and projecting a good image to shareholders, the accounting rules should not be permitted to harm the firm's business prospects or methods of conducting operations. For this reason, a third dimension of exposure management is crucial.

Each enterprise must have a strategy for exposure management. After taking into account both short-term accounting and longer-term funds-flow implications, the firm must judicially conclude how much and what types of foreign exchange exposure it is prepared to assume. In virtually all situations it is impossible or prohibitively expensive to insure against all foreign exchange risk. How much risk is an enterprise willing to accept to improve its return on capital? The philosophy of management and stockholders determines the answer to this question.

A fourth dimension to exposure management is a method of forecasting the amount, timing, pattern, and probability of changes in foreign exchange rates, as was suggested in Chapter 16. The forecasts suggest the magnitude of possible gains or losses resulting from given levels of exposure. Thus, they provide an indispensable ingredient in calculating whether it pays to buy protection against given exposures. Many of the multinationals noted for their international financial expertise have hired their own specialists to make currency predictions. Other firms rely on international banks and international advisory services for insights into probable currency movements.

A final exposure component is the implementation system. Given the analysis of the firm's exposures and the forecast of foreign exchange rates, the financing manager can work out a protection strategy making use of the growing body of quantitative and model-building work available on managing foreign exchange risk.[2] Many

---

[2]For example, see Bernard A. Lietaer, *Financial Management of Foreign Exchange* (Cambridge, Mass.: The M.I.T. Press, 1971); Alan Shapiro, "Hedging Against Devaluation—A Management Science Approach," *In International Business Systems Perspectives,* ed. C. Alexandrides (Atlanta: Georgia State University Press, 1973); Gunter Dufey, "Corporate Finance and Exchange Rate Variations," *Financial Management,* Summer 1972; William R. Folks, Jr., "Decision Analysis for Exchange Risk Management," *Financial Management,* Winter 1972; William R. Folks, Jr., "The Optimal Level of Forward Exchange Transaction," *Journal of Financial and Quantitative Analysis,* January 1973; Richard K. Goeltz, "Managing Liquid Funds Internationally," *Columbia Journal of World Business,* July–August 1972; Don S. Gull, "Corporate Foreign Exchange Risk," *Columbia Journal of World Business,* Fall 1975; Newton H. Hoyt, Jr., "The Management of Currency Exchange Risk by the Foreign Company," *Financial Management,* Spring 1972; Bernard A. Lietaer, "Managing Risks in Foreign Exchange," *Harvard Business Review,* March–April 1970; David Rutenberg, "Maneuvering Liquid Assets in a Multinational Corporation," *Management Science,* June 1970; Alan C. Shapiro, "Optimal Inventory and Credit-Granting Strategies under Inflation and Devaluation," *Journal of Financial and Quantitative Analysis,* January 1973.

means of minimizing foreign exchange losses are available to the financial manager, including financing alternatives and foreign exchange contracts. The manager can accelerate payments of accounts and remittances to hard-currency countries. He or she can delay dollar inflows and try to delay obligations such as accounts payable, loans, and taxes due in local currency. He or she can try to accelerate local currency receivables through intensive collection efforts, reduction of credit terms, and offers of generous discounts. The manager can use currency or credit swaps when local financing cannot be arranged. For a short list of international financing instruments commonly used and their hedging implications, see Figure 21–6.

After calculating net exposure and working out financing alternatives and reduction of exposure, the financial manager will try to use

FIGURE 21–6
Typical International Transactions and Their Financing and Hedging Implications

Dollar financing: Credits repayable in U.S. dollars.

Foreign currency credits: Financing repayable in foreign currency, such as foreign bank loans, overdrafts, or other lines of credit.

Discounting or factoring of foreign bills or promissory notes: The borrowing technique by which the company draws a bill or note on its commercial bank (discounting); alternatively, the sale of receivables to a factor (factoring), which accelerates the conversion of foreign currency claims into cash.

Forward exchange contracts: The purchase or sale of foreign currency at a given rate for future delivery.

Financial swaps: Transactions in which equivalent amounts of dollars and foreign currencies are swapped for a given period, at the end of which both parties return the original amounts of each currency.

Arbi loans (International Interest Arbitrage Loans): Transactions that enable a company to increase financing in a scarce currency by supplementing it with capital from a country where money is abundant and cheap. (Money is borrowed in the cheap-money market and simultaneously transferred to the tight-money country, and a forward exchange contract is arranged that bears the same maturity as the loan itself.)

Here is a summary of the effects that these various transactions have:

	Cash availability	Net exposure
Dollar financing	Increases	No effect
Foreign currency credits	Increases	Decreases
Discounting or factoring	Increases	Decreases
Forward exchange contracts	No effect	Decreases
Financial swaps	Increases	Decreases
Arbi loans	Increases	Decreases

Source: Bernard A. Lietaer, "Managing Risks in Foreign Exchange," *Harvard Business Review,* March–April 1970, p. 128.

the forward exchange market to cover the rest of the exposure, providing the cost of such cover compares favorably with the prospective loss. In some cases the cost of insurance will be too high or nonfinancial considerations such as local goodwill are involved so that the company itself will absorb the foreign exchange loss. To use a simple example, suppose that the forecaster gives an estimated devaluation size of 20 percent and a probability of occurrence of 75 percent, and suppose the forecaster has been wrong 10 percent of the time.[3] These three factors multiplied together ($0.20 \times 0.75 \times 1.10$) equal 16.5 percent. This result is multiplied by the company treasurer's safety factor which reflects the company's willingness to accept risk, say, a 15 percent safety factor. Then, 16.5 percent multiplied by 1.15 equals 18.98 percent. This number can be compared with the market cost of cover to reach a decision. Suppose the annual market discount rate on forward contracts is 15 percent. The treasurer would spin off the risk because the cover cost is less than the expected loss indicated by the analysis. If the market price of cover is 22 percent, the company would self-insure because the cost of the cover would be more expensive than the probable loss.

INVESTMENT DECISIONS AND CAPITAL BUDGETING

Investment decisions represent ultimate control over the operating subsidiaries and a principal means of implementing the global strategy of a multinational enterprise. Although decisions to establish new operations or expand existing ones are based on many considerations, the financial manager invariably plays a key role through his responsibility for analyzing and comparing the expected returns and other financial features of alternative proposals. This financial management activity is normally performed within a capital-budgeting framework, that is, through a process of matching advantages from possible uses of funds against the cost of alternative ways to obtain the needed resources.

In domestic business, capital budgeting has become highly developed, with sophisticated analytical approaches available for investment decisions.[4] In the international field, however, the use of capital-budgeting techniques is still in an early stage because of the additional complications and uncertainties that must be handled once national boundaries are crossed. As Brooke and Remmers have reported from their survey of multinational firms, the usual difficulties in applying

---

[3] R. B. Shulman, "Are Foreign Exchange Risks Measurable?" *Columbia Journal of World Business*, May–June 1970, pp. 59–60.

[4] For a standard reference on capital budgeting, see Harold Bierman, Jr. and Seymour Smidt, *The Capital Budgeting Decision*, 2d ed. (New York: Macmillan Co., 1966).

capital-budgeting techniques for the appraisal of investment projects in foreign operations "are compounded by the generally poor quality of information that is obtainable, the added risks, and the different costs of capital which arise from operating in a multiple business environment."[5] Another survey of 92 U.S. and 18 foreign multinational corporations concluded that financial investment criteria were used most often in evaluating relatively small projects which fell under the purview of local managers. "For relatively large or strategic investments, however, financial investment criteria were used only as a rough screening device to prevent obviously unprofitable projects from wasting the time of the board of directors."[6]

Another prevailing pattern has been for foreign-investment decisions to be made on a country-by-country basis.[7] Each country is considered as a separate entity and investments in that country have been justified largely in terms of the potential size and profitability of operations within the country. New operations, therefore, are proposed when conditions in a single national market seem justified, without evaluation of possible alternative schemes for supplying that market and without basing investment decisions on the return to the total multinational system. Increasingly, however, companies have been recognizing that investment decisions should be based on the net benefits that any additional investment will bring to the multinational system as a whole rather than to any unit of the system taken separately. Chapter 18 on global planning shows one way this might be done. Beyond this, financial evaluation techniques are being developed for taking a systems approach, as illustrated in Figure 21–7, that allow for tax and financial cost variations among countries as well as tariff differences.[8]

The return-on-investment analysis for an international project follows essentially the same general form used for domestic business but with several additional international elements to be considered. These arise at each of three stages in the analysis. In the first stage, the estimated receipts and disbursements for the project are analyzed by including problems of exchange rates, financial costs, and risk measurement. In the second stage, the analysis moves from the subsidiary to the headquarters level. This requires estimating (1) what amounts

[5]Michael Z. Brooke and H. Lee Remmers, *The Strategy of Multinational Enterprise* (New York: American Elsevier Publishing Co., 1970), p. 102.

[6]Arthur Stonehill and Leonard Nathanson, "Capital Budgeting and the Multinational Corporation," *California Management Review,* Summer 1968, p. 40.

[7]Jack Zwick, "Models for Multicountry Investments," *Business Horizons,* Winter 1967, p. 73.

[8]A pioneering study emphasizing the systems approach is Sidney M. Robbins and Robert B. Stobaugh, *Money in the Multinational Enterprise* (New York: Basic Books, 1973).

FIGURE 21–7
A Systems Approach to Financial Optimization (an example)

Characteristics of the Multinational System (by country)			
Three fully owned system companies	*A*	*B*	*C*
Local corporation tax rates	50%	20%	40%
Import duty rates for system transfers	10	30	80
Local interest rates	9	7	8

Each company transfers some production to the other two.
Each company has local profits and incurs corporation tax.

Possibilities for System Savings over Independent Operation

1. *Alter source of capital*
    Independent decision: Raise capital from cheapest source and pay local taxes. Net cost = (*A*) 3.5% (*B*) 5.6% (*C*) 4.2%
    System decision: Company with highest tax rate (*A*) to raise capital from cheapest source and advance interest free to others. Net cost = (*A,B,C,*) 3.5%.
2. *Alter transfer prices*
    Independent decision: Price somewhere between supplier company cost and receiving company revenue.
    System decision: Adjust prices as indicated on the table below. Gains would continue until lowered prices reached zero and increased prices eliminated all the profits of the receiving company, but there will be practical limitations in the real world.

		Gains from $100 Change			
Goods Transferred From:	*Direction of Price Change*	*Source Country Tax ($)*	*Destination Country Tax ($)*	*Import Duty ($)*	*Net System Gain ($)*
A to B	.Lower	+50	−20	+30	+60
B to C	.Lower	+20	−40	+80	+60
C to A	.Adjust to give desired company profits				0
A to C	.Lower	+50	−40	+80	+90
C to B	.Lower	+40	−20	+30	+50
B to A	.Raise	−20	+50	−10	+20

3. *Alter royalty charges and transfer prices*
    Independent decision: Combined total to fall between supplier company cost and receiving company revenue.
    System decision: Lower *all* transfer prices to minimize import duties, and charge royalties from lowest taxed company to minimize corporation tax.

will be transferred, at what time, and in what form from the subsidiary to the parent company, (2) what taxes and other expenses will be incurred due to these transfers, and (3) what incremental revenues and costs will result elsewhere in the system. In a third and last stage, the project is evaluated and compared with other investment projects on the basis of incremental net cash flow accruing to the system as a return on the investment.

The projection of receipts and disbursements begins, of course, from the market forecasts, including export possibilities from the project. A unique aspect of projecting receipts and disbursements for a foreign project is the need to develop schedules of relevant, anticipated exchange rates for each type of transaction involved. This task goes beyond the general requirement for foreign exchange forecasting. Some countries will have both an official and a free rate of exchange, each applying to different transactions. Many transactions involving foreign exchange are subject to duties, special taxes, and exemptions. Equipment exports, for example, may be exempted or receive exchange rate concessions. In some instances, foreign exchange rates are subject to negotiations between the government and the international enterprise. Consequently, the international financial manager may need separate projections over time of exchange rates for equipment imports, raw material imports, and export sales, and he will have to evaluate the importance of such rates to the revenues and costs of the project.

A second international consideration may be the need to consider alternative financial structures for the proposed project, which in turn will affect projected receipts and disbursements. Local debt financing, for example, tends to reduce both foreign exchange and inflation risk. But the availability of local credit for international enterprises varies greatly among countries for national policy or other reasons. In certain countries, the international firm may be required to finance up to certain limits by local sales of equity. Or the country may offer special incentives if external rather than local financing is used for imported equipment, in order to encourage foreign investment inflows. By considering such matters, the firm may want to develop separate receipts and disbursement forecasts for several alternative financial plans that are feasible for a particular national situation.

Still another international consideration is the need to include risk elements of a political- or national-controls nature in the investment analysis. As an extreme example, high probabilities of expropriation or confiscation can markedly change the projections of receipts and disbursements. These risks have been discussed in Chapters 13 and 14, where techniques for handling such risk elements have been suggested. In addition to their impact on projected receipts and disbursements for a project analyzed at a national level, these risk elements must be considered at the headquarters level from the standpoint of how they might affect income flows such as dividend remittances and royalty payments available to the parent and the rest of the system.

In the second stage, where the analysis moves to the headquarters level, the principal additional issues become the availability to headquarters of income flows from the project and the net incremental benefits, if any, to the system. Operations within the same country can reasonably assume that cash flows from one unit of an enterprise are freely available to another unit. In many countries, the repatriation of cash flows above a certain percentage return is not allowed or is heavily taxed and forecasts of remittance policies are required in such cases. Profits that are freely available to the parent concern have a different value than profits that must be reinvested. Forced reinvestment may, however, have desirable and beneficial results in cases where opportunities are growing or where the firm has initially set up a new venture on a narrow financial base to minimize its exposure. In any event, the firm will have to decide whether it should assign lower values to project flows that cannot be converted into home-country currency or transferred freely to other countries, or whether all earnings from the project should be considered as available inflows to the parent company. It will also have to take into account the tax and other costs of transferring income to the parent companies. The estimated inflows must also be translated into home-country currency units on the basis of foreign exchange forecasts over the planning period.

The incremental benefits to the rest of the system should be imputed as additional available income from the proposed project. These can be profits from increased export sales from the parent company; payments of license fees, royalties, or management services; or even transfers of technological or marketing know-how available to the rest of the system from the activities of the new venture.

At the third and last stage, the alternative investment projects are compared with each other and ranked on the basis of expected return on investment, in which order they will be accepted up to the limit of the investment sums considered available for the capital-budgeting period. One of the issues at this stage may be the method used for comparing projects. Another will be the criterion used for the cost of capital.

The "net present value" method has become most widely used for evaluating investments. The method takes into account earnings over the life of a project. It discounts the expected future net cash flows, using the cost of capital as the discount rate, and then deducts the original cost of capital to determine the present net value of the project.[9]

Policies on cost of capital may range from a *pool-of-funds concept* with a presumed single pool of corporate funds and a single target rate

---

[9] See Bierman and Smidt, *Capital Budgeting Decision*, pp. 18–38, for a discussion of alternative techniques such as the payback method and average rate of return method, and for an explanation of the way to apply the alternative methods.

to the use of separate costs of capital for each country of operation or each project.[10] The pool-of-funds approach assumes that funds are raised on a worldwide basis with debt incurred where the terms are most favorable and transferred to the places where funds are most desired. This concept obviously does not apply where a philosophy of "every tub on its own bottom" is being followed and a subsidiary is responsible for its own financing after the initial phase. In such cases, the cost of capital must be estimated separately for each project. Also, where special sources of financing are available for specific projects, such as through financial incentives uniquely available to projects located in the depressed region of southern Italy, such special costs would most likely be taken into account by using separate target rates for the cost of capital. Ordinarily, however, a single, company-wide cost of capital measure should be used as the discount factor in evaluating foreign-investment projects.[11]

The principal international risk elements—foreign exchange, national controls, and political risk—have already been incorporated into the analysis. The recommended risk-adjustment procedures are to analyze the specific sources of risk and through the use of subjective probabilities to estimate the specific impact of the possible outcomes to produce an expected return on the investment. In making a final selection, the enterprise will have its estimates of the net present value of available inflows and a measure of risk for each alternative. The alternatives may consist of different projects or the same projects financed in different ways. The final choices from the financial point of view will then depend upon the firm's attitudes toward taking risks.[12]

FINANCIAL STRUCTURES AND FINANCING TECHNIQUES

The choice among alternative financial structures and financing plans for affiliates, as previously noted, may influence significantly the attractiveness of new projects and expansions. The choice can also affect the degree of foreign exchange and political risk incurred in multinational operations. The options will differ, of course, in the case of a wholly owned subsidiary from those related to a joint venture.

In choosing optimal financing plans for foreign affiliates, the financial manager will have to decide such questions as the appropri-

[10]Dan T. Smith, "Financial Variables in International Business," *Harvard Business Review*, January–February, 1966, pp. 97–98.

[11]David B. Zenoff and Jack Zwick, *International Financial Management* (Englewood Cliffs, N.J.: Prentice-Hall, 1969), pp. 186–203.

[12]For an example of the large amount of literature on portfolio selection covering this point, see Alexander A. Robichek and Stewart C. Myers, *Optimal Financing Decisions* (Englewood Cliffs, N.J.: Prentice-Hall, 1965).

ate mix of debt and equity and the extent to which debt should be local or imported. The alternatives will depend on the local and foreign sources of capital available for financing projects in specific countries, national governmental regulations regarding financing and ownership arrangements, relative costs of the various options, and other factors.[13]

What constitutes an appropriate mix of debt and equity has long been debated by financial experts. Debt constitutes a fixed obligation to pay interest and repay principal regardless of business conditions. Because the cost of debt is generally fixed and tax deductible, it gives the suppliers of equity leverage for maximizing their earnings. There are limits to the amount of debt that can be used, however, because as the proportion of debt increases, both lenders and purchasers of new equity may demand a higher return because of the risk that the firm may not meet its fixed obligations in periods of bad business conditions. But the tolerable limits of debt will vary from country to country. A study of 463 corporate financial structures in nine selected industries showed that the average debt to total assets in each of the industries was consistently higher in Japan, Italy, Sweden, and West Germany than in the United States or France.[14] In Japan, for example, steel companies had debt/equity ratios on the order of 4:1 (80 percent debt to 20 percent equity), whereas U.S. steel companies had debt ratios on the order of 3:1. Or to take a more extreme case, the share of equity in the total capital structure of major Japanese trading companies ranged from 3 to 7 percent as compared to 45 percent for Sears, Roebuck in the United States and 71 percent for A&P, the large food distributor.[15]

Also, the international manager must consider the effect of the financial structure of the affiliate on the total enterprise, where the parent's and affiliates financial statements will be consolidated.[16] High debt ratios may be acceptable in the country of the subsidiary, but the consolidated balance sheet may show a higher debt ratio than is considered appropriate in the country of the parent. The result may be that the cost of financing for the parent company is increased because the optimal financing plan for the affiliate is suboptimal for the total enterprise. Such a problem would be less common for Japanese than for U.S. multinational enterprises.

---

[13]For an analysis of the external financing experience of 115 subsidiaries over the period 1960 to 1967, see Brooke and Remmers, Strategy of Multinational Enterprise, pp. 179–210; also see Zenoff and Zwick, International Financial Management, pp. 185–204 on criteria for selection of affiliate financial structures.

[14]Arthur Stonehill and Thomas Stitzel, "Financial Structure and Multinational Corporations," California Management Review, Fall 1969, pp. 257–61.

[15]James C. Abegglen, ed., Business Strategies for Japan (Tokyo, Japan: Sophia University, 1970), pp. 57–68.

[16]Rita M. Rodriguez and E. Eugene Carter, International Financial Management (Englewood Cliffs, N.J.: Prentice-Hall, 1976), pp. 336–48.

In international business, a high debt ratio for a foreign subsidiary has important advantages beyond the usual benefit from leverage. Local debt financing in weak-currency countries tends to reduce both devaluation and inflation risks. When devaluations occur, servicing requirements on debts denominated in outside currencies increase because larger amounts of local currency are required to meet interest payments and retire principal. In contrast, the servicing requirements on local debt are not affected by devaluation. For this reason, firms are frequently willing to borrow locally even though the cost is higher than imported funds, and the additional cost is considered an insurance payment against devaluation risk. With revaluations, as occurred in Germany and Japan in the early 1970s, the ability to meet external obligations will, of course, increase.

The advantage of local debt in reducing inflation risk is that repayment obligations may remain fixed in local currency while revenues and profits rise along with inflation. In other words, debt is being paid off with "cheaper" money. The inflation advantage of local debt, however, has been eliminated in some countries with traditionally high rates of inflation. Brazil, for example, has widely adopted the device of "monetary correction" in order to make long-term financing available in a country with continuing inflation. Under this system, called *indexing,* debts are readjusted upward on an annual basis by the amount of inflation as determined by an official index. The practice is followed in cases of mortgages and even government bonds.

Debt imported from strong-currency countries has the disadvantage already mentioned that the amount of local currency required to meet interest and repayment obligations will increase in the case of devaluation. But even where devaluations are anticipated, nonlocal debt may have advantages from the standpoint of providing greater freedom for foreign remittances where exchange controls prevail. Most countries give preference in the allocation of foreign exchange to remittances of interest and debt repayment over the remittance of dividends on equity.

Many companies prefer high debt ratios and a minimum of equity capital for their foreign subsidiaries for still other reasons. The parent company may feel that local managers will be more highly motivated to meet repayment obligations than to earn profit on equity. Debt obligations exert greater pressure than equity, which is sometimes classified more in the category of a "free" good.

It is important for the enterprise to determine its financial structure preferences for affiliates, but it should also be recognized that in some countries these preferences cannot be implemented. Companies prefer to use locally borrowed funds in areas that appear to be politically and economically unstable. Yet it is the risky areas that chronically lack loan capital. Furthermore, certain countries restrict foreign companies in their local borrowing on the grounds that one justification for admitting foreign firms is that they can increase the total amount of local investment by bringing in capital. Another reason is that the growth of local enterprise should not be stunted by having to compete for scarce funds with large, profitable, and well-known international enterprises which have easier access to outside capital markets. Some less developed countries that are greatly concerned with their balance-of-payments situation object to high debt proportions when it appears that such a financial structure is intended to support high levels of foreign exchange remittances to the parent companies.

The preference for minimizing the amount of equity capital supplied to the affiliate by the parent company frequently leads to the subsidiaries being seriously undercapitalized. This problem has been met in many cases by open account inventory financing. The parent company sells merchandise to the subsidiary but does not require payment until much later even though the goods have been sold by the subsidiary. This method allows the parent company to increase and develop its foreign operations without actually sending either additional equity capital or formal cash loans. Furthermore, the length of the credit is flexible.

The desire to minimize equity is not characteristic of the large and internationally committed multinational enterprises. They typically use a guideline such as "let equity equal fixed assets" in order that host countries do not become concerned about excessive local borrowing or unduly high dividend remittances. This strong equity base facilitates local borrowing after the subsidiary has become established and gives it greater independence in the future from the parent's central source of funds.

The decision to enter into a joint-venture arrangement with a group of local partners or to sell equity shares in the subsidiary locally can also reduce the financial burden on the multinational enterprise and increase access to other local sources of capital. If the outside ownership groups have similar expectations, equity costs would be unaffected, but where expectations are dissimilar among the participants, equity costs of the financial plan can be increased. Outside shareholders, for example, may expect to receive larger dividends than are traditional for the international enterprise. If so, the larger (or smaller) return expectations should be included explicitly in the flow projections used to appraise the desirability of a project.

Business firms operating internationally differ greatly in their knowledge of and willingness to use the numerous sources of funds available to multinational enterprises.[17] The more highly developed capital markets of the United States were for many decades the best source for both large quantities of capital and low cost of capital. U.S. firms, in particular, generally limited their source of funds alternatives to the United States, the local country in which a project was being established, or foreign funds generated by the company in other foreign projects.[18] But the international situation has changed rapidly as to availability and comparative cost of capital, and many international firms have become accustomed to considering an ever-wider variety of capital sources and financing techniques in their decisions about financial structures for affiliates.[19]

To the extent that local financing is undertaken in the country in which a subsidiary is operating, the principal requirement at the headquarters level is for the international financial manager to become familiar with and expert in domestic financing patterns. He must become informed on patterns of commercial banking, the functioning of securities markets, and government policies and controls which may vary greatly from country to country. The American firm when going international will have to learn about overdraft lending by commercial banks, which permits a customer to write checks in excess of amounts he has deposited, up to some previously agreed upon limit. The U.S. firm will have to become familiar with government financing institutions such as Nacional Financiera in Mexico and Kreditanstalt fur Wiederaufbau (KFW) in Germany, which are major sources for local financing and for which there is no American counterpart. Likewise, Shell, the Anglo-Dutch international oil enterprise, had to develop special skills for using the highly regulated U.S. securities markets in providing local financing for its U.S. subsidiary, Shell Oil Company.

The financing function becomes much more complex when cross-border financing is required, that is, when funds are secured in one country and transferred to another, because of the national controls in many countries over capital transfers. Where controls are placed on direct investment outflow, only a limited range of devices such as short-term loans, open inventory financing, or swap loans can be used for cross-border financing from the home country.

---

[17]Clovis de Faro and James V. Jucker, "The Impact of Inflation and Devaluation on the Selection of an International Borrowing Source," *Journal of International Business Studies*, Fall 1973.

[18]Stefan H. Robock, "Overseas Financing For U.S. International Business." *Journal of Finance*, May 1966, pp. 297–307.

[19]For detailed current information on financing techniques, sources for cross-border financing, and the domestic financing situation in a large number of countries, see the monthly service, *Financing Foreign Operations* of Business International, or other similar services.

Aside from capital sources in the home country and in the country in which an affiliate is operating, multinational firms can also look to international institutions, private and public regional financing agencies, and international capital markets—particularly the Euro-currency markets.[20]

The future of the Euro-currency market may be affected negatively by reforms in the international monetary system. Nevertheless, the market offers great attractions to both borrowers and investors which have become strong motives for its continuance. Euro-bonds are always issued in such a way that interest is paid free of withholding tax. When they are issued in bearer form, the holder has additional means to defer or avoid income taxes. The freedom from taxation, the diversification opportunities for both borrowers and currencies, and the absence of interference by national governments are features of the Euro-bond market that appeal to investors. From the standpoint of the borrower, many of the attractive features are similar. In addition to offering a choice of currencies, interest rates in the Euro-bond market have generally been at levels little different from the prevailing rates in the home country of the currency.

In summary, the financial structure of affiliates will depend first on the willingness of the parent company to assume equity risk. Although many companies prefer to minimize their equity commitments, for new foreign projects or expansions the hard-core financing will have to come from within the multinational enterprise. It must show a willingness to risk its own funds in order to tap external sources. A common pattern has been to finance fixed assets with company funds and long-term loan capital, and for working capital to use local borrowings to the maximum extent. The mix between local and imported debt depends on local availability, the relative costs of alternative sources, the degree of operating freedom associated with funds from different sources, and local government constraints on excessive debt ratios. Where local money costs exceed imported costs, a company will have to decide how much it wants to pay for risk avoidance. Tax factors and the effect of the financing plan on both the financial situation of the parent company and the total system will be additional considerations.

INTERNATIONAL MONEY MANAGEMENT

Given a multinational enterprise as it exists at any point of time, the international financial manager also plays a major role in the manage-

---

[20]See Gunter Dufey, "The Eurobond Market: Its Significance For International Financial Managements." *Journal of International Business Studies,* Summer 1970, pp. 65–77.

ment of short-term assets and liabilities so as to optimize financial goals on a systemwide basis. This function, referred to as international money management, has gone undeveloped in many small firms with limited international experience. The survey presented in Chapter 19 of recent patterns followed by U.S. multinational companies in organizing and managing the international function revealed that many firms view each subsidiary as an independent operation and make little or no attempt to optimize the financial function on a systemwide basis. But a strong trend is clearly in the direction of adopting a systems view and using relatively sophisticated international financial management techniques.

This trend has been supported by three factors. First, the relatively new international business companies have been accumulating the necessary international experience which they previously lacked. Second, the relatively calm and stable international financial environment that characterized the post–World War II period was irrevocably disrupted by the world monetary crises of the early 1970s. As a result, international firms became more keenly aware of the need and opportunities for more rational and efficient responses to rapidly changing conditions in national and international financial markets. A third factor has been the rapid development of improved techniques for financial management on a global basis.

A Systems Approach

The more advanced approaches to international money management that have been emerging are all systems approaches. The system consists of units in different countries, each of which operates in a different environment and has an accounting system of its own. The units are connected to each other by a series of links through which assets and liabilities can be shuttled. Inter-unit flows are subject to policy control within certain limits, and the challenge is to make use of the policy tools to produce the best results for the system as a whole.[21]

This section summarizes the results of one pioneering study by Robbins and Stobaugh. The primary links between the different units are equity flows, generally from the parent to the subsidiary. Dividends flow in the opposite direction. Other links are the provision of services and technology by the parent to the subsidiary, which results in return flows in the form of management fees, royalty payments, and the sale of goods, which result in payments for merchandise received.

---

[21]Robbins and Stobaugh, *Money in the Multinational Enterprise.*

Finally, the units have credit links in the form of intercompany short- and long-term loans, accounts payable, and interest flows. Matching each of these links are financial policy tools which can be adjusted to set the level at which the link will operate. Dividend policy, for example, is the tool associated with the equity link and the amount and timing of dividends to be paid can be adjusted. The relationships between links, tools, and the variables they control can be seen in Figure 21-8.

FIGURE 21-8

Financial Links, Associated Policy Tools, and Affected Variables

Link	Policy Tool	Variables Controlled
1. Equity............	Dividend policy	Amount of dividends accruing
2. Services		
Management........	Management fee policy	Amount (or rate and specified base) of fees accruing
Know-how.........	Royalty policy	Amount (or rate and specified base) of royalties accruing
3. Merchandise.........	Transfer-pricing policy	Intrasystem's sales price or deviation of intrasystem price from arm's-length price
4. Credit		

a. Accounts payable ⎫
   b. Mgt. fees payable ⎪
   c. Royalties payable ⎬   Payables policy
   d. Dividends payable ⎪
   e. Interest payable ⎭
	Payables policy	Amount outstanding, terms, and interest charged

f. Short-term lending	Short-term lending policy	Amount outstanding, terms, and interest charged
g. Long-term lending	Long-term lending policy	

Source: Sidney M. Robbins and Robert B. Stobaugh, *Money in the Multinational Enterprise* (New York: Basic Books, 1973).

Limitations to the use of these policy tools arise out of government regulations, different patterns and mores of different financial markets, and internal constraints such as a desire to avoid disrupting the system of performance evaluation. Other limitations are the cost of having complete information at the optimization center, the difficulties of securing accurate information, and the need to make forecasts that handle future uncertainties such as foreign exchange risks.

A complex strategy under a systems approach would synchronize all the policy tools available to the various units of the multinational enterprise to maximize after-tax profits for the system as a whole. Although the use of complex strategies through a systems approach has not yet become common, exploratory work in this field has demonstrated that significant gains might be achieved as compared to a situation where units function as a collection of unrelated enterprises dealing with each other at arm's length. In a hypothetical case, for example, the systems approach has been demonstrated to produce consolidated profits after taxes of 15 percent higher than when the strict rules of arm's-length behavior are followed.[22]

In applying a strategy in practice, modifications may be needed to reduce conflicts between the subgoals of the various units and also to allow for international factors difficult to introduce into a systems calculation. For example, a higher interest rate source of credit to one unit may be preferred because it gives more protection against devaluation and is better for the system as a whole.

Although the use of a full systems approach is in the future, a series of less comprehensive techniques that focus on certain subgoals in international money management are in wide use.[23]

International Cash Management

International cash management is concerned with the mechanics of money transfers, collections, and disbursements. Systems have been developed for accelerating the collection of receipts arising from exports, rationalizing transfers between affiliates, and netting certain intercompany payments. Allowing for mail time and processing at the several banks in a collection chain, delays of one or two weeks are common for payments via international mail transfers between two European countries, or between Europe and the United States. As one example of accelerating the payment process where large sums or very lengthy delays are involved, the payer may be requested to remit payments by cable directly to the exporter's bank account in the country of the currency involved. By accelerating payments, less working capital is required and sizable savings can be realized.

The availability of funds to the multinational corporation can also be increased through the rationalization of internal transfers. Techniques range from the use of cable transfers to obtain immediate value on payments to the development of elaborate netting programs. Given the delays and expense incurred in making international payments, netting systems attempt to offset transactions among units of the enterprise on either a bilateral or a multilateral basis. By analyzing the transactions of every affiliate with other units in the system, it is possible to arrange for the participants to remit or receive only their net debit or credit positions under the directions of a central control point. The volume of actual transfers is cut sharply, with a consequent reduction in working capital requirements and foreign exchange costs

---

[22]Ibid.

[23]See "Developments in International Money Management," *World Financial Markets* (New York: Morgan Guaranty Trust Co., June 24, 1971).

and commissions. These savings are commonly estimated at up to 0.5 percent of the amount of the transfers eliminated.

Management of Working Capital and Liquidity

The control of liquidity—liquid assets and short-term debt or credit facilities—is based in large part on the concept of pooling, which aims at offsetting liquidity differences between affiliates so that the cash deficit of one is financed by the cash surplus of another, thus minimizing aggregate interest costs. Any net surplus or deficit for the pool as a whole can then either be directed into short-term investments or financed by drawing on central credit facilities. When pooling is attempted on a multicountry, multicurrency basis, tax considerations and exchange controls may preclude the actual pooling of funds in communal accounts. The same constraints may also limit direct intercompany lending. However, indirect financing between affiliates can be achieved through the leading and lagging of intercompany payments—usually trade, but sometimes dividends, royalties, fees, and loan payments. Cash-poor affiliates are allowed to lag on payments to a cash-rich affiliate; or cash-rich affiliates are directed by the central control point to prepay or lead their obligations to the others. In some cases, affiliates may be directed to draw funds available to them under low-cost credit facilities, and to prepay their obligations to those affiliates with higher-cost borrowings outstanding. In order to determine the optimum course of action, the international financial manager must be appraised of all intercompany transactions, as well as each affiliate's liquidity position and its local money market conditions.[24]

Protection against Inflation

In managing working capital and controlling liquidity, the international manager will be particularly concerned with the problem of protecting assets in countries with high rates of inflation. The physical assets such as property, plant, and equipment generally maintain their value in real terms during inflation. But the value of working capital, particularly cash and receivables, is highly vulnerable to erosion through inflation. And the international financial manager is concerned about profits and the value of assets as measured in the home-country currency or some other strong convertible currency.

---

[24]Ibid., pp. 3–4. Also, for two model-building approaches, see Dileep Mehta and Isik Inselbag, "Working Capital Management of a Multinational Firm," in *Multinational Business Operations,* ed. S. Prakash Sethi and J. N. Sheth (Pacific Palisades, Calif.: Goodyear Publishing Company, 1972); David P. Rutenberg, "Maneuvering Liquid Assets in a Multinational Company," *Management Science,* June 1970, pp. B671–B684.

The traditional local strategy for protecting working capital in an inflationary situation is to operate with a minimum amount of liquidity by minimizing cash balances, reducing receivables, lagging in the payment of local expenses, and maximizing local borrowing. Where the penalties for tax delinquency are low, some companies try to lag as much as possible in local tax payments. The value of inventories, particularly imported goods, is less likely to suffer from inflation. Where a local unit is part of a multinational system, it has additional possibilities for protecting assets by accelerating cash remittances to the parent company or elsewhere in the system where inflation rates are lower and by delaying the receipt of payments from low-inflation countries. Such policies of taking advantage of leads and lags is similar to the strategy for protection against devaluation to be discussed below.

Traditional anti-inflation strategy, however, has shortcomings which result from treating individual components of working capital in isolation although they are in fact interrelated. For example, when credit and receivables are treated in isolation, the usual policy is to restrict credit to reduce the holding of monetary assets that lose buying power. But an optimal policy under a systems approach which recognizes the interrelationships may be to increase rather than reduce credit. Inflation adds to the attraction of credit as part of the marketing mix and, by continuing to offer credit, the firm may generate a substantial increase in sales. The increase in profit margins that can result where large-scale economies can be exploited and where costs lag behind prices may more than offset the additional costs of increasing credit in an inflationary situation.[25]

REMITTANCE POLICIES

The management of international remittances has already been discussed in relation to international money management and foreign exchange risk. The subject of remittance policies, however, deserves some additional comment. The actual practice of many multinational companies in the recent past has been to make their decisions on dividend remittances separately from the decisions regarding other remittances or flows from royalties, management fees, interest on intercompany loans, and repayments of such loans.[26]

[25]Lee A. Travis, "The Management of Short-Term Funds Under Conditions of Inflation: A Systems Approach" (D.B.A. diss., Graduate School of Business, Indiana University, 1969).

[26]See David B. Zenoff, "Profitable, Fast Growing, But Still the Stepchild," *Columbia Journal of World Business,* July–August 1967; and "Remitting Funds from Foreign Affiliates," *Financial Executive,* March 1968, pp. 46–63.

One dominant consideration has been to have subsidiaries help the parent company meet its dividend payments to stockholders by remitting a fixed percentage of their earnings after foreign taxes. Another important consideration has been to establish a record of regular remittances in the operating country in order to improve the company's chances for continuing to remit during difficult balance-of-payments periods for the country. Still another motivation for having local managers remit substantial amounts on a regular basis to the parent company is a feeling that local managers need to be reminded that the parent company supplied the capital and that the controlling objectives are set by headquarters. Where a company does not consolidate its accounts, only the remittances from the affiliates are recorded as income by the parent company and dividend remittance policies can be used to influence the profits reported by the parent.

When the local subsidiary is a joint venture with local shareholders, the problem of remittances becomes more complicated. When dividends are declared by local subsidiaries, local shareholders, as well as the parent company, share in the payments. While funds remitted to headquarters may still be available wholly or net of taxation to the multinational enterprise, dividends paid locally will generally leave the system and come back only through new financing. Also, it is not uncommon for local shareholders to expect high dividends, whereas the multinational enterprise may prefer to reinvest a large share of earnings and declare only modest dividends.

THE TAX VARIABLE

In a world of independent taxing authorities, the enterprise conducting business within many nations and across national boundaries faces an almost infinite variety of types of taxes, levels of tax burdens, tax incentives, patterns of tax administration, and possible overlaps in tax systems.[27] Because of the pervasive importance of the tax variable in financial management and because of the diversity and complexity of taxes, the multinational enterprise requires great expertise to anticipate tax burdens with accuracy and to minimize tax obligations within legal limits. As has already been noted, taxes are an important variable in capital-budgeting decisions, in the choice of the business form for foreign operations (for example, branch versus subsidiary), in selecting the financing strategy for an affiliate, and in the formulation of remittance policies.

---

[27]Various tax guides are published periodically by some international accounting firms such as Price, Waterhouse and Co. and Arthur Anderson and Co. These give detailed information on the tax treatment of foreign income and related matters and are available for most countries where international business is a significant activity.

At the subsidiary level, differential tax burdens can change greatly the profitability of similar operations in different countries. The United States relies heavily at the federal level on direct taxes, mainly personal and corporate income taxes. In contrast, European countries depend mainly on indirect or turnover taxes such as the tax on value added (TVA). Corporation income tax rates differ somewhat among countries in both statutory and effective rates. The differences in effective rates reflect the varying treatment of depreciation and other expenses, investment allowances and credits, and undistributed profits. The way in which such differences can alter the profitability and financial management practices of a subsidiary can be illustrated by the case of Germany. Profits not distributed to shareholders but retained by the corporation are taxed at 51 percent. Profits distributed to shareholders are taxed at only 15 percent. Under such a system, the pressures are to distribute profits to shareholders and meet needs for additional capital through new financing rather than through retained earnings.

The tax issue at the local level is mainly one of becoming fully informed on the characteristics of the system and its administration and adapting accordingly. In some cases, though, a special problem may arise through discrimination against foreign enterprises under the tax laws or through the administration of such laws. At the second stage of the multinational level the tax variable becomes increasingly complex. When profits are transferred from the subsidiary to the parent company or to other units of the multinational enterprise, the firm must cope with overlapping tax jurisdictions and possible double taxation. Also, additional local tax obligations are frequently imposed when profits are remitted out of a country.

The international firm must recognize and adjust to the attempts of different taxing authorities to collect taxes from activities that take place outside their territory. The policies of the major industrial countries toward foreign income that is repatriated range from complete exemption to full taxation at domestic rates, with a range from full credit down to no deduction for taxes paid to a foreign jurisdiction. The Netherlands, Belgium, and France, for example, may exempt foreign earnings from income tax or tax them at a reduced rate under certain specified or negotiated conditions. In contrast, the United States even taxes the parent company for certain undistributed profits of some foreign-based companies.

In a practical sense, the different national policies reflect the potential importance of foreign-earned income as a source of taxation and the inevitable desire of taxing authorities to maximize their tax revenues. Such taxation of foreign-earned income has been justified as necessary for securing an equitable division of tax revenues among taxing authorities and on the grounds that the total corporate enterprise, rather than the corporation as a legal entity, should be the unit subject to tax. In the debate over the tax changes adopted in the Internal Revenue Act of 1962, the U.S. government argued that history shows that U.S. parent companies are willing to overlook the nationality of a subsidiary when it is advantageous to do so and yet expect the U.S. government to protect their foreign interests in whatever form they may be in case of confiscation or expropriation by a foreign government.

Since the adoption of its Federal Income Tax Law in 1913, the policy of the United States has been to impose its income taxes both on income arising within its boundaries, regardless of the nationality or residence of the earner, and on income received from foreign sources by resident individuals and corporations chartered within the United States. Initially, foreign taxes were deductible from taxable income. Later, the policy was changed to permit income taxes paid abroad to be deductible from income taxes due the U.S. government.

A few countries known as "tax havens" have exceptionally low tax rates and liberal interpretations of taxable income. Income "sourced" in tax-haven countries could until 1962 avoid the U.S. tax and that of other relatively high-taxing authorities by being retained in the low-rate country and by not being paid out as dividends to owners in the United States. The Internal Revenue Act of 1962, however, sharply reduced the importance of tax havens.

In the tax field, as previously discussed in Chapter 8, governments have taken steps to avoid double taxation through bilateral treaties. Under such treaties, a country agrees to share with another on a prearranged basis the taxes imposed on business operations in the territory of one country by nationals of another country. Tax treaties may also provide for information exchanges between the governments that will aid each other in tax collection. The negotiation of a network of tax treaties has resulted in more tax uniformity among countries.

Another tax topic that deserves mention is the matter of "tax sparing." Some countries offer special tax incentives to attract foreign investment. Such incentives may temporarily spare the multinational enterprise the imposition of part or all of certain taxes which it would otherwise have to pay. Tax sparing in a foreign country offers little advantage to the business enterprise if the income is taxable at the same or higher rate in the home country of the parent company. Some countries permit a tax credit for taxes that have been spared in a foreign country. But others, particularly the United States, do not. The effect of policies such as that of the United States is to reduce or cancel the attractiveness of foreign tax incentives in influencing the investment decisions of U.S. multinational enterprises.

IMPORT AND EXPORT FINANCING

In the traditional field of importing and exporting, an extensive range of financial services has been developed for financing international transactions. Whether for transactions within an international firm or with suppliers or customers, these offer the international manager important opportunities for extending the funds available to him.

There are two broad categories of credits. "Supplier" credit is extended by the exporter to the foreign importer from his own funds, and the exporter in turn is refinanced with credit from external sources. "Buyer" credit is granted directly to the foreign buyer to be used by him for stipulated imports. Supplier credit generally covers short-term credits and some medium-term transactions. Buyer credit is usually available only for medium and long-term credits of large amounts, normally for purchasing capital goods.

In extending supplier credit, the seller is primarily concerned with credit risk, the protection of export proceeds against currency fluctuations, and political risk. In recent years, many countries have developed export credit insurance-guarantee programs to expand the country's export earnings by reducing these risks. Export-guaranteed paper may then be financed more easily and at a lower financing cost.

Financing may be with or without recourse. If the importer fails to pay the note or the bill when due, the financing institution may or may not have recourse to the exporter for the amount due. Most export credit is granted with recourse to the exporter. However, an insurance policy or guarantee issued by a government export credit insurance agency limits the financing without recourse to the extent that risks and losses are covered by the insurance.

Commercial banks are the principal source of short-term export financing. Private commercial finance firms are also important in export financing but the growth of export guarantees has encouraged the use of commercial banks because the private finance houses usually charge more than banks. Traditionally, commercial banks have been reluctant to grant medium-term financing, but as a result of government export promotion programs, sponsorship of new institutions, and guarantee programs, commercial banks and other private sources for medium-term financing have been increasing rapidly.

For long-term financing, public sources and lending agencies are the most important. The U.S. Export-Import Bank is the biggest and most diversified export-credit institution in the world. It offers programs of long-term project financing, direct medium-term export financing, medium-term guarantees, short-term insurance through the affiliated FCIA, a banking program for export financing, and a rediscount facility.

A special form of payment increasingly used in trade with communist and some developing countries is the use of clearing currencies within the framework of currency-clearing arrangements between two countries. In the case of an export switch, the importer in a communist or developing market pays the exporter from a clearing balance held against a third country. The exporter then has the possibility, with the assistance of specialized agents (mainly in Austria, Germany, the Netherlands, and Switzerland) to use the clearing funds in the country holding the balance or to sell the bilateral funds at a discount.

SUMMARY

International financial management is primarily concerned with the maximization of profits after taxes for the multinational system as a whole, within the framework of a wider pursuit of corporate objectives. International operations add many complexities to the financial management function, ranging from the difficulties of developing an adequate financial information system, where the initial data input into the system must necessarily be shaped by varying patterns in national accounting systems, to the problems of dealing in multiple currencies and managing foreign exchange risks. At the same time, a multinational system affords opportunities to minimize interest costs, tax liabilities, and the effects of differential inflation rates among countries, and to reduce working capital needs through pooling liquidity among affiliates.

Thus, the major challenge and opportunity in international financial management are to optimize on a systemwide basis. Toward this end, major progress has been achieved in the development of concepts and tools for complex strategies that reveal profit-taking opportunities that normally do not become apparent under simple strategies focused on subgoals of financial management. But the use of complex and sophisticated techniques can be expensive in terms of required data, personnel, and experience. Given these cost and other limitations, many international firms deal with each subsidiary as an independent operation and make little or no effort to optimize the financial function on a systemwide basis.

Under most circumstances, however, the investment and capital-budgeting decisions above certain financial limits are a centralized responsibility for the multinational firm. The international financial manager has also become increasingly involved in decisions on financial structures of affiliates, financing techniques, and management of foreign exchange risk. The management of cash flows and liquidity on an international basis has been growing rapidly as an international financial management function.

EXERCISES AND DISCUSSION QUESTIONS

1. What are the special accounting problems of multinational operations? Why is it unlikely that uniform international accounting standards will be adopted?

2. Why might a multinational firm decide to invest in a project that shows a low expected rate of return on the basis of the first-level analysis at the local country level?

3. Which source of funds would be the cheapest—a loan in the United Kingdom at 11 percent annually on an overdraft basis or a loan from a U.S. bank at 9 percent annually but with the requirement of a 20 percent compensating balance?

4. A U.S. multinational enterprise has three subsidiaries, each located in a different European country. The British subsidiary imports semi-finished products from its Dutch affiliate for further processing and distribution. Part of the British subsidiary's output is exported to its German affiliate, and the rest is sold in the British home market. Normal trade credit terms on all transactions are 60 days. In anticipation of British sterling depreciation during 1975, the British subsidiary was directed to give its German affiliate 110 days to pay and to reduce its liabilities to the Dutch affiliate to zero, that is, to pay for its imports C.O.D. How can such tactics provide a hedge against one-time exchange losses?

5. The chief financial officer of a U.S. multinational company says, "Our foreign exchange strategy is to avoid risk. We pursue the practice of offsetting all balance sheet exposures with foreign exchange hedges, thus neutralizing the exposures." Comment on the wisdom of such a strategy.

22

Information and Control in the Multinational Firm

HOW DOES A MULTINATIONAL FIRM monitor the progress of its foreign subsidiaries in accomplishing the strategic (policy) and tactical (operational) objectives of the enterprise? Building a global strategy is a process by which the activities of the foreign subsidiaries are molded to achieve a common goal for the enterprise. The task of headquarters management, however, does not end with the approval of the objectives and implementation plans of the subsidiaries. The center must also have an information and control system for keeping informed as to the progress of the subsidiaries, for receiving warning signals that certain situations are not in equilibrium, for evaluating performance, and for taking effective remedial action when necessary. In addition, the total enterprise and the individual subunits of the firm must have information systems that respond to external control requirements, particularly those of the different countries in which the firm operates.

In order for the control process to be operational, objectives must be specified in a way that makes it possible for performance toward achieving these objectives to be measured, and meaningful standards must be established as a basis for evaluating progress. The objectives and the standards should be formulated jointly by top management and the subsidiary head as discussed in Chapter 18. The standards are applied regularly against performance through a system of information flows and reports to identify variances from tactical plans and operating budgets. In some cases, variances will require remedial action. In other cases, actual performance experience will result in revisions in the strategic plans of the enterprise.

The choice of performance criteria is an especially crucial issue for the multinational enterprise because of the many inherent conflicts of interest between units of the enterprise, such as those previously discussed in relation to transfer-pricing policy (Chapter 20), and because of the added problem of complying with the multiple and varied external control pressures, to be discussed below. The conflicts cannot be eliminated, but they can be explicitly recognized and evaluated as to the effects of the trade-offs. If this is not done, the performance criteria selected for the control process can unnecessarily pit groups within the company against each other and reduce the effectiveness of the firm's operations.

SPECIAL INTERNATIONAL FACTORS

The managerial control process in multinational operations is complicated by special international factors. Among these are the following:

1. *Outside ownership interests.* Multinational firms frequently have subsidiaries where ownership and control are shared with local partners whose objectives and motivations may conflict with the global goals of the enterprise.
2. *Communications.* Cross-national communications increase the time cycle, expense, possibility of errors, and the likelihood of distortions in information flows.
3. *Diversity.* Variations among countries in accounting procedures and in economic, political, and social features complicate the task of setting standards, evaluating performance, and designing effective corrective measures.
4. *Uncertainties.* The accuracy and completeness of economic and industry data will vary greatly among countries. Also, political and economic conditions in some countries can change rapidly from the situation on which global planning was based.
5. *Host-country goals.* In some countries, particularly the less developed countries, the firm's control objectives and methods of control may be on a collision course with host-country goals.

THE REPORTING AND REVIEW OF PROGRESS

Most large firms operate a formal planning and control system. The need for such a system, therefore, is not uniquely related to international operations. Nevertheless, the planning and control systems frequently cited as examples of advanced practices are those of multinational firms. This reflects the special importance in multinational operations of an effective planning and control system as a tool for knitting the entity together across national boundaries.

The formal planning process is usually constructed around an annual planning cycle, beginning with the submission to the subsidiaries of planning guidelines from the central office, as discussed in Chapter 18. These guidelines emerge from the development of a global strategy and are designed to move the plans of the enterprise from a strategic to a tactical level. After receiving the guidelines, the subsidiary managers prepare their own plans, and the process of review and consultation between central offices and subsidiary management begins.

Some corporations have formal review meetings which pit the functional specialists at headquarters against the line managers who have submitted the plans. At such meetings, the chief executive may play the role of grand inquisitor cum adjudicator. In the case of ITT, somewhat of a legendary example in this respect, the review sessions are attended by the top managers of other subsidiaries.[1] The purpose of such attendance is to facilitate coordination between the subsidiaries or divisions, avoid repetition of similar planning problems, and generally raise the standard of planning. The transfer of standards obtained in this way can be particularly valuable when the subsidiaries are of comparable size and situation.

The formal acceptance of plans gives the line executive a license to implement the proposals in the plans and acknowledges the targets as reasonable expectations of achievement. Seldom are plans formally rejected. They may, however, be referred back for amendment or review. In this way, the planning cycle tries to avoid any implication of failure.[2]

International Standardization

In one form or another, multinational firms have a standard planning or budget manual specifying a standard presentation of data in subsidiary plans. These standards may require that all data, from market demand assessment to profit and balance sheet items, be presented in one corporate currency. In such cases, the rules relating to conversion of currencies can have a significant effect on the results reported, particularly when there have been fluctuations in the exchange rate between the local and the corporate currency.

In recent years, the trend in international manuals has been to increase the requirements for detailed information and to move from accounting figures to much more data on markets and the business and economic environment. Some multinational firms have set standard

---

[1] *Business Week,* November 3, 1973, p. 46.

[2] Michael Z. Brooke and H. Lee Remmers, *The Strategy of Multinational Enterprise* (New York: American Elsevier Publishing Co., 1970), pp. 91–150.

requirements for cost reductions from subsidiaries and for the treatment of price inflation in their plans. An example of the emphasis placed on accurate reporting is the memorandum sent by Harold Geneen, chief executive officer of ITT, to all company executives, in which he said,

> The highest art of professional management requires the literal ability to "smell" a real fact from all the others—and moreover to have the temerity, intellectual curiosity, guts, and/or plain impoliteness, if necessary, to be sure that what you have is indeed what we will call an unshakable fact.[3]

Reporting Requirements

Periodic reporting and review of progress during the year are standard requirements. Most firms require monthly reports on sales and certain financial items. Other types of reports may be required quarterly or semiannually.

There are several channels for reporting within the multinational system. The prime channel is reporting by managers up the line ultimately to the chief executive officer. Controllers or financial officers frequently report directly to their headquarters counterpart on certain aspects of performance without going through their own chief executive. There may be as many as four or five types of input from the subsidiary to corporate staff from such functions as factory management, engineering, or research and development. As a headquarters official of ITT explained, "On every company we get four or five inputs and the problems can't fail to surface."[4]

In some companies, the various reports are an input for periodic monthly management meetings where progress is evaluated and trouble spots identified. Where problems have been identified, plans may be revised or, when appropriate, a task force may be dispatched from headquarters or some other subsidiary to make repairs.

Control through People

Where operations are in different countries and managers have different cultural and language backgrounds, control through programs of "corporate acculturation" and "people transfer" can be important and effective. Corporate acculturation is the process of training subsidiary managers extensively so that they understand and

---

[3]*Business Week,* November 3, 1973, p. 46.
[4]Ibid.

generally accept the company's way of doing business.[5] Part of this process is to have key people who will be assigned to positions of responsibility in the subsidiaries spend part of their career at the head office. Likewise, headquarters personnel should have some experience working in the subsidiaries.

Personnel contacts through either short-term or long-term people transfers or through periodic group meetings of headquarters and subsidiary personnel greatly increase the ability of managers with diverse backgrounds to understand each other's viewpoints. A serious problem can arise, however, when short-term people transfers are viewed by the subsidiaries as a "half-spying" tactic.

INFORMATION FOR SYSTEM CONTROL

Clearly, to operate a multinational enterprise as a system, the center and the other units need continuing flows of data. Thus the firm's system for collection and dissemination of data on a global basis becomes a key element in the control system. The information system will normally include two categories of communications between home-office management and subsidiary management: (1) personal exchanges such as telephone conversations, visits, and meetings, and (2) impersonal communications such as budgets, plans, and regular reports. Communications covering performance measurement generally follow established organization channels, whereas those involving educational, advisory, or coordinating functions frequently bypass lines of authority or organizational hierarchy.

Modern technology has provided the means for rapid and efficient transmission of information to any point of the globe. For example, Mitsui, the giant Japanese trading company, has a private cable and telex system linking more than 120 overseas offices in over 70 countries and extending over 260,000 kilometers, or eight times around the world, and in 1974 was handling 30,000 telex messages daily at Tokyo headquarters. The problems of an information system, therefore, are not technological but improving the quality of information flows and translating such flows into more effective management decisions.[6] In many cases a mountain of routine standardized reports become an easy substitute for rigorous planning of what is essential and for making more effective use of information flows.

Most multinational enterprises are relatively sophisticated in ob-

---

[5]Ulrich Wiechmann, "Integrating Multinational Marketing Activities," *Columbia Journal of World Business,* Winter 1974, pp. 13–14.

[6]See Sune Carlson, "International Transmission of Information and the Business Firm," *ANNALS of the American Academy of Political and Social Science,* March 1974, pp. 55–63.

taining the internal corporate information they use in planning and control. The quality of such flows can be assured through "systems transfers," which refer to the use of a uniform framework for planning, budgeting, and performance reporting in all parts of the enterprise.[7] The transfer of a well-developed uniform system to the subsidiaries serves several purposes. It provides headquarters with comparable data from all subsidiaries. It ensures that all managers, regardless of background or nationality, can speak a common "company language" on professional and business matters.

Multinational enterprises, however, are generally less effective in developing information flows on the external environment.[8] Yet, extensive and rapid changes occurring outside the corporation can be extremely critical for global operations and control. Key external environmental intelligence variables must be identified, evaluated, and communicated to management so that important decisions and evaluations will not be made in ignorance of them.

Determining the right kind, amount, and frequency of information flows is one component of an effective information system. Another equally important aspect of information flows is the ability of personnel at both the sending and receiving sides to communicate with each other.

The importance of people transfers in improving the communications system is strongly underlined in a study of the Brazilian subsidiaries of 63 European, Japanese, and U.S. multinational firms.[9] As was reported by the subsidiary managers, two factors that strongly influenced the effectiveness of communications with headquarters were (1) whether a superior at headquarters had worked in the Brazilian subsidiary and (2) the tenure with the company of the chief executive officer of the subsidiary. The communications patterns differed, however, with the nationality of the parent firms. The U.S. companies more frequently employed Brazilian nationals for managerial positions in the subsidiary than did either European or Japanese firms. This employment policy explains in part the fact that most U.S. companies held annual meetings for the chief executive officer of their affiliates, whereas less than half of the European and Japanese firms held such meetings annually. Also, visits between the head of the Brazilian subsidiary and his or her home office superior averaged 4.8 times per year for the U.S. firms as compared to 3.4 and 2.9 for the European and Japanese companies, respectively.

[7]Wiechmann, "Integrating Multinational Marketing Activities," p. 14.

[8]Kyung-Il Ghymn, *Strategic Intelligence System for Multinational Corporations,* (Ph.D. diss., University of Pittsburgh, 1974) p. 1.

[9]William K. Brandt and James M. Hulbert, "Patterns of Communications in the Multinational Corporation: An Empirical Study," *Journal of International Business Studies,* Spring 1976, pp. 17–30.

Still another aspect of the communications and control system is the feedback pattern. In this respect, the study of Brazilian subsidiaries revealed nationality differences. Most subsidiaries of U.S. firms received a monthly response to their reports, whereas less than 10 percent of the European and Japanese subsidiaries received regular feedback. This suggests that the non-U.S. companies have a more relaxed attitude to minor deviations from plans.

MULTINATIONAL FINANCIAL CONTROLS

Because of their crucial importance in monitoring the operations of the multinational enterprise, financial controls warrant special attention. The demands on the financial information system and the difficulties in meeting these demands are greatly increased for the multinational firm over those involved in domestic operations because of the multiple currency problem and major variations in the accounting systems that must be used by different units of the system.

An accounting system for multinational enterprises has to satisfy several requirements simultaneously.[10] It must provide financial data for information and decision purposes that are understandable both in the country in which a particular unit of the system is operating and in the headquarters country where decisions involving more than one country have to be made. In addition, the accounting system must provide financial statements that can be consolidated on an enterprise-wide basis. To fulfill the consolidation requirements, the labeling and content of accounts must be uniform throughout the system and major difficulties inherent in translating values from one currency to another must be resolved.

At the subsidiary level, understandability must be guaranteed within the national environment. National accounting principles and procedures, prescribed either by law or by local professional organizations, must be followed in order that financial reports can be understood by tax and other government officials. And national accounting systems will vary with the legal, tax, and other features of the environment that are decided independently by each national government.[11] Adherence to national accounting standards also permits each local manager to manage on the basis of data and concepts with which he is familiar, lets him compare his performance with that of local

---

[10]This section draws heavily from Hanns-Martin Schoenfeld, "Some Special Accounting Problems of Multinational Enterprises," *Management International Review* 9, nos. 4–5 (1969): 3–11.

[11]For example, see *Professional Accounting in 25 Countries* (New York: American Institute of Certified Public Accountants, 1964); Stephen A. Zeff, *Forging Accounting Principles in Five Countries: A History and an Analysis of Trends* (Champaign, Ill.: Stipes Publishing Co., 1972).

competitors, and permits evaluation of his results against local rather than parent-company standards. Furthermore, many managerial decisions are dependent on national environmental constraints and have to be based on pertinent relevant data. For example, price-level adjustments for company expenses or sales for different time periods may be locally essential because of inflationary conditions even though such accounting practices are not typical in the country of the parent. Other examples of differences from U.S. practice are shown in Figure 22–1.

To secure understandability of accounting data in the decision center of the home office presents many difficult problems. Because the financial information system must be based on data retaining their various local characteristics, the accounting data that flow from the units within the system to headquarters normally contain only part of the pertinent variables and may be based on different environmental decision parameters. Understandability thus requires that top manage-

FIGURE 22–1

Accounting Principles and Practices That Are Different from Those Generally Accepted in the United States (some examples)

Accounting	*Explanation of Difference*	*Selected Countries Following Different Practice*
Exchange losses	Exchange losses arising on foreign currency liabilities incurred for importation of items of inventories are added to the cost of inventories if the corresponding items are unsold when the exchange losses arise. (A lower cost or market test is applied to the inventory after the exchange losses, if any, are added to the inventories.)	Argentina, Chile, India, Mexico, Peru, Philippines
Surplus entries	Capital reserves generally include items constituting capital gains which are carried to equity reserves without passing through (crediting) income.	Australia, Belgium, Ireland, New Zealand, Peru, Spain, United Kingdom
Disclosure		
Rental commitments	Material rental commitments on long-term leases (say, over one year) are seldom disclosed.	Argentina, Australia, Belgium, Brazil, Chile, Colombia, France, Germany, Italy, Japan
Consolidation of financial statements	In the case of a parent company having subsidiaries, consolidated (or group) accounts are not included in local statutory financial statements. Further, the parent's equity in subsidiaries, carried at cost, is not disclosed.	Colombia, Germany, Italy, Japan, Spain, Switzerland, Venezuela

Source: Price, Waterhouse and Co., USA, *Guide For the Readers of Foreign Financial Statements,* 2d ed., January 1975.

ment cultivate a multiple currency consciousness, a facility with multiple report forms and multiple analysis devices, and a general awareness of the assumptions, biases, or other distortions that may be inherent in the different national accounting systems. In many situations, the decision center may need several parallel financial information systems to provide the information required for divergent purposes.

An obvious solution is to develop internationally accepted accounting principles or move national regulations toward this goal. With the founding of the International Accounting Standards Committee (IASC) in 1973 by national accounting groups from nine major countries, and with representation from 35 countries, some progress had been made by 1976 toward setting internationally uniform accounting standards.[12] The barriers to a single set of generally accepted accounting principles, however, are not primarily the difficulties of securing agreement by representatives of many different nations. The basic difficulty is that accounting systems must be consistent with the economic and business systems prevailing in different countries. Only where environments are similar can a particular single body of accounting principles give meaningful results.[13] As one example, in the United States with a highly developed capital market, accounting practices must recognize the special needs of security analysts and the disclosure requirements of government regulatory agencies.

Even though a trend toward greater uniformity in accounting standards may eventually reduce some of the complexities of international financial management, the problem of multiple currencies is likely to remain for some time. Transactions are conducted and records kept in one currency and the parent company must ultimately see the results in its own currency. Over any given time period, the relationship of the two standards to each other may change because of differential rates of inflation and devaluations or revaluations. The operations of a foreign subsidiary may be highly successful when measured in local currency but may actually involve losses to the multinational enterprise system because of devaluation. Action taken to reduce potential devaluation losses to the system may also reduce the income of the subsidiary in local currency. Consequently, the currency problem produces complications in using the financial information system for appraising operation results and may require that performance responsibility be assigned in each of the two standards.

---

[12]See *Accountants Weekly*, September 3, 1976, pp. 10–12.

[13]Gerhard G. Mueller, "Accounting Principles Generally Accepted in the United States Versus Those Generally Accepted Elsewhere," *The International Journal of Accounting, Education, and Research*, Spring 1968, pp. 91–103.

The manager of the subsidiary, for example, may be expected to maximize profits in the local currency and the financial office of the parent company be responsible for minimizing losses through devaluation.

The problems of translation and consolidation of accounts were discussed in Chapter 21 as key issues in international financial management. Other accounting problems arise with transfer pricing, service charges of various sorts, and the allocation of headquarters and research expenses to the subsidiaries. Generally, the parent-company management reserves final authority in such decisions and attempts to make them in terms of systemwide optimization. Thus, financial comparisons and evaluations of local operating companies may be determined as much by parent-company decisions as by the actual operating results of the subsidiaries. In many cases, therefore, it is extremely difficult to make the necessary adjustments for a fair evaluation of the profitability of individual units of the enterprise.

Given the multiple purposes that must be served simultaneously by financial reporting and the variations in accounting principles, multinational enterprises are finding it necessary to use three or four different sets of financial statements. National financial statements are prepared on the basis of nationally accepted accounting principles. A second set of financial statements is prepared by each unit of the system which complies with the accounting principles and the translation methods that are accepted in the country of the home office. Still another set may be prepared to comply with the regulations of the various tax authorities involved. And finally, separate financial statements may be prepared which present a picture of the enterprise for management. In such a statement, for example, uniform valuation methods for assets of all subsidiaries might be used, regardless of the different legal regulations or locally accepted accounting practices.

CONTROL PROBLEMS IN RELATION TO JOINT VENTURES

Joint ventures present a special control problem in multinational business operations. By desire or by necessity, multinational firms commonly have joint-venture affiliates as part of their multinational operations. And if the firm tries to implement a global strategy and realize the special advantages of multinational operations, it has to deal with conflicts that are likely to exist between the interests of the local partners and the global objectives and opportunities for the enterprise. Frequently joint ventures are located in the less developed countries where the governments enforce a joint-venture policy as a means of increasing local control over business decisions to ensure that these decisions are compatible with national objectives.[14]

In the case of joint ventures, the experience of Japanese multinationals is of special interest because Japanese firms have had a much higher ratio of joint ventures than have U.S., European, or Canadian firms. The extent to which a joint-venture subsidiary can be controlled by the parent, according to one study, depends upon the control the parent has over key resources required by the subsidiary.[15] These key resources are informational (technology and management know-how), financial, and input-output leverage. The informational resources are controlled through technical assistance contracts and through placing parent-company personnel in subsidiary managerial positions. The so-called input-output leverage exists when the subsidiary is dependent upon the parent for securing components, equipment, and replacement parts or for marketing a significant share of the subsidiary's output.

For Japanese firms, the most important source of control has been the technical assistance contract and information and know-how flows. The second most important means has been the placing of home-country personnel in the subsidiary. The production manager position was more heavily relied upon than the financial manager position as a means of control.

Control through home-country personnel frequently ran into difficulties because of the desire of foreign countries to have local nationals in managerial posts. Host governments in Malaysia, Singapore, Indonesia, and Thailand, for example, have been unwilling at times to issue visas or work permits to financial officers from Japan. The country motivation was not only to promote local financial talent but also to try to make accounting information more accessible so that local demands for higher wages could be supported. At one time Malaysia and Singapore also attempted to control the assignment of home-country engineers and technical personnel but had to reverse this policy because qualified local personnel was not available.[16]

There is no easy solution to the joint-venture control problem. In many cases, multinational firms have had to resolve the difficulties and

---

[14]Richard W. Wright and Colin S. Russel, "Joint Ventures in Developing Countries: Realities and Responses," *Columbia Journal of World Business,* Summer 1975, pp. 74–80.

[15]Kichiro Hayashi, "Japanese Management of Multinational Operations: Sources and Means of Control" (Paper presented at the annual meetings of the Academy of International Business in Dallas, Texas, December 1975).

[16]Ibid, pp. 16–17.

frustrations associated with control attempts by increasing their ownership position or by selling out to local interests.

EXTERNAL REPORTING AND CONTROLS

In recent years, the pressures on all business firms for external reporting to stockholders, government agencies, and the general public have increased greatly, and the pressures on multinational enterprises have escalated most dramatically.[17] Multinationals must respond to the numerous and varied demands of many different national environments, and in many countries they are often subjected to unusually stringent demands because of the foreign nationality of the parent.

Outside auditing, required of publicly held corporations in most countries, is one major form of external reporting. In the United States, the coverage of outside auditing and external reporting is particularly extensive for firms interested in raising capital in the U.S. capital markets or having their shares listed on the U.S. stock exchanges. Many European firms have great difficulties with the U.S. requirements because they are unaccustomed by national tradition to making so much detailed information publicly available.

During the mid-1970s, a combination of outside auditing, congressional investigations, and security regulation in the United States resulted in extensive information becoming publicly available on the foreign bribery practices of many U.S. multinationals. These revelations showed that foreign government officials and foreign companies had participated in bribery and caused governments outside of the United States to establish reporting and control systems in the bribery area.

Another trend in external reporting may emerge in the area of capital flows. The Swiss National Bank in 1976 requested foreign and Swiss multinationals to provide monthly forecasts of international capital flows. With the shift in the international financial system from fixed exchange rates to a managed float, the Swiss government wanted to avoid big swings in the value of its currency by being prepared to intervene in the marketplace when capital shifts are anticipated.

The broadest pressures for external reporting have been from the movement for establishing guidelines for multinational enterprises already discussed in Chapter 8. The guidelines agreed to by the OECD countries (Figure 22-2) illustrate the extensive information and reporting objectives of national governments.[18] The guidelines, for example,

---

[17]See J. J. Boddewyn, *Corporate External Affairs: Blueprint for Survival* (New York: Business International, December 1975).

[18]See Karl P. Sauvant and Farid G. Lavipour, eds., *Controlling Multinational Enterprises: Problems, Strategies, Counterstrategies* (Boulder, Colorado: Westview Press, 1976).

FIGURE 22–2
OECD Guidelines for Multinational Enterprise

Disclosure of Information

Enterprises should, having due regard to their nature and relative size in the economic context of their operations and to requirements of business confidentiality and to cost, publish in a form suited to improve public understanding a sufficient body of factual information on the structure, activities, and policies of the enterprise as a whole, as a supplement, insofar as necessary for this purpose, to information to be disclosed under the national law of the individual countries in which they operate. To this end, they should publish within reasonable time limits, on a regular basis, but at least annually, financial statements and other pertinent information relating to the enterprise as a whole, comprising in particular:

1. The structure of the enterprise, showing the name and location of the parent company, its main affiliates, its percentage ownership, direct and indirect, in these affiliates, including shareholdings between them.

2. The geographic areas* where operations are carried out and the principal activities carried on therein by the parent company and the main affiliates.

3. The operating results and sales by geographical area and the sales in the major lines of business for the enterprise as a whole.

4. Significant new capital investment by geographical area and, as far as practicable, by major lines of business for the enterprise as a whole.

5. A statement of the sources and uses of funds by the enterprise as a whole.

6. The average number of employees in each geographic area.

7. Research and development expenditure for the enterprise as a whole.

8. The policies followed in respect of intragroup pricing.

9. The accounting policies, including those on consolidation, observed in compiling the published information.

---

*For the purposes of the guideline on disclosure of information the term "geographic area" means groups of countries or individual countries as each enterprise determines is appropriate in its particular circumstances. While no single method of grouping is appropriate for all enterprises or for all purposes, the factors to be considered by an enterprise would include the significance of operations carried out in individual countries or areas as well as the effects on its competitiveness, geographic proximity, economic affinity, similarities in business environments and the nature, scale, and degree of interrelationships of the enterprises' operations in the various countries.

Source: Organization for Economic Co-Operation and Development, *International Investment and Multinational Enterprises* (Paris, 1976), pp. 14–15.

---

require multinational firms to report operating results and sales by geographic area, sales by major lines of business, transfer-pricing policies, and financial flows. The guidelines are voluntary and require implementing national legislation in the OECD countries to be compulsory. Yet, the existence of the guidelines, even though "voluntary," exerts strong pressure on the multinationals to comply.

Another important trend has been the growing demands and expectations that business firms act in a socially responsible fashion.[19] It may be further in the future, but there is a strong probability that multinational firms may have to publish a social audit and report on their relationship to the social environment and the effects of this relationship. As some business leaders have predicted, "in addition to their independently audited annual statements, firms will some day be legally obliged to submit audited social utility accounts—even if the definitive form of such accounts is not yet clear."[20]

SUMMARY

The complexity, scale, and diversity of multinational operations make the control function in multinational business both extremely important and unusually difficult. Because information systems cross national boundaries and varied cultures, special efforts are required to improve the effectiveness of communications. It is difficult to develop performance standards that are meaningful and do not interfere significantly with operating objectives. The environments and the ground rules for operations change rapidly in both the home and host countries. Control systems, therefore, must be flexible and continuously adapted to new circumstances.[21]

The external reporting and control situation is particularly complicated for the multinational enterprise. The firm uses its information and control system to accomplish its global objectives. National governments increasingly are demanding more extensive external reporting so that they can exert greater control over multinationals toward achieving national objectives. Thus, from the standpoint of both internal and external controls, the information and control function in the multinational enterprise is one of management's most challenging responsibilities.

EXERCISES AND DISCUSSION QUESTIONS

1. The principles, procedures, and general problems of planning, information systems, and control appear to be fundamentally the same for operating in one or many national environments. Discuss.

---

[19]Isaiah A. Litvak and Christopher J. Maule, "Foreign Corporate Social Responsibility in Less Developed Economies," *Journal of World Trade Law*, March/April 1975; Melvin Anshen, ed., *Managing the Socially Responsible Corporation* (New York: Macmillan, 1974).

[20]*Vision (Europe)*, February 1975, p. 55.

[21]See James Milano and Philip D. Grub, "Problems Associated with a World-Wide Information and Control System in the Multinational Environment" (Paper presented at the Academy of International Business meetings, New York, December 1973).

2. How will the OECD guidelines on disclosure of information affect the information and control system of a multinational enterprise operating in industrialized countries? In less-developed countries?

3. For purposes of external reporting, what items would you include in Social Utility Accounts?

4. In choosing performance criteria, what are examples of potential conflicts of interest among units of the enterprise that must be considered?

5. The International Accounting Standards Committee (IASC) has made some progress toward developing internationally uniform accounting standards. What are some of the major difficulties inherent in reaching agreement on uniform standards and what are some of the advantages that can result?

23

Multinational Management of Human Resources

THE QUALITY OF A FIRM'S EXECUTIVES is almost certain to be the single most important determinant of its success in international business. An aggressive global strategy implies managerial resources of a caliber to think out and implement such policies. More broadly, as one international executive has observed, ". . . virtually any type of international problem, in the final analysis, is either created by people or must be solved by people. Hence, having the right people in the right place at the right time emerges as the key to a company's international growth. If we are successful in solving that problem, I am confident we can cope with all others . . ."[1]

Multinational business brings with it many unique problems in the management of human resources, the most fundamental of which is the necessity for managers raised and experienced in one culture to play bicultural or multicultural roles. The managers of foreign subsidiaries play a boundary or middleman role between two sets of cultural patterns.[2] To their subordinates and customers, they are "the company" and represent headquarters. To headquarters, they are the "local manager" who belongs to the subsidiary. They must know the local culture and language and they must understand the foreign cultural assumptions underlying the technology and business practices being introduced into the local environment. Whether a national or an expatriate, the local manager is sandwiched between his or her own culture and the foreign cultures.[3]

---

[1]Michael G. Duerr, "International Business Management: Its Four Tasks," *Conference Board Record,* October 1968, p. 43.

[2]See Chapter 15.

[3]Chul Koo Yun, "Role Conflicts of Expatriate Managers: A Construct," *Management International Review* 13 (1973/76): 106.

Managers at headquarters or the regional level play a multicultural role. They must integrate and coordinate activities taking place in many cultural environments that are being directed by managers with diverse cultural orientations. Furthermore, they must deal with the natural tendency of local managers to identify with the national interests of their unit.

Another set of management problems arises out of the necessity to transfer some employees across cultural and national boundaries. The selection of those who are to be transferred involves choice among the various nationalities involved; raises questions concerning desirable characteristics, education, and renumeration; and requires procedures to facilitate the adjustment of those who switch cultures and residence.

Finally, the international extension of a firm involves widely varying manpower environments in terms of the available supply and skills of workers,[4] many different patterns of labor-management relations, and the emerging issue of international union collaboration for multinational bargaining.

GENERAL POLICY ON INTERNATIONAL EXECUTIVES

What policy should the multinational firm adopt for the recruitment and development of international executives? Essentially, the international firm can choose from among three alternative policies for staffing management positions, or design some combination of the three. It can fill key positions everywhere in the world with personnel from the home country of the parent company—an ethnocentric policy. It can use local nationals to manage foreign subsidiaries and home-country nationals as headquarters managers—a polycentric policy. Or it can recruit and develop the best persons without regard to nationality for key positions anywhere in the multinational system—a geocentric policy. Each of the alternatives has advantages and disadvantages.

At first glance, the most effective policy would appear to be a geocentric one, where the best person is sought for a job, regardless of the person's nationality and the location of the job. Such a policy would be consistent with the unique strength of multinational business, namely its ability to rationalize on an international basis the use of natural resources, financial resources, and technology. Why shouldn't it also rationalize on an international basis the use of managerial resources? To some degree and for a period of time, expatriate managers might be handicapped by not being fully immersed in the national cultural, political and economic situation. But these disadvan-

---

[4]John C. Shearer, "The External and Internal Manpower Resources of MNCs," *Columbia Journal of World Business*, Summer 1974, pp. 9–17.

534 International Business and Multinational Enterprises

tages would be more than offset by his or her superior ability and experience. Even more important, the tendency of national identification of managers with units of the system will be reduced so that the firm will be better able to realize its multinational potentials.

Yet there have been only modest beginnings by a relatively few international firms toward developing a truly international executive force. The factors explained the limited popularity of a geocentric policy indicate the disadvantages of this alternative. First, host countries want foreign subsidiaries to be staffed by their local nationals and frequently adopt national controls to achieve this goal. Second, an international executive policy can be expensive because it requires widespread recruitment, a substantial investment in language training and cultural orientation programs for managers and their families, substantial costs in transferring executives and their families into and away from foreign posts, and a willingness to pay international salary levels which are significantly higher than national levels in many countries. Third, such a pattern would require a high degree of centralization in the control of personnel and their career patterns, and undercut the cherished prerogative of local managers to choose their own personnel. A fourth reason is that the policy would take a long time to implement. Finally, firms have discovered that adaptations to a general policy of using nationals can achieve many of the advantages of a truly international executive policy.

Foreign Nationals for Managing Subsidiaries

Hiring nationals has many obvious advantages, which are mainly the obverse of the disadvantages of an international executive-career policy. Hiring nationals largely eliminates the language barriers, expensive training periods, and the cross-cultural adjustment problems of managers and their families. It lowers the profile of a foreign firm in sensitive political situations. It permits the firm to take advantage of lower national salary levels, while still paying a premium over local norms to attract high-quality personnel. And since the career of nationals will be in their home country, they will give continuity to the management of foreign subsidiaries.

Nevertheless, there is a price to be paid in following a policy of hiring nationals. At the overseas subsidiary level, nationals will adapt well to the local environment, but they are likely to have difficulties in bridging the gap between the subsidiary and the rest of the system. The education, business experience, and cultural environment to which they have been exposed all their lives may not have prepared them to work as part of a multinational enterprise. They may experience cross-cultural problems because of different concepts as to business practices, differences in personal values such as a reluctance to "dirty one's hands," and many other cultural variables. They may identify with their country as against the spirit and advantages of multinationalism. They are not likely to be fully knowledgeable about the management techniques, products, and technology developed in the parent firm's home country on which the firm's international expansion is based. There is an inbuilt immobility. Once a foreign manager reaches the top position in the overseas subsidiary, he has nowhere to go. The narrow focus of his career can affect his own morale and block the promotion of those underneath him.[5] In turn, some of the most promising foreign nationals may be difficult to recruit and to retain because of the limited promotion possibilities within the total enterprise. Also, many nationals are interested in only a limited tour of duty with foreign firms in order to get training and experience.

Japanese multinationals, because their international business language is generally Japanese, have unusual difficulties in finding nationals with the necessary language ability. Even if the language gap is bridged by hiring nationals of Japanese ancestry, the culture gap may still remain. As a Japanese executive complained about his company's experience in Brazil, where there is a large nisei population, "They look Japanese, they speak Japanese, but they think Brazilian."

For most U.S. multinationals, the advantages of hiring nationals in their foreign operations clearly outweigh the disadvantages. In 1974, General Motors had 185,000 employees outside of the United States, of which only 350 were Americans. IBM had 115,000 employees overseas, including only 400 Americans. At the same time, IBM had more than 1,000 foreigners working in the United States.

Patterns appear to vary with the nationality of the multinationals. A study in Brazil of the local subsidiaries of U.S., European, and Japanese multinationals showed that the median proportion of Brazilian officers to total officers in U.S. subsidiaries was 56 percent compared with 38 percent for the Europeans and 16 percent for the Japanese. Also, despite the chronic shortage of management personnel in this rapidly developing country, 24 percent of the U.S. subsidiaries were headed by Brazilian citizens as compared with 8 percent for European subsidiaries and none for the Japanese.[6] These differences, of course, reflect in part the longer operating experience of U.S. companies in Brazil.

[5]See Yoram Zeira, "Overlooked Personnel Problems of Multinational Corporations," Columbia Journal of World Business, Summer 1975, pp. 96–103.

[6]William K. Brandt and James M. Hulbert, "Managing the Multinational Subsidiary in Brazil: A Preliminary Summary," Research Paper No. 65 (New York: Graduate School of Business, Columbia University, July 1974).

Headquarters Managers

Discussions of executive employment policies have generally focused on the management of overseas subsidiaries, with only relatively minor attention devoted to the implications of alternative policies to filling management positions at headquarters. Just as local nationals in foreign subsidiaries will have cross-cultural problems in communicating and dealing with headquarters, home-country nationals at headquarters will have even larger problems in cross-cultural dealings with a large number of foreign countries. A study of the communication barrier in 55 companies of U.S. and non-U.S. nationality concluded that two major causes of communication problems in international management were (1) the lack of multinational working experience by the corporate top executives who are assigned to run the international operations, and (2) the limited number of experienced international executives on the boards of directors of these companies.[7]

A policy of employing nationals makes it difficult for young executives from headquarters or from foreign subsidiaries to get experience working outside of their home country and to develop their capacity to communicate, coordinate, and effectively supervise in a multicultural setting. Such a policy is unlikely to create a body of international executives able to switch between units of the multinational firm as the need arises. It also reinforces the dominance of home-country executives, frequently with little actual foreign working experience, in the higher corporate posts dealing with strategy and capital allocations decisions between subsidiary units dominated by local nationals. The almost complete domination of top-management echelons of U.S. international companies by U.S. personnel in the middle 1960s was demonstrated by a study showing that out of almost 4,000 top managers of the 150 largest U.S. industrial corporations, only 59, or 1.6 percent, were foreigners, and half of this foreign group was Canadian.[8] Although the situation has changed somewhat since the time of the study, the general pattern still persists.

A 1972 study of Britain's 86 largest industrial companies revealed that out of 1,126 directors, only 57 were foreign nationals, including 12 cross-directorships of three binational companies—Unilever, Shell, and Dunlop. Only one company, Rio Tinto-Zinc, approached true multinationality with 10 foreign directors out of a total of 27.[9]

---

[7]Dimitri N. Chorafas, *The Communication Barrier in International Management* (New York: American Management Association, 1969), p. 63.

[8]Kenneth Simmonds, "Multinational? Well, Not Quite," *Columbia Journal of World Business*, Fall 1966, pp. 115–22.

[9]Kenneth Simmonds and Richard Connell, "Breaking the Boardroom Barrier: The Importance of Being British," *The Journal of Management Studies*, May 1974, pp. 85–95.

Retention of top corporate management at headquarters in the hands of nationals of the parent country has a number of advantages. The executives come from a reasonably similar cultural background and have little trouble in communicating with each other. They are likely to have experienced the buildup of the parent unit and to have developed skills and evolved a working pattern in the management of an international operation. In the longer run, however, a firm with this sort of management pattern can become a grouping of virtually independent national units with the prime responsibility for transfer of ideas and for general cohesion falling on executives of the parent unit who are not sufficiently prepared for this task.

Criteria for Choosing a Policy

Clearly, none of the alternative policies—including the use of home-country personnel around the world—provides a complete answer to the complexities of managing multinational enterprises. But subprograms which complement or modify a basic policy of favoring nationals can go a long way toward giving the firm the "best of both worlds." One technique is to identify replacement candidates for key executives throughout the system and arrange at least one cross-cultural assignment of generally two years' duration as part of their international career plan. This will expose headquarters executives to the challenges of field operations and expand the experience of foreign nationals, while still keeping them in a career path toward top management in their home country. Another approach is to hire local nationals for foreign subsidiaries who have had academic training in the country of the parent company. Many foreign students graduating from U.S. business schools have become a significant source of management personnel for U.S. multinational companies.[10] Still another practice that has been followed by only a few advanced companies is to develop a small group of truly international career managers who will have several cross-cultural assignments and be considered for assignments throughout the enterprise.[11] In addition, most companies carry on training or management-development programs designed to transfer technical and managerial skills to promising local national

---

[10]G. G. Alpander, "Foreign MBA: Potential Managers for American International Corporations," *Journal of International Business Studies,* Spring 1973.

[11]For examples of two of the most advanced programs for internationalizing management personnel, see Charles K. Campbell, *Cross Cultural and Cross Functional Development of Personnel in IBM World Trade Corporation,* mimeographed (New York: National Foreign Trade Council, February 1970), NFTC ref. no. M-9292; Donald N. Leich, *Transnational Executive Development in the Royal Dutch Shell Group of Companies,* mimeographed (New York: National Foreign Trade Council, February 1970), NFTC ref. no. M-9293.

managers and other candidates for middle- and upper-management positions.

But even when a policy of employing nationals is supplemented by cross-cultural training assignments and other programs, some companies still feel that they must have a home country "presence" in each foreign subsidiary. In practice, this presence for U.S. firms which follow such a policy is the local general manager or chief finance officer. Some companies go even further in insisting on home-country personnel as essential for transferring technological strength from the parent company and feedback from the subsidiaries. As one manager of a European company claimed, "There should be a European at the head of the U.S. operation. I have a rapport with our parent that dates back over 33 years. This rapport is terribly useful for communication back and forth. How could an American develop such a rapport . . . particularly with a French mother company?"[12]

Given the various alternatives, how does a multinational company decide on its policy as to the desired nationality mix for its international executives? Its choice depends heavily on an evaluation of the following five factors.

1.   The nature of a firm's business and its product strategy.
2.   National controls and policies favoring the hiring of local nationals.
3.   National controls over the transfer of personnel and the mobility of managers.
4.   The supply of managerial personnel in the countries of operations.
5.   The costs of alternative policies, including the cost of remedying the deficiencies of the policies.

Most multinational firms follow a policy that favors hiring local nationals for foreign subsidiaries, home-country nationals at headquarters,[13] and, where a regional organization exists, a mix of foreign and home-country managers for regional positions.[14] Within this general policy, the nationality mix will vary with the nature of a firm's business and its product strategy. Where area expertise plays a major role, as in the case of consumer goods and/or a limited product line, the use of home-country personnel for overseas assignments will be minimal. Where product expertise is highly important and/or industrial markets are being served, home-country personnel will be used more

---

[12]*European Strategies in the United States* (Geneva, Switzerland: Business International, S.A., 1971), p. 42.

[13]Michael G. Duerr and James Greene, *Foreign Nationals in International Management* (New York: National Industrial Conference Board, 1968), p. 3.

[14]National Foreign Trade Council, *Regional Personnel Management: Survey of Company Practice* (New York, October 1973).

extensively for foreign assignments because they generally have quick access to the home-country sources of supply and technical information. Service industries also tend to have more home-country personnel in foreign posts, particularly where the firm is serving home-country multinationals in foreign areas, as in the case of banking.

Whatever policy or combination of policies is adopted, the international firm must have a long-range and continuing program of management recruitment and development that is integrated with its global strategy and business planning.[15] It needs to work constantly toward internationalizing the experience and outlook of all executive personnel including the higher echelons of corporate power. Promising managerial talent must be discovered early so that young managers can secure cross-national experience and be moved in the middle of their careers either to regional or global headquarters where they can make the jump from a "functional" to a "general" manager. Any strategies directed toward greater internationalism of managerial resources will, of course, be constrained by national laws. However, within this framework, much can be done. The most compelling argument for developing multinational executives is that it will avoid inbreeding and narrowness at the top. For the firm of the future, truly international management will have greater sensitivity to changes in the world environment and flexibility in adapting to them.

PROBLEMS OF CROSS-NATIONAL TRANSFERS

All international firms transfer employees across cultural or national boundaries to some extent. Cross-national transfers may be part of an international career-development program, a result of a borrowing and lending concept between countries, or a means of supplying experienced personnel for a new subsidiary while local nationals are being trained. In any event, managers who are assigned to foreign posts for extended periods are likely to encounter special problems of working in a foreign environment, living in a different culture, and maintaining satisfactory relations with the parent company.

New Working Relationships

The executive transferred will, of course, have to establish new working relationships within a cultural environment vastly different from the one to which he or she is accustomed. The executive will have to be aware of the cultural variations discussed in Chapter 15 as they

---

[15]Lawrence G. Franko, "Who Manages Multinational Enterprises?" *Columbia Journal of World Business*, Summer 1973, pp. 30–42.

affect local patterns of decision making, issuing and accepting instructions, and conducting many other day-to-day aspects of management and business operations. He or she must deal with local foreign personnel with backgrounds, languages, attitudes, values, and points of view different from his own; adapt technical and managerial know-how to an unfamiliar environment; and cope with economic and political environments that are unfamiliar and often more complicated than those encountered at home.[16]

A number of studies have investigated the kinds of problems encountered in cross-national assignments, mainly of Americans in less developed country settings.[17] Anecdotes and case examples abound. European and Japanese expatriate managers undoubtedly face numerous similar problems in cross-national transfers, although their experiences have not yet been well documented. However, one study reports that a number of European managers transferred to the United States discovered that dealing with U.S. labor unions was too traumatic for them and that this task was best left to Americans.[18] But the emphasis on problems, as Skinner cautions, "should in no sense imply that all men sent abroad fail to perform well, that most assignments abroad are unhappy ones, or that expatriate managers always present difficult and absorbing problems for executives in the home office. This is not so."[19]

Family and Social Adjustments

Outside his working situation, the foreign executive and his or her family encounter environmental differences that are even more marked than the on-the-job differences. Social contacts may be severely curtailed, for example, if the expatriate's wife cannot speak the local language. Wives of local business and social acquaintances are unlikely to be able to speak anything other than the local language, and significant relationships are not likely to be built up across a language barrier. Wives in some countries will have several servants and with some relief from household duties have considerable free time. Bore-

---

[16]See Wickham Skinner, *American Industry in Developing Economies* (New York: John Wiley and Sons, 1968), pp. 222–48.

[17]For example, see John Fayerweather, *The Executive Overseas* (Syracuse, N.Y.: Syracuse University Press, 1969); John C. Shearer, *High-Level Manpower in Overseas Subsidiaries* (Princeton, N.J.: Industrial Relations Section, Princeton University, 1960); Richard F. Gonzalez and Anant R. Negandhi, *The United States Overseas Executive: His Orientations and Career Patterns* (East Lansing, Mich.: Michigan State University, 1967).

[18]*European Strategies in the United States*, p. 43.

[19]Skinner, *American Industry in Developing Economies*, p. 222.

dom, excessive drinking, and high spending are not uncommon results. A broad study of almost 2,000 employees of a multinational firm on cross-national assignments, of whom about 20 percent were of American nationality, concluded that an employee's satisfaction with his foreign assignment depended mainly on his wife's adjustment to the assignment. The wife's satisfaction ranked as the most important element among the American group and only slightly lower than job-related elements in the total group.[20]

The stress of cross-national transfers on an executive and the executive's family may produce behavior patterns that prejudice the manager's job performance. Rejection of the new culture and glorification of the old is not uncommon. Frequently referred to as "culture shock," this can result in the establishment of tight groups of expatriates from the home country who devote themselves to recreating the home culture and dwelling on the "weaker" points of that in which they reside. This is what a Shell executive calls "those bloody people" syndrome.

> The expatriate goes young and fresh to his first "new" country and he makes a big effort to integrate. He learns about local culture, he travels the country, and he tries to learn the language. Then he is moved. The next country is a little more difficult. Those people in his first overseas assignment were pretty unreliable anyway. The new lot are worse. He makes some kind of effort, but it's not such a big effort. By the fourth or fifth country, he may have given up. He locks himself up with expatriate colleagues and he doesn't want to see anything of the local scene except when he is actually working. That man, I submit, is a major liability in any multinational operation . . . for him, they are only "those bloody people."[21]

Career Patterns

Other problems raised by cross-national transfers have to do with career patterns and relationships with parent-company headquarters. Unless international assignments are part of a planned cross-pollination program, that is, the process of moving high-potential professionals between foreign affiliates for management-development purposes, the executive who undertakes such an assignment may experience amplified feelings of insecurity and concern over his or her future career. As the distance and time away from headquarters

---

[20]Gillian Purcer-Smith, *Studies of International Mobility (in IBM World Trade Corp.)*, mimeographed (New York: National Foreign Trade Council, 1971), NFTC ref. no. M-9936.

[21]Leich, *Transnational Executive Development in the Royal Dutch Shell Group of Companies,* p. 22.

increase, an "exile complex" may develop and the manager will begin to ask such questions as: "Will I be forgotten at the home office?" and "Where is my next assignment going to be?" Even if the person is scheduled to return to the parent company or the home subsidiary, the manager may be concerned about the reentry problem.

To reduce the potential dissatisfaction of executives being transferred, the international firm should have a policy for repatriation. If the firm always repatriates the executives concerned and finds them a post with equally high status in the parent company, unhappy executives will expect to be taken care of. The cost can be high. Not only are transfer costs large, but the foreign subsidiary must find a replacement with additional transfer costs and lack of continuity in the job. It is not always easy to find a job for a returning expatriate when the person is ready to return. Some firms make it clear that those going overseas do so on a career basis and will be returned only if they are asked to take another position in the firm. Other firms argue that even the more successful and experienced managers within the firm will have failures in foreign posts due to factors outside their control, and that these managers are worth retaining despite the cost of repatriation. The more important task is to minimize the failures through careful selection and prior training.

RECRUITMENT AND SELECTION OF INTERNATIONAL EXECUTIVES

If a firm is to develop a truly international management team, the best place to start is with recruitment policies. When a firm takes its first steps toward becoming international, it normally has not had the opportunity to develop a cadre of international managers. Its middle- and top-level managers would have been recruited in earlier periods when selection criteria were based on domestic business needs. Its recruitment would almost certainly have been limited to persons living in the home country. Prior to going international, the firm could not offer internal opportunities for managers to gain international experience except in the exporting field. Thus at such an early stage, managers for international operations have been mainly recruited from within the organization without having had any previous experience in foreign operations.[22] Where international expansion occurred through acquisitions, some firms were able to add key executives of the

---

[22]Enid Baird Lovell, *The Changing Role of the International Executive* (New York: National Industrial Conference Board, 1966), p. 26. A study of 144 U.S. companies concluded that "In a substantial proportion of the companies the incumbent (international) executive was transferred to the top executive position without having had any prior experience in its foreign operations."

acquired companies to their international management staff. A third source may have been "buy-ins," or experienced international managers hired from outside the company.

Such makeshift methods, however, must be replaced by a continuing system of management development and career planning for international operations. Such a system, of course, is not uniquely international. It begins with a forecast of future management manpower needs on an annual basis for at least a five-year forward period. Given the long lead time necessary to develop top and middle management within an enterprise, a company such as Royal Dutch Shell works with 15-year forecasts based on the firm's long-term planning.[23] The forecasts estimate future demand for different regions and for different functions. The forecasts are matched against an annual inventory of staff with potential to qualify for forecasted vacancies. The shortfall or deficiency then becomes the recruitment target. With a total employment in 1970 of more than 170,000 in the Royal Dutch Shell group of companies, except for the United States and Canada, the number of top- and middle-management positions with which the company's executive development program was concerned totaled about 5,000.

With recruitment targets specified as to positions to be filled, the location of these positions, and the type of personnel required, the international firm can follow conventional recruitment practices, except for several additional international complications. Some of the international issues on which it must decide are as follows:

1. In what countries should the company recruit?
2. Where recruitment is planned in countries other than the home country, what new techniques and sources will have to be used?
3. To what extent should recruitment decisions and activities be centralized in the parent company or decentralized in foreign subsidiaries?
4. What special selection criteria should be used because of the international nature of the company?
5. To what extent, if any, will the general policies on international executives assist or act as an obstacle in recruitment?

Recruitment for international managers should extend beyond the universities or business schools of the developed countries and should include universities wherever the firm operates. Outside the United States, management training is a relatively new educational field, but the amount and quality of such academic training began to expand

---

[23]Leich, *Transnational Executive Development in the Royal Dutch Shell Group of Companies,* p. 4–A.

rapidly in most developed countries and in many less developed countries by the late 1960s. In many countries, universities have not yet developed adequate facilities for assisting firms in their recruitment. In such cases, recruitment techniques may have to rely heavily on newspaper advertising, executive recruitment companies, or special efforts to contact young people when they finish their military service.

An enterprise-wide executive development and recruitment program will necessarily be a cooperative effort between the foreign subsidiaries and regional and global headquarters. But for the larger corporation, a central inventory of international executives will be needed to assure that promising executives do not become lost in a foreign posting. This in turn will lead to some surrender of power to make appointments on the part of individual units of the organization. Without a central voice in appointments, continued career development of the international executive might be sacrificed to the interests of individual units or jeopardized by preferred promotion of those known locally.

Actual recruitment activities, however, can be decentralized and the managers of foreign subsidiaries should have a voice in the final decision on the hiring of personnel that will work under their direction. A company like Proctor and Gamble has its subsidiaries establish their recruitment needs which are then consolidated at the division level, for example, the European Division, which has responsibility for recruitment. Foreign nationals studying in the United States are recruited by the parent company for the foreign subsidiaries but only up to a preselection phase. Such candidates are then interviewed by the manager of the division or the subsidiary, which makes the final offer. In some cases, the prospective candidate may even be flown back to his or her home country at company expense so that the local manager can interview the person and make the final decision.

In selecting executives for international management and for cross-national postings, it must be borne in mind that few firms have large numbers of executives competent and available for such posts, and a highly complex selection system is likely to be unnecessary. Moreover, so little is known about measuring characteristics that make for success in cross-cultural management and foreign postings that the accuracy of such systems is questionable. One fairly reliable characteristic is previous cross-cultural experience. For this reason, many U.S. firms aggressively recruit foreigners who have become familiar with U.S. culture through studying in the United States or young Americans with overseas Peace Corps experience.

Listings of the qualities needed for success in a foreign posting seem very like those needed anywhere for success as an executive. The requirements, anyway, vary from situation to situation and country to country so that no single set of standards would be adequate.[24] Because of these difficulties in predicting success in foreign environments, the failure rate can be high and the costs so great that some care is warranted in searching for factors that are likely to lead to failures. Measurement becomes more a check for weakness than an absolute testing. As one recruitment expert has observed, "Most selection methods . . . are in effect rejection schemes."[25] Inflexibility, and insensitivity to others' views and to new political situations have been cited as frequent characteristics of failures. But failures can be equally caused by strong attachments to a family grouping left behind in the home country, health problems, or basic marital instability. Long interviews with executives who are being considered for foreign appointments are perhaps the best means of drawing out potential problems.[26] Of course, the most difficult time will be the first overseas posting, but then many executives will be younger and their pattern of life less rigidly established.

A final issue relevant to the success of recruitment programs is the firm's policies on promotion. In order to secure good managers for foreign assignments, the international firm must make clear by its actions that cross-national service is of importance to the firm. And in order to recruit promising executives to work with the subsidiaries, the firm must have a policy of open career opportunities for top-management positions. The view of many ambitious and able young foreign nationals was expressed as follows by an international manager:

> He must feel that if he has the ability he can aspire to any job in the company, apart perhaps from the presidency. It may be that when he is faced with the prospect of going on the main board, and so spending the rest of his working life outside his home country he will decide to reject the opportunity. If so that will be his decision. But he must feel that his nationality does not, of itself, disqualify him from aiming for the stars."[27]

----

[24]Richard D. Hays, "Expatriate Selection: Insuring Success and Avoiding Failure," *Journal of International Business Studies*, Spring 1974, pp. 25–37; and Edwin L. Miller, "The Selection Decision for an International Assignment: A Study of the Decision Maker's Behavior," *Journal of International Business Studies*, Fall 1972, pp. 49–65.

[25]A. T. M. Wilson, "Management Recruitment for the Multinational Company," *Prospect 3, Journal of AIESEC International*, Autumn 1969, p. 25.

[26]See William Alexander, Jr., "Mobil's Four Hour Environmental Interview," *Worldwide P & I Planning*, January–February 1970, pp. 18–27. Alexander reports that Mobil has had "only 5 complete failures out of 750 employees placed abroad."

[27]Christopher Tugendhat, *The Multinationals* (London: Eyre & Spottiswoode, 1971), p. 197. See also John D. Daniels, "The Non-American Manager, Especially as Third Country National in U.S. Multinationals: A Separate but Equal Doctrine?" *Journal of International Business Studies*, Fall 1974, pp. 25–40.

TRAINING FOR THE INTERNATIONAL EXECUTIVE

Training programs have a special importance for the international firm. They can be the key to developing national managers in countries where management and technical skills are in short supply. They may be a necessary step for indoctrinating foreign employees in the products, policies, and procedures of the parent company. They can be a principal means of preparing managers to deal with the special cross-cultural challenges posed by international business operations. Special training for cross-national transfers can significantly reduce the failure rates in such assignments. In recognition of these needs and opportunities, multinational firms have developed a wide range of formal and informal training approaches.

The use of training programs to develop local management talent can be illustrated by the case of Celanese in Mexico.[28] When it decided in 1944 to build a synthetic fiber plant in Mexico, Celanese had to import technicians and managers from the United States. At the same time, Celanese recruited 12 recently graduated chemical engineers from the National University of Mexico and brought this group to the company's plant in Virginia for a year's training program in handling the process technology on which the Mexican plant was based. Through this and other training programs, by 1972 Celanese Mexicana with more than 6,000 employees was able to operate with only 14 foreigners, some of whom were on temporary assignments.

Even where the supply of personnel is adequate for the needs of foreign subsidiaries, the international company invariably needs to use training programs to familiarize its foreign staff with the company's products, policies, and procedures. There is no substitute for this type of training in a multinational company. It transfers knowledge; it improves communications; it helps impart the parent company's way of operating. Frequently, this type of training is conducted at corporate headquarters so that foreign and headquarters personnel can also become personally acquainted.

For all managers, whether at headquarters or working in foreign subsidiaries, training can be a valuable means of increasing their sensitivity to cultural patterns that are foreign to their own experience and values. Such training should have at least two dimensions. It should develop in the individual an awareness of his or her own cultural assumptions and the nature of his or her cultural conditioning. It should also develop a special kind of intellectual and emotional radar that alerts the manager to situations where cultural assumptions

---

[28]See Richard W. Hall, *Putting Down Roots: 25 Years of Celanese in Mexico* (New York: Vantage Press, 1969).

other than his or her own are present. If culture sensitivity could be achieved simply through intellectual awareness that cultural patterns differ, the task of developing cultural sensitivity might be accomplished through readings and lectures. But the problem is more difficult. Human reactions are likely to be emotional, visceral, or psychological motor responses. One can be fully aware in an intellectual sense that time has a different meaning and value in Latin America, and yet have unkind and unfriendly reactions when forced to wait hours rather than minutes beyond the previously fixed time for an appointment.

Foreign language training can be extremely useful for developing cultural sensitivity. Other valuable measures are sensitivity training and cross-cultural living experiences. These approaches, of course, are generally relevant for all kinds of cross-cultural work, be it as a businessperson, religious missionary, government diplomat, or technician in development-assistance work.

The most lasting means of achieving culture sensitivity comes through a sustained experience of living and working in one or more foreign environments. Such living experience may strain a person emotionally, regardless of his or her adaptability and preparation. The learning process may be painful and agonizing but out of it is likely to come the behavior changes needed to deal with cultural variables.

Training for cross-national appointments will, of course, heavily emphasize language study. Even though both a husband and wife may be required to devote several months on a full-time basis to language study, the benefits to the firm invariably justify the investment. In the process of such language training, moreover, there will be a considerable amount of learning about the characteristics of the new culture. If only a short period of time is available, an executive can still develop a considerable understanding of a language through an intensive language training course.

Multinational firms also use training programs to fit special needs arising out of a company's business strategy or the nature of its product. In firms that rely on a worldwide network of independent distributors, training programs have been used to develop a corps of what amounts to international consultants who can advise and service distributors in a large number of countries. In other firms where the nature of the product has led to logistically interdependent manufacturing units in a number of foreign locations, teams have been specially trained to assist in the establishment of new units and to build them into an international production network.

In designing management-training programs to fit its needs, the international firm has many alternatives available and will encounter numerous problems. Much of the training is best handled by the company itself either at corporate headquarters or in foreign locations.

Companies may also rely on educational institutions in the home or foreign countries for specialized or custom-designed training programs.[29] Outside programs in which many firms participate have the advantage of exposing participants either formally or informally to the experience of other companies. Whatever the approach, the wide range of problems peculiar to international business that can be resolved through training make the training function a crucial element for achieving the benefits of multinational operations.

COMPENSATION POLICIES

Compensation policies can produce some of the sharpest international conflicts within an international firm. They can also influence the pattern of promotion that executives seek within the corporation. Overpaid posts in peripheral foreign activity, for example, might attract good executives away from more important but lower paid posts in the mainstream of the firm's development or, worse still, discourage them from returning to mainstream jobs later on. International compensation policies thus deserve the careful attention of top management.[30]

Why is it difficult to develop a satisfactory international compensation policy? The principal problem has to do with expatriates and the fact that salary levels invariably differ among countries in which the international firm operates. What policy should be followed when executives are transferred? Executives on the higher rates will not want any reduction when transferred. If they continue to receive their national salary level (plus allowances) they will be higher paid in the new post than local nationals with comparable responsibilities. If executives going to higher-wage areas are remunerated at the high-level rates, problems arise when they return to their home country. Do they revert to their old salary scales?

These fundamental questions of compensation policy have no one answer. The compensation policy is not an end in itself but a means of achieving company objectives. When a top executive wants to accomplish some goal over a short-term horizon, he or she may be little concerned with the long-term implications of a salary decision designed to get the best managers into new markets.

---

[29]See Nancy G. McNulty, *Training Managers: The International Guide* (New York: Harper and Row, 1969).

[30]For surveys of the practices and problems of international companies in the compensation field, see Hans Schollhammer, "The Compensation of International Executives," *MSU Business Topics,* Winter 1969, pp. 19–30; *Worldwide Executive Compensation* (New York: Business International, 1967); *Setting Up An Overseas Compensation Package* (New York: Business International, 1970).

Ideally, an effective compensation policy for expatriates should try to meet the following objectives:

1. Attract and retain employees qualified for overseas service.
2. Facilitate transfers between foreign affiliates and between home-country and foreign affiliates.
3. Establish and maintain a consistent and reasonable relationship between the compensation of all employees of any affiliate whether posted at home or abroad and between affiliates.
4. In the various locations, compensation must be reasonable in relation to the practices of leading competitors.

Most U.S. companies construct their international compensation policies for expatriates with three components: base salary, premiums to work overseas, and overseas allowances.

Base Salaries

In order to be competitive, multinationals normally follow local salary patterns in each country. Thus, rates of pay for roughly comparable jobs will differ between nations. If the firm attempted to maintain the same salary levels in all countries, it would cost itself out of markets where lower salary levels prevail and it would not be able to attract managers in high-salary countries.

Managers are usually hired in their home countries, as previously noted, and at salaries comparable to those paid for domestic assignments. When a manager is transferred cross-nationally, the base salary of the expatriate continues to be that of his or her home country. The basic underlying philosophy is that in order to facilitate reassimilation into the home-base company, all personnel are tied to their respective home-country payrolls no matter where they are working.

For many years, this policy worked reasonably well for U.S. companies. Most expatriates were U.S. employees and U.S. salaries were the highest in the world. The principal difficulty inherent in this policy was the fact that employees of the same affiliate with similar responsibilities would be compensated differently due to nationality. Also, as the use of third-country nationals in the overseas operations of U.S. companies has grown substantially, new elements have been injected into the compensation equation. Third-country nationals are nationals of a country other than the United States who are working for the U.S. company in a country other than the one of which they are citizens.

Additional problems have arisen with the devaluation of the U.S. dollar beginning in 1971, the realignment of the major world currencies that has ensued, and the escalation of salaries in some foreign countries to levels above those in the United States.[31] With shifting exchange rates, most companies have tried to maintain constant salary rates in U.S. dollars to facilitate reassimilation in the parent company, and have offset foreign-currency losses by other means. But the solutions to these and other emerging problems are difficult to find. One recommended approach is to have more than one international compensation program in the same company.[32]

Premiums

Two types of premiums or inducements are commonly used: those to encourage mobility and those to compensate for the hardship of living in undesirable locations. Generally, the places where hardship premiums must be paid are not numerous and have few nonlocal employees. More important is the premium paid to encourage overseas mobility. This premium is usually a fixed percentage of base salary (10–20 percent) and is paid for the duration of a foreign assignment.

The disadvantage of the traditional pattern of continuing the premium payment as long as the employee is assigned abroad is that the employee has no financial incentive to move from one foreign country to another and that moves back to the parent country usually mean a substantial reduction in income. Several approaches have been adopted by some companies to resolve these problems and to increase the mobility of international personnel. One approach is the "premium phase-out," whereby after *x* years (usually three to five) the premium is phased out in increments. Another approach is the single payment "mobility premium," which ties the premium to the move instead of to the assignment. In both cases, the premium is paid each time a move is made.

If the company's objective is to keep employees abroad for long assignments, it makes sense to pay a continuous premium. On the other hand, if the company is aiming at mobility and rapid movement, it will prefer the single-payment or phase-out premium.

Allowances

Allowances are intended to assist those managers assigned to foreign posts to continue their normal pattern of living. The most

---

[31]See "Living Costs Soar for Executives Abroad," *Business Week,* May 19, 1973; and "Europe: 'The Poor Underpaid American Executives'," *Business Week,* May 26, 1973.

[32]Calvin Reynolds, "Career Paths and Compensation in the MNCs," *Columbia Journal of World Business,* November –December 1972, pp. 77–87.

common allowances are for cost of living, housing, education, and tax protection. The two largest items are usually taxes and housing.

With taxes, many international firms follow a policy of deducting taxes at the rate for residents in the employee's home country and then paying the actual tax assessment. Generally speaking, it is only worth equalizing taxes if the differences are more than marginal and the differences in benefits, such as lower medical costs in the United Kingdom, fail to account for most of the variation. If the situation of double taxation arises and the firm is responsible for this through the timing of its transfer, it should clearly reduce an employee's tax obligation to that of residence in one country or the other.

In the case of other allowances, most U.S. companies adopt in varying degrees the allowance program of the U.S. Department of State. There are many problems, however, in developing international comparisons of the cost of living on which allowances are based, including changing exchange rates.[33] Also, as companies increase their mix of third-country nationals in foreign posts, the allowance schedules of the parent country become less relevant. The latter problem is being handled by some companies through making use of the United Nations allowance system, which has been designed for professionals of many nationalities stationed throughout the world.

LABOR RELATIONS IN THE MULTINATIONAL FIRM

The multinational firm operates in and across many different labor market and industrial relations environments.[34] Thus, important general characteristics of any industrial relations system, such as strike propensities and collective bargaining structures, become variables at the global planning level. In some nations, the employer may be forced into a paternalistic relationship with his employees whether he likes it or not. At the other end of the spectrum, employers are required by law to share management responsibilities with representatives of the workers in such important countries as West Germany, Sweden, Norway, Denmark, Austria, and Peru.[35] Labor unions vary greatly in strength, in their degrees of political activism, and in the issues

---

[33]See Henri-J. Ruff and Graham I. Jackson, "Methodological Problems in International Comparisons of the Cost of Living," *Journal of International Business Studies,* Fall 1974, pp. 57–67.

[34]For a representative comparative study of industrial relations environments, see Everett M. Kassalow, *Trade Unions and Industrial Relations: An International Comparison* (New York: Random House, 1969).

[35]"Co-determination: When Workers Help Manage", *Business Week,* July 17, 1975; "Employees on the Board", *Sweden Now,* February 1976.

considered appropriate for negotiation with the employer. Furthermore, many features of national labor relations environments have
been changing significantly in recent years.[36]

Work Force Management

In recognition of the unique cultural, legal, and institutional settings in different nations which affect labor relations through varying
social values, psychic needs of workers, the peculiar industrial relations lore, pertinent legal intricacies, and so forth, multinational firms
have generally delegated the task of work-force management to the
managers of foreign subsidiaries. In the negotiation of agreements,
local managers know the local situation in more detail, and as they will
have to manage under the terms of the agreement, they should be
responsible for its final arrangements. For international management
to hold the final authority in negotiations would, moreover, tend to
lower the status, authority, and efficiency of the local management.

In the view of one experienced multinational company, the affiliated companies must have continuing responsibility and authority for
handling industrial relations. "Without this responsibility it would be
extremely difficult, if not impossible, for the affiliates to develop and
maintain the kinds of relationships with their employees and employee
representatives that are a key factor to the success of their operations."[37] Such a policy assumes, of course, that local managers have
been competently trained for administering labor affairs.

There are strong arguments, though, for international management
exercising some central coordination.[38] In new units, acquired as going
concerns, local management experience in labor management may not
be extensive nor up to the standard expected of a multinational
corporation. Also, agreements made in one country may affect the
international plans of the corporation or create precedents for negotiations in other countries. The more unions cooperate across country
boundaries, the more need there will be for the firm to present a
consistent front. The case for central labor relations coordination is

[36]See Jean-Daniel Reynaud, "The Future of Industrial Relations in Western Europe,"
Bulletin, International Institute for Labour Studies (Geneva, February 1968), pp.
88–115; B. J. Widick, "The New Look in Labor Relations," *Columbia Journal of World
Business,* July–August 1971, pp. 63–67; Robert W. Cox, "Approaches to a Futurology of
Labor Relations," *Bulletin, International Institute for Labour Studies* (Geneva, 1971),
pp. 139–64.

[37]Malcolm L. Denise, "Industrial Relations and the Multinational Corporation: The
Ford Experience," in *Bargaining Without Boundaries,* ed. Robert J. Flanagan and
Arnold R. Weber (Chicago: The University of Chicago Press, 1974), p. 140.

[38]See Duane Kujawa, *International Labor Relations Management in the Automotive
Industry* (New York: Praeger Publishers, Inc., 1971).

thus strong, but such coordination should involve full participation by local management and infringe as little as possible on local autonomy.

Coordination does not necessarily mean that the international firm should have common policies in all countries. A whole range of elements may differ from environment to environment, leading to different arrangements in each. Any attempt to impose parent-company policies on new situations where they do not fit would be wrong. To have a worldwide policy to avoid unionization simply because this had worked in the parent company would be one example. Many companies who are not unionized in the parent unit have successfully followed unionization in subsidiaries and vice versa.

In fulfilling its coordination role and managing its own responsibilities, headquarters staff needs to develop considerable understanding and a continuing flow of information on national labor-management patterns. Assessments and forecasts of the labor relations component of national environments are a necessary input for decisions on the location and expansion of facilities. They are also necessary for evaluating the performance of subsidiaries and local managers. Where transnational sourcing patterns have been developed and a subsidiary in one country relies on a subsidiary in another country as a source of components or as a user of its output, labor relations throughout the system become of direct importance to central management for maintaining its global production strategy.

Transnational Labor Union Collaboration

The most recent consideration, however, pressing for headquarters involvement in labor-management affairs has been the move toward internationalization of the labor movement as a direct reaction to the growth of the multinational corporation. Unions around the world have felt increasingly threatened by powerful multinational employers and have made major strides in cooperation across national boundaries in organizing, bargaining, and striking. In essence, their situation parallels that of national governments: They are national institutions facing an international challenge.

Many trade unionists are firmly convinced that multinational companies make their decisions on all important matters on a highly centralized basis, with central headquarters concerned with only global goals. Others feel seriously handicapped because of what they describe as a floating and invisible decision center for labor relations matters. Subsidiary companies, so the complaint goes, claim that decisions are made at central headquarters, and central headquarters respond that decisions are made by their subsidiaries. Another belief is that international companies can shift their investment at will and will do so if a trade union is found "unreasonable" in its demands. Still another problem they see in collective bargaining is the ability of the firm to call on plants in another country to meet production needs when there is a strike in one particular location.[39]

While the internationalization of business has been going on for many years, the response of labor union organizations has begun to crystallize only since the middle 1960s. Although strong environmental forces favor local labor-relations patterns and mitigate against the internationalization of the labor movement, transnational collaboration among unions has expanded and operated with considerable effectiveness in several areas. Four general types of union strategies have already emerged in response to the multinational corporation. These strategies are the collection and dissemination of information, international consultation, coordination of union policies and tactics with respect to specific international firms, and a drive for controls over multinational corporations.[40]

The collection and dissemination of information have become highly developed and widely utilized activities. The United Auto Workers, as only one example, recently developed a computer guide to collective bargaining and national social security provisions in the Latin American automobile industry, which it was hoped would support the international harmonization of wages and working conditions. International consultation has occurred through worldwide meetings focusing on a specific multinational enterprise as well as through small meetings between representatives of two specific unions. In 1969, for example, the International Federation of Chemical and General Workers' Union, known as the ICF, held a precollective bargaining strategy meeting concerned with the worldwide operations of the French company, St. Gobain. This consultation led to agreements by the various unions to adopt coordinated negotiating policies. While all the unions did not follow the strategy recommendations, several did. As an example of coordinating tactics, the International Metalworkers' Federation (IMF) has been attempting to organize procedures for a simultaneous ending of all labor agreements with a particular multinational company, thus possibly taking away from the firm the opportunity of using its subsidiaries in various countries to

---

[39]Harry Weiss, "The Multinational Corporation and Its Impact on Collective Bargaining," *Collective Bargaining Today* (Washington, D.C.: Bureau of National Affairs, Inc., 1971), pp. 287–312; see also Duane Kujawa, ed., *International Labor and Multinational Enterprise* (New York: Praeger Publishers, Inc., 1975).

[40]David H. Blake, "Corporate Structure and International Unionism," *Columbia Journal of World Business,* March–April 1972, pp. 19–26; David H. Blake, "International Labor and the Regulation of Multinational Corporations: Proposals and Prospects," *San Diego Law Review,* November 1973, pp. 179–205.

help break strikes elsewhere.[41] The fourth tactic, the drive for controls, has been used at the international and national levels. A June 1971 meeting of the International Confederation of Free Trade Unions (ICFTU) passed a resolution urging the adoption of international and national standards for regulating international firms. On the national level, the U.S. union movement sponsored and supported legislation in 1971 that would lead to complete government regulation of the outflow of direct investment and the export of technology.

Unions are basically nationalistic, and strong political and ideological cleavages exist between different national labor movements. Consequently, the degree of success that unions can achieve through international collaboration is uncertain. Nevertheless, attempts at cooperation in one form or another are bound to increase, and the management of the multinational firm must develop policies for meeting international requests as well as partisan requests from labor in individual companies which are concerned with their position vis-a-vis employees in other countries. Local labor strategies will continue to be dominant, but supplementary global labor strategies will also be required. Cooperative efforts by unions across national frontiers will probably occur first within the European Economic Community area.[42]

SUMMARY

In international business, as in most other activities, human resources are the critical elements. The peculiar problem that international firms face is that people are usually raised, educated, and indoctrinated in one culture, whereas international business management requires cross-cultural communication, coordination, and supervision. The challenge is to develop managers who can think globally or at least biculturally.

The multinational firm has various options in choosing a policy that will develop international managers with this ability. It can follow a policy of hiring local nationals to manage its subsidiaries, but it will then have to rely on training programs to internationalize its personnel.

---

[41]For many specific details on the trade union response, see Tugendhat, *Multinationals*, pp. 180–92; Charles Levinson, *Capital, Inflation, and the Multinationals* (New York: Macmillan Co., 1971); International Labour Organisation, Metal Trades Committee, *General Report* (Geneva: International Labour Office, 1970), pp. 145–80.

[42]Lloyd Ulman, "The Rise of the International Union?" in *Bargaining Without Boundaries,* ed. Flanagan and Weber, p. 66; see also B. C. Roberts, "Multinational Collective Bargaining: A European Prospect?" *British Journal of Industrial Relations,* March 1973, pp. 1–19.

It will have to invest in training programs to prepare executives and their families for cross-national transfers. One of the most perplexing problems faced by multinational companies has been the matter of compensation policies, but with increasing experience most companies have been able to work out reasonably satisfactory solutions even for handling cross-national transfers.

The management of labor relations must necessarily be delegated largely to local management because of innumerable local variations in worker attitudes, labor union roles, and the degree of governmental participation in labor-management affairs. However, the growing internationalization of the labor movement, in response to a perceived threat from the multinational enterprise, has tended to bring headquarters management increasingly into the formulation and implementation of labor strategies, and is likely to continue to do so in the future.

EXERCISES AND DISCUSSION QUESTIONS

1. What are the advantages and limitations of a policy that favors hiring nationals as managers of subsidiaries?

2. Many international companies recruit potential managers for their home-country domestic operations and later look to this staff for their international managers, particularly at headquarters. Under what conditions, if any, would you advise a company to do specialized outside recruiting for its international management personnel?

3. You have been asked to design an orientation program for personnel being transferred on a two-year assignment to a less developed country (you select the country). The program must be completed by the participants in three weeks of full-time study. What are the several most important subjects that should be included in the program and why?

4. How would the local labor situation affect your location decision for a new foreign plant that produced a product whose characteristics or technology would have to change rapidly to meet competitive conditions?

5. How would you answer the fear of labor unions that the multinational corporation can easily transfer its operations to a different country if it feels that the demands of labor unions in a specific area of operations are "unreasonable"?

part six

Cases and Problems in International Business

Working within the International Framework

Which Company Is Truly Multinational?*

FOUR SENIOR EXECUTIVES of the world's largest firms with extensive holdings outside the home country speak:

Company A: "We are a multinational firm. We distribute our products in about 100 countries. We manufacture in over 17 countries and do research and development in three countries. We look at all new investment projects—both domestic and overseas—using exactly the same criteria."

The executive from Company A continues, "Of course most of the key posts in our subsidiaries are held by home-country nationals. Whenever replacements for these men are sought, it is the practice, if not the policy, to look next to you at the head office and pick someone (usually a home-country national) you know and trust."

Company B: "We are a multinational firm. Only 1 percent of the personnel in our affiliate companies are nonnationals. Most of these are U.S. executives on temporary assignments. In all major markets, the affiliate's managing director is of the local nationality."

He continues, "Of course there are very few non-Americans in the key posts at headquarters. The few we have are so Americanized that we usually don't notice their nationality. Unfortunately, you can't find good foreigners who are willing to live in the United States, where our headquarters is located. American executives are more mobile. In addition, Americans have the drive and initiative we like. In fact, the

*Copyright 1971 by Professor Warren J. Keegan. This case is adapted with permission from Howard V. Perlmutter, "The Tortuous Evolution of the Multinational Corporation," *Columbia Journal of World Business,* January–February 1969.

European nations would prefer to report to an American rather than to some other European."

Company C: "We are a multinational firm. Our product division executives have worldwide profit responsibility. As our organizational chart shows, the United States is just one region on a par with Europe, Latin, America, Africa, etc., in each division."

The executive from Company C goes on to explain, "The worldwide product division concept is rather difficult to implement. The senior executives in charge of these divisions have little overseas experience. They have been promoted from domestic posts and tend to view foreign consumer needs as really basically the same as ours. Also, product division executives tend to focus on the domestic market because the domestic market is larger and generates more revenue than the fragmented foreign markets. The rewards are for global perform-ance, but the strategy is to focus on domestic. Most of our senior executives simply do not understand what happens overseas and really do not trust foreign executives, even those in key positions."

Company D (non-American): "We are a multinational firm. We have at least 18 nationalities represented at our headquarters. Most senior executives speak at least two languages. About 30 percent of our staff at headquarters are foreigners."

He continues by explaining that "since the voting shareholders must by law come from the home country, the home country's interest must be given careful consideration. But we are proud of our nationali-ty; we shouldn't be ashamed of it. In fact, many times we have been reluctant to use home-country ideas overseas, to our detriment, espe-cially in our U.S. subsidiary. Our country produces good executives, who tend to stay with us a long time. It is harder to keep executives from the United States."

1. Which company is truly multinational?
2. What are the attributes of a truly multinational company?
3. Why quibble about how multinational a firm is?

Freelandia

FREELANDIA'S MAIN EXPORTS came from its primary industries and included wool, meat, butter, timber, fruit, and a variety of less advanced manufactures. For 1972 the total exported was $1,120 million.

Imports totaled $1,103 million, made up mainly of heavy manufactured goods such as machinery and transport equipment, while an additional $12 million was spent on transport and travel and $5 million on other services.

The country had recently begun to encourage foreign industry to invest in new factories and plants, provided that the output either substituted for imports or had export potential and included at least 40 percent of Freelandian content. This campaign had proven quite successful and during 1972 a total of $116 million was remitted for direct investment in Freelandia. The policy was beginning to meet resistance from the opposition political parties, however, because the considerable income these companies were earning was payable to them in overseas funds and placed a strain on the balance of payments. In 1972 a total of $66 million was repatriated by overseas companies, out of their net earnings of $98 million.

The Freelandian government had also been encouraging its major domestic producers to establish processing plants overseas to increase their receipts from primary exports. A total of $42 million was invested in this way in 1972 and was expected to add significantly to the future inflow from overseas business investments, which totaled only $18 million 1972.

There was an additional reinvested income of $22 million from these direct investments overseas during 1972, but it was still true, as the opposition argued, that foreign firms' ownership in Freelandia far outweighed Freelandia's overseas business activities—in cumulative figures at the end of 1971, a comparison of $963 million to $242 million. This comparison, moreover, was similar for holdings of investment securities. Foreign investment in Freelandian securities totaled $360 million at the end of 1971 and increased in value by $44 million during 1972, while Freelandian holdings of overseas stocks and bonds were only valued at $122 million in 1971, increasing in value by $13 million over the year. Heavy restrictions permitted only $5 million to be remitted by Freelandia for further purchases during 1972, but foreigners purchased a further $42 million in comparison.

The government's policies had also led them to borrow $28 million from overseas investors during the year in order to finance new container facilities at the major ports, but their indebtedness to the IMF was reduced to $321 million with a repayment of $25 million. Total interest payments to service the government's liabilities were $56 million, including the interest on government debentures floated overseas which totaled $403 million at the end of 1971. The central bank's holdings of convertible currencies overseas increased during the year by $19 million to $126 million.

Shorter-term commercial finances were less important to the Freelandian situation but local holdings of foreigners again more than offset Freelandian holdings overseas. Short-term overseas holdings by Freelandian companies were $80 million at the end of 1971 and liquid holdings $6 million, while overseas companies held $56 million short-term claims and $48 million in liquid funds within Freelandia. By the end of 1972, the net change on short-term nonliquid funds was $14 million. Overseas companies had increased their claims by $6 million, and Freelandian companies had increased their claims by $20 million. There was no change over the year in Freelandian liquid claims, but foreign banks increased their holdings by $18 million.

1. From the above particulars prepare balance-of-payments accounts for Freelandia for 1972 and show the country's international investment position at the end of 1971 and 1972.

2. What do you think might happen if Freelandia's currency were to be devalued against other currencies by 20 percent? Do you think this devaluation is likely?

Staven Electronics

STAVEN ELECTRONICS was a large U.S. multinational manufacturer of electronic components and consumer durables. In 1975, worldwide sales equaled $1 billion; approximately half of sales and profits were derived from operations of 40 wholly owned subsidiaries.

The subsidiaries manufactured primarily for the markets in which they were located, although each of them exported to third-country markets and a few exported to sister subsidiaries located in other countries. Materials required for manufacture were purchased by subsidiaries from local suppliers, the U.S. parent company, third-country suppliers, and in a few cases from sister subsidiaries in third countries.

The respective subsidiaries were financed through a mixture of: (1) initial equity investment by the parent company, (2) occasional U.S. dollar loans by the parent, (3) retained earnings, and (4) local currency credits. Normally, subsidiaries relied largely on retained earnings and local borrowings. Dividend payments to the parent company were usually budgeted to be 60 percent of current earnings. When local credit conditions were unusually restrictive and currency conditions unstable, the parent company allowed cash-poor subsidiaries to lengthen their payment terms on intercompany accounts.

Staven Electronics faced competition from its two major multinational competitors and several local manufacturers in almost every market. Competition normally focused on: (1) retail prices, (2) product quality, and (3) credit and discount terms to distributors.

In early 1976, Berent Riker was appointed managing director of the small Staven subsidiary in the United Kingdom. The United Kingdom was continuing to experience 10–15 percent price inflation, and a continuation of periodic falls in the value of sterling was widely referred to in the newspapers. Riker had extensive experience in marketing management and administration but no experience in finance or accounting. As managing director he was expected by the parent company to evaluate the 6–12 month outlook for sterling, minimize his subsidiary's probability of incurring foreign exchange loss, and produce increased U.S. dollar profits for Staven Electronics.

As he assumed his new duties, Berent Riker was preoccupied with the following issues and questions:

1. Suppose another fall in sterling occurred soon; what would be the possible implications of the exchange-rate change to his business?

2. Of what possible consequence and relevance to the parent company was a reduction in the value of sterling?

3. Of what possible consequence and relevance to thousands of stockholders of the publicly owned parent company was a sterling devaluation?

The Clifford Company

IN EARLY 1975, THE CLIFFORD COMPANY, a Swiss-based company with extensive overseas investments, began to develop a generalized formula approach for measuring the degree of risk in any foreign currency at a given point in time. The technique was devised as a consequence of continuing concern among executives of the company about foreign currency devaluation and the accompanying Swiss franc value erosion of certain company assets. A formula approach was chosen for ease of application and consistency. Basically, the system as described below involves five economic indicators, each having a weighting factor that is granted in various numerical degrees according to favorable or unfavorable trends within each indicator. Accompanying the five factor descriptions are the values given for significant trend categories. A perfect score signifying overall excellent currency health, would be 100; however, of 22 actual situations analyzed, in no case did a total exceed 85.

The specific weights were arbitrarily assigned although not completely without basis, for this study involved detailed observation of a number of indicators and their interrelationships. It was felt by the analysts who developed the approach that the assigned weights reflected properly the relative importance of the factors.

The factors chosen for presentation, the thinking that led to their choice, and the weights assigned each (Exhibit 1) are as follows:

1. ***Reserves.*** Monetary gold, SDRs, foreign exchange, and the IMF gold trance position are a reflection of the solvency of a country in regard to its ability to meet international obligations. These can, of course, be represented by debt repayment obligations, profits,

EXHIBIT 1
Currency Risk

Factors	Relative Weight
1. Reserves	40
2. Cost of living	20
3. Money supply	20
4. Exchange	10
5. Balance of trade	10

Reserves
(past three years)

Rising trend	40
Consistent stability	35
Sporadic or improving	30
Slow decline	20
Rapid decline	10
Rapid decline (no IMF assistance)	5
Negative (chaos)	0

Cost of Living: Five-Year Trend
(compound percent per annum)

Stable (0–1.5%)	20
Rising (1.5–3.5%)	15
Rising (3.5–6%)	10
Rising (6–15%)	5
Rising (more than 15%)	0

Money Supply: Five-Year Trend
(compound percent per annum increase)

Stable	20
Rising (2–4%)	15
Rising (6–10%)	10
Rising (more than 10%)	5
Chaos	0

Balance of Trade: Three-Year Trend

Export surplus	10
Stability (with exchange cushion)	10
Deficit (stable, slight)	5
Deficit (expanding rapidly)	5

Exchange (spread between official and free market*): Six-Month Trend

Less than 10%	10
More than 10%	5
No correlation	0

*Where a fluctuating free market governs all transactions, the trend over six months is used.

royalty remittances, and so on. A foreign investor's direct concern is whether or not he will be able to retrieve the proceeds derived from proposed Swiss franc investments quite apart from the investment proposal's internal attractiveness.

The IMF gold tranche position is included (gold tranche being the maximum amount that can be borrowed without having to make unusual arrangements) because it acts as a reserve which can be drawn upon with virtual certainty. However, there are circumstances in which the IMF may refuse to lend. For this reason, a category, given five points, is included to reflect a deteriorating situation where no outside assistance is available.

Reserves are assigned a total of 40 out of 100 because of their clearly critical effect upon the external value of a given currency. In no observed situation did a nation avoid devaluation, or the institution of other measures tantamount to devaluation, when a severe drop in reserves was experienced.

2. Money Supply. Currency in circulation plus demand deposits are the factors here. Normally, there is a close correlation between the internal supply of money and cost of living. In the ideal classical sense a nation should experience an increase in production to match increases in demand at home. With increases in production there is usually a reduction in unemployment and, as a result, a higher level of real income. Theoretically, it can happen without inflation. However, actual experience suggests that wages and other forms of payment tend to move upward at a more rapid rate than output. This leads to a supply of money, usable for making payments, that grows faster than the supply of goods. Generally a situation results that leaves too much money available to buy too few goods. Hence, prices are bid up and inflation results. The events of 1973–74 were a good example of this pattern.

In countries where capital and consumer goods must be imported, the value of the goods is inflated in internal currency terms while it remains stable in Swiss francs, dollar, or other hard-currency terms. Eventually the dollar becomes increasingly expensive, causing further import price increases and, in addition, making it increasingly more difficult for the exporter to find markets and thus to earn foreign exchange. If this kind of situation continues, an adjustment must eventually be made, probably via the introduction of trading obstructions or devaluation.

The situation is particularly likely in countries where it is considered politically advantageous for governments to embark on vast deficit spending programs financed by the printing press.

Money supply is assigned a total of 20 out of 100 points. The frequently direct correlation between this factor and cost of living is accounted for by weighting them equally. They are mentioned separately, however, because there are a number of situations where the correlation is not evident. Excessively unfavorable trends in either category may or may not undermine the other, although the existence of either at rates deemed excessive can lead to external pressures on a currency.

3. Cost of Living. The significance of the internal purchasing power of a given currency is self-evident. An erosion of value at home cannot help but be eventually reflected externally, provided there is not a similar relative decline in the internal value of important trading currencies.

There may or may not be a direct correlation between cost of living and money supply. Because of the inconsistency of the interrelationship between the two, each is assigned 20 out of 100 points.

Some general conclusions as to the rate of deterioration in the internal value of a given currency were derived from the annual First National City Bank Monthly Economic Letter review of currency value erosion. The relative weights were obtained from an analysis of this review as to frequency and extent of devaluations in the numerous countries reported.

4. Trade Balance. This involves the dollar volume of international trading activities. For most countries, the relationship between these items is critical to the reserve position. Exports frequently form the most important source of foreign exchange earnings, and imports the most important source of drainage. While it may not be possible to state categorically that a continuing deficit is intolerable, it is probably safe to say that in the long run such a situation is unhealthy. A trend toward a deficit position in international trading accounts is, in a vast majority of cases, an indication of troubled times ahead.

A value of 10 points was given to this category because of the usual importance of trade to the foreign exchange balance. Countries were classified as either good, indifferent, or bad, depending upon their trade balance.

5. Official versus Free-Market Rates of Exchange (Exchange Spread). The "official" rate in this comparison is that rate at which most government-authorized transactions take place. It should not be equated with the IMF established rate, which is meaningless in some countries where the official rate is set in the free market. In countries using a fluctuating free-market rate for all transactions, trends in this rate over the month are used.

The purpose of the comparison is to observe the value placed upon a given currency by outsiders whose interests are neither politically nor emotionally tied to overvaluing their currencies, whereas outside traders tend to exaggerate their weaknesses by undervaluing the currencies. Nevertheless, a sudden or persistent widening of this spread would serve as an indication of increasing apprehension over the near future, thus providing a signal that may be useful in timing new investments.

A total value of 10 points was assigned to the exchange spread, with intermediate values for variations up to 10 percent discount and more than 10 percent discount. The 10 percent bench mark is an arbitrary one that, by observation, seems to indicate a significant shift in outside value appraisals.

In the 22 countries studied by the Clifford Company, the following significance can be attached to various formula results:

Total Score	*Overall Evaluation*
75–100	Strong
65–75	Bears watching, perhaps closer analysis
45–65	Definite risk, some adjustment necessary
0–45	High risk, devaluation or equivalent expected

1. How might the Clifford Company use the measurement formula?
2. What problems might arise in its use?

Stability, Inc.

STABILITY, INC. WAS FOUNDED in the mythical republic of Bellerivia on January 1, 1971. On December 31, 1974, its condensed balance sheet was as shown in Exhibit 1. All figures are stated in Bellerivian doubloons, a decimal currency represented by the dollar symbol ($).

EXHIBIT 1

STABILITY, INC.
Condensed Balance Sheet
December 31, 1974
(in thousands)

Assets

Current assets		
Cash...	$ 400	
Accounts and notes receivable	1,500	
Inventories.....................................	2,500	
Total current assets.......................		$4,400
Fixed assets		
Plant and equipment	$2,000	
Deduct accumulated depreciation	400	
Total fixed assets		1,600
Total assets................................		$6,000

Liabilities

Current liabilities		
Accounts and notes payable......................	$1,300	
Total liabilities		$1,300

Stockholders' Equity

Capital stock....................................	$2,000	
Retained earnings...............................	2,700	
Total stockholders' equity		4,700
Total equities		$6,000

Stability, Inc. does only wholesale business, with no manufacturing operations. All wages and salaries are charged to expense as earned. Inventory is valued on the first in, first out (FiFo) basis. Prices were stable during the first four years of the company's life. The general price index on December 31, 1974 was 100—the same as it had been on January 1, 1971. Early in 1975, however, the government of Bellerivia launched large-scale rearmament and social-welfare programs. These activities were financed mainly by government borrowing from the Bellerivian central bank, which was allowed to treat the government's promissory note as part of its required legal reserves. Taking prices at January 1, 1971 as 100, the general price index changed as follows during the year:

Date	General Price Index
January 1, 1975	100
First quarter average	110
Second quarter average	130
June 30, 1975	140
Third quarter average	150
Fourth quarter average	170
December 31	180
1975 average	140

The company's trial balance on an original cost basis, was as follows on December 31, 1975 (in thousands of doubloons):

	Debits	Credits
Cash	190	
Accounts and notes receivable	1,400	
Inventories	4,250	
Plant and equipment	2,210	
Accumulated depreciation		521
Accounts and notes payable		1,550
Capital stock		2,000
Retained earnings, Dec. 31, 1974		2,700
Sales		15,400
Cost of goods sold expense	12,250	
Salaries and other current expenses	1,750	
Depreciation expense	121	
Total	22,171	22,171

Purchases during 1975 were as follows (in thousands of doubloons):

Quarter	Historical Cost
1	2,750
2	3,250
3	3,750
4	4,250
Total	14,000

Under the Fifo inventory method, the goods in the December 31, 1975 inventory were those purchased at various times during the final quarter of 1975. The ending inventory represented the same physical quantity as the January 1, 1975 figure. During the year, purchases and sales of physical units of goods were the same in each quarter.

The major part of the plant and equipment, costing $2 million, was acquired on January 1, 1971 when the business was founded. Depreciation had been recorded on this part of the asset account at the rate of 5 percent per year. On June 30, 1975 additional equipment costing $210,000 was acquired. It was expected to have a useful life of five years, but depreciation was recorded for only one-half year in 1975.

At a meeting early in 1976 the board of directors was considering the question of how large a cash dividend to pay.

1. Prepare a balance sheet, income statement, source and application of funds statement, and a cash receipts and disbursements statement for 1975 on the basis of historical cost.

2. Prepare the same statements for 1975 on a price-level adjustment basis.

3. Compute the gain or loss from holding monetary assets in 1975.

4. Compute the gain or loss from holding inventories and fixed assets during 1975. What is the meaning of your answer?

5. How do the procedures used for adjusting account balances for general price-level changes resemble the procedures for translating the accounts of a foreign business subdivision into the domestic currency? In what major ways do the two types of procedures differ?

6. What policy should Stability, Inc. follow if it wishes to minimize the gain or loss on monetary accounts?

7. How can the management of Stability, Inc. use the adjusted financial information? What are its shortcomings?

Peters Brass Company*

PETERS BRASS COMPANY, a rapidly growing Pittsburg casting company, invested $2,350,000 in 1966 to establish a local unit in Argentina. The investment represented a 65 percent share in a new Argentinian company established in partnership with Sr. Pedro Gomez y Silvo of Buenos Aires. At the time of the initial investment, the Argentinian peso was worth 1.2 U.S. cents, but periodic devaluations of the Argentinian currency brought the exchange rate to a point in mid-April 1971 when it fell from 180 pesos to 205 pesos to the U.S. dollar.

For four years the parent company had shown the Argentinian operation in its books at the original investment cost, recording the profits (which were all paid out as dividends) as investment income. At the time of the April 1971 devaluation, the new president had been thinking about consolidating the subsidiary accounts for 1971 (see Exhibit 1). He asked Bill Adams, the controller, to calculate for him what the effect of consolidation would be and what the recent devaluation would mean.

*Adapted from a case written by Professor Richard N. Farmer, Graduate School of Business, Indiana University.

EXHIBIT 1

PETERS BRASS COMPANY OF ARGENTINA

Cuadro Demostrativo de Ganancias y Perdidas al 31 de marzo de 1971
(Profit and Loss—Year Ending March 31, 1971)

Entrada (Revenues)   *Pesos*

Ventas menos costo de la mercaderia vendida   220,500,000
(Sales less cost of goods sold)
Comision   40,000,000
(Commissions)
Renta.   50,000,000
(Rental income)
Varias entrada   30,000,000
(Miscellaneous income)

    Total entrada (Total revenue).   340,500,000

Gastos (Expenses)
Remuneraciones al personal   130,500,000
(Wages and salaries)
Gastos de operacion   40,000,000
(Fuel, heat, and light)
Amortizaciones.   15,500,000
(Depreciation)
Gastos de comision y regalias   35,000,000
(Commission expenses and royalties)
Impuestos.   50,500,000
(Taxes)

    Total gastos (Total expenses)   271,500,000

Utilidad del Ejercicio (Net profit)   69,000,000

EXHIBIT 1 (*continued*)

Balance General al 31 marzo de 1971
(Balance Sheet, March 31, 1971)

Activos (Assets)	*Pesos*
Caja y bancos	
(Cash on hand)	8,100,000
Deudores en cuenta	
(Accounts receivable)	32,700,000
Bienes de cambio	
(Inventories)	90,700,000
Maquinarias y accesorios	
(Machinery and equipment)	142,400,000
Immuebles (menos amortizacion)	
(Buildings, less depreciation)	253,400,000
Terreno	
(Land)	129,800,000
Total	657,100,000

Pasivos (Liabilities)

Deudas (Debts)

Comerciales	
(Accounts payable)	40,000,000
Bancarias	
(Bank overdraft)	25,000,000
Equipo hipotecarios	
(Equipment notes payable)	55,000,000

Capital, reserves y resultados
(Shareholders' equity)

Suscripto	
(Common stock)	300,000,000
Reservas y utilidades	
(Capital surplus)	237,100,000
Total	657,100,000

American Level Corporation

ON GRADUATION FROM BUSINESS SCHOOL, James Bennett joined American Level Corporation in July 1971 as assistant to the corporate treasurer in the New Jersey headquarters.

American Level had two wholly owned manufacturing subsidiaries, one in Brazil and one in Germany, but apart from a quarterly review of the foreign exchange situation by the corporate finance committee, there had been no regular procedure for avoiding the foreign exchange risks arising from the international operations. The treasurer was aware of the gaps in the American Level procedures and asked Bennett as his first major assignment to outline a methodology for forecasting exchange-rate changes as well as a set of decision rules to be followed for minimizing foreign exchange costs. The treasurer thought it would be wise to prepare the way for the procedure recommendations with a clear statement of the foreign exchange exposure of the two subsidiaries, based on their accounts to June 30. This was to be ready for the finance committee meeting on August 25, along with the usual estimate of the previous month's foreign exchange gains or losses.

The spot rate on June 30 for the German mark was DM 3.65 = U.S. $1, and for the Brazilian cruzeiro 5.20 = U.S. $1. During July, however, the German mark had been "floated" with the end-of-month rate quoted as DM 3.35 = U.S. $1. The exchange rate of the cruzeiro had also been changed to an official rate of 5.40 = $1.

The balance sheets of the two subsidiaries on June 30, 1971, are shown in Exhibit 1. In the case of the Amel S.A. about 50 percent of the raw material and packaging material was imported from the United States, mainly from the parent company.

576

EXHIBIT 1

AMERICAN LEVEL CORPORATION
Subsidiary Balance Sheets
As of June 30, 1971

Assets	*Amel Gmbh, (DM 000)*	*Amel S.A. (Cruzeiro 000)*
Cash.	4,419	415
Accounts receivable: trade other	25,134	13,078
Inventories		
Raw materials.	9,807	15,972
Packaging material	744	3,221
Work in process	10,323	5,321
Finished goods.	3,525	1,972
Total current assets.	53,952	39,979
Fixed assets	11,246	3,106
Less depreciation	1,479	916
Net fixed assets	9,767	2,190
Deferred expenses	—	1,121
Total assets	63,719	43,290

Liabilities		
Notes payable.	3,418	8,876
Accounts payable: trade and intercompany	18,259	13,808
Accrued expenses.	1,369	473
Accrued taxes, miscellaneous	7,803	4,367
Total current liabilities.	30,849	27,524
Reserve for patent infringement	186	—
Capital	16,508	6,527
Retained earnings	11,075	8,189
Current profit	5,101	1,050
Total net worth	32,684	15,766
Total liabilities	63,719	43,290

Meeting the Interests of Nation-States

Flexoid Carribia*

THE FLEXOID CORPORATION wished to invest in a new plant in Carribia to manufacture Myoprene, a specialty chemical. The company held the patents for the process and had several plants on-stream in Europe. Myoprene imports had been prohibited from Carribia for some years as they were not included within the local government's category of "essential imports," but Flexoid management had come to the conclusion that a plant solely to serve the Carribian market could be justified.

The company analysts had worked out a pro forma income statement for a typical year of expected operations, as shown in Exhibit 1, and were preparing a note for management as a basis for negotiations with the Carribian government's Foreign Investment Review Board. Management had asked for an evaluation of the advantages of alternative financing plans and an outline of the arguments that might be used to justify the project to the Review Board.

Carribia was still basically an agricultural country, relying on the export of agricultural commodities for foreign exchange earnings. Mechanisation in agriculture and a high birth rate, however, had combined to produce widespread underemployment, and the creation of new jobs in manufacturing had been given high priority by the government.

To spur the development of import-replacing investments, many infant-industry tariffs had been introduced. Normally only one investor was permitted to manufacture a given product, and the tariffs were set sufficiently high to give the manufacturer at least a temporary

*This case was prepared by Professor John Stopford and Professor Kenneth Simmonds of the London Graduate School of Business Studies. Copyright 1976 by John Stopford.

EXHIBIT 1
Pro Forma Income Statement for a Typical Year's Operations in Carribia

		Pesos (000s)
Sales.		1,000
Cost of goods sold		
Labor—local	200	
Raw materials—local	400	
imported	100	700
Gross margin		300
Indirect expenses—maintenance, depreciation, selling, administration, etc.		100
Profit before interest and 50% local taxation.		200

monopoly. Myoprene from a Carribian plant would be priced at 20 percent above the prevailing world supply price, but preliminary discussions with Carribian trade officials had indicated that a tariff of 30 percent ad valorem would be imposed on Myoprene and substitutes in the event of the plant being authorized.

As yet there was no important chemical investment in Carribia. The recent government five-year development plan, however, called for such investment. The establishment of a Myoprene facility would provide local demand for several base chemicals and would certainly add to the interest of major international chemical companies in further Carribian investment.

Carribia had numerous development options, and it was known that the government planners had been using a rate of 20 percent per annum as a gauge of the opportunity cost of capital in determining priorities among competing projects.

The total capital cost for the new Myoprene operation was estimated at 900,000 pesos and would be financed by 400,000 pesos of equity from Flexoid and 500,000 pesos of long-term debt. Flexoid's founder, recently retired as president, had viewed minority partners as "getting a free ride on profits" and had shaped Flexoid's financial policy to retain full ownership of all subsidiaries with maximum use of fixed-interest debt. If Flexoid raised the debt finance outside Carribia and secured it against its home-base assets, the interest rate would be 10 percent per annum. Money raised in Carribia solely against the security of the proposed plant, however, would cost 15 percent per annum. The peso was valued on a par with the U.S. dollar and the Carribian government had followed a policy, which seemed unlikely to change, of maintaining this parity.

The American Aluminum Corporation*

BY THE END OF JULY 1974, Charles M. Hall, a recent MBA graduate from a leading U.S. business school, had been on his first assignment with American Aluminum Corporation (AMAL) for only two weeks and he found himself facing the first important problem of his very brief career. Hall's boss had assigned him the responsibility for the petroleum coke aspects of the primary aluminum production process and with this responsibility came two related problems with important long-run consequences. The first problem was whether or not to accept an offer from British Columbia Aluminum, Ltd., a Canadian company, to supply 50,000 tons of petroleum coke at a delivered price of 10 percent less than the delivered price of the best alternative source of petroleum coke from U.S. sources. American used large quantities of petroleum coke and needed to purchase 50,000 tons in order to tide it over for the next six months. The second problem was to establish and justify a price at which a new long-run source of petroleum coke should be transferred from a newly formed Canadian subsidiary to AMAL's U.S. smelting operation. But before deciding what to do about these two problems, Hall reviewed what he knew about AMAL operations.

---
*Prepared by J. Frederick Truitt, Associate Professor of International Business, with the assistance of Rex Loesby, MBA student, of the Graduate School of Business Administration, University of Washington. This material was prepared as the basis for classroom discussion rather than as an illustration of an effective or ineffective handling of an administrative situation.

EXHIBIT 1
The Aluminum Refining Process: Raw Materials Required

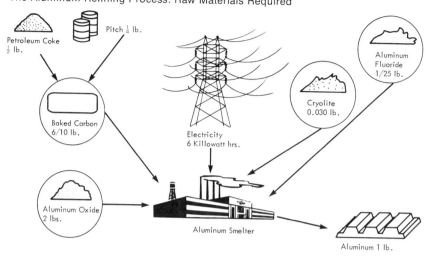

The Company Structure

American Aluminum Corporation, a U.S. corporation located on the West Coast of the Pacific Northwest, refines high-quality aluminum ingot from aluminum oxide (alumina) which is transported in bulk ocean carriers from bauxite mines in western Australia to AMAL's smelter. The aluminum smelting process combines a few basic raw materials, (alumina, cryolite, aluminum fluoride, pitch, and petroleum coke), with large quantities of electric power to produce aluminum ingot (see Exhibit 1). AMAL's smelter is located so that it has access to a deep-water harbor for unloading the alumina, as well as convenient rail service and relatively inexpensive hydroelectric power.

AMAL is owned by two U.S. corporations, Eastern Metals Corporation and North American Metals Corporation. Each owns 50 percent of AMAL. Eastern Metals Corporation is in turn 40 percent owned by European Resources, Ltd., a French corporation (see Exhibit 2).

The Petroleum Coke Supply Problem

During the two years immediately preceding Hall's assignment, AMAL had been experiencing problems securing dependable supplies of petroleum coke[1] at a stable and reasonable price. AMAL used a

---

[1]Petroleum coke is the last product resulting from the petroleum refining process after all the higher-grade fuels and chemicals are taken off. Before the coke is suitable for use in the aluminum smelting process, it must go through a calcining process which removes the impurities in the coke.

EXHIBIT 2
Corporate Ownership Structure: American Aluminum Corporation

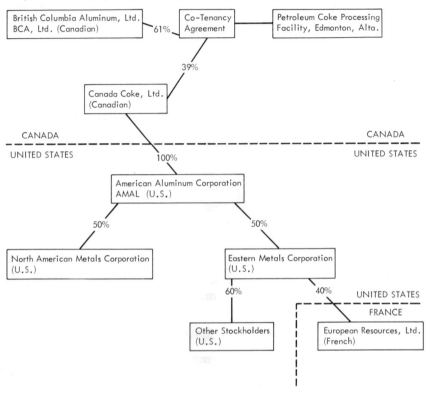

maximum of 110,000 tons of petroleum coke per year, and between late 1973 and December 1974 the delivered price of petroleum coke had increased from $45 to $90 per ton. This dramatic increase in price along with interruptions in supply and decrease in the quality of petroleum coke available from U.S. West Coast refineries led AMAL to seek an alternative source of supply for a substantial portion of its petroleum coke requirements.

Canada Coke, Ltd.

AMAL management decided in late 1973 to procure their petroleum coke from Canada and had entered into a venture with British Columbia Aluminum, Ltd. (BCA, Ltd.) to construct a petroleum coke processing facility near the petroleum refineries in Edmonton, Alberta. Canada Coke, Ltd. was formed as a wholly owned Canadian subsidiary to carry out the details of the venture with BCA, Ltd. Canada Coke was a corporate facade or "nonfirm" in the sense that no management personnel were employed by Canada Coke, Ltd. in Canada. All managerial decisions involving Canada Coke, Ltd. were made by AMAL personnel in the United States.

Hall found the nature of the agreement between AMAL's Canada Coke, Ltd. and BCA, Ltd. interesting because it did not seem to fit into any of the familiar categories (wholly owned subsidiary, joint venture, licensing arrangement, etc.) he had studied in his MBA program. AMAL (through Canada Coke, Ltd.) and BCA, Ltd. shared the output of the newly constructed petroleum coke processing facility proportional to the contribution each partner made to financing the construction of the facility. The arrangement was in many ways similar to a joint venture between AMAL and BCA, Ltd., but was in fact called a "co-tenancy" agreement. The petroleum coke producing facility had no separate legal identity and the co-tenancy form allowed each of the participating companies to write down their respective shares in the assets at different depreciation schedules. AMAL had decided to write down its share in the new facility using the straight-line method of depreciation over a 20-year period.

BCA, Ltd. contributed 61 percent of the cost of constructing the petroleum coke processing facility and was scheduled to take 61 percent of its annual 180,000 ton production. AMAL, through Canada Coke, Ltd., contributed 39 percent of the construction cost and was scheduled to take 39 percent of the annual 180,000 ton production when the facility came on-stream sometime in the next six months (see Exhibits 2 and 3). BCA, Ltd. was the operating partner in the co-tenancy arrangement and was to provide coke to AMAL through Canada Coke, Ltd. at a cost determined by the following schedule:

Actual operating cost of calcining process (does not include depreciation)	$ 5.00 per ton (US$)
Management fee	0.50
Coke purchasing commission	0.40
Total	5.90
Cost of green coke from refineries	40.00
Total cost charged by BCA, Ltd., the operating company of the co-tenancy arrangement, to Canada Coke, Ltd.	$45.90 per ton (US$)

Transporting the refined Canadian coke from the Edmonton facility to the AMAL smelter would cost $13.00 per ton. The U.S. tariff on petroleum coke imports was 7.5 percent ad valorem.

Canada Coke, Ltd. was financed with $850,000 in capital stock and

EXHIBIT 3
Flow of Petroleum Coke from Edmonton

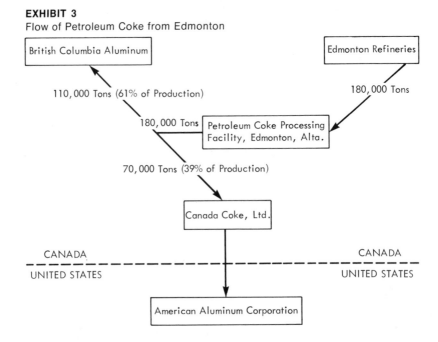

$2,000,000 in loans at the prime rate of 12 percent from a major Canadian bank; that is, AMAL's 39 percent participation in the Edmonton coke facility was through Canada Coke, Ltd. in the amount of $2,850,000.

The Transfer-Pricing Decision

The decision to go to Canada in this particular arrangement had been put into motion before Hall had joined AMAL. What remained for Hall to decide was the price at which Canada Coke, Ltd. sold its 39 percent share of the petroleum coke output from the calcining facility to AMAL. Since Canada Coke, Ltd.'s profits, and hence Canadian income tax liability, were dependent almost entirely on this transfer price, Hall saw the need to proceed carefully, lest AMAL run afoul of Canadian (let alone U.S.) income tax authorities. Therefore he sought the assistance of tax lawyers on the corporate staff. Summarized, this assistance told Hall the following:

1. Since AMAL is a subsidiary of two large, complex U.S. corporations, the tax rates of the parent corporations must be taken into account when calculating AMAL's effective tax rate. The effective rate of U.S. income tax turns out to be in the 30–35 percent range.

2. The effective tax rate for Canada Coke, Ltd. is 41 percent.
3. Canadian tax authorities' judgment on the propriety of transfer-pricing decisions would be based upon the "arm's length" guideline, i.e., the transfer price had to be close to the price that would be used by two unrelated organizations. The two basic methods for determining an arm's length transfer price favored by Canadian authorities are:

    a. A *market* price between unrelated organizations, or if a market price is not available as a guideline;

    b. Comparison of rates of return on assets, i.e.,

    $$\text{RTA} = \frac{\text{Net profit before interest and tax}}{\text{Total assets}}$$

    of similar independent operations with the expectation that a foreign-owned subsidiary in transfer-pricing relationships with its parent company should earn a return on assets comparable to independent firms.

Earlier in the week Hall took a day off from the smelter and drove down to a large university library in order to look up some more information on the petroleum coke industry in Canada. He found that the RTA (return on total assets) for petroleum coke operations in Canada averaged a surprisingly low 5–6 percent. Later he verified this figure by telephone with the Canadian consulate nearest AMAL's smelter. He also found that to the best of his and the consulate's knowledge there was no market price for petroleum coke in western Canada, because there were no sales of petroleum coke between independent companies in western Canada.

It was Friday morning, the weather was promising, and Hall was looking forward to a good relaxing weekend. But the weekend would be all the more relaxing if in the next couple of hours he could make the decisions on the BCA, Ltd. offer and Canada Coke, Ltd. transfer price, write the two-page justification for his decisions, and wrap up these two problems before leaving for the weekend.

Russell Karagosian*

WINGING SOUTH TO LATIN AMERICA aboard Pan American, Russell
Karagosian had five hours flying time and an evening in his hotel room
to prepare a presentation to the Minister for Industry outlining the
basic characteristics of a scheme for evaluating new foreign investments.

Russell was a principal consultant for a Boston firm of business
consultants. He had worked with this firm since completing his degree
at a leading business school and had been mainly engaged in international market surveys and feasibility studies for multinational corporations. The current assignment stemmed from a Christmas party in 1969
at which Russell was introduced to Senor da Silva, a prominent lawyer
from one of the smaller Latin American countries. On learning that
Russell was an international business consultant, this gentleman had
inferred that perhaps Russell's specialty was inventing ways to get
higher profits out of Latin America and referred to the topical editorial
from *Worldwide P & I Planning* shown in Appendix 1. Defending
himself, Russell argued that any problems stemmed from the countries
themselves. They had not made up their minds precisely what was in
their best interests and then given a clear indication of what they
wanted and how they would measure it. It was not too difficult, Russell
asserted, to develop a standard set of questionnaire forms that would
require potential investors to show clearly the benefits and disadvantages of any proposal from the viewpoint of the recipient country.

Three months later, after a change of government, Senor da Silva

---

was appointed Minister for Industry of his country. Shortly thereafter, Russell Karagosian received a telephone call inviting him to meet the minister the following day to discuss his ideas further with a view to a more formal assignment to develop them into operative plans. There was no time to build a careful presentation but Russell was able to put his hands on two papers in his files as he left for the airport. One of these was a set of measurements introduced in the Philippines some years previously as a guide for profit remittance, shown as Appendix 2. The other was an extract from a Council of the Americas study discussing the measurable effects of U.S. direct investment in Mexico, shown as Appendix 3.

APPENDIX 1

The Latin American Repatriation Game[1]

"If I were a Minister of Finance in South America, I'd get me a good tough audit staff of young guys trained in Uncle Sugar Able. Then I'd comb the books of the bigger *Yanqui* subs in my country . . . and I'd sock it to 'em, sock it to 'em, sock it to 'em."

With this malediction my international controller buddy, Chuck McGregor slid into place next to me at *Charlie Brown's* in the Pan Am Building. He certainly was more than slightly steamed (and oiled) as he flipped open a copy of the October 1969 *Fortune* to the article "Threatening Weather in Latin America."

"Here's someone who says U.S. subsidiaries in Latin America contribute 20 percent of that area's tax revenues. If I had the job, I could get that up to at least 35 to 40 percent, without half trying. Hell, in some subs, my company is taking out its original investment every year or more and there are others like us."

I chastised him for being un-American, unpatriotic, and warned him, with loose talk like that he could be drummed out of the National Foreign Trade Council as well as the Council for Latin America and the International Executives Association. And, if he kept on blithering that he wanted to repatriate less money from South of the Border, he would soon talk his way out of the cushiest controller job in mid-Manhattan.

Didn't he know, I emphasized, that U.S. subs "down there" accounted for 12 percent of all Latin production? And 20 percent of that area's exports? Or didn't he care?

"Sure I know these things and I care," he sniffed. "But I'm running scared. What with the anti-*norteamericano* climate in Peru and

---

[1] *Worldwide P & I Planning,* November December 1969.

Bolivia—and rumblings elsewhere—I don't want our five Latin plants to be expropriated. So we damn well better come up with some more loot for the locals—and fast. I hate to say it, but as *Fortune* hinted, they're beginning to wise up."

But hadn't his firm done a lot for local Latin economies? I mentioned a double-page ad spread in *Time* which dramatically showed what his company's sub had done for a small Latin town "before" and "after." Money was pumped in with no promise of return. And look what happened. New schools, new roads, with illiteracy down, disease down, and employment up.

"I remember that ad," he chuckled. "Our local guys had a helluva time rounding up enough good-looking Indians for the photo. Sure we did something for them. But we're doing a lot more for us. Do you remember what the copy said? 'We are again proving our faith in_____ by reinvesting profits for our workers' future.' "

"But," Chuck went on, "do you want to know the real score? After our 'allowable' repatriation and after we took our several hundred thou' more in pre-tax 'expenses,' then we're glad to invest the little that's left. Because in weak-currency countries, we've been taking out 50 to 100 percent R.O.I. every year."

Was he intimating U.S. subsidiaries in Latin America kept two sets of books?

"Well, it isn't two sets of books in the classic Tuscan sense. We only have one, but we make it do the work of two. Any local tax man can see we carry 'expenses' on the books. But they're just a neat device to siphon off as much pre-tax income as we can."

I cautioned him not to give away company secrets as I looked around to see if any of his competitors or Latin tax authorities were tuning in. Chuck tends to get boisterous after his third Tanqueray.

"The only trouble is," he said, ignorning my blunt warning, "that we're weakening, not shoring up, the economies of these countries by scarfing off all the foreign exchange the traffic will bear. Let's take a hypothetical case. I'll exaggerate somewhat but I'll show you how to play the Latin American repatriation game.

"Let's say our investment is $500,000 . . . and local authorities fix our repatriation ratio at 10 percent of investment. Then we quick pump in a $2 million loan from our Mexican sub at 20 percent interest for fixed asset expansion. We 'convince' Exchange Control that our fixed assets are now $2.5 million—and 10 percent of *that* begins to look pretty good. With our true return of $1 million on $6 million sales, then I can 'legitimately' get out $250,000—50 percent of our original investment—as our allowable dollar repatriation.

"But," Chuck grinned slyly, "I'm still way ahead of the game because I'm getting 400 thou' as interest on our $2 million Mexican loan. Then I work up some nifty Home Office charges such as technical management advice, special research, packaging design, etc. We figure these at 4 percent of sales, so this is a cool $240,000."

Are the charges real, I wanted to know.

"Of course not," he said spiritedly. "You sure are green. But who's to prove me wrong? And aren't our trademark and name worth something? Of course, they are," he said, answering his own question. "And I value these at 3 percent of sales, which is another $180,000.

"When I have loaded on all the hard currency pre-tax expenses, I have one final fillip left. I make the local sub pay $500 a month toward the salary of our regional Latin Vice President in Coral Gables. It's a real check, but he never sees it.

"Let's total up," Chuck said briskly, writing on the bar with his Cross ball-point.

Home office charges. . . $	240,000
Trademark value.	180,000
Share of "salary".	6,000
Interest on loan.	400,000
Repatriation.	250,000
Total. . . . . $	1,076,000

"So here I am repatriating just over twice our original $500,000 investment! Not bad for a country boy from Indiana. By the way, we never go through with expansion. We'll cancel the loan quietly, but it's served its real purpose—to really jump our investment base. The authorities won't catch on for some time—if ever—as we'll finance expansion out of local accounts."

As I reached for the check, he made one final point. "But we just have to cut back. Most Latin countries are training some sharp MBA types up here. And, remember, they have a legitimate bitch. A lot of us haven't left *that* much behind in the local economy—and I'm afraid we'll have to pay the piper and dance to the Finance Minister's tune."

How much would he pay and how fast would he dance, I asked.

"A lot more. On our Baton Rouge tank farm, we went for 10 percent R.O.I. over 10 years. I'd settle for 20 percent in five in Latin America. This should keep the wolves at bay for awhile. It's less for us, but it's better than losing everything. The good old carpetbagging days are done."

APPENDIX 2

Central Bank of the Philippines, Manila—Memorandum to All Authorized Agents

As a result of continuing analytical studies, the system of measurements has been amended to improve the method of implementing the

Central Bank's policy on investment remittance. Under this policy, which applies equally to precontrol investments as well as to approved postcontrol investment, Philippine companies and branches of foreign companies are allowed to remit profits and dividends due to their nonresident stockholders or head offices on the basis of the net contributions of the companies to (a) national income and employment or "the national income effect," (b) strengthening the balance-of-payments position of the country or "the balance-of-payments effect," and (c) supply of goods and services to serve the basic needs of the economy or "the product essentiality." The system of measurements, as amended, is indicated below.

I.   NATIONAL INCOME EFFECT
  A.   The national income effect is the ratio of the net domestic value added by the firm to the amount of scarce resources utilized in production and is expressed by the equation:

$$Y = (V_g/I_t) \times 100\%$$

where:

Y = national income effect, percent.
V_g = net domestic value added by the firm, pesos.
I_t = amount of scarce resources utilized in production, pesos.

  B.   Net domestic value added consists of the sum of the shares of the four factors of production in the income of the firm. This is obtained by adding the shares of:
    1.   Labor—consisting of salaries and wages, bonuses, and commissions received by the employees and wage earners of the firm.
    2.   Land—rent of land and buildings used by the firm in production.
    3.   Entrepreneur—profits before income tax.
    4.   Capital—interest payments on loans.
  C.   Scarce resources consist of:
    1.   Replacement of fixed assets—current amortization (depreciation) of fixed assets of both domestic and imported origin.
    2.   Maintenance of fixed assets—cost of spare parts, labor, supplies, and other costs incurred in maintenance. (If maintenance is done by an outside firm, the total charges of the outside firm plus the cost of spare parts and supplies provided by the firm will be deducted.)
    3.   Foreign exchange utilized—the foreign exchange cost of raw materials and supplies (including fuel) directly

imported and indirectly (domestically purchased) imported, salaries of foreign personnel remitted abroad, and all other foreign exchange costs (royalties, service charges, expenses of business trips abroad, and so forth).

D. Automatic rating for firms producing intermediate products. Firms producing intermediate products necessary for the production processes of other essential industries are credited a minimum 3-point rating in the national income effect. Necessity is established if the intermediate product possesses either or both of the following characteristics:

1. It forms an integral part, physically or chemically, of the product of the other essential industry.

2. It is a necessary accessory for handling or merchandising, that is, containers, of the final product.

E. The rating accruing from contribution to national income effect is obtained by the following schedule:

SCHEDULE 1

National Income Effect (percent)	Accrued Rating* (points)
Above 300	5
251–300	4
201–250	3
151–200	2
101–150	1
100 and below	0

*Except for firms producing intermediate products which are credited a minimum 3-point rating.

II. BALANCE-OF-PAYMENTS EFFECT

A. The balance-of-payments effect is measured by the ratio of the net foreign exchange earned and saved to the amount of scarce resources utilized during the period and is expressed by the following equation:

$$B = (F_n/I_t) \times 100\%$$

where:

B = balance-of-payments effect, percent.

F_n = net foreign exchange earned and saved, pesos.

I_t = amount of scarce resources utilized in production, pesos.

B. The net foreign exchange earned and saved is determined by subtracting the foreign exchange costs of production from the foreign exchange value of the product.

C. The foreign exchange costs consist of the foreign exchange utilized in production [I (C)(3) above] plus the current amortization of imported fixed assets. Generally, land, furniture, and buildings are considered domestic fixed assets; and all the rest, imported fixed assets.

D. The foreign exchange value is determined by:
　1. Earnings—foreign exchange received for payment of exports.
　2. Savings—in the case of import substitute, the foreign exchange cost of the product if it were imported (CIF value of the product shall be used). A product shall be considered as an import substitute if it is an essential commodity or its manufacture began subsequent to the imposition of exchange control (December 9, 1949) and it displaces products imported prior to the import control.

E. The rating accruing from the strengthening of the balance of payments position of the country is given by the following schedule:

SCHEDULE 2

Balance-of-Payments Effect (percent)	Accrued Rating (points)
Above 200	5
166–200	4
131–165	3
96–130	2
61– 95	1
60 and below	0

III. PRODUCT ESSENTIALITY
　A. Products are first classified according to (1) export products and (2) products for domestic consumption.
　B. Export products are further classified according to the degree of processing they have undergone as:
　　1. Manufactured products.
　　2. Semi-manufactured products.
　　3. Raw materials.
　C. Products for domestic consumption are further classified into:
　　1. Highly essential products.
　　2. Essential producer products.
　　3. Essential consumer products.
　　4. Nonessential producer products.
　　5. Nonessential consumer products.

The Central Bank Commodity Classification shall be used as the primary basis of classifying products for domestic consumption. For this purpose, the unclassified items in the Central Bank Commodity Classification shall be reclassified. The criteria to be used in the reclassification shall be "utility" of the product.

D. The corresponding rating accruing from the essentiality of the product is determined by the following schedule:

SCHEDULE 3

Products for Domestic Use	Export Products	Category	Accrued Rating (points)
Highly essential	Manufactured	I	5
Essential producer		II	4
Essential consumer	Semi-manufactured	III	3
Nonessential producer		IV	2
Nonessential consumer	Raw materials	V	1

IV. SCHEDULE OF ALLOWABLE REMITTANCES

A. A straight 40 percent of the nonresident's share in the net profits shall be allowed to be remitted by the following firms:

1. Firms operating under a government franchise wherein the output is of the character of a public service.

2. Banks and insurance companies.

B. Beginning with profits realized for financial years ending in 1958, all other companies are allowed to remit dividends or profits to their nonresident stockholders or head offices abroad according to the following schedule of allowable annual remittances:

SCHEDULE 4

Social Productivity Rating (SPR)	Allowable Remittances (whichever is lower)	
	Percent of the Nonresident's Share in Current Net Profit	Percent of Foreign Capital Invested*
13–15	100	60
10–12	80	50
7– 9	60	40
4– 6	40	30
1– 3	25	20

*As of the beginning of the period for which the profit is realized.

The Social Productivity Rating of a firm is the sum of the ratings accruing from the national income effect, balance-of-payments effect, and product essentiality. For non-Philippine companies, the depreciated or net book value of capital assets as at the beginning of the fiscal year for which the profit is realized will be used instead of capital invested.

C. Withholding taxes on dividends are to be deducted from the remittable amounts as determined.

APPENDIX 3
THE IMPACT OF FOREIGN INVESTMENT IN MEXICO[2]

The Measurable Effects of United States Direct Investment on Mexico's Balance of Payments

No reliable estimate can be made about the collective effects of all foreign investment on Mexico's balance-of-payments since the necessary information is available on only U.S. direct investments. However, it is estimated that U.S. direct investments bolstered the balance-of-payments position of Mexico during 1965–68 by an annual average of about $1,552 million. U.S. manufacturing investments provided balance of payments support averaging $1,140 million per year, or almost three fourths of the total support by all U.S. direct investments. Investments by mining and smelting companies and by petroleum companies provided annual balance-of-payments support of $191 million and $13 million, respectively. The annual support provided by all other U.S. investments averaged about $208 million.

Exports by all U.S. affiliates aggregated about $446 million in 1966. Moreover, the gross import savings derived from part of the domestic sales by U.S. affiliates that year amounted to about $1,305 million. The combined export earnings and gross import savings of the affiliates are therefore estimated at $1,751 million. However, they imported goods and services worth about $190 million to help fulfill their production requirements. Accordingly, the combined export earnings and net import savings of all U.S. affiliates amounted to about $1,561 million in 1966—a year that is assured here to represent the average annual operational results of the affiliates for the four-year period, 1965–68.

Net new U.S. direct investment in Mexico averaged $106 million during 1965–68. Addition of the amount to the net annual balance-of-payments support provided by the affiliates through their export

---

[2]Extracted from *Impact of Foreign Investment in Mexico* (New York: Council of the Americas, n.d.).

earnings and net import savings resulted in gross balance-of-payments support averaging $1,667 million per year. The earnings derived by U.S. investors averaged $115 million. It is therefore estimated that the *net* support provided by all U.S. investments to the balance of payments of Mexico during 1965–68 averaged $1,552 million annually. The importance of U.S. investments to Mexico's balance of payments may be evaluated in part by the following:

Total exports from Mexico averaged $1,180 million per year during 1965–68. Exports by U.S. affiliates amounted to about $446 million in 1966, or 37.8 percent of the average annual total.

Total imports by Mexico averaged $1,718 million per year during the same period. The additional imports necessary to meet the production needs of domestically owned enterprises and the consumption needs of the Mexican people would have averaged about $1,115 million annually—64.9 percent in excess of actual imports—if U.S. affiliates had not provided import substitutions of that amount. (The gross import savings provided by U.S. affiliates, about $1,305 million, were offset by imports of about $190 million that they effected for their own production purposes.)

Other Effects of U.S. Direct Investment

Taxes. Total tax payments to the government of Mexico by all U.S. affiliates are estimated to have amounted to 2,288 million pesos in 1966. This was 11.8 percent of the government's total tax revenues, as compared with 16.9 percent in 1957. Tax payments by the U.S. manufacturing affiliates alone amounted to 1,175 million pesos in 1966.

Employment. The estimated employment in 1966 by the U.S. manufacturing, mining and smelting, and petroleum affiliates was 104,430 people, only 685 of whom (less than 0.7 percent) were U.S. employees. The total managerial staffs numbered 1,072 people, of whom 432 (40.3 percent) were U.S. employees. The total number of technical and professional employees was 7,876, of whom 253 (3.3 percent) were U.S. employees. All the other 95,482 employees were Mexicans.

Technological and Other Effects

We have concentrated in this study on the measurable economic effects of foreign investments primarily because those effects have been important to the people of Mexico and because reliable information is available with regard to them. However, we do not wish to imply an exclusive interest in quantitative measurements or in economic or material values. Foreign investments have had important social, cultural, psychological, and political consequences. Each deserves extensive and intensive analysis by competent and dispassionate professionals in those fields, but interested as we are in these matters, we cannot claim to be such professionals. Moreover, even with regard to the "strictly economic" effects of foreign investment, it must be acknowledged that many of those effects simply cannot be demonstrated other than quantitatively, or cannot be demonstrated at all.

It is, for example, particularly difficult to *demonstrate* (rather than merely to assert or to deny) the extent to which foreign investment has been a significant medium for the transfer to Mexico of important technological and managerial expertise. Many individual examples of the effective transfer of such expertise can be cited,[3] but it is ordinarily very difficult or impossible to evaluate the full economic consequences of the separate examples. Moreover, we know of no way to determine and evaluate the economic consequences of all, or even of most, of the infinite number of transfers of knowledge that may in fact have taken place. Nevertheless, we shall list below some of the innovations that have reportedly been introduced into Mexico by various foreign investors: Polyester and its applications, ester gums (hydrogenated) for chewing gum, acrylic resins and their applications, chain-stopped alkyd resins, thermo-setting resins, thermo-plastic resins, chlorobenzenes, ammonium chloride, disc plows, pull-type planters and rotary cutters, commercial credit reporting, handling methods in explosives production, wire-connection techniques, aircraft loading and unloading equipment, nonferrous smelting and refining processes, automatic radiator shutters, automotive heaters, activated carbon manufacture processes, trisodium phosphate anhydrous, water-repellant tube greases, low-temperature soldering fluxes, cheese, butter, and margarine color, aerosol cans, pull tabs for cans, powered iron cores, ferrites, grinding mills, wet-milling techniques, tools and fixtures in vehicle assembly, concrete improvement techniques, coated abrasives, direct-selling methods, fiber molds for round concrete columns, data processing input equipment, offset composition equipment, plastic binding methods, laminating machines, automotive wire harness, automotive and truck transmissions, forging steel, mass gear cutting, spline rolling, continuous automatically controlled heat treating, tool making, cutter grinding, gear shaving, gear honing, aspirin crystallization process, selection herbicides.

---

[3]Reference can be made, for example, to the book, *Putting Down Roots,* by Richard W. Hall, published for and by the Celanese Corporation, New York, 1969.

Inland Metals*

THE VICE PRESIDENT INTERNATIONAL of Inland Metals, a nationally known U.S. corporation, in 1966 received an urgent call from a Lebanese-American importer and exporter in New York who on previous occasions had assisted the company in getting raw materials in short supply from producing countries. This cosmopolitan operator had just received an offer from a high official of a Latin American country (apparently with the full sanction of the president of the country) to obtain exclusive buying rights to all antimony produced in the country. Prices would be at least 10 percent less than world market wholesale prices, but 20 percent of the funds were to be deposited in a numbered account in a Swiss bank. Antimony had been in scarce supply for over a year and with the escalation of defense spending following the Vietnam engagement, the demand was increasing.

The Lebanese-American was now in turn offering that Inland Metals buy from him the total antimony output of the Latin American country. While he would be the party formally contracting with the unnamed official and would presumably get a commission on the transaction, the antimony would be shipped to Inland Metals and not through his warehouse. Payment, however, could be made through his firm.

*This case was prepared by Professor Kenneth Simmonds, London Business School. It is not intended to illustrate the policies or practice of any particular firm. Copyright 1976 by Kenneth Simmonds.

Assessing Differences in National Environments

British Airborne*

DR. AMAR SINGH, an Indian national who had been in Canada for four weeks at the invitation of the government to lecture on some obscure aspects of neurosurgery—a subject on which he was a leading expert—was going back to Delhi. He had, in fact, been on his way to Montreal's airport at Dorval, when he decided that he would like to stop in London for a day or two on his way home to meet his old friend and teacher, Sir Michael Shannon.

On arrival at Dorval Airport, the 5′ 4″ disheveled and untidy doctor made his way to the counter of British Airborne. There was a well-groomed and charming lady in attendance with "Jane Smith" boldly splashed on her name tag.

"Yes, sir?"

"I want a booking on your evening flight—to London and on to Delhi," said Dr. Singh.

Miss Smith punched a few keys. "Yes, we can manage that, sir."

Dr. Singh handed over his ticket. "I would like to stop in London for about 12 hours."

Miss Smith looked at the ticket, her brows furrowed, and she consulted a manual on her desk. "You have an excursion ticket, sir, and there's no way we can permit you to break your journey in London."

"But when I came to Montreal, Trans Am permitted me to stop over

*This case was prepared by Mr. Shiv Mathur, Research Fellow, and Professor Kenneth Simmonds of the London Graduate School of Business Studies. It is not intended to illustrate the policies or practice of any particular firm. Financial support was provided by the British Overseas Trade Board. Copyright 1976 by London Business School.

in London. Perhaps I can speak to someone in your organisation who could assist me."

"I can't speak for Trans Am, sir. It may have been an oversight on their part, but we don't do it. The airline's rules are very specific and the answer is no. There's nobody else who could help you," said Miss Smith firmly but suavely, adding with a smile, "Should I make a reservation straight to Delhi?"

Dr. Singh was slightly taken aback. "Perhaps I could pay the difference."

"We can't accept that ticket in part exchange. You will have to buy an entirely new ticket and perhaps you wouldn't want to do that, sir."

Dr. Singh looked at her.

"I am afraid the answer remains definitely no." With these words Miss Smith looked over Dr. Singh's head at the tall American hippie next in the queue.

Dr. Singh looked around, seemed upset, then picked up his bags and walked over to the Mediterranean Airways counter.

Later that evening when Miss Smith was having a cup of tea with John Parry-Green, British Airborne's marketing manager for eastern Canada, she recounted the incident with Dr. Singh.

"Quite right, too," agreed Mr. Parry-Green when he heard the stand she had taken. But when Miss Smith had returned to her counter, Mr. Parry-Green continued to think about the matter.

Since his appointment to the region six months previously, Mr. Parry-Green had been trying to drum up business for British Airborne in the eastern provinces of Canada. He had had talks with travel agents and some of the larger business houses in the province of Quebec and he felt that negotiations had, by and large, been satisfactory. However, he had been unable to come to terms with the two Indian travel agents who made the majority of bookings for the large population of Indians and other Asians resident in eastern Canada. Mr. Parry-Green had invited them to his office and quite specifically laid down his attractive terms on discounts and commission, but they had, in his opinion, taken an extreme bargaining position and it all seemed of little use. The two travel agents had telephoned him on several occasions to ask him if he would contact British Airborne's London office to explain their position, but Mr. Parry-Green had assured them that though he could not alter his terms he quite understood the nature of their demands and would advise them if his airline was ever in a position to change its policy. As he felt quite competent to deal with the situation, he did not think it necessary to refer the question to London and negotiations had now been deadlocked for a few weeks.

Asians and Arabs with their extended families were frequent travellers and British Airborne could certainly do with their business. But

Mr. Parry-Green felt that they wanted him to bend not only British Airborne, but also IATA (International Air Transport Association) rules. He suspected other airlines, and especially Mediterranean Airways, of making illegal concessions to passengers. These concessions could take many forms, such as overlooking excess baggage and giving unallowed stopovers and large discounts.

Of course, local managers of other airlines denied this, and Jean Cohen of Mediterranean Airways was most vociferous in his denials. But could one trust that lot? Mr. Parry-Green had, on his own initiative, once or twice tried to check on Mediterranean Airways activities, but had been unable to document any irregularity. However, such concessions were almost impossible to detect on a cursory check and would require a much more thorough investigation. Mr. Parry-Green had himself been tempted to make some concessions to his passengers that would technically infringe IATA rules and had, in fact, noted this as a point of serious discussion at the forthcoming marketing managers' conference in London. If London did not permit him to try some concessions, he had almost decided that he would register a complaint anonymously with the IATA authorities regarding Mediterranean Airways' activities. IATA would surely uncover many irregularities and although the substantial fines that would be imposed following the detection of such offenses might not worry an airline of Mediterranean Airways' standing, it would at least give Jean Cohen something to account for to his head office and customers. The International Air Transport Association had not been lenient in recent years about infringement of rules.

Over the last three months, British Airborne's comparative load factor from Dorval had fallen at an increasing rate, in spite of the additional facilities and staff that Mr. Parry-Green had employed to serve customers. Mr. Parry-Green felt that this was partly due to the growing recession and consequent excess capacity on flights and competition for customers. Still, it did not look good in the first year of his appointment, and the incident with Dr. Singh made him wonder again whether he should not suggest that counter staff fail to notice excursion rates when passengers held British Airborne's own tickets and wanted to stop over.

Bell Schönheitsprodukte GmbH*

THE MANAGEMENT OF BELL SCHÖNHEITSPRODUKTE GmbH decided in January 1972 to give serious consideration to undertaking a major plant expansion outside of Germany. The year 1971 had seen the formal revaluation of the once-floating German mark to a parity of 0.3106 U.S. dollars. This revaluation represented an increase of 13.6 percent in the value of the deutsch mark (DM) over the DM–dollar rate of May 1971. The year 1971 had also seen an increase in the wage bill (including social benefits) at Bell GmbH of nearly 15 percent. As Bell exported over 60 percent of its rather labor-intensive German production, these events threatened to reduce unpleasantly the firm's profitability.

Internationalizing Bell's sources of production appeared to be the most interesting route out of this predicament. A U.S.-owned competitor, which had previously been producing most of its output in Germany, had just opened a plant in France and had proceeded to start a price war. Wages in France were on the order of five to six francs per hour. Wages in Germany were 6 DM per hour.[1] The unanswered question, however, was "Where should Bell put the new plant?"

The Company and Its Products

Bell Schönheitsprodukte GmbH was a German, family-owned company with a total Europe-wide turnover of 22 million DM in 1971. The

---

*This case is based on the experience of a company that wishes to remain anonymous. Various data have been disguised. This case was written for class discussion rather than to illustrate effective or ineffective handling of an administrative situation. Copyright 1972 by Dr. Lawrence G. Franko, faculty member, Centre d'Etudes Industrielles (CEI), Geneva, Switzerland.

[1]One franc equaled 0.627 DM in January 1972.

product line consisted entirely of special opening, closing, sliding, and spring packagings for the cosmetic industry. Among Bell's over 200 customers were several very large multinational companies such as Unilever, Colgate-Palmolive, and L'Oreal. The single largest customer purchased 10 percent of Bell's sales.

Bell's American name derived from the fact that its product line was produced under an exclusive license of an American company, Bell Industries, Inc. The American licensor, however, had no ownership position in Bell GmbH. Although Bell GmbH was a relatively small firm, it had already opened a plant in Great Britain in the mid-1960s. The United Kingdom plant had a capacity of 25 million units as compared to the 200 million unit capacity of the main German plant, located in Hanover. Both plants ordinarily produced at 90–95 percent of capacity. About 18.8 million DM of sales came from the German plant's production; the remaining 2.3 million were accounted for by United Kingdom production. Because of the 9.6 percent EEC common tariff, United Kingdom production went only to the United Kingdom. All other European markets (including other EFTA markets) were supplied by Germany. Indeed, the United Kingdom plant had only been set up because of the 9.6 percent ad valorem EFTA tariff facing German output. Thirty people were employed in the United Kingdom plant, compared to 120 in Germany. Of the German personnel, 90 were women workers who assembled and decorated packages. The remainder consisted of administrative personnel plus technicians who designed and built much of Bell GmbH's machinery and who handled

EXHIBIT 1
Market Size for Closable Cosmetic Packaging

	Approximate Market Size (1971) in Units (millions)
United Kingdom	150
Germany	360
France	200
Benelux	90
Greece	5
Italy	150
Scandinavia	60
Spain	25
Portugal	5
Switzerland	40
Austria	10
Yugoslavia	5
Total Europe	1,100
United States	2,400

the very important (indeed critical) quality-control aspects of the business. None of Bell's employees were union members. According to management, "we are too small to have attracted the attention of the unions."

Sales were made in all countries of Western Europe plus Yugoslavia. Under the terms of its American license, the company was restricted to selling in Europe and the socialist countries. Exhibit 1 shows the total 1971 European and U.S. markets for the kind of special cosmetic-packaging products produced by Bell, in units. Given normal economic conditions, that is 4 to 5 percent yearly growth in GNP, management expected 20 percent per years sales growth in the more developed areas of Europe and somewhat higher growth in countries such as Greece, Portugal, and Spain.

Competition and Prices

Bell GmbH's competitors have the characteristics shown below:

Competitor	Ownership	Output of Plants by Country—1971	
A (large)	U.K. group	France	80%
		U.K.	15
		Italy	5
B (large)	U.S. company	Germany	65
		England	30
		France	5
C (small)	U.S. (recently acquired)	Germany	100
D (small)	Italian	Italy	100
E (small)	Italian	Italy	100

Bell's management suspected that the two small Italian firms (*D* and *E*) were secretly backed by their government; all the more so since the Italian price level was 10–15 percent lower than that elsewhere in the EEC. *D* and *E* had tried to export a part of their production. However, their quality standards were apparently not as high as those of Bell, *A*, and *B*. Moreover, their plants were unionized and subject to occasional strikes. Thus, they had a poor reputation for meeting delivery dates outside of Italy. Still, they totally dominated the local market. Bell had once had 30 percent of the Italian market and was well known there. With practically nonexistent margins, however, Bell found it increasingly impossible to compete in Italy. Nevertheless, in late 1971, just as the Italian situation began to look really hopeless, the President of Bell, Herr Kahler, had received a letter from two ex-managers of Italian competitor *E* suggesting that Bell start up a plant in Italy—under their direction, of course.

EXHIBIT 2
Comparative Market Shares (in percent)*

	Bell	Competitor A	Competitor B	Others	Total
Europe total.........	19	35	25	21	100
France.............	7	70	20	3	100
United Kingdom.......	15	30	45	10	100
Germany............	22	30	30	18	100

*Rough estimates. No one in the industry publishes sales figures.

With the exception of the Italian situation, prices elsewhere in Europe were relatively uniform: Bell's ex-factory price was 100 DM per thousand in the EEC. Competitor *B,* who had started the price war that had recently pushed prices down to 95 DM from a previous higher level also billed in DM. Competitor *A,* who because of its dominant French position, billed in francs, by and large charged a similar price once value-added tax adjustments were made. According to one Bell manager, "we tend to react immediately to what *A* and *B* do, and vice versa. Everyone tries to differentiate their product other than by price, but finally, one packaging is like another."

Exhibit 2 summarizes estimates for the market share of Bell and its competitors in France, Germany, England, and the whole of Europe.

Alternative Courses of Action

In the face of competition, unfavorable exchange-rate movements, wage increases in Germany, and the Italian proposal, management felt that action would be needed soon. Herr Kahler had received a phone call from competitor *A* suggesting that they try to counter *B's* price cutting by "an arrangement." The virtues of such an arrangement from Bell's point of view, however, seemed questionable. *A,* after all, was sitting with 80 percent of its production in France, where wages were favorable and devaluation more often the rule than not.

Putting up a new plant in France, of course, seemed a most tempting possibility; all the more so since the French government offered very interesting incentives in certain parts of the country. In addition, some technical and design tasks could eventually be performed in France since indigenous skills were available. Ninety percent of the component needs would be supplied initially from Bell's usual outside suppliers in Germany. However, by the second year of operations, perhaps 30 percent could be obtained locally, and, if necessary, all materials could be obtained locally after the third year. Last, but not least, in regions such as Alsace, French technicians and workers generally were fluent in German. Thus there would be few language difficulties during the plant start-up. But management could not help wondering whether or not the French wage and exchange-rate situations would remain as favorable to exports in the future as they had in the past. Moreover, the investment incentives picture had recently been altered by the EEC agreement to limit incentive grants to 20 percent of project costs as of January 1972. And what if another May 1968 were around the corner?

In some ways, adding 25 or 50 million units of capacity to the United Kingdom plant seemed about the easiest thing to do. A plant and trained people were already in existence. Incentives might be available. The pound might devalue again. And perhaps wages would not increase as fast as elsewhere in the now expanding EEC. Still, the United Kingdom might be less attractive for the time being because it would probably take five years before tariff barriers would finally disappear between the United Kingdom and the EEC. As in France, local components could eventually be substituted for German-made goods.

The request from the Italians reminded Bell management that a local plant might well help it to capture back its once 30 percent market share. Technical skills and components would be as easily available as in the United Kingdom and France. Moreover, Italy could conceivably provide a relatively low wage base for exports. And the lira had depreciated against the mark in recent times. But could any country that had taken 23 ballots to elect a president in 1971 be a stable place in which to invest?

One final alternative that appeared interesting to Herr Kahler and other members of Bell's management was that of setting up a plant in Spain. Perhaps such a move might give the company a much greater and longer lasting competitive advantage than would the other possibilities. Whether or not components could ever be obtained locally was simply unknown. Still, wage rates were thought to be low enough to easily jump the EEC common tariff. Although a 10 percent duty might have to be paid on components imported from Germany, it seemed probable that a rebate arrangement for re-exported components could be negotiated with the Spanish authorities.

The plant sizes that appeared most interesting for Italian, Spanish, United Kingdom, or French operations were either 25 million or 50 million units per year. Factory buildings could be leased for very similar yearly rentals throughout Europe. Details of the capacity and cost alternatives considered are given in Exhibit 3. The necessary machinery would either be made at Bell's main plant or purchased in Germany. Tentatively, it was thought best to finance a foreign plant by an equity stake equal to the cost of machinery. Working capital

EXHIBIT 3
Capacity and Cost Alternatives

	Alternative 1	Alternative 2
Annual plant capacity (million units)	25	50
Space requirements.	600 m²	1000 m²
Approximate yearly rental cost for leased plant* . . .	28,000 DM	48,000 DM
Cost of machinery (to be purchased in Germany). . .	300,000 DM	500,000 DM†
Working capital requirements	100,000 DM	220,000 DM
Components cost (per million units)	46,000 DM	46,000 DM
Direct labor (per million units produced in Germany).	7,000 DM	7,000 DM
General administration and overhead (per year). . . .	100,000 DM	150,000 DM†
Transport costs	2% sales price	2% sales price

*Similar in all countries.
†For plants above 50 million units, machinery and overhead costs are roughly proportional to capacity.

requirements could be met either by local borrowing or by the extension of account-payable terms (for components) to the foreign plant.

As Bell management was preparing to draw up pro forma economic forecasts and cash-flow projections for the French, United Kingdom, Spanish, and Italian alternatives, Herr Kahler reminded his colleagues of a letter he had received in November 1971. He suggested that this letter should stimulate Bell to examine the German economy a bit more carefully, too. The letter was from a Yugoslavian company that was soliciting Bell's participation in a joint venture—whose aim would be to export back to Europe. Herr Kahler rejected serious consideration of such an alternative for the time being on the grounds that Bell was too small to enter into protracted negotiations with a prospective partner in a venture that might end up competing with already existing wholly owned facilities. Still, he felt it might be useful to look at the medium-term outlook for Germany and the competitiveness of the headquarters plant. If a firm in a country like Yugoslavia were to enter into the packaging business, perhaps continued German revaluations and steep wage increases could make the position of the main 200 million unit capacity plant less and less tenable over the years. Up to this point, it had been assumed that German production would still account for most of Bell's sales, even after the new plant were added. It was quite true that the German stockholders might not want to shift a lot of Bell's current production to a foreign country. But efforts at automation could only go so far. Bell had reduced the number of its women workers from 150 to 90 between 1970 and 1971 while increasing output. However, productivity increases could not be obtained at this rate in the future. Would some existing German plant capacity eventually have to be transferred elsewhere?

EXHIBIT 4
Exchange Rates, Money Supply, and Prices—Selected European Countries 1965–1971*

	1965	1966	1967	1968	1969	1970	1971
Italy							
Rate of exchange (lira per dollar)	624.70	624.45	623.86	623.50	625.50	623.00	581.5
Money supply (1963 = 100)	125	142	164	184	213	273	
Cost-of-living index (1963 = 100)	109	112	115	117	121	128	
France							
Rate of exchange (francs per dollar)	4.902	4.952	4.908	4.948	5.558	5.520	5.116†
Money supply (1963 = 100)	118	127	133	145	146	157	
Cost-of-living index (1963 = 100)	105	108	112	118	124	131	
United Kingdom							
Rate of exchange (pound per dollar)	0.357	0.358	0.415	0.419	0.416	0.418	0.383
Money supply (1963 = 100)	113	118	131	140	144	157	
Cost-of-living index (1963 = 100)	109	114	116	123	129	139	
Germany							
Rate of exchange (marks per dollar)	4.006	3.977	3.999	4.000	3.690	3.648	3.223
Money supply (1963 = 100)	117	119	131	142	150	165	
Cost-of-living index (1963 = 100)	107	109	110	113	116	120	
Spain							
Rate of exchange (peseta per dollar)	59.99	60.00	69.70	69.82	70.06	69.72	64.47
Money supply (1963 = 100)	139	155	178	198	229	250	
Cost-of-living index (1963 = 100)	123	130	138	142	147	157	

*Year end.
†Commercial rate.
Source: IMF, *International Financial Statistics*, January 1972.

EXHIBIT 5

International Financial Data—Selected European Countries (millions of U.S. dollars)*

	1965	1966	1967	1968	1969	1970	1971 (Nov.)
Italy							
Official reserves	4,800	4,911	5,463	5,341	5,045	5,352	6,431
Balance on goods and services†	1,883	1,779	1,273	2,336	2,013	679	
Trade (goods) balance only	646	331	-21	1,048	542	-340	
France							
Official reserves	6,343	6,733	6,994	4,201	3,833	4,960	7,494
Balance on goods and services†			732	-238	-971	1,148	
Trade (goods) balance only			356	-158	-1,223	726	
United Kingdom							
Official reserves	3,004	3,099	2,695	2,422	2,527	2,827	5,572
Balance on goods and services†	378	801	-115	-118	1,613	1,911	
Trade (goods) balance only	-664	-204	-1,446	-1,543	-338	7	
Germany							
Official reserves	7,430	8,029	8,153	9,948	7,129	13,610	17,371
Balance on goods and services†	-86	1,593	3,970	4,554	3,780	3,225	
Trade (goods) balance only	248	1,878	4,116	4,485	3,902	4,024	
Spain							
Official reserves	1,422	1,253	1,100	1,150	1,282	1,817	3,104
Balance on goods and services†	-846	-983	-907	-709	-959		
Trade (goods) balance only	-1,759	-1,992	-1,781	-1,574	-1,871		

*End of year.

†Not including transfer payments.

Source: IMF, *International Financial Statistics.*

EXHIBIT 6

Wage Increases Related to Output Increases in Industry—Selected European Countries*

	1966	1967	1968	1969	1970	1971	(forecast) 1972†
Italy							
Percent increase in industrial output	11.3	8.5	6.3	2.9	4.0	-2.6	8.0
Percent increase in wages§.		5.2	3.6	7.5	21.4	14.5	15.0
Ratio of output to wage increases		(1.64)	(1.75)	(0.36)	(0.14)	(0.19)	(0.53)
France							
Percent increase in industrial output	4.3	2.6	4.1	12.7	5.6	2.5	5.0
Percent increase in wages§.	5.9	6.0	12.4	11.3	10.5	11.1	10.0
Ratio of output to wage increases	(1.24)	(0.43)	(0.33)	(1.13)	(0.53)	(0.22)	(0.50)
United Kingdom							
Percent increase in industrial output	1.8	-0.9	5.3	3.4	1.6	0.8	3.5
Percent increase in wages§.	6.7	4.0	6.8	9.2	9.6	12.1	12.0
Ratio of output to wage increases	(0.27)	(-0.22)	(0.78)	(0.37)	(0.17)	(0.07)	(0.29)
Germany							
Percent increase in industrial output	1.8	-1.7	12.3	12.5	6.3	3.2	0
Percent increase in wages‡.	7.3	3.9	4.3	9.1	12.8	13.3	6.5
Ratio of output to wage increases	(0.25)	(-0.44)	(2.9)	(1.4)	(0.49)	(0.24)	(0)
Spain							
Percent increase in industrial output	15.0	6.2	6.5	14.5	7.9		6.6
Percent increase in wages‡.	16.0	15.0	7.0	9.0	17.0		12.0
Ratio of output to wage increases	(0.94)	(0.42)	(0.93)	(1.61)	(0.47)		(0.55)

*Calculated from OECD, *Main Economic Indicators*, various issues.
†Eurofinance-Vision Projections, *Vision*, January 1972, p. 38.
‡Hourly earnings.
§Hourly rates.

EXHIBIT 7

Wages in Manufacturing (All Industries) in Local Currencies—Selected European Countries

	Austria per month Schilling†	Belgium per day Male B. Franc†	Denmark per hour (M & F)* Ore†	France per hour (wage rate) Francs†	W. Germany per hour (M & F)* D. Mark†	Italy per hour Lira†	Spain per hour pesetas†	Switzerland per hour Sw. Fr.†	U.K. per hour Male s.d.†
1965	3,141	359.0	923	3.00	4.12	386	21.57	5.20	8/9
1966	3,514	389.7	1,040	3.18	4.42	401	25.13	5.58	9/3
1967	3,781	414.2	1,128	3.37	4.60	426	28.81	5.94	9/8
1968	4,018	438.7	1,283	3.79	4.79	445	31.16	6.24	10/4
1969	4,263	474.1	1,407	4.21	5.28	489	34.69	6.64	11/2
1970	5,074	—	—	4.56	5.77	—	—	—	—

*Male and female.
†Earnings.
‡Rates.

Source: *ILO Yearbook of Labor Statistics*, 1970.

EXHIBIT 8

Indices of Industrial Capacity Utilization—Selected European Countries

Year*	Belgium	France	Germany	Italy	Nether-lands	United Kingdom
1965	95.3%	91.7%	92.1%	86.8%	89.7%	
1966	90.6	90.0	85.8	88.5	87.6	93.6%
1967	90.2	87.0	86.7	89.4	86.7	
1968	90.6	96.8	93.0	80.0	91.2	96.9
1969	94.2	94.7	97.3	79.1	93.2	95.8
1970	92.8	95.6	94.0	87.3	94.0	94.5
1971 . . . . (1)	94.7	96.1	97.1	86.1	96.5	93.6
(2)	92.2	93.2	95.4	82.1	94.8	94.2
(3)	92.9	95.5	93.1	79.4	93.6	93.4

*Year end 1965–70, and first three quarters 1971.
Source: "Wharton Indices of Industrial Capacity Utilization in Europe," *Wharton Quarterly,* various issues. (Available from The Wharton School, University of Pennsylvania, Philadelphia, Pa.)

EXHIBIT 9

Sample Cash-Flow Projection for an Italian Investment*

Projected cash flows: Italian investment in 50 million-unit plant

Investment

Machinery	500,000 DM
Working capital	220,000
Total.	720,000
Less: 70% debt	(504,000)
Net investment	216,000 DM

Annual Cash Flows	*Before Devaluation*	*After 10% Devaluation*
Sales revenue (95 × 50,000 DM)	4,750,000 DM	4,750,000 DM
Expenses†		
Building rental	48,000	43,000
Components	2,300,000	1,970,000
Direct labor.	170,000	153,000
General overhead	150,000	135,000
Transport costs.	75,000	68,000
Interest (5%)	25,000	23,000
Net cash flow	1,982,000 DM	2,358,000 DM

*Showing results assuming: (1) no devaluation and (2) a 10% devaluation.
†Major assumptions:

1. All components supplied locally.
2. Income tax holiday provided by Italian government.
3. All production is for export.
4. Depreciation not included in overhead charges.

Expanding and Adjusting within a Global Market

P. T. Indol*

ON JUNE 8, 1973 MR. BRIAN MANVILLE, Portfolio Manager of the Overseas Investment Company (OIC), a London-based investment bank, received an urgent telex from his Singapore office indicating that if an immediate decision was not taken to invest in P. T. Indol in Indonesia, it was likely that the sponsors of the project would look elsewhere and almost certainly, successfully, for funds. The telex went on to suggest that attractive terms for investment had been made possible by "cultivation and subsequent exploitation of friendship" and requested an urgent and affirmative reply.

The Overseas Investment Company had been originally set up to serve as a vehicle for providing overseas loan and equity funds for projects in the developing countries of the world. However, the company was extremely careful to invest in projects that seemed commercially viable and over the years had gathered a worldwide portfolio of more than £100 million of industrial, trading, and agricultural investment. OIC was well known in the developing countries, well thought of in the City of London, and its board included city bankers and heads of international companies.

The company was generally willing to make equity and loan investment for overseas development projects, provided it felt that the project was fundamentally sound and had a return on OIC funds in the region of 12 percent before U.K. taxes. Most of OIC's investment was classified as development projects in the host country with conse-

*This case was prepared by Mr. Shiv Mathur, Research Fellow, and Professor Kenneth Simmonds of the London Graduate School of Business Studies with the cooperation of an organization which chooses to remain anonymous. Some facts and figures have been altered to preserve corporate confidentiality. Financial support was provided by The British Overseas Trade Board. Copyright by London Business School, 1976.

quent tax and other benefits. The U.K. government had made some funds available to OIC at a concessionary interest rate as part of its aid programme to developing countries, making a target rate of 12 percent quite attractive to OIC's investment managers.

INDONESIAN INVESTMENT

P. T. Indol had been brought to the attention of the London office of OIC in March 1973 by Gerald Carter of the Singapore office. OIC had been actively looking for profitable investment opportunities in Southeast Asia and Mr. Carter had spent over two years developing contacts in Indonesia. Indonesia had lately been identified by OIC and other investors as a country with ample natural resources and attractive investment opportunities. Brian Manville had commissioned Paul Harrison, OIC's economic and market analyst, to prepare a political and economic report on Indonesia (Exhibit 1). When compared with the economies of other developing countries, Indonesia appeared quite favorable to overseas investors. The recent discovery of substantial oil resources was forecast to give Indonesia an enviable position in Southeast Asian trade.

Mr. Carter had recently been introduced to three Indonesian businessmen planning to set up a plantation and factory, trading as P. T. Indol, to grow and distil patchouli oil—an essential oil used extensively in the production of perfumes and toiletries. Patchouli oil had been used in the Orient and India since time immemorial. It was through Indian shawls carrying with them the odour of patchouli that Europe had become familiar with the perfume. In the days of the East India Company, patchouli oil was considered to be a fine perfume by itself. Gradually patchouli oil became an important raw material for the perfumer and one of the best fixatives for heavy perfumes: an essential, though inexpensive, ingredient for any perfume of quality.

The three Indonesian sponsors of P.T. Indol were of Chinese extraction, settled on the island of Java, and were also partners in an Indonesian trading company which had a turnover of more than U.S. $100,000 a month. The trading company was extremely well thought of on the Indonesian business scene and had received glowing testimonials from trading associates as far away as Australia. Its main business was in the export of essential oils, such as sandalwood, nutmeg, citronella, and patchouli oil. The three partners had been exporting patchouli oil from Indonesia for the last four years. In their experience almost all patchouli oil sold to them by small holdings for export was adulterated with gurjin (another herb oil) to increase the volume of "patchouli oil." Following continuing complaints from European and American importers that the quality of patchouli oil being sold was substandard, the partners decided that there was money in the business if they could supply a high-grade product on a continuing basis.

The quality of patchouli leaves was affected by various soil and climatic conditions. These variables and the precise method of distillation gave the extracted oil a distinctive smell and other required chemical characteristics. Oil distilled in Southeast Asia was generally extracted by traditional methods—mainly in iron drums—which contributed to impurities in the final product. Better skills and methods of distillation were available in the United Kingdom and France and were used in these countries to distill oil for high-quality perfumes from imported leaves. European-distilled patchouli had a less woody and earthy odour and a fruitier top than Southeast Asian distillates and was used for the most expensive perfumes. Inferior Asian distillates were used for the manufacture of soaps, soap powder, and cheaper cosmetics.

The sponsors of P. T. Indol had firm plans to import from France a stainless steel distillation plant to obtain pure distillates. By using a better and more efficient distillation process than hitherto installed in Southeast Asia, they hoped to gain a reputation for unadulterated oil and save on both production costs and the freight costs of bulky leaf export to Europe. They were convinced that in this manner they would become a prestigious and reliable source of supply and their product command the substantial price premium that was paid for pure patchouli oil.

P. T. INDOL

P. T. Indol had been incorporated under Indonesian domestic investment law and officially recognised by the Indonesian government as a development project. A tax holiday for four years and concessions on custom duties for imported equipment had been granted.

Gerald Carter had gone thoroughly into the commercial and financial aspects of P. T. Indol and by early April 1973 Mr. Manville had received a full investment analysis and this is reproduced below:

INVESTMENT COMMITTEE PAPER
(SUBMITTED BY G. CARTER, APRIL 1, 1973)

Introduction

P. T. Indol will grow patchouli leaves, distill them, and export oil to traders in the United States, United Kingdom, France, and Japan, etc. The project will be the world's first large-scale integrated patchouli oil production operation using modern distillation equipment.

Market

The total 1972 world trade in patchouli of all grades is about 400–500 tonnes per year, of which it is estimated that good-quality oil accounts for 25 percent. The larger portion of patchouli oil is distilled incorrectly or adulterated with cheaper oil and there is a general scarcity of good-quality oil. Consequently, the price of oil fluctuates widely for all but a few producers and these producers sell at a substantial premium.

P. T. Indol will produce at full capacity 66 tonnes of good-quality oil annually. Part of this production will be absorbed by natural growth (estimated at 7–9 percent per year), but the bulk will replace producers and suppliers offering poor-quality oil. Although Indonesian oil may not achieve the quality of French/U.K.-distilled oil, it is likely to attract a better price than the low-quality East Indian (Sumatran) oil now marketed.

Prevailing prices per kilo in April 1973 in the U.K. were:

East Indian	£6–7 for low-quality oil
Seychelles	£9.20
English	£22.00
French	£20.30
Singapore distilled	£7.50
Penang	£9.00

Future Markets

The world output of perfume and toiletries has been increasing in volume at the rate of 7–9 percent per annum. In a trade survey carried out by an English merchant, it seems that a potential demand exists for East Indian unadulterated high-quality oil and this would command a premium of about 50 percent more than the price of the virtually pure native oil, which sells at £6–7 per kilo. In fact, some U.K. brokers have already expressed a desire to negotiate with P. T. Indol regarding contracted supplies, subject to guarantees of quality.

Prices of East Indian oil have been rising steadily from £2.71 per kilo in 1963 to £4 in 1971 and to about £7 in 1973, and the price trend appears firm. There is at the moment no indication of any other Indonesian supplier attempting to set up a combined plantation and distillation unit.

Production Details

P. T. Indol has already bought a plantation of about 1,152 hectares near Medan in north Sumatra in the heart of patchouli-growing territory, of which 960 hectares are considered suitable for planting patchouli. Fifty hectares have already been planted for experimentation and roads have been constructed. In fact, some leaves have already been plucked and the sponsors feel they are of more than acceptable quality. Leaf yield is good and is very likely to reach the suggested "normal" yield of 2.3 tons per hectare, with an oil yield of about 3. 2 percent.

The sponsors hope to plant the entire 960 hectares within a period of two years, and they have the staff, equipment, and expertise to do so. Patchouli plants are allowed to grow for six months after planting, during which time they are fertilized, sprayed, and weeded. They are then cut for the first time and this is followed by two more harvests with three months for growth between each. After the third cutting the plants are removed, and the ground is allowed to lie fallow for six months before the cycle begins again.

The plantation is situated 60 kilometers from the factory where a warehouse capable of storing two months of production will be provided. Adequate transport arrangements have been made to import the distillation plant from a leading equipment manufacturer in France, and appropriate processing machinery will be imported from France, Germany, and Denmark, and will be erected by French engineers. The plant will be capable of producing well over 90 tonnes of oil per annum on a three-shift basis. The factory is due for completion by the end of 1973 and will go commercial by early March 1974.

Financial

It is estimated that the total funds required by the project are on the order of Rupiahs 420 million (Rp 1,045 = 1). This includes capitalization of pre-operation costs and interest charges and also a contingency

	Rp Millions	*Remarks*
Sponsors	84	Sponsors' funds
State bank (SB) loans	146	Already committed at 12% per annum—an extremely low rate as the project is classified as a development project. Loan secured by first claim on fixed assets.
Others (recommended OIC) . . .	190	Bearing a coupon rate of 12% and a profit sharing right of 9% of profit before tax. Loan secured by guarantees from the shareholders.

budget of about Rp 60 million. The funds required will be financed as follows:

Attached are some financial details regarding P. T. Indol's projected operation. Exhibit 2 gives the assumptions on which the projected profit-and-loss statements and P. T. Indol's cash flows over the next five years have been calculated. As Exhibit 2 makes clear, these assumptions are far too conservative. The total yield is assumed to be only 46 percent of what "normal yield" for similar plantations in Sumatra should be. Selling prices have been assumed to be only 67 percent of what one would expect high-quality East Indian oil to sell for. These two assumptions imply that total revenue from P. T. Indol has been assumed to be only 31 percent of what would be expected to be the normal revenue from such a plantation. In addition, as also shown in Exhibits 2 and 3, fairly substantial contingency provisions have been made for possible cost underestimation and inflation.

Exhibit 4 gives the projected profit-and-loss statement for the period 1974–75 to 1978–79, and Exhibit 5 shows that the sponsors of P. T. Indol will be comfortably off after having met all their commitments. Exhibit 6 shows the repayment schedule for the state bank loan and Exhibit 7 the repayment schedule on the suggested OIC loan. A discounted internal rate of return of more than 18 percent is estimated to be the return on Overseas Investment Company's involvement. However, it is worthwhile pointing out that since the total revenue that is likely to accrue to P. T. Indol has been underestimated by about 70 percent, the actual return on OIC's involvement could be substantially higher.

Management

The management of P. T. Indol are highly thought of in the Indonesian trading community. They have ample experience in overseas trade of essential oils and good connections with patchouli brokers. Australian connections have spoken highly of their adherence to agreements and delivery dates. The three sponsors of the project have been operating efficiently in the Indonesian economic climate, and know their way around many bureaucratic tangles. This is of considerable importance to any Indonesian operation.

One of the three partners would be responsible for day-to-day administration of the distillation plant. A plantation manager with long experience in rubber, tobacco, and coconut plantations has already been selected along with a qualified agronomist. Attempts are being made to recruit an overall general manager and a factory manager.

In the Dutch fashion there would be a two-tier board, one executive, the other nonexecutive. The executive board itself would look after the marketing of Indol products and the company's operational details. The nonexecutive board, which will include the three partners and possibly representatives from the other two financially interested parties, would oversee the entire operation and also assist in the formulation of long-term company policy.

An Australian-based consultant John Hawkes & Co. has been appointed to help the sponsors with the initial phases of the project. The consultant had earlier conducted a feasibility study for the entire project and commented very favourably on it. It is possible that their services will be retained to assist the executive board during the initial phases of the project.

Conclusions

As mentioned earlier, the sponsors of the project are influential and competent. They have a viable management plan and excellent manpower for the project. Even under the most adverse conditions the investment is likely to be very profitable. What is even more important to OIC is that it could be a very safe and rewarding introduction to the Indonesian market and would open up various other opportunities in an economy that is likely to be of growing importance in Southeast Asia. It is recommended that an investment in P. T. Indol be made without further delay as there are rumors that an American bank is very interested in this business.

FURTHER VIEWS

Brian Manville had been impressed with the report and was seriously considering the investment. He had been disturbed by the fact that Gerald Carter recommended a debt/equity ratio of about 80:20, which seemed to be very high by British capital structure standards. However, Gerald Carter had explained that such ratios were not unknown in development projects and especially in Southeast Asia. What really mattered was whether they were within the debt-bearing capacity of P. T. Indol, and there was ample proof that this was so even under the most adverse conditions outlined in this investment proposal. Gerald Carter had further argued that the loan investment in Indol should be considered to be partially an equity investment as it would be entitled to a share of the profits. To call it a loan was in some ways misleading as it was essentially a method of overcoming the bureaucratic difficulties in making foreign equity investments under the local laws. Not only would the OIC loan have the right to share profits in P. T. Indol, but returns would be safeguarded from a downturn in business. OIC's investment would be entitled to a 12 percent interest from the first year onwards, thus ensuring an early and continuing return, and also 9 percent of the profits before tax when they materialised. Therefore, the investment should qualify as less-risky equity. The entire remittance to OIC would be free of tax for four years. After that time there would still be no withholding tax on dividends remitted abroad and withholding taxes on interest payments would be nominal. However, if OIC still wanted to be represented on the board of P. T. Indol, the sponsors would be very willing to agree to this.

Almost on receipt of Gerald Carter's investment analysis from Singapore, Brian Manville had instructed Paul Harrison, OIC's economic and marketing consultant, to have a close look at the whole business of patchouli oil. On probable projects, OIC almost invariably undertook a U.K.-based study in an attempt to check on the assessments submitted by regional offices. Mr. Harrison spent the better part of the month talking to brokers who bought oil and leaves from Southeast Asia and other sources and sold them to consumers world-wide. He had also been in touch with expert bodies like the Tropical Products Institute in London for their opinion.

Mr. Paul Harrison summarised the salient points of his findings as follows:

> The principal producers and exporters of patchouli oil are Malaysia, Singapore, Indonesia, and the Seychelles. Indonesian patchouli is grown mainly in Sumatra, which accounts for perhaps 70–80 percent of world production. Attempts to grow patchouli in Java have not been highly successful as the oil produced smelt different and was unacceptable to the trade. The oil is largely produced by small holdings in Sumatra which are financed by merchants in Singapore and Malaysia and sell leaf and oil to them. These Southeast Asian merchants, in turn, sell to essential oil brokers in Europe, the United States, and Japan. Western brokers deal in a variety of essential oils and maintain close contact with their customers. Perfumeries and cosmetic manufacturers rarely attempt to set up their own channels to buy direct from Southeast Asian merchants as the small quantities of various oils required do not justify the setting up of independent buying organisations.
>
> The main buyers of patchouli oil are the United States and France. The matrix in Exhibit 9 gives some idea of the pattern of trade of patchouli oil in 1962—the latest year for which such figures were available. A fair amount of Indonesian oil was re-exported from Malaysia and Singapore and therefore the figures are only useful as a measure of magnitude. France, in addition to oil, imported leaves which were distilled and used in the French perfume industry. Very little is known about re-exports from the developed countries.

In his discussion with brokers, Mr. Harrison had been unable to get very precise information regarding buying preferences. Brokers were aware that Southeast Asian oil was sometimes adulterated and preferred high-quality and unadulterated oil from reliable sources. In this respect French buyers were the most fussy and to ensure a high-quality product preferred to distill the leaves themselves.

Brokers as a matter of policy did not involve themselves with the production of oil. But interest in selling high-quality oil was evident from all brokers contacted. English brokers were very keen on exchanging contracts with an Indonesian supplier who would sell an oil of consistent quality. A British broker commented:

> We would suggest that the marketing agents for the high-quality oil from Indol be kept as few as possible so that the price level can be kept up. As selling patchouli oil requires close contact and co-operation with the actual user, it would be better to have a good international broker on a long-term basis. I believe we could find outlets for such oil provided we were not tied to marketing it solely through the U.K.

Mr. Harrison found that prices of oil quoted in the London market depended not only on the quality of the product but the politics of the supplying nation. In fact, there was often a London quote and no oil available for supply. The steep rise in 1965 and 1966 prices (Exhibit 10) for some East Indian oil was explained by a reputed broker to be "a result of the Indonesian-Malaysian confrontation. This led to a short supply of oil and consequently high prices which in turn produced further adulteration of existing supplies. There followed a loss of confidence in East Indian supplies and a sharp fall in prices from 1966 to 1969." Brokers felt that fairly wide price fluctuations "were inevitable as demand for oil was inelastic in response to price changes in the short run, whereas a sharp rise in prices resulted in increases in supply as small holders in Indonesia responded to high and attractive prices." Mr. Harrison had also been able to check on London contracts of Indol's three sponsors and they were thought of as competent trading partners. By and large, brokers were quite keen on buying from an Indonesian supplier of high-quality oil, and on examining samples of Indol oil a few were willing to exchange long-term contracts, subject to guarantees of quality.

Late in April Mr. Harrison had submitted his report to Brian Manville. He agreed with Gerald Carter's assessment that a high-quality product would command a premium and felt that the projected figures on the financial details were adequately conservative. Overall, Mr. Harrison had found Gerald Carter's report quite attractive and recommended that Indol would be a worthwhile project, provided a suitable marketing strategy was evolved. The addition of 66 tonnes of high-quality oil a year could pose problems of absorption. To some extent high-quality oil would displace low-quality oil and this would require some re-organisation of channels and markets. Mr. Harrison felt that the channel decision was of considerable importance and should be decided at an early stage. He felt the following questions should be given particular attention:

1. Should Indol use the existing merchant-broker link or establish its own marketing organisation?
2. If Indol did decide to use the existing channels, should it negotiate with one or many brokers?
3. If Indol decided to set up its own marketing channel, what should this look like?
4. Should Indol enter into a long-term contract with one broker? This would protect it from wide price fluctuations and guarantee a certain offtake, or should it play the market?

By early June, Mr. Manville had referred the various Indol papers to his colleagues in OIC. The general attitude had been favourable but they in substance agreed with Mr. Harrison's views. Mr. Manville realised that OIC could play a significant role in helping Indol select a suitable strategy. In fact, the sponsors had already indicated that they would welcome OIC's suggestions. He was thinking of putting his own ideas on marketing the Indol produce to Gerald Carter for discussion with Indol's sponsors and asking a few more questions about the project, when the telex from Singapore arrived.

EXHIBIT 1
Indonesia—Foreign Investment (prepared by Mr. Paul Harrison, Economic and Market Analyst)

Background

In the mid-1960s, Indonesia was going through a period of hyperinflation, with 1966 inflation running at around 65 percent a year. By 1971 this figure had dropped to 2.5 percent and it seemed that the economic chaos that had existed was gradually being brought under control.

Indonesia, with a population of 120 million of whom 80 million live in congested slum conditions on the island of Java and another 20 million in Sumatra, is a poor country with a per capita annual income of US $100 or less. It is, however, in the Southeast Asian context a promising economy with a strategic geographical situation. It has substantial forest wealth on its 13,000 islands. Rubber and tin are exported and the recent large exports of oil have done much to alter Indonesia's economic situation. Sulphur-free Indonesian oil commands a premium over Middle East oil and is exported, largely, to the Japanese market. In early 1972 it was estimated that Indonesian oil would attract foreign earnings of US $1,400 million a year. In fact, all targets set for oil exports have been exceeded for the past 2–3 years.

EXHIBIT 1 *(continued)*
Foreign Investment

It was only in 1967 that a foreign investment policy was coherently voiced. A Foreign Investment Law was promulgated to attract foreign capital, especially of the type that would process industrial raw materials and use Indonesia's large surplus of labour.

Investment in Indonesia can now be made under three different schemes: (1) Companies Law (CA), (2) Domestic Investment Law (DOIL), and (3) Foreign Investment Law (FIL). The Domestic Investment Law had originally been brought in to attract back Indonesian money which had fled the country. Only Indonesians may hold equity in companies formed under this scheme and such companies would qualify for various economic incentives like tax holidays, investment grants, etc. These incentives are not available to domestic companies incorporated under Company Law.

Under the new Foreign Investment Law it is possible for foreigners to make equity investments in Indonesia. But in the experience of most investors the bureaucracy and red tape associated with a foreign equity investment are formidable. To incorporate a company under the Foreign Investment Law a preliminary application has to be made to the concerned government department and through it to the Foreign Investment Board. When this is approved, a final direct application has again to be made to the board and if it is accepted then the President of Indonesia himself signs a document authorising the investment. The whole process can take 12–18 months or more, even with the help of local middlemen who abound and multiply in the Indonesian climate. The whole process is indicative of the bureaucratic and cultural problems that are likely to be encountered with ongoing Indonesian operations.

However, Foreign Equity Investments, when finally approved, qualify for various economic incentives like tax holidays, waiver of import duties, etc. Owing to the formidable red tape involved, foreign investors are reluctant to invest in equity unless there are strong reasons for doing so. However, large equity investments have been made by U.S. and Japanese companies in petroleum extraction and agriculture.

It is generally believed by foreigners that a great deal can be accomplished in Indonesia by knowing the right way or person and that almost everything is negotiable. In spite of all these problems, Indonesian foreign exchange regulations are quite mild, by developing-country standards. It is possible to make foreign-currency loans to Indonesian firms and have the proceeds returned in the original currency with very little formal documentation. With minor reservations, the government guarantees the repatriation of capital and profits and gives an understanding not to nationalise the investment for a period of 30 years, and even then there is resort to independent arbitration.

In conclusion, it seems that if the bureaucratic problems can be resolved, then there are less currency, business, and political risks in Indonesia than encountered in a whole host of developing countries.

EXHIBIT 2
Assumptions Made

	1974/75	1975/76	1976/77	1977/78	1978/79
Effective hectares planted*	1,500+200†	1,920	1,920	1,920	1,920
Leaf yield (tonnes)	2,125	2,400	2,400	2,400	2,400
Tonnes/hectare	1.25	1.25	1.25	1.25	1.25
Oil yield (tonnes)	58.4	66	66	66	66
Percent yield	2.75	2.75	2.75	2.75	2.75
Agricultural costs‡ (Rp million)	87	96	105	115	127
Sales price (£/kg)	6	6	6	6	6

*Effective hectares are calculated on the basis of area producing one crop per year. As some areas produce 2–3 crops per year, effective hectares can be larger than total area under cultivation.
†Produce from 200 effective hectares produced during 1973–74 will be available for sale during 1974–75.
‡Agricultural costs, in addition to increase in size of operation, have been assured to increase at 10 percent per annum to account for inflation.

EXHIBIT 3
Conservative Nature of Assumptions

		Normal	Assumed	Percent Conservatism (assumed/normal %)
Yields:				
Leaves	Tonnes / Effective hectare	2.30	1.25	54
Oil	Oil in tonnes % / Leaves in tonnes	3.2	2.75	86
Total yield	Oil in tonnes / Effective hectare	0.074	0.034	46
Prices	East Indian oil—			
	high quality (£/kilo)	9*	6	67
	low quality (£/kilo)	6–7	—	—

Costs . . . . 1. A contingency provision of 10% has been added to all costs. In addition, all costs are budgeted to increase at 10% per annum.
2. It has been further assumed that new seeds and fertilizers will be needed after each cutting. This is not ordinarily required and implies an additional contingency provision of Rp 15 million to agricultural costs.

Sensitivity . . . . . . The price of Indol oil must fall to well below £4/kg at assumed yields for the breakeven point to be reached. This implies a fall in sales price of 33% below that used in forecasts and 40% below current price for adulterated oil.

*No market quote but based on discussions with oil brokers.

EXHIBIT 4
Projected Profit and Loss Account (Rp million, year ending July 30)

	1974/75	1975/76	1976/77	1977/78	1978/79
Sales	366	413	413	413	413
Cost of sales					
Agricultural costs	87	96	105	115	127
Variable costs	23	29	31	35	38
Fixed operating costs	34	37	41	45	50
Depreciation	45	45	45	45	45
Total	189	207	222	240	260
Trading profit	177	206	191	173	153
Interest	52	38	26	14	—
Profit before tax	125	168	165	159	153
OIC's share @ 9%	11	15	15	14	—
Profit before tax attributable to sponsors	114	153	150	145	153
Tax	—	—	—	—	69
Profit after tax attributable to sponsors	114	153	150	145	84

EXHIBIT 5
Cash-Flow Forecasts (Rp million)

	1973/74	1974/75	1975/76	1976/77	1977/78	1978/79
Sources						
Sponsors	84					
State bank loan	146					
OIC loan	190					
Net profit		114	153	150	145	84
Depreciation		45	45	45	45	45
Total sources	420	159	198	195	190	129
Applications						
Fixed assets	296	—	—	—	—	38*
Pre-op expenses	44	—	—	—	—	—
Increase in working capital	60	31	12	—	—	—
Loan repayment—State bank	—	20	30	40	56	—
OIC	—	—	63	63	64	—
Total Applications	400	51	105	103	120	38
Net balance	20	108	93	92	70	91
Cumulative balance	20	128	221	313	383	474

*Provision for improvement of distillation plant.

EXHIBIT 6
State Bank Loan—Interest and Repayment Schedule (Rp million)

	5/73	2/74	8/74	2/75	8/75	2/76	8/76	2/77	8/77	2/78	8/78
State bank loan	(146)										
Interest at 12%		11.7*	8.8	8.8	7.6	7.6	5.8	5.8	3.4	3.4	—
Repayment				20		30		40		56	

*Interest of Rp 11.7 million falling due in February 1974 will be payable during the financial year 1974/75. However, there will be no further interest on this sum.

EXHIBIT 7
OIC Loan Repayment Schedule and Return on Investments (Rp million)

	8/73	2/74	8/74	2/75	8/75	2/76	8/76	2/77	8/77	2/78	8/78
Discounting year	0	½	1	1½	2	2½	3	3½	4	4½	5
Loan	(190)										
Interest @ 12%		11.4*	11.4	11.4	11.4	11.4	7.6	7.6	3.8	3.8	—
Profit share					11		15		15		14
Loan repayment						63		63		64	
Total cash flow	(190)	11.4	11.4	11.4	22.4	74.4	22.6	70.6	18.8	67.8	14
Discounts @ 18% discount factor	1	0.92	0.84	0.77	0.71	0.65	0.60	0.55	0.51	0.46	0.43

Rate of return of just over 18%

*Payment of Rp 11.4 million has been capitalized as pre-operating expenses.

EXHIBIT 8

P. T. Indol Organisation Chart

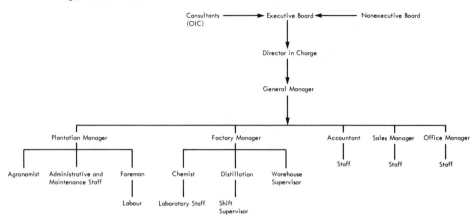

EXHIBIT 9

Leaf and Oil Exports—1962 (figures in tonnes)

		Importing Nations					
	Malaysia/ Singapore	*France*	*United Kingdom*	*United States*	*Japan*	*India*	*Other*
Exporters							
Indonesia......	180* +170 L†						
Malaysia/ Singapore		40 +70 L	25	150	5 +5 L	25 +3 L	50 +4 L
Seychelles		15 +25 L					3 L
France........					7	1	
United Kingdom						1	

*Of this amount it is suspected that about 80 tonnes were re-exported.
†L After a figure signifies leaf exports.
Source: Trade Information.

EXHIBIT 10

Patchouli Oil Prices in United Kingdom (quoted forward prices CIF; in shillings and decimal per pound)

	Quarterly Averages				Annual Range	
	1	*2*	*3*	*4*	*Low*	*High*
Chinese						
1958	—*	27.3	27.3	27.3	27.3	27.3
1959	25.1	30.3	34.0	34.0	20.8	35.0
1960	34.0	—	—	—	—	—
1961	—	—	—	—	—	—
1962	—	—	19.0	19.0	19.0	19.0
1963	19.0	19.0	19.0	19.0	19.0	19.0
1964	19.0	19.0	19.0	19.0	19.0	19.0
1965	19.0	19.0	19.0	19.0	19.0	19.0
1966	15.9	12.8	12.8	—	12.8	19.0
1967	—	—	—	—	—	—
1968	—	—	—	—	—	—
East Indian						
1958–60	—	—	—	—	—	—
1961	—	—	32.0	27.3	25.0	32.0
1962	24.3	21.8	20.7	18.4	18.0	25.0
1963	19.0	18.2	17.8	25.0	16.3	25.5
1964	23.0	20.0	21.4	39.0	19.0	39.0
1965	39.0	48.3	64.4	76.3	39.0	85.0
1966	104.2	119.5	92.5	56.7	45.0	125.0
1967	37.5	29.2	22.2	19.5	18.5	42.5
1968	22.0	—	—	—	—	—
English†						
Malaysia						
1958	28.8	27.6	24.9	21.8	20.0	28.8
1959	20.1	30.5	36.2	35.0	18.8	38.5
1960	37.0	44.8	46.5	46.5	35.0	46.5
1961	42.3	35.5	34.7	—	32.0	46.5
1962–67	—	—	—	—	—	—
Penang						
1958	33.0	28.0	26.5	26.3	24.5	34.0
1959	20.4	32.7	33.8	33.4	18.8	38.5
1960	33.6	37.6	39.3	36.5	33.0	40.0
1961	36.7	35.0	34.0	—	33.4	38.0
1962–67	—	—	—	—	—	—
Seychelles						
1958	32.0	34.0	34.0	34.0	31.0	34.0
1959	—	—	34.0	38.0	34.0	40.0
1960	45.0	47.5	47.5	47.5	40.0	47.5
1961	47.5	47.5	47.5	47.5	47.5	47.5
1962	47.5	50.8	57.3	57.3	47.5	57.3
1963	57.3	57.3	57.3	57.3	57.3	57.3
1964	57.3	57.3	57.3	57.3	57.3	57.3
1965	57.3	60.5	60.5	60.5	57.3	60.5
1966	60.5	60.5	60.5	60.5	60.5	60.5
1967	60.5	60.5	60.5	60.5	60.5	60.5
1968	60.5	—	—	—	—	—

*—indicates price not quoted.
†Note: Prices are quoted consistently as 140/-throughout the period.
Source: Trade Information.

Rediplant*

EARLY IN 1971 John Bryant, owner and chairman of a successful English timber products firm, was asked by his close friend Martin Nievelt whether he would consider becoming a commisar of Rediplant N.V.—a company being formed to exploit the new Rediplant method for packaging bulbs. Commisars of Dutch corporations are outside directors appointed by the shareholders to oversee the employee directors. They have a number of specific powers and their consent must be obtained for all borrowing by the company. Nievelt also wanted Bryant's opinion on the number of sealing machines that should be purchased in advance of the first full season of Rediplant sales. This was a particularly difficult decision as there was little guide to the volume of sales that could be expected and most of the packaging would have to be carried out during the month of August.

Martin Nievelt and Walter Praag were owners and joint managing directors of Hans Praag & Company, an old-established Dutch bulb exporter based on Hillegom, Holland. Before the Rediplant development, Praag had concentrated on bulb sales to France, United Kingdom, Switzerland, and Germany, selling to nurserymen, wholesalers, and large retailers, as well as directly to the public through mail-order catalogs. There were two seasons each year. The larger was for spring bulbs which were lifted from the bulb fields and distributed in the autumn for planting up to mid-winter. This season represented 70

*This case was prepared by Kenneth Simmonds, professor, London Graduate School of Business Studies, with the cooperation of Rediplant management. Copyright 1971 by Kenneth Simmonds.

percent of the bulb market and covered tulips, crocuses, narcissi, and hyacinths.

Performance of many firms in the bulb business had been poor and there had been numerous failures over the previous two years. There were some 600 exporting houses and although they belonged to an industry association and argued the need to hold price levels, competition among them resulted in continual margin cutting. Praag had recorded losses both years mainly because of low response to their mail-order catalogs attributed by Nievelt to cold, wet weekends discouraging customers from thinking about gardening. While substantial profits could still be made in a good mail-order season, the response rates had been dropping at an average rate of 8 percent per year and increased order size had not grown in step. The development of the Rediplant system therefore came at a particularly opportune time and gave Praag an opportunity to differentiate its product and increase its margins. Praag decided to withdraw from the direct mail-order side of the business and concentrate on building the broadest possible sales of Rediplant packed bulbs. Sale of the mail-order lists, moreover, would provide finance for the new effort and avoid surrender of ownership interest which was usually required in order to obtain long-term bank lending for small private companies.

The French, German, and Swiss mailing lists were sold to Beinum & Company late in 1970. Beinum was the largest Dutch bulb merchant, with a turnover of around 50 million guilders (Fl 50m)[1] and a mailing list of 5 million catalogs. Praag's United Kingdom mail-order list and the United Kingdom wholesale business was sold to Sutcliffe Seeds Ltd. of Norwich. Sutcliffe were moving into the bulb market as an extension from their traditional seed activities and the agreement provided for Praag to supply all Sutcliffe's requirements for Dutch bulbs while retaining the right to go directly to a selected list of retail chains and large stores in the United Kingdom.

Development of the Rediplant System

The idea for Rediplant was first conceived in November 1969 by Praag, who concentrated on the engineering and production sides of the business, leaving the commercial side to Nievelt. Rediplant was basically a transparent plastic strip molded to hold bulbs in equally spaced blisters open at the top and bottom. It was designed as a usage container that could be planted directly in the soil without removing the bulbs, giving them protection from frost, birds, rodents, and slugs,

---

[1]The standard abbreviation for a Dutch guilder, or florin, is Fl. Exchange rates in January 1971 were $1 (US) = Fl 3.60; £1 (Sterling) = Fl 8.60; 1 deutschemark = Fl 1.00.

and enabling the bulbs to be easily retrieved for planting in subsequent seasons.

Praag explained the development in this way:

> I got the idea at the end of 1969 and aimed only to make our competitive position easier and to solve planting problems for the buyer. We ran trials and found that it made not only for easier planting but also gave protection and a better flower, though it was not invented for that purpose. We tested a great quantity with a sensitive control test and the packaged bulbs showed up better than bulbs planted by hand. We limited our tests to hyacinths, tulips, narcissi, crocuses, and gladioli because the others have extra difficulties for packaging and these are the main selling items. With gladioli we had some trouble, and I had to redesign the pack as the sprouts came out of the side of the bulb rather than at the top. We make our own prototype wooden molds and have our own cabinetmaker for this. When we told people the name of our new pack was Rediplant, many remarked that it was not a very good name—but minutes later they would all use the name without any prompting. We decided it must be a very good name.

The bulbs were packed automatically into previously formed plastic strips which were then sealed and fitted into a cardboard sleeve printed with details of the bulbs and planting instructions. After considerable experimentation the new pack was ready for launching and in May 1970 a vacuum-forming machine was purchased to make quantities of the strips. At this stage the pack was comparatively crude with a single-colored cardboard sleeve that totally enclosed the plastic strip, which was in turn stapled together to hold the bulbs.

Nievelt did his own market research by asking friends, acquaintances, and the general public what they thought of the packs, and if they would buy them. On his frequent sales trips to England, for example, he asked customers in garden centers and large stores he visited whether they would buy the packs and they all said they would. The packs contained six tulips with a suggested retail price of 32^{1}/2p as against a price of 25p for similar loose bulbs. Nievelt also asked retailers in England what they thought of the packaging. He recalled, "Large retail chains, Woolworths, Boots, Debenhams, and John Lewis liked it, and after a while the larger garden centers would say that they would buy it. Small centers and garden stores, however, generally said they did not like Rediplant. They gave few reasons, but they seemed worried that it would mean other types of stores would find it easier to sell bulbs." Nievelt also persuaded three different outlets to test market the strips—a store on a U.S. air force base at Woodbridge, a seed shop in Ipswich, and a garden center at Ramsey, Essex. Each received 100 strips, without charge, and each quickly sold the entire assignment at 32^{1}/2p.

Rediplant packaging was next featured in Praag mail-order catalogs for spring bulbs sent out in autumn 1970. These were mailed to some 300,000 customers in England, France, and Germany at a cost, including postage, of £0.05 each. Prices for a Rediplant package of six bulbs were set about 30 percent below the catalog prices for a standard quantity of ten loose bulbs, making the price for a Rediplant bulb 15 percent higher than an equivalent loose bulb. Rediplant packaging featured on the cover and the catalog started with a two-page spread outlining the Rediplant system and offering a 200 percent guarantee to replace every nonflowering Rediplant bulb with two new bulbs. The spread also showed how Rediplant strips could be planted in evenly spaced rows or in cartwheel or zigzag patterns. Walter Praag commented that this sort of thing seemed to appeal particularly to the Germans, who were also much more concerned with rodent and insect damage than were other nationalities. He thought the British tended to be keener gardners and more knowledgeable about bulbs, while many more potential customers in France and Germany would avoid buying loose bulbs that they did not understand or else buy some and plant them upside down. With Rediplant packages these customers would find it much easier. Praag experience had been, too, that the British tended to be much more price conscious than the others, while the French tended to identify value with the price charged.

As orders began to come in during the early winter months, Praag was very encouraged by the high proportion of Rediplant sales. Final figures were as follows:

| Country | Catalogs Posted | No. of Orders Received | Average Order Size | % of Total Ordered in Rediplant Packs | | |
				Tulips	Hyacinths	Narcissi
United Kingdom	150,000	8,056	£3.50	18	20	10
France	101,000	5,581	£5.20	27	32	13
Germany.	50,000	2,091	£5.45	44	39	39

Examination of 160 United Kingdom orders at random showed the average order for Rediplant to be £2, representing an average 50 percent of the customer's total order.

Walter Praag continued work on the Rediplant design and at this stage employed a local firm of two young design consultants with excellent reputations in the textile and packaging markets. The cardboard sleeve was redesigned with full-color pictures of the blooms and better instructions, and the strips were made narrower and extended to include seven bulbs rather than six in a new pack measuring 40 centimeters. Nievelt thought this might discourage price comparison

EXHIBIT 1

Assortment 180 s

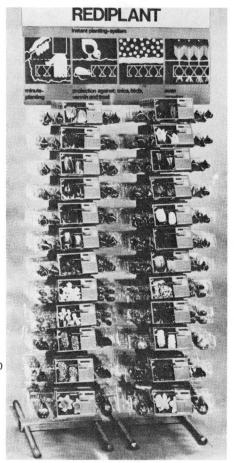

An exclusive new pre-assembled Assortment for You!

112 packs of tulips in 14 varieties 7 bulbs
     per pack
24   packs of hyacinths in 4 varieties
     5 bulbs per pack
12   packs of narcissi in 2 varieties
     5 bulbs per pack
32   packs of crocus in 4 varieties
     14 bulbs per pack
180 packs in 24 well-chosen varieties

Floor space: 15" x 33"
Height display: 63"
Size display poster: 31½" x 18½"
Weight case: 59 lbs.

This display offers an easy and fast set-up
with a minimum of floor space

Advantages:
REDIPLANT is unique (patent pending)
Honest presentation in see-through packs
Optimal ventilation preserves the quality
of the bulbs
Packs are delivered on pegs, saving labour
in setting up display (except assortment 180
and 90)
REDIPLANT has been successfully tested
Over a century of successful bulb-growing
experience guarantees a high quality
product
Your Department as well as the Dutch Dept.
of Agriculture inspects all bulbs before
they are exported

with loose bulbs sold in dozens. These new strips can be seen on the
display stand in Exhibit 1.

For sale through retail outlets, special units of 90 and 180 strips
were designed with wire pegs for each six strips. These pegs could be
fitted onto pegboards or specially designed Rediplant display stands
for floor or counter displays. The mix of varieties for the units was
based on a statistical analysis of the historical proportions of bulb sales
and would not be varied for individual orders. The "180" unit
contained 112 strips of tulips in 14 varieties, 24 strips of hyacinths in 4
varieties, 12 strips of narcissi in 2 varieties, and 32 strips of crocuses in

4 varieties. Large display posters illustrating the planting of Rediplant strips were designed to accompany each unit, which would be boxed with or without a display stand as required.

Patents for the Rediplant system of packaging were applied for and obtained in the Benelux countries, the United Kingdom, France, Germany, Canada, and the United States. This patent was granted for a "usage" package and competitors would find it difficult to break through simply by altering the design. Moreover, anyone wishing to compete would find it essential on a cost basis to package in Holland rather than to ship, pack, and then redirect the bulbs—and Praag was sure that it would be advised by the Dutch customs if its patent was infringed.

Partnership with Van Diemen Bros.

In early 1970 when the new designs were being developed, Praag was approached by Van Diemen Bros. who had seen the packages and wanted to explore ways to which they too could use the new packaging method. Discussions led to the idea of a partnership for developing the system. Van Diemen had the largest sales force in the Dutch bulb industry, owned their own bulb fields and research laboratories, and were suppliers by appointment to the Netherlands royal family. "The idea went against the mentality of the industry that it is not right to work together," said Martin Nievelt. "We had the idea but the other firm had 40 sales people against Praags' two, as well as contacts with wholesalers all round the world. A partnership would provide resources and backing at the same time as it removed one of the major sources of potential competition. Another reason was that the product had to be kept secret while patents were applied for and Van Diemen was one of the few companies with its own laboratories." Nievelt believed that the fragmented nature of the industry and the lack of product differentiation were the prime causes of low prices and small or nonexistent profits, and he hoped that the combined strength of the two firms would enable them to make a much larger impact on the bulb market and eventually claim a significant proportion of Dutch bulb sales at higher margins.

The arrangement worked out on a friendly basis with Van Diemen was that Rediplant N.V. would be formed as a limited company with Hans Praag & Co. and Van Diemen Bros. each owning 50 percent of the equity. Rediplant would lease Praag's storage and packing facilities in Hillegom and manufacture for the two sales companies, invoicing them at cost after payment of a royalty to Praag of Fl.02 per strip. Praag would retain the right to all sales anywhere in the world destined for customers via mail order and also to wholesale sales in the

United Kingdom, Holland, and Switzerland. Van Diemen would cover wholesale sales in all remaining countries. This arrangement meant that there would be little change from past concentration because Praag had had very little wholesale revenue from France or Germany. The direct-mail market, moreover, accounted for some 20 percent of Dutch bulb exports for dry sales. Martin Nievelt and the senior Van Diemen agreed to act as commisars for the new firm and to ask John Bryant to act as a third neutral commisar. Solicitors were asked to draw up formal agreements, and as at the end of February 1971 the drafts had not yet been received.

Meanwhile, Walter Praag and Dik Van Diemen, son of the Van Diemen president, had agreed to become joint managing directors of Rediplant and had become immersed in detailed planning of the production requirements for the 1971 spring bulb season. The elder Van Diemen had also applied to the Dutch government for a grant to develop the invention—on the basis of its potential contribution of Dutch exports—and Rediplant had received a nonreturnable grant of 65,000 guilders.

Meeting the Demand

The period for selling spring bulbs to intermediate outlets ran from January through August, but delivery requirements would be very tight. Excluding mail-order business, 55 percent of all sales must be packed by August 17, the next 30 by the end of August, and the last 15 percent by the end of September. All U.S. sales were included in the intitial 55 percent because of the need to meet shipping dates, but another week could be saved by air freight, although it would increase the freight cost for a standard shipment from $6 per 180 unit to $18. After September, mail-order business could then be supplied fairly evenly until early December. Delivery commitments were regarded as very important by all the Rediplant executives. The retail buying season was concentrated, and a supplier who failed to meet his commitments would ruin his chance of repeat business. Nievelt considered it would be better to take a limited amount of Rediplant orders in the first season rather than run the risk of not being able to meet orders on time and ruining the Rediplant name.

The supply of bulbs themselves presented few problems. Most bulbs were bought from the growers on a contract basis in the spring while still in the ground. A buyer would contract to buy all the production of a given acreage at a fixed price per bulb. As he sold to his customers before he knew how many bulbs he would receive from this acreage, he had to buy any additional requirements or sell any excess on the free market where the price could fluctuate wildly, depending on whether there was a glut or a poor season. Although the average price of bulbs could usually be predicted within 10 percent, a given tulip had fluctuated in price between Fl 14 and Fl 22 per hundred over the previous few years. By industry agreement, payment to growers was required promptly on November 1, and for a merchant to retain a good name amongst suppliers this could not be delayed.

The real problems in supply stemmed from the short packaging season after the bulbs were taken from the fields. Crocuses might not be ready to be packed until July 25, narcissi and hyacinths until the end of July, and tulips between July 25 and August 10, depending on the variety. Packaging, therefore, had to be very carefully planned.

When bulbs arrived for packaging, they would be inspected and sorted before being placed in the polyvinyl chloride (PVC) strips by semiautomatic filling machines. The strips would then pass along conveyors to an automatic radio-frequency sealing machine and from there to a station where they would be fitted with the cardboard sleeve and packed into cartons. While the vacuum-forming machine making the PVC strips could produce only 900 strips per hour, stocks could be built up well before packaging began. The sorting machines worked rapidly and could take large quantities of bulbs so they did not limit the output in any way. The speed of the filling machines could also be increased if needed. Four filling machines, moreover, had been built and these could keep at least four sealing machines busy. The limiting factor, then, seemed to be the number of sealing machines. These operated with an output of 900 strips per hour and at Fl 16,500 were the most expensive items. One machine had been specially designed for Rediplant and modified after tests. Orders for further units would have to be placed immediately as there was a three-month delivery time and orders placed after the beginning of March might not be received in time for the packaging season if there was any delay. The machines were believed to be reliable, but if an electronic component should break down, an engineer from the manufacturer would be required.

Praag and Van Diemen were annoyed that the manufacturer of the sealing machine was insisting on payment before delivery, had raised the price to Fl 16,500 from a verbally agreed figure of Fl 12,500, and would not make any effort to schedule shorter delivery. They had, therefore, investigated other methods of sealing that did not require expensive equipment. All had major disadvantages. Adhesives and stapling were much slower and stapling spoilt the look of the package while adhesives attracted the dust from the bulbs and were not 100 percent effective.

Nievelt argued that only one further sealing machine should be ordered. He pointed out that there was no guarantee that huge volumes

EXHIBIT 2
Rediplant Costings

Equipment		Fl
Vacuum-forming plant.	42,000	
Transformer and electrical installation	10,000	
Molds	20,000	
Sorting machines (5,000 × 4)	20,000	
Filling machines (3,750 × 4).	15,000	
Transport lines	10,000	
Sealing machines (16,500 × 2).	33,000	150,000

Packaging Cost		
Electricity and maintenance	5,000	
Rent	20,000	
Labor (25,000 hours @ Fl 6)	150,000	
Other overheads.	50,000	
Depreciation @ 20%	30,000	
Interest		
On equipment.	15,000	
On materials and working capital	10,000	280,000

		Per	Per Unit
Packaged Cost (excluding display stands)		Strip	(180 Strips)
Bulbs		0.62	111.6
PVC		0.04	7.9
Sleeve		0.06	10.8
Royalties (all sales).		0.02	3.6
Packaging (@ 1m strips).		0.28	50.4
Carton packaging, including labor		0.04	7.0
Point-of-sale advertising (display posters and pegs)		0.03	4.3
Packaged cost.		1.09	195.6

of Rediplant could be sold in the first season when the buyers knew it to be experimental; moreover, financial difficulties could limit the opportunity to expand in later years. Hans Praag & Co. had little finance available and this had been a further reason for the partnership with Van Diemen. The total requirement for subscribed capital had to be kept to 200,000 guilders (see Exhibit 2) if Praag's share in the partnership was not to fall below 50 percent. There was no chance of credit from the machinery supplier and at this stage banks would only advance capital if there was a surrender of some of the ownership equity.

During the busy season it was usual to work two shifts seven days a week, using mainly student labor. For the peak period from July 27 until August 17, Nievelt calculated that two sealing machines would enable a production of 605,000 strips—21 days × 16 hours × 900 strips × 2 machines. As this period would represent 55 percent of the season's activity, this would mean a total production limit of 1.1

million strips. To be on the safe side he set a first tentative limit of 4,750 units (855,000 strips) for the season's selling activity.

Rediplant Sales

While Walter Praag and Dik Van Diemen concentrated on the production planning, Martin Nievelt took on the task of coordinating the Rediplant sales commitments. With Van Diemen agreement, he had in January allocated the tentative target limit of 4,750 units on the following basis:

United Kingdom	1,500
United States	1,000
Germany	1,000
Sweden	500
France	250
Holland	250
Switzerland	250

Nievelt was quick to admit that these were little more than rough guesses based on what he thought the salesmen would achieve, but he felt that the overall demand figures offered even less help. These are shown in Exhibit 3.

By the end of February the sales force was just commencing its main effort and there was still very little sales feedback to go on. One large order of 1,000 units without stands, however, had just been confirmed by the largest garden supply wholesaler in Germany who had placed this initial order against a request that he be the sole German

EXHIBIT 3
Dutch Bulb Exports, 1969

	Total Exports (Fl millions)	Exported for Dry Sales* (%)
Germany	118	31
United States	48	70
Sweden	35	35
United Kingdom	34	64
France	31	59
Italy	21	42
Switzerland	8	68
Canada	6	64
Austria	5	55
(all other markets less than Fl 5 million)		

*Dry sales refer to the proportion of the sales going to the general public either directly or through outlets. Wet sales refer to sales to nurserymen for forcing cut flowers.

distributor next year. This firm employed a sizeable sales force calling on both garden supply outlets and major retail chains. The price negotiated by the Van Diemen sales force was Fl 1.33 per strip net ex Praag warehouse. The retail price the wholesaler would aim for was not known, but the German retail markup was usually 35 percent on sales, and the Van Diemen sales representative had gained the impression that the wholesaler himself would take a 20 percent markup on retail price. Transport costs to be met by the wholesaler, moreover, would be small, and there was no duty into Germany.

There had also been other inquiries for large-volume supplies, but Nievelt had argued against pursuing these for 1971. For example, Beinum, the mail-order house that had purchased Praag's mailing lists, had inquired about Rediplant. Beinum would supply its own bulbs and purchase only the packing—but the volumes required could be very large indeed. After initial discussions that ranged around a figure of Fl 0.6 per strip it was decided not to do anything until the following season. A very large U.S. mail-order firm, Henry Field Seed Nursery Company of Iowa, also showed interest but would have required delivery for September when their mail-order packing commenced. Several of the large U.S. retail chains had expressed interest. Other than arrangements for a modified test by A & P, the supermarket chain, however, these were not followed up because this one firm alone could absorb all Rediplant output in just one of its regions. Van Diemen's U.S. salesmen were instead concentrating on the suburban garden centers which mainly purchased loose bulbs. One of them had reported that by chaining the size of the Rediplant order he would accept to the amount of loose bulbs ordered he had been able to gain a substantial increase in sales of loose bulbs.

Nievelt felt that he could safely leave the Van Diemen sales effort to the Van Diemen management, which was well organized, with a worldwide sales director and four area managers. He had, however, provided sets of Rediplant brochures and price sheets drawn up in five languages. The prices Van Diemen chose were set to allow them around 20 percent on sales and meet the usual trade margins in the particular country. In the United States, for example, the wholesale price for a strip had been set at U.S. $0.46 (Fl. 1.65) to cover such a margin, 12$\frac{1}{2}$ percent duty, and delivery costs.

Van Diemen salesmen were paid a basic salary of Fl 12,500 plus a commission of 2 percent for the first Fl 400,000 increasing by $\frac{1}{2}$ percent for each additional Fl 100,000. A detailed technical training was given and maintained on all aspects of bulb culture, although there was no special sales training. A geographical breakdown of Van Diemen's sales is shown in Exhibit 4, together with the numbers of salesmen concentrating on each country. Scandinavia, with a 5 percent

EXHIBIT 4
Van Diemen Bros.—Geographical Performance

	Percentage of 1969 Turnover	*No. of Salesmen*
Sweden	.20.1	4
West Germany	.19.7	4
Finland	.16.7	1 + 1 agent
France	.10.7	6 + 3 agents
Italy	8.2	1
Norway	7.0	1 + 6 agents
United States	4.5	5
Denmark	3.8	1
Switzerland	3.0	1
Canada	1.4	—
Austria	1.2	1
Iran	1.1	—
England	0.9	1
Greece	0.4	—
South America	0.4	—
Belgium	0.4	—
Japan	0.1	—
Portugal	0.1	—
Hong Kong	0.1	—
Others	0.1	—

growth rate, was the fastest growing market as well as bringing Van Diemen its largest sales.

United Kingdom Market

Having reserved 1,500 units for the United Kingdom market, Nievelt was anxious to meet this figure and was awaiting news from Jan Straten, Praag's only other salesman, who was currently on a sales trip in England. Nievelt expected him to come back with some good orders for Rediplant, some of which would be test orders from the major chains.

Praag's United Kingdom bulb turnover in 1970 had been £90,000, of which £40,000 was direct mail. Nievelt had built this turnover steadily since the end of World War II, even shifting his home to England for the first few years in order to get a good start. At this level of activity Praag was sixth or seventh in the ranking of about 300 Dutch bulb exporters to the United Kingdom. It was this entire turnover that Praag had sold to Sutcliffe Seeds Ltd. at the end of 1970. As part of the agreement Sutcliffe undertook to purchase all its Dutch bulbs from Praag at an agreed formula, whether sold by direct mail or through outlets. Prices were to be set to cover packing and shipping costs and give Praag a 20 percent markup on the packaged cost. The suggested retail price would then be set at a 100 percent markup on the price to Sutcliffe (50 percent on sales). Sutcliffe would give its outlets a discount of 33.3 percent off this suggested retail price plus an additional 5 percent for payment within 30 days.

Praag's agreement with Sutcliffe had been reached at a time when Sutcliffe was actively looking for ways of expanding its sales of bulbs. Sutcliffe had recently taken over the garden seed division of Charles Gibb & Sons and now held over 30 percent of the retail seed market in the United Kingdom. With a total United Kingdom seed market of only £6 million, however, further growth would be difficult. Against this the United Kingdom bulb market of around £10 million offered more opportunity, and Paul Duke, managing director of Sutcliffe, had set his sights on 10 percent of this market by 1975. Although Sutcliffe had bulb sales of only £40,000 at this time and there were a great number of competitors, Duke planned to develop into the quality end of the market using Sutcliffe's name and selling only the best Dutch bulbs. Local bulb growing had expanded considerably in recent years and Dutch mail-order firms had been undercut by local suppliers, but there were still many bulb varieties better provided from Holland and direct container shipment in bulk could offset almost all the location advantage.

Paul Duke had also asked if Sutcliffe could have an exclusive distributorship for Rediplant in the United Kingdom. Nievelt knew that Praag would not have the resources to set up a significant sales force and had agreed to Duke's proposal subject to Praag retaining the right to visit a number of its existing outlets and 20 of the largest chain stores and department stores in the United Kingdom. Nievelt undertook not to sell to these outlets at a price lower than Sutcliffe's net price to its outlets less 2 percent cash discount, on the understanding that Sutcliffe would use the same markups as for loose bulbs.

Nievelt was very pleased with the agreement made with Sutcliffe. He thought that in the first year Sutcliffe's sales force of 60, which called on all the garden centers and hardware and garden stores in the United Kingdom, would take orders for somewhere in the vicinity of 600 units. The top salesmen sold between £50,000 and £60,000 of merchandise each year. Sutcliffe planned, moreover, to spend £20,000 on advertising its bulbs in the ensuing year and were planning to hold a cocktail and dinner party to announce their venture, which would be widely covered in the trade papers.

With the major demands of the Rediplant development, Nievelt had been unable to manage a selling visit to the major outlets he had retained for Praag, and had sent Straten in his place. Straten had started with Praag eight years ago at the age of 18 and with the exception of a two-year spell in the Dutch army had worked with them ever since. He was paid a fixed salary of Fl 12,000 and received £6.50 a day to cover his expenses while in the United Kingdom. He retained his home in Hillegom, seldom being away from home for more than a month at a time, and had sold £25,000 last year, which Nievelt thought was fairly good for a younger man.

The price at which Straten was seeking Rediplant sales in the United Kingdom was 22p per strip delivered to the customer, less 2 percent discount for payment within 10 days. This price was based on a suggested retail selling price of 33p per strip which Nievelt had decided would be necessary to give Sutcliffe the same markup as for loose bulbs and still leave a reasonable profit for Praag. Costs of packing, freight, insurance, duty (10 percent), delivery, and so forth would amount to about 20 percent of the packaged cost, although this percentage might be reduced for full-container deliveries. Nievelt would have preferred the retail price to be 29p, which would have about equalled the price for similar loose bulbs in garden stores, but was convinced that at 33p Straten should be able to persuade several of the chains to place orders.

Dexion Overseas Limited*

In November 1975, Mr. John Foster, recently appointed managing director, and Mr. Keith Galpin, Marketing Manager of Dexion Overseas Limited (DOS), were attempting to give new direction to Dexion's overseas activities. Dexion had, over the years, grown substantially but somewhat haphazardly in its export markets and it seemed to the two managers that it was time for a full review of the company's present position and future overseas activities. They were particularly concerned with DOS's operations in Africa and the Middle East as these regions characterised the changing political and economic conditions in most of Dexion's overseas markets.

DEXION-COMINO INTERNATIONAL LTD.

Dexion (the word is Greek for "right"), or Dexion-Comino International Ltd. to give it its full name, was founded before the Second World War to manufacture slotted angles invented by Demetrius Comino—Greek by origin, Australian by upbringing, and British by residence—as a solution to the recurring need for easily erectible and demountable industrial structures. What was initially jokingly referred to as "industrial meccano" soon acquired wide acceptance. Mr. Comino's initial investment of £14,000 in a 4,000-square foot

*This case was prepared by Mr. Shiv Mathur, Research Fellow of London Graduate School of Business Studies. It was written with the cooperation of Dexion management. Facts and figures have been disguised to preserve corporate confidentiality. Financial support was provided by The British Overseas Trade Board. Copyright 1976 by London Business School.

factory in North London with a turnover of £40,000 in 1948 had by 1968 grown into a 200,000 square-foot site at Hemel Hempstead producing well over 50 million feet of slotted angles. By 1973, Dexion was well established as a worldwide name with wholly owned subsidiaries in North America, Europe, and Australia, with exports accounting for over 60 percent of the U.K. factory's total turnover.

Product Range

As the group's turnover and geographic coverage had increased so had the company's range of products. What had started as ordinary slotted angles (known as DCP—Dexion Catalogue Products), that could be erected by almost anybody, had gradually grown in sophistication. By 1975, Dexion was a world leader in manufacturing and installing complete materials handling systems. Exhibit 1 gives an idea of the main products marketed by the company.

In the developed countries the continuing search for more efficient techniques of storage and materials handling resulted in a rapid growth of the "unit load concept" (various small parts being containerized for efficient storage)—and in particular the use of pallets. Dexion systems like "Speedlock" adjustable pallet racking—which were developed to cater for unit loads—understood and emphasised this need. The Speedlock range and other similar products permitted vertical storage to a height limited only by the height of the building itself. When fitted with wheels the racks, then known as "Poweracks," could be mounted on steel rails which permitted the closing down of an old aisle and opening up of a new one at the touch of a switch. These novel design concepts, among others, not only made materials handling much faster and more efficient but also contributed to long run production economics.

By 1975, Dexion manufactured a whole family of products that served particular applications. "Apton" square tube framing had been designed for the smarter display of goods and for a wide variety of other applications, many outside the industrial field; "Clearspan" and "Impex" shelving for better storage of hand loaded goods; and "Maxi" for storing small items. Not only had the basic DCP range been modified and extended to meet specific requirements, but often the same product had been used for entirely new applications. For example, DCP products that were usually used for storage had been modified to facilitate the construction of prefabricated housing units in the developing economies.

The development of new products and systems had benefited from a two way dialogue with customers. The growth of new products in many instances had meant a concurrent growth for DCP products as

EXHIBIT 1

Dexion
shelving

Choose the *precise* answer to
your need from the six Dexion
shelving systems shown here.

1. With **Dexion slotted angles**
2. With the **Dexion Speedlock** heavy-duty construction system
3. With **Apton** square tube
4. With the **Dexion Impex** boltless shelving system
5. With the **Dexion cantilever shelving** system
6. With the **Dexion mobile storage** system

1. Dexion slotted angle shelving

The world's first, finest and best-selling range of slotted angles, steel shelves and accessories. Dexion slotted angles give you shelving precisely tailored to your goods, your space, your operations — the right answer at a price that makes real sense. And very often Dexion slotted angles are not just the best answer, but the only answer to specialised storage requirements.

2. Dexion Speedlock heavy-duty shelving

Europe's leading heavy duty shelving system. Gives you long, strong shelf spans — up to 16ft (4876mm) — with tough clip-over shelf panels for loads up to 560lb (254kg) each. Heavy goods — like the motor engineering parts here — can be safely stored in bulk. The strength of the uprights, and the long, clear spans, mean you can put more weight in less space than with other systems. And to meet changing needs, beams are quickly, easily adjustable up and down at 3in (76mm) centres.

3. Apton shelving

For smart, snag-free storage of light-weight goods. Apton is a simple square steel tube construction system. The tube is finished in hard, smooth stove-enamel. The neat, compact shelving shown here, built using the 1in (25mm) Apton system, provides safe storage for costly equipment. ¾in (19mm) Apton tube is also available — particularly suitable for light-duty storage.

EXHIBIT 1 *(continued)*

4. Dexion Impex boltless shelving

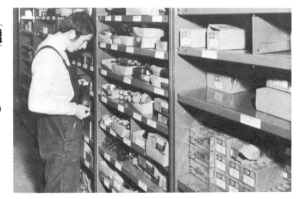

Faster and easier to build, faster and easier to adjust than any other shelving available. Shelves clip into place at any of 50 or more levels in a bay; dividers give compartments of virtually any sizes to suit different items. Impex shelving can be open or clad, in 3ft (915mm) or 6ft (1828mm) bays, in free-standing units or continuous runs. And you adjust shelf levels, adapt the layout, add to runs quickly and simply — whenever necessary.

5. Dexion cantilever shelving

The ideal system for any company handling uniformly-sized boxed or packaged goods. Absence of uprights along the loading face means that boxes can be stored along the entire length of the shelves instead of being fitted into separate compartments. (The installation shown has completely clear shelves 30ft (9.2m) long). Cantilever shelving can carry up to 25 per cent more stock than conventional shelving. Absence of uprights also means faster loading and unloading, easier stock control.

6. Dexion mobile storage

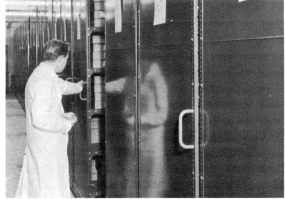

No shelving system can pack more stock into a smaller space — and still ensure easy selection and control of stock. Dexion mobile storage eliminates almost all the gangways needed with static shelving. Racks are mounted on mobile bases, running on precision laid rails (really precision laid — to an accuracy of 0.41mm over 1m). A gentle push opens up the gangway wherever needed to give access to any item. Racks are made of Dexion slotted angles, Speedlock or Apton to suit your goods. Loads up to 3 tons per rack can be stored in perfect safety, moved smoothly and easily.

EXHIBIT 1 *(continued)*

Dexion pallet storage

1. With **Dexion Speedlock pallet racking**

2. With **Dexion Poweracks**

3. With **Dexion Pallet Glidestock**

4. With **Dexion Speedlock drive-in racking**

These four systems, either individually or combined, provide the best answer to most pallet storage problems.

1. Dexion Speedlock pallet racking

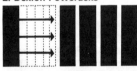

The most widely specified pallet racking in Europe. Speedlock reaches virtually any height, with beams at any levels on a 3in (76mm) module. Design of the beam-to-upright connector ensures easy adjustability.

A range of accessories allow storage of barrels, drums, coils, non-palletised loads . . .

2. Dexion Poweracks

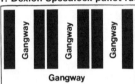

Speedlock racking on powered mobile bases. Only one gangway is needed for every 8, 10, 12 . . . double-entry racks — racks up to 35ft (10.7m) high that can carry up to 24 tons per bay in perfect safety. Touch a button, and electric motors move racks smoothly and safely on pre-cision-laid steel rails — closing the old aisle, opening up the new one wherever needed. Poweracks can as much as double storage capacity compared with static pallet racking, and still ensure 100 per cent stock selectivity.

EXHIBIT 1 *(continued)*

3. Dexion Pallet Glidestock

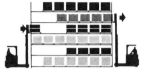

The most reliable of all live storage systems — and more widely used than all other live storage systems put together. Pallet Glidestock consists of a number of conveyors built up in a single framework to form a compact storage block. Pallets are fed through the block, loaded into conveyor lanes at one face and withdrawn in strict rotation from the opposite face. Only two gangways are needed, one for input, one for withdrawal. Dexion Pallet Glidestock makes intense use of space, gives automatic stock rotation, simplifies stock selection and control.

4. Dexion Speedlock drive-in racking

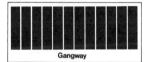

Gangway

The only system specifically developed to meet the special loading and safety requirements of drive-in racking. Speedlock drive-in racking consists of storage lanes in a single framework. Fork-lift trucks drive into the lanes, placing pallets one behind the other on rails each side of the lanes. Only one access gangway is needed — so storage capacity is virtually twice that of conventional racking. Speedlock drive-in racking can be up to 24ft (7.2m) high, and gives safe storage for pallet loads up to 2 tons in weight.

EXHIBIT 1 *(continued)*

Dexion multi–level storage

1. With **Dexion slotted angles**
2. With the **Dexion Speedlock** heavy-duty construction system
3. With the **Dexion Impex** boltless shelving system

Put another level of storage between ground and roof — and you can double your usable storage space.

1. Dexion slotted angle multi-tier storage

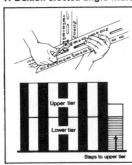

Three levels of storage in a single installation, each level designed for different types of stock. At ground level, Dexion slotted angle bar racking, for compact storage of steel tube; above that, steel shelving for maintenance materials; and, to use the space below the roof, a wooden platform for storage of light, bulky materials. Dexion slotted angles provide a made-to-measure structure, quickly and economically built, to use every foot of space from floor to ceiling.

they constituted a basic ingredient of the more advanced design and were also in demand in their own right.

Overseas Activities

In the pre-1970 period overseas growth of Dexion's activities had been largely organic. As Dexion products had gained popularity, the company had set up subsidiaries in North America, Europe, and Australia. In many other countries of the world Dexion had appointed distributors to stock and retail the products. In economies where local demand was fairly substantial but import restrictions prevented direct export and circumstances did not justify a subsidiary, local manufacturers had been licensed to produce and sell some products in the Dexion range. By the early 1970s Dexion had licensing arrangements with manufacturers in various parts of the world (Exhibit 2). Licensing arrangements in Africa and the Middle East were few and confined in product range to DCP and in some cases Apton square tube and Speedlock pallet racking systems.

The actual agreement varied from licensee to licensee and reflected the company's attitude to overseas markets at the time the agreement was actually signed. In principle, each agreement specified a royalty income based on a percentage of turnover and often subject to a minimum annual payment. Dexion had little control over the pricing and marketing policies of its licensees though sometimes restrictions were placed on their export activities. As the majority of licensees were mainly concerned with building up strong positions in their home markets, pressure to export to third countries in competition with Dexion's own direct export activities was not a major factor. The problems as seen at Dexion headquarters, were not so much of licensee exports to third country markets but of ensuring that they developed their home markets and that licensee income due was in fact repatriated. Since many of the licensee markets had recurring balance of payment problems the actual collection of royalties was of continuing concern.

Over the years, competition with Dexion products both in the U.K. and overseas had multiplied manifold. Dexion had maintained its market leadership in the U.K. and in many overseas territories, in particular where associated companies had been set up. Overseas, especially in Europe, there had been for quite some years a large number of competitors. Further afield, in the Middle East and Africa, in addition to budding indigenous manufacturers, Dexion was facing growing competition from Italian and Continental exporters and lately the Japanese and Indians. Dexion products were, however, well established and the company prided itself on having a much more comprehensive product range and better design and other back up services than the non-European competition. The fact that British steel was cheaper gave Dexion exports a very real advantage. But it seemed that the position was gradually changing and Mr. Foster was getting increasingly concerned about Japanese and subsidised Indian competition in the Middle East and the gradual erosion of the cost advantage of using U.K. made steel.

EXHIBIT 2
Licensed Product Sales, Royalty Income and Products Licensed

Country (year of agreement)	Licensee 1974 Sales (£s)	Royalty Rates*	Products Licensed
Mexico (1964).	1,170,000	2%	DCP, Apton, Speedlock
Canada (1964)	1,950,000	£25,000 per annum (fixed sum)	DCP and accessories
S. Africa (1971).	325,000	4%	DCP, Apton, Speedlock
Portugal (1957).	620,000	2%	DCP, Apton, Speedlock
Spain (1957).	650,000	£13,000 per annum (fixed sum)	DCP, pallet racking
Brazil (1966)	490,000	4%	DCP, Apton, Speedlock
Nigeria (1970).	490,000	4%	DCP and accessories
Argentina (1966)	160,000	4%	DCP, Speedlock
Jamaica (1968)	87,000	4%	DCP
New Zealand (1959). . . .	210,000	2%	DCP
Peru (1967)	230,000	£4,000 per annum (fixed sum)	DCP
El Salvador (1961).	50,000	4%	DCP
India (1960)	420,000	Profit participation agreement	DCP, Apton
Hungary (1971).	650,000	£65,000 (lump sum royalty)	DCP

*Expressed as percentage of turnover unless otherwise indicated.

DEXION OVERSEAS LIMITED

In 1970, Dexion Comino International Ltd. had set up Dexion Overseas Limited (DOS) as a separate company within the organisation to look after and coordinate its entire overseas export and licensing activities. Markets where Dexion had established subsidiaries or associates were excluded. In order to closely supervise distribution DOS had divided the overseas market into five regions and during the early 1970s appointed a regional sales manager (RSM) located in London to oversee Dexion's interests in each of these areas. The five regions were: (1) the Middle East and North Africa, (2) Europe, (3) the Rest of Africa, (4) the Far East and Southeast Asia, (5) the Caribbean and South America. Of all these regions Africa and the Middle East had accounted for over 55 percent of the turnover in direct exports and 60 percent of gross profits for the financial year 1973–74. Exhibit 3 (*a*) gives DOS results for the previous three years and Exhibit 3 (*b*) gives a break-up of 1974–75 results by region.

EXHIBIT 3(*a*)
DOS Operating Results (£1,000s)

	1972–73	*1973–74*	*1974–75*
Invoiced sales................	5,672	6,444	6,914
Gross profits*................	1,076	1,770	2,088
Variable distribution costs........	156	221	290
Gross profit (after distribution costs)........	920	1,549	1,798
Home office and regional expenditure................	565	560	703
Operating profit...............	355	989	1,095
Miscellaneous income (including royalties)...........	94	122	136
Interest....................	(13)	(75)	(75)
Profit before tax..............	436	1,036	1,156

*After deducting transfer prices payable to Dexion-Comino International Ltd.

EXHIBIT 3(*b*)
Allocation of 1974–1975 DOS Results by Region (£1,000s)

	Invoiced Sales	*Gross Profit*	*Regional Expenses*
Middle East and North Africa......	3,016	1,006	96
Europe....................	1,829	378	33
Africa....................	1,090	408	42
Far East...................	257	61	26
Caribbean, etc...............	426	142	49
Miscellaneous...............	296	93	13
Total...................	6.914	2,088	259
Variable distribution expenses.....		290	
Gross profit (after distribution).....		1,798	
Less:			
Regional expenses............	259		
Central expenses.............	133		
Marketing and promotion.......	104		
Administration and rent.........	130		
Technical................	77		
Total.....................		703	
Operating profit...........		1,095	

Direct exports and involvement in the Far East and Central and South America were comparatively small. Dexion's operations in Europe were mature in nature and the increasing similarity between the U.K. and continental Europe in terms of competition, products and customers had gradually resulted in most of Western Europe being treated as an extension of the home market at least so far as the existing product range was concerned. With U.K. entry into the EEC in 1973, this similarity between the home market and continental Europe was becoming even more obvious, although differences in channels of distribution remained.

DOS was of the opinion that during the next five years the company's business in the oil-rich countries of the Middle East and North Africa would expand much more rapidly than elsewhere. This called for a strategy that took into account the prominent position of the region. But the company felt that such a strategy would be applicable in principle to almost all other overseas activities of the company.

DOS'S INTERNATIONAL POLICY

Markets and Organisation

DOS had carried out a detailed analysis of the various international markets that could provide it with substantial business in the future. This analysis had incorporated not only informed views within the company but also interpreted demographic and economic data. The attempt was to highlight not only those markets which would continue to grow but also select those which could become major profit generators in future. This exercise had brought to light some Southeast Asian and Middle Eastern countries which could be the target for more concentrated attacks.

The company's marketing manager was of the view that the entire Dexion market in Africa and the Middle East could be broken up, very roughly, into three kinds of buyers which though overlapping in many situations were distinct enough to be considered separately:

1. Bazaar buyers.
2. Small installation buyers.
3. Project buyers.

Bazaar buyers were customers who bought mostly DCP type products to erect small and fairly crude storage and other structural units. Though DOS had no hard data on the buying behaviour of these customers, it was generally believed that they designed their requirements themselves or with some help from local Dexion dealers. Their main criteria for buying Dexion products in preference to those of other suppliers were price and availability. The demand was more for the less sophisticated Dexion products and an important characteristic of the buyer was his lack of awareness and perhaps need for more sophisticated storage and material handling systems.

A second group of buyers was in the market for installation. These installations could vary from small simple racking units (similar to those put up by the bazaar buyer himself) to complete warehouse units made up of products such as Speedlock pallet racking and Impex hand loaded shelving. This type of business was invariably handled by local distributors, sometimes with the help of Dexion staff, and often required detailed designs and site construction. This design and construction service was increasingly being provided by the local distributor although Dexion's U.K.-based units assisted with jobs which were outside the resources and capability of a particular distributor.

Even in poorer countries and to a growing extent in the oil-rich Middle East, there was occasional demand for relatively large and sophisticated systems requiring special resources such as system analysis, structural design, subcontracting, contract negotiation, financing, project management, etc., outside the scope of any distributor. DOS referred to this third type of business as project business and it invariably involved sales and implementation resources not available locally from a distributor even when supported by a local Dexion salesman, the support of the local distributor being enlisted by the payment of a negotiated commission.

In order to serve the growth in both installation and project business, DOS had established in London a special design and technical services cell (see Exhibit 4 for organisation chart). The regional sales managers could refer their design problems to this unit and the cell itself undertook some marketing activities. It stayed in touch with U.K.-based architects, specifiers, and designers to influence them to use Dexion equipment in projects they were associated with. The cell had gradually developed over the years to a stage where it had established the expertise to quote for and supervise a wide variety of overseas projects. Its links with the regional sales managers were close and there was frequent exchange of information on how activities on a particular assignment could be coordinated.

As part of its central marketing function, the DOS staff at headquarters attempted to coordinate the advertising and sales promotion campaign for Dexion products in various national markets. Films, pamphlets, and information material in various languages had been prepared. The marketing department together with regional staff undertook to arrange seminars in various overseas capitals aimed at

EXHIBIT 4
DOS Organisation Chart

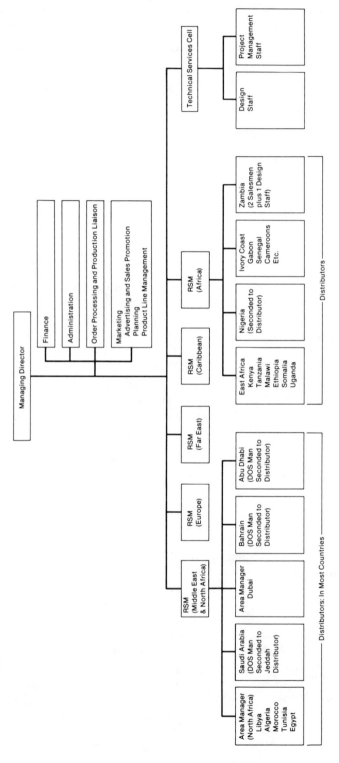

NB: Full-time distributor staff looking after DOS sales and design in Kuwait, Oman, and Lebanon.

specific audiences. The marketing department also looked after the promotion of individual products and retained staff members who coordinated the activities of a particular product in various regions acting as product managers.

Distributors, Pricing and Margins

DOS as part of group policy was supplied by the plant at Hemmel Hempstead at a transfer price that reflected the direct costs of production and an allocation of works and general overheads. DOS, in turn, set prices for its distributors by adding a percentage markup to cover the cost of its own operations and provide a satisfactory profit.

In Mr. Foster's view, the essence of DOS's policy on distributor pricing was:

> A question of competitive activity—we should evaluate what price competitive products are selling at and adjust our margins to account for the comparative advantages and disadvantages of Dexion goods.

In effect, distributors in different national markets were quoted different prices to take into account expected local distributor markup, the prices of competitive products, and the local customers' ability to pay. The company's differential pricing policy was exemplified by the fact that though during the inflationary period of 1973–74 when transfer prices charged to DOS rose by 15 percent (Exhibit 5(a)), there was no corresponding across-the-board increase in prices charged to customers. For example, European customers paid an extra 5 percent but those in the Middle East paid an extra 15 percent in sterling prices. When the effective devaluation of sterling had been accounted for, the price increases were considerably reduced to most of DOS's overseas customers.

As part of its policy of value pricing, the markups charged on various Dexion products were considerably different depending on the product range sold. Exhibit 5 (b) gives an indication of gross margins by product category. Though DOS did, informally, indicate to its distributors in various national markets the price at which they should retail their products, it did not, and in management's view could not, lay down firm directives. This policy had both its advantages and disadvantages. The disadvantages were fairly obvious as the company did not retain any firm control on its prices and occasionally found distributors in well-protected or prosperous markets charging exorbitant markups. But by pricing competitively, DOS had set up for itself a vast distributor network with at least one stocklist in almost all national markets in which it operated. The distributor, it was hoped,

EXHIBIT 5(*a*)
Increase in Transfer Price 1973–1974

	Increase		Contents of Costs	Increase
Steel.	−5%	on	40%	−2.0%
Auxillary material	20	on	35	7.0
Accessories	10	on	10	1.0
Other costs	0	on	15	0
Volume down 30% on budget.				9.0
Total increase				15.0%

EXHIBIT 5(*b*)
Product Margins (excluding project sales; in £1,000s)

	1972–73			1973–74		
	Sales	Gross Profits	Percent	Sales	Gross Profits	Percent
DCP	2,079	610	29.3	2,530	874	34.5
Apton.	305	120	39.3	481	164	34.1
Speedlock	1,120	238	21.3	1,347	393	29.2
Others	590	108	18.3	570	107	18.8
Total	4,094	1,076	26.3	4,928	1,538	31.2

would in turn set retail prices to maximise his own and consequently DOS's profits. The fact that this did not always happen was seen as a largely unavoidable consequence of using independent companies as part of the distributor system.

AFRICA

The regional sales manager (Africa) had for administrative convenience divided all the countries south of the area of Arab influence into four regions: (*a*) East Africa and Sudan, (*b*) Zambia, (*c*) Nigeria, and (*d*) the erstwhile French West Africa. The four regions were seen as being almost equal in terms of market potential and would thus impose an equivalent workload on the four area managers who were based in convenient local capitals.

It was apparent (Exhibit 6) that besides Zambia, Nigeria, and South Africa, the continent of Africa could be described as comprised largely of developing countries with foreign exchange problems and complicated systems of tariff and exchange controls. Though Dexion had a distributor in virtually every African capital, the choice was restricted and determined more by the distributor's general business standing and connections with the local government than by any previous experience of selling products related to storage and materials handling.

EXHIBIT 6

Africa—Orders Received (£1,000s)

	1972-73				1973-74				1974-75			
	DCP	Speedlock	Others	Total	DCP	Speedlock	Others	Total	DCP	Speedlock	Others	Total
Ethiopia	32	—	—	32	25	1	1	27	16	—	—	16
Ivory Coast	12	—	—	12	5	—	3	8	38	3	4	45
Kenya	26	—	—	26	18	3	2	23	55	8	—	63
Nigeria	44	3	58	105	60	22	57	139	103	60	49	212
South Africa	3	3	5	11	11	5	4	20	16	—	56	72
Sudan	44*	—	—	44	—	—	—	—	—	—	—	—
Tanzania	—	—	—	—	5	—	—	5	18	—	—	18
Zambia	74*	—	35*	109	61*	21*	50*	132	140*	256*	23*	419
Zaire	5	13	—	18	1	2	—	3	—	—	—	—
Others												
Cameroons												
Gabon												
Ghana												
Gibraltar	85	5	21	111	72	22	7	101	49	4	4	57
Senegal												
Niger												
Etc.												
Total	325	24	119	468	258	76	124	458	435	331	136	902

*Project activity.

This criterion of selection was justified as often there was no dearth of demand for Dexion products but a noticeable lack of buying power for foreign produce. This was in the regional sales manager's view the single most important impediment in exporting to the African market. Consequently, the whole region was fragmented, with few areas where concentrated marketing effort could be justified. Not only was the entire region plagued by controls but it was also in a state of constant economic and political flux. The regional sales manager commented:

> Extreme situations such as the anti-Asian policy in Uganda and the war in Ethiopia can close entire markets overnight, and there is no way of accurately forecasting such incidents.

Competition and Users

Many suppliers besides those in the developed countries had found it possible to meet the less sophisticated level of African demand. Continental, Japanese, and Indian exports abounded, but Dexion with its wide and well-established network of distribution had a firm grip and in some countries like Tanzania had almost wiped out the use of competitive products. In virtually all markets, small local manufacturers making a restricted range of generally low quality products were a continuing threat.

In the regional sales manager's opinion, what Dexion had and the competition did not, was the local contacts and a name for quality and service that was well established. It was not really the overseas exporters that provided the major threat in African markets but the growing desire in most developing countries to set up their own production units. As the outlay for such a project would be about £500,000 it was well within the reach of most governments, if not individual entrepreneurs. It was possible that the small African markets would not support economical production units. But there was always the possibility of some countries getting together to come to tariff arrangements to form a quasi common market or to look actively for regional exports. Some countries in East Africa and the erstwhile French West Africa had shown just this sort of inclination and this was seen as the thin end of the wedge at DOS headquarters.

The regional sales manager felt that the richer countries of Africa—Nigeria, Zambia, and South Africa—were different in their purchasing behaviour. The presence of areas of industrial concentration had resulted in a demand for a whole host of Dexion products and services. To South Africa and specially Nigeria, in spite of the presence of local licensees, Dexion directly exported the more modern systems, which were not manufactured locally. In Zambia, the company had obtained a large contract to design, supply, and erect a complete materials handling and storage system. The Zambian case characterised an obvious trend in buying behaviour. Developing country governments keen to put up large industrial complexes, often with the help of overseas funds, increasingly contracted out for the supply, design, and erection of complete turnkey projects often preferring that not only the plant but also the civil engineering part of the project be done by one main contractor.

MIDDLE EAST AND NORTH AFRICA

The regional sales manager (Middle East) held the view:

> The Middle East is a fascinating region. In spite of popular beliefs it's not all gold. For us there are three to four countries that contribute most of the sales. And it would be fair to say that in most countries the results are directly proportional to the effort we put in. When I say "we," I mean "we"—the local distributors have far too much on their plates and are often so badly organised that they need all the assistance we can give. The real selling force is frequent visits and resident expatriate staff— people who are willing to live in Arab countries and promote the Dexion name. And they are harder to find that you would imagine.

Markets

In many surprising ways, the Middle East market was similar to the African one. In spite of the massive oil revenues there was a growing inclination in some Arab countries to ban foreigners from setting up purely trading companies. The U.A.E, Iraq, Iran, and Algeria had formulated, or were in the process of formulating, controls for limiting the activities of foreigners. Others like Libya, who were at that moment big customers of DCP products, had already outlined their intention to set up their own slotted angle plants to reduce the economy's dependence on imports.

In many other ways, the Middle East was very different from the poorer countries of Africa. There was an explosive industrialisation programme underway. All over the Middle East new plants were being constructed and the host countries, while embarrassingly rich financially, lacked almost all the human skills and infrastructural facilities to cope with this phenomenon. Even countries like Iraq and Algeria, while attempting to lower their reliance on foreign companies, recognised the necessity to permit foreigners to bid for and undertake large projects. In fact, almost all Dexion's business in Iraq, Algeria, Iran, and a substantial portion of that in Saudi Arabia had been obtained by negotiating large contracts.

The regional sales manager estimated that in 1974–75 about 25 percent of turnover was accounted for by project sales. A similar ratio was indicated by a rough break-up of orders received figures (Exhibit 7). Though the dynamic growth in project activity was generally welcomed by Dexion management, it had, especially in the Middle East, created some organisational problems. The fact that contract negotiation took a comparatively long time and resulted more often than not in "next year's sales and this year's expenses" was not always welcome. The regional sales managers, who were always under considerable pressure to maintain expenditure within agreed budgets, treated project activity with mixed emotions. Though when the organisational problems, both within DOS and with distributors in whose territory the project was located, had been overcome, this form of activity was very welcome. It was estimated that gross profits on successful tenders in the Middle East were broadly similar to those obtained on the sale of hardware alone.

Competitors and Distribution

With the growth in oil revenue it appeared that almost all the world's businessmen were on flights to Jeddah and Abu Dhabi. But often not only business but hotel accommodations were difficult to find. In spite of this, many international companies had established a very definite presence in the Middle East.

DOS considered that competition was strongest from the Japanese, Italians, and Indians in the supply of DCP-type hardware and from Japan and Germany in the project market. The Japanese and Germans often had a slight edge on Dexion as they had been able to quote for complete turnkey projects. In the supply of hardware, Dexion had a wide network of distributors capable of handling day-to-day design problems often with the help of DOS's local representative. In Libya, DOS's distributor had established very good links with the local government and Dexion products had reached a large market share, but only by pricing below DOS's normal markup to offset the price advantage of Italian products.

In the other main markets such as Saudi Arabia and the U.A.E., which still constituted the bulk of the hardware (as distinct from project) business, there was again a proliferation of competitive products. DOS's response had been twofold—first to pare margins and second to promote slightly more advanced systems like Speedlock. In spite of the presence of overseas and, at times, local manufacturers crowding these markets, there was still ample opportunity for all. The fact that countries like Saudi Arabia and the U.A.E. had five-year plans that budgeted a threefold increase in public expenditure was justification enough for the most forceful of selling efforts.

EXHIBIT 7

Middle East and North Africa—Orders Received (£1,000s)

	1972–73				1973–74				1974–75			
	DCP	Speedlock	Others	Total	DCP	Speedlock	Others	Total	DCP	Speedlock	Others	Total
Abu Dhabi	73	—	7	80	155	9	16	180	285	26	7	318
Dubai	32	7	4	43	78	—	3	81	85	19	8	112
Iraq	147*	—	—	147	478*	—	2	480	209*	—	4*	213
Libya	377*	3*	18*	398	356*	4*	13*	373	252*	57*	3*	312
Oman	18	13	2	33	58	2	78	138	130	6	98*	234
Saudia Arabia	65	44	4	113	134	247		381	257	75	294†	626
Bahrain	18	2	7	27	35	8	26	69	25	—	21	46
Qatar	9	—	—	9	17	—	3	20	25	—	—	25
Algeria	—	—	1,235†	1,235		43*	4*	47	—	—	—	—
Others												
Cyprus												
Egypt												
Iran												
Jordan												
Kuwait												
Lebanon	94	14	—	108	294	13	16	323	91	7	2	100
Malta												
Pakistan												
Syria												
Tunisia												
Yemen												
Total	833	83	1,277	2,193	1,605	326	161	2,092	1,359	190	437	1,986

*Project activity.

†Projects not broken up by product groups.

ALTERNATIVE POSSIBILITIES

With this background of the marketplace, and the target of achieving a 15 percent annual increase in sales and profits, the management was aware that a series of long-term strategic decisions had to be made. These decisions would have to encompass almost all the activities of the company but were of the following nature.

Production Decisions

In view of the fact that 100 percent owned subsidiaries would be difficult to establish overseas:

1. Should the company continue to license overseas manufacturers to produce the DCP range in areas of high tariffs and foreign exchange problems, or should the licensing policy be extended to cover more products and markets? In particular, should DOS agree to permit the manufacture of the Speedlock and Apton range in Nigeria?
2. If licensing was not a viable option, in view of local government hostility to royalties, should DOS look to joint ventures?
3. Another possibility could be to discontinue all overseas manufacture and cancel where possible the existing licensing arrangements and manufacture and export from the U.K., or another suitable European base.

Marketing and Product Decisions

1. Which markets to focus on and with what products?
2. To change and modify the existing pricing policy, if necessary.
3. To consider if there was any need to restructure the distribution strategy.

The list of issues which needed to be questioned and sorted out seemed endless. DOS management was also aware of the fact that it would be impossible to put hard figures on many of these options but Mr. John Foster felt that the data he had were reliable, in the sense that they were indicative of the situation. He was particularly aware that the issues were interrelated (e.g., the company could not have a production policy that required licensing arrangements and a marketing strategy that required distributors) and the direction that DOS's total strategy took should at least be compatible within itself.

John Marshall*

FOLLOWING THE SUDDEN DEATH of the chief accountant of General Engineers Proprietary, John Marshall was promoted to fill the vacancy. The position reported directly to the firm's vice president of finance and entailed responsibility for the commercial side of the firm's operations, including invoicing, costing, accounts payments, and financial accounting, and full control of an office staff of over 100. John, who was only 29, was a chartered accountant and for two years previously had been an assistant accountant responsible for the development and installation of a new cost-control system.

General Engineers Proprietary carried out a range of engineering activities in Australia, operating from headquarters in Brisbane. In a section of its works on the Brisbane waterfront, some 300 men were regularly engaged in ship repair and maintenance work. This work was largely undertaken at cost plus a fixed percentage to cover overheads and profit. The fixed percentage was usually 8 to 10 percent and usually negotiated with the Australian offices or agents of the shipping companies owning the vessels.

Two days after taking up his new post, John was brought an invoice for signature by Bill Brady, the chief shipping clerk. It amounted to A$59,587 and was for repair work just being completed on the M. V. Hull. Bill explained to John that the invoice must be signed in quintuplicate by the chief accountant and then taken for countersigning by the captain and chief engineer before the ship sailed.

---

*This case was prepared by Professor Kenneth Simmonds, Manchester Business School. Persons, places, and corporations are fictitious and the case is not intended to illustrate the policies or practices of any particular firms. Copyright 1969 by Kenneth Simmonds.

663

John immediately requested to see the cost sheets backing up the cost-plus invoice. Bill, who was an older man of over 60 and had always seemed to John to be reliable and helpful, if perhaps a little fatherly, was reluctant to bring the cost sheets. He first argued that Mr. Knox, the previous chief accountant, had never bothered to check the cost sheets. Then he explained that the last two days' costs were not yet posted and had been taken from time records and material requisitions and purchase orders. Nevertheless, John insisted and Bill brought him the records and rapidly demonstrated the transfer of cost sheet totals onto the summary sheet shown in Exhibit 1. When these were checked, Bill left John with the summary sheet, suggesting he add it and compare the totals with the invoice.

As John added the summary sheet, the last entry for unposted wages caught his eye. He could not understand why the activity had jumped on the last day. He called the time office to check the figure and was told that the unposted cost was A$515, including an estimate for work still being completed.

When Bill came back to pick up the signed invoice copies John raised this point:

John: That's fine, Bill, but where do the unposted wages of $2,625 come from?

Bill: Well, those are for ship's crew that helped us with the work instead of taking shore leave.

John: How do we pay them?

Bill: Well, I draw up a list of names and amounts, have it countersigned by the shipping manager, draw cash, and then make the payment when I take the invoice.

John: Does anybody audit these payments?

Bill: No. There is no need.

John: Well, I would like to come down today.

Bill: It's not really practical. You see, I usually give it to the chief engineer for distribution.

John: But how do we know the right men get it?

Bill: We don't—and it might be best for you not to worry further. What you have no cause to pursue can never hurt you.

It finally dawned on John that this was probably a payoff to ship's officers. He sat thinking for a while. Should he sign the invoice or should he push for more accurate particulars?

If he was not going to sign, he would have to take immediate action before the ship sailed—find out exactly to whom the amounts were paid, insist on an amended invoice, and take whatever consequences the likely loss on the job would bring. With a rueful smile he signed the five copies and handed them to Bill, thinking as he did that it would be best to take a few days to look into things and think it through.

EXHIBIT 1

Cost Summary Sheet

	Job No. and Particulars	Hours	Wages	Material and Supplies	Machinery and Transport Cost	Total Cost
8064	M. V. Hull—engine room.	5,444	$10,009.64	$2,964.13	$1,167.79	$14,141.56
8065	M. V. Hull—engine room.	2,939	5,123.15	822.65	756.29	6,702.09
8066	M. V. Hull—deck repairs	1,497	2,896.15	964.21	326.11	4,186.47
8073	M. V. Hull—pump and winch overhaul.	2,329	5,093.60	1,064.22	3,421.61	9,579.43
8074A	M. V. Hull—shipwrights	1,261	2,939.20	1,745.50	491.27	5,175.97
8074B				405.00		405.00
8076	Electricians.	2,413	4,762.79	980.73	1,731.32	7,474.84
		15,883	$30,824.53	$8,946.44	$7,894.39	$47,665.36
Above jobs			515.00	2,175.25	165.00	2,855.25
	Unposted		2,625.00			2,625.00
			$33,964.53	$11,121.69	$8,059.39	$53,145.61

That evening and the following day John considered the alternatives. He could do nothing and continue to sign invoices as the chief accountant had done in the past. Taking this approach he could always argue that he knew nothing of any payoffs, but then it was his responsibility to know what he was signing and to ensure adequate internal checking. Moreover, referring to the code of ethics of his accountancy institute he read quite clearly: "No member shall make, prepare, or certify as correct any statement which he knows to be false, incorrect or misleading. . . ." And John reasoned he would be no less unethical because no one could prove he knew what was going on. As a second alternative he considered the possibility of delegating responsibility for signing invoices to one of the accountants reporting to him. He felt they might have less ethical qualms than he, and everything work out much better. Third, he could acknowledge the practice and set up an occasional audit check to make sure the cash was actually reaching the ship's officers. And finally he might make an ethical stand on the issue and insist that the practice either be discontinued or he be formally exonerated in writing. He suspected, however, that neither would be done and he would have to leave or live with the situation. At the very least there would be considerable annoyance and embarrassment at what many would consider a youngster's Sunday School idealism.

The evening after this discussion with Bill Brady, John happened to enter the elevator with George Mitchell, the assistant shipping manager, so he suggested they call in for a drink on the way home. During the conversation John asked George what percentage of an invoice was usually paid ship's officers and how it was distributed, endeavouring to convey at the same time that he knew all about the practice. George explained that it varied with the officers, but rarely went as high as 10 percent, and that it might be distributed between as many as ten engineers on a large vessel. The arrangements as to percentage were part custom, part bantering negotiation over drinks, and part intuition by General Engineers' executives. George claimed that payoffs existed all around the world, although some firms operated their own ship repair yards where they insisted on major overhauls being done. However, the ship's officers frequently had plenty of latitude for repairs and could always have storm damage, corroded pipes, winches, and refrigeration equipment repaired wherever it suited them. George also pointed out that most of the superintendents of the shipping companies knew all about the practice—having been ship's captains or chief engineers themselves at one time.

John could see that any action might affect the livelihood of the 300 men in the ship repair section. This was the biggest ship repair unit in Brisbane, and in all likelihood the work would go to another port,

EXHIBIT 2
Ship Repair Section, 1964–1969

Year	Average No. of Men Employed	Ships Repaired	Total Invoiced ($000s)	Markup On Total Cost	Payments To Ship's Crews ($000s)
1964 351		108	$2,419	12.1%	$162
1965 337		101	2,386	11.8	157
1966 341		93	2,435	11.4	143
1967 331		99	2,264	11.3	127
1968 309		94	2,161	11.1	110
1969 305		85	2,216	11.0	102

possibly outside Australia, if officers were not remunerated. The men employed could of course be absorbed over time in other work but many were specially trained and had spent their working lifetime in ship repair. Before he made his final decision, John decided to have a look at the figures for ship repair activity to see what profits, volume, and payoffs were involved. The day after his conversation with George Mitchell, John had the tabulation shown in Exhibit 2 prepared for him.

Organizing and Controlling the Multinational Enterprise

Hamesin International*

THE ISRAELI PERIOD (1960-1969)

Hamesin, Ltd. was founded in 1960, as a joint venture of Geha chemicals company (70 percent) and Rimon, Inc. (30 percent). Hamesin, Ltd. was intended to penetrate the Israeli veterinary products market in the area of special food additives. As a main entry into that market, the company would use a license obtained a short time before by Rimon from a French company named Solar, producing a chicken-feed enriching compound.

Nine years later, at a board meeting held in October 1969, the company's situation was reviewed by the chairman of the board and general manager, Mr. Eli Yahalomi. The balance sheet for September 30, 1969 was presented, and future prospects for the company were discussed. The following are highlights from Mr. Yahalomi's presentation:

Areas of Activity

The company markets two types of products in Israel (1) a chicken-feed enriching compound and (2) special additives for poultry and cattle feed.

Chicken-Feed Enriching Compound. The enrichment compound is produced by Hamesin under license. The product is used for the

---

*This case was prepared by Mr. Yoav Eizenberg under the direction of Dr. Igal Ayal of the Leon Recanati Graduate School of Business Administration, Tel-Aviv University. Reprinted with permission of the authors.

feeding of broilers. It is also used to increase the yield of egg-laying hens. Hamesin holds 60 percent of this market and has only one competitor.

Special Feed Additives. The product is produced through a rather simple process. It is a small ingredient in the feed produced by kibbutzim and by regional feed-processing plants for feeding poultry and livestock. The market includes two other firms, the leader being Tiv-Tov, with a 70 percent market share. The trend in recent years has been away from small processing plants and toward concentration of feed processing in large regional plants. This trend, if continued, could severely cut down the size of the existing market due to backward integration by the large plants producing their own premixes.

Financial and Sales Data

Annual Sales Volume (in tons)

Product	1966	1967	1968	1969
Feed enrichment compound. .	1,921.3	2,245.9	2,597.9	2,857.7
Special additives	199.4	300.4	321.1	324.5

Distribution of sales revenues in 1969:

Feed enrichment compound: 73.3%

Special additives: 26.7%

Income Statements

	1966	1967	1968	1969
Gross margin (000 Israeli £s.)	3,570	4,760	5,950	6,970
Expenses	3,060	3,400	5,780	6,885
Income before taxes	510	1,360	170	85

Reviewing the company's financial situation, Mr. Yahalomi pointed out the gap between the rates of growth for expenses and for the gross margin. The outlook for sales growth in both areas of activity was not encouraging, since the market was well established and in fact may have reached a saturation level for Israel. There also did not appear to be much chance of increasing Hamesin's share of the market.

The best alternative, unanimously adopted by the board, was to develop export markets for the company.

Export Potential—Existing Capabilities

Existing Export Licenses—Feed Enriching Compound.   The license agreement signed in 1960 with Solar, Inc. gave Rimon the right to produce and market the feed enriching compound in several foreign markets, including Turkey, Greece, Iran, and all of South America. The use of such compounds was not common in any of these markets in 1969. The main provisions of the agreement were:

1. Raw materials would be purchased from Solar.
2. Royalties would be paid on all sales in all markets, according to a specified formula.
3. The product should never fall below Solar's quality standards and would be marketed everywhere, except in Israel, under the Solar brand.

Existing Marketing Channels.   The Geha Corp. had branches in several South American countries, including Argentina, Brazil, Chile, and Uruguay. The branches marketed pesticides in these countries. None of the branches amounted to much in the way of marketing power, and in fact they were company representatives, marketing the pesticides through local channels in each country. The main point, though, was that there existed a highly experienced export administration system within the Geha home office. This system could be utilized to organize planned exports by Hamesin.

Professional Know-How.   Professional personnel developed and employed by Hamesin for marketing its products in Israel were divided into two main groups:

The Field Group.   This included seven agronomists who operated as the company's main selling force. Each agronomist, who really served as a combination extension agent and salesman, had a separate territory. Each one of these agronomists was highly experienced in animal feeding, with some of them specializing in livestock feed and the others in poultry feed. Special skills acquired during eight years of work for Geha were:

1. Experience in "selling" the benefits of using feed enriching compound to farmers using regular feed.
2. The capability of explaining professionally the advantages of the Solar compound over a rival compound.
3. The ability to handle all the economic and nutritional elements involved in selecting feed for poultry and for livestock.

The Development Group.   This was an ad hoc working group of well-known experts on animal feeding. The group gathered technical information on building and operating feed processing plants, and particularly on new developments in this area. Through this group,

Hamesin hoped to be able to sell to the large plants complete feed formulations designed to achieve stated nutritional objectives at a minimum cost.

Productive Capacity. Forty percent of Hamesin's productive capacity for feed enrichment compound was not utilized during 1969. It was clear that production could be substantially increased without any capital investment, and with only a very small increase in work force.

The situation was somewhat different for special additives, but even there export operations could be started without additional investments since the company could use subcontractors' plants.

Operational Alternatives

The immediate problems before the board of directors were what to export, to what markets, and how. It was decided to conduct a basic market research study and decide according to the findings.

Ideal market conditions for introducing the feed enriching compound, as presented to the market researchers, were:

1. A well-developed egg industry. Production by economic units which produce a maximum for the market and a bare minimum for local consumption.
2. Egg production in large, intensive chicken farms, utilizing relatively advanced technology.
3. A well-developed market for meat, so that a broiler industry either exists already or has good chances of developing.
4. Feed prices should be above a certain minimum, so that the use of enriching compound to increase the broiler food conversion index will be worthwhile for the farmer, while leaving a reasonable profit for the compound manufacturer.

Target markets surveyed were Turkey, Iran, and the South American markets. Market potentials for special additives were also examined. The survey concluded:

> *Argentina:* Right from the beginning it was clear to the market researchers that this market holds the best promise for their products. Argentina has a highly developed farm industry and is one of the largest livestock producers. Agricultural production is concentrated in large farms managed according to economic criteria. While production in Argentina is mainly in large chicken farms, the yield of eggs per hen is much lower than in Israel. In general, agricultural technology in Israel is substantially more developed than in Argentina. This means that Israel can professionally contribute to Argentinian chicken farming, and on the other hand Argentina has farm personnel capable of assimilating new knowledge.

The chicken farms in Argentina are organized in cooperatives, which buy raw materials for the members and market their output. The market potential for feed enrichment compound amounts to 6,800 tons per year, or almost twice the Israeli market size.

ESTABLISHING AN INTERNATIONAL MARKETING SYSTEM

Strategy Formulation

On the basis of the market survey, an export strategy for Hamesin was formulated during late 1969 and early 1970, as follows:

Target Markets.   In the first phase, the company would build a marketing system based on exporting to a single market—Argentina. While operating in this market for several years, the company would develop personnel and a management system capable of conducting business in faraway markets. At the same time, the company would learn to deal with the problems of operating as a foreign company in a market and competing with local companies, and would develop appropriate control and information systems. These capabilities would be utilized in the second phase for extension in other markets.

Products.   It was decided that international operations would not be limited to a single product. On the other hand, the initial thrust would concentrate on the feed enriching compound as a base for building export activities.

Economic Objectives.   It was agreed between the partners that all of Hamesin's operations abroad would be based on exports from Israel. In this manner, the company hoped to circumvent currency exchange and capital transfer problems, and to solve the Hamesin profitability problems.

Organizational Structure.   It was decided that the organizational structure for operations abroad would be tailored to each market. It was clear that the Geha branch in Argentina would not be usable for Hamesin because of its limited nature. On the other hand, it was agreed that the administration of export activities would be handled by the Geha export department, which was well versed in dealing with the banks and government agencies, as required.

Application to Argentina

In March 1970, Mr. Avraham Eshed, formerly sales manager for Hamesin, was sent to Argentina to examine the possible methods for marketing feed enrichment compound in Argentina. The following are the main conclusions reached by him during the first two months of his stay:

1. There was no possibility to market the product through local channels, since such channels did not exist for a product of this nature and the product requires development of basic awareness of its value throughout the farming community.

2. An independent distribution system fully controlled by Hamesin had to be established. It should be based on regional warehouses, holding sufficient inventories and serving farms up to 300 kilometers distant from the warehouse.

3. Distribution should be based on selling to the farm cooperatives. These would buy for their members and handle payments. Thus, the firm would only have to ship the product from the regional warehouse to the cooperative warehouse rather than to individual farms. The procedure would also simplify collections and reduce the risk of bad debts.

4. Following the Israeli format, two fieldmen should be assigned to each regional distribution centre. Their function would be to establish product awareness among farmers and to conduct business with merchants. Regarding the cooperatives, the fieldmen would seek to increase "pull" from below. Actual transactions with cooperatives would be concluded at the enterprise management level.

5. The product was marketed in Israel in three versions: (*a*) high-energy feed enrichment compound for rapid fattening of special high-grade broilers, (*b*) high-protein feed enrichment compound for raising reasonable quality broilers on farms where the care and maintenance level was mediocre, and (*c*) low-protein feed enrichment compound for enriching egg-laying hens on farms with good maintenance and care levels. Mr. Eshed concluded that there was no need in Argentina for the first version of the compound, since the existence of a well-developed beef industry limited the potential for high-grade broilers. He also concluded that there was no need to differentiate between the other two versions. The general care and maintenance level in Argentina was quite low, due to availability of cheap labour. Under these conditions, only the second high-protein version was capable of producing good results.

6. Language problems convinced Mr. Eshed that the company should look for local, Spanish-speaking agricultural experts.

7. His conclusions regarding the appropriate distribution system pointed to the need for a sizable level of local expenditures. It became clear to Mr. Eshed that substantial bank financing would be necessary. Since Argentinian law drastically limited credit availability for foreign-owned firms, Mr. Eshed recommended the establishment of a

joint venture with a local company. The local partner would hold 75 percent of the stock, giving the firm maximal access to local bank financing.

These recommendations led Hamesin's board of directors to adopt the following operational decisions:

1. A new company, named Hamesin Argentina, would be set up. Twenty-five percent of the stock would be owned by Hamesin (Israel) and 75 percent by local investors.

2. The company manager would always be an Israeli, appointed by Hamesin. The firm would issue voting stock, giving Hamesin the lion's share of voting power.

3. A founding team would be sent to Argentina. The team would be comprised of Mr. Eshed as general manager, two Israeli fieldmen with substantial experience, and one new agronomist hired for this purpose. The Israeli fieldmen would be assigned for the first six months to different chicken-farming areas in Argentina. Each one of the fieldmen would do missionary selling in his area, convincing the local farmers of the benefits attendant to the use of feed enrichment compounds. At the same time, the general manager would recruit six local agronomists, and these would be trained by the Israeli fieldmen.

4. Twenty tons of feed enrichment compound, worth $8,700, would be allocated for demonstrations, samples, and experiments in the initial periods.

5. All policy-level decisions (including pricing, recruitment, and unusual contracts) by the local general manager would require authorization from the management in Israel. A monthly reporting system was established, covering the financial situation, sales, and inventory levels.

6. A three-year plan and budget were drawn up as follows:

a. Start-up period: January 1, 1970–September 31, 1970.
Revenues from sales: None.
Expenses: Samples (20 tons) . . $ 8,700
            Salaries and wages. .   60,000
            Other expenses   11,300
            Total investment . . . $80,000

b. Sales were budgeted after the six-month start-up period as follows:

	Sales per Month (tons)	Sales for Period (tons)
Next six months of operation	110	660
Second year of operation	200	2,400
Third year of operation	270	3,240

c. Expected monthly expenditure levels were:

	Second Half of First Year	Second Year	Third Year
Fieldmen wages	$ 4,400	$ 7,000	$ 9,000
Office salaries and wages	4,500	5,000	5,500
Transportation	6,380	9,800	10,500
Financing and miscellaneous	2,500	5,000	6,000
Total monthly expenditure	$17,780	$26,800	$31,000

d. The feed enrichment compound price to the final consumer could not exceed $650 per ton, considering feed prices in the local market. Price after a 10 percent discount to various distributors, including the cooperatives and independent merchants, was $585 per ton, net to the company.
e. Cost-accounting data in Israel showed that production and shipping costs (to Buenos Aires) would amount to $383 per ton.
f. In accordance with these data, the following sales and profit plan was developed (all in 1970 prices):

Item	First Six Months of Sales ($)	Second Year of Operation ($)	Third Year of Operation ($)
Net selling price in Argentina/ton	585	585	585
Net selling price to Hamesin Argentina/ton	435	435	435
Cost to Hamesin Israel/ton	383	383	383
Profit/ton, Hamesin Israel	52	52	52
Contribution/ton, Hamesin Argentina	150	150	150
Total sales for period, in tons	660	2,400	3,240
Profit for period, Hamesin Israel	34,320	124,800	168,480
Total contribution for period, Hamesin/Argentina	99,000	360,000	486,000
Forecasted expenses for period, Hamesin/Argentina	106,680	321,600	372,000
Profit (loss) for period, Hamesin/Argentina	(7,680)	38,400	114,000

From these data, it appeared that Hamesin would recover its initial investment of $80,000 in the middle of the second year of operations. Hamesin Argentina was planned to show an accumulated profit of $145,000 by the end of the third year. This budgeted profit should provide sufficient reserve against unforeseen developments and present a reasonably attractive image to banks and to the local government.

THREE YEARS LATER

Early in 1973 Mr. Eshed was summoned to Israel to participate in a series of discussions regarding the situation of Hamesin Argentina, and plans for the continuation of Hamesin operations in Argentina, and possible expansion to other markets. Some serious charges were made against Mr. Eshed during these discussions.

Mr. Yahalomi, Hamesin's chief executive officer, urged that sales in Argentina were far below expectations. Average sales in the second year were only 185 tons per month, and only 230 tons per month in the third year. According to him, most of Mr. Eshed's time was spent in trying to develop local business in partnership with some operators in the animal feed market, which prevented him from reaching budgeted sales levels. Mr. Yahalomi insisted that the Argentinian venture was established in order to promote Hamesin's exports—not to develop the Argentinian economy.

Mr. Shamir, Hamesin's export manager, stated that throughout the period he had to fight with Mr. Eshed in order to receive updated inventory reports and other reports that were included in the planned information system. Finally, personal relations between himself and Mr. Eshed had deteriorated to the point where they could no longer work together.

Mr. Tidhar, Geha general manager, stated that he was severely disappointed with Hamesin Argentina's inability to utilize its distribution system to market Geha pesticides in Argentina. He charged Mr. Eshed with attempting to increase Hamesin Argentina's sales volume through local business deals, thereby increasing his bonus (which was based on total sales volume). Mr. Tidhar suggested that Mr. Eshed's contract should be changed, to give him a bonus on sales from Israeli imports only.

Mr. Yahalomi summarized the charges by stating that while the Argentinian operation exceeded budgeted profit levels, the company was no longer directed by the shareholders' aims and objectives, and its operations were being extended too far afield by its general manager.

Responding to the charges, Mr. Eshed reviewed the first three years of operations, and presented the following arguments:

1. Management in Israel does not understand the complications involved in operating in a foreign country so far from headquarters. The initial definition of his responsibilities and authority was wrong, leaving too many policy decisions to the Israeli management. Hamesin management should have decided on central policy guidelines and then let him manage the company, rather than trying to manage Hamesin Argentina from Israel.

2. The far-reaching market development activities conducted during the start-up period attracted two other firms with foreign technical know-how to enter the market. These firms offered lower-quality products at lower prices. Since the product offered by Hamesin had not had a chance to prove its superior quality in the field prior to the outset of competition, price became a critical variable. Using painstaking comparative feed conversion experiments, Hamesin Argentina personnel succeeded in proving the superiority of the Israeli feed enrichment compound. This success, however, did not prevent the competitors from selling, and Hamesin Argentina was obliged to reduce its price to the final consumer to $629 per ton. Mr. Eshed argued that the three-month delay between the time he reached his conclusion regarding the necessary price change and the time of obtaining concurrence from the Israeli management was crucial, enabling the competitors to establish a strong market position.

3. Another major problem was personnel. As it turned out, "job-hopping" is the accepted custom among young Argentinian university graduates. Labor turnover was high throughout the period, and even now there are only two satisfactory fieldmen out of a crew of six. Mr. Eshed explained that the phenomenon results from a wealth of job opportunities facing educated young people in Argentina, and an absence of "patriotic" feelings toward an employer (such as exists in Israel).

4. Midway through the second year of operations it became clear to Mr. Eshed that he could not meet planned profit levels. Sales of 185 tons per month at a net price of $566 would cause the firm losses of over $2,500 per month, since expenses ran at about the forecasted level. His repeated requests to reduce his purchase price for enrichment compound were denied. Thus, he felt he had to search urgently for additional local sources of revenue for the company. Early in 1971 he reached separate agreements with three large feed processors. It was agreed that his fieldmen, who had to meet chicken farmers in any case while selling the compound, would promote feed sales for the processing plants. Within six months, sales commissions on feed were providing

25 percent of the total contribution, and total profits exceeded budgeted levels by 30 percent.

5. Mr. Eshed tried to impress upon the listeners that a management information system between parent company and subsidiary should be designed to promote the common interests—not to hinder operations. According to him, informational demands placed upon him were never ending, including subjects that were totally irrelevant to the solution of his pressing problems and even Hamesin problems. On the other hand, all of his requests for sending experts on nutrition and feed technology (experts that were available among Hamesin personnel) went unanswered. Even his requests for special products that could easily be marketed in Argentina (but had to be developed in Israel) did not receive proper treatment. On the other hand, he was always asked to use his fieldmen to market pesticides, an area that was completely out of their sphere of operations.

6. Summing up his arguments, Mr. Eshed stated that there is certain internal logic in the evolution of a business venture. In the long run, a business must retain flexibility and adaptability in order to survive. It cannot operate in a very rigid and unyielding framework, and the farther away from the centre it is, the more it needs independence.

Adjourning the meeting, Mr. Yahalomi announced the agenda for the next board meeting:

1. What form should future operations in Argentina take, and under what guidelines?
2. What actions have to be taken to prepare for entrance to the Iranian market?
3. Should Mr. Eshed be kept on as Hamesin Argentina's general manager?

Meridian Electric*

Early in 1963 Mr. Donald Bennett was appointed general manager of Meridian Electric. Meridian was the fully owned British subsidiary of International Electric Corporation and distributed International products in Britain along with a number of lines from other manufacturers. Mr. Bennett's appointment had been made by Mr. G. C. Sakuda, who as vice president international of International Electric was responsible to the board of directors for all foreign subsidiaries. The previous general manager had retired early for health reasons and Sakuda had persuaded Bennett to transfer to Meridian Electric from an engineering supply firm in which he held the position of assistant to the managing director.

Sakuda pointed out to Bennett that the past results of Meridian were poor and the board did not want to see the company continuing with lines which had an after-tax return on the assets it held below the company minimum target of 10 percent.

Meridian was organized into four product lines as shown in Exhibit 1. Small appliances covered radios, television sets, record players, tape recorders, and hand appliances such as mixers, electric irons, and hair dryers. Large appliances covered domestic refrigerators, washing machines, etc. Industrial appliances were sold to hotels, hospitals, restaurants, and works canteens, and covered larger and more substantial appliances than those sold for domestic use. The parts and replacements line covered all replacements for the other three lines.

The sales staff were responsible directly to the sales manager, not to the four product line managers, and worked through wholesalers, or in the case of industrial appliances, direct with the potential customer. Each salesman had a specific territory to cover.

Bennett began his appointment by requesting the product line managers to prepare a full-scale report on their product lines and their plans for the future. Three weeks later, Mr. Grey, the manager of the small appliances line, presented the report set out in Exhibit 2. The small appliances line had been showing the lowest return of the four lines and accounted for 35 percent of Meridian's total sales.

Mr. Grey had received an International Electric Group circular noting that the central office had imposed a 10 percent minimum return on assets for lines of activity to be continued, and in commenting on his report he said that Mr. Bennett should be careful in interpreting the figures shown because they tended to make his line look worse than it really was.

Approximately 85 percent of the costs in my profit and loss are allocated costs rather than direct costs. The accounting practice has been simply to total all the expenses for the company—advertising, sales promotion, rent, heat, light, warehousing, provisions for bad debts and inventory losses, allocated corporate overhead, and so on—and to allocate these expenses to the product line on the basis of their sales budgets. Only sales, inventory, and gross margin are broken out by specific product lines. The way the accounts are set up, it is impossible to find out what the small appliances line is actually spending. It also seems to me that prorating the costs among product lines on the basis of sales budgets is wrong. If a manager has budgeted low and has a good year, this method of allocating makes him look doubly good because he is charged with less than his proper share of expenses. Likewise, if he has been too optimistic with his sales projections, he looks doubly bad because he's carrying more than his load of costs.

Another problem concerns sundry debtors. The accounting practice has been to report sundry debtors for the firm as a whole, by customer and by type of account—such as special terms account, regular open account, installment contract account, and so on. For purposes of calculating the return on assets of the various product lines the account-ants first compute the ratio that total debtors bear to total sales. Then they apply this ratio to the sales of each product line, and come up with an allocated debtors figure for each. The same sort of formula has been used to allocate cash and fixed assets to the product lines, although these items aren't quite as large as debtors and therefore not as important. I would say that the actual overall sundry debtors for small appliances does not exceed 120 days' sales and is probably closer to 90 days' sales. Yet my allocated debtors are reflecting the experience of the other product lines. Also some of the products within the line are doing much better than others on asset return. Some may be doing 10 percent or more. But because I can't get exact or detailed debtors figures, the whole product line is made to look bad.

Bennett decided that he should discuss some of these points with other Meridian executives, to help him in his interpretation of Grey's report. He discovered that a number of these executives had strong reservations about the validity or usefulness of the product line studies, particularly about the return on investment as a measure of a product line's performance. One product line manager said:

> We're merchandisers, not accountants. You can't tell just from looking at figures what makes a good product mix, and you certainly cannot expect every product to turn the same profit. What about the loss leaders? They're as old as the history of merchandise. I'm not saying we should carry a line that shows a steady loss, but neither do I think we should consider dropping it just because its profit doesn't come up to some arbitrarily established level. The small appliances line helps us to sell other lines. I think that, especially in going into new markets, we should regard consumer products as the calling cards of our business. They're a way of getting the International Electric trademark known and respected so that later, when we try and sell industrial lines and International's other products, people will know who we are.

When asked what value he thought carried over from his line to the others, Grey observed that while it was difficult for him to assess the role that small appliances played in cultivating markets for other Meridian product lines, he had found that a given product frequently helped generate consumer preference for other products in his own line. He pointed to the relation between radio receivers and television receivers as a case in point. In areas where Meridian radio receivers enjoyed popularity, they had paved the way with the beginning of television broadcasting, for the introduction of Meridian television receivers. He added that possessing a full line of consumer products was important in establishing and maintaining Meridian's position with distributors and dealers.

Another of the product line managers, who had been with Meridian for many years, told Bennett that within the firm the size of gross margins had traditionally been the measure of the value of a product line and that, in his opinion, gross margins were still the soundest index. He thought this was particularly true since gross margins were based entirely on *actual* figures, completely avoiding the question of allocated costs or assets. He pointed out that the average gross margin on small appliances had risen from 15 percent in 1961 to 16.2 percent in 1962, and that it would probably exceed 18 percent in 1963.

Yet another product line manager expressed the view that while return on assets might be a valid measure of a product line's perform-

682   *International Business and Multinational Enterprises*

ance in some business organizations, it was not a valid measure at Meridian because product line managers did not have complete control of either the assets for which they were responsible or of certain cost elements which affected profits. He pointed out, for example, that the purchasing function was not under the direction of the product line manager.

> I have no complaint against our purchasing people, and I know that they make purchases only on orders from the product line managers. But anyone knows that a purchasing agent who's got his heart in it can save a lot of money and help keep inventory levels down. The problem is that the purchasing people aren't on the product manager's team. They aren't under the manager's control. Since the product manager doesn't have purchasing under his administrative control, I don't see how he can be held responsible for asset management.
>
> More important, though, is the fact that the sales operation isn't under the product line manager's control. While sales aren't as removed from the product managers as purchasing, still the sales people don't share the product managers profit-and-loss responsibility, with the result that they may not try as hard on a sale or press for terms the way they might if they were on the marketing team. This matter of credit terms also affects the manager's performance in asset management. We all know that the product manager has the right of final approval on variations from established credit terms, but he has to rely largely on the sales organization's appraisal of what terms it's going to take to close a deal. If a salesman is a little too liberal in his estimate, the product managers get tied down to higher debtors which, of course, reduces return on assets. I think if the salesmen were on the product manager's team and shared his profit responsibility, they'd be more hard-headed about credit terms. Finally, the fact that sales aren't under the product manager's control means he may not have the sales force he would like to have representing his line or that the sales force isn't administered in the way he thinks best.
>
> These are all factors that affect a product line's return on assets, and they're outside the manager's control. So I don't see how you can consider return on assets an accurate measure of a product line's performance.

Meridian's controller expressed the view that return on assets, though a useful financial yardstick in determining the effectiveness of a given product line, was not the only measure to be considered.

> I think that before you drop a line you have to take into account how much it contributes to the total sales volume and how much overhead it may be carrying, especially if you don't have any other product to replace it. Small appliances provide the second largest sales volume among Meridian's product lines and accounted for 35 percent of 1962 sales. At

this level, small appliances absorb significant amounts of Meridian's administrative expenses, of corporate administrative expenses allocated by International Electric, and of the manufacturing division's factory overhead and product engineering expenses. If one were to estimate these figures, which is perfectly possible, it would be seen that the small appliances line is making an important corporate-wide contribution to fixed expenses. If the line were dropped, these expenses would continue and would simply have to be reallocated.

Since this argument called for estimates of overhead that would not be eliminated if the product line was dropped, Bennett asked the controller to obtain for him the appropriate figures for 1962 to 1964. These estimates are shown in Exhibit 3.

EXHIBIT 1
Organization Chart

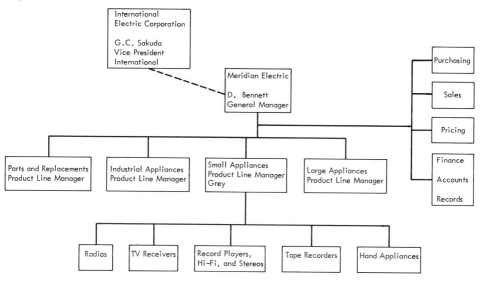

EXHIBIT 2

TO: Bennett
FROM: Grey
SUBJECT: Small Appliances Line Plan

Analysis of sales volume and gross margin for the period 1960–63 shown in Table 1 points up the following facts.

1.   The decrease in sales has been most noticeable since the peak year 1961. In 1961 gross margins were cut and longer credit terms were

EXHIBIT 2 *(continued)*

extended to distributors. In addition, many distributors bought more goods during this period than they were able to move and consequently went into 1962 with large overstocks. Other factors hindering sales in 1962 were higher prices and shortened credit terms. These moves were taken with a view toward increasing gross margins, reducing receivables, and thereby increasing profits. Despite the lower sales, figures show that this move was successful and profits have increased.

2. In mid-year 1962, large appliances were transferred out of the line, but the figures for the two lines are shown together until December 31. After that date figures include only small appliances. This change, of course, affects the validity of trend-line figures.

3. Television sales reached a peak in 1961 but the market is becoming more saturated.

4. International radios have decreased in volume mainly because of increased competition from foreign producers. Other brand radios were successful until foreign manufacturers moved into the market with similar, lower-priced goods.

5. Tape recorder sales were hurt critically because poor products were shipped in 1961–62. With this problem now out of the way, there should be no difficulty in making up lost ground.

6. Record player and hi-fi volume has increased since 1960 and has remained fairly constant. There has been some hesitancy to purchase because of the advent of stereo. However, orders are coming in now and we may exceed last year's figures.

Table 2 shows the overall operation for the years 1960 through 1962 and estimates for 1963–64.

1. Gross margins are improving and will continue upward. Low grosses were taken in 1961. Since then they have improved measurably despite sizable markdowns and write-offs due to defective tape recorders and slow-moving other brand radio stocks.

2. Expenses have been cut appreciably; where there were 17 people engaged in the marketing function a year ago, we now have only seven. Mechanization of order handling has also helped cut expenses.

3. Net profit, which was in the red in 1961 and broke even in 1962, will be well in the black in 1963, despite lower volume. With the expenses further pared down, lower inventories, and the write-offs on tape recorders and markdowns on other brand radio receivers behind us, we can expect a greatly improved net profit in 1964.

4. Total assets peaked in 1961–62 due to large debtors and other brand radio inventory. Here again good progress has been made and the assets will be brought down to a point more consistent with volume and profit potential.

5. Great progress will be made as far as the sundry debtors' picture is concerned. This will be due in great measure to having shortened our terms and eliminated large appliances. There still remains a problem so far as overdue debts are concerned. An estimated £100,000 will be difficult to collect.

6. Return on assets will show great improvement this year and the 2.9 percent return is conservative, as we see a good possibility of 7.0 percent for 1964. With continued progress on inventories, gross margins, expenses, and receivables, we should within the next few years realize 10 percent return on assets.

EXHIBIT 2 *(continued)*

Table 1

Small Appliances Line Sales (£000s) and Gross Margin (%)

		1960	1961	1962	Budget 1963	Budget 1964
Radios: International						
Electric brand	Sales	231	296	159	117	107
	GM	n.a.*	14.8	14.6	14.0	13.6
Other brands	Sales	176	228	322	89	—
	GM	n.a.	20.0	14.2	10.1	—
TV receivers.	Sales	433	1,053	610	537	556
	GM	n.a.	14.6	18.2	18.2	18.4
Record players and hi-fi	Sales	143	254	241	228	236
	GM	n.a.	14.3	17.6	23.8	26.8
Tape recorders	Sales	121	154	95	101	128
	GM	n.a.	16.4	16.2	16.8	19.8
Hand appliances (large appliances until end of 1962).	Sales	634	729	553	62	43
	GM	n.a.	13.8	15.0	20.0	24.8
Product line total.	Sales	1,738	2,714	1,980	1,134	1,070

*n.a. = not available.

Table 2

Small Appliance Line Selected Operating Figures (in £000s)

	1960	1961	1962	Budget 1963	Budget 1964
Sales.	1,738	2,714	1,980	1,134	1,070
Cost of sales.	1,464	2,307	1,659	928	857
Gross margin,.	274	407	321	206	213
% to sales	15.8	15.0	16.2	18.2	20.0
Expenses, ...	229	418	321	159	126
% to sales	13.3	15.4	16.2	14.0	11.8
Net profit (after taxes of 50%), ...	22	(5)	—	24	44
% to sales	1.3	(0.2)	—	2.1	4.1
Average inventories	338	669	594	192	132
Sundry debtors	654	1,122	1,152	645	478
Total assets	1,022	1,809	1,801	872	629
Current liabilities	n.a.*	n.a.	509	289	270
Asset turnover.	1.7	1.5	1.1	1.3	1.7
Return on assets (%).	2.1	(0.3)	0	2.9	7.0

*n.a. = not available.

EXHIBIT 3

Controller's Estimate of Overhead That Would Not Be Eliminated by Dropping the
Small Appliance Line (£000s)*

	1962	1963	1964
Included in Cost of Sales			
Manufacturing divisions' overhead			
including depreciation.	55	23	21
Amortization of product engineering expenses	15	6	6
Included in Product Line Expenses			
International Electric's allocated corporate			
expense	13	7	7
Meridian Electric's fixed administrative			
expenses.	62	26	25
Total	145	62	59

*These figures are based on actual 1962 volume and budgeted 1963 and 1964 volumes.

Dorcas International Corporation*

DORCAS INTERNATIONAL manufactured a line of electric razors and over the years had built a significant market position in most of the more developed countries. There had been recent signs, however, that the electric razor market had matured to a point where competition on price, and therefore cost, would be the outstanding characteristic of the industry over the next half-dozen years. Recognizing the changed situation, Jorg Moroney, the Dorcas president, had established a central management services group to look into the question of concentrating further expansion of production into a smaller number of sites in order to gain greater scale economies.

In setting up this group, however, Moroney indicated that he did not intend to dispense with a policy of holding operating units to profit achievement. While profit achievement had always been applied quite loosely, each manufacturing unit had been free to set its own price for its local markets and for supply to other marketing units.

The task of proposing a plan for future plant expansion fell to Stephan Morse as head of the new management services group. He decided that the first essential in preparing his recommendations was to collect basic cost and revenue data for the Dorcas International system. This he did, and as he considered the current situation irrelevant to the problem, he projected market growth, alternative price-sales figures, and cost estimates for four years ahead in current dollars. These are summarised in Exhibit 1. All this involved many

*This case was prepared by Kenneth Simmonds, professor, London Graduate School of Business Studies. Copyright 1972 by Kenneth Simmonds.

simplifications, but Morse felt they would not materially affect a decision. For example:

1. Export duties and rebates were ignored as immaterial.
2. Any new capacity would take about two years to build and cost variations among alternative sites were unpredictable.
3. About 30 percent of fixed production cost was represented by depreciation in the first year (15 percent of plant cost). As depreciation reduced, it would be more or less offset by increased repair cost. The three existing plants could continue production at the indicated figures indefinitely. Plants would have little scrap value.
4. Tax rates applied to nonremitted funds only, but as Dorcas had large borrowings in each country no profit remittances were envisaged in the foreseeable future.

The next task seemed to be to calculate some sort of approximation to an optimum and then to mold this into reasonable management recommendations.

EXHIBIT 1
Summary of Cost and Revenue Data for Dorcas International System

					Country			
	Unit	General	A	B	C	D	E	F
1. Annual sales volume in four years' time for alternative average prices to wholesale	000 units							
$9.00			50	150	250	80	250	50
8.50			55	160	320	120	300	60
8.00			60	180	340	160	350	70
7.50			65	210	370	190	500	80
7.00			75	250	400	200	600	100
2. Variable cost of local marketing, selling, and distribution per average unit	$		0.50	0.60	0.40	0.40	0.20	0.50
3. Corporation tax rate	%		30	50	40	20	50	40
4. Customs tariff on imports based on transfer price	%		40	60	25	25	10	25
5. Transport costs per unit of transfers								
Among A, B, C, F	$	0.10						
Between D and others	$	0.20						
Between E and others	$	0.20						
6. Existing production capacity Volume limit	000 units			400	300		400	
7. Fixed production cost per annum (including interest and depreciation)	$000			800	1,100		1,200	
8. Variable production cost per average unit	$			3.00	2.00		2.00	
9. Additional production capacity Fixed production cost for plant with annual volume								
200,000 units	$000	800						
300,000 units	$000	1,100						
400,000 units	$000	1,350						
500,000 units	$000	1,500						
10. Variable production cost per average unit from new plant	$		1.50	2.00	1.80	1.80	1.50	1.80

The Widget*

THE WIDGET WAS AN IMPORTANT COMPONENT in the electronics industry: its two major uses were in *Product A,* a consumer end item, and in *Product B,* an industrial end item. Seven European companies made the widget, which was well standardized in design. There were no duties on the widget and shipping costs were a negligible proportion of its selling price.

The largest European widget maker was Lamar Electronics, which made nearly 50 percent of the total European annual volume of 98 million units. One of the smallest widget makers was Electronic Products Incorporated (EPI), one of four European subsidiaries of Western Electronics (WE). Each of the WE houses maintained a separate profit-and-loss statement and balance sheet and had decentralized profit responsibility. (See Exhibit 1 for a partial organization chart of WE and its subsidiaries.)

All four WE subsidiaries made *Product A* and three made *Product B,* but EPI was the only WE subsidiary that made the widget. The WE policy on intercompany transfers stated that the subsidiaries were free to purchase their component needs from outside the WE system if they could obtain a lower price commensurate with good quality and dependable supply. (See Exhibit 2 for excerpts from WE's transfer policy.)

EPI had offered to supply each of the three other WE subsidiaries

---

*This case has been prepared and copyrighted 1963 by Harbridge House, Inc., and is designed for teaching purposes only. The case does not necessarily indicate the policy or practice of any company or corporation, and is not necessarily intended to illustrate either correct or incorrect, desirable or undesirable, management procedures.

EXHIBIT 1
Western Electronics Partial Organization Chart

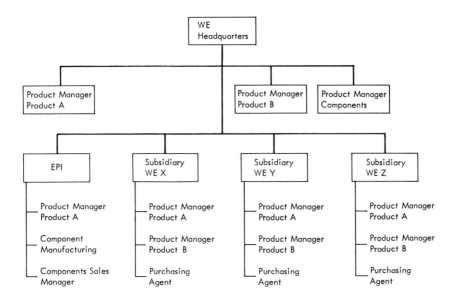

with their annual widget requirements, but its sister houses claimed that they could purchase their requirements more cheaply from Lamar, and in fact they all bought from Lamar. Each of the subsidiaries admitted that EPI's quality was comparable with Lamar's.

EPI made 3 million widgets a year, using 1 million for its own production of *Product A* (these were transferred to the *Product A* division at an intrahouse price of $0.66) and selling the remainder to a variety of small manufacturers at prices averaging $0.68 per unit.

EXHIBIT 2
Excerpts from Western Electronics' Intercompany Transfer Policy

1. Purchases should be made from other system houses rather than from outside competitors if price, quality, delivery, and service are competitive. . .
2. Where the parts in question are of standard design, are obtainable from outside the system, and are being used in manufacture by the buying company, they should be transferred at cost plus 10 percent, but not to exceed the lesser of market or most favored customer trade price for like quality, . . . less discount for sales and advertising expense not incurred in interhouse business.
3. As used in paragraph 2, cost is to include material, labor, and manufacturing overhead, but not administrative or marketing expenses.

The annual widget requirements of the WE subsidiaries, the prices at which they purchased from Lamar, and the prices offered to them by EPI were as follows:

Subsidiary	Annual Purchases	Lamar Unit Price	EPI Price Offer
WE X	1 million units	$0.49	$0.55
WE Y	2 million units	0.44	0.50
WE Z	3 million units	0.42	0.49

EPI's manufacturing costs at various volumes were as follows:

Annual Volume (million units)	Total Fixed Manufacturing Cost (million dollars)	Fixed Cost/Unit ($)	Variable Cost/Unit ($)	Total Cost/Unit ($)
3	1.0	0.33	0.27	0.60
4	1.0	0.25	0.26	0.51
5	1.0	0.20	0.25	0.45
6	1.5	0.25	0.24	0.49
7	1.5	0.21	0.22	0.43
8	1.5	0.19	0.21	0.40
9	1.5	0.17	0.20	0.37
10	1.5	0.15	0.18	0.33

Total widget sales for the year were $2.02 million, of which $1.36 million were to customers outside the WE system. EPI's marketing expenses for the year were 14 percent of widget sales to outside customers. General and administrative overhead was charged at 4 percent of total sales. Thus, the widget line operated at a before-tax loss of about $60,000.

Managing Personnel in Cross-National Situations

Raze Limited*

THE SENIOR MANAGEMENT OF RAZE LTD. had got together in a large conference room. The setting was obviously American with potted plants and nameplates to identify the various members. Bill Waters, the managing director, called the meeting to order.

"I need hardly remind you that the decision to appoint a new marketing manager for the Data Equipment Division was taken about six months back. Since then, we have advertised in the national press and even in the English-language papers on the Continent. All of us have had the opportunity of meeting the candidates who had been short-listed and they in turn have seen the company and the people they may be working with. In spite of the fact that there has been a fair amount of activity, we have not made a final offer and this, in my view, is long overdue. I suggest we decide today." Bill Waters looked pointedly at Ray Ryston, General Manager of the Data Equipment Division, before he continued.

"The result of the previous months' activity has been that we have identified two candidates for the position. You have all seen Mark Davies and Anwar Latif. I have all their papers and our own interview comments, in case you wish to refresh your memories." He indicated two slim files on the table in front of him, "the two seem fairly similar in experience, they are both about 30 and have been involved in marketing activities for the last five to six years. But there are a few significant differences. Anwar has been to a business school and has

*This case was prepared by Mr. Shiv Mathur, Research Fellow, London Graduate School of Business Studies, in association with Professor Kenneth Simmonds. Copyright 1976 by Shiv Mathur.

been involved for the past couple of years in marketing planning. Marketing planning will be of crucial importance to our organisation over the next five years."

"Doesn't that make him an obvious choice," said Keith Cameron, who held the post of controller and treasurer. "I have often complained to both you and Ray that our planning systems are a shambles. If we are going to expand overseas at the rate the two of you hope, the most important attribute of the man we get in will be his ability to put some order and method into planning the expansion. Latif's experience in this area should decide the issue."

"It should and it shouldn't," said Ray Ryston. "One point that Bill has not mentioned is that Latif is of Pakistani extraction. The fact that he had lived here all his life and been to Cambridge does not alter the fact that his colour is going to raise problems." He waved John Davidson, the personnel officer who was trying to come in on the discussion, back into his chair. "I know what you are going to say. I know we have an equal employment policy. I also know that we inherited it from our American parent along with these potted plants. Now don't get me wrong, I am wholeheartedly in support of having such a policy. As far as the factory was concerned, we have Asian chargehands and even a supervisor or two. But we have all agreed that attitudes cannot be changed overnight. A coloured manager would raise problems with all other sales and marketing staff. I suppose that might be overcome. But we are an international company with 20 percent of our products being exported to South Africa and Eastern Europe. How can a marketing manager looking after only 80 percent of the market be held to be really responsible? And who's going to carry through all the negotiations with these countries, which are precisely where our expansion programme is really likely to be aimed?" He looked around the table. "The customer is always right, and if our South African distributors do not wish to deal with a coloured Englishman, then we'll have to take that into account."

John Davidson, who had been listening with an impatience he could hardly conceal, spoke, "Does that imply that as long as we keep selling to South Africa or Russia our equal opportunity policy has to be confined to the shop floor and no further?"

"You tell me," said Ray Ryston, "and it is fair to add that it is not only a problem connected with colour. My own sister is married to a Jew and I wouldn't select him to be our area representative in the Middle East. These are the age-old problems of dealing internationally and when doing so all our policies and strategies must reflect an international stance. Latif's business school would be the first one to tell him that."

"Living in South Africa for two years has changed you considerably," said John Davidson in a heated tone.

"I call myself a realist and that's what one wants to be if one wishes to remain in industry," retorted Ray Ryston.

"Gentlemen, gentlemen," said Bill Waters, "this discussion is getting a bit out of hand. Let's get back to the issue. The points that Ray has raised are valid but in conflict with an equal opportunity policy. I believe that there are two problems. Firstly within our organisation and secondly with our customers. It stands to reason that the new recruit, if he is coloured, will have to work under pressure that a white candidate would not feel. I am firmly committed to this company's policy of racial equality and am sure that we can come to some arrangement over the customer problem. But before we make Anwar Latif a final offer, I think it's only fair that we appraise him of the problems his background may cause and we should also try to ascertain whether he would cope with this kind of hostility. I suggest that you have another chat with him, Ray."

Two days later Ray Ryston walked into Bill Waters' office, lit a cigarette, and said, "I have now come to the conclusion that when it comes to the question of race and cultural differences in interviewing situations, it is best to bring the issue out into the open. There are only two ways of dealing with this problem and it definitely is a problem; the first is to ignore it and that is unrealistic from the point of view of the interviewed candidate and ourselves, and the other is to mention it candidly and go on from there."

Bill Waters nodded. Ray Ryston went on, "Take the case of Anwar Latif. There's no point in telling a man with that kind of educational background that we have not noticed that he's coloured. He knows it and I know it and no matter what the world says, it does make a difference. As you suggested, I invited him for lunch and another chat. I told him that I was going to be absolutely frank and he didn't seem to mind. I mentioned that he was going to be the first senior coloured manager in our company and probably one of the very few in the U.K. Such a position would present various opportunities and challenges. The opportunities were obvious but the challenges were just as great. In the U.K., where at times even accent and education arouse great hostility, the addition of colour to this mixture would make a fairly volatile situation. In fact, I told him that I am not even sure if my more socialistic colleagues have forgiven me Harrow, Christchurch, and the Coldstream Guards."

Ray paused as Bill Waters smiled, then continued. "A coloured manager could arouse great hostility amongst our senior staff, some of whom with their colonial backgrounds have never been ordered around by Asians, and possibly also among our customers. Without stressing the South African connection, I asked Latif how he would cope with this sort of problem. He muttered about each situation being different, but produced no satisfactory answer. He did ask, rather feebly, how the company would react. I told him in no uncertain terms that no company could prevent personal prejudices and interpersonal clashes of this nature. The coloured person, if employed, will by and large have to sort this problem out for himself. What is essential, and I didn't tell him this, is that the candidate's personality is not incompatible with that of the company and that he is able to get on in this culture."

Ray lit a cigarette, then continued, "The best way to judge a coloured candidate's suitability is to find out about his background. What nationality are his friends? Where has he lived and how closely does he associate with people of his own ethnic background? This could be a way to minimise hostility and could also serve other useful purposes as it would give some indication of where the candidate finally wanted to live. We don't want to recruit a person for a managerial position only to find him leaving for, say, Nigeria at the end of the year. I believe that the best way to do this is to speak fairly frankly when we consider candidates from alien cultures. The real question is when and how a discussion of this nature should take place. Perhaps it is best done in the early stages of the battery of interviews that we hold, when some senior manager could rate the candidate on his compatibility and form a considered opinion. After that it would be possible to treat the candidate absolutely equally with other applicants. It may be unwise to leave this screening too late as then we may quite unjustly be accused of prejudice. Anyway, perhaps you should think about this and we should establish some policy."

When Ray Ryston had left, Bill Waters sat back to think about the problem. The number of coloured applicants for managerial positions was increasing and he did feel that this was in many ways different from recruiting shop-floor workers from an immigrant community. Bill Waters himself felt no racial bias but agreed that there was a lot of truth in what Ray had said about the futility of ignoring the issue. But if the company did decide to subject candidates from alien cultures to compatability tests and there was merit in the suggestion, there arose a whole host of issues. What form should the tests take? Who should conduct them and at what stage? What questions should be asked and what answers expected? And how much should the company's customers influence the final choice?

As Bill Waters thought, he looked once again at the letter he had been reading when Ray Ryston had come in—a brief one from Anwar Latif withdrawing his application.

Dahl Systems Incorporated*

"SALARY POLICY has got to be the main item on the board agenda. What I want the board to agree on is the principle of local salary levels for all those on the payroll of any subsidiary, and a shift of the international headquarters staff in London out of the United Kingdom division and into a separate company for pay purposes." Ronald Cunningham was speaking by telephone in October 1976 to Brent Wojciekowski, Vice President International of Dahl Systems Incorporated. As managing director of Dahl's German subsidiary, Ronald Cunningham sat on the international board which met bimonthly in London at Brent's headquarters for all of Dahl's operations outside the Americas. Cunningham went on, "We have lost two English team heads to our competitors in the last month. With the deutsch mark revaluation of 6 percent this week and more to come, and the fall in sterling with more to come too, we will probably need a 30 percent increase in salary level to keep any non-Germans. An increase in housing subsidies and education allowances may be needed as well."

Himself an Englishman, Ronald Cunningham had nearly 20 expatriate Englishmen and Americans in his managerial team in Frankfurt. This had come about because Dahl had expanded to London from its Chicago base very early in the development of the specialist computer and systems services industry. It was only four years ago, however, that the company had moved into Germany in any strength. To establish the unit Dahl had moved a senior team to Frankfurt,

---

*This case was prepared by Professor Kenneth Simmonds of the London Graduate School of Business Studies. Copyright 1976 by Kenneth Simmonds.

including many who had already been handling some German business from the London office. While the proportion of expatriates in Germany was especially large, the international movement of management and systems specialists would remain at a high rate throughout Dahl. Dahl was in a fast-moving business and the transfer of state-of-the-art knowledge of systems and applications was best achieved through transferring individuals who had built up the appropriate expertise and proved they could sell it.

Dahl's salary policy for those transferred internationally was to set the salary in the currency of the executive's home country at a level that would be appropriate in the home country and to translate this base salary at the current exchange rate. With fluctuating exchange rates, the sum received could change dramatically from month to month. On top of this base salary, though, a local sum was established yearly for each executive to cover increased cost of living. This sum covered actual increases in the cost of housing, including local taxes, heating, telephones, etc., plus costs of children's schooling and a further percentage of base salary set annually for the country of residence. The percentages allowed for each country were reviewed at the main board each year and tended to reflect both differences in relative price levels and subjective assessments of the costs felt by the various executives who were affected. Currently the percentage allowed for expatriates in Germany was 30 percent and for expatriates in the United Kingdom it was 20 percent. Differential movement in price levels and exchange rates during 1976, as shown in Exhibit 1, indicated that some trenchant memoranda would be arriving at the head office over the next few months arguing for increases in these rates. To date, no foreign executives had been transferred to the U.S. parent company for other than short visiting periods, so there was as yet no U.S. residence percentage.

Dahl's policy was quite new. It had been reshaped under considerable pressure from expatriate U.S. executives in London barely three years previously. The U.S. executives had also pressed for taxation equalization to reduce the impact of United Kingdom taxes down to the U.S. levels, and Brent Wojciekowski had himself been a prime mover in making these demands. The taxation equalization privilege had not been extended beyond U.S. expatriates, however, as others had not presented a specific case for it. Moreover, Dahl's treasurer in Chicago said that he was not prepared to have corporate staff diverted from their main function into a morass of calculations concerning taxation differences between third countries.

Following his telephone conversation with Cunningham, Brent Wojciekowski had a long luncheon discussion with John Jones, the managing director of the United Kingdom division. "I think Ronnie is

EXHIBIT 1

	United Kingdom	West Germany	United States
Consumer price index (1970 = 100)			
1973	127	119	114
1974	147	127	127
1975	182	135	138
1976 (second quarter)	208	141	145
Exchange rate	£1 =	1DM =	
March 1973	$2.48	$0.354	
March 1974	2.39	0.387	
March 1975	2.41	0.426	
March 1976	1.91	0.392	
October 1976	1.57	0.415	
Representative local salary of a Dahl senior systems specialist in 1976	£9,500	DM130,000	$36,000
Marginal tax rate (on last $1,000 of an income of $40,000 after deductions)	83%*	45%	58%

*Ninety-eight percent on interest and dividends over $1,600.

really thinking about himself," said John. "He already receives 50 percent more than I do, for instance. And that's before tax. If we followed Ronnie's suggestion we would have an even greater outflow of U.K. staff to cope with. Before we do anything on salaries we should first change the policy of internal advertisement of all job openings internationally. We really promote transfers by selecting the best-qualified applicants and paying relocation costs. It is a ridiculous situation when over-qualified Englishmen apply in large numbers for any continental job opening at all. Our bread and butter still comes from the U.K. division and if we are going to continue to perform against our competition here, we just have to hang on to the key people we still have. What's more, we should bring some back on salaries that bear some relationship to British levels. We really need David Symes back here. But I can never forgive him bragging to everyone before he went off to join Ronnie last year that his children would now get a good English public school education."

Some Additional Cases

AN EXTENSIVE RANGE OF CASES is available through the Intercollegiate Case Clearing House, Soldiers Field, Boston, Massachusetts 02163. Listed below is a selection of those that have proved of significant teaching value and that might be used to further supplement the text. The Clearing House code numbers are quoted following the case titles.

Working within the International Framework:
Banque de Bruxelles   9-305-063
   Decision to pay spot rates or cover forward.
Weiss Appliance Co. Inc.   9-312-011
   Plant relocation against an assessment of changing import-export patterns for household appliances.
American Drug Corporation   9-302-043
   Decision as to treatment of Colombian distributors against a background of foreign exchange difficulties.
The Log Export Problem   9-374-896
   Can a sensible case be made for restricting the U.S. export of logs?

Meeting the Interests of Nation-States:
United Fruit Company   9-302-039/40
   What policies should (a) United Fruit and (b) the Central American republics have adopted in the late 1950s?
Mallory Batteries Inc.   9-572-658
   How should the company react to the U.K. Monopolies Commission request for a price rollback?

Panelec Argentina, S.A.   4-370-077 ICR 470R
Policy toward a government hearing to raise tariffs at the request of a questionable local component manufacturer.

Expropriation of Alcan's Bauxite Mining Subsidiary in Guyana, Parts A–E   9-375-661/5
Evaluation of company and government tactics and motivations leading up to expropriation.

Assessing Differences in National Environments:

Polaroid France, S.A.   9-513-119
Reassessment of the marketing strategy adopted for introduction of the Polaroid Swinger in France.

Showa-Packard Ltd. (*A*), (*B*)   9-373-348/9
Negotiations with Japanese partners over managerial patterns and control of a joint venture.

General Motors Malaysia Sdn. Bhd.   9-574-065
Strategy for market introduction of the Basic Transportation Vehicle.

Expanding and Adjusting within a Global Market:

Gordon Machine Corporation   1-575-049
How should a manufacturer of couplings and clutches go international?

Kenics Corporation   9-574-036
Developing a marketing strategy for Europe with the U.S. strategy as reference.

Two-Ply Manufacturers Inc.   9-371-349 ICR 545
Review of international joint-venture policies of a tire manufacturer and strategy within the Mexican market.

Organizing and Controlling the Multinational Enterprise:

Perkins Engines (*B*)   4-574-069
Evaluating role and performance of product marketing managers in increasing global market share.

Svenska Ackumulator AB Jungner   9-574-809
Introducing marketing planning into a multinational company.

Royal Dutch Chemical N.V.   9-574-033
Matrix organization and the introduction of new products in a global corporation.

Managing Personnel in Cross-National Situations:

Collision on the A12   9-372-685
What steps should the company take with regard to employees and their families following a serious accident involving the local police?

Bibliography

Bibliography

Part one
The Nature and Scope of International Business

Aharoni, Yair. *The Foreign Investment Decision Process.* Boston: Division of Research, Graduate School of Business Administration, Harvard University, 1966.

Aho, D. Michael. *Bibliography on Foreign Direct Investment.* Cambridge, Mass.: International Business Research Center for International Studies, Massachusetts Institute of Technology, May 1974.

Behrman, Jack N. *Some Patterns in the Rise of the Multinational Enterprise.* Chapel Hill: Graduate School of Business Administration, University of North Carolina, 1969.

Brooke, Michael Z., and H. Lee Remmers. *The Multinational Company in Europe.* London: Longman, 1972.

Daniels, John D., Ernest W. Ogram, Jr., and Lee H. Radebaugh. *International Business: Environments and Operations.* Reading, Mass.: Addison-Wesley Publishing Co., 1976.

Dunning, John H., ed. *Economic Analysis and the Multinational Enterprise.* New York: Praeger Publishers, Inc., 1974.

Fayerweather, John. *International Business Management: A Conceptual Framework.* New York: McGraw-Hill Book Co., Inc., 1969.

Franko, Lawrence G. *The European Multinationals: A Renewed Challenge to American and British Big Business.* Stamford, Conn.: Greylock Publishers, 1976.

Hays, Richard D., Christopher M. Korth, and Manucher Roudiani. *International Business.* Englewood Cliffs, N.J.: Prentice-Hall, Inc., 1972.

705

Knickerbocker, F. *Oligopolistic Reaction and Multinational Enterprises.* Boston: Division of Research, Graduate School of Business Administration, Harvard University, 1973.

Kolde, Endel J. *International Business Enterprise.* 2d ed. Englewood Cliffs, N.J.: Prentice-Hall, Inc., 1972.

Lall, Sanjaya. *Foreign Private Manufacturing Investment and Multinational Corporations: An Annotated Bibliography.* New York: Praeger Publishers, Inc., 1975.

Lauter, Geza P., and Paul M. Dickie. *Multinational Corporations and East European Socialist Economies.* New York: Praeger Publishers, Inc., 1975.

Mason, R. Hal, Robert R. Miller, and Dale R. Weigel. *The Economics of International Business.* New York: John Wiley & Sons, 1975.

Reuber, Grant, H. Crookell, M. Emerson, and G. Gallais-Hamonno. *Private Foreign Investment in Development.* New York: Oxford University Press, 1973.

Turner, Louis. *Multinational Companies and the Third World.* New York: Hill & Wang, 1973.

United Nations. *Multinational Corporations in World Development.* New York, 1973.

U.S. Department of Commerce. *Foreign Investment in the United States.* Washington, D.C.: U.S. Government Printing Office, 1976.

Vaupel, James W., and Joan P. Curhan. *The World's Multinational Enterprises.* Boston: Division of Research, Graduate School of Business Administration, Harvard University, 1973.

Vernon, Raymond. *The Economic and Political Consequences of Multinational Enterprise: An Anthology.* Boston: Division of Research, Graduate School of Business Administration, Harvard University, 1972.

Vernon, Raymond, and Louis T. Wells, Jr. *Economic Environment of International Business.* 2d ed. Englewood Cliffs, N.J.: Prentice-Hall, Inc. 1976.

Wilkins, Mira. *The Emergence of Multinational Enterprise.* Cambridge, Mass.: Harvard University Press, 1970.

———— *The Maturing of Multinational Enterprise.* Cambridge, Mass.: Harvard University Press, 1974.

Part two
The Framework for International Transactions

Aliber, Robert Z., ed. *The International Market for Foreign Exchange.* New York: Praeger Publishers, Inc., 1969.

————. *National Monetary Policies and the International Financial System.* Chicago: The University of Chicago Press, 1974.

————. *The International Money Game.* 2d ed. New York: Basic Books, 1976.

Baker, James C. *The International Finance Corporation.* New York: Frederick A. Praeger, Inc., 1968.

Baldwin, Robert E. *Nontariff Distortions of International Trade.* Washington, D.C.: The Brookings Institution, 1970.

Bell, Geoffrey. *The Euro-Dollar Market and the International Financial System.* New York: Halsted Press/John Wiley & Sons, Inc., 1974.

Bergsten, C. Fred, ed. *Toward a New World Trade Policy.* Lexington, Mass.: D. C. Heath & Co., 1975.

Bergsten, C. Fred, and Lawrence B. Krause, eds. *World Politics and International Economics.* Washington, D.C.: The Brookings Institution, 1975.

Bergsten, C. Fred, Thomas Horst, and Theodore H. Moran. *American Multinationals and American Interests.* Washington, D.C.: The Brookings Institution, 1977.

Brenner, Michael J. *The Politics of International Monetary Reform: The Exchange Crisis.* Cambridge, Mass.: Ballinger Publishing Co., 1976.

Caves, Richard E., and Ronald W. Jones. *World Trade and Payments.* Boston: Little, Brown and Company, 1973.

Dam, Kenneth W. *The GATT—Law and International Organization.* Chicago: The University of Chicago Press, 1970.

Einzig, Paul. *The Euro-Dollar System.* 5th ed. New York: St. Martin's Press, Inc., 1973.

Friedman, Milton. *The Balance of Payments: Free versus Fixed Exchange Rates.* Washington, D.C.: American Enterprise Institute for Public Policy Research, 1967.

Grubel, Herbert G. *International Economics.* Homewood, Ill.: Richard D. Irwin, Inc., 1977.

Heller, H. Robert. *International Monetary Economics.* Englewood Cliffs, N.J.: Prentice-Hall, Inc., 1974.

Hewson, John, and E. Sakakibara. *The Eurocurrency Markets and Their Implications.* Lexington, Mass.: D. C. Heath & Co., 1975.

Holmes, Alan R., and Francis H. Schott. *The New York Foreign Exchange Market.* New York: Federal Reserve Bank of New York, 1965.

Johnson, Harry G. *The Problem of International Monetary Reform.* London: Athlone Press, 1974.

Kindleberger, Charles P. *International Economics.* 5th ed. Homewood, Ill.: Richard D. Irwin, Inc., 1973.

Kreinin, Mordecai E. *International Economics.* 2d ed. New York: Harcourt Brace Jovanovich, Inc., 1975.

Law, Alton D. *International Commodity Agreements.* Lexington, Mass.: D. C. Heath & Co., 1975.

Lees, F. A. *International Banking and Finance.* New York: Halsted Press, 1974.

Machlup, Fritz. *Economic Integration: Worldwide, Regional, Sectoral.* New York: Halsted Press, 1963.

Maizels, Alfred. *Industrial Growth and World Trade.* Cambridge: Cambridge University Press, 1963.

Malmgren, Harald B.   *Trade for Development.* Washington, D.C.: Overseas Development Council, 1971.

McKenzie, George W.   *The Economics of the Eurocurrency System.* New York: Halsted Press, 1976.

Meier, Gerald M.   *Problems of World Monetary Order.* New York: Oxford University Press, 1974.

Organization for Economic Cooperation and Development.   *Export Cartels.* Paris, 1974.

Paxton, John.   *The Developing Common Market: The Structure of the EEC in Theory and in Practice.* Boulder, Colo.: Westview Press, 1976.

Root, Franklin R.   *International Trade and Investment.* 3d ed. Cincinnati, Ohio: South-Western Publishing Co., 1973.

Scammell, W. M.   *International Monetary Policy: Bretton Woods and After.* New York: Halsted Press, 1975.

Smith, David N., and Louis T. Wells, Jr.   *Negotiating Third World Mineral Agreements.* Cambridge, Mass.: Ballinger Publishing Co., 1975.

Stern, Robert M.   *The Balance of Payments: Theory and Economic Policy.* Chicago: Aldine Publishing Co., 1973.

Tuerck D., and L. Yeager.   *Foreign Trade and U.S. Policy: The Case for Free International Trade.* New York: Praeger Publishers, Inc., 1976.

Wallace, Don Jr., and Helga Ruof-Koch, eds.   *International Control of Investment,* New York: Praeger Publishers, Inc., 1974.

Wolf, Thomas A.   *United States East-West Trade Policy.* Lexington, Mass.: D. C. Heath and Co., 1973.

Part three
The Nation-State and International Business

Baerrensen, Donald W.   *The Border Industrialization Program of Mexico.* Lexington, Mass.: D. C. Heath & Co., 1971.

Baranson, Jack.   *Automotive Industries in Developing Countries.* Baltimore: The Johns Hopkins Press, 1969.

———.   *Industrial Technologies for Developing Economies.* New York: Frederick A. Praeger, Inc., 1969.

Barnet, Richard J., and Ronald Müller.   *Global Reach: The Power of the Multinational Corporation.* New York: Simon and Schuster, 1974.

Behrman, Jack N.   *National Interests and the Multinational Enterprise.* Englewood Cliffs, N.J.: Prentice-Hall, Inc., 1970.

Behrman, Jack N., J. J. Boddewyn, and Ashok Kapoor.   *International Business-Government Communications.* Lexington, Mass.: D. C. Heath & Co., 1975.

Behrman, Jack N., and Harvey W. Wallender.   *Transfers of Manufacturing Technology Within Multinational Enterprises.* Cambridge, Mass.: Ballinger Publishing Co., 1976.

Boddewyn, J. J. *Western European Policies Toward U.S. Investors.* New York: Graduate School of Business Administration, Institute of Finance, New York University, 1974.

Bos, H. C., M. Sanders, and C. Secchi. *Private Foreign Investment in Developing Countries: A Quantitative Study on the Evaluation of the Macro-economic Effects.* Holland: Reidel, 1974.

Brash, Donald T. *American Investment in Australian Industry.* Canberra: Australian National University Press, 1966.

Cohen, Benjamin I. *Multinational Firms and Asian Exports.* New Haven, Conn.: Yale University Press, 1975.

Cooper, Richard N. *The Economics of Interdependence: Economic Policy in the Atlantic Community.* New York: McGraw-Hill Book Co., 1968.

Delupis, I. *Finance and Protection of Investment in Developing Countries.* New York: Halsted Press, 1974.

Drysdale, P. *Direct Foreign Investment in Asia and the Pacific.* Toronto: University of Toronto Press, 1972.

Duncan, W. C. *American Direct Investment in the Japanese Automobile Industry.* Cambridge, Mass.: Ballinger Publishing Co., 1973.

Dunning, John H. *Studies in International Investment.* London: George Allen & Unwin, Limited, 1970.

———. *The Multinational Enterprise.* London: George Allen & Unwin, Limited, 1971.

Faith, Nicholas. *The Infiltrators.* New York: E. P. Dutton & Co., Inc., 1972.

Fayerweather, John. *Foreign Investment in Canada: Prospects for National Policy.* White Plains, N.Y.: International Arts and Sciences Press, Inc., 1973.

Feinschreiber, Robert. *Tax Incentives for U.S. Exports.* Dobbs Ferry, N.Y.: Oceana Publications, Inc., 1975.

Gabriel, Peter P. *The International Transfer of Corporate Skills.* Boston: Division of Research, Graduate School of Business Administration, Harvard University, 1967.

Goldman, Marshall I. *Detente and Dollars: East-West Trade.* New York: Basic Books, 1975.

Goodsell, Charles T. *American Corporations and Peruvian Politics.* Cambridge, Mass.: Harvard University Press, 1974.

Gordon, Lincoln, and Englebert Grommers. *United States Manufacturing Investment in Brazil.* Boston: Division of Research, Graduate School of Business Administration, Harvard University, 1962.

Gray, H. Peter. *The Economics of Business Investment Abroad.* London: The Macmillan Press, 1972.

Gunnemann, Jon P. *The Nation-State and Transnational Corporations in Conflict.* New York: Praeger Publishers, Inc., 1975.

Haendel, Dan, Gerald T. West, and Robert G. Meadow. *Overseas Investment and Political Risk.* Philadelphia: Foreign Policy Research Institute, 1975.

Hahlo, H. R., J. Smith and Richard W. Wright. *Nationalism and the Multinational Enterprise.* Dobbs Ferry, N.Y.: Oceana Publications, 1973.

Hodges, Michael. *Multinational Corporations and National Government: A Case Study of the United Kingdom's Experience 1964–1970,* London: Heath and Saxon House, 1974.

Hufbauer, G. C., and F. M. Adler. *Overseas Manufacturing and the Balance of Payments.* Washington, D.C.: U. S. Treasury Department, 1968.

International Labor Office. *Multinational Enterprises and Social Policy,* Geneva. 1973.

Johnson, Harry G. *Economic Policies Towards Less Developed Countries.* New York: Frederick A. Praeger, Inc., 1967.

———. *Technology and Economic Interdependence.* New York: St. Martin's Press, 1975.

Johnstone, Allan W. *United States Direct Investment in France: An Investigation of the French Charges.* Cambridge, Mass.: The M.I.T. Press, 1965.

Kapoor, A., and James E. Cotten. *Foreign Investments in Asia: A Survey of Problems and Prospects in the 1970s.* Princeton, N.J.: The Darwin Press, Inc., 1972.

Kindleberger, Charles B. *The International Corporation.* Cambridge, Mass.: The M.I.T. Press, 1970.

Kujawa, Duane, ed. *International Labor and Multinational Enterprise.* New York: Praeger Publishers, Inc., 1975.

Lal, Deepak. *Appraising Foreign Investment in Developing Countries.* New York: Homes & Meier Publishers, Inc., 1975.

Layton, Christopher. *Trans-Atlantic Investments.* Boulogne-Sur-Seine: The Atlantic Institute, 1968.

Levinson, Charles. *Capital, Inflation and the Multinationals.* New York: The Macmillan Co., 1971.

Levitt, Kari. *Silent Surrender: The American Economic Empire in Canada.* New York: Liverwright, 1971.

Litvak, Isaiah A., and Christopher J. Maule.*Foreign Investment: The Experience of Host Countries.* New York: Frederick A. Praeger, Inc., 1970.

Litvak, I. A., C. J. Maule, and R. D. Robinson. *Dual Loyalty: Canadian/U.S. Business Arrangements.* Toronto: McGraw-Hill Ryerson, Ltd., 1971.

May, Herbert K. *The Contributions of U.S. Private Investment to Latin America's Growth.* New York: Council of the Americas, 1970.

May, Stacy, and Galo Plaza. *The United Fruit Company in Latin America.* Washington, D.C.: National Planning Association, 1958.

Mikesell, R. F. *Foreign Investment in the Petroleum and Mineral Industries: Case Studies of Investor-Host Relations.* Baltimore: The Johns Hopkins Press, 1971.

Moran, Theodore H. *Multinational Corporations and the Politics of Dependence: Copper in Chile.* Princeton, N.J.: Princeton University Press, 1975.

National Industrial Conference Board. *Obstacles and Incentives to Private Foreign Investment 1962–1964.* New York, 1965.

Nwogugu, Edwin I. *The Legal Problems of Foreign Investment in Developing Countries.* New York: Oceana Publications, 1965.

Poh, E. Lim. *Multinational Corporations and Their Implications for Southeast Asia.* Moscow: Institute of Oriental Studies.

Reddaway, W. B., S. J. Potter, and C. T. Taylor. *Effects of U.K. Direct Investment Overseas.* Cambridge: Cambridge University Press, 1968.

Safarian, A. E. *Foreign Ownership of Canadian Industry.* Toronto: McGraw-Hill Book Co. of Canada Limited, 1966.

Sauvant, Karl P., and Farid G. Lavipour, eds. *Controlling Multinational Enterprises: Problems, Strategies, Counter-strategies.* Boulder, Colo.: Westview Press, 1976.

Servan-Schreiber, Jean-Jacques. *The American Challenge.* New York: Atheneum House, Inc., 1968.

Skinner, Wickham. *American Industry in Developing Economies.* New York: John Wiley & Sons, Inc., 1968.

Stephenson, R. *The Impact of the International Corporation on the Nation State.* London: Weidenfeldt and Nicholson, 1972.

Torneden, Roger L. *Foreign Disinvestment by U.S. Multinational Corporations.* New York: Praeger Publishers, Inc., 1975.

United Nations Commission on Transnational Corporations. *National Legislation and Regulations Relating to Transnational Corporations.* New York: United Nations, January 26, 1976.

Vernon, Raymond, ed. *Big Business and the State: Changing Patterns in Western Europe.* Cambridge, Mass.: Harvard University Press, 1974.

———.*Sovereignty at Bay.* New York: Basic Books, Inc., 1971.

Watkins, Melville H. et al. *Foreign Ownership and the Structure of Canadian Industry. Report of the Task Force on the Structure of Canadian Industry.* Ottawa: Queen's Printer, 1968.

Wilczynski, Josef. *The Multinationals and East-West Relations: Towards Transideological Collaboration.* Boulder, Colo.: Westview Press, 1976.

Zink, Dolph Warren. *The Political Risks for Multinational Enterprise in Developing Countries.* New York: Praeger Publishers, Inc., 1973.

Part four
Assessing National Environments

Abegglen, James C. *The Japanese Factory.* Glencoe, Ill.: The Free Press, 1960.

Alsegg, Robert J. *Researching the European Market, AMA Research Study 95.* New York: American Management Association, Inc., 1969.

Apter, David E., and Louis W. Goodman, ed., *The Multinational Corporation and Social Change.* New York: Praeger Publishers, Inc., 1976.

Arensberg, Conrad, and Arthur H. Niehoff. *Introducing Social Change.* Chicago: Aldine Publishing Co., 1964.

Davis, Stanley M. *Comparative Management—Organizational and Cultural Perspectives.* Englewood Cliffs, N.J.: Prentice-Hall, Inc., 1971.

Dickerman, Allen. *Training Japanese Managers.* New York: Praeger Publishers, Inc., 1974.

England, George W. *The Manager and His Values.* Cambridge, Mass.: Ballinger Publishing Co., 1975.

Farmer, Richard N., and Barry M. Richman. *Comparative Management and Economic Progress.* Homewood, Ill.: Richard D. Irwin, Inc., 1965.

Gilpin, Robert G., Jr. *U.S. Power and the Multinational Corporations: The Political Economy of Foreign Direct Investment.* New York: Basic Books, 1975.

Glazer, Herbert. *The International Businessman in Japan.* Tokyo: Sophia University, 1968.

Granick, David. *Managerial Comparisons of Four Developed Countries.* Cambridge, Mass.: The M.I.T. Press, 1972.

Hagen, Everett E. *The Economics of Development.* Rev. ed. Homewood, Ill.: Richard D, Irwin, Inc., 1975.

Hall, Edward T. *The Silent Language.* New York: Doubleday & Co., Inc., 1959.

Hamblin, Robert L., R. Brooke Jacobsen, and Jerry L. L. Miller. *A Mathematical Theory of Social Change.* New York: John Wiley & Sons, Inc., 1973.

Henle, Paul. *Language, Thought and Culture.* Ann Arbor: The University of Michigan Press, 1958.

Hill, T. P. *The Measurement of Real Product.* Paris: OECD, 1971.

Hirschman, Albert O. *The Strategy of Economic Development.* New Haven, Conn.: Yale University Press, Inc., 1958.

Horowitz, Irving L. *The Three Worlds of Development. The Theory and Practice of International Stratification.* New York: Oxford Univeristy Press, Inc., 1966.

Johnson, R. J. et al. *Business Environment in an Emerging Nation.* Evanston, Ill.: Northwestern University Press, 1969.

Kamarck, A. M. *The Economics of African Development.* New York: Frederick A. Praeger, Inc., 1967.

Kravis, Irving B. et al., eds. *A System of International Comparisons of Gross Product and Purchasing Power.* Baltimore: The Johns Hopkins University Press, 1975.

McClelland, David C. *The Achieving Society.* Princeton, N.J.: D. Van Nostrand Co., Inc., 1961.

Marris, Peter, and Anthony Somerset. *African Businessmen.* London: Routledge & Kegan Paul, Limited, 1971.

Matus, G. L. *International Stratification and Underdeveloped Countries.* Chapel Hill: University of North Carolina Press, 1963.

Meier, Gerald M. *Leading Issues in Economic Development.* 3d ed. New York: Oxford University Press, Inc., 1976.

Merrett, Richard L., and Stein Rokkan, eds. *Comparing Nations: The Use of Quantitative Data in Cross-National Research.* New Haven, Conn.: Yale University Press, 1966.

Mikdashi, Zuhayr. *The International Politics of Natural Resources.* Ithaca, N.Y.: Cornell University Press, 1976.

Palubinskas, Feliksas. *Guidebook to Worldwide Marketing.* Westport, Conn.: Technomic Publishing Co., 1975.

Richman, Barry M. *Management Development and Education in the Soviet Union.* East Lansing: Institute for International Business, Michigan State University, 1967.

Robinson, Richard D. *National Control of Foreign Business Entry.* New York: Praeger Publishers, Inc., 1976.

Rogers, Everett M. *Diffusion of Innovations.* New York: The Free Press of Glencoe, 1962.

Sommers, Montrose S., and Jerome B. Kernan, eds. *Comparative Marketing Systems.* New York: Appleton-Century-Crofts, 1968.

Thorelli, Hans B., and Sarah V. Thorelli. *Consumer Information Handbook: Europe and North America.* New York: Praeger Publishers, Inc., 1974.

United Nations. *The Impact of Multinational Corporations on Development and International Relations.* New York, 1974.

Urquidi, Victor L. *The Challenge of Development in Latin America.* New York: Frederick A. Praeger, Inc., 1962.

Waterston, Albert. *Development Planning: Lessons of Experience.* Baltimore: The Johns Hopkins Press, 1965.

Webber, Ross A. *Culture and Management.* Homewood, Ill.: Richard D. Irwin, Inc., 1969.

Part five
Managing the Multinational Enterprise

Aggarwal, Raj. *Financial Policies for Multinational Companies.* New York: Praeger Publishers, Inc., 1976.

Aitken, T. *The Multinational Man: The Role of the Manager Abroad.* New York: Halsted Press, 1973.

Alexandrides C.G., and George P. Moschis. *Export Marketing Strategy.* New York: Praeger Publishers, Inc., 1977.

Auderieth, Stephen, and Elmer M. Pergament. *Tax Guide to International Operations.* New York: Panel Publishers, 1975.

Bartels, Robert. *Comparative Marketing: Wholesaling in Fifteen Countries.* Homewood, Ill.: Richard D. Irwin, Inc., 1963.

Berg, Kenneth B., Gerhard C. Mueller, and Lauren M. Walker, eds. *Readings in International Accounting.* Boston: Houghton Mifflin Co., 1969.

Boddewyn, J. *Comparative Management and Marketing.* Glenview, Ill.: Scott, Foresman & Co., 1969.

Brooke, Michael Z., and H. Lee Remmers. *The Strategy of Multinational Enterprise: Organisation and Finance.* New York: American Elsevier, 1970.

Bursk, E. C., John Dearden, David E. Hawkins, and Victor Longstreet. *Financial Control of Multinational Operations.* New York: Financial Executives Research Foundation, 1971.

Carlson, Sune. *International Financial Decisions: A Study of the Theory of International Business Finance.* Amsterdam: North-Holland Publishing, 1969.

Chown, John F. *Taxation and Multinational Enterprise.* New York: Longman, Inc., 1973.

Chruden, Herbert J. *Personnel Practices of American Companies in Europe.* New York: American Management Association, Inc., 1972.

Colebrook, P. *Going International: A Handbook of British Direct Investment Overseas.* New York: Halsted Press, 1973.

deHoghton, Charles. *Cross-Channel Collaboration: A Study of Agreements between British and Continental Firms.* London: Political and Economic Planning, 1967.

Duerr, Michael G. *R & D in the Multinational Company.* New York: National Industrial Conference Board, 1970.

Duerr, Michael G., and James Greene. *Foreign Nationals in International Management.* New York: National Industrial Conference Board, 1968.

Dymsza, William A. *Multinational Business Strategy.* New York: McGraw-Hill Book Co., Inc., 1972.

Eiteman, David K., and Arthur I. Stonehill. *Multinational Business Finance.* Reading, Mass.: Addison-Wesley Publishing Co., Inc., 1973.

Fayerweather, John. *Management of International Operations.* New York: McGraw-Hill Book Co., Inc., 1960.

Fayerweather, John, and Ashok Kapoor. *Strategy and Negotiations for the International Corporation: Guidelines and Cases.* Cambridge, Mass.: Ballinger Publishing Co., 1976.

Franko, Lawrence G. *The European Multinationals.* Stamford, Conn.: Greylock Publishers, 1976.

Gennard, John. *Multinational Corporations and British Labour.* London: British-North American Committee, 1972.

Gonzalez, Richard F., and Anant R. Negandhi. *The United States Overseas Executive: His Orientations and Career Patterns.* East Lansing: Michigan State University, 1967.

Greene, James, and Michael G. Duerr. *Intercompany Transactions in the Multinational Firm.* New York: National Industrial Conference Board, 1970.

Gunther, Hans, ed. *Transnational Industrial Relations.* London: The Macmillan Co., Limited, 1972.

Haner, Frederick. *Multinational Management.* Columbus, Ohio: C. E. Merrill, 1973.

Hawkins, Robert F., and Walter Ingo, eds. *The United States and International Markets.* Lexington, Mass.: D. C. Heath and Co., 1972.

Kassalow, Everett M. *Trade Unions and Industrial Relations: An International Comparison.* New York: Random House, Inc., 1969.

Keegan, Warren J. *Multinational Marketing Management.* Englewood Cliffs, N.J.: Prentice-Hall, Inc. 1974.

Kolde, E.J. *The Multinational Company: Behavior and Managerial Analysis.* Lexington, Mass.: D. C. Heath and Co., 1974.

Kubin, Konrad W., and Gerhard G. Mueller. *A Bibliography of International Accounting.* 3d ed. Seattle: International Accounting Studies Institute, University of Washington, 1975.

Kujawa, Duane, ed. *International Labor and Multinational Enterprise.* New York: Praeger Publishers, Inc., 1975.

Lamont, Douglas F. *Managing Foreign Investment in Southern Italy: U.S. Business in the Developing Areas of the EEC.* New York: Praeger Publishers, Inc., 1973.

Lietaer, Bernard A. *Financial Management of Foreign Exchange.* Cambridge, Mass.: The M.I.T. Press, 1971.

Lovell, Enid B. *Appraising Foreign Licensing Performance.* New York: National Industrial Conference Board, 1969.

McNair, Malcolm P. et al. *Distribution Costs—An International Analysis.* Boston: Harvard Business School, 1961.

Manser, W. A. P. *Financial Management of Multinational Enterprises.* London: Cassell & Co., Ltd., 1973.

Moxon, Richard W. *Offshore Production in the Less Developed Countries.* New York: NYC Graduate School of Business Administration, 1974.

Mueller, Gerhard G. *International Accounting.* New York: The Macmillan Co., 1967.

Nehrt, Lee C. *International Finance for Multinational Business.* 2d ed. Scranton, Pa.: International Textbook Co., 1971.

Neufeld, E. P.   *A Global Corporation: A History of the International Development of Massey-Ferguson Limited.* Toronto: University of Toronto Press, 1969.

Phatak, Arvind V.   *Managing Multinational Corporations.* New York: Praeger Publishers, Inc., 1974.

Prasad, S. Benjamin, and Krishna Y. Shetty.   *An Introduction to Multinational Management.* Englewood Cliffs, N.J.: Prentice-Hall, Inc., 1976.

Richman, Barry M., and Melvyn R. Copen.   *International Management and Economic Development.* New York: McGraw-Hill Book Co., 1972.

Robbins, Sydney, and Robert B. Stobaugh.   *Money in the Multinational Enterprise.* New York: Basic Books, Inc., 1973.

Robinson, Richard D.   *International Business Policy.* New York: Holt, Rinehart & Winston, Inc., 1964.

————.   *International Business Management.* New York: Holt, Rinehart and Winston, Inc., 1973.

Rodriguez, Rita M., and E. Eugene Carter.   *International Financial Management.* Englewood Cliffs, N.J.: Prentice-Hall, 1976.

Root, Franklin R.   *Strategic Planning for Export Marketing.* Scranton, Pa.: International Textbook Co., 1966.

Rueschoff, Norlin G.   *International Accounting and Financial Reporting.* New York: Praeger Publishers, Inc., 1976.

Schwendiman, John S.   *Strategic and Long Range Planning for the Multinational Corporation.* New York: Praeger Publishers, Inc., 1973.

Sethi, S. Prakash.   *Advanced Cases in Multinational Business Operations.* Pacific Palisades, Calif.: Goodyear Publishing Co., Inc., 1972.

Sethi, S. Prakash, and Richard H. Holton, eds.   *Management of the Multinationals.* New York: The Free Press, 1974.

Shearer, John C.   *High Level Manpower in Overseas Subsidiaries.* Princeton, N.J.: Goodyear Publishing Co., Inc., 1972.

Steiner, George A., and Warren M. Cannon.   *Multinational Corporate Planning.* New York: The Macmillan Co., 1966.

Stopford, John, and Louis T. Wells.   *Managing the Multinational Enterprise.* New York: Basic Books, Inc., 1972.

Terpstra, Vern.   *International Marketing.* New York: Holt, Rinehart & Winston, Inc., 1972.

Thorelli, H. B., ed.   *International Marketing Strategy.* Baltimore: Penguin Books, Inc., 1973.

Tindall, Robert E.   *Multinational Enterprises.* Dobbs Ferry, N.Y.: Oceana Publications, Inc., 1975.

Tsurumi, Yoshi.   *Multinational Management: Texts, Readings and Cases.* Cambridge, Mass.: Ballinger Publishing Co., 1976.

Weston, J. Fred, and Bart W. Sorge.   *International Managerial Finance.* Homewood, Ill.: Richard D. Irwin, Inc., 1972.

Wiechmann, Ulrich E. *Marketing Management in Multinational Firms.* New York: Praeger Publishers, Inc., 1976.

Wilkins, Mira, and Frank E. Hill. *American Business Abroad: Ford on Six Continents.* Detroit: Wayne State University Press, 1964.

Wilson, Charles. *The History of Unilever.* London: F. Cassell, 1954.

———. *Unilever 1945–1965.* London: F. Cassell, 1968.

Wilson, Charles, and J.C. Scheffer. *Multinational Enterprises: Financial and Monetary Aspects.* Leiden: A. Sijthoff, 1974.

Wood, Richard, and Virginia Keyser. *Sears, Roebuck de Mexico, S.A.* Washington, D.C.: National Planning Association, 1953.

Zenoff, David B. *International Business Management.* New York: The Macmillan Co., 1971.

Zenoff, David B., and Jack Zwick. *International Financial Management.* Englewood Cliffs, N.J.: Prentice-Hall, Inc., 1969.

Indexes

Author Index

Subject Index

A

This book has been set in 10 point and 9 point Caledonia, leaded 2 points. Part numbers are 22 point Helvetica Medium. Part titles are 20 point Helvetica. Chapter numbers are 28 point Helvetica Medium, and chapter titles are 16 point Helvetica. The size of the type page is 27 × 45 picas.